Spanish
Phrasebook
and Dictionary
Second Edition

New York Chicago San Francisco Lisbon London Madrid Mexico City
Milan New Delhi San Juan Seoul Singapore Sydney Toronto

The **McGraw·Hill** Companies

VOX (y su logotipo) es marca registrada de Larousse Editorial
www.vox.es

1 2 3 4 5 6 7 8 9 10 11 12 13 14   QFR/QFR   1 9 8 7 6 5 4 3 2

ISBN 978-0-07-178867-0
MHID   0-07-178867-0

Library of Congress Cataloging-in-Publication Data

Vox Spanish phrasebook and dictionary / by Vox. — 2nd ed.
        p.   cm. — (Vox dictionaries)
    Text in English and Spanish.
    Previous ed.: New York : McGraw-Hill, c2002.
    ISBN-13: 978-0-07-178867-0 (acid-free paper)
    ISBN-10: 0-07-178867-0 (acid-free paper)
    1. Spanish language—Dictionaries—English.   2. English language—
Dictionaries—Spanish.   3. Spanish language—Conversation and phrase
books—English.   I. McGraw-Hill Companies.

    PC4640.V6975   2012
    463'.21—dc23   2011052487

Editorial Director: Jordi Induráin Pons
Editorial Coordinator: Mª José Simón Aragón
Phrasebook:
Editor: Arthur Barry Kench
© 1996 Larousse Editorial, S.L.
Dictionary:
Project Manager: Andrew Hastings
Lexicographers: Isabel Ferrer Marrades, Victoria Ordóñez Diví, Jose Mª Ruiz Vaca,
Stephen Waller

CONTENTS

HOW TO USE THIS BOOK

The *Vox Spanish Phrasebook and Dictionary*, second edition, is designed to provide language assistance for all your travel needs.

The **Phrasebook** section presents in convenient thematic sections the Spanish words and phrases required for most typical travel situations, from arrival to shopping, from sightseeing to emergencies. Each expression and phrase in Spanish is followed by an easy-to-read transliteration. Italics indicate the syllable to be stressed in each word. On occasion, alternative expressions are provided in parentheses to reflect regional differences in Spanish. Try these alternatives if the first term has not been understood.

Where appropriate, Spanish terms are listed first: for help in reading menus (pages 32–35), filling out forms (page 85), and understanding doctor's instructions (pages 85–86). For more advanced speakers of Spanish, extended dialogs provide examples of conversations in typical travel situations. The English translation is provided on the facing page.

The **Dictionary** section includes more than 15,000 terms, providing travelers with the information they need in a most manageable and concise form. The lexicon in this remarkably compact bilingual dictionary has been specially edited to include only the most frequently used words and their most common meaning in Spanish and English.

In every way, the *Vox Spanish Phrasebook and Dictionary*, second edition, is ideal for anyone who needs a complete, comprehensive, and truly portable language aid for travel.

ARRIVAL

At the airport

Where do I check in?	**¿Dónde puedo chequear (facturar) mis boletos (billetes)?** *don*deh *p*wedo chekeyar (faktoorar) mees boletos (beel-yetes)?
Where is the check-in desk for Iberia Airlines, please?	**¿Dónde está el mostrador del check-in (de facturación) de la Aerolínea Iberia, por favor?** *don*deh esta el mostrador del chek-een (deh faktooratheeyon) deh la ayeroleeneya eebereeya, por favor?
I'd like a window/aisle seat, please.	**Quisiera un asiento junto a la ventana/al pasillo, por favor.** keeseeyera oon aseeyento hoonto a la ventana/al pasil-yo, por favor
Is there a weight limit for luggage?	**¿Hay límite de peso para el equipaje?** ay leemeeteh deh peso para el ekeepaheh?
How many carry-on items am I allowed?	**¿Cuánto equipaje de mano se permite?** kwanto ekeepaheh deh mano se permeeteh?
Where is gate 8B?	**¿Dónde está la sala (puerta de embarque) 8B?** *don*deh esta la sala (pwerta deh embarkeh) ocho beh?
Why has the plane been delayed?	**¿Por qué está el avión retrasado?** porkeh esta el aveeyon retrasado?
Is there someone here who speaks English?	**¿Hay alguien aquí que hable inglés?** ay algeeyen akee keh ableh eengles?

On the plane

I'd like a vegetarian meal, please.	**Quisiera una comida vegetariana, por favor.** keeseeyera oona komeeda vehetareeyana, por favor
Is there going to be a movie?	**¿Va a haber una película?** va a aber oona peleekoola?
My seatbelt won't fasten.	**Mi cinturón no abrocha.** mee seentooron no abrocha
My headphones don't work.	**Mis audífonos (auriculares) no sirven.** mees aoodeefonos (aooreecoolares) no seerven
I feel sick. Can I have some water, please.	**Me siento mal. ¿Puedo tomar tantita (un poco de) agua, por favor?** meh seeyento mal. pwedo tomar tanteeta (oon poko deh) agwa, por favor?
What time are we scheduled to land?	**¿Para qué hora está programado el aterrizaje?** para keh ora esta programado el aterrisaheh?
I have a connection to Cuernavaca.	**Tengo una conexión a Cuernavaca.** tengo oona konekseeyon a kwernavaka

Customs & security

Do you need my passport?	**¿Necesita mi pasaporte?** neseseeta mee pasaporteh?
I'm here on vacation/business.	**Estoy aquí de vacaciones/de negocios.** estoy akee deh vakaseeyones/deh negoseeyos
I'll be here for ten days.	**Estaré aquí diez días.** estareh akee deeyes deeyas
I'll be staying at the Intercontinental Hotel.	**Me voy a quedar en el Hotel Intercontinental.** meh voy a kedar en el otel eenterkonteenental

I have nothing to declare.	**No tengo nada que declarar.**
	no *tengo na*da keh dekla*rar*

Directions

How do you get to Plaza Santa Ana?	**¿Cómo se llega a la Plaza Santa Ana?**
	*ko*mo seh *l-ye*ga a la *pla*sa santa ana?
Am I going in the right direction for...?	**¿Voy en la dirección correcta para...?**
	voy en la deerekseeyon korrecta para...?
I think I'm a little lost.	**Creo que ando un poco perdido.**
	*kre*yo keh *an*do oon *po*ko perdeedo
Could you help me with this map?	**¿Me podría ayudar con este mapa?**
	meh po*dree*ya a*yoo*dar kon *es*teh *ma*pa?
north	**el norte** el *nor*teh
south	**el sur** el soor
east	**el este** el *es*teh
west	**el oeste** el o*es*teh
ahead	**derecho** de*re*cho
behind	**detrás de** de*tras* deh
next to	**junto a** *hoon*to a
across from	**enfrente de** en*fren*teh deh
Turn...	**Voltee... (Gire...)** vol*te*yeh (*hee*reh)
to the right	**a la derecha** a la de*re*cha
to the left	**a la izquierda** a la eeskee*yer*da
Follow the signs	**Siga las señales (los letreros)**
	*see*ga las se*nya*les (los le*tre*ros)

Arrival

arrival	**la llegada** la l-ye*g*ada
baggage trolley	**el carrito de equipaje** el ka*rree*to deh eke*e*paheh
baggage	**el equipaje** el eke*e*paheh
baggage reclaim hall	**la sala de reclamación (recogida) de equipajes** la *sa*la deh reklamasee*yon* (reko*hee*da) deh eke*e*pahes
boarding card	**el pase de abordar (la tarjeta de embarque)** el *pa*seh deh abor*dar* (la tar*he*ta deh em*bar*keh)
boarding gate	**la sala de abordar (la puerta de embarque)** la *sa*la deh abor*dar* (la *pwer*ta deh em*bar*keh)
bus station	**la estación de autobuses** la estasee*yon* deh aooto*boo*ses
check-in desks	**los mostradores de check-in (facturación)** los mostra*do*res deh chek-*een* (faktoorathee*yon*)
customs	**la aduana** la ad*wa*na
departure	**la salida** la sa*lee*da
departure lounge	**la sala de abordar (embarque)** la *sa*la deh abor*dar* (em*bar*keh)
duty free	**libre de impuestos** *lee*breh deh eem*pwes*tos
elevator	**el ascensor** el as-sen*sor*
entrance/exit	**la entrada/la salida** la en*tra*da/la sa*lee*da
escalator	**la escalera eléctrica (mecánica)** la eska*le*ra e*lek*treeka (me*ka*neeka)
flight number	**el número de vuelo** el *noo*mero deh *vwe*lo
form of identification	**la forma de identificación** la *for*ma deh eedenteefeekasee*yon*
gate	**la puerta** la *pwer*ta
gents	**caballeros** kaba*l-ye*ros
goods to declare	**algo que declarar** *al*go keh dekla*rar*
information desk	**la oficina de información** la ofee*see*na deh eenformasee*yon*
ladies	**señoras** se*nyo*ras
left baggage	**la consigna de equipaje** la kon*seeg*na deh eke*e*paheh
lost baggage	**el equipaje extraviado** el eke*e*paheh ekstravee*ya*do
lost property	**los objetos perdidos** los ob*he*tos per*dee*dos

mail box	**el buzón** el boo*son*
moving walkways	**las cintas transportadoras** las *seen*tas transporta*do*ras
nothing to declare	**nada que declarar** *na*da keh decla*rar*
passport control	**el control de pasaportes** el kon*trol* deh pasa*por*tes
personal items	**los artículos personales** los ar*tee*koolos personales
post office	**la oficina de correos** la ofee*see*na deh ko*rre*yos
restroom	**los baños (servicios)** los *ban*yos (ser*bee*theeyos)
security control	**el control de seguridad** el kon*trol* deh segooree*dad*
skycap	**el mozo de equipaje** el *mo*so deh ekee*pa*heh
stairs	**las escaleras** las eska*le*ras
ticket	**el boleto (billete)** el bo*le*to (bee*l-yeh*teh)
e-ticket	**el boleto (billete) electrónico** el bo*le*to (bee*l-yeh*teh) elek*tro*neeko
trolley	**el carrito** el ka*rre*eto
walkway	**el pasillo** el pa*seel*-yo

On the plane

air hostess	**la azafata** la asa*fa*ta
baggage rack	**el portaequipajes** el portaekee*pa*hes
boarding card	**el pase de abordar (la tarjeta de embarque)** el *pa*seh deh abor*dar* (la tar*he*ta deh em*bar*keh)
crew	**la tripulación** la treepoolasee*yon*
emergency exit	**la salida de emergencia** la sa*lee*da deh emer*hen*seeya
fasten seat belt	**abróchense el cinturón** a*bro*chenseh el seentoo*ron*
hand baggage	**el equipaje de mano** el ekee*pa*heh deh *ma*no
landing	**el aterrizaje** el aterree*sa*heh
life jacket/life vest	**el chaleco salvavidas** el cha*le*ko salva*vee*das
row 21 seat C	**fila 21 asiento C** *fee*la veyeenteh-oono asee*yen*to seh
seat belt	**el cinturón de seguridad** el seentoo*ron* de segooree*dad*
seat	**el asiento** el asee*yen*to
steward	**el sobrecargo** el sobre*kar*go
stewardess	**la sobrecargo** la sobre*kar*go
take-off	**el despegue** el des*pe*gheh

Dialog: At the airport

Hombre	¿Dónde puedo comprar revistas y periódicos?
Señorita	En el puesto (quiosco), allí a la derecha.
Señora	¿Hay alguna cafetería aquí?
Señorita	Sí, señora; a la izquierda subiendo las escaleras.
Joven	¿Para chequear los boletos (facturar los billetes)?
Señorita	Abajo, señor; enfrente de la entrada principal.
Anciana	Perdone, ¿podría decirme dónde está el mostrador de check-in (facturación) de la compañía Mexicana, por favor?
Señorita	Sí, señora; baje las escaleras eléctricas (mecánicas) y voltee (gire) a la izquierda; está justo enfrente de la entrada principal.
Jovencita	Perdone, ¿podría decirme dónde están los baños (aseos), por favor?
Señorita	Sí; enfrente de la cafetería, subiendo las escaleras.
Hombre	¿Para cambiar dinero?
Señorita	En el banco que hay nada más pasando las escaleras eléctricas (mecánicas).
Joven	¿Alquiler de coches?
Señorita	Al fondo a la izquierda.
Señora	¿Hay algún teléfono público aquí?
Señorita	Por allí a la derecha, al lado del puesto (quiosco).

Man	Where can I get magazines and newspapers?
Girl	At the bookstall over there on the right, sir.
Lady	Is there a cafeteria here?
Girl	Yes, madam; on the left at the top of the stairs.
Young man	Where do I check in?
Girl	Downstairs, sir; opposite the main entrance.
Old lady	Excuse me. Could you tell me where the check-in desk for Mexicana Airlines is, please?
Girl	Yes, madam; down the escalator, turn left and it is opposite the main entrance.
Young lady	Excuse me. Could you tell me where the toilets are, please?
Girl	Yes; opposite the cafeteria at the top of the stairs.
Man	To change money?
Girl	At the bank counter just past the escalator.
Yong man	Rent-a-car?
Girl	On the left at the far end.
Lady	Are there any public telephones here?
Girl	Over there on the right next to the bookstall.

ACCOMMODATION

Checking in

Could you recommend a good moderately-priced hotel?	**¿Podría recomendarme un buen hotel de precio moderado?** pod*ree*ya rekomend*ar*meh oon bwen o*tel* deh *pre*seeyo mode*ra*do?
We have a reservation.	**Tenemos una reservación.** te*ne*mos *oo*na reservasee*yon*
We'll be staying for five nights.	**Nos vamos a quedar cinco noches.** nos *va*mos a ke*dar seen*ko *no*ches
We'd like a double bed, not twin beds.	**Quisiéramos cama matrimonial (de matrimonio), no camas individuales.** keesee*ye*ramos *ka*ma matree*mo*neeyal (deh matree*mo*neeyo), no *ka*mas eendeeveed*wales*
The room has air conditioning, right?	**La habitación tiene aire acondicionado, ¿no?** la abeetasee*yon* tee*ye*neh *ay*reh akondeeseeyo*na*do, no?
Could you give us a wake-up call?	**¿Nos podría hablar (llamar) para despertarnos?** nos pod*ree*ya a*blar* (l-ya*mar*) para desper*tar*nos?
How do you make an outside call?	**¿Cómo se marca para la calle?** *ko*mo seh *mar*ka para la *kal*-yeh?
Could someone help us with our bags?	**¿Hay alguien que nos pueda ayudar con nuestras maletas?** ay alg*ee*yen keh nos *pwe*da ayoo*dar* kon *nwe*stras ma*leh*tas?
What floor is the dining room on?	**¿En qué piso está el comedor?** en keh *pee*so es*ta* el kome*dor*?

What time does breakfast begin/end?	**¿A qué hora empieza/termina el desayuno?** a keh *o*ra empee*yes*a/ter*mee*na el desa*yoo*no?

Complaints

The air conditioning/heating doesn't work.	**El aire acondicionado/La calefacción no funciona.** al *ay*reh akondeeseeyo*na*do/ la kalefaksee*yon* no foonsee*yo*na
My room hasn't been cleaned.	**No han limpiado mi cuarto.** no han leempee*ya*do mee *kwar*to
Our neighbors are too noisy.	**Nuestros vecinos son muy ruidosos.** *nwes*tros ve*see*nos son mwee rwee*do*sos
This charge is incorrect.	**Este cargo no está correcto.** *es*teh *kar*go no es*ta* kor*rek*to

Departure

We're ready to check out.	**Estamos listos para desocupar.** es*ta*mos *lees*tos *pa*ra desokoo*par*
Can you get my bill ready and send someone up to collect our baggage, please?	**¿Puede preparar la cuenta y enviar a alguien para que baje nuestro equipaje, por favor?** *pwe*deh prepa*rar* la *kwen*ta ee envee*yar* a al*ghe*yen *pa*ra keh *ba*heh *nwes*tio ekee*pa*heh, por fa*vor*?
Can I have my bill, please?	**¿Me puede dar la cuenta, por favor?** me *pwe*deh dar la *kwen*ta, por fa*vor*?
Could we leave our baggage here for a short time?	**¿Podríamos dejar nuestro equipaje aquí un rato?** podree*ya*mos de*har* *nwes*tro ekee*pa*heh a*kee* oon *ra*to?
Could you get me a taxi, please?	**¿Me podría pedir un taxi, por favor?** me podree*ya* pe*deer* oon *tak*see, por fa*vor*?

Dialog: In the hotel

Recepcionista	Buenos días, señor. Buenos días, señora. ¿En qué puedo servirles?
Sr. Austen	Tenemos reservadas dos habitaciones para cinco días. El nombre es Austen.
Recepcionista	Señores Austen e hija. Sí, aquí está: una habitación doble con baño y una individual con regadera (ducha). Cinco días, desde hoy hasta el doce de abril.
Sra. Austen	¿Está cerca la habitación de nuestra hija de la nuestra?
Recepcionista	De hecho, señora, están casi pegadas. Ustedes tienen la habitación 612 y su hija la 614.
Recepcionista	¿Le importaría llenar esta forma (rellenar este impreso), señor? Ponga su nombre, dirección y número de pasaporte y firme aquí, por favor.
Sra. Austen	¿A qué hora se sirve el desayuno?
Recepcionista	El desayuno se sirve en el comedor desde las siete y media hasta las diez, señora.
Sr. Austen	¿Está correcto?
Recepcionista	Perfecto, señor, gracias. El botones tiene sus llaves. Les subirá el equipaje y les enseñará las habitaciones. Espero que tengan una estancia agradable. Si necesitan algo, les ruego que no duden en pedirlo.
Sr. Austen	Muchas gracias.

Clerk	*Good morning, sir. Good morning, madam. Can I help you?*
Mr. Austen	*Yes. We have two rooms booked here for five days. The name is Austen.*
Clerk	*Mr. and Mrs. Austen and daughter. Yes, here we are, sir: one double room with bathroom en suite and one single room with shower. Five days from today till the 12th of April.*
Mrs. Austen	*Is our daughter's room near ours?*
Clerk	*As a matter of fact, madam, it's almost next door. You have room 612 and your daughter has room 614.*
Clerk	*Would you mind filling in this card, sir? Just your name, home address and passport number. Then sign it here.*
Mrs. Austen	*What time is breakfast?*
Clerk	*Breakfast is served in the restaurant from 7.30 to 10.00 madam.*
Mr. Austen	*Is this correct?*
Clerk	*Perfect, sir. Thank you. The porter has your keys. He will take your luggage up and show you to your rooms. I hope you have a pleasant stay. If there is anything you need, please don't hesitate to ask.*
Mr. Austen	*Thank you very much.*

In the hotel

air conditioning	**el aire acondicionado** el *a*yreh akondeeseeyo*na*do
ashtray	**el cenicero** el see*nee*sero
bathroom	**el cuarto de baño** el *kwa*rto deh *ba*nyo
bed	**la cama** la *ka*ma
double bed	**la cama matrimonial (de matrimonio)** la *ka*ma matreemonee*ya*l (deh matree*mo*neeyo)
twin beds	**las camas individuales** las *ka*mas eendeeveed*wa*les
bedside table	**la mesita de noche** la me*see*ta de *no*cheh
bell	**el timbre** el *tee*mbreh
bill	**la cuenta** la *kwen*ta
blanket	**la cobija (manta)** la ko*bee*ha (*man*ta)
central heating	**la calefacción central** la kalefaksee*yon* sen*tral*
chambermaid	**la camarera** la kama*re*ra
concierge	**el conserje** el kon*ser*heh
door	**la puerta** la *pwer*ta
electric socket	**el enchufe** el en*choo*feh
envelopes	**los sobres** los *so*bres
faucet	**la llave (el grifo)** la *l-ya*veh (el *gree*fo)
fax machine	**la máquina de fax** la *ma*keena deh faks
floor	**el suelo/el piso** el *swe*lo/el *pee*so
bedroom floor	**el suelo de la habitación** el *swe*lo de la abeetasee*yon*
second floor	**el primer piso** el pree*mer pee*so
full board	**la pensión completa** la pensee*yon* kom*ple*ta
gymnasium	**el gimnasio** el heem*na*seeyo
hairdryer	**el secador de pelo** el seka*dor* deh *pe*lo
internet connection	**la conexión para el internet** la koneksee*yon* *pa*ra el *een*ternet
lamp	**la lámpara** la *lam*para
bedside lamp	**la lámpara de la mesita de noche** la *lam*para deh la me*see*ta deh *no*cheh
laundry	**la lavandería** la lavande*ree*ya

light	**la luz** la loos
luggage/baggage	**el equipaje/las maletas** el ekee*pah*eh/las ma*l*etas
manager	**el gerente/el director** el he*ren*teh/el deerek*tor*
meal	**la comida** la ko*mee*da
pillow case	**la funda de almohada** la *foon*da deh almo*a*da
pillow	**la almohada** la almo*a*da
radio	**el (la) radio** el (la) *ra*deeyo
reservation	**la reservación (reserva)** la reserva*seeyon* (re*ser*va)
room	**la habitación** la abeeta*seeyon*
single	**individual** eendeeveedoo*al*
double	**doble** *dob*leh
with bath	**con baño** kon *ban*yo
with shower	**con regadera (ducha)** kon rega*de*ra (*doo*cha)
number	**el número** el *noo*mero
key	**la llave** la *l-ya*veh
service	**el servicio** el ser*vee*seeyo
shampoo	**el champú** el cham*poo*
sheet	**la sábana** la *sa*bana
soap	**el jabón** el ha*bon*
swimming pool	**la alberca (piscina)** la al*ber*ka (pees*thee*na)
telephone	**el teléfono** el te*le*fono
television	**la televisión/la tele** la televee*seeyon*/la *te*leh
toilet	**el escusado (wáter)** el eskoo*sa*do (*ba*ter)
toilet paper	**el papel higiénico** el *pa*pel eeheey*enee*ko
towels	**las toallas** las to*yal*-yas
hand towel	**la toalla para las manos** la to*yal*-ya *pa*ra las *ma*nos
face towel	**la toalla para la cara** la to*yal*-ya *pa*ra la *ka*ra
bath towel	**la toalla de baño** la to*yal*-ya deh *ban*yo
sink	**el lavabo** el la*va*bo
cold water	**el agua fría** el *ag*wa *free*ya
hot water	**el agua caliente** el *ag*wa kalee*yen*teh
window	**la ventana** la ven*ta*na
writing paper	**el papel de escribir** el *pa*pel deh eskree*beer*

Dialog: Checking out

Sr. Austen	¿Me podría dar la cuenta, por favor?
Recepcionista	Naturalmente, señor. Habitaciones seiscientos doce y seiscientos catorce: una habitación doble y una individual durante cinco días; cena para tres el viernes y el domingo. Cinco llamadas de teléfono, todas a los Estados Unidos. ¿Está correcto, señor?
Sr. Austen	Sí, mi mujer llama a su madre todas las noches.
Recepcionista	Servicio de habitaciones: nada. ¿El minibar, señor?
Sr. Austen	Sí, tomé dos de esas botellas miniaturas de whisky.
Recepcionista	Gracias. Eso es todo. ¿Paga usted en efectivo o con tarjeta de crédito?
Sr. Austen	Con tarjeta de crédito, Visa.
Recepcionista	Gracias, señor. ¿Podría firmar aquí, por favor? Gracias. Su tarjeta, su comprobante y la cuenta. Gracias, señor. Espero que hayan disfrutado de su estancia.
Sr. Austen	Sí, muchísimo. ¿Podríamos dejar aquí las maletas durante media hora aproximadamente?
Recepcionista	Naturalmente, señor. ¿Son sólo esas dos maletas?
Sr. Austen	Esas dos maletas y este paquete.
Recepcionista	Estarán aquí en recepción cuando vuelvan, señor.
Sr. Austen	Gracias. Otra cosa más, ¿Podría pedirnos un taxi cuando volvamos?
Recepcionista	Sí, no hay ningún inconveniente.

Mr. Austen	*Could I have the bill, please.*
Receptionist	*Certainly, sir. That's room 612 and 614: one double room and one single room for five days. Dinner for three on Friday and Sunday. Telephone calls five, all to the United States. Is that correct?*
Mr. Austen	*Yes, my wife phones her mother every night.*
Receptionist	*Room service: nothing. Room bar, sir?*
Mr. Austen	*Yes, I had two of those miniature bottles of whiskey.*
Receptionist	*Thank you, sir. That's all. Are you paying in cash or with a credit card, sir?*
Mr. Austen	*With a credit card. Visa.*
Receptionist	*Thank you, sir. Could you just sign here, please? Thank you. Your card, your credit card receipt, and your bill. Thank you, sir. I hope you have all enjoyed your stay here.*
Mr. Austen	*Yes, very much. Could we leave our baggage here for half an hour or so?*
Receptionist	*Certainly, sir. Is it just the two suitcases?*
Mr. Austen	*Two suitcases and this package.*
Receptionist	*They will all be here in reception when you come back, sir.*
Mr. Austen	*Thank you. Just one other thing. Can you get us a taxi when we come back?*
Receptionist	*Yes, no trouble at all, sir.*

TRANSPORTATION

What is the best way to get to Plaza Mayor?	**¿Cuál es la mejor forma de ir a la Plaza Mayor?** kwal es la me*hor for*ma de eer a la *pla*sa ma*yor*?
Have you any maps of central Santiago?	**¿Tienen mapas (planos) del centro de Santiago?** teeyenen *ma*pas (*pla*nos)del *sen*tro deh santee*ya*go?
Where can I get information about train times?	**¿Dónde puedo obtener información de los horarios de trenes?** *don*deh *pwe*do ob*te*ner eenformasee*yon* deh los ora*ree*yos deh *tre*nes?

Taxi

Please take us to...?	**¿Nos puede llevar a...?** nos *pwe*deh l-ye*var* a?
How much will it cost to...?	**¿Cuánto cuesta a.../al...?** *kwan*to *kwes*ta a/al?
The corner ahead is fine.	**La siguiente esquina está bien.** la seegee*yen*teh es*kee*na es*ta* bee*yen*
What's the total?	**¿Cuánto es el total?** *kwan*to es el to*tal*?
Can you wait for two minutes?	**¿Puede esperar dos minutos?** *pwe*deh espe*rar* dos mee*noo*tos?
fare	**el precio del viaje** el *pre*seeyo del vee*ya*heh
for hire	**libre** *lee*breh
suitcase	**la maleta** la ma*le*ta
surcharge	**el suplemento** el soople*men*to
taxi/cab	**el taxi** el *tak*see
taxi driver	**el taxista** el tak*sees*ta

taxi rank	**la parada de taxis** la pa*r*ada de *tak*sees
taximeter	**el taxímetro** el tak*see*metro
tip	**la propina** la pro*pee*na

Bus

Is this the right bus for...?	**¿Éste es el camión (autobús) para...?** *esteh* es el kamee*yon* (aooto*boos*) *pa*ra?
How often does the bus run?	**¿Cada cuándo pasa el camión (autobús)?** *ka*da *kwan*do *pa*sa el kamee*yon* (aooto*boos*)?
bus	**el camión (autobús)** el kamee*yon* (aooto*boos*)
bus fare	**el precio del boleto (billete)** el *pre*seeyo del bo*le*to (bee*l-ye*teh)
bus stop	**la parada de camión (autobús)** la pa*r*ada de kamee*yon* (aooto*boos*)
driver	**el conductor** el kondoo*ktor*
exact fare	**el cambio exacto** el *kam*beeyo esa*k*to
next stop	**la próxima parada** la *prok*seema pa*r*ada
no standing	**prohibido estar de pie** proee*bee*do es*tar* deh pee*yeh*
ticket	**el boleto (billete)** el bo*le*to (bee*l-ye*teh)

Train

Is this the platform for the train to Valparaiso?	**¿Éste es el andén para el tren de Valparaiso?** *esteh* es el an*den* *pa*ra el tren de valpa*ray*so?
Is this seat taken?	**¿Está ocupado este asiento?** es*ta* okoo*pa*do *esteh* asee*yen*to?
What station is this?	**¿Qué estación es ésta?** keh estasee*yon* es *es*ta?
arrival	**la llegada** la l-ye*ga*da
booking office	**la taquilla** la ta*keel*-ya

destination	**el destino** el des*tee*no
luggage rack	**el portaequipajes** el portaekee*pa*hes
no smoking	**prohibido fumar** proee*bee*do foo*mar*
passengers	**los pasajeros** los pasa*he*ros
platform	**el andén** el an*den*
rail station	**la estación de ferrocarril** la estasee*yon* dch ferroka*rreel*
ticket	**el boleto (billete)** el bo*le*to (bee*l-ye*teh)
one-way	**el boleto sencillo (billete de ida)** el bo*le*to sen*seel*-yo (bee*l-ye*teh deh *ee*da)
roundtrip	**el boleto (billete) de ida y vuelta** el bo*le*to (bee*l-ye*teh) deh *ee*da ee *vwel*ta
train	**el tren** el tren

Subway

Which line should I take to get to…?	**¿Qué línea debo tomar para llegar a...?** keh *lee*neya *de*bo to*mar* para l-ye*gar* a?
Is this the correct platform to go to…?	**¿Ésta es la plataforma correcta (el andén correcto) para ir a...?** *es*ta es la plata*for*ma ko*rrek*ta (el an*den* ko*rrek*to) *pa*ra eer a?
What's the next station?	**¿Cuál es la siguiente estación?** kwal es la seegee*yen*teh estasee*yon*?
escalator	**la escalera eléctrica (mecánica)** la eska*le*ra e*lek*treeka (me*ka*neeka)
platform	**el andén** el an*den*
station	**la estación** la estasee*yon*
subway	**el metro** el *me*tro
ticket machine	**la máquina expendedora de boletos (billetes)** la *ma*keena ekspende*do*ra deh bo*le*tos (bee*l-ye*tes)
train fare	**el precio del boleto (billete)** el *pre*seeyo del bo*le*to (bee*l-ye*teh)

Car rental

We have a reservation for a compact for three days.	**Tenemos una reservación (reserva) de un coche compacto para tres días.** tenemos oona reservaseeyon (reserba) deh oon kocheh kompakto para tres deeyas
What does the insurance cover?	**¿Qué cubre el seguro?** keh koobreh el segooro?
There will be two drivers.	**Serán dos conductores.** seran dos kondooktores
I would like to drop the car off at the airport.	**Me gustaría entregar el coche en el aeropuerto.** meh goostareeya entregar el kocheh en el ayropwerto
Does the car take regular or diesel?	**¿Qué gasolina usa el coche?** keh gasoleena oosa el kocheh?
How do I undo the gas cap?	**¿Cómo se quita la tapa del tanque de la gasolina?** komo seh keeta la tapa del tankeh deh la gasoleena?
accident report form	**el parte de accidentes** el parteh deh akseedentes
breakdown	**la avería** la avereeya
car rental	**la renta (el alquiler) de coches** la ronta (el alkeeler) deh koches
collision damage waiver	**el renunciante a daños de colisión** el renoonseeyanteh a danyos deh koleeseeyon
dent	**la abolladura** la abol-yadoora
driver's license	**la licencia de manejar (el carné de conducir)** la leesenseeya deh manehar (el carneh deh condootheer)
excess miles	**las millas de exceso** las meel-yas deh ekseso
insurance policy	**la póliza de seguro** la poleesa deh segooro
rental rate	**la tarifa de alquiler** la tareefa deh alkeeler

Dialog: Getting Around

Sr. Austen	Buenos días. ¿Me puede decir cuál es la mejor forma de moverse por la ciudad?
Empleado	Bueno, pues generalmente tomo el metro. Es muy extenso. Lo deja a unas cuantas cuadras (manzanas) de donde quiera ir.
Sra. Austen	¿Cada cuándo hay trenes?
Empleado	En las líneas principales, cada cinco o diez minutos. Ya en la noche, los trenes son cada quince o veinte minutos.
Sr. Austen	¿Cuál es la forma más barata de comprar boletos (billetes)? ¿Hay algún descuento por comprar más de un boleto (billete)?
Empleado	Yo le recomendaría comprar un boleto que se llama de "diez viajes". Es un boleto que se puede usar diez veces.
Sra. Austen	¿Y los camiones (autobuses)?
Empleado	Yo creo que pueden ser complicados si no está usted familiarizado con la ciudad. En primer lugar, no se alcanzan a ver los letreros de las calles desde el camión (autobús), y el conductor casi nunca anuncia los nombres de las calles.
Sr. Austen	¿Y los taxis? Me imagino que deben ser muy caros.
Empleado	Pueden llegar a serlo. Yo casi siempre evito tomar taxis excepto cuando ya es de noche.
Sr. Austen	Supongo que mejor tomamos el metro entonces. ¿Nos puede decir cómo llegamos al nuevo museo de arte?
Empleado	¡Ah! No sabía que querían ir ahí. Mire este mapa. Pueden llegar ahí caminando en menos de diez minutos.
Sra. Austen	Es un día muy bonito así que yo creo que la mejor idea es ir caminando.

Mr. Austen	Good morning. Can you tell us what's the best way to get around the city?
Hotel clerk	Well, I usually take the subway. It's really extensive. It'll take you within blocks of almost anywhere you want to go.
Mrs. Austen	How often do the trains run?
Clerk	The main lines run every five to ten minutes. Later at night the trains run every fifteen to twenty minutes.
Mr. Austen	What's the cheapest way to buy tickets? Is there some kind of discount for buying more than one?
Clerk	I'd recommend getting a ticket called "ten trips". One ticket that can be used ten times.
Mrs. Austen	What about the buses?
Clerk	I think it might be confusing if you're not familiar with the city. For one thing, you can't really see the street signs from the bus, and the driver often doesn't call out the street names.
Mr. Austen	And taxis? I imagine that they're quite expensive.
Clerk	They can be. I usually avoid taking taxis except when it's late at night.
Mr. Austen	I suppose we'll take the subway then. Could you tell us how to get to the new art museum?
Clerk	Oh, I didn't know you wanted to go there. Here, look at this map. You could walk there in less than ten minutes.
Mrs. Austen	It's a nice day too, so I think a walk is the best idea.

MAKING FRIENDS

Greetings

Hi	**Hola** *ola*
Good morning	**Buenos días** *bwenos deeyas*
Good afternoon	**Buenas tardes** *bwenas tardes*
Good evening/night	**Buenas noches** *bwenas noches*
My name is John. Pleased to meet you.	**Me llamo John. Encantado de conocerlo.** *meh l-yamo jon. enkantado deh konoserlo*
Sorry, I didn't catch your name.	**Perdón, no escuché su nombre.** *perdon, no eskoocheh soo nombreh*

Farewells

Goodbye	**Adiós** *adeeyos*
See you later.	**Hasta luego.** *asta lwego*
See you tomorrow.	**Hasta mañana.** *asta manyana*

Arranging meetings

Let's meet at 6:30.	**Nos vemos a las seis y media.** *nos vemos a las seyees ee medeeya*
I'll meet you at the fountain in the plaza.	**Nos vemos en la fuente de la plaza.** *nos vemos en la fwenteh deh la plasa*
I'll call if I'm going to be late.	**Te llamo si voy a llegar tarde.** *teh l-yamo see voy a l-yegar tardeh*
What do you want to do?	**¿Qué quieres hacer?** *keh keeyeres aser?*
Let's get a drink.	**Vamos a tomar algo.** *vamos a tomar algo*

Family
___

| This is my wife and daughter. | **Ésta es mi mujer y mi hija.** |
| | esta es mee mooher ee mee eeha |

How old is your daughter?	**¿Cuántos años tiene su hija?**
She is seven.	**Tiene siete años.** kwantos anyos teeyeneh
	soo eeha? teeyeneh seeyeteh anyos

| Our son goes to college. | **Nuestro hijo va a la universidad.** |
| | nwestro eeho va a la ooneeverseedad |

| My daughter/son is married. | **Mi hija está casada./Mi hijo está casado.** |
| | mee eeha esta kasada/mee eeho esta kasado |

| I have one sister and two | **Tengo una hermana y dos hermanos.** |
| brothers. | tengo oona ermana ee dos ermanos |

mother	**la madre** la madreh
father	**el padre** el padreh
sister	**la hermana** la ermana
brother	**el hermano** el ermano
aunt	**la tía** la teeya
uncle	**el tío** el teeyo
grandmother	**la abuela** la abwela
grandfather	**el abuelo** el abwelo
wife	**la mujer** la mooher
husband	**el marido** el mareedo
girlfriend	**la novia** la noveeya
boyfriend	**el novio** el noveeyo

Professions/Jobs
___

| What area of work are you in? | **¿En qué trabaja?** en keh trabaha? |

| What company do you work for? | **¿Para qué compañía trabaja?** |
| | para keh kompanyeeya trabaha? |

I'm an engineer and I work for General Motors.	**Soy ingeniero y trabajo para la General Motors.** soy eenheneeyero ee trabaho para la 'General Motors'
My girlfriend is studying to become an architect.	**Mi novia está estudiando para ser arquitecta.** mee noveeya esta estoodeeyando para ser arkeetekta
We're students but we have part-time jobs.	**Somos estudiantes pero trabajamos medio tiempo.** somos estoodeeyantes pero trabahamos medeeyo teeyempo
I'm looking forward to my retirement.	**Ya tengo ganas de retirarme.** ya tengo ganas deh reteerarmeh
accountant	**el contador/la contadora (el/la contable)** el kontador/la kontadora (kontableh)
civil servant	**el funcionario/la funcionaria** el foonseeyonareeyo/la foonseeyonareeya
dentist	**el/la dentista** el/la denteesta
doctor	**el médico/la médica** el medeeko/la medeeka
editor	**el redactor/la redactora** el redaktor/la redaktora
engineer	**el ingeniero/la ingeniera** el eenheneeyero/la eenheneeyera
housewife	**el ama de casa (pl. las amas de casa)** el ama deh kasa (las amas deh kasa)
journalist	**el/la periodista** el/la pereeyodeesta
manager	**el/la gerente** el/la herenteh
mechanic	**el mecánico/la mecánica** el mekaneeko/la mekaneeka
musician	**el músico/la música (la músico)** el mooseeko/la mooseeka (la mooseeko)
pharmacist	**el farmacéutico/la farmacéutica** el farmaseyooteeko/la farmaseyooteeka
physicist	**el físico/la física** el feeseeko/la feeseeka
police officer	**el/la policía** el/la poleeseeya

programmer	**el programador/la programadora**
	el programa*dor*/la programa*dora*
teacher	**el maestro/la maestra** el *may*stro/la *may*stra
salesman/woman	**el vendedor/la vendedora**
	el vende*dor*/la vende*dora*
technician	**el técnico/la técnica** el *tek*neeko/la *tek*neeka
writer	**el escritor/la escritora**
	el eskree*tor*/la eskree*tora*

Meetings and plans

Are you here with anyone?	**¿Está aquí con alguien?**
	es*ta* a*kee* kon algee*yen*?
I'm here on my own.	**Estoy aquí solo.** es*toy* a*kee* *solo*
Are you married or single?	**¿Es casado o soltero?** es ka*sa*do o sol*tero*?
My boyfriend/husband and I are here on vacation.	**Mi novio/marido y yo estamos aquí de vacaciones.** mee no*veeyo*/ma*ree*do ee yo es*ta*mos a*kee* deh vakasee*yo*nes
Can I buy you a drink?	**¿Le puedo invitar algo para tomar?** leh *pwe*do eenvee*tar* *al*go *para* to*mar*?
Would you like to meet for some coffee?	**¿Le gustaría vernos para tomar un café?** leh goosta*reeya* *ver*nos *para* to*mar* oon ka*feh*?
Would you like to go for a walk in the park?	**¿Le gustaría ir a dar una vuelta al parque?** leh goosta*reeya* eer a dar *oona* *vwel*ta al *parkeh*?
Let's go dancing tonight.	**Vamos a bailar hoy en la noche.** *va*mos a bay*lar* oy en la *no*cheh
Call me at my hotel.	**Llámeme a mi hotel.** *l-ya*memeh a mee o*tel*

Countries & languages

Where do you live?	**¿Dónde vive?** *don*deh *vee*veh?
I come from...	**Soy de...** soy deh
I don't speak Spanish very well.	**No hablo español muy bien.** no *a*blo espa*nyol* mwee bee*yen*
I'd like to practice my Spanish.	**Me gustaría practicar mi español.** meh goosta*ree*ya prakee*kar* mee espa*nyol*
Do you speak English?	**¿Habla (usted) inglés?** *a*bla (*oo*sted) een*gles*?
America (U.S.)	**Estados Unidos** es*ta*dos oo*nee*dos
American	**estadounidense** estado-oonee*den*seh
Argentina	**Argentina** arhen*tee*na
Argentinian	**argentino** arhen*tee*no
Chile	**Chile** *chee*leh
Chilean	**chileno** chee*le*no
Colombia	**Colombia** ko*lom*beeya
Colombian	**colombiano** kolombee*ya*no
Costa Rica	**Costa Rica** *kos*ta *ree*ka
Costa Rican	**costarricense** kostarree*sen*seh
Cuba	**Cuba** *koo*ba
Cuban	**cubano** koo*ba*no
Dominican	**dominicano** domeenee*ka*no
Dominican Republic	**República Dominicana** re*poob*leeka domeenee*ka*na
Ecuador	**Ecuador** ekwa*dor*
Ecuadorian	**ecuatoriano** ekwatoree*ya*no
England	**Inglaterra** eengla*ter*ra
English	**inglés** een*gles*
Europe	**Europa** eyoo*ro*pa
European	**europeo** eyoore*pe*yo
France	**Francia** *fran*seeya
French	**francés** fran*ses*

Honduran	**hondureño** ondoo*r*enyo
Honduras	**Honduras** on*doo*ras
Italy	**Italia** ee*ta*leeya
Italian	**italiano** eetaleeya*n*o
Latin America	**América Latina/Latinoamérica** amereeka la*t*eena/lateenoamereeka
Latin American	**latinoamericano** lateenoamere*e*kano
Mexican	**mexicano (mejicano)** mekseekano (meheekano)
Mexico	**México** *m*ekseeko
Nicaragua	**Nicaragua** neekara*g*wa
Nicaraguan	**nicaragüense** neekaragwe*n*seh
North America	**América del Norte** amereeka del *n*orteh
North American	**norteamericano** norteyamereekano
Paraguay	**Paraguay** paragwa*y*
Paraguayan	**paraguayo** paragwayo
Peru	**Perú** pe*r*oo
Peruvian	**peruano** perooano
Puerto Rican	**puertorriqueño/por̦torriqueño** pwertorree*k*enyo/portorree*k*enyo
El Salvador	**El Salvador** el salva*d*or
Salvador(i)an	**salvadoreño** salvado*r*enyo
South America	**Sudamérica/América del Sur** sooda*m*ereeka/amereeka del soor
South American	**sudamericano** soodamereekano
Spain	**España** es*p*anya
Spanish	**español** espan*yo*l
Spanish (Hispanic) America	**Hispanoamérica** eespanoa*m*ereeka
Spanish (Hispanic) American	**hispanoamericano** ee*s*panoamereekano
United States (of America)	**Estados Unidos (de América)** es*t*ados oo*n*eedos (deh a*m*ereeka)
Uruguay	**Uruguay** ooroogwa*y*
Uruguayan	**uruguayo** ooroogwayo
Venezuela	**Venezuela** venes*w*ela
Venezuelan	**venezolano** veneso*l*ano

EATING OUT

What type of cuisine does
this restaurant serve?

**¿Qué clase de cocina sirve este
restaurante?** keh *kla*seh deh ko*see*na
*seer*veh este restaoo*ran*teh?

Can we make a reservation?

**¿Podemos hacer una reservación
(reserva)?** po*de*mos a*ser oo*na
reservasee*yon* (re*ser*ba)?

A reservation for four people
at 8 pm.

**Una reservación (reserva) para cuatro
personas a las ocho de la noche.**
*oo*na reservasee*yon* (re*ser*ba) para *kwa*tro
per*so*nas a las *o*cho deh la *no*cheh

A table for two, please.

Una mesa para dos, por favor.
*oo*na *me*sa *pa*ra dos, por fa*vor*

Do you have a menu in English?

¿Tiene el menú en inglés?
tee*ye*neh el me*noo* en een*gles*?

I'd like to try some typical
regional cooking.

**Quisiera probar unos platos típicos de
la región.** keesee*ye*ra pro*bar oo*nos *pla*tos
*tee*peekos deh la rehee*yon*

What's the difference between
enchiladas and tortillas?

**¿Qué diferencia hay entre las
enchiladas y las tortillas?**
keh deefe*ren*seeya ay *en*treh las enchee*la*das
ee las tor*teel*-yas?

Can you tell me what this is?

¿Me puede decir qué es esto?
me *pwe*deh de*seer* keh es *es*to?

Can you tell me how this
is prepared?

¿Me puede decir cómo se prepara esto?
me *pwe*deh de*seer* *ko*mo seh pre*pa*ra *es*to?

Is the food very hot?

¿Es muy picante la comida?
es mwee pee*kan*teh la ko*mee*da?

How would you like your steak: **¿Cómo quiere el filete: poco cocido,**
rare, medium, or well done?   **término medio (en su punto) o bien**
                                   cocido (muy hecho)? *ko*mo kee*ye*reh el
                                   fee*le*teh: *po*ko ko*see*do, *ter*meeno *me*deeyo
                                   (en soo *poon*to) o bee*yen* ko*see*do (mwee
                                   *e*cho)?

Could you bring another glass?   **¿Podría traer otro vaso?**
                                   po*dree*ya tra*yer* otro va*so*?

Have you any olive oil?   **¿Tiene aceite de oliva?**
                                   *tee*yene a*see*yee*teh* deh o*lee*va?

Black or white coffee, sir?   **¿Café (solo) o café con leche?**
                                   *Ka*feh (*so*lo) o *ka*feh kon *le*cheh?

Could I have the bill, please?   **¿Puede traerme la cuenta, por favor?**
                                   *pwe*deh tra*yer*meh la *kwen*ta, por fa*vor*?

Can I pay with my credit card?   **¿Puedo pagar con mi tarjeta de crédito?**
                                   *pwe*do pa*gar* kon mee tar*he*ta deh *kre*deeto?

What time do you close?   **¿A qué hora cierran?** a keh *o*ra see*ye*rran?

Are you open on Sundays?   **¿Están abiertos los domingos?**
                                   es*tan* abee*ye*rtos los do*meen*gos?

In the restaurant

Flatware/Cutlery

dessert spoon   **la cucharita (cuchara) de postre**
                         la koocha*ree*ta (koo*cha*ra) deh *pos*treh

fork   **el tenedor** el tehneh*dor*

knife   **el cuchillo** el koo*cheel*-yo

soup spoon   **la cuchara sopera** la koo*cha*ra so*pe*ra

spoon   **la cuchara** la koo*cha*ra

teaspoon   **la cucharita (cucharilla)**
                         la koocha*ree*ta (koochа*reel*-ya)

Meals

meal	**la comida** la ko*mee*da
breakfast	**el desayuno** el desa*yoo*no
lunch	**el almuerzo (la comida)** el al*muerzo* (la ko*mee*da)
dinner	**la cena** la *se*na

Menu

cheese	**el queso** el *ke*so
coffee	**el café** el ka*feh*
white	**con leche** con *le*cheh
black	**solo** *so*lo
dessert	**el postre** el *pos*treh
fish dishes	**el pescado** el pes*ka*do
main course	**el plato principal (el segundo plato)** el *pla*to preensee*pal* (el se*goon*do *pla*to)
meat	**la carne** la *kar*neh
menu	**la carta, el menú** la *kar*ta, el me*noo*
fixed-price meal	**el menú del día** el me*noo* del *dee*ya
salad	**la ensalada** la ensa*la*da
soups	**la sopa** la *so*pa
starter	**para empezar (el primer plato)** *pa*ra empe*sar* (el pree*mer pla*to)
tea	**el té** el teh

Service

wine list	**la carta de vinos** la *kar*ta de *vee*nos
bill	**la cuenta** la *kwen*ta
table for two	**la mesa para dos** la *me*sa *pa*ra dos
tip	**la propina** la pro*pee*na
service charge	**el servicio** el ser*vee*seeyo

Staff

waitress	**la mesera (la camarera)** la me*se*ra (la kama*re*ra)

waiter	**el mesero (el camarero)**
	el mesero (el kama*r*ero)
chef	**el cocinero** el kosee*n*ero
manager	**el/la gerente** el/la he*r*enteh

Tableware

cup	**la taza** la *t*asa
glass	**el vaso** el *v*aso
jug of water	**la jarra de agua** la *h*arra de a*g*wa
mayonnaise	**la mayonesa** la mayo*n*esa
napkin	**la servilleta** la servee*l*-yeta
oil	**el aceite** el ase*y*eeteh
pepper	**la pimienta** la peemee*y*enta
plate	**el plato** el *p*lato
salt	**la sal** la sal
sauce	**la salsa** la *s*alsa
saucer	**el plato para la taza**
	el *p*lato *p*ara la *t*asa
seasoning	**los condimentos** los kondee*m*entos
table cloth	**el mantel** el man*t*el
vinegar	**el vinagre** el vee*n*agreh
wine glass	**la copa de vino** la *k*opa deh *v*eeno

Breakfast

butter	**la mantequilla** la mante*k*eel-ya
cereal	**los cereales** los sere*y*ales
coffee	**el café** el ka*f*eh
jelly	**la mermelada** la merme*l*ada
milk	**la leche** la *l*echeh
orange juice	**el jugo (zumo) de naranja**
	el *h*oogo (*th*oomo) deh na*r*anha
sugar	**el azúcar** el a*s*ookar
toast	**el pan tostado (la tostada)**
	el pan tos*t*ado (la tos*t*ada)

Alcoholic drinks

bebida f. **alcohólica** be*bee*da al*ko*leeka	alcoholic drink
cerveza f. ser*ve*sa	beer
champán m. cham*pan*	champagne
coñac m. *ko*nyak (*ko*nyak)	brandy
ginebra f. hee*ne*bra	gin
jerez m. he*res*	sherry
oporto m. o*por*to	port
ron m. ron	rum
tequila f. te*kee*la	tequila
vino m. *vee*no	wine

Food items

aceite m. **de oliva** a*se*yeeteh deh o*lee*va	olive oil
cacao m. ka*ka*yo	cocoa
caramelos mpl. kara*me*los	candy
champiñón m./**seta** f. champee*nyon*/se*ta*	mushroom
chocolate m. choko*la*teh	chocolate
galleta f. gal-*ye*ta	cookie
gelatina f. hela*tee*na	jelly
helado m. e*la*do	ice cream
huevo m. *we*vo	egg
leche f. *le*cheh	milk
mantequilla f. mante*keel*-ya	butter
mermelada f. merme*la*da	jam
miel f. mee*yel*	honey
nata f. *na*ta	cream
pan m. pan	bread
pastel m. pas*tel*	cake
queso m. *ke*so	cheese
salchicha f. sal*chee*cha	sausage
sopa f. *so*pa	soup

zumo m. **de naranja**   *soo*mo deh na*ran*ha   orange juice

Fish and shellfish

almejas fpl. al*me*has	clams
anchoas fpl. an*cho*as	anchovies
atún m. a*toon*	tuna
bacalao m. baka*la*o	cod
cangrejo m. kan*gre*ho	crab
gambas fpl. *gam*bas	shrimp
gambas rebozadas fpl. *gam*bas rebo*sa*das	scampi
langosta f. lan*gos*ta	lobster
lenguado m. len*gwa*do	sole
mejillones mpl. mehee*l-yo*nes	mussels
merluza f. mer*loo*sa	hake
ostras fpl. *os*tras	oysters
salmón m. sal*mon*	salmon
trucha f. *troo*cha	trout

Herbs

acedera f. ase*de*ra	sorrel
ají m. a*hi*	red pepper
ajo m. *a*ho	garlic
canela f. ka*ne*la	cinnamon
estragón m. estra*gon*	tarragon
menta f./**hierbabuena** f. *men*ta/eeyerba*bwe*na	mint
perejil m. pere*hil*	parsley

Nuts

almendras fpl. al*men*dras	almonds
avellanas fpl. avel-*ya*nas	hazel nuts
cacahuetes mpl. kaka*we*tes	peanuts
castañas fpl. kas*ta*nyas	chestnuts
nueces fpl. *nwe*ses	walnuts

Fruit

albaricoques fpl. albaree*k*okes	apricots
ananá(s)/piña f. anan*a*(s)/*peenya*	pineapple
cerezas fpl. se*resas*	cherries
ciruelas fpl. see*r*welas	plums
dátiles mpl. *d*ateeles	dates
frambuesas fpl. fram*bwe*sas	raspberries
fresas fpl. *freh*sas	strawberries
fruta f. *froo*ta	fruit
higos mpl. *ee*gos	figs
limones mpl. lee*mo*nes	lemons
mango m. *ma*ngo	mango
manzanas fpl. man*sa*nas	apples
melocotones mpl. meloko*to*nes	peaches
melón m. me*lon*	melon
naranjas fpl. na*ra*nhas	oranges
plátanos mpl. *pla*tanos	bananas
uva f. *oo*va	grapes

Meat

carne f. **de vaca/buey** *ka*rneh deh *va*ka/bwey	beef
carne f. **de cerdo** *ka*rneh deh *ser*do	pork
carne m. *ka*rneh	meat
conejo m. ko*ne*ho	rabbit
cordero m. **lechal** kor*de*ro le*chal*	lamb
ganso m. *ga*nso	goose
jamón m. ha*mon*	ham
pato m. *pa*to	duck
pavo m. *pa*vo	turkey
pollo m. *pol*-yo	chicken
ternera f. ter*ne*ra	veal
tocino/bacon m. to*see*no/*bay*kon	bacon

Vegetables

alcachofa f. alca*ch*o*f*a	artichoke
apio m. a*p*eeyo	celery
arroz m. a*rros*	rice
berenjena f. beren*h*ena	eggplant
calabacín m. kalaba*seen*	zucchini
cebollas mpl. se*b*ol-yas	onions
col f. kol	cabbage
espinacas fpl. espee*n*akas	spinach
guisantes mpl. gees*a*ntes	peas
judías fpl. hoo*d*eeyas	beans
lechuga f. leh*ch*ooga	lettuce
lentejas fpl. len*t*ehas	lentils
patatas fpl. pa*t*atas	potatoes
pepino m. peh*p*eeno	cucumber
pimientos mpl. peemee*ye*ntos	peppers
tomates mpl. to*m*ates	tomatoes
zanahorias fpl. sanaoreeyas	carrots

Typical dishes and drinks

antojitos mpl. anto*h*eetos	appetizers
arroz m. **con leche** a*rros* kon *l*echeh	rice pudding
caldo m. *k*al/do	a broth-like soup
ceviche m. se*v*eecheh	raw fish with lemon juice
chorizo m. *ch*o*r*eeso	a spicy sausage
cocido m. ko*se*edo	a meat and vegetable stew
gazpacho m. gas*p*acho	a cold tomato soup
paella f. pa*ye*l-ya	a rice dish
mole m. *m*oleh	chili cocoa, and peanut sauce
sangría f. sangreeya	red wine, soda and fruit
tapas fpl. *t*apas	popular bar snacks (Sp)
tortilla f. tor*t*eel-ya	a potato omelet (Sp); a thin pancake (Mex)

Dialog: In the restaurant

Maitre	Buenas noches, señor. Buenas noches, señora. ¿Una mesa para cenar?
Sr. Austen	Sí, por favor. Una mesa para tres. Nuestra hija está por llegar.
Sra. Austen	¿Podríamos sentarnos en aquella mesa de la esquina?
Maitre	Naturalmente, señora.
Sra. Austen	Queremos cenar algo típicamente español esta noche.
Sr. Austen	Así podremos decirles a nuestros amigos en casa lo que pensamos de la comida española.
Maitre	Creo que les gustarán los platos de nuestra carta. ¿Con qué les gustaría empezar?
Sra. Austen	Mi marido y yo tomaremos el caldo gallego y nuestra hija la ensalada.
Maitre	Gracias, señora. ¿Y como plato principal? (¿Y de segundo?)
Sr. Austen	Tengo que probar la paella.
Sra. Austen	Yo voy a probar el pollo al chilindrón; Carmen quiere el bacalao a la riojana.
Maitre	¿Qué verduras quieren usted y su hija, señora?
Sra. Austen	Yo judías verdes y Carmen tomará los chícharos (guisantes).
Maitre	Gracias, señora. El mesero (camarero) les atenderá cuando quieran pedir los postres. ¿Desea beber vino, señor?
Sr. Austen	Sí, por favor. Una botella de vino tinto.
Maitre	Gracias, señor. Espero que disfruten de la cena.

Head waiter	*Good evening, sir. Good evening, madam. A table for dinner?*
Mr. Austen	*Yes, please. A table for three. Our daughter's just coming.*
Mrs. Austen	*Could we have that table over there in the corner?*
Head waiter	*Certainly, madam.*
Mrs. Austen	*We want to have something typically Spanish this evening.*
Mr. Austen	*Then we can tell our friends back home what we think of Spanish food.*
Head waiter	*I think you will like the dishes on our menu. What would you like to start with?*
Mrs. Austen	*My husband and I will have the caldo gallego and our daughter will have the salad.*
Head waiter	*Thank you, madam. And for the main course?*
Mr. Austen	*I must have paella.*
Mrs. Austen	*I'm going to try the chicken dish with red peppers and ham. Carmen wants the cod with tomatoes.*
Head waiter	*What vegetables would you and your daughter like, madam?*
Mrs. Austen	*I'll have green beans and Carmen will have peas.*
Head waiter	*Thank you madam. The waiter will take your order when you are ready for dessert. Would you like wine, sir?*
Mr. Austen	*Yes, please. A bottle of red wine.*
Head waiter	*Thank you, sir. I hope you enjoy your meal.*

MONEY

Can I cash traveller's checks here?	**¿Puedo cambiar cheques de viajero (viaje) aquí?** *pwe*do kam*bee*yar *che*kes deh veeya*he*yar (bee*ya*he) a*kee*?
Do you charge commission?	**¿Cobran comisión?** *kob*ran komee*see*yon?
How much do you charge to cash traveller's checks?	**¿Cuánto cobran por cambiar cheques de viajero (viaje)?** *kwan*to *kob*ran por kam*bee*yar *che*kes deh veeya*he*ro (bee*ya*he)?
Can I change these pesos for pounds?	**¿Puedo cambiar estos pesos por dólares?** *pwe*do kam*bee*yar *es*tos *pe*sos por *do*lares?
Can I see your passport, please?	**¿Puedo ver su pasaporte, por favor?** *pwe*do ver soo pasa*por*teh, por fa*vor*?
How would you like the money, sir?	**¿Cómo quiere el dinero, señor?** *ko*mo *kee*yere el dee*ne*ro, se*nyor*?
Fifty dollars in tens, forty in fives and the rest in ones, please.	**Cincuenta dólares en billetes de diez, cuarenta de cinco y el resto de un dólar, por favor.** seen*kwen*ta *do*lares en bee-*ye*tes deh dee*yes*, kwa*ren*ta deh *seen*ko ee el *res*to deh oon *do*lar, por fa*vor*
I'd like to exchange some money please.	**Me gustaría cambiar dinero, por favor.** meh goosta*ree*ya kam*bee*yar dee*ne*ro, por fa*vor*
Can you tell me what the exchange rate for pesos/euros is?	**¿Me puede decir a cómo está el peso/euro contra el dólar?** meh *pwe*deh de*seer* a *ko*mo es*ta* el *pe*so/e*yoo*ro *kon*tra el *do*lar?
What is the fee for exchanging money?	**¿Cuánto es la comisión por cambiar dinero?** *kwan*to es la komee*see*yon por kam*bee*yar dee*ne*ro?

In the bank

automatic teller machine	**cajero automático** kahero aootomateeko
bank clerk	**el empleado de banco** el empleyado deh *ban*ko
bank manager	**el director de banco** el deerek*tor* deh *ban*ko
bank notes	**los billetes de banco** los bil*-yetes deh *ban*ko
buy/sell	**comprar/vender** kom*prar*/ven*der*
cash a check	**cobrar un cheque** ko*brar* oon *che*keh
change money	**cambiar dinero** kambee*yar* dee*ne*ro
check	**el cheque** el *che*keh
coins	**las monedas** las mo*ne*das
commission	**la comisión** la komeesee*yon*
counter	**el mostrador** el mostra*dor*
credit card	**la tarjeta de crédito** la tar*he*ta deh *kre*deeto
exchange rate	**la tasa de cambio** la *ta*sa deh *kam*beeyo
identification	**la identificación** la eedenteefeekasee*yon*
passport number	**el número de pasaporte** el *noo*mero deh pasa*por*teh
receipt	**el recibo** el re*see*bo
signature	**la firma** la *feer*ma
traveller's checks	**los cheques de viajero** los *che*kes deh veeya*he*ro (beeya*he*)

Dialog: In the bank

Empleado	Buenos días.
Sr. Austen	Buenos días. ¿Podría cambiar unos cheques de viajero (viaje) aquí?
Empleado	Sí, naturalmente, señor. ¿Son de euros?
Sr. Austen	Sí. Quislera cambiar cien euros.
Empleado	Estos cheques de viajero (viaje) son de otro banco.
Sr. Austen	¿No se pueden cambiar estos cheques aquí?
Empleado	Sí podemos cambiárselos señor, pero tendrá que pagar por el servicio.
Sr. Austen	¿Quiere decir una comisión?
Empleado	Sí. Cargamos un uno por ciento con un mínimo de cinco euros. Le costará cinco euros cambiar el número que desee de cheques de viajero (viaje) hasta quinientos euros. Si cambia seiscientos euros, tendrá que pagar seis euros. Si va usted directamente a su banco, se los cambiarán sin cobrarle comisión.
Sr. Austen	Ya iré la próxima vez. Hoy los cambiaré aquí y pagaré la comisión.
Empleado	¿Cómo quiere el dinero?
Sr. Austen	Ochenta en billetes de diez y el resto de cinco.
Empleado	Cien euros menos cinco euros de comisión son noventa y cinco euros. Así que serán ocho de diez y tres de cinco. Gracias, señor. ¿Le puedo dar un consejo?
Mr. Austen	¡Por supuesto!
Bank clerk	Yo que usted consideraría usar los cajeros automáticos. Dan el mejor tipo de cambio y son mucho más fáciles de usar.

Bank clerk	Good morning.
Mr. Austen	Good morning. Can I cash some traveller's checks here, please?
Bank clerk	Yes, of course, sir. Are they in euros?
Mr. Austen	Yes, they are. I want to cash 100 euros.
Bank clerk	These traveller's checks are from a different bank.
Mr. Austen	Isn't it possible to cash these checks here?
Bank clerk	We can cash them for you, sir; but you will have to pay for the service.
Mr. Austen	Commission, you mean.
Bank clerk	Yes. We charge 1% with a 5 euro minimum. It will cost you 5 euros to cash any number of travellers checks up to 500 euros. If you cash 600 euros, you pay 6 euros. If you take these checks to your own bank, they will cash them without charge.
Mr. Austen	I will next time. Today I'll cash them here and pay the commission.
Bank clerk	How would you like the money, sir?
Mr. Austen	I'll have eighty in ten-euro notes and the rest in fives.
Bank clerk	100 euros less 5-euro commission is 95 euros. That's eight tens and three fives. Thank you, sir. Can I give you some advice, sir?
Mr. Austen	Yes, please do.
Bank clerk	You might consider using an automatic teller machine. They give the best exchange rates and are much easier to use.

SHOPPING

Have you a list of shops specializing in…?	**¿Tienen una lista de tiendas especializadas en…?** teeyenen oona leesta deh teeyendas espeseeyaleesadas en?
Do you sell toys?	**¿Venden juguetes?** venden hooghetes?
Have you a doll for a girl of six?	**¿Tienen muñecas para una niña de seis años?** teeyenen moonyekas para oona neenya deh seys anyos?
How much is this?	**¿Cuánto vale esto?** kwanto valeh esto?
How much is it a meter (a kilo, etc.)?	**¿A cuánto es el metro (el kilo, etc.)?** a kwanto es el metro (el keelo, etc.)?
Could you tell me where I could find a shop selling maps?	**¿Podría decirme donde hay una tienda que venda mapas (planos)?** podreeya deseermeh dondeh ay oona teeyenda keh venda mapas (planos)?
Could you recommend a good shop for china and glass?	**¿Podría recomendarme una buena tienda de porcelana y cristalería?** podreeya rekomendarmeh oona bwena teeyenda deh porselana ee kreestalereeya?

Paying

Could you put it in a bag, please?	**¿Puede ponerlo en (darme) una bolsa, por favor?** pwedeh ponerlo en (darmeh) oona bolsa, por favor?
Can I change this for a larger one, please?	**¿Puedo cambiarlo por uno más grande, por favor?** pwedo kambeeyarlo por oono mas grandeh, por favor?
Could you wrap it up, please?	**¿Me lo puede envolver, por favor?** meh lo pwedeh envolver, por favor?

Can I pay with credit card?	**¿Puedo pagar con tarjeta de crédito?** *pwedo pagar kon tarheta deh kredeeto?*
Can I pay for it now and pick it up later?	**¿Puedo pagarlo ahora y pasar a recogerlo más tarde?** *pwedo pagarlo aora ee pasar a rekoherlo mas tardeh?*
Can you deliver it to the hotel?	**¿Puede enviarlo al hotel?** *pwedeh enveeyarlo al otel?*
Is sales tax/VAT included?	**¿Está incluído el I.V.A. (Impuesto sobre el valor añadido)?** *esta eenklooyeedo el eeva (eempwesto sobreh el valor anyadeedo)?*
Is there a guarantee?	**¿Tiene garantía?** *teeyeneh garanteeya?*
Can I order this by Internet?	**¿Puedo encargar esto por Internet?** *pwedo enkargar esto por eenternet?*

Containers

una caja de (a box/carton of):	**cerillos (cerillas)** (matches), **puros** (cigars), **chocolates (bombones)** (chocolates), **leche** (milk), **jugo (zumo) de frutas** (fruit juice), **crema (nata)** (cream)
un paquete de (a packet of):	**cigarrillos** (cigarettes), **galletas** (biscuits), **servilletas de papel** (paper napkins)
una bolsa de (a bag of):	**papas (patatas) fritas** (chips), **caramelos** (candy)
una lata de (a tin/can of):	**sopa** (soup), **pintura** (paint), **grasa** (grease), **cerveza** (beer)
un bote de (a pot of):	**jalea (mermelada)** (jelly), **mermelada de naranja** (marmalade)
una botella de (a bottle of):	**vino** (wine), **limonada** (lemonade)
un saco de (a sack of):	**papas (patatas)** (potatoes), **carbón** (coal), **madera** (wood)

Shops and stores

Shops

antique shop	**el anticuario**	el anteekwareeyo
baker's	**la panadería**	la panadereeya
bookstore	**la librería**	la leebrereeya
butcher's	**la carnicería**	la karneesereeya
cake shop	**la pastelería**	la pastelereeya
camera shop	**la tienda de fotografía** la teeyenda de fotgrafeeya	
china and glass shop	**la cristalería**	la kreestalereeya
dress shop	**la boutique**	la booteek
dry cleaner's	**la tintorería**	la teentorereeya
fish shop	**la pescadería**	la peskadereeya
flower shop	**la florería (floristería)** la florereeya (floreestereeya)	
furniture shop	**la tienda de muebles** la teeyenda deh mwebles	
greengrocer's	**la verdulería**	la verdoolereeya
grocer's	**el ultramarino**	el ooltramareeno
hair salon	**la peluquería**	la pelookereeya
hardware store	**la ferretería**	la ferretereeya
jewelry store	**la joyería**	la hoyereeya
liquor store	**la tienda de licores (la bodega)** la teeyenda deh leekores (la bodega)	
menswear shop	**la tienda de ropa de caballero** la teeyenda deh ropa deh cabal-yero	
music store	**la tienda de discos** la teeyenda deh deeskos	
newsstand	**el puesto de periódicos (quiosco)** el pwesto deh pereeyodeekos (keeyosko)	
pharmacy	**la farmacia**	la farmaseeya
shoe store	**la zapatería**	la sapatereeya
stationer's	**la papelería**	la papelereeya

tobacco shop	**el estanquillo (estanco)** el estan*keel*-yo (es*tan*ko)
toy store	**la juguetería** la hoogete*ree*ya
travel agency	**la agencia de viajes** la a*hen*seeya deh vee*ya*jes

Other establishments

department store	**el almacén (los grandes almacenes)** el alma*sen* (los *gran*des alma*the*nes)
gas station	**la gasolinera** la gasolee*ne*ra
post office	**el correo (correos)** el ko*rre*yo (ko*rre*yos)
supermarket	**el supermercado** el soopermer*ka*do

Camera

Can you repair this camera?	**¿Puede componer esta cámara?** *pwe*deh kompo*ner* esta *ka*mara?
Do you have film for this video camera?	**¿Tiene película para esta cámara de video (vídeo)?** tee*ye*neh pe*lee*koola *para* esta *ka*mara deh vee*de*yo?
camera	**la cámara** la *ka*mara
camera film	**el rollo de película** el *rrol*-yo deh pe*lee*koola
video camera	**la cámara de video (vídeo)** la *ka*mara deh vee*de*yo (*vee*deyo)
exposures	**las exposiciones (fotografías)** las eksposeesee*yo*nes (fotogra*fee*yas)
15-minute video film	**una película de video (vídeo) de quince minutos** *oo*na pe*lee*koola deh vee*de*yo (*vee*deyo) deh *keen*seh mee*noo*tos

Gas station

Please fill up the tank.	**¿Me puede llenar el tanque, por favor?** meh *pwe*deh l-ye*nar* el *tan*keh, por fa*vor*?

Is this gas station self-service?	**¿Esta gasolinera es de autoservicio?** *esta gasoleenera es deh aootoserveeseeyo?*
regular/super	**regular/super** *regoolar/sooper*
unleaded/diesel	**sin plomo/diesel** *seen plomo/deesel*

Newstand

newspaper	**el periódico** el *pereeyodeeko*
magazine	**la revista** la *reveesta*
cigarettes	**los cigarrillos** los *seegarreel-yos*

Pharmacy

analgesic	**el analgésico** el *analheseeko*
aspirin	**la aspirina** la *aspeereena*
bandages	**las vendas** las *vendas*
compresses	**las compresas** las *kompresas*
condom	**el condón/el preservativo** el *kondon*/el *preservateevo*
cotton wool	**el algodón** el *algodon*
disinfectant	**el desinfectante** el *deseenfektanteh*
ear drops	**las gotas para los oídos** las *gotas para* los *oyeedos*
eye drops	**las gotas para los ojos** las *gotas para* los *ohos*
gauze	**la gasa** la *gasa*
insect cream	**la loción contra insectos** la *loseeyon kontra eensektos*
ointment	**la pomada** la *pomada*
for cuts	**para cortadas (cortes)** *para kortadas (kortes)*
for burns	**para quemaduras** *para kemadooras*
oxygenated water	**el agua oxigenada** el *agwa okseehenada*
plaster/bandage	**la bandita (tirita)** la *bandeeta (teereeta)*
sanitary towels	**los paños higiénicos (las compresas)** los *panyos eeheeyeneekos (las kompresas)*

sticking plaster/adhesive bandage	**la cinta adhesiva (el esparadrapo)** la *seen*ta adhe*seeva* (el esparadrapo)
suppository	**el supositorio** el sooposee*to*reeyo
syrup	**el jarabe** el ha*ra*beh
thermometer	**el termómetro** el ter*mo*metro
toothpaste	**la pasta de dientes** la *pas*ta deh dee*yen*tes

Post office

How much to send a postcard to the U.S.?	**¿Cuánto cuesta mandar una postal a los Estados Unidos?** *kwan*to *kwes*ta man*dar oo*na pos*tal* a los es*ta*dos oo*nee*dos?
I want to send this parcel to Canada.	**Quiero mandar este paquete a Canadá.** kee*ye*ro man*dar es*teh pa*ke*teh a kana*da*
stamp	**la estampilla/el timbre (el sello)** la estam*peel*-ya/el *teem*breh (el *sel*-yo)
letter	**la carta** la *kar*ta
postcard	**la postal** la pos*tal*
parcel	**el paquete** el pa*ke*teh
by airmail	**por correo aéreo** por ko*rre*yo a*ye*reyo
registered mail	**correo registrado (certificado)** ko*rre*yo rehees*tra*do (therteefee*ka*do)

Souvenirs

book	**el libro** el *lee*bro
blanket	**la cobija (manta)** la ko*bee*ha (*man*ta)
castanets	**las castañuelas** las kasta*nywe*las
ceramics	**la cerámica** la se*ra*meeka
fan	**el abanico** el aba*nee*ko
guitar	**la guitarra** la ghee*ta*rra
poster	**el póster** el *pos*ter
hat	**el sombrero** el som*bre*ro
tee shirt	**la camiseta** la kamee*se*ta
textiles	**los textiles** los teks*tee*les

Dialog: Going shopping

Sra. Austen	¿Qué te parece esta tienda?
Dependiente	Tenemos una gran variedad de productos tradicionales aquí.
Sr. Austen	Que no se nos olvide que tenemos que llevarle un souvenir a mi madre.
Sra. Austen	Mira toda esta exposición de cerámica. ¿Crees que a tu madre le gustaría algo así?
Dependiente	Tengo muchos tamaños y estilos. Tenemos platos de todas las regiones del país.
Sra. Austen	Los colores son hermosísimos.Quizá le compre uno a mi tía.
Sr. Austen	No estoy seguro de que a mi madre le vaya a gustar este tipo de cosas.
Sra. Austen	Está bien. ¿Qué tal uno de estos chales?
Dependiente	¡El trabajo es increíble! ¡La tela es de lo más suave!
Sr. Austen	No estoy seguro de que jamás se lo pondría.
Sra. Austen	¿Qué tal uno de estos abanicos?
Sr. Austen	¿No tiene algo más barato?
Dependiente	Pero considere todo el trabajo que tienen. Son hechos a mano.
Sr. Austen	¿Ves algo más que le podríamos llevar a mi madre?
Dependiente	Aquí hay mucha joyería. Vamos a ver. Tenemos collares, aretes (pendientes) y pulseras.
Sr. Austen	No creo que mi madre use mucha joyería. No creo que le gustara nada de eso tampoco.
Sra. Austen	¡Yo creo que están preciosos! Me voy a comprar una pulsera para mí.
Sr. Austen	¿Pero qué va a pasar con lo que le tenemos que llevar a mi madre?
Dependiente	Yo creo que a este paso va a terminar con una esferita de cristal.

Mrs. Austen	*How about this store?*
Assistant	*We offer lots of traditional things here.*
Mr. Austen	*Don't forget that we have to get a souvenir for my mother.*
Mrs. Austen	*Look at this pottery display. Do you think your mother would like something like this?*
Assistant	*I have lots of sizes and styles. We have plates from every region of the country.*
Mrs. Austen	*The colors are gorgeous. Maybe I'll get one for my aunt.*
Mr. Austen	*I'm not sure that my mother would like that kind of thing.*
Mrs. Austen	*Okay. How about these shawls?*
Assistant:	*The craftsmanship is amazing! The fabric is so soft!*
Mr. Austen	*I'm not sure that she'd ever wear it.*
Mrs. Austen	*What about one of these fans?*
Mr. Austen	*Do you have anything cheaper?*
Assistant:	*But consider all the work that went into them! They're handmade.*
Mr. Austen	*Do you see anything else we could get my mother?*
Assistant	*Over here is a lot of jewelry. Let's see. We have necklaces, earrings, and bracelets.*
Mr. Austen	*I don't think that my mother wears a lot of jewelry. I'm not sure that she'd like those either.*
Mrs. Austen	*I think they're adorable! I'm going to buy a bracelet for myself.*
Mr. Austen	*But what about something for my mother?*
Assistant	*I think at this rate that she's going to end up with a snowglobe.*

Departments

Ropa de señora (ladieswear): **vestidos** (dresses), **blusas** (blouses), **faldas** (skirts), **abrigos** (coats), **impermeables** (raincoats)

Ropa de caballero (menswear): **trajes** (suits), **sacos (americanas)** (jackets), **pantalones** (pants/trousers), **abrigos** (overcoats), **impermeables** (raincoats), **camisas** (shirts), **corbatas** (ties), **calcetines** (socks)

Ropa de niños (childrenswear): **chaquetas y pantalones para niños** (jackets and pants for boys), **vestidos y faldas para niñas** (dresses and skirts for girls)

Calzado (footwear): **botas** (boots), **zapatos** (shoes), **sandalias** (sandals), **pantuflas (zapatillas)** (slippers)

Medias y calcetines (hosiery): **medias** (stockings), **pantimedias (medias)** (tights), **calcetines** (socks)

Ropa deportiva (sportswear): **ropa de playa** (beachwear), **ropa (de) sport** (leisurewear)

Productos de belleza: (cosmetics) **agua de colonia** (toilet water), **jabón de tocador** (toilet soap), **polvos para la cara** (face powder), **lápiz (barra) de labios** (lipstick)

Porcelana y cristalería: (china and glassware) **tazas** (cups), **platitos** (saucers), **platos** (plates), **platones (fuentes)** (dishes), **jarrones** (vases), **vasos/copas** (glasses)

Ropa blanca (household linen): **sábanas** (sheets), **fundas de almohadas** (pillow cases), **cobijas (mantas)** (blankets), **manteles** (table cloths)

Utensilios de cocina: (kitchenware) **cacerolas** (saucepans), **sartenes** (frying pans), **charolas (bandejas)** (trays)

Joyería (jewelry): **collares** (necklaces), **anillos** (rings), **aretes (pendientes)** (earrings)

Accesorios (accessories):	**bolsos de señora** (handbags), **bufandas y pañuelos** (scarves), **guantes** (gloves), **paraguas** (umbrellas)
Mercería (fabric store):	**lana** (wool), **agujas de tejer (hacer punto)** (knitting needles), **hilo** (thread), **alfileres y agujas** (pins and needles)
Telas (dress fabrics):	**algodón** (cotton), **lana** (wool), **seda** (silk), **telas para trajes** (suitings)
Artículos de viaje: (travel goods)	**maletas** (suitcases), **baúles** (trunks), **bolsas** (bags), **portafolios (maletines)** (brief cases)
Artículos de escritorio: (stationery)	**papel de escribir** (writing paper), **plumas** (pens), **máquinas de escribir** (typewriters), **cuadernos** (notebooks)
Tapicería (furnishings):	**cortinas** (curtains), **alfombras** (carpets), **cojines** (cushions)
Relojería (clocks and watches):	**despertadores** (alarm clocks), **relojes de pulsera** (wrist watches)
Radio y televisión: (radio and television)	**sistemas de estéreo** (stereo systems), **radios portátiles** (portable radios)
Electrodomésticos: (household appliances)	**refrigeradores (frigoríficos)** (refrigerators), **hornos microondas** (microwave ovens), **aspiradoras** (vacuum cleaners)
Can you tell me where the men's clothing is?	**¿Me puede decir donde está la ropa de caballero?** meh *pwe*deh de*seer don*deh es*ta* la *ro*pa deh kabal*-yero*?
I'm looking for an umbrella	**Estoy buscando un paraguas.** es*toy* boos*kan*do oon para*g*was
Do you sell cosmetics?	**¿Venden cosméticos?** *ven*den kos*mee*teekos?
Can I pay for these here?	**¿Puedo pagar esto aquí?** *pwe*do pa*gar* esto a*kee*?

In the store

Building

basement	**el sótano**	el *so*tano
doors	**las puertas**	las *pwer*tas
elevator	**el ascensor**	el as-sen*sor*
emergency exit	**la salida de emergencia**	la sa*lee*da deh emer*hen*seeya
entrance/exit	**la entrada/salida**	la en*tra*da/sa*lee*da
escalator	**la escalera eléctrica (mecánica)**	la eska*le*ra e*lek*treeka (me*ka*neeka)
floors	**las plantas**	las *plan*tas
first floor	**la planta baja**	la *plan*ta *ba*ha
second floor	**la primera planta**	la pree*mer*a *plan*ta
third floor	**la segunda planta**	la se*goon*da *plan*ta
main door	**la puerta principal**	la *pwer*ta preensee*pal*
main entrance	**la entrada principal**	la en*tra*da preensee*pal*
rear entrance	**la entrada trasera**	la en*tra*da tra*se*ra
side door	**la puerta lateral**	la *pwer*ta late*ral*
side entrance	**la entrada lateral**	la en*tra*da late*ral*
stairs	**las escaleras**	las eska*le*ras
shop window	**el escaparate**	el eskapa*ra*teh

Counter

assistant	**el dependiente/la dependienta**	el dependee*yen*teh/la dependee*yen*ta
bag	**la bolsa**	la *bol*sa
by check	**con cheque**	kon *che*keh
cash register	**la caja**	la *ka*ha
counter	**el mostrador**	el mostra*dor*
exchange goods	**cambiar artículos**	kambee*yar* ar*tee*koolos
display	**la exposición**	la eksposee*see*yon
in cash	**en efectivo**	en efek*tee*vo
to pay	**pagar**	pa*gar*

receipt	**el recibo** el re*see*bo
with credit card	**con tarjeta de crédito** kon tar*het*a deh *kred*eeto
to wrap	**envolver** envol*ver*

Departments

childrenswear	**la ropa de niños** la *r*opa deh *nee*nyos
china and glass	**la porcelana y la cristalería** la porse*lan*a ee la kreestale*ree*ya
clocks and watches	**la relojería** la relohe*ree*ya
cosmetics	**la perfumería** la perfoome*ree*ya
dress material	**las telas para ropa** las *tel*as *par*a *r*opa
fabrics	**los tejidos** los te*heed*os
footwear	**la zapatería** la sapate*ree*ya
furniture	**los muebles** los *mw*ebles
hosiery	**las medias y los calcetines** las *med*eeyas ee los kalse*teen*es
jewelry	**la joyería** la hoye*ree*ya
kitchenware	**los utensilios de cocina** los ootensee*leey*os deh ko*seen*a
ladieswear	**la ropa de señora** la *r*opa deh se*ny*ora
menswear	**la ropa de caballero** la *r*opa deh kaba*l-yer*o
music	**los discos** los *dees*kos
pets	**los animales domésticos** los anee*mal*es do*mest*ockos
radio and television	**el (la) radio y la televisión** el (la) *r*adeeyo ee la televeese*eey*on
sports equipment	**los deportes** los de*por*tes
sportswear	**la ropa de deportes** la *r*opa deh de*por*tes
stationery	**la papelería** la papele*ree*ya
toys	**la juguetería** la hooghete*ree*ya

Sale

sale	**las rebajas** las re*ba*has
discount	**el descuento** el des*kwen*to

Dialog: In the department store

Sr. Austen	Perdone, ¿podría decirme dónde puedo comprar pañuelos de caballero, por favor?
Dependiente	Departamento de caballeros, segunda planta, señor.
Sra. Austen	¿Dónde puedo encontrar ropa de playa?
Dependiente	Ropa de señora, primera planta, señora.
Carmen	¿Los baños (servicios)?
Dependiente	Los baños (servicios) de señora están en la cuarta planta, señora. Puede subir en el ascensor que hay allí.
Joven	¿A qué hora cierran ustedes?
Dependiente	A las seis.
Joven	¿Todos los días?
Dependiente	No, señor; los jueves, viernes y sábados estamos abiertos hasta las ocho.
Extranjero	¿Aceptan cheques de viajero (viaje)?
Dependiente	Si son en euros, sí, señor.
Extranjero	¿Y tarjetas de crédito?
Dependiente	Sí, todas las tarjetas principales (más conocidas).
Extranjero	Muchas gracias. Ah, otra cosa; ¿tienen ustedes un departamento donde vendan piezas para rasuradoras (maquinillas de afeitar) eléctricas?
Dependiente	Tendrá que ir al departamento de electro-domésticos, en el sótano, señor. Baje por esas escaleras, voltee (gire) a la derecha y verá el mostrador a la izquierda.
Extranjero	Muchas gracias.

Mr. Austen	Excuse me, could you tell me where I can find men's handkerchiefs, please?
Assistant	Men's department on the third floor, sir.
Mrs. Austen	Where can I find beachwear?
Assistant	Ladieswear, second floor, madam.
Carmen	The restroom?
Assistant	The ladies' restroom is on the fifth floor, madam. You can go up in the elevator over there.
Young man	What time do you close?
Assistant	Six o'clock.
Young man	Every day?
Assistant	No, sir; on Thursdays, Fridays and Saturdays we're open till eight.
Foreigner	Do you accept traveller's checks here?
Assistant	If they are in euros, yes, sir.
Foreigner	And credit cards too?
Assistant	Yes, all the main credit cards.
Foreigner	Thank you very much. Oh, one more thing: have you a department where they sell spare parts for electric shavers?
Assistant	That will be in electrical goods in the basement, sir. Go down those stairs over there, turn right and you'll see the counter on the left.
Foreigner	Thank you very much.

CLOTHING

Where could I find a pair of boots like these?

¿Dónde podría encontrar un par de botas como éstas? *dondeh* podreeya enkon*trar* oon par deh *botas komo* estas?

Are there any shops that specialize in children's clothes?

¿Hay alguna tienda especializada en ropa de niños? ay al*goona* tee*yenda* espeseeyalee*sada* en *ropa* deh *neenyos?*

The sleeves are too long.

Las mangas están (son) demasiado largas. las *mangas* es*tan* (son) demasee*yado largas*

The pockets are too small.

Los bolsillos están (son) demasiado pequeños. los bol*seel-yos* es*tan* (son) demasee*yado* pe*kenyos*

The lapels are too wide.

Las solapas están (son) demasiado anchas. las solapas es*tan* (son) demasee*yado anchas*

The jacket is too big.

El saco (La chaqueta) está (es) demasiado grande. el *sako* (la cha*keta)* es*ta* (es) demasee*yado grandeh*

The trousers are too short.

Los pantalones están (son) demasiado cortos. los panta*lones* es*tan* (son) demasee*yado kortos*

Can you shorten/lengthen the sleeves?

¿Pueden acortar/alargar las mangas? *pweden* akor*tar*/alar*gar* las *mangas?*

Can you take in/let out the hem?

¿Pueden coger (meter)/sacar el dobladillo? *pweden* ko*her* (me*ter*)/sa*kar* el dobla*deel*-yo?

Can you alter the collar?	**¿Pueden cambiar el cuello?** pweden kambeeyar el kwel-yo?
Can you change the buttons?	**¿Pueden cambiar los botones?** pweden kambeeyar los botones?
Can you take in/let out the waist?	**¿Pueden coger (meter)/sacar la cintura?** pweden koher (meter)/sakar la seentoora?
Haven't you got this dress in a darker blue?	**¿Tiene este vestido en un azul más oscuro?** teeyeneh este vesteedo en oon asool mas oskooro?
Have you got this blouse in any other colors?	**¿Tiene esta blusa en otros colores?** teeyeneh esta bloosa en otros kolores?
Have you got a blouse in a larger size?	**¿Tiene una blusa en una talla más grande?** teeyeneh oona bloosa en oona tal-ya mas grandeh?
Have you got a blouse to match this skirt?	**¿Tiene una blusa que haga juego con esta falda?** teeyene oona bloosa keh aga hwego kon esta falda?
Could I change this for a size smaller?	**¿Podría cambiar éste por una talla más chica (menor)?** podreeya kambeeyar este por oona tal-ya mas cheeka (menor)?

Clothing sizes

(Shirt) What size, sir?	**¿Qué talla, señor?** keh tal-ya, senyor?
(Shoes) What size, sir?	**¿Qué número, señor?** keh noomero, senyor?
(Dress) What size, madam?	**¿Qué tamaño (talla), señora?** keh tamanyo (tal-ya), senyora?

Colors

beige	**beige** bej (beyj)
black	**negro** *ne*gro
blue	**azul** a*sool*
brown	**café (marrón)** *ka*feh (ma*rron*)
fuchsia	**fucsia** *fook*seeya
gold	**dorado** do*ra*do
green	**verde** *ver*deh
grey	**gris** grees
khaki	**caqui** *ka*kee
mauve	**lila (malva)** *lee*la (*mal*va)
orange	**naranja** na*ran*ha
pink	**rosa** *ro*sa
red	**rojo** *ro*ho
silver	**plateado** plate*ya*do
white	**blanco** *blan*ko
yellow	**amarillo** ama*reel*-yo
a red pleated skirt	**una falda roja plisada** *oo*na *fal*da *ro*ha plee*sa*da
a light green silk dress	**un vestido de seda verde claro** oon ves*tee*do deh *se*da *ver*deh *kla*ro
black patent leather shoes	**unos zapatos de charol negros** *oo*nos sa*pa*tos deh cha*rol ne*gros

Materials

algodón	cotton	**hilo**	linen
ante	suede	**lana**	wool
charol	patent leather	**nilon**	nylon
cheviot	cheviot	**pana**	corduroy
crepé (crespón)	crepe	**poliéster**	polyester
cuero	leather	**popelina**	poplin
estambre	worsted	**rayón**	rayon
fieltro	felt	**satín (satén)**	satin
franela	flannel	**seda**	silk
gasa	gauze	**terciopelo**	velvet

Items of clothing

abrigo	overcoat	**shorts**	shorts
bata de baño (albornoz)	bathrobe	**sombrero**	hat
		traje de baño	trunks, swimsuit
bata	dressing gown		
blusa	blouse	**traje**	suit
brasier (sujetador)	bra	**vestido de noche**	evening dress
		vestido	dress/frock
bufanda	scarf		
calcetines	socks	Footwear	
calzoncillos	underwear (pants)	**botas**	boots
		de tacón alto	high heels
calzones (bragas)	panties	de tacón bajo	low heels
camisa	shirt	**pantuflas** (zapatillas)	slippers
camiseta	undershirt		
camisón	nightdress	**sandalias**	sandals
capa	cape	**zapatos** de deporte	sports shoes
chaleco	waistcoat		
corbata	tie	Accessories	
falda	skirt	**bolsillo**	pocket
guantes	gloves	**botón**	button
impermeable	raincoat	**cinturón**	belt
lencería	lingerie	**cremallera**	zip
medias	stockings	**cuello**	collar
pantalones	pants	**dobladillo**	hem
pantalones vaqueros	jeans	**faja**	sash
		forro	lining
pantimedias (medias)	tights	**hebilla**	buckle
		manga	sleeve
pijama	pajamas	**olán (volante)**	frill
ropa interior	underwear	**puño**	cuff
saco (americana)	jacket	**solapa**	lapel

Dialog: Shopping for clothes

Dependiente	Buenos días, señor. ¿En qué puedo servirle?
Sr. Austen	Quisiera ver uno de los trajes del escaparate. Es azul.
Dependiente	¿Es éste señor?
Sr. Austen	Sí, ése es.
Dependiente	¿Qué talla usa?
Sr. Austen	No estoy seguro. Cada vez que me compro un traje es distinta.
Dependiente	No se preocupe caballero. Puedo tomar sus medidas. Primero su pecho: treinta y ocho pulgadas. Ahora la cintura: treinta y ocho también. Ahora el largo de pierna: treinta y cuatro. Este traje debería de quedarle bien, señor.
Sra. Austen	Pruébate primero el saco (la chaqueta), John.
Dependiente	Las mangas le quedan un poco largas.
Sra. Austen	¿Tiene algo más claro, en gris, por ejemplo?
Dependiente	Sí, tenemos esos trajes en gris; éstos en café (marrón); y aquéllos verdes de allí. ¿Qué le parece éste?
Sr. Austen	Me gusta. La tela es muy suave.
Sra. Austen	No me gustan los bolsillos; están demasiado grandes. Los pantalones están demasiado estrechos y no tienen valenciana (vuelta).
Dependiente	Hoy en día muchos trajes tienen bolsillos grandes. Los pantalones rara vez llevan valenciana (vuelta). ¿Qué opina de este traje gris con raya, señor?
Sr. Austen	No, no me gustan los trajes con rayas. ¿Tiene sacos (americanas) de sport?
Dependiente	Los sacos (Las americanas) están en aquel departamento, señor.
Sr. Austen	Creo que voy a ir a echarles una ojeada.
Dependiente	Muy bien, señor.

Assistant	Good morning, sir. Can I help you?
Mr. Austen	I'd like to see one of the suits in the window. It's blue.
Assistant	Is it this one, sir?
Mr. Austen	Yes, it is.
Assistant	What size to you take?
Mr Austen	I'm not sure. It changes every time I buy a suit.
Assistant	Don't worry, sir. I can measure you. First your chest – thirty-eight inches. Now your waist – that's thirty-eight too. Now your trouser leg – thirty-four. This suit should fit you, sir.
Mrs Austen	Try the jacket on first, John.
Assistant	The sleeves are a little too long.
Mrs Austen	Have you anything lighter, in grey perhaps?
Assistant	Yes, we have those grey suits; these brown ones; and the green ones over there. What do you think of this one?
Mr Austen	I like it. The material is very smooth.
Mrs Austen	I don't like the pockets; they are too big. The trousers are too narrow and they have no cuffs.
Assistant	Most suits have big pockets nowadays and trousers rarely have cuffs. What do you think of this grey pin striped one, sir.
Mr Austen	No, I don't like pin striped suits. Have you any sports jackets?
Assistant	Sports jackets are in that department there, sir.
Mr Austen	I think I'll go and have a look at them.
Assistant	Certainly, sir.

ENTERTAINMENT

Where could I find the
program of concerts for
this month?

**¿Dónde podría encontrar el programa
de conciertos de este mes?**
*don*deh po*dree*ya enkon*trar* el programa deh
konsee*yer*tos deh *es*teh mes?

Is it possible to book tickets
for the theater here?

**¿Se pueden reservar localidades
(entradas) del teatro aquí?**
seh *pwe*den reser*var* lokalee*da*des (en*tra*das)
del te*ya*tro a*kee*?

Can you recommend a
good movie?

**¿Puede recomendarme una buena
película?** *pwe*deh rekomen*dar*meh *oo*na
*bwe*na peh*lee*koola?

What's on at the Palace theater?

¿Qué dan en el teatro Palacio?
keh dan en el te*ya*tro pa*la*seeyo?

Have you two good seats in
the stalls?

**¿Tiene dos buenas butacas en (de)
platea?** tee*ye*neh dos *bwe*nas boo*ta*kas en
(deh) pla*te*ya?

There are two in the middle
of the fifth row – row E.

**Hay dos en el centro (medio) de la
quinta fila, fila E.** ay dos en el *sen*tro
(*me*deeyo) deh la *keen*ta *fee*la, *fee*la eh

How much are the seats in
the balcony?

**¿Cuánto cuestan las localidades en la
galería?** *kwan*to *kwes*tan las lokalee*da*des
en la gale*ree*ya?

Have you anything cheaper?

¿Tiene algo más barato?
tee*ye*neh *al*go mas ba*ra*to?

What time does the show begin?	**¿A qué hora empieza el espectáculo?** a keh *o*ra empee*yesa* el espek*ta*koolo?
Where can I get a program?	**¿Dónde puedo conseguir un programa?** *don*deh *pwe*do konse*gheer* oon pro*gra*ma?
Could I book a table for dinner after the concert?	**¿Podría reservar una mesa para cenar después del concierto?** po*dree*ya reser*var* *oo*na *me*sa para se*nar* des*pwes* del konsee*yer*to?
Is there any charge for admission?	**¿Hay que pagar entrada?** ay keh pa*gar* en*tra*da?
What sort of music do they play here?	**¿Qué tipo de música ponen aquí?** keh *tee*po deh *moo*seeka ponen a*kee*?
Can we get a taxi after the show?	**¿Podemos coger un taxi después de la función?** po*de*mos ko*her* oon *tak*see des*pwes* deh la foonsee*yon*?

Booking by phone

Can I pay for these over the phone?	**¿Puedo pagar por teléfono?** *pwe*do pa*gar* por te*le*fono?
My credit card number is…	**El número de mi tarjeta de crédito es…** el *noo*mero deh mee tar*he*ta deh *kre*deeto es
The expiry date is...	**La fecha de vencimiento (caducidad) es el…** la *fe*cha deh venseemee*yen*to (kadoothee*dad*) es el
Is there a confirmation number?	**¿Hay algún número de confirmación?** ay al*goon* *noo*mero deh konfeermasee*yon*?

General

box office	**la taquilla** la ta*k*eel-ya
entertainment	**los espectáculos** los espe*ct*akoolos
coatcheck	**el guardarropa** el gwarda*rr*opa
seats at the front	**las butacas delanteras** las boo*t*akas delan*t*eras
in the middle	**centrales** sen*t*rales
at the back	**traseras** trase*r*as
upstairs/downstairs	**arriba/abajo** a*rr*iba/a*b*aho
orchestra	**orquesta** or*k*esta
dress circle	**la platea** a pla*t*eya
gallery	**la galería** la gale*r*eeya
row C	**la fila C** la *f*eela seh
ticket	**la entrada** la en*t*rada

Classical music

concert hall	**la sala de conciertos** la *s*ala deh konsee*y*ertos
opera house	**la ópera** la *o*pera
orchestra	**la orquesta** la or*k*esta
conductor	**el director/la directora** el deere*kt*or/la deere*kt*ora
singer	**el/la cantante** el/la kan*t*anteh
musician	**el músico/la música (la músico)** el *m*ooseeko/la *m*ooseeka (la *m*ooseeko)

Theater

intermission	**el entreacto/el descanso (el intermedio)** el entre*y*akto/el des*k*anso (el eenter*m*edeeyo)
play	**la obra de teatro** la *o*bra deh te*y*atro
program	**el programa** el pro*g*rama
comedy	**la comedia** la ko*m*edeeya
drama	**el drama** el *d*rama

Movie theater

film	**la película** la pe*lee*koola
movie theater	**el cine** el *see*neh
actor/actress	**el actor/la actriz** el ak*tor*/la ak*trees*
screen	**la pantalla** la pan*tal*-ya
subtitles	**los subtítulos** los soob*tee*toolos
dubbed	**doblada** dob*la*da

Bars, etc.

discotheque	**la discoteca** la deesko*te*ka
bar	**el bar** el bar
live music	**la música viva (en directo)** la *moo*seeka *vee*va (en dee*rek*to)
night club	**night club** "night club"
dance	**bailar** bay*lar*
identification	**identificación** eedenteefeekasee*yon*

Sport

baseball	**el béisbol** el *bey*eesbol
basketball	**el básquetbol (baloncesto)** el *bás*quetbol (balon*thes*to)
bullfight	**la corrida de toros** la ko*rree*da deh *to*ros
game	**el partido** el par*tee*do
golf	**el golf** el golf
horseback riding	**montar a caballo** mon*tar* a ka*bal*-yo
ice-skating	**el patinaje sobre hielo** el patee*na*heh *so*breh *ee*yelo
skiing	**esquiar** eskee*yar*
soccer	**el fútbol** el *foot*bol
stadium	**el estadio** el es*ta*deeyo
team	**el equipo** el e*kee*po
tennis	**el tenis** el *te*nees
working out	**el ejercicio** el eher*see*seeyo

Dialog: Going out for the evening

Sr. Austen	¿Podría decirnos algo sobre las diversiones que hay aquí?
Recepcionista	Para eso les aconsejo que hablen con Ricardo. Es nuestro experto en el tema. Ric, ¿te importaría informar a estos señores acerca de las diversiones que hay aquí en la ciudad?
Sr. Austen	¿Hay algo que usted recomendaría a dos turistas norteamericanos y su hija de dieciséis años?
Ricardo	Bueno, tenemos el Auditorio Nacional, donde puede encontrar muchos espectáculos si le gustan la música clásica o el teatro.
Sr. Austen	Nos gusta la música clásica pero tenemos que excluir el teatro si está en español.
Sra. Austen	No nos importan las películas con subtítulos.
Ricardo	El cine que está en la plaza aquí cerca a menudo tiene películas con subtítulos.
Sr. Austen	¿Qué más hay aquí cerca?
Ricardo	Hay dos salas de conciertos y también hay otro lugar que es para recitales.
Sra. Austen	¿Los tres para música clásica?
Ricardo	No siempre, depende. Vamos a ver el periódico. El Ballet Nacional pone (representa) «El lago de los Cisnes» en el Festival Hall; hay un concierto de jazz de los años treinta en el Music Hall y hay un concierto de música popular (folk) en el Folkloric Center.
Sr. Austen	¿Qué más hay ahí?
Ricardo	También está el teatro pero está (es) en español . También está el museo de arte contemporáneo. Tienen dos exposiciones estos días, una del pintor y escultor Gerardo Rueda.
Sra. Austen	Vamos a la plaza, John.

Mr. Austen	*Could you give us some idea about entertainment here?*
Receptionist	*You had better ask Ricardo here about that, sir. He's our expert on that subject. Ric, would you like to tell this lady and gentleman about the city's entertainment?*
Mr. Austen	*Is there anything you could recommend to two U.S. visitors and their 16-year-old daughter?*
Ricardo	*Well, there's the performing arts center, where you will find plenty to entertain you if you like classical music or theater.*
Mr. Austen	*We like classical music, but we must exclude theater if it's in Spanish.*
Mrs. Austen	*We don't mind films with subtitles.*
Ricardo	*The cinema in the nearby plaza often has films with subtitles.*
Mr. Austen	*What else is nearby?*
Ricardo	*There are two concert halls; then there is another place, which is for recitals.*
Mrs. Austen	*All three for classical music?*
Ricardo	*Not always, it depends. Let's have a look at the newspaper. The National Ballet are doing Swan Lake at the Festival Hall; there's a 1930's jazz concert at the Music Hall; and there's traditional folk music at the Folkloric Center.*
Mr. Austen	*What else is there?*
Ricardo	*There's the theater, but that's in Spanish. Then there's the contemporary art museum. They've got two exhibitions there at the moment, one of the painter and sculptor Gerardo Rueda.*
Mrs. Austen	*Let's go to the plaza, John.*

SIGHTSEEING

Which are the best museums for modern art?	**¿Cuáles son los mejores museos de arte moderno?** *kwa*les son los me*ho*res moo*se*yos deh *ar*teh mo*der*no?
What style was this built in?	**¿En qué estilo fue construído este edificio?** en keh es*tee*lo fweh konstroo*yee*do *es*teh edee*fee*seeyo?
Who was the architect?	**¿Quién fue el arquitecto?** kee*yen* fweh el arkee*tek*to?
Is there a guided tour?	**¿Hay visitas con guía?** ay vee*see*tas kon *ghee*ya?
Do you have a commentary in English?	**¿Tienen la explicación (cinta) en inglés?** tee*yen*en la ekspleekasee*yon* (*seen*ta) en een*gles*?

Historic buildings

battlements	**las almenas** las al*me*nas
castle	**el castillo** el kas*teel*-yo
drawbridge	**el puente levadizo** el *pwen*teh leva*dee*so
dungeons	**las mazmorras** las mas*mor*ras
fountains	**las fuentes** las *fwen*tes
minaret	**el minarete** el meena*re*teh
moat	**el foso** el *fo*so
monument	**el monumento** el monoo*men*to
mosque	**la mezquita** la mes*kee*ta
palace	**el palacio** el pa*la*seeyo
pyramid	**la pirámide** la peera*mee*deh
ruin	**la ruina** la roo*ee*na

site	**sitio arqueológico** *see*teeyo arkeyo*lo*heeko
square	**la plaza** la *pla*sa
street	**la calle** la *ka*l-yeh
walls	**los muros** los *moo*ros

Churches

aisle	**la nave lateral (el pasillo)** la *na*veh late*ra*l (el pa*see*l-yo)
altar	**el altar** el al*ta*r
arches	**los arcos** los *ar*kos
bell tower	**el campanario** el kampa*na*reeyo
cathedral	**la catedral** la kate*dra*l
chancel	**el presbiterio** el presbee*te*reeyo
chapel	**la capilla** la ka*pee*l-ya
choir stalls	**las sillas del coro** las *see*l-yas del *ko*ro
church	**la iglesia** la ee*gle*seeya
churchyard	**el cementerio** el semen*te*reeyo
cloister	**el claustro** el *kla*wstro
crypt	**la cripta** la *kreep*ta
dome	**la cúpula** la *koo*poola
font	**la pila bautismal** la *pee*la baootees*mal*
nave	**la nave** la *na*veh
organ	**el órgano** el *or*gano
pews	**los bancos** los *ban*kos
portico	**el pórtico** el *por*teeko
pulpit	**el púlpito** el *pool*peeto
spire	**la aguja** la a*goo*ha
steeple	**el campanario** el kampa*na*reeyo
tombs	**los sepulcros** los se*pool*kros
transept	**el crucero** el kroo*se*ro

Buildings

ceiling	**el techo** el *te*cho
courtyard	**el patio** el *pa*teeyo
doors	**las puertas** las *pwer*tas
façade	**la fachada** la fa*cha*da
fireplace	**la chimenea** la cheeme*ne*ya
floor	**el suelo** el *swe*lo
gates	**las rejas (verjas)** las *re*has (*ber*has)
passage	**el pasillo** el pa*seel*-yo
roof	**el tejado** el te*ha*do
rooms	**las salas/las habitaciones** las *sa*las/las abeetasee*yo*nes
windows	**las ventanas** las ven*ta*nas

Art galleries

ceramics	**la cerámica** la se*ra*meeka
drawing	**el dibujo** el dee*boo*ho
engraving	**el grabado** el gra*ba*do
miniature	**la miniatura** la meeneeya*too*ra
mosaic	**el mosaico** el mosa*yee*ko
mural	**el mural** el moo*ral*
oil painting	**el óleo** el *o*leyo
paintings	**las pinturas** las peen*too*ras
landscape	**el paisaje** el paye*esa*heh
portrait	**el retrato** el re*tra*to
seascape	**la marina** la ma*ree*na
still life	**el bodegón** el bode*gon*
pottery	**la cerámica** la se*ra*meeka
sculpture	**la escultura** la eskool*too*ra
bust	**el busto** el *boos*to

Period

art nouveau	**modernista** moder*nee*sta
Aztec	**azteca** as*te*ka
colonial	**colonial** koloneey*al*
contemporary	**contemporáneo** kontempor*a*neyo
Gothic	**gótico** *go*teeko
impressionist	**impresionista** eempreseeyo*nee*sta
Inca	**incaico (inca)** een*kay*eeko (*een*ka)
Mayan	**maya** *ma*ya
mission	**misión** meese*eyon*
Mozarabic	**mozárabe** mo*sa*rabeh
neoclassical	**neoclásico** neyo*kla*seeko
pre-Columbian	**precolombino** prekolom*bee*no
renaissance	**renacentista** renasen*tee*sta
Roman	**romano** ro*ma*no
romanesque	**románico** ro*ma*neeko

Museum

art exhibitions	**exposiciones de arte** eksposeesee*yo*nes deh *a*rteh
audio visual material	**el material audio-visual** el matereey*al* aoodeeyo-veeso*al*
collection	**la colección** la koleksee*yon*
exhibit	**el objeto expuesto/la exhibición** el ob*he*to eks*pwe*sto/la ekseebeesee*yon*
guided tour	**la visita con guía** la vee*see*ta kon *ghee*ya
lecture	**la conferencia** la konfe*ren*seeya
library	**la biblioteca** la beebleeyo*te*ka
modern art	**el arte moderno** el *a*rteh mo*de*rno
museums	**los museos** los moo*se*yos
painting	**la pintura** la peen*too*ra
sculpture	**la escultura** la eskool*too*ra
tableau	**el cuadro viviente** el *kwa*dro veeveey*en*teh

Dialog: Sightseeing

Sr. Martínez	Si tienen tiempo podrían ir a pasar una mañana o una tarde al río.
Sr. Austen	¿Y qué haríamos tanto tiempo?
Sr. Martínez	Muchas cosas. Si quieren pasar todo el día paseando, les aconsejo que empiecen por el palacio.
Sra. Austen	Siempre he querido visitar el palacio.
Sr. Martínez	Después del palacio, pueden ir al puente que está al lado que es uno de los más famosos del mundo. Luego, al otro lado del río, pueden visitar el buque de guerra.
Sra. Austen	¿Cree que eso le interesará a mi hija?
Sr. Austen	Un barco así resulta interesante para todo el mundo.
Sr. Martínez	Después, pueden coger el ferry y ver un velero del siglo diecinueve.
Sra. Austen	¿Y a dónde vamos desde ahí?
Sr. Austen	Río arriba.
Sr. Martínez	Así es. Si bajan del ferry en el embarcadero pueden echar un vistazo a la Corte Suprema y al Congreso. Luego, crucen la plaza hasta la abadía y, para terminar, sigan hasta la catedral.
Sra. Austen	Es mucho para un sólo día.
Sr. Austen	Creo que es mucho mejor organizar una visita turística de un día que visitar solamente un sitio cada día.
Sr. Martínez	Estoy de acuerdo con usted, incluso si no hacen más visitas turísticas durante su estancia.
Sr. Austen	Después del recorrido que usted ha sugerido, ¡no creo que tenga fuerzas para más visitas!

Mr. Martínez	*If you have time, you could spend a morning or afternoon on the river.*
Mr. Austen	*But what would we do in all that time?*
Mr. Martínez	*Lots of things. If you want to spend the whole day going round, then I suggest you begin at the palace.*
Mrs. Austen	*I have always wanted to visit the palace.*
Mr. Martínez	*After the palace you can visit the nearby bridge, one of the most famous bridges in the world. After that, on the opposite side of the river, you can visit the warship.*
Mrs. Austen	*Do you think our daughter would be interested?*
Mr. Austen	*A ship like that is interesting for everyone.*
Mr. Martínez	*Then you can take the riverbus and see a nineteenth-century sailing ship.*
Mrs. Austen	*Where do we go from there?*
Mr. Austen	*Up the river.*
Mr. Martínez	*That's right. You get off the riverbus at the pier. Have a look at the supreme court and congress. Then walk across the plaza to the abbey and finally to the cathedral.*
Mrs. Austen	*It's a lot to do in one day.*
Mr. Austen	*I think it is much better to plan an organised day's sightseeing than to visit just one place a day.*
Mr. Martínez	*I quite agree, even if you don't do any more sightseeing for the rest of the holiday.*
Mrs. Austen	*After the itinerary you have suggested for one day, I wouldn't have the strength!*

OUTDOOR EXCURSIONS

I'd like a hike suitable for beginners.	**Me gustaría una excursión apropiada para principiantes.** meh goostar*ee*ya *oo*na ekskoorsee*yon* apropee*ya*da *pa*ra preenseepee*ya*ntes
Stop, please. I need to take a rest.	**Pare, por favor. Necesito descansar.** *pa*reh, por fa*vor*. neses*ee*to deskan*sar*
What type of animal/bird/plant is that?	**¿Qué clase de animal/pájaro/planta es ése/ésa?** keh *kla*seh deh anee*mal*/ *pa*haro/*pla*nta es *e*seh/*e*sa?
How deep is the pool?	**¿Qué tan honda es la alberca? (¿Cómo es de profunda la piscina?)** keh tan *on*da es la al*ber*ka? (*ko*mo es deh pro*foon*da la pees*thee*na?)
Is it safe to swim here?	**¿Es seguro nadar aquí?** es se*goo*ro na*dar* a*kee*?
How much is it to rent scubagear for an hour?	**¿Cuánto cuesta rentar (alquilar) el equipo para buceo por hora?** *kwan*to *kwe*sta ren*tar* (alkee*lar*) el e*kee*po *pa*ra boo*se*yo por *o*ra?

In the park

park	**los parques** los *par*kes
bushes	**los arbustos** los ar*boo*stos
fish pond	**el estanque** el es*tan*keh
flowerbeds	**las jardineras (los parterres)** las hardee*ne*ras (los par*teh*rres)
gardens	**los jardines** los har*dee*nes
grass	**el pasto (la hierba)** el *pa*sto (la ee*yer*ba)
lake	**el lago** el *la*go

paths	**los senderos/los caminos** los senderos/los kameenos
refreshments	**los refrescos** los refreskos
seats	**los asientos** los aseeyentos
benches	**los bancos** los bankos
tennis courts	**las canchas (pistas) de tenis** las kanchas (peestas) deh tenees
trees	**los árboles** los arboles
water birds	**los pájaros acuáticos** los paharos akwateekos
wild flowers	**las flores silvestres** las flores seelvestres

At the zoo

zoo	**el parque zoológico** el parkeh soh-oloheeko
apes house	**la casa de los changos (monos)** la kasa deh los changos (monos)
aquarium	**el acuario** el akwareeyo
aviary	**el aviario** el aveeyareeyo
cages	**las jaulas** las hawlas
insect house	**la casa de los insectos** la kasa deh los eensektos
lion and tiger house	**la casa de las fieras** la kasa deh las fecyeras
mammals	**los mamíferos** los mameeferos
reptile house	**el serpentario (terrario)** el serpentareeyo (terrareeyo)

By the river

river	**el río** el reeyo
barge	**la barca (la barcaza)** la barka (la barkasa)
bridge	**el puente** el pwenteh
docks	**los muelles** los mwel-yes

ferry	**el ferry** el *fe*rree
flood barrier	**el dique contra inundaciones** el *dee*keh *kon*tra eenoondasee*yo*nes
island	**la isla** la *ees*la
motorboat	**el barco (a) motor** el *bar*ko (a) mo*tor*
pier	**el embarcadero** el embarka*de*ro
rapids	**los rápidos** los *ra*peedos
river cruise	**el crucero por el río** el kroo*se*ro por el *ree*yo
riverbank	**la orilla del río** la o*ree*l-ya del *ree*yo
riverbus	**el ferry** el *fe*rree
sailing boat	**el barco de vela** el *bar*ko deh *ve*la
sailing club	**el club de vela (club náutico)** el kloob deh *ve*la (kloob na*oo*teeko)
tide	**la marea** la ma*re*ya
high tide	**marea alta** ma*re*ya *al*ta
low tide	**marea baja** ma*re*ya *ba*ha
wharf	**el muelle** el *mwel*-yeh

Resorts

amusement park	**el parque de atracciones** el *par*keh deh atraksee*yo*nes
roller coaster	**la montaña rusa** la mon*ta*nya *rroo*sa
beach	**la playa** la *pla*ya
pier	**el embarcadero** el embarka*de*ro
promenade	**el paseo marítimo** el pa*se*yo ma*ree*teemo
sea	**el mar** el mar
spa	**el balneario** el balney*a*reeyo
tourist information center	**la oficina de información turística** la ofee*se*ena deh eenformasee*yon* too*ree*steeka
town	**el pueblo** el *pwe*blo
village	**la aldea** la al*de*ya

Excursions

countryside	**el paisaje/el campo** el payeesaheh/el kampo
excursions/trips	**las excursiones** las ekskoorseeyones
guide book	**la guía** la gheeya
map	**el mapa (plano)** el mapa (plano)
street plan	**el plano de calles** el plan deh kal-yes
historical tours	**visitas a los lugares históricos** veeseetas a los loogares eestoreekos

Hiking

canyon	**el cañón** el kanyon
cave	**la cueva** la kweva
cliff	**el acantilado** el akanteelado
desert	**el desierto** el deseeyerto
forest	**el bosque** el boskeh
hill	**la colina** la koleena
jungle	**la selva** la selva
lake	**el lago** el lago
meadow	**el prado** el prado
mountain	**la montaña** la montanya
national park	**el parque nacional** el parkeh naseeyonal
picnic	**el picnic** el peekneek
volcano	**el volcán** el volkan

Weather

What's the weather forecast?	**¿Qué dice el boletín meteorológico?** keh deeseh el boleteen meteyoroloheeko?
It's sunny.	**Hace sol.** aseh sol
It's freezing.	**Hace mucho frío.** aseh moocho freeyo
It's pouring.	**Está diluviando.** esta deelooveeyando

cloud	**la nube** la *noo*beh
fog	**la niebla** la nee*ye*bla
lightning	**el relámpago** el re*lam*pago
rain	**la lluvia** la *l-yoo*veeya
thunder	**el trueno** el *trw*eno
thunderstorm	**la tormenta** la tor*men*ta
wind	**el viento** el vee*yen*to

Flora

branch	**la rama** la *ra*ma
bush	**el arbusto** el ar*boo*sto
cactus	**el cactus** el *kak*toos
flower	**la flor** la flor
leaf	**la hoja** la *o*ha
pine tree	**el pino** el *pee*no
plant	**la planta** la *plan*ta
tree	**el árbol** el *ar*bol

Fauna

ant	**la hormiga** la or*mee*ga
bear	**el oso** el *o*so
bee	**la abeja** la a*be*ha
bird	**el pájaro** el *pa*haro
butterfly	**la mariposa** la maree*po*sa
cow	**la vaca** la *va*ka
deer	**el ciervo** el see*ye*rvo
ducks	**los patos** los *pa*tos
eagle	**el águila** el a*ghee*la
fox	**el zorro** el *so*rro
frog	**la rana** la *rra*na
goat	**la cabra** la *ka*bra
hen	**la gallina** la ga*l-yee*na
insect	**el insecto** el een*sek*to

lizard	**el lagarto** el la*ga*rto
parrot	**el loro** el *lo*ro
rabbit	**el conejo** el ko*ne*ho
sheep	**la oveja** la o*ve*ha
snake	**la serpiente** la serpee*yen*teh
spider	**la araña** la a*ra*nya
stork	**la cigüeña** la see*gwe*nya
swans	**los cisnes** los *sees*nes

Seaside

bathingsuit	**el traje de baño (bañador)** el *tra*heh deh *ba*nyo (banya*dor*)
beach	**la playa** la *pla*ya
coast	**la costa** la *kos*ta
fish	**el pescado (pez)** el pes*ka*do (pes)
to go diving	**ir a bucear** eer a boose*yar*
island	**la isla** la *ees*la
jet ski	**la moto acuática** la *mo*to akwa*tee*ka
ocean	**el océano** el o*se*yano
reef	**el arrecife** el arre*see*feh
sand	**la arena** la a*re*na
sea	**el mar** el mar
shark	**el tiburón** el teeboo*ron*
sun	**el sol** el sol
sunglasses	**los anteojos (las gafas) de sol** los ante*yo*hos (las *ga*fas) deh sol
sunscreen	**el protector contra el sol** el protek*tor* *kon*tra el sol
surf	**surf, las olas rompientes** soorf, las *o*las rompee*yen*tes
to swim	**nadar** na*dar*
swimming pool	**la alberca (piscina)** la al*ber*ka (pees*thee*na)
wave	**la ola** la *o*la

EMERGENCIES & HEALTH

Where is the restroom?	**¿Dónde están los baños (servicios)?** *don*deh es*tan* los *ban*yos (ser*vee*see*yos*)?
Help!	**¡Socorro!** so*korro*!
Stop, thief!	**¡Alto, (Al) ladrón!** *al*to, (al) lad*ron*!
Leave me alone!	**¡Déjeme en paz!** *de*hemeh en pas!
Please call the police!	**Llame a la policía, por favor.** *l-ya*meh a la po*lee*see*ya*, por fa*vor*
Fire!	**¡Fuego!** *fwe*go!
I feel sick.	**Estoy enfermo(-a).** es*toy* en*fermo*(-a)
Call an ambulance.	**Llame a una ambulancia.** *l-ya*meh a *oo*na ambo*olan*seeya
It's an emergency.	**Es una emergencia.** es *oo*na emer*hen*seeya
May I borrow your mobile phone.	**¿Me presta su celular (móvil)?** meh *presta* soo selo*olar* (*mo*beel)?
There's been an accident.	**Ha habido un accidente.** a a*bee*do oon akse*edenteh*
Someone has been injured.	**Alguien está herido.** al*gee*yen es*ta* e*ree*do

Police

Where is the nearest police station?	**¿Dónde está la estación de policía más cercana?** *don*deh es*ta* la estase*eyon* deh po*lee*see*ya* mas ser*kana*?
I need an English-speaking lawyer.	**Necesito un abogado que hable inglés.** nese*see*to oon abo*gado* keh *ableh* een*gles*

Can you give me the address of the American Embassy, please? | **¿Me puede dar la dirección de la Embajada de los Estados Unidos, por favor?** meh *pwe*deh dar la deereksee*yon* deh la emba*ha*da deh los es*ta*dos oo*nee*dos, por fa*vor*?

I need to call... | **Necesito llamar...** nese*see*to l-ya*mar*

I want to report... | **Quiero reportar... (denunciar...)** kee*ye*ro repor*tar* (denoon*thee*yar)

  an assault | **un asalto** oon a*sal*to

  a rape | **una violación** *oo*na veeyolasee*yon*

  a theft | **un robo** oon *rro*bo

My handbag has been stolen. | **Me robaron la bolsa. (Me han robado el bolso.)** meh rro*ba*ron la *bol*sa (meh an rro*ba*do el *bol*so)

I have lost my credit card. | **Perdí mi tarjeta de crédito.** per*dee* mee tar*he*ta deh *kre*deeto

Where is the lost and found? | **¿Dónde está la oficina de objetos perdidos?** *don*deh es*ta* la ofee*see*na deh ob*he*tos per*dee*dos?

Can I have a report for my insurance company? | **¿Me puede dar un reporte (informe) para mi compañía de seguros?** meh *pwe*deh dar oon re*por*teh (een*for*meh) *pa*ra mee compan*yee*ya deh se*goo*ros?

Lost and stolen

car keys | **las llaves del coche** las *l-ya*ves del *ko*cheh

credit card | **la tarjeta de crédito** la tar*he*ta deh *kre*deeto

driver's license | **la licencia (el permiso) de conducir** la lee*sen*seeya (el per*mee*so) deh kondoo*seer*

handbag	**el bolso**	el *bol*so
money	**el dinero**	el dee*ne*ro
passport	**el pasaporte**	el pasa*por*teh
purse	**el monedero**	el mone*de*ro
rental car	**el coche rentado (alquilado)**	
	el *ko*cheh rren*ta*do (alkee*la*do)	
suitcase	**la maleta**	la ma*le*ta
ticket	**el boleto (billete)**	el bo*le*to (bi*l-ye*te)
traveler's checks	**los cheques de viajero (viaje)**	
	los *che*kes deh veeya*he*ro (beeya*he*)	
visa	**la visa**	la *vee*sa
wallet	**la cartera**	la kar*te*ra

Missing

My daughter is missing.	**No encuentro a mi hija.**
	no en*kwen*tro a mee *ee*ha
She wears glasses.	**Usa anteojos. (Lleva gafas.)**
	*oo*sa ante*yo*hos (*l-ye*ba *ga*fas)
I last saw my wife 4 hours ago.	**La última vez que vi a mi esposa fue**
	hace cuatro horas. la *ool*teema ves keh
	vee a mee es*po*sa fweh aseh *kwa*tro oras
She has black hair.	**Tiene (el) pelo negro.**
	tee*ye*neh (el) *pe*lo *ne*gro
He is 5'8 tall.	**Mide 1.74 m.**
	*mee*deh oon *me*tro se*ten*ta ee *kwa*tro

Parts of the body

skin	**la piel**	la pee*yel*
hair	**el pelo**	el *pe*lo
blonde	**rubio**	*roo*beeyo
brown	**moreno**	mo*re*no

black	**negro** *ne*gro
gray	**canoso** ka*no*so
curly	**rizado** ree*sa*do
straight	**lacio (liso)** *la*seeyo (*lee*so)
balding	**está perdiendo el pelo (calvo)** es*ta* perdee*yen*do el *pe*lo (*kal*bo)
beard	**la barba** la *bar*ba
moustache	**el bigote** el bee*go*teh
chin	**la barbilla** la bar*beel*-ya
head	**la cabeza** la ka*be*sa
face	**la cara** la *ka*ra
nose	**la nariz** la na*rees*
ear	**la oreja** la o*re*ha
hearing aid	**el audifono** el aoodee*fo*no
eyes	**los ojos** los *o*hos
eyebrow	**la ceja** la *se*ha
mouth	**la boca** la *bo*ka
throat	**la garganta** la gar*gan*ta
tongue	**la lengua** la *len*gooa
teeth	**los dientes** los *dee*yentes
gums	**las encías** las en*see*yas
body	**el cuerpo** el *kwer*po
neck	**el cuello** el *kwel*-yo
shoulder	**el hombro** el *om*bro
back	**la espalda** la es*pal*da
chest	**el pecho** el *pe*cho
breasts	**los pechos** los *pe*chos
nipples	**los pezones** los pe*so*nes
stomach	**el estómago** el es*to*mago
hip	**la cadera** la ka*de*ra
bottom	**el trasero** el tra*se*ro
arm	**el brazo** el *bra*so

elbow	**el codo** el *ko*do
hand	**la mano** la *ma*no
fingers	**los dedos** los *de*dos
leg	**la pierna** la *pee*yerna
knee	**la rodilla** la rro*deel*-ya
ankle	**el tobillo** el to*beel*-yo
foot	**el pie** el pee*yeh*
heel	**el talón** el ta*lon*
toe	**el dedo del pie** el *de*do del pee*yeh*
lungs	**los pulmones** los pool*mo*nes
heart	**el corazón** el kora*son*
digestive system	**el sistema digestivo** el sees*te*ma deehes*tee*vo
testicles	**los testículos** los tes*tee*koolos
penis	**el pene** el *pe*neh
vagina	**la vagina** la va*hee*na
blood	**la sangre** la *sa*ngreh
vein	**la vena** la *ve*na
muscle	**el músculo** el *moo*skoolo
bone	**el hueso** el *we*so

Getting treatment

Can I make an appointment to see...?	**¿Podría darme una cita (hora) para ver a...?** po*dree*ya *dar*meh *oo*na *see*ta (*o*ra) *pa*ra ver a?
the doctor	**el doctor/la doctora** el dok*tor*/la dok*to*ra
the nurse	**la enfermera** la enfer*me*ra
the dentist	**el dentista** el den*tee*sta
the hospital	**el hospital** el ospee*tal*
health insurance plan	**el plan de seguro médico** el plan deh se*goo*ro *me*deeko
insurance card	**la tarjeta del seguro** la tar*he*ta del se*goo*ro

inoculations	**las vacunas** las va*koo*nas
doctor's office	**el consultorio (la consulta) del doctor** el konsool*toreeyo* (la konsoo*lta*) del dok*tor*
the waiting room	**la sala de espera** la *sala* deh es*pera*
I have an appointment to see...	**Tengo una cita para ver a...** *ten*go *oo*na *seeta para* ver a

Filling out forms

Por favor ¿Podría rellenar esta ficha?	Can you fill in this form, please?
Apellido	Surname
Nombre	First Name
Edad	Age
Fecha de nacimiento	Date of Birth
Lugar de nacimiento	Place of Birth
Nacionalidad	Nationality
Dirección	Address
Número de teléfono	Telephone Number
Familiar más cercano	Next of Kin
Historial médico	Medical History
Detalles sobre previas operaciones	Details of previous operations
Enfermedades	Serious illnesses
Alergias	Allergies
¿Ha tenido alguna de estas enfermedades?	Have you ever had any of the following illnesses?

The consultation

Voy a...	I am going to...
tomarle la presión sanguínea	to take your blood pressure
tomarle el pulso	to take your pulse
tomar una muestra de sangre	to take a blood sample
hacerle una prueba de orina	to do a urine test

auscultarle el corazón/el pecho	to listen to your heart/chest
mirarle la garganta	to look down your throat
comprobar los reflejos	to test your reflexes
Podría...	Could you ...
subirse las mangas	roll up your sleeves
levantarse la camisa	lift up your shirt
qitarse la ropa	take off your clothes
quitarse todo salvo la ropa interior	take everything off except your underwear (pants)
ponerse esta bata	put this gown on
subirse a la cama	climb on the bed
acostarse	lie down
abrir la boca	open your mouth wide
hacer una muestra de orina/feces	do a urine/stool sample

Doctor's questions and instructions

¿Dónde le duele?	Where does it hurt?
Muéstreme dónde le duele.	Show me where it hurts.
¿Le duele aquí mucho?	Does it hurt much?
¿Puede mover...?	Can you move your...?
Debe guardar cama.	You should stay in bed.
No debe ir al trabajo/al colegio/de viaje.	You should not go to work/school/travel.
Me gustaría hacer más pruebas.	I would like to do further tests.
Necesito tomarle unos rayos X.	You need an X-ray.
Necesita un scan.	You need a scan.
Le voy a arreglar una cita para que vaya al hospital.	I will make an appointment at the hospital for you.
No es nada grave.	It is nothing serious.
Se pondrá bien pronto.	You will be better soon.
¿Tiene alguna alergia a algo?	Are you allergic to anything?

Conditions

allergy	**una alergia** *oo*na a*ler*heeya
arthritis	**la artritis** la ar*tree*tees
asthma	**el asma** el *as*ma
backache	**los dolores de espalda** los do*lo*res deh es*pal*da
bronchitis	**la bronquitis** la bron*kee*tees
bruise	**un moretón (cardenal)** oon more*ton* (karde*nal*)
cancer	**el cáncer** el *kan*ser
constipation	**el estreñimiento** el estrenyeemee*yen*to
cough	**la tos** la tos
cut	**una cortada (un corte)** *oo*na kor*ta*da (oon *kor*teh)
flu	**la gripa (gripe)** la *gree*pa (*gree*peh)
heart mumur	**un murmullo (soplo)en el corazón** oon moor*mool*-yo (*so*plo) en el kora*son*
heartburn	**la acidez** la asee*des*
hemorrhoids	**las hemorroides** las emor*roy*eedes
hernia	**una hernia** *oo*na *er*neeya
hip replacement	**un reemplazo de la cadera** oon re-em*pla*so deh la ka*de*ra
indigestion	**la indigestión** la eendeeheestee*yon*
infection	**la infección** la eenfeeksee*yon*
insect bite	**un piquete (una picadura) de insecto** oon pee*ke*teh (*oo*na peeka*doo*ra) deh een*sek*to
kidney stone	**un cálculo renal** oon *kal*koolo rre*nal*
migraine	**una migraña** *oo*na mee*gran*ya
nosebleed	**una hemorragia nasal** *oo*na emor*ra*heeya na*sal*
pacemaker	**un marcapasos** *oo*na marka*pa*sos
rash	**un sarpullido** oon sarpool*-yee*do
rheumatism	**el reumatismo** el reyooma*tees*mo

sciatica	**la ciática** la see*y*ateeka
swelling	**una hinchazón** *oo*na eenchaso*n*
sunstroke	**una insolación** *oo*na eensolasee*y*on
tetanus	**el tétano** el *te*tano
tonsillitis	**la amigdalitis** la ameegda*lee*tees
toothache	**el dolor de muelas** el do*lor* deh *mw*elas
ulcer	**una úlcera** *oo*na *oo*lsera
vomiting	**vómitos** *vo*meetos
wound	**una herida** *oo*na e*ree*da

The treatment

una receta	a prescription
la medicina	medicine
los antibióticos	antibiotics
la aspirina	aspirin
una cápsula	a capsule
una crema antihistamínica	antihistamine cream
una crema antiséptica	antiseptic cream
un inhalador	an inhaler
una pastilla	a tablet
la penicilina	penicillin
un supositorio	a suppository
el ungüento	ointment
untar	to rub on
la dosis	the dosage
tragar/tomar	to swallow/take
Agitar la botella antes de usar.	Shake the bottle before use.
tres veces al día	three times a day
antes/después de la comidas	before/after meals
Tómese con las comidas.	Take with food.
Tómese en ayunas.	Take on an empty stomach.
No tome esto en caso de embarazo.	Do not take if pregnant.

GENERAL INFORMATION

Days of the week

on Monday	**el lunes** el *loo*nes
next Tuesday	**el próximo martes** el *prok*seemo *mar*tes
last Wednesday	**el miércoles pasado** el mee*yer*koles pa*sa*do
the Thursday before last	**el jueves antepasado (hace dos jueves)** el *hwe*ves antepa*sa*do (*a*the dos *hwe*bes)
Friday	**viernes** vee*yer*nes
Saturday	**sábado** *sa*bado
Sunday	**domingo** do*meen*go

Months of the year

In January	**en enero** en e*ne*ro
February	**febrero** fe*bre*ro
March	**marzo** *mar*so
April	**abril** *abril*
May	**mayo** *ma*yo
June	**junio** *hoo*neeyo
July	**julio** *hoo*leeyo
August	**agosto** a*gos*to
September	**septiembre** septee*yem*breh
October	**octubre** ok*too*breh
November	**noviembre** novee*yem*breh
December	**diciembre** deesee*yem*breh

Seasons

Spring	**primavera** preema*vera*
Summer	**verano** ve*ra*no
Fall/Autumn	**otoño** o*ton*yo
Winter	**invierno** eenvee*yer*no

Holidays

New Year's Day	**Año Nuevo** *anyo nwevo*
Mardi Gras	**Martes de Carnaval** *martes deh karnaval*
Easter	**Pascua** *paskwa*
May Day/Labor Day	**Día del Trabajo** *deeya del trabajo*
Christmas	**Navidad** *naveedad*
New Year's Eve	**Nochevieja** *nocheveeyeha*

Time expressions

It's one o'clock.	**Es la una.** *es la oona*
It's ten past two.	**Son las dos y diez.** *son las dos ee deeyes*
before three o'clock	**antes de las tres** *antes deh las tres*
around quarter to four	**alrededor del cuarto para las cuatro (de las cuatro menos cuarto)** *alrededor del kwarto para las kwatro (deh las kwatro menos kwarto)*
after five o'clock	**después de las cinco** *despwes deh las seenko*
twenty to six	**veinte para las seis (las seis menos veinte)** *veynteh para las seys (las seys menos veynteh)*
at seven thirty	**a las siete y media** *a las seeyeteh ee medeeya*
between eight to nine	**entre las ocho y las nueve** *entreh las ocho ee las nweveh*
from ten til eleven	**desde las diez hasta las once** *desdeh las deeyes asta las onseh*
midnight	**medianoche** *medeeyanocheh*
noon	**mediodía** *medeeyodeeya*
in the morning	**por la mañana** *por la manyana*
in the afternoon	**por la tarde** *por la tardeh*
this evening	**esta noche** *esta nocheh*
at night	**por la noche** *por la nocheh*

On January 23rd	**El 23 de enero** el veynteh*tres* deh e*n*ero
From the 6th to the 7th February	**Del 6 al 7 de febrero** del seys al seeyeteh deh fe*br*ero
March 9th, 2004	**el 9 de marzo del 2004** el *n*weveh deh *m*arso del dos meel *kw*atro
In 2003	**en el 2003** en el dos meel tres
In the nineties	**en los años noventa** en los a*n*yos no*v*enta
today	**hoy** oy
tomorrow	**mañana** ma*ny*ana
the day before yesterday	**antier (anteayer)** antee*yer* (anteya*yer*)
next week	**la semana que viene** la se*m*ana keh vee*y*eneh
ten years ago	**hace diez años** aseh dee*y*es a*ny*os
yesterday afternoon	**ayer por la tarde** a*y*er por la *t*ardeh
last night	**anoche** a*n*ocheh
nowadays	**hoy en día** oy en *d*eeya
day after tomorrow	**pasado mañana** pasado ma*ny*ana
every day	**todos los días** *t*odos los *d*eeyas
at this moment	**en este momento** en esteh mo*m*ento
early	**temprano** tem*pr*ano
late	**tarde** *t*ardeh
on time	**a tiempo** a tee*y*empo
in 10 minutes	**en (durante) diez minutos** en (doo*r*anteh) dee*y*es mee*n*ootos
for two hours	**por (desde hace) dos horas** por (*d*esdeh aseh) dos oras
20 minutes ago	**hace veinte minutos** aseh *v*eynteh mee*n*ootos

Numbers

one half	**una mitad** oona mee*t*ad
one quarter	**un cuarto** oon *kw*arto
one third	**un tercio** oon *t*erseeyo

0	**cero** *sero*	60	**sesenta** se*sen*ta
1	**uno** *oo*no	70	**setenta** se*ten*ta
2	**dos** dos	80	**ochenta** o*chen*ta
3	**tres** tres	90	**noventa** no*ven*ta
4	**cuatro** *kwa*tro	100	**cien/ciento** see*yen*/see*yen*to
5	**cinco** *seen*ko	101	**ciento uno**
6	**seis** seys		see*yen*to *oo*no
7	**siete** see*ye*teh	200	**doscientos/-as**
8	**ocho** *o*cho		dosee*yen*tos/-as
9	**nueve** *nwe*veh	300	**trescientos/-as**
10	**diez** dee*yes*		tresee*yen*tos/-as
11	**once** *on*seh	400	**cuatrocientos/-as**
12	**doce** *do*seh		*kwa*tro-see*yen*tos/-as
13	**trece** *tre*seh	500	**quinientos/-as**
14	**catorce** ka*tor*seh		keenee*yen*tos/-as
15	**quince** *keen*seh	600	**seiscientos/-as**
16	**dieciséis** deeyesee-*seys*		seys-see*yen*tos/-as
17	**diecisiete** deeyesee-see*ye*teh	700	**setecientos/-as**
18	**dieciocho** deeyesee-*yo*cho		seteh-see*yen*tos/-as
19	**diecinueve**	800	**ochocientos/-as**
	deeyesee-*nwe*veh		*o*cho-see*yen*tos/-as
20	**veinte** *veyn*teh	900	**novecientos/-as**
21	**veintiuno** *veyn*tee-*oo*no		*no*veh-see*yen*tos/-as
22	**veintidós** *veyn*tee-*dos*	1,000	**mil** meel
23	**veintitrés** *veyn*tee-*tres*	1st	**1º primero** pree*me*ro
24	**veinticuatro** *veyn*tee-*kwa*tro	2nd	**2º segundo** se*goon*do
30	**treinta** *treyn*ta	3rd	**3º tercero** ter*se*ro
31	**treinta y uno** *treyn*ta-ee-*oo*no	4th	**4º cuarto** *kwar*to
32	**treinta y dos** *treyn*ta-ee-*dos*	5th	**5º quinto** *keen*to
40	**cuarenta** kwa*ren*ta	6th	**6º sexto** *seks*to
41	**cuarenta y uno**	7th	**7º séptimo** *sep*teemo
	kwa*ren*ta-ee-*oo*no	8th	**8º octavo** ok*ta*vo
50	**cincuenta** seen*kwen*ta	9th	**9º noveno** no*ve*no
		10th	**10º décimo** *de*seemo

English-
Spanish

ABREVIATURAS USADAS
EN ESTE DICCIONARIO

adj., adj.	adjetivo	*def.*	definido;
adv., adv.	adverbio		defectivo
AGR.	agricultura	DEP.	deportes
AJED.	ajedrez	DER.	derecho; forense
ÁLG.	álgebra	desus.	desusado
ANAT.	anatomía	DIB.	dibujo
ant.	antiguamente;	*dim.*	diminutivo
	anticuado		
ARIT.	aritmética	ECLES.	eclesiástico;
ARQ.	arquitectura		iglesia
ARQUEOL.	arqueología	ECON.	economía
art.	artículo	E. U.	Estados Unidos
ARTILL.	artillería	ELECT.	electricidad
ASTR.	astronomía;	ENT.	entomología
	astrología	EQUIT.	equitación
AUTO.	automóvil;	ESC.	escultura
	automovilismo	ESGR.	esgrima
aux.	verbo auxiliar	esp.	especialmente
AVIA.	aviación		
		f.	femenino; nombre
B. ART.	bellas artes		femenino
BIB.	Biblia	fam.	familiar
BIOL.	biología	FARM.	farmacia
BOT.	botánica	FERROC.	ferrocarriles
BOX.	boxeo	fig.	figurado
		FIL.	filosofía
CARN.	carnicería	FÍS.	física
CARP.	carpintería	FISIOL.	fisiología
CERÁM.	cerámica	FORT.	fortificación
CINEM.	cinematografía	FOT.	fotografía
CIR.	cirugía		
COC.	cocina	GEOGR.	geografía
COM.	comercio	GEOL.	geología
compar.	comparativo	GEOM.	geometría
Cond.	Condicional	ger., GER.	gerundio
conj.	conjunción	gralte.	generalmente
CONJUG.	Conjugación	GRAM.	gramática
contr.	contracción		
CRIST.	cristalografía	HIST.	historia

i., i.	verbo intransitivo	PERSP.	perspectiva
ICT.	ictiología	*pl.*	plural
impers.	verbo impersonal	poét.	poético
IMPR.	imprenta	POL.	política
IND.	industria	pop.	popular
indef.	indefinido	*pos.*	posesivo
INDIC.,	indicativo	*p. p.*, p. p.	participio pasivo
indic.		*pref.*	prefijo
inf.	infinitivo	*prep.*	preposición
ING.	ingeniería	Pres., *pres.*	presente
Ingl.	Inglaterra	Pret., *pret.*	pretérito
interj.	interjección	*pron.*	pronombre
irreg.	irregular		
		QUÍM.	química
JOY.	joyería		
		RADIO.	radiotelefonía;
LIT.	literatura		radiotelegrafía
LITUR.	liturgia	*ref.*	verbo reflexivo
LÓG.	lógica	REL.	religión
m.	masculino; nombre	S.	sur
	masculino	*s.*	nombre
MAR.	marina; marítimo		substantivo
MAT.	matemáticas	SUBJ.	Subjuntivo
may.	mayúscula	*superl.*	superlativo
MEC.	mecánica		
MED.	medicina	*t.*, t.	verbo transitivo
METAL.	metalurgia	TEAT.	teatro
METEOR.	meteorología	TEJ.	tejeduría
MÉTR.	métrica	TELEF.	telefonía
MIL.	militar; milicia	TELEGR.	telegrafía
MIN.	minería	TELEV.	televisión
min.	minúscula	TEOL.	teología
MINER.	mineralogía	TOP.	topografía
MIT.	mitología	TRIG.	trigonometría
MÚS.	música		
		us.	usado
NAT.	natación		
n. pr.	nombre propio	V.	Véase
		vulg.	vulgarismo
ORN.	ornitología	VET.	veterinaria
PART. PAS.	Participio pasivo	ZOOL.	zoología
pers.	persona(s);		
	personal		

SIGNOS DE LA A.F.I. EMPLEADOS EN LA TRANSCRIPCIÓN FONÉTICA DE LAS PALABRAS INGLESAS

Vocales

[i]	como en español en *vida*, *tigre*.
[e]	como en español en *guerra*, *dejar*, pero aún más abierta.
[æ]	sin equivalencia en español. Sonido intermedio entre la *a* en *caso* y la *e* en *perro*.
[ɑ]	como en español en *laurel*, *ahora*, pero enfatizada y alargada.
[ɔ]	como en español en *roca*, *manojo*, pero aún más abierta.
[u]	como en español en *uno*, pero con el sonido más prolongado.
[ʌ]	sin equivalencia en español. Sonido intermedio entre la *o* y la *e*.
[ə]	sin equivalencia en español. Parecida a la [ə] francesa en *venir*, *petit*.

Semiconsonantes

[j]	como en español en *labio*, *radio*.
[w]	como en español en *luego*, *huevo*.

Consonantes

[p]	como en español en *puerta*, *capa*, pero aspirada.
[t]	como en español en *todo*, *tienda*, pero aspirada.
[k]	como en español en *copa*, *queso*, pero aspirada.
[b]	como en español en *barco*, *vela*, pero aspirada.

[d]   como en español en *conde, candado,* pero aspirada.

[ð]   como en español en *adivinar, adorar.*

[g]   como en español en *guerra, gato,* pero aspirada.

[f]   como en español en *fuerza, fuego.*

[θ]   como en español en *hacer, ácido.*

[s]   como en español en *saber, silencio.*

[ʃ]   sin equivalencia en español. Fricativa palato-alveolar sorda. Parecida a la pronunciación de *chico,* si se alarga la consonante y se redondean los labios.

[v]   sin equivalencia en español. Fricativa labiodental. Al pronunciarla los incisivos superiores tocan el labio inferior y hay vibración de las cuerdas vocales. Es la pronunciación del francés en *avec.*

[z]   como en español en *mismo, asno.*

[ʒ]   sin equivalencia en español. Fricativa palato-alveolar sonora. Parecida a la pronunciación argentina de la *ll* pero con proyección de los labios.

[tʃ]   como en español en *chico, chocolate.*

[dʒ]   sin equivalencia exacta en español. Africada palato-alveolar sonora. Sonido semejante al de la *y* española en *conyuge, yugo.*

[l]   como en español en *labio, cola.*

[m]   como en español en *madre, lima.*

[n]   como en español en *nota, notable.*

[ŋ]   como en español en *cuenca, ángulo.*

[r]   sonido fricativo parecido al de la *r* española en *pero.*

[h]   sonido parecido al de la *j* española en *jerga,* pero mucho más suave.

Otros signos

[']   indica el acento tónico primario.

[,]   indica el acento tónico secundario.

[:]   indica un alargamiento de la vocal.

English - Spanish

A

a [eɪ, ə] *det* un, una.
A [eɪ] *abbr* **1** sobresaliente *(calificación)*. **2** la *(nota musical)*.
abandon [əˈbændən] *vt* abandonar.
abattoir [ˈæbətwɑːʳ] *n* matadero.
abbey [ˈæbɪ] *n* abadía.
abbreviation [əbriːvɪˈeɪʃən] *n* abreviatura.
abdomen [ˈæbdəmən] *n* abdomen.
abduct [æbˈdʌkt] *vt* raptar, secuestrar.
ability [əˈbɪlɪtɪ] *n* **1** capacidad. **2** talento, aptitud.
able [ˈeɪbəl] *adj* hábil, capaz. • **to be able to 1** poder. **2** saber: *he was able to drive when he was sixteen*, sabía conducir a los dieciséis años.
abnormal [æbˈnɔːməl] *adj* **1** anormal. **2** inusual.
aboard [əˈbɔːd] *adv* a bordo.
abort [əˈbɔːt] *vi* abortar.
abortion [əˈbɔːʃən] *n* aborto *(provocado)*.
about [əˈbaʊt] *prep* **1** de, sobre, acerca de. **2** por, en: *he's somewhere about the house*, está por algún rincón de la casa. ► *adv* **1** alrededor de. **2** por aquí, por ahí: *there was nobody about*, no había nadie. • **to be about to...** estar a punto de...
above [əˈbʌv] *prep* **1** por encima de. **2** más de, más que: *above 5,000 people*, más de 5.000 personas. ► *adv* arriba. • **above all** sobre todo.
abridged [əˈbrɪdʒd] *adj* abreviado,-a.
abroad [əˈbrɔːd] *adv* **1** al extranjero. **2** en el extranjero.
absent [ˈæbsənt] *adj* ausente.
absent-minded [æbsəntˈmaɪndɪd] *adj* distraído,-a.
absolute [ˈæbsəluːt] *n* absoluto,-a.
absorb [əbˈzɔːb] *vt* absorber
abstain [əbˈsteɪn] *vi* abstenerse.
abstract [ˈæbstrækt] *adj* abstracto,-a. ► *n* resumen, sinopsis.
abundant [əˈbʌndənt] *adj* abundante.
abuse [əˈbjuːs] *n* **1** insultos. **2** malos tratos. **3** abuso.
abyss [əˈbɪs] *n* abismo.
academic [ækəˈdemɪk] *adj* académico,-a. ► *n* profesor, -ra de universidad. ■ **academic year** curso escolar.
academy [əˈkædəmɪ] *n* academia.

accelerate [æk'seləreɪt] *vt-vi*
acelerar.

accelerator [ək'seləreɪtəʳ] *n*
acelerador.

accent ['æksənt] *n* acento.

accept [ək'sept] *vt* aceptar.

access ['ækses] *n* acceso. ▶ *vt*
COMPUT acceder a.

accessory [æk'sesərɪ] *n* **1** accesorio. **2** cómplice.

accident ['æksɪdənt] *n* accidente.

accident-prone ['æksɪdəntprəʊn] *adj* propenso,-a a los accidentes.

acclaim [ə'kleɪm] *vt* aclamar.

accommodation [əkɒmə'deɪʃən] *n* alojamiento.

accompany [ə'kʌmpənɪ] *vt*
acompañar.

accomplish [ə'kɒmplɪʃ] *vt* lograr, conseguir.

according to [ə'kɔːdɪŋtʊ] *prep*
según.

accordion [ə'kɔːdɪən] *n* acordeón.

account [ə'kaʊnt] *n* **1** cuenta.
2 relato, versión. **3** importancia. • **on account** a cuenta;
on account of por, a causa de.

to account for *vi* explicar.

accounting [ə'kaʊntɪŋ] *n* contabilidad.

accumulate [ə'kjuːmjʊleɪt] *vt-vi* acumular(se).

accurate ['ækjʊrət] *adj* exacto,-a, preciso,-a.

accusation [ækjuː'zeɪʃən] *n*
acusación.

accuse [ə'kjuːz] *vt* acusar.

accustom [ə'kʌstəm] *vt* acostumbrar.

accustomed [ə'kʌstəmd] *adj*
acostumbrado,-a. • **to get accustomed to** acostumbrarse a.

ace [eɪs] *n* as.

ache [eɪk] *n* dolor. ▶ *vi* doler.

achieve [ə'tʃiːv] *vt* lograr.

acid ['æsɪd] *n* ácido. ▶ *adj* ácido,-a. ■ **acid rain** lluvia ácida.

acknowledge [ək'nɒlɪdʒ] *vt*
1 reconocer. **2** agradecer.

acknowledgement [ək'nɒlɪdʒmənt] *n* **1** reconocimiento. **2** acuse de recibo.

acne ['æknɪ] *n* acné.

acorn ['eɪkɔːn] *n* bellota.

acoustic [ə'kuːstɪk] *adj* acústico,-a.

acquaint [ə'kweɪnt] *vt* informar, poner al corriente.

acquaintance [ə'kweɪntəns] *n* conocido,-a.

acquire [ə'kwaɪəʳ] *vt* **1** adquirir *(posesiones)*. **2** obtener, conseguir *(información)*.

acquit [ə'kwɪt] *vt* absolver.

acre ['eɪkəʳ] *n* acre.

acrobat ['ækrəbæt] *n* acróbata.

acronym ['ækrənɪm] *n* sigla.

across [ə'krɒs] *prep* **1** a través de: *to swim across a river*, cruzar un río a nado. **2** al otro lado de: *they live across the*

road, viven enfrente. ► *adv* de un lado a otro.

act [ækt] *n* **1** acto. **2** número: *tonight's first act is a clown*, el primer número de la noche es un payaso. **3** (*Act of Parliament*) ley. ► *vi* actuar. ■ **act of God** fuerza mayor.

acting ['æktɪŋ] *n* actuación. ► *adj* en funciones.

action ['ækʃən] *n* acción. ● **out of action** fuera de servicio; **to bring an action against** SB entablar una demanda contra ALGN.

active ['æktɪv] *adj* activo,-a.

activity [æk'tɪvɪti] *n* actividad.

actor ['æktər] *n* actor.

actress ['æktrəs] *n* actriz.

actual ['æktjuəl] *adj* **1** real. **2** exacto,-a: *those were her actual words*, esas fueron sus palabras exactas.

actually ['æktjuəli] *adv* **1** en realidad, de hecho. **2** de verdad: *have you actually seen a ghost?*, ¿de verdad que has visto un fantasma?

acute [ə'kjuːt] *adj* agudo,-a.

ad [æd] *n fam* anuncio.

adamant ['ædəmənt] *adj* firme, inflexible.

adapt [ə'dæpt] *vt-vi* adaptar(se).

adaptor [ə'dæptər] *n* ladrón (*enchufe*).

add [æd] *vt* añadir. ► *vt-vi* sumar.

to add to *vt* aumentar.

to add up *vt-vi* sumar. ► *vi fig* cuadrar: *his version doesn't add up*, su versión no cuadra.

adder ['ædər] *n* víbora.

addict ['ædɪkt] *n* adicto,-a.

addition [ə'dɪʃən] *n* adición. ● **in addition to** además de.

additive ['ædɪtɪv] *n* aditivo.

address [ə'dres] *n* **1** dirección. **2** discurso. **3** conferencia. ► *vt* dirigirse a. ■ **address book** agenda.

adept [ə'dept] *adj* experto,-a.

adequate ['ædɪkwət] *adj* adecuado,-a, satisfactorio,-a.

adjective ['ædʒɪktɪv] *n* adjetivo.

adjourn [ə'dʒɜːn] *vt* aplazar.

adjust [ə'dʒʌst] *vt* ajustar (*temperatura*). ► *vi* adaptarse.

adjustable [ə'dʒʌstəbəl] *adj* regulable. ■ **adjustable spanner** llave inglesa.

adjustment [ə'dʒʌstmənt] *n* ajuste.

administration [ədmɪnɪs'treɪʃən] *n* administración.

administrator [əd'mɪnɪstreɪtə'] *n* administrador,-ra.

admiral ['ædmərəl] *n* almirante.

admiration [ædmɪ'reɪʃən] *n* admiración.

admire [əd'maɪə'] *vt* admirar.

admission [əd'mɪʃən] *n* **1** ingreso (*en hospital, institución*). **2** entrada: *"Admission free"*, "Entrada gratuita".

admit [əd'mɪt] *vt* **1** admitir. **2** ingresar *(en hospital)*.
adolescent [ædə'lesənt] *adj-n* adolescente.
adopt [ə'dɒpt] *vt* adoptar.
adore [ə'dɔːʳ] *vt* adorar.
adorn [ə'dɔːn] *vt* adornar.
adrift [ə'drɪft] *adj* a la deriva.
adult ['ædʌlt] *adj-n* adulto,-a.
adulterate [ə'dʌltəreɪt] *vt* adulterar.
advance [əd'vɑːns] *n* **1** avance. **2** anticipo, adelanto *(de dinero)*. ▶ *vt* **1** avanzar *(tropas)*. **2** ascender *(empleado)*. **3** adelantar *(reunión)*. **4** anticipar *(dinero)*. ▶ *vi* avanzar. • **in advance** por adelantado.
advantage [əd'vɑːntɪdʒ] *n* ventaja.
adventure [əd'ventʃəʳ] *n* aventura. ■ **adventure playground** parque infantil.
adverb ['ædvɜːb] *n* adverbio.
adversary ['ædvəsəri] *n* adversario,-a.
adversity [əd'vɜːsɪti] *n* adversidad.
advert ['ædvɜːt] *n fam* anuncio.
advertise ['ædvətaɪz] *vt* anunciar. ▶ *vi* hacer publicidad.
advertisement [əd'vɜːtɪsmənt] *n* anuncio.
advice [əd'vaɪs] *n* consejos.
advise [əd'vaɪz] *vt* aconsejar. • **to advise against** STH desaconsejar algo.
adviser [əd'vaɪzəʳ] *n* asesor,-a.

advocate ['ædvəkət] *n* partidario,-a.
aerial ['eərɪəl] *n* antena.
aerodynamic [eərəʊdar'næmɪk] *adj* aerodinámico,-a.
aeroplane ['eərəpleɪn] *n* avión.
aerosol ['eərəsɒl] *n* aerosol.
aesthetic [iːs'θetɪk] *adj* estético,-a.
affair [ə'feəʳ] *n* **1** asunto. **2** caso: *the Watergate affair*, el caso Watergate. **3** lío, aventura *(amorosa)*.
affect [ə'fekt] *vt* afectar.
affection [ə'fekʃən] *n* afecto.
affectionate [ə'fekʃənət] *adj* afectuoso,-a.
affiliated [ə'fɪlieɪtɪd] *adj* afiliado,-a.
affirmative [ə'fɜːmətɪv] *adj* afirmativo,-a.
affluent ['æfluənt] *adj* rico,-a, próspero,-a.
afford [ə'fɔːd] *vt* permitirse: *I can't afford to pay £750 for a coat*, no puedo permitirme pagar 750 libras por un abrigo.
afraid [ə'freɪd] *adj* temeroso,-a. • **to be afraid** tener miedo.
afresh [ə'freʃ] *adv* de nuevo.
after ['ɑːftəʳ] *prep* **1** después de. **2** detrás de: *the police are after us*, la policía nos está persiguiendo. ▶ *adv* después. ▶ *conj* después de que. • **after all** al fin y al cabo.
after-effect ['ɑːftərɪfekt] *n* efecto secundario.

afternoon [ɑːftə'nuːn] *n* tarde: *good afternoon*, buenas tardes.

after-sales ['ɑːftə'seɪlz] *adj* posventa.

aftershave ['ɑːftəʃeɪv] *n* loción para después del afeitado.

afterwards ['ɑːftəwədz] *adv* después, luego.

again [ə'gen, ə'geɪn] *prep* de nuevo, otra vez.

against [ə'genst, ə'geɪnst] *prep* contra.

age [eɪdʒ] *n* edad. ▶ *vi-vt* envejecer. • **of age** mayor de edad; **under age** menor de edad.

aged [eɪdʒd] *adj* **1** de… años: *a boy aged ten*, un niño de diez años. **2** viejo,-a, anciano,-a.

agency ['eɪdʒənsɪ] *n* agencia.

agenda [ə'dʒendə] *n* orden del día.

agent ['eɪdʒənt] *n* agente.

ages ['eɪdʒɪz] *npl* años, siglos: *it's ages since she left*, hace años que se marchó.

aggressive [ə'gresɪv] *adj* agresivo,-a.

agility [ə'dʒɪlɪtɪ] *n* agilidad.

agitate ['ædʒɪteɪt] *vt* agitar.

ago [ə'gəʊ] *adv* hace: *a long time ago*, hace mucho tiempo.

agonize ['ægənaɪz] *vi* atormentarse, angustiarse.

agony ['ægənɪ] *n* **1** dolor. **2** angustia.

agree [ə'griː] *vi-vt* **1** estar de acuerdo. **2** ponerse de acuerdo, acordar. **3** acceder, consentir: *will he agree to our request?*, ¿accederá a nuestra petición? **4** concordar, encajar: *the two men's stories don't agree*, las historias de los dos hombres no encajan. **5** sentar bien *(comida)*.

agreeable [ə'griːəbəl] *adj* agradable.

agreement [ə'griːmənt] *n* acuerdo.

agriculture ['ægrɪkʌltʃə'] *n* agricultura.

ahead [ə'hed] *adv* delante.

aid [eɪd] *n* ayuda, auxilio. ▶ *vt* ayudar, auxiliar.

AIDS [eɪdz] *abbr* SIDA.

ailment ['eɪlmənt] *n* dolencia, achaque.

aim [eɪm] *n* **1** puntería. **2** meta, objetivo. • **to take aim** apuntar.

to aim at *vt* apuntar a.

to aim to *vt* tener la intención de, proponerse.

air [eə'] *n* aire. ▶ *vt* **1** airear. **2** ventilar. ■ **air hostess** azafata.

airbag ['eəbæg] *n* airbag.

air-conditioned [eəkən'dɪʃənd] *adj* con aire acondicionado, climatizado,-a.

aircraft ['eəkrɑːft] *n* avión. ■ **aircraft carrier** portaaviones.

airline ['eəlaɪn] *n* compañía aérea.

airplane ['eəpleɪn] *n* US avión.

airport ['eəpɔːt] *n* aeropuerto.

airsick ['eəsɪk] *adj* mareado,-a *(en el avión)*.

airstrip ['eəstrɪp] *n* pista de aterrizaje.

airtight ['eətaɪt] *adj* hermético,-a.

airy ['eərɪ] *adj* bien ventilado,-a.

aisle [aɪl] *n* **1** pasillo. **2** nave lateral.

alarm [ə'lɑːm] *n* alarma. ► *vt* alarmar. ▪ **alarm clock** despertador.

album ['ælbəm] *n* álbum.

alcohol ['ælkəhɒl] *n* alcohol.

alcoholic [ælkə'hɒlɪk] *adj* alcohólico,-a.

ale [eɪl] *n* cerveza.

alert [ə'lɜːt] *adj* alerta. ► *n* alarma, aviso: *bomb alert*, aviso de bomba. ► *vt* alertar.

algae ['ældʒiː] *npl* algas.

alibi ['ælɪbaɪ] *n* coartada.

alien ['eɪlɪən] *adj* **1** extranjero,-a. **2** extraterrestre.

alight [ə'laɪt] *adj* encendido,-a.

to alight on *vt* **1** posarse en. **2** darse cuenta de.

align [ə'laɪn] *vt-vi* alinear(se).

alike [ə'laɪk] *adj* igual. ► *adv* igual, de la misma forma. • **to look alike** parecerse.

alimony ['ælɪmənɪ] *n* pensión alimenticia.

alive [ə'laɪv] *adj* vivo,-a.

all [ɔːl] *adj* todo,-a, todos,-as. ► *pron* **1** todo, la totalidad. **2** lo único. **3** todos, todo el mundo. ► *adv* **1** completamente, muy: *you're all dirty!*, ¡estás todo sucio! **2** empatados, iguales: *the score was three all*, empataron a tres. • **after all** después de todo; **all right 1** bueno,-a. **2** bien: *are you all right?*, ¿estás bien?; **at all** en absoluto; **not at all 1** en absoluto. **2** no hay de qué, de nada: *Thank you very much. –Not at all*, Muchas gracias. –De nada.

allege [ə'ledʒ] *vt* alegar.

alleged [ə'ledʒd] *adj* presunto,-a, supuesto,-a.

allergy ['ælədʒɪ] *n* alergia.

alley ['ælɪ] *n* callejuela, callejón.

alligator ['ælɪgeɪtə'] *n* caimán.

allocate ['æləkeɪt] *vt* asignar.

allow [ə'laʊ] *vt* **1** permitir, dejar. **2** admitir: *dogs are not allowed in*, no se admiten perros. **3** conceder, dar, asignar.

to allow for *vt* tener en cuenta.

allowance [ə'laʊəns] *n* **1** prestación, subsidio, dietas. **2** US paga semanal.

alloy ['ælɔɪ] *n* aleación.

ally ['ælaɪ] *n* aliado,-a. ► *vt-vi* aliar(se).

almond ['ɑːmənd] *n* almendra.

almost ['ɔːlməʊst] *adv* casi.

alone [ə'ləʊn] *adj* solo,-a.

along [ə'lɒŋ] *prep* a lo largo de, por. ► *adv* hacia delante:

she was walking along, iba caminando. • **all along** desde el principio; **along with** junto con; **come along!** ¡ven!, ¡venid!

alongside [əlɒŋ'saɪd] *prep* al lado de. ► *adv* al costado.

aloof [ə'luːf] *adj* distante.

aloud [ə'laʊd] *adv* en voz alta.

alphabet ['ælfəbet] *n* alfabeto.

already [ɔːl'redɪ] *adv* ya.

also ['ɔːlsəʊ] *adv* también.

altar ['ɔːltəʳ] *n* altar.

alter ['ɔːltəʳ] *vt* **1** cambiar, modificar. **2** arreglar *(ropa)*.

alternate [*(adj)* ɔːl'tɜːnət, *(vb)* 'ɔːltɜːneɪt] *adj* alterno,-a. ► *vt-vi* alternar(se).

alternative [ɔːl'tɜːnətɪv] *adj* alternativo,-a. ► *n* alternativa.

although [ɔːl'ðəʊ] *conj* aunque.

altogether [ɔːltə'geðəʳ] *adv* **1** del todo, completamente. **2** en conjunto, en total. • **in the altogether** en cueros.

always ['ɔːlweɪz] *adv* siempre.

amateur ['æmətəʳ] *adj-n* aficionado,-a.

amaze [ə'meɪz] *vt* asombrar.

amazing [ə'meɪzɪŋ] *adj* asombroso.

ambassador [æm'bæsədəʳ] *n* embajador,-ra.

amber ['æmbəʳ] *n* ámbar.

ambience ['æmbɪəns] *n* ambiente.

ambiguous [æm'bɪgjʊəs] *adj* ambiguo,-a.

ambition [æm'bɪʃən] *n* ambición.

ambitious [æm'bɪʃəs] *adj* ambicioso,-a.

ambulance ['æmbjʊləns] *n* ambulancia.

ambush ['æmbʊʃ] *n* emboscada. ► *vt* tender una emboscada a.

ameba [ə'miːbə] *n* US ameba.

amend [ə'mend] *vt* enmendar.

amenities [ə'miːnɪtɪz] *npl* servicios, instalaciones.

amiable ['eɪmɪəbəl] *adj* amable.

amid [ə'mɪd] *prep* en medio de, entre.

ammonia [ə'məʊnɪə] *n* amoníaco.

ammunition [æmjʊ'nɪʃən] *n* municiones.

amoeba [æ'miːbə] *n* ameba.

among [ə'mʌŋ] *prep* entre.

amongst [ə'mʌŋst] *prep* entre.

amount [ə'maʊnt] *n* cantidad.

to amount to *vt* ascender a.

ampere ['æmpeəʳ] *n* amperio.

amphibian [æm'fɪbɪən] *n* anfibio.

ample ['æmpəl] *adj* **1** abundante. **2** amplio,-a *(habitación)*.

amplifier ['æmplɪfaɪəʳ] *n* amplificador.

amplify ['æmplɪfaɪ] *vt* amplificar.

amputate ['æmpjʊteɪt] *vt* amputar.

amuse [ə'mjuːz] *vt* entretener, divertir.

amusement [ə'mjuːzmənt] *n* diversión, entretenimiento. ■ **amusement park** parque de atracciones.

amusing [ə'mjuːzɪŋ] *adj* divertido,-a.

an [ən, æn] *det* un,-a.

anaemia [ə'niːmɪə] *n* GB anemia.

anaesthesia [ænəs'θiːzɪə] *n* GB anestesia.

anal ['eɪnəl] *adj* anal.

analgesic [ænəl'dʒiːzɪk] *adj* analgésico,-a. ► *n* analgésico.

analyse ['ænəlaɪz] *vt* analizar.

analysis [ə'næləsɪs] *n* análisis.

anarchy ['ænəkɪ] *n* anarquía.

anatomy [ə'nætəmɪ] *n* anatomía.

ancestor ['ænsəstə'] *n* antepasado.

anchor ['æŋkə'] *n* ancla. ► *vt-vi* anclar.

anchovy ['æntʃəvɪ] *n* anchoa.

ancient ['eɪnʃənt] *adj* antiguo, -a, histórico,-a.

and [ænd, ənd] *conj* y, e.

anecdote ['ænɪkdəut] *n* anécdota.

anemia [ə'niːmɪə] *n* US anemia.

anesthesia [ænəs'θiːzɪə] *n* US anestesia.

angel ['eɪndʒəl] *n* ángel.

anger ['æŋgə'] *n* cólera, ira.

angle ['æŋgəl] *n* ángulo.

angler ['æŋglə'] *n* pescador,-ra *(de caña)*. ■ **angler fish** rape.

angling ['æŋglɪŋ] *n* pesca *(con caña)*.

angry ['æŋgrɪ] *adj* enfadado,-a.

anguish ['æŋgwɪʃ] *n* angustia.

animal ['ænɪməl] *n* animal.

animate ['ænɪmeɪt] *vt* animar.

ankle ['æŋkəl] *n* tobillo.

annex [*(vb)* ə'neks*(n)* 'aneks] *vt* anexar. ► *n* US anexo.

annexe ['ænəks] *n* GB anexo.

annihilate [ə'naɪəleɪt] *vt* aniquilar.

anniversary [ænɪ'vɜːsərɪ] *n* aniversario.

announce [ə'nauns] *vt* anunciar.

announcement [ə'naunsmənt] *n* anuncio.

announcer [ə'naunsə'] *n* presentador,-ra, locutor,-ra.

annoy [ə'nɔɪ] *vt* molestar.

anonymous [ə'nɒnɪməs] *adj* anónimo,-a.

anorexia [ænə'reksɪə] *n* anorexia.

another [ə'nʌðə'] *adj-pron* otro,-a.

answer ['ɑːnsə'] *n* respuesta. ► *vt-vi* responder, contestar.

to answer back *vt-vi* replicar *(con insolencia)*.

to answer for *vt* responder por, responder de.

answering machine ['ɑːnsərɪŋməʃiːn] *n* contestador automático.

ant [ænt] *n* hormiga. ▪ **ant hill** hormiguero.

antelope ['æntɪləup] *n* antílope.

antenna [æn'tenə] *n* antena.

anthem ['ænθəm] *n* himno.

antibiotic [æntɪbaɪ'ɒtɪk] *n* antibiótico. ► *adj* antibiótico,-a.

antibody ['æntɪbɒdɪ] *n* anticuerpo.

anticipate [æn'tɪsɪpeɪt] *vt* **1** esperar: *we anticipate problems*, esperamos problemas. **2** prever: *as anticipated*, de acuerdo con lo previsto.

anticlockwise [æntɪ'klɒkwaɪz] *adj* en el sentido contrario al de las agujas del reloj.

antifreeze ['æntɪfriːz] *n* anticongelante.

antique [æn'tiːk] *adj* antiguo, -a. ► *n* antigüedad. ▪ **antique shop** anticuario, tienda de antigüedades.

antiseptic [æntɪ'septɪk] *adj* antiséptico,-a. ► *n* antiséptico.

antivirus [æntɪ'vaɪrəs] *adj* antivirus.

antlers ['æntləʳ] *npl* cornamenta.

anus ['eɪnəs] *n* ano.

anvil ['ænvɪl] *n* yunque.

anxious ['æŋkʃəs] *adj* ansioso,-a.

any ['enɪ] *adj* algún,-una, ningún,-una *(con el verbo negativo)*, cualquier,-ra, todo,-a: *any fool knows that*, cualquier tonto sabe eso. ► *pron* alguno,-a, ninguno,-a *(con el verbo negativo)*, cualquiera: *I asked for some records, but they hadn't got any left*, pedí unos discos pero ya no quedaba ninguno. ► *adv*: *I don't work there any more*, ya no trabajo allí.

anybody ['enɪbɒdɪ] *pron* alguien, alguno,-a, nadie *(con el verbo negativo)*, cualquiera: *don't tell anybody*, no se lo digas a nadie.

anyhow ['enɪhau] *adv* **1** en todo caso. **2** bueno, pues. **3** de cualquier forma.

anyone ['enɪwʌn] *pron* → anybody.

anything ['enɪθɪŋ] *pron* algo, alguna cosa, nada *(con el verbo negativo)*, cualquier cosa, todo cuanto: *do you want anything else?*, ¿quieres algo más?

anyway ['enɪweɪ] *adv* → anyhow.

anywhere ['enɪweəʳ] *adv* **1** (en) algún sitio, a algún sitio. **2** (en) ningún sitio, a ningún sitio *(con el verbo negativo)*. **3** donde sea, en cualquier sitio, a donde sea, a cualquier sitio: *I'd go anywhere with you*, iría a cualquier sitio contigo.

aorta [eɪ'ɔːtə] *n* aorta.

apart [ə'pɑːt] *adv* separado,-a. ● **apart from** aparte de, excepto, menos.

apartment [ə'pɑːtmənt] n piso, apartamento.
apathy ['æpəθɪ] n apatía.
ape [eɪp] n simio. ► vt imitar.
aperitif [əperɪ'tiːf] n aperitivo.
apiece [ə'piːs] adv cada uno,-a.
apologize [ə'pɒlədʒaɪz] vi disculparse, pedir perdón.
apology [ə'pɒlədʒɪ] n disculpa.
appal [ə'pɔːl] vt GB horrorizar.
appall [ə'pɔːl] vt US horrorizar.
apparatus [æpə'reɪtəs] n equipo, aparatos.
apparent [ə'pærənt] adj 1 evidente. 2 aparente.
appeal [ə'piːl] n 1 llamamiento. 2 petición, súplica. 3 atractivo. 4 apelación (contra sentencia judicial). ► vi 1 pedir, solicitar, suplicar. 2 atraer: it doesn't appeal to me, no me atrae. 3 apelar (contra sentencia judicial).
appealing [ə'piːlɪŋ] adj atractivo.
appear [ə'pɪəʳ] vi 1 aparecer. 2 parecer: this appears to be a mistake, parece que esto es un error.
appearance [ə'pɪərəns] n 1 aparición. 2 apariencia, aspecto.
appendicitis [əpendɪ'saɪtɪs] n apendicitis.
appendix [ə'pendɪks] n apéndice.
appetizer ['æpɪtaɪzəʳ] n aperitivo.

appetizing ['æpɪtaɪzɪŋ] adj apetitoso,-a.
applaud [ə'plɔːd] vt-vi aplaudir.
applause [ə'plɔːz] n aplausos.
apple ['æpəl] n manzana. ▪ **apple pie** tarta de manzana.
appliance [ə'plaɪəns] n aparato.
applicant ['æplɪkənt] n candidato,-a, solicitante.
application [æplɪ'keɪʃən] n 1 solicitud. 2 aplicación. ▪ **application form** impreso de solicitud.
apply [ə'plaɪ] vt aplicar. ► vi 1 aplicarse. 2 dirigirse, presentarse, solicitar: to apply for a job, solicitar un trabajo.
appointment [ə'pɔɪntmənt] n 1 cita, hora: I've got an appointment with the doctor, tengo hora con el médico. 2 nombramiento.
appraise [ə'preɪz] vt valorar.
appreciate [ə'priːʃɪeɪt] vt 1 agradecer. 2 entender. 3 valorar, apreciar.
apprehension [æprɪ'henʃən] n 1 detención, captura. 2 aprensión, recelo.
apprehensive [æprɪ'hensɪv] adj aprensivo.
apprentice [ə'prentɪs] n aprendiz,-za.
approach [ə'prəʊtʃ] n 1 aproximación, acercamiento. 2 entrada, acceso (a un lugar). 3 enfoque (de un problema). ► vt 1 acercarse a, aproximarse a.

2 enfocar, abordar *(un problema)*. ▪ **approach road** vía de acceso.

appropriate [əˈprəʊprɪət] *adj* apropiado,-a.

approval [əˈpruːvəl] *n* aprobación. ▪ **on approval** a prueba.

approve [əˈpruːv] *vt* aprobar.

to approve of *vt* aprobar.

approximate [əˈprɒksɪmət] *adj* aproximado,-a.

apricot [ˈeɪprɪkɒt] *n* albaricoque.

April [ˈeɪprɪl] *n* abril. ▪ **April Fool's day** el día de los Inocentes *(celebrado el 1 de abril)*.

apron [ˈeɪprən] *n* delantal.

apt [æpt] *adj* apropiado,-a.

aquarium [əˈkweərɪəm] *n* acuario.

Arab [ˈærəb] *adj* árabe. ► *n* árabe.

arbitrate [ˈɑːbɪtreɪt] *vt-vi* arbitrar.

arc [ɑːk] *n* arco.

arcade [ɑːˈkeɪd] *n* **1** galería comercial. **2** salón recreativo. ▪ **arcade game** videojuego.

arch [ɑːtʃ] *n* arco.

archaeology [ɑːkɪˈɒlədʒɪ] *n* arqueología.

archery [ˈɑːtʃərɪ] *n* tiro con arco.

archipelago [ɑːkɪˈpelɪgəʊ] *n* archipiélago.

architect [ˈɑːkɪtekt] *n* arquitecto,-a.

architecture [ˈɑːkɪtektʃəʳ] *n* arquitectura.

archive [ˈɑːkaɪv] *n* archivo.

are [ɑːʳ, əʳ] *pres* → be.

area [ˈeərɪə] *n* área.

arena [əˈriːnə] *n* **1** estadio. **2** ruedo *(de plaza de toros)*.

argue [ˈɑːgjuː] *vi* **1** discutir. **2** argüir, argumentar.

argument [ˈɑːgjʊmənt] *n* **1** discusión, disputa. **2** argumento.

arise [əˈraɪz] *vi* **1** surgir, provenir de. **2** presentarse.

aristocrat [ˈærɪstəkræt] *n* aristócrata.

arithmetic [əˈrɪθmətɪk] *n* aritmética.

ark [ɑːk] *n* arca.

arm [ɑːm] *n* **1** brazo. **2** manga. **3** arma.

armchair [ˈɑːmtʃeəʳ] *n* sillón.

armour [ˈɑːməʳ] (US **armor**) *n* **1** armadura. **2** blindaje.

armpit [ˈɑːmpɪt] *n* sobaco, axila.

army [ˈɑːmɪ] *n* ejército.

aroma [əˈrəʊmə] *n* aroma.

arose [əˈrəʊz] *pt* → arise.

around [əˈraʊnd] *adv* alrededor. ► *prep* alrededor de.

arouse [əˈraʊz] *vt* despertar.

arrange [əˈreɪndʒ] *vt* **1** arreglar, colocar, ordenar. **2** planear, organizar, concertar.

arrangement [əˈreɪndʒmənt] *n* **1** arreglo *(floral, musical)*. **2** acuerdo, arreglo. ► *npl* **arrangements** planes, preparativos.

arrears [əˈrɪəz] *npl* atrasos.

arrest [əˈrest] *n* arresto. ▶ *vt* arrestar, detener: *to be under arrest*, estar detenido.

arrival [əˈraɪvəl] *n* llegada.

arrive [əˈraɪv] *vi* llegar.

arrow [ˈærəʊ] *n* flecha.

arse [ɑːs] *n* GB *vulg* culo.

arson [ˈɑːsən] *n* incendio provocado.

art [ɑːt] *n* arte. ▶ *npl* **arts** letras. ■ **arts and crafts** artes y oficios.

artery [ˈɑːterɪ] *n* arteria.

artichoke [ˈɑːtɪtʃəʊk] *n* alcachofa.

article [ˈɑːtɪkəl] *n* artículo. ■ **leading article** editorial.

artificial [ɑːtɪˈfɪʃəl] *adj* artificial.

artisan [ˈɑːtɪzæn] *n* artesano,-a.

artist [ˈɑːtɪst] *n* artista.

as [æz, əz] *prep* como. ▶ *conj* **1** mientras, cuando: *she sang as she painted*, cantaba mientras pintaba. **2** como, ya que, puesto que: *as the hotel was full, we had to look for another*, como el hotel estaba completo, tuvimos que buscar otro. **3** como: *as you know*, como sabes. ● **as… as 1** tan… como: *as big as an elephant*, tan grande como un elefante. **2** tanto como: *he works as little as possible*, trabaja lo mínimo posible; **as for** en cuanto a; **as if** como si; **as of** desde; **as though** como si; **as yet** hasta ahora.

asbestos [æsˈbestəs] *n* amianto.

ascend [əˈsend] *vt-vi* ascender, subir.

ascent [əˈsent] *n* subida.

ascribe [əsˈkraɪb] *vt* atribuir.

ash[1] [æʃ] *n* ceniza.

ash[2] [æʃ] *n* fresno.

ashamed [əˈʃeɪmd] *adj* avergonzado,-a.

ashore [əˈʃɔːʳ] *adv* en tierra, a tierra. ● **to go ashore** desembarcar.

ashtray [ˈæʃtreɪ] *n* cenicero.

aside [əˈsaɪd] *adv* al lado, a un lado. ▶ *n* aparte *(en teatro)*.

ask [ɑːsk] *vt* **1** preguntar. **2** pedir. **3** invitar, convidar: *they asked me to dinner*, me invitaron a cenar.

to ask after *vt* preguntar por.

to ask for *vt* pedir.

to ask out *vt* invitar a salir.

asleep [əˈsliːp] *adj-adv* dormido,-a: *to fall asleep*, dormirse.

asparagus [əsˈpærəgəs] *n* espárragos.

aspect [ˈæspekt] *n* **1** aspecto. **2** orientación *(de edificio)*.

asphalt [ˈæsfælt] *n* asfalto.

aspire [əsˈpaɪəʳ] *vi* aspirar.

aspirin® [ˈæspɪrɪn] *n* aspirina®.

ass [æs] *n* burro,-a, asno,-a.

assailant [əˈseɪlənt] *n* agresor,-ra.

assault [əˈsɔːlt] *n* **1** asalto *(militar)*. **2** agresión *(a persona)*.

assemble [əˈsembəl] *vt* montar, armar. ▶ *vi* reunirse.

assembly [ə'semblɪ] *n* **1** reunión, asamblea. **2** montaje, ensamblaje. ▪ **assembly hall** salón de actos.

assert [ə'sɜːt] *vt* **1** afirmar. **2** imponer *(autoridad)*.

assess [ə'ses] *vt* valorar.

asset ['æset] *n* ventaja, baza. ▶ *npl* **assets** bienes.

assign [ə'saɪn] *vt* asignar.

assignment [ə'saɪnmənt] *n* **1** misión. **2** tarea, trabajo.

assist [ə'sɪst] *vt* ayudar.

assistant [ə'sɪstənt] *n* ayudante. ▪ **assistant manager** subdirector,-ra.

associate [*(n)* ə'səʊsɪət, *(vb)* ə'səʊsɪeɪt] *n* socio,-a. ● *vt-vi* asociar(se). ● **to associate with SB** relacionarse con ALGN.

association [əsəʊsɪ'eɪʃən] *n* asociación.

assortment [ə'sɔːtmənt] *n* surtido.

assume [ə'sjuːm] *vt* **1** suponer. **2** tomar, asumir *(responsabilidad)*. **3** adoptar *(actitud)*.

assurance [ə'ʃʊərəns] *n* **1** garantía. **2** seguro.

assure [ə'ʃʊə'] *vt* asegurar.

asthma ['æsmə] *n* asma.

astonish [əs'tɒnɪʃ] *vt* asombrar.

astray [ə'streɪ] *adj-adv* extraviado,-a. ● **to go astray 1** extraviarse. **2** descarriarse.

astrology [əs'trɒlədʒɪ] *n* astrología.

astronaut ['æstrənɔːt] *n* astronauta.

astronomy [əs'trɒnəmɪ] *n* astronomía.

astute [əs'tjuːt] *adj* astuto,-a, sagaz.

asylum [ə'saɪləm] *n* **1** asilo, refugio. **2** manicomio.

at [æt, ət] *prep* en, a: *at home*, en casa; *at night*, por la noche; *at the beginning/end*, al principio/final; *at 50 miles an hour*, a 50 millas la hora.

ate [et, eɪt] *pt* → eat.

atheist ['eɪθɪɪst] *n* ateo,-a.

athlete ['æθliːt] *n* atleta.

athletics [æθ'letɪks] *n* atletismo.

atlas ['ætləs] *n* atlas.

atmosphere ['ætməsfɪə'] *n* atmósfera.

atom ['ætəm] *n* átomo. ▪ **atom bomb** bomba atómica.

atrocity [ə'trɒsɪtɪ] *n* atrocidad.

attach [ə'tætʃ] *vt* **1** sujetar. **2** atar. **3** pegar. **4** adjuntar.

attachment [ə'tætʃmənt] *n* **1** accesorio. **2** archivo adjunto, anexo. **3** cariño, apego.

attack [ə'tæk] *n* ataque. ▶ *vt* atacar.

attain [ə'teɪn] *vt* lograr.

attempt [ə'tempt] *n* intento. ▶ *vt* intentar.

attend [ə'tend] *vt* asistir a.

to attend to *vt* ocuparse de

attendance [ə'tendəns] *n* **1** asistencia. **2** asistentes.

attention [ə'tenʃən] n atención.

attic ['ætɪk] n desván.

attitude ['ætɪtjuːd] n actitud.

attorney [ə'tɜːnɪ] n US abogado,-a. ■ **Attorney General** GB Fiscal General.

attract [ə'trækt] vt atraer.

aubergine ['əʊbəʒiːn] n GB berenjena.

auction ['ɔːkʃən] n subasta. ► vt subastar.

audience ['ɔːdɪəns] n **1** público, espectadores. **2** audiencia (de televisión).

audit ['ɔːdɪt] n auditoría. ► vt auditar.

August ['ɔːgəst] n agosto.

aunt [ɑːnt] n tía.

authentic [ɔː'θentɪk] adj auténtico,-a.

author ['ɔːθəʳ] n autor,-ra.

authority [ɔː'θɒrɪtɪ] n autoridad. ● **on good authority** de buena tinta.

authorize ['ɔːθəraɪz] vt autorizar.

automatic [ɔːtə'mætɪk] adj automático,-a.

automaton [ɔː'tɒmətən] n autómata.

automobile ['ɔːtəməbiːl] n automóvil.

autopsy ['ɔːtɒpsɪ] n autopsia.

autoteller ['ɔːtəʊtələʳ] n cajero automático.

autumn ['ɔːtəm] n otoño.

auxiliary [ɔːg'zɪljərɪ] adj auxiliar.

available [ə'veɪləbəl] adj disponible.

avalanche ['ævəlɑːnʃ] n alud, avalancha.

avenge [ə'vendʒ] vt vengar.

avenue ['ævənjuː] n avenida.

average ['ævərɪdʒ] n promedio, media. ► adj medio,-a. ● **on average** por término medio.

aviation [eɪvɪ'eɪʃən] n aviación.

avocado [ævə'kɑːdəʊ] n aguacate.

avoid [ə'vɔɪd] vt evitar.

awake [ə'weɪk] adj despierto, -a. ► vt-vi despertar(se).

awaken [ə'weɪkən] vt-vi → awake.

award [ə'wɔːd] n **1** premio. **2** beca. ► vt otorgar, conceder.

aware [ə'weəʳ] adj consciente. ● **to be aware of** ser consciente de.

away [ə'weɪ] adv lejos, fuera: **he lives 4 km away**, vive a 4 km de aquí.

awful ['ɔːfʊl] adj horrible.

awkward ['ɔːkwəd] adj **1** torpe (gesto). **2** difícil, complicado, -a. **3** embarazo-so,-a, delicado,-a (situación).

awning ['ɔːnɪŋ] n toldo.

awoke [ə'wəʊk] pt → awake.

awoken [ə'wəʊkən] pp → awake.

ax [æks] n US hacha.

axe [æks] n GB hacha.

axis ['æksɪs] n eje.

axle ['æksəl] n eje.

B

baa [bɑː] *vi* balar.

B & B ['biːənˈbiː] *abbr (bed and breakfast)* hostal familiar.

babble ['bæbəl] *vt-vi* balbucear.

baby ['beɪbɪ] *n* bebé, niño,-a.

baby-sitter ['beɪbɪsɪtəʳ] *n* canguro.

bachelor ['bætʃələʳ] *n* soltero.

back [bæk] *adj* trasero,-a, posterior. ► *n* **1** espalda. **2** lomo *(de animal)*. **3** respaldo *(de silla)*. **4** fondo, parte de atrás. **5** defensa *(en deportes)*. ► *adv* **1** atrás, hacia atrás, hace. **2** de vuelta. ► *vt* **1** apoyar, respaldar. **2** financiar. **3** dar marcha atrás a *(coche)*. ► *vi* retroceder. ●**back to front** al revés. ■**back pay** atrasos; **back street** callejuela.

backbone ['bækbəun] *n* columna vertebral.

background ['bækɡraund] *n* **1** fondo *(de imagen)*. **2** *fig* origen, formación.

backhand ['bækhænd] *n* revés.

backpack ['bækpæk] *n* mochila.

backstroke ['bækstrəuk] *n* espalda *(en natación)*.

backup ['bækʌp] *n* apoyo. ■ **backup copy** copia de seguridad.

backward ['bækwəd] **1** *adj* hacia atrás. **2** atrasado,-a, retrasado. ► *adv* → backwards.

backwards ['bækwədz] *adv* **1** hacia atrás. **2** al revés. ● **backwards and forwards** de acá para allá.

bacon ['beɪkən] *n* beicon.

bad [bæd] *adj* **1** malo,-a, mal. **2** grave: *a bad accident*, un accidente grave. **3** fuerte *(dolor de cabeza)*. ● **to go bad** echarse a perder, pudrirse; **to go from bad to worse** ir de mal en peor.

bade [beɪd] *pt* → bid.

badge [bædʒ] *n* **1** insignia. **2** chapa.

badger ['bædʒəʳ] *n* tejón.

bad-tempered [bædˈtempəd] *adj*. ● **to be bad-tempered** tener mal carácter, estar de mal humor.

bag [bæɡ] *n* **1** bolsa, saco. **2** bolso.

baggage ['bæɡɪdʒ] *n* equipaje.

baggy ['bæɡɪ] *adj* holgado,-a.

bagpipes ['bæɡpaɪps] *npl* gaita.

bail [beɪl] *n* fianza.

bait [beɪt] *n* cebo.

bake [beɪk] *vt* cocer al horno. ■ **baked beans** alubias cocidas con salsa de tomate.

baker ['beɪkəʳ] *n* panadero,-a.

baker's ['beɪkəz] *n* panadería.

bakery ['beɪkərɪ] *n* panadería.

balance ['bæləns] *n* **1** equilibrio. **2** balanza. **3** saldo, balance. ► *vi* mantenerse en equilibrio.

balcony ['bælkənɪ] *n* balcón.

bald [bɔːld] *adj* calvo,-a.

ball [bɔːl] *n* **1** pelota, balón, bola. **2** ovillo. **3** baile, fiesta.

ballet ['bæleɪ] *n* ballet. ■ **ballet dancer** bailarín, bailarina.

balloon [bə'luːn] *n* globo.

ballot ['bælət] *n* **1** votación. **2** papeleta. ■ **ballot box** urna.

ballpoint pen ['bɔːlpɔɪnt pen] *n* bolígrafo.

ballroom ['bɔːlruːm] *n* sala de baile.

balm [baːm] *n* bálsamo.

ban [bæn] *n* prohibición. ▶ *vt* prohibir.

banana [bə'naːnə] *n* plátano.

band [bænd] *n* **1** banda. **2** cinta, tira. **3** raya, franja.

bandage ['bændɪdʒ] *n* venda, vendaje. ▶ *vt* vendar.

bandit ['bændɪt] *n* bandido,-a.

bandstand ['bændstænd] *n* quiosco de música.

bang [bæŋ] *n* **1** golpe. **2** porrazo, estampido, estallido, portazo. ▶ *vt-vi* golpear.

banger ['bæŋə'] *n* **1** petardo. **2** GB *fam* salchicha.

bangle ['bæŋgəl] *n* pulsera.

banish ['bænɪʃ] *vt* desterrar.

banister ['bænɪstə'] *n* barandilla.

bank[1] [bæŋk] *n* banco. ■ **bank account** cuenta bancaria; **bank holiday** GB día festivo.

bank[2] [bæŋk] *n* **1** banco *(para sentarse)*. **2** ribera, orilla *(de río)*.

banker ['bæŋkə'] *n* banquero,-a.

banknote ['bæŋknəʊt] *n* billete de banco.

bankrupt ['bæŋkrʌpt] *adj* en quiebra, en bancarrota.

banner ['bænə'] *n* **1** estandarte. **2** pancarta.

banquet ['bæŋkwɪt] *n* banquete.

baptize [bæp'taɪz] *vt* bautizar.

bar [baː'] *n* **1** barra. **2** pastilla *(de jabón)*. **3** tableta *(de chocolate)*. **4** bar.

barb [baːb] *n* **1** púa. **2** lengüeta.

barbecue ['baːbəkjuː] *n* barbacoa.

barber's ['baːbəs] *n* barbería.

barbiturate [baː'bɪtʃərət] *n* barbitúrico.

bare [beə'] *adj* **1** desnudo,-a, descubierto,-a. **2** mero,-a: *a bare 10%*, solo el 10%.

barely ['beəlɪ] *adv* apenas.

bargain ['baːgən] *n* **1** trato. **2** ganga. ▶ *vi* **1** negociar. **2** regatear.

bark[1] [baːk] *n* ladrido. ▶ *vi* ladrar.

bark[2] [baːk] *n* corteza *(de árbol)*.

barley ['baːlɪ] *n* cebada.

barmaid ['baːmeɪd] *n* camarera.

barman ['baːmən] *n* camarero, barman.

barn [baːn] *n* granero.

barnacle ['baːnəkəl] *n* bálano.

baroque [bə'rɒk] *adj* barroco,-a.

barracks ['bærəks] *n* cuartel.
barrel ['bærəl] *n* **1** barril, tonel, cuba. **2** cañón *(de fusil)*.
barren ['bærən] *adj* estéril.
barricade [bærɪ'keɪd] *n* barricada
barrier ['bærɪəʳ] *n* barrera.
barrister ['bærɪstəʳ] *n* abogado,-a *(en tribunales superiores)*.
barter ['bɑːtəʳ] *n* trueque.
base [beɪs] *n* base. ▶ *vt* basar.
baseball ['beɪsbɔːl] *n* béisbol.
basement ['beɪsmənt] *n* sótano.
basic ['beɪsɪk] *adj* básico,-a.
basin ['beɪsən] *n* **1** cuenco. **2** lavabo. **3** cuenca.
basis ['beɪsɪs] *n* base: *on a weekly basis*, semanalmente.
basket ['bɑːskɪt] *n* cesta, cesto.
basketball ['bɑːskɪtbɔːl] *n* baloncesto.
bass¹ [bæs] *n* lubina.
bass² [beɪs] *n* bajo *(cantante, instrumento)*.
bassoon [bə'suːn] *n* fagot.
bat¹ [bæt] *n* murciélago.
bat² [bæt] *n* bate.
batch [bætʃ] *n* lote.
bath [bɑːθ] *n* **1** baño. **2** bañera. ▶ *vt* bañar. ▶ *vi* bañarse. ▶ *npl* **baths** piscina *(pública)*.
bathe [beɪð] *vi* bañarse. ▶ *vt* lavar *(herida)*.
bathing ['beɪðɪŋ] *n* baño. ■ **bathing costume** traje de baño, bañador; **bathing suit** traje de baño.

bathrobe ['bɑːθrəʊb] *n* albornoz.
bathroom ['bɑːθruːm] *n* cuarto de baño.
bathtub ['bɑːθtʌb] *n* bañera.
baton ['bætən] *n* **1** porra *(de policía)*. **2** batuta *(música)*. **3** testigo *(carrera de relevos)*.
batter¹ ['bætəʳ] *n* rebozado.
batter² ['bætəʳ] *vt* apalear.
battery ['bætəri] *n* **1** batería. **2** pila.
battle ['bætəl] *n* batalla.
battlements ['bætəlmənts] *npl* almenas.
battleship ['bætəlʃɪp] *n* acorazado.
bauble ['bɔːbəl] *n* baratija.
baulk [bɔːk] *vt* → balk.
bay¹ [beɪ] *n* bahía, golfo.
bay² [beɪ] *n* laurel.
bay³ [beɪ] *n* hueco. ■ **loading bay** cargadero; **parking bay** plaza de parking.
be [biː] *vi* **1** ser: *she's clever*, es inteligente. **2** estar: *how are you?*, ¿cómo estás? **3** tener: *I'm cold*, tengo frío. **4** hacer: *it's sunny*, hace sol. ▶ *aux* **1** **be** + *pres participle* estar: *it is raining*, está lloviendo. **2** **be** + *past participle* ser: *he was sacked*, fue despedido, lo despidieron. **3** **be** + *infinitive*: *the King is to visit Egypt*, el Rey visitará Egipto. ●**there is/are** hay.
beach [biːtʃ] *n* playa. ▶ *vt* varar, embarrancar.

bead [biːd] *n* **1** cuenta *(de collar)*. **2** gota *(de sudor)*.
beak [biːk] *n* pico.
beam [biːm] *n* **1** viga. **2** rayo *(de luz)*. ► *vi* sonreír.
bean [biːn] *n* **1** alubia, judía, haba. **2** grano *(de café)*.
bear¹ [beəʳ] *n* oso.
bear² [beəʳ] *vt* soportar.
beard [bɪəd] *n* barba.
bearer [ˈbeərəʳ] *n* **1** portador, -ra. **2** titular.
bearing [ˈbeərɪŋ] *n* cojinete.
beast [biːst] *n* bestia, animal.
beat [biːt] *vt* **1** golpear. **2** batir *(huevos, alas, récord)*. **3** vencer, derrotar. ► *vi* latir *(corazón)*. ► *n* **1** latido. **2** ritmo. ► *adj fam* agotado,-a.
beautician [bjuːˈtɪʃən] *n* esteticista.
beautiful [ˈbjuːtɪfʊl] *adj* **1** bonito,-a. **2** maravilloso,-a.
beauty [ˈbjuːtɪ] *n* belleza. ■ **beauty contest** concurso de belleza; **beauty spot 1** lunar. **2** lugar pintoresco.
beaver [ˈbiːvəʳ] *n* castor.
became [bɪˈkeɪm] *pt* → become.
because [bɪˈkɒz] *conj* porque. ► *prep* **because of** a causa de.
become [bɪˈkʌm] *vi* **1** convertirse en. **2** volverse. • **to become of** ser de.
bed [bed] *n* **1** cama. **2** macizo *(de flores)*. **3** lecho, cauce *(de río)*, fondo *(del mar)*.

bed and breakfast [bedənˈbrekfəst] *n* hostal familiar.
bedroom [ˈbedruːm] *n* dormitorio.
bedside [ˈbedsaɪd] *n* cabecera. ■ **bedside table** mesita de noche.
bedspread [ˈbedspred] *n* colcha.
bee [biː] *n* abeja.
beech [biːtʃ] *n* haya.
beef [biːf] *n* carne de vaca.
beefburger [ˈbiːfbɜːgəʳ] *n* hamburguesa.
beefsteak [ˈbiːfsteɪk] *n* bistec.
beehive [ˈbiːhaɪv] *n* colmena.
been [biːn, bɪn] *pp* → be.
beer [bɪəʳ] *n* cerveza.
beetle [ˈbiːtəl] *n* escarabajo.
beetroot [ˈbiːtruːt] *n* remolacha.
before [bɪˈfɔːʳ] *prep* **1** antes de. **2** delante de, ante. ► *conj* antes de + *inf*, antes de que + *subj*: *before you go*, antes de irte, antes de que te vayas. ► *adv* **1** antes. **2** anterior.
beforehand [bɪˈfɔːhænd] *adv* de antemano.
beg [beg] *vi* mendigar. ► *vt* pedir, suplicar, rogar.
began [bɪˈgæn] *pt* → begin.
beggar [ˈbegəʳ] *n* mendigo,-a.
begin [bɪˈgɪn] *vt-vi* empezar, comenzar. • **to begin with** para empezar.
beginner [bɪˈgɪnəʳ] *n* principiante.

beginning [bɪˈgɪnɪŋ] *n* principio.

begun [bɪˈgʌn] *pp* → begin.

behave [bɪˈheɪv] *vi* comportarse, portarse. • **to behave oneself** portarse bien.

behaviour [bɪˈheɪvjəʳ] (US **behavior**) *n* conducta, comportamiento.

behead [bɪˈhed] *vt* decapitar.

behind [bɪˈhaɪnd] *prep* detrás de. ▶ *adv* **1** detrás. **2** atrasado, -a: *he's behind with his work*, va atrasado con el trabajo.

beige [beɪʒ] *adj-n* beige.

belch [beltʃ] *n* eructo.

belief [bɪˈliːf] *n* creencia.

believe [bɪˈliːv] *vt-vi* creer.

bell [bel] *n* **1** campana. **2** timbre: *to ring the bell*, tocar el timbre.

bellboy [ˈbelbɔɪ] *n* botones.

bellow [ˈbeləʊ] *n* bramido.

belly [ˈbelɪ] *n* vientre, barriga. ■ **belly button** *fam* ombligo.

belong [bɪˈlɒŋ] *vi* **1** pertenecer. **2** ser socio,-a.

belongings [bɪˈlɒŋɪŋz] *npl* pertenencias.

below [bɪˈləʊ] *prep* debajo de, por debajo de. ▶ *adv* abajo. • **below zero** bajo cero.

belt [belt] *n* **1** cinturón. **2** correa.

bench [bentʃ] *n* **1** banco *(asiento)*. **2** banquillo.

bend [bend] *n* curva. ▶ *vt* doblar. ▶ *vi* **1** doblarse. **2** torcer.

to bend over *vi* inclinarse.

beneath [bɪˈniːθ] *prep* bajo, debajo de, por debajo de. ▶ *adv* abajo, debajo.

benefit [ˈbenɪfɪt] *n* **1** beneficio. **2** subsidio. ▶ *vt-vi* beneficiar(se).

benign [bɪˈnaɪn] *adj* benigno,-a.

bent [bent] *pt-pp* → bend.

bequest [bɪˈkwest] *n* legado.

beret [ˈbereɪ] *n* boina.

berry [ˈberɪ] *n* baya.

berth [bɜːθ] *n* **1** amarradero. **2** litera.

beside [bɪˈsaɪd] *prep* al lado de, junto a.

besides [bɪˈsaɪdz] *prep* **1** además de. **2** aparte de. ▶ *adv* además.

besiege [bɪˈsiːdʒ] *vt* sitiar.

best [best] *adj* mejor. ▶ *adv* mejor. ▶ *n* lo mejor. • **all the best!** ¡que te vaya bien!; **at best** en el mejor de los casos; **to do one's best** esmerarse. ■ **best man** ayudante del novio *(en boda)*.

bet [bet] *n* apuesta. ▶ *vt-vi* apostar.

betray [bɪˈtreɪ] *vt* traicionar.

better [ˈbetəʳ] *adj* mejor. ▶ *adv* mejor. ▶ *vt* mejorar. • **had better** más vale que + *subj*: *we'd better be going*, más vale que nos vayamos, deberíamos irnos; **to get better** mejorar, ponerse mejor. ■ **better half** media naranja.

betting [ˈbetɪŋ] *n* apuestas.

between [bɪ'twiːn] *prep* entre. ► *adv* en medio, entre medio.

beverage ['bevərɪdʒ] *n* bebida.

beware [bɪ'weəʳ] *vi* tener cuidado.

bewilder [bɪ'wɪldəʳ] *vt* desconcertar, confundir.

bewitch [bɪ'wɪtʃ] *vt* hechizar.

beyond [bɪ'jɒnd] *prep* más allá de, al otro lado de. ► *adv* más allá.

bias ['baɪəs] *n* parcialidad, prejuicio.

bib [bɪb] *n* babero.

biceps ['baɪseps] *n* bíceps.

bicycle ['baɪsɪkəl] *n* bicicleta.

bid [bɪd] *n* **1** puja. **2** intento. **3** oferta. ► *vt-vi* pujar.

bidet ['biːdeɪ] *n* bidé.

big [bɪg] *adj* grande, gran. ■ **big brother** hermano mayor; **big game** caza mayor; **big sister** hermana mayor.

bike [baɪk] *n* **1** *fam* bici. **2** *fam* moto.

bikini [bɪ'kiːnɪ] *n* biquini.

bile [baɪl] *n* bilis, hiel.

bill [bɪl] *n* **1** factura, cuenta. **2** proyecto de ley. **3** US billete de banco. **4** cartel, póster. ● **to top the bill** encabezar el reparto. ■ **bill of exchange** letra de cambio.

billboard ['bɪlbɔːd] *n* US valla publicitaria.

billiards ['bɪlɪədz] *n* billar.

billion ['bɪlɪən] *n* mil millones.

bin [bɪn] *n* cubo de la basura, papelera.

bind [baɪnd] *vt* **1** atar. **2** ligar *(salsa)*. **3** obligar. **4** encuadernar.

binder ['baɪndəʳ] *n* carpeta.

binoculars [bɪ'nɒkjʊləz] *npl* gemelos.

biography [baɪ'ɒgrəfɪ] *n* biografía.

biology [baɪ'ɒlədʒɪ] *n* biología.

birch [bɜːtʃ] *n* abedul.

bird [bɜːd] *n* ave, pájaro. ■ **bird of prey** ave de rapiña.

birdseed ['bɜːdsiːd] *n* alpiste.

bird's-eye view [bɜːdzaɪ'vjuː] *n* vista aérea.

Biro® ['baɪrəʊ] *n* GB boli.

birth [bɜːθ] *n* nacimiento. ● **to give birth to** dar a luz a. ■ **birth certificate** partida de nacimiento.

birthday ['bɜːθdeɪ] *n* cumpleaños.

birthmark ['bɜːθmɑːk] *n* antojo.

birthplace ['bɜːθpleɪs] *n* lugar de nacimiento.

biscuit ['bɪskɪt] *n* GB galleta.

bishop ['bɪʃəp] *n* **1** obispo. **2** alfil *(en ajedrez)*.

bison ['baɪsən] *n* bisonte.

bit¹ [bɪt] *n* trozo, pedacito. ● **a bit** un poco, algo.

bit² [bɪt] *n* bit.

bit³ [bɪt] *n* broca.

bit⁴ [bɪt] *pt* → bite.

bitch [bɪtʃ] *n* **1** hembra, perra. **2** *pej* bruja, arpía.

bite [baɪt] *n* **1** mordisco. **2** picadura. **3** mordedura. **4** bocado. ► *vt-vi* **1** morder(se). **2** picar.

bitten ['bɪtən] *pp* → bite.

bitter ['bɪtə'] *adj* amargo,-a *(sabor)*. ► *n* cerveza amarga. ► *npl* **bitters** bíter.

black [blæk] *adj-n* negro,-a. ■ **black coffee** café solo; **black eye** ojo morado.

blackberry ['blækbərɪ] *n* mora, zarzamora.

blackboard ['blækbɔːd] *n* pizarra.

blackhead ['blækhed] *n* espinilla.

blackmail ['blækmeɪl] *n* chantaje.

blacksmith ['blæksmɪθ] *n* herrero.

bladder ['blædə'] *n* vejiga.

blade [bleɪd] *n* **1** hoja, filo, cuchilla. **2** pala *(de remo)*. **3** brizna *(de hierba)*.

blame [bleɪm] *n* culpa. ► *vt* culpar, echar la culpa a. • **to put the blame on** echar la culpa a.

bland [blænd] *adj* soso,-a.

blank [blæŋk] *adj* en blanco. ■ **blank cartridge** cartucho de fogueo.

blanket ['blæŋkɪt] *n* manta.

blast [blɑːst] *n* **1** ráfaga *(de aire)*. **2** chorro *(de agua)*. **3** explosión, voladura. • **at full blast** a todo volumen. ■ **blast furnace** alto horno.

blaze [bleɪz] *n* **1** incendio. **2** fogata, hoguera. ► *vi* **1** arder. **2** brillar con fuerza.

bleach [bliːtʃ] *n* lejía.

bleat [bliːt] *n* balido.

bled [bled] *pt-pp* → bleed.

bleed [bliːd] *vi* sangrar.

bleep [bliːp] *n* pitido.

bleeper ['bliːpə'] *n* busca.

blend [blend] *n* mezcla ► *vt-vi* mezclarse.

blender ['blendə'] *n* batidora.

bless [bles] *vt* bendecir.

blew [bluː] *pt* → blow.

blind [blaɪnd] *adj* ciego,-a. ► *n* persiana. ► *vt* cegar.

blink [blɪŋk] *vi* parpadear.

blister ['blɪstə'] *n* ampolla.

block [blɒk] *n* bloque. ► *vt* **1** obstruir, cegar. **2** bloquear. ■ **block letters** mayúsculas.

blog [blɒg] *n* blog.

blond [blɒnd] *adj-n* rubio,-a.

blood [blʌd] *n* sangre. ■ **blood group** grupo sanguíneo; **blood pressure** tensión arterial.

bloodhound ['blʌdhaʊnd] *n* sabueso.

bloom [bluːm] *n* flor. ► *vi* florecer.

blossom ['blɒsəm] *n* flor. ► *vi* florecer.

blot [blɒt] *n* borrón.

blotch [blɒtʃ] *n* **1** mancha. **2** borrón.

blouse [blaʊz] *n* blusa.

blow[1] [bləʊ] *n* golpe.

blow² [bləʊ] *vi* **1** soplar *(viento)*. **2** sonar *(silbato)*. **3** fundirse *(fusible)*. ► *vt* tocar *(cláxon, trompeta, etc)*. • **to blow one's nose** sonarse la nariz.

to blow up *vt* **1** hacer explotar. **2** hinchar, inflar. **3** ampliar *(foto)*. ► *vt* hacer explosión, explotar.

blowout ['bləʊaʊt] *n* reventón.

blue [bluː] *adj* **1** azul. **2** triste, deprimido,-a. **3** verde *(película)*. ► *n* azul. • **out of the blue** de forma inesperada, como llovido del cielo. ▪ **the blues 1** melancolía. **2** el blues *(música)*.

blueberry ['bluːbərɪ] *n* arándano.

bluff [blʌf] *n* farol.

blunder ['blʌndə'] *n* metedura de pata.

blunt [blʌnt] *adj* **1** desafilado,-a. **2** franco,-a.

blurred [blɜːd] *adj* borroso,-a.

blush [blʌʃ] *n vi* ruborizarse.

boar [bɔː'] *n*. ▪ **wild boar** jabalí.

board [bɔːd] *n* **1** tabla, tablero. **2** tablón de anuncios. **3** junta, consejo. ► *vt* subirse a, embarcar en. • **on board** a bordo. ▪ **full board** pensión completa; **half board** media pensión.

boarding ['bɔːdɪŋ] *n*. ▪ **boarding card** tarjeta de embarque; **boarding house** casa de huéspedes.

boast [bəʊst] *vi* jactarse.

boat [bəʊt] *n* barco, barca.

bobbin ['bɒbɪn] *n* bobina.

body ['bɒdɪ] *n* **1** cuerpo. **2** organismo, entidad.

body-building ['bɒdɪbɪldɪŋ] *n* culturismo.

bodyguard ['bɒdɪgɑːd] *n* guardaespaldas.

bodywork ['bɒdɪwɜːk] *n* carrocería.

bog [bɒg] *n* pantano.

boil¹ [bɔɪl] *n* furúnculo.

boil² [bɔɪl] *vt-vi* hervir.

boiler ['bɔɪlə'] *n* caldera.

boiling ['bɔɪlɪŋ] *adj* hirviente.

bold [bəʊld] *adj* valiente. ▪ **bold type** negrita.

bolt [bəʊlt] *n* **1** cerrojo, pestillo. **2** perno, tornillo.

bomb [bɒm] *n* bomba. ► *vt* bombardear. ▪ **bomb scare** amenaza de bomba.

bombshell ['bɒmʃel] *n* **1** obús. **2** bombazo, bomba.

bond [bɒnd] *n* **1** lazo, vínculo. **2** bono, obligación.

bone [bəʊn] *n* **1** hueso. **2** espina *(de pescado)*.

bonfire ['bɒnfaɪə'] *n* hoguera.

bonnet ['bɒnɪt] *n* **1** gorro, gorra. **2** capó.

bonus ['bəʊnəs] *n* prima.

bony ['bəʊnɪ] *adj* **1** huesudo,-a. **2** lleno,-a de espinas.

boo [buː] *vt-vi* abuchear.

booby trap ['buːbɪtræp] *n* trampa explosiva.

book [bʊk] *n* libro. ► *vt* **1** reservar. **2** multar, amonestar.

bookcase ['bʊkkeɪs] *n* librería, estantería.

booking ['bʊkɪŋ] *n* reserva. ■ **booking office** taquilla.

booklet ['bʊklət] *n* folleto.

bookshelf ['bʊkʃelf] *n* estante. ► *npl* **bookshelves** librería, estantería.

bookshop ['bʊkʃɒp] *n* librería.

bookstore ['bʊkstɔːʳ] *n* librería.

boom¹ [buːm] *n* estruendo.

boom² [buːm] *n fig* boom, auge.

boost [buːst] *n* empuje. ► *vt* **1** aumentar *(ventas)*. **2** estimular, impulsar *(producción)*.

boot [buːt] *n* **1** bota. **2** GB maletero. ► *vt-vi* arrancar *(ordenador)*. ● **to boot** además.

booth [buːð] *n* **1** cabina. **2** barraca, caseta *(de feria)*.

bootlegger ['buːtlegəʳ] *n* contrabandista.

border ['bɔːdəʳ] *n* **1** frontera. **2** borde, margen.

bore¹ [bɔːʳ] *pt* → bear.

bore² [bɔːʳ] *n* calibre. ► *vt* horadar, taladrar.

bore³ [bɔːʳ] *n* **1** pelmazo,-a. **2** lata.

bored [bɔːd] *adj* aburrido,-a.

boring ['bɔːrɪŋ] *adj* aburrido,-a.

born [bɔːn] *pp* → bear. ● **to be born** nacer.

borne [bɔːn] *pp* → bear.

borough ['bʌrə] *n* **1** distrito. **2** municipio.

borrow ['bɒrəʊ] *vt* tomar prestado,-a, pedir prestado,-a.

boss [bɒs] *n* jefe,-a.

botany ['bɒtəni] *n* botánica.

botch [bɒtʃ] *n* chapuza.

both [bəʊθ] *adj-pron* ambos, -as, los/las dos. ► *conj* tanto.

bother ['bɒðəʳ] *n* molestia. ► *vt* **1** molestar. **2** preocupar. ► *vi* molestarse. preocuparse. ● **not to be bothered** dar igual, no tener ganas.

bottle ['bɒtəl] *n* **1** botella. **2** biberón. ► *vt* embotellar. ■ **bottle bank** contenedor de vidrio; **bottle opener** abrebotellas.

bottom ['bɒtəm] *n* **1** fondo *(del mar, calle)*. **2** culo *(de botella, trasero)*. **3** bajo *(de vestido)*. ► *adj* de abajo.

bought [bɔːt] *pt-pp* → buy.

bounce [baʊns] *n* bote. ► *vi* **1** rebotar. **2** ser rechazado por el banco *(cheque)*.

bound¹ [baʊnd] *pt-pp* → bind.

bound² [baʊnd] *adj* seguro: *it's bound to happen*, tiene que pasar. ● **bound for** con destino a, con rumbo a.

bound³ [baʊnd] *vi* saltar.

boundary ['baʊndəri] *n* límite, frontera.

bounds [baʊndz] *npl* límites.

bouquet [buːˈkeɪ] *n* **1** ramillete. **2** aroma.

boutique [buːˈtiːk] *n* boutique.

bow¹ [baʊ] *n* reverencia.

bow² [bəʊ] *n* arco. ■ **bow tie** pajarita.

bow³ [baʊ] *n* proa.

bowel [ˈbaʊəl] n intestino.
bowl¹ [bəʊl] n **1** escudilla, cuenco. **2** palangana, barreño.
bowl² [bəʊl] n bocha.
bowler [ˈbəʊləʳ] n lanzador,-ra (críquet). ■ **bowler hat** bombín.
bowling [ˈbəʊlɪŋ] n bolos. ■ **bowling alley** bolera.
box¹ [bɒks] n **1** caja, cajón, cajetilla, estuche. **2** palco (en teatro). ■ **box office** taquilla.
box² [bɒks] vi boxear.
boxing [ˈbɒksɪŋ] n boxeo.
boy [bɔɪ] n niño, chico, muchacho, joven.
boyfriend [ˈbɔɪfrend] n novio.
brace [breɪs] n aparato (de dientes). ► npl GB **braces** tirantes.
bracelet [ˈbreɪslət] n pulsera.
bracket [ˈbrækɪt] n **1** paréntesis. **2** soporte.
brag [bræg] vi fanfarronear.
braid [breɪd] n US trenza.
brain [breɪn] n cerebro.
brake [breɪk] n freno. ► vt-vi frenar.
bramble [ˈbræmbəl] n zarza.
branch [brɑːntʃ] n **1** rama. **2** sucursal. ► vi bifurcarse.
brand [brænd] n marca.
brand-new [bræn'njuː] adj completamente nuevo.
brandy [ˈbrændɪ] n brandy.
brass [brɑːs] n **1** latón. **2** instrumentos de metal.
brassiere [ˈbræzɪəʳ] n sujetador, sostén.
brave [breɪv] adj valiente

brawl [brɔːl] n reyerta, pelea.
breach [briːtʃ] n **1** brecha. **2** incumplimiento (de contrato).
bread [bred] n pan.
breadth [bredθ] n anchura.
break [breɪk] n **1** ruptura. **2** interrupción, pausa, descanso. ► vt **1** romper. **2** batir (récord). **3** no cumplir (promesa). **4** comunicar (noticias). ► vi **1** romperse. **2** estallar (tormenta).
to break down vt **1** echar abajo, derribar. **2** desglosar. ► vi averiarse.
to break in vt domar. ► vi entrar a robar.
to break out vi **1** escaparse (prisioneros). **2** estallar (guerra).
to break up vi **1** disolverse (multitud). **2** separarse. **3** empezar las vacaciones.
breakdown [ˈbreɪkdaʊn] n **1** avería. **2** crisis nerviosa
breakfast [ˈbrekfəst] n desayuno. • **to have breakfast** desayunar.
breakwater [ˈbreɪkwɔːtəʳ] n rompeolas.
breast [brest] n **1** pecho. **2** pechuga (de pollo).
breaststroke [ˈbreststrəʊk] n braza.
breath [breθ] n aliento. • **out of breath** sin aliento; **to hold your breath** contener la respiración.
Breathalyser® [ˈbreθəlaɪzəʳ] n alcoholímetro.

breathe [bri:ð] *vt-vi* respirar.
breathing ['bri:ðɪŋ] *n* respiración.
bred [bred] *pt-pp* → breed.
breed [bri:d] *n* raza. ▸ *vt* criar.
breeze [bri:z] *n* brisa.
brew [bru:] *n* brebaje. ▸ *vt* **1** hacer *(cerveza)*. **2** preparar *(té)*. ▸ *vi* reposar *(té)*.
brewery ['bruəri] *n* cervecería.
bribe [braɪb] *n* soborno.
brick [brɪk] *n* ladrillo.
bricklayer ['brɪkleɪəʳ] *n* albañil.
bride [braɪd] *n* novia *(el día de la boda)*.
bridegroom ['braɪdgru:m] *n* novio *(el día de la boda)*.
bridesmaid ['braɪdzmeɪd] *n* dama de honor.
bridge [brɪdʒ] *n* puente.
bridle ['braɪdəl] *n* brida.
brief [bri:f] *adj* breve. ▸ *n* informe.
briefcase ['bri:fkeɪs] *n* maletín, cartera.
briefs [bri:fs] *npl* **1** calzoncillos. **2** bragas.
brigade [brɪ'geɪd] *n* brigada.
bright [braɪt] *adj* **1** brillante. **2** despejado *(día)*. **3** vivo,-a *(color)*.
brilliant ['brɪljənt] *adj* **1** brillante. **2** *fam* estupendo,-a.
brim [brɪm] *n* borde.
bring [brɪŋ] *vt* **1** traer. **2** llevar.
to bring about *vt* causar.
to bring back *vt* devolver.
to bring down *vt* derribar.

to bring in *vt* **1** introducir. **2** producir.
to bring on *vt* provocar.
to bring out *vt* sacar.
to bring round *vt* hacer volver en sí.
to bring up *vt* **1** criar, educar. **2** plantear. **3** devolver, vomitar.
bristle ['brɪsəl] *n* cerda.
brittle ['brɪtəl] *adj* quebradizo,-a, frágil.
broad [brɔ:d] *adj* ancho,-a, amplio,-a, extenso,-a. ▪ **broad bean** haba.
broadcast ['brɔ:dkɑ:st] emitir, transmitir.
broadcasting ['brɔ:dkɑ:stɪŋ] *n* **1** radiodifusión. **2** transmisión,
broccoli ['brɒkəli] *n* brécol.
brochure ['brəʊʃəʳ] *n* folleto.
broil [brɔɪl] *vt* US asar a la parrilla.
broke [brəʊk] *pt* → break. ▸ *adj fam* sin blanca.
broken ['brəʊkən] *pp* → break. ▸ *adj* **1** roto,-a. **2** chapurreado,-a *(lenguaje)*.
bronchitis [brɒŋ'kaɪtəs] *n* bronquitis.
bronze [brɒnz] *n* bronce.
brooch [brəʊtʃ] *n* broche.
brook [brʊk] *n* arroyo.
broom [bru:m] *n* escoba.
broth [brɒθ] *n* caldo.
brother ['brʌðəʳ] *n* hermano.
brother-in-law ['brʌðərɪnlɔ:] *n* cuñado.
brought [brɔ:t] *pt-pp* → bring.

brow [braʊ] *n* **1** ceja. **2** frente. **3** cresta, cima.

brown [braʊn] *adj* **1** marrón. **2** castaño,-a *(pelo)*. **3** moreno,-a *(piel)*. **4** integral *(arroz, pan)*.

browse [braʊz] *vi* mirar, hojear. • **to browse the Web** navegar por la Web.

browser ['braʊzəʳ] *n* navegador *(programa)*.

bruise [bruːz] *n* morado.

brunette [bruːˈnet] *n* morena.

brush [brʌʃ] *n* **1** cepillo. **2** pincel. **3** brocha. **4** maleza. ▶ *vt* cepillar.

Brussels sprouts ['brʌsəlz] *n pl* coles de Bruselas.

brutal ['bruːtəl] *adj* brutal.

bubble ['bʌbəl] *n* burbuja. ■ **bubble bath** gel de baño; **bubble gum** chicle.

buck [bʌk] *n* US *fam* dólar.

bucket ['bʌkɪt] *n* cubo.

buckle ['bʌkəl] *n* hebilla. ▶ *vt* abrochar *(con hebilla)*. ▶ *vi* combarse, doblarse.

bud [bʌd] *n* yema, capullo.

buddy ['bʌdɪ] *n* US *fam* colega.

budgerigar ['bʌdʒərɪgaːʳ] *n* periquito.

budget ['bʌdʒɪt] *n* presupuesto. ▶ *vt-vi* presupuestar.

buffalo ['bʌfələʊ] *n* búfalo.

buffer ['bʌfəʳ] *n* **1** tope *(para trenes)*. **2** memoria intermedia.

buffet ['bʌfeɪ] *n* **1** bar, cantina. **2** bufet libre. ■ **buffet car** vagón restaurante.

bug [bʌg] *n* **1** bicho. **2** error *(en programa)*.

build [bɪld] *vt* construir.

to build up *vt-vi* acumular(se).

building ['bɪldɪŋ] *n* edificio. ■ **building site** obra; **building society** sociedad de ahorro para la vivienda.

built [bɪlt] *pt-pp* → build.

built-in [bɪltˈɪn] *adj* **1** empotrado,-a. **2** incorporado,-a.

bulb [bʌlb] *n* **1** bulbo. **2** bombilla.

bulk [bʌlk] *n* mayor parte. • **in bulk** a granel, al por mayor.

bull [bʊl] *n* toro.

bullet ['bʊlɪt] *n* bala.

bulletin ['bʊlɪtɪn] *n* boletín.

bullfight ['bʊlfaɪt] *n* corrida de toros.

bullfighter ['bʊlfaɪtəʳ] *n* torero,-a.

bullring ['bʊlrɪŋ] *n* plaza de toros.

bumblebee ['bʌmbəlbiː] *n* abejorro.

bump [bʌmp] *n* **1** chichón. **2** bache *(en carretera)*. **3** choque, golpe. ▶ *vt-vi* chocar.

to bump into *vt* tropezar con.

bumper ['bʌmpəʳ] *n* GB parachoques.

bun [bʌn] *n* **1** panecillo, bollo. **2** moño.

bunch [bʌntʃ] *n* **1** manojo. **2** ramo. **3** racimo. **4** grupo.

bundle ['bʌndəl] *n* **1** fardo. **2** haz. **3** fajo.

bung [bʌŋ] n tapón.
bunion ['bʌnjən] n juanete.
bunk [bʌŋk] n litera (en un barco o tren). ▪ **bunk bed** litera (en una habitación).
buoy [bɔɪ] n boya.
burden ['bɜːdən] n carga. ► vt cargar.
bureaucracy [bjʊə'rɒkrəsɪ] n burocracia.
burger ['bɜːgəʳ] n hamburguesa.
burglar ['bɜːgləʳ] n ladrón,-ona.
burglary ['bɜːglərɪ] n robo.
burial ['berɪəl] n entierro.
burn [bɜːn] n quemadura. ► vt quemar. ► vi arder, quemarse.
burner ['bɜːnəʳ] n quemador.
burnt [bɜːnt] pt-pp → burn.
burrow ['bʌrəʊ] n madriguera.
burst [bɜːst] n 1 explosión. 2 reventón. ► vt-vi reventar(se).
bury ['berɪ] vt enterrar.
bus [bʌs] n autobús. ▪ **bus stop** parada de autobús.
bush [bʊʃ] n arbusto.
business ['bɪznəs] n 1 los negocios. 2 negocio, empresa. 3 asunto.
businessman ['bɪznəsmən] n hombre de negocios, empresario.
businesswoman ['bɪznəswʊmən] n mujer de negocios, empresaria.
bust[1] [bʌst] n busto.
bust[2] [bʌst] vt-vi fam romper, romperse.

busy ['bɪzɪ] adj 1 ocupado,-a. 2 concurrido,-a (calle). 3 que comunica (teléfono).
but [bʌt] conj 1 pero. 2 sino: **not two, but three**, no dos, sino tres. ► prep excepto, salvo, menos. • **but for** si no hubiese sido por, si no fuese por.
butane ['bjuːteɪn] n butano.
butcher ['bʊtʃəʳ] n carnicero,-a.
butler ['bʌtləʳ] n mayordomo.
butt [bʌt] n 1 colilla. 2 culata.
butter ['bʌtəʳ] n mantequilla.
butterfly ['bʌtəflaɪ] n mariposa.
buttock ['bʌtək] n nalga.
button ['bʌtən] n botón. ► vt-vi abrochar(se).
buttonhole ['bʌtənhəʊl] n ojal.
buy [baɪ] vt comprar.
buyer ['baɪəʳ] n comprador,-ra.
buzz [bʌz] n.
buzzer ['bʌzəʳ] n timbre.
by [baɪ] prep 1 por. 2 en: **by car/train**, en coche/tren. 3 para: **I need it by ten**, lo necesito para las diez. 4 de: **by day/night**, de día/noche. 5 junto a, al lado de: **sit by me**, siéntate a mi lado. ► adv de largo. • **by and by** con el tiempo.
bye [baɪ] interj fam ¡adiós!, ¡hasta luego!
bypass ['baɪpɑːs] n 1 variante (carretera). 2 by-pass.
by-product ['baɪprɒdʌkt] n subproducto, derivado.
byte [baɪt] n byte.

C

cab [kæb] *n* **1** taxi. **2** cabina.
cabbage ['kæbɪdʒ] *n* col.
cabin ['kæbɪn] *n* **1** cabaña. **2** camarote. **3** cabina.
cabinet ['kæbɪnət] *n* **1** gabinete. **2** armario, vitrina.
cable ['keɪbəl] *n* cable. ▪ **cable car** teleférico; **cable television** televisión por cable.
cache [kæʃ] *n* **1** alijo. **2** caché.
cactus ['kæktəs] *n* cactus.
café ['kæfeɪ] *n* cafetería.
cafeteria [kæfə'tɪərɪə] *n* cafetería.
cage [keɪdʒ] *n* jaula.
cagoule [kə'guːl] *n* chubasquero.
cake [keɪk] *n* pastel, tarta.
calculate ['kælkjəleɪt] *vt* calcular.
calculating ['kælkjəleɪtɪŋ] *adj* calculador,-ra. ▪ **calculating machine** calculadora.
calendar ['kælɪndə'] *n* calendario.
calf¹ [kɑːf] *n* ternero,-a.
calf² [kɑːf] *n* pantorrilla.
call [kɔːl] *n* **1** grito. **2** llamada. **3** demanda: *there's not much call for it*, no tiene mucha demanda. **4** visita. ▶ *vt-vi* **1** llamar. *vi* **2** llamar. **3** pasar: *call at the butcher's*, pásate por la carnicería. **4** efectuar parada: *this train calls at Selby and*

York, este tren efectúa parada en Selby y York. ● **on call** de guardia. ▪ **call box** GB cabina telefónica.
to call for *vt* pasar a buscar.
to call off *vt* suspender.
to call on *vt* visitar.
to call out *vt-vi* gritar.
caller ['kɔːlə'] *n* **1** visita, visitante. **2** persona que llama.
calm [kɑːm] *adj* **1** en calma *(mar)*. **2** tranquilo,-a *(persona)*. ▶ *vt* calmar.
calorie ['kælərɪ] *n* caloría.
camcorder ['kæmkɔːdə'] *n* videocámara.
came [keɪm] *pt* → come.
camel ['kæməl] *n* camello.
camera ['kæmərə] *n* cámara.
camomile ['kæməmaɪl] *n* manzanilla.
camouflage ['kæməflɑːʒ] *n* camuflaje. ▶ *vt* camuflar.
camp [kæmp] *n* campamento. ▶ *vi* acampar. ▪ **camp bed** cama plegable; **camp site** camping, campamento.
campaign [kæm'peɪn] *n* campaña.
camper ['kæmpə'] *n* **1** campista. **2** US caravana.
can¹ [kæn] *aux* **1** poder. **2** saber.
can² [kæn] *n* lata.
canal [kə'næl] *n* canal.
canary [kə'neərɪ] *n* canario.
cancel ['kænsəl] *vt* **1** cancelar *(pedido)*. **2** anular *(contrato)*.

care

cancer ['kænsə'] *n* cáncer.

candidate ['kændɪdət] *n* candidato,-a.

candle ['kændəl] *n* vela.

candy ['kændɪ] *n* US caramelo.

cane [keɪn] *n* 1 caña. 2 bastón, vara.

canine ['keɪnaɪn] *adj* canino,-a.

canister ['kænɪstə'] *n* bote, lata.

cannon ['kænən] *n* cañón.

cannot ['kænɒt] *aux* → can.

canoe [kə'nuː] *n* canoa.

canopy ['kænəpɪ] *n* dosel.

can't [kɑːnt] *aux* contracción de **can** + **not**.

canteen [kæn'tiːn] *n* cantina.

canvas ['kænvəs] *n* 1 lona. 2 lienzo.

canyon ['kænjən] *n* cañón.

cap [kæp] *n* 1 gorro, gorra. 2 capuchón, chapa, tapa.

capable ['keɪpəbəl] *adj* capaz.

capacity [kə'pæsɪtɪ] *n* capacidad.

cape[1] [keɪp] *n* capa corta.

cape[2] [keɪp] *n* cabo.

caper ['keɪpə'] *n* alcaparra.

capital ['kæpɪtəl] *n* 1 capital. 2 mayúscula.

capitalism ['kæpɪtəlɪzəm] *n* capitalismo.

capricious [kə'prɪʃəs] *adj* caprichoso,-a.

capsize [kæp'saɪz] *vi* volcar.

capsule ['kæpsjuːl] *n* cápsula.

captain ['kæptɪn] *n* capitán.

caption ['kæpʃən] *n* leyenda, pie de foto.

captive ['kæptɪv] *adj-n* cautivo,-a.

captivity [kæp'tɪvɪtɪ] *n* cautiverio, cautividad.

capture ['kæptʃə'] *n* captura. ► *vt* capturar.

car [kɑː'] *n* 1 coche, automóvil. 2 vagón, coche *(de ferrocarril)*. ■ **car park** aparcamiento; **car wash** túnel de lavado.

caramel ['kærəmel] *n* caramelo.

carat ['kærət] *n* quilate.

caravan [kærə'væn] *n* caravana.

carbon ['kɑːbən] *n* carbono.

carburettor [kɑːbə'retə'] *n* carburador.

carcass ['kɑːkəs] *n* res muerta.

card [kɑːd] *n* 1 carta, naipe. 2 tarjeta, felicitación. 3 ficha. 4 carnet, carné *(de socio)*. 5 cartulina.

cardboard ['kɑːdbɔːd] *n* cartón.

cardiac ['kɑːdɪæk] *adj* cardíaco,-a. ■ **cardiac arrest** paro cardíaco.

cardigan ['kɑːdɪgən] *n* rebeca.

cardphone ['kɑːdfəʊn] *n* teléfono de tarjeta.

care [keə'] *n* 1 cuidado. 2 asistencia: *health care*, asistencia sanitaria. ► *vi* preocuparse: *I don't care*, me tiene sin cuidado. ● **take care!** ¡cuidado!; **to take care of** 1 cuidar, cuidar de. 2 ocuparse de.

to care for *vt* cuidar.

career [kəˈrɪəʳ] n carrera.

careful [ˈkeəfʊl] adj cuidadoso,-a. • **to be careful** tener cuidado.

caress [kəˈres] n caricia. ► vt acariciar.

caretaker [ˈkeəteɪkəʳ] n conserje.

cargo [ˈkɑːgəʊ] n carga.

caries [ˈkeərɪz] n caries.

carnation [kɑːˈneɪʃən] n clavel.

carol [ˈkærəl] n villancico.

carp [kɑːp] n carpa (pez).

carpenter [ˈkɑːpɪntəʳ] n carpintero.

carpet [ˈkɑːpɪt] n moqueta, alfombra.

carriage [ˈkærɪdʒ] n 1 carruaje. 2 vagón, coche (de ferrocarril). ■ **carriage paid** portes pagados.

carrier [ˈkærɪəʳ] n 1 transportista. 2 portador,-ra (de enfermedad). ■ **carrier bag** bolsa (de plástico o papel).

carrot [ˈkærət] n zanahoria.

carry [ˈkærɪ] vt llevar.

to carry on vt seguir.

to carry out vt llevar a cabo.

carsick [ˈkɑːsɪk] adj mareado, -a (en un coche).

cart [kɑːt] n 1 carro. 2 carretilla.

cartilage [ˈkɑːtɪlɪdʒ] n cartílago.

carton [ˈkɑːtən] n 1 envase de cartón. 2 cartón.

cartoon [kɑːˈtuːn] n 1 caricatura. 2 dibujos animados. 3 historieta, tira cómica.

cartridge [ˈkɑːtrɪdʒ] n 1 cartucho. 2 recambio (para estilográfica).

carve [kɑːv] vt 1 tallar. 2 trinchar (carne).

case¹ [keɪs] n caso. • **in any case** en cualquier caso; **in case** por si; **in case of** en caso de; **just in case** por si acaso.

case² [keɪs] n 1 maleta. 2 caja. 3 estuche, funda.

cash [kæʃ] n dinero en efectivo. ► vt cobrar (talón). • **cash down** al contado; **cash on delivery** contra reembolso. ■ **cash desk** caja; **cash dispenser** cajero automático; **cash register** caja registradora.

cash-and-carry [kæʃənˈkærɪ] n autoservicio al por mayor.

cashier [kæˈʃɪəʳ] n cajero,-a.

cashmere [kæʃˈmɪəʳ] n cachemira.

casino [kəˈsiːnəʊ] n casino.

cask [kɑːsk] n tonel, barril.

casserole [ˈkæsərəʊl] n 1 cazuela. 2 guiso.

cassette [kəˈset] n casete. ■ **cassette player/ recorder** casete.

cast [kɑːst] n 1 reparto (de película, etc). 2 molde.► vt 1 lanzar. 2 dar el papel de. 3 moldear. • **to be cast away** naufragar. ■ **cast iron** hierro colado.

castle [ˈkɑːsəl] n 1 castillo. 2 torre (ajedrez).

casual ['kæʒjʊəl] *adj* **1** fortuito,-a, casual *(encuentro)*. **2** informal *(ropa)*.

casualty ['kæʒjʊəltɪ] *n* **1** víctima. **2** baja *(soldado)*. ▪ **casualty department** urgencias.

cat [kæt] *n* gato,-a.

catalogue ['kætəlɒg] (US **catalog**) *n* GB catálogo.

cataract ['kætərækt] *n* catarata.

catarrh [kəˈtɑːʳ] *n* catarro.

catastrophe [kəˈtæstrəfɪ] *n* catástrofe.

catch [kætʃ] *vt* coger. ▶ *n* **1** parada *(de pelota)*. **2** pesca. **3** cierre, pestillo.

category ['kætəgərɪ] *n* categoría.

cater ['keɪtəʳ] *vt* **1** proveer comida. **2** atender.

caterpillar ['kætəpɪlə'] *n* oruga.

cathedral [kəˈθiːdrəl] *n* catedral.

Catholic ['kæθəlɪk] *adj-n* católico,-a.

cattle ['kætəl] *n* ganado vacuno.

caught [kɔːt] *pt-pp* → catch.

cauliflower ['kɒlɪflaʊəʳ] *n* coliflor.

cause [kɔːz] *n* causa. ▶ *vt* causar.

caution ['kɔːʃən] *n* **1** precaución. **2** aviso, advertencia.

cautious ['kɔːʃəs] *adj* prudente.

cavalry ['kævəlrɪ] *n* caballería.

cave [keɪv] *n* cueva. ▪ **cave painting** pintura rupestre.

cavern ['kævən] *n* caverna.

caviar ['kævɪɑːʳ] *n* caviar.

cavity ['kævɪtɪ] *n* cavidad.

CD ['siːˈdiː] *abbr (compact disc)* disco compacto, CD. ▪ **CD player** reproductor de discos compactos.

cease [siːs] *vt-vi* cesar.

cease-fire [siːsˈfaɪəʳ] *n* alto el fuego.

cedar ['siːdəʳ] *n* cedro.

ceiling ['siːlɪŋ] *n* techo.

celebrate ['selɪbreɪt] *vt-vi* celebrar.

celebration [selɪˈbreɪʃən] *n* celebración.

celery ['selərɪ] *n* apio.

cell [sel] *n* **1** celda. **2** célula.

cellar ['seləʳ] *n* **1** sótano. **2** bodega *(para vino)*.

cello ['tʃeləʊ] *n* violoncelo.

cellophane® ['seləfeɪn] *n* celofán®.

cellphone ['selfəʊn] *n* teléfono móvil.

cement [sɪˈment] *n* cemento. ▪ **cement mixer** hormigonera.

cemetery ['semətrɪ] *n* cementerio.

censorship ['sensəʃɪp] *n* censura.

census ['sensəs] *n* censo.

cent [sent] *n* centavo, céntimo. ● **per cent** por ciento.

centigrade ['sentɪgreɪd] *adj* centígrado.

centimetre ['sentɪmiːtəʳ] (US **centimeter**) n centímetro.

central ['sentrəl] adj central. ▪ **central heating** calefacción central.

centre ['sentəʳ] (US **center**) n centro. ► vt-vi centrar. ▪ **centre forward** delantero centro.

century ['sentʃərɪ] n siglo.

ceramics [səˈræmɪks] npl cerámica.

cereal ['sɪərɪəl] n cereal.

cerebral ['serɪbrəl] adj cerebral.

ceremony ['serɪmənɪ] n ceremonia.

certain ['sɜːtən] adj 1 seguro,-a. 2 cierto,-a, alguno,-a. ● **for certain** con toda seguridad; **to make certain of** asegurarse de.

certificate [səˈtɪfɪkət] n certificado.

cesspit ['sespɪt] n pozo negro.

chafe [tʃeɪf] vt rozar, escoriar.

chain [tʃeɪn] n cadena.

chair [tʃeəʳ] n 1 silla. 2 sillón. ▪ **chair lift** telesilla.

chairman ['tʃeəmən] n presidente.

chairwoman ['tʃeəwʊmən] n presidenta.

chalet ['ʃæleɪ] n chalet, chalé.

chalk [tʃɔːk] n tiza.

challenge ['tʃælɪndʒ] n reto, desafío. ► vt retar, desafiar.

challenger ['tʃælɪndʒəʳ] n rival.

chamber ['tʃeɪmbəʳ] n cámara.

chambermaid ['tʃeɪmbəmeɪd] n camarera.

chameleon [kəˈmiːlɪən] n camaleón.

champion ['tʃæmpɪən] n campeón,-ona.

championship ['tʃæmpɪənʃɪp] n campeonato.

chance [tʃɑːns] n 1 azar. 2 oportunidad. ● **by chance** por casualidad; **to take a chance** arriesgarse.

chancellor ['tʃɑːnsələʳ] n canciller. ▪ **Chancellor of the Exchequer** GB ministro,-a de Economía y Hacienda.

change [tʃeɪndʒ] n cambio. ► vt-vi cambiar. ► vi cambiarse de ropa. ● **for a change** para variar; **to change into** convertirse en, transformarse en.

changing ['tʃeɪndʒɪŋ] adj. ▪ **changing room** vestuario.

channel ['tʃænəl] n canal (cauce de agua). ► vt canalizar.

chaos ['keɪɒs] n caos.

chap [tʃæp] n fam tío, tipo.

chapel ['tʃæpəl] n capilla.

chapter ['tʃæptəʳ] n capítulo.

character ['kærəktəʳ] n 1 carácter. 2 personaje.

characteristic [kærəktəˈrɪstɪk] adj característico,-a. ► n característica.

charcoal ['tʃɑːkəʊl] n 1 carbón vegetal. 2 carboncillo.

charge [tʃɑːdʒ] n 1 precio, coste. 2 cargo, acusación *(formal)*. 3 carga. ▶ vt 1 cobrar. 2 acusar *(de delito)*. 3 cargar. • **to be in charge of** estar a cargo de; **to bring a charge against** SB formular una acusación contra ALGN; **to take charge of** hacerse cargo de.

charger ['tʃɑːdʒəʳ] n cargador *(de batería)*.

charity ['tʃærɪtɪ] n caridad.

charm [tʃɑːm] n 1 encanto. 2 amuleto *(de la suerte)*. ▶ vt encantar.

chart [tʃɑːt] n 1 tabla, gráfico, diagrama. 2 carta de navegación. • **the charts** los cuarenta principales.

charter ['tʃɑːtəʳ] n 1 carta, estatutos. 2 flete. ▶ vt fletar. • **charter flight** vuelo chárter.

chase [tʃeɪs] n persecución. ▶ vt perseguir.

chassis ['ʃæsɪ] n chasis.

chat [tʃæt] n charla. ▶ vi 1 charlar. 2 chatear. • **chat show** programa de entrevistas.

chatter ['tʃætəʳ] n 1 cháchara, parloteo. 2 castañeteo *(de dientes)*. ▶ vi 1 charlar, parlotear. 2 castañetear *(dientes)*.

chauffeur ['ʃəʊfəʳ] n chófer.

cheap [tʃiːp] adj barato,-a.

cheat [tʃiːt] n tramposo,-a. ▶ vi 1 hacer trampa. 2 copiar *(en un examen)*. ▶ vt-vi engañar, timar.

check [tʃek] n 1 comprobación, verificación. 2 US → cheque. 3 US nota, cuenta. 4 jaque. ▶ vt 1 comprobar, verificar. 2 dar jaque a.

to check in vi 1 facturar *(en aeropuerto)*. 2 dejar los datos *(en hotel)*.

checkbook ['tʃekbʊk] n US talonario de cheques.

checked [tʃekt] adj a cuadros.

checkers ['tʃekəz] npl US damas.

checkmate ['tʃekmeɪt] n jaque mate. ▶ vt dar mate a.

checkout ['tʃekaʊt] n caja.

checkup ['tʃekʌp] n chequeo.

cheek [tʃiːk] n 1 mejilla. 2 *fig* descaro.

cheekbone ['tʃiːkbəʊn] n pómulo.

cheer [tʃɪəʳ] n viva. ▶ vt-vi vitorear.

to cheer up vt-vi animar(se).

cheerful ['tʃɪəfʊl] adj alegre.

cheers [tʃɪəz] interj 1 ¡salud! 2 ¡gracias! 3 ¡adiós!, ¡hasta luego!

cheese [tʃiːz] n queso.

cheesecake ['tʃiːzkeɪk] n tarta de queso.

cheetah ['tʃiːtə] n guepardo.

chemist ['kemɪst] n 1 químico,-a. 2 GB farmacéutico,-a.

chemistry ['kemɪstrɪ] n química.

chemist's ['kemɪsts] n farmacia.

cheque [tʃek] n cheque, talón.

chequebook ['tʃekbʊk] n talonario de cheques.

cherish ['tʃerɪʃ] *vt* **1** apreciar, valorar. **2** abrigar *(esperanza)*.

cherry ['tʃerɪ] *n* cereza.

chess [tʃes] *n* ajedrez.

chessboard ['tʃesbɔːd] *n* tablero de ajedrez.

chest [tʃest] *n* **1** pecho. **2** cofre, arca. ■ **chest of drawers** cómoda, cajonera.

chestnut ['tʃesnʌt] *n* **1** castaña *(fruto)*. **2** castaño *(color)*.

chew [tʃuː] *vt* masticar.

chewing gum ['tʃuːɪŋgʌm] *n* chicle.

chicken ['tʃɪkɪn] *n* **1** pollo *(carne)*. **2** gallina *(ave)*.

chickenpox ['tʃɪkɪnpɒks] *n* varicela.

chickpea ['tʃɪkpiː] *n* garbanzo.

chicory ['tʃɪkərɪ] *n* achicoria.

chief [tʃiːf] *n* jefe.

chilblain ['tʃɪlbleɪn] *n* sabañón.

child [tʃaɪld] *n* **1** niño,-a. **2** hijo, hija. ■ **only child** hijo,-a único,-a.

childbirth ['tʃaɪldbɜːθ] *n* parto.

childhood ['tʃaɪldhʊd] *n* infancia.

children ['tʃɪldrən] *npl* → child.

chill [tʃɪl] *adj* frío,-a. ► *n* resfriado. ► *vt-vi* enfriar(se).

chimney ['tʃɪmnɪ] *n* chimenea.

chimpanzee [tʃɪmpæn'ziː] *n* chimpancé.

chin [tʃɪn] *n* barbilla, mentón.

china ['tʃaɪnə] *n* porcelana.

chip [tʃɪp] *n* **1** patata frita. **2** chip. **3** astilla, lasca *(de madera)*. **4** ficha *(en casino)*. ► *vt-vi* **1** astillarse *(madera)*. **2** resquebrajarse *(piedra)*. **3** descoharse *(pintura)*.

chiropodist [kɪ'rɒpədɪst] *n* podólogo,-a.

chitchat ['tʃɪttʃæt] *n* cháchara.

chocolate ['tʃɒkələt] *n* **1** chocolate. **2** bombón.

choice [tʃɔɪs] *n* elección.

choir ['kwaɪə'] *n* coro.

choke [tʃəʊk] *n* estárter. ► *vi* ahogarse.

cholera ['kɒlərə] *n* cólera.

choose [tʃuːz] *vt* escoger.

chop [tʃɒp] *n* chuleta *(carne)*. ► *vt* cortar.

chopsticks ['tʃɒpstɪks] *npl* palillos chinos.

chord [kɔːd] *n* acorde.

chorus ['kɔːrəs] *n* **1** coro. **2** estribillo.

chose [tʃəʊz] *pt* → choose.

chosen ['tʃəʊzən] *pp* → choose.

christen ['krɪsən] *vt* bautizar.

christening ['krɪsənɪŋ] *n* bautizo.

Christian ['krɪstɪən] *adj-n* cristiano,-a. ■ **Christian name** nombre de pila.

Christmas ['krɪsməs] *n* Navidad. ■ **Christmas card** tarjeta de Navidad, christmas; **Christmas Eve** Nochebuena.

chronic ['krɒnɪk] *adj* crónico,-a.

chronicle ['krɒnɪkəl] *n* crónica.

chronology [krə'nɒlədʒɪ] *n* cronología.

chuck [tʃʌk] *vt* **1** tirar *(objeto)*. **2** dejar *(novio, trabajo)*.

chunk [tʃʌŋk] *n fam* cacho.

church [tʃɜːtʃ] *n* iglesia.

chute [ʃuːt] *n* tobogán.

cider ['saɪdəʳ] *n* sidra.

cigar [sɪ'gɑːʳ] *n* puro.

cigarette [sɪgə'ret] *n* cigarrillo.

■ **cigarette case** pitillera; **cigarette holder** boquilla; **cigarette lighter** encendedor.

cinder ['sɪndəʳ] *n* ceniza.

cinema ['sɪnəmə] *n* cine.

cinnamon ['sɪnəmən] *n* canela.

cipher ['saɪfəʳ] *n* código.

circle ['sɜːkəl] *n* **1** círculo. **2** anfiteatro *(en teatro)*.

circuit ['sɜːkɪt] *n* circuito.

circumference [sə'kʌmfərəns] *n* circunferencia.

circumstance ['sɜːkəmstəns] *n* circunstancia.

circus ['sɜːkəs] *n* **1** circo. **2** GB glorieta, rotonda.

cistern ['sɪstən] *n* cisterna.

citizen ['sɪtɪzən] *n* ciudadano,-a.

citric ['sɪtrɪk] *adj* cítrico,-a.

city ['sɪtɪ] *n* ciudad.

civil ['sɪvəl] *adj* **1** civil. **2** cortés, educado,-a. ■ **civil servant** funcionario,-a; **civil service** administración pública.

civilization [sɪvɪlaɪ'zeɪʃən] *n* civilización.

claim [kleɪm] *n* **1** reivindicación. **2** derecho. **3** afirmación. ▶ *vt* **1** afirmar. **2** reclamar.

clam [klæm] *n* almeja.

clap [klæp] *n* **1** aplauso. **2** ruido seco. **3** palmada. ▶ *vt-vi* aplaudir.

clarinet [klærɪ'net] *n* clarinete.

clash [klæʃ] *n* **1** choque. **2** estruendo. ▶ *vi* **1** chocar. **2** coincidir *(fechas)*. **3** desentonar *(colores)*.

class [klɑːs] *n* clase.

classic ['klæsɪk] *adj* clásico,-a.

classification [klæsɪfɪ'keɪʃən] *n* clasificación.

classify ['klæsɪfaɪ] *vt* clasificar.

classmate ['klɑːsmeɪt] *n* compañero,-a de clase.

classroom ['klɑːsruːm] *n* clase.

clause [klɔːz] *n* **1** cláusula. **2** oración.

clavicle ['klævɪkəl] *n* clavícula.

claw [klɔː] *n* **1** garra *(de ave)*. **2** uña *(de gato)*. **3** pinza *(de cangrejo)*.

clay [kleɪ] *n* arcilla, barro.

clean [kliːn] *adj* limpio,-a. ▶ *vt* limpiar.

cleaner's ['kliːnəz] *n* tintorería.

cleanse [klenz] *vt* limpiar.

clear [klɪəʳ] *adj* **1** claro, a. **2** transparente *(vidrio)*. **3** despejado,-a *(cielo, vista)*. ▶ *vt* **1** despejar. **2** levantar, recoger *(mesa)*. **3** absolver *(acusado)*. **4** salvar *(obstáculo)*. ● **in the clear 1** fuera de peligro. **2** fuera de toda sospecha.

to clear up *vt* **1** aclarar. **2** ordenar, recoger. ▶ *vi* mejorar, despejarse *(tiempo)*.

clearance ['klɪərəns] *n*. ■ **clearance sale** liquidación.

clearing ['klɪərɪŋ] *n* claro.

cleavage ['kliːvɪdʒ] *n* escote.

clef [klef] *n* clave *(música)*.

clerk [klɑːk, US klɜːrk] *n* **1** oficinista. **2** US dependiente,-a.

clever ['klevəʳ] *adj* listo,-a.

click [klɪk] *n* chasquido.

client ['klaɪənt] *n* cliente.

cliff [klɪf] *n* acantilado.

climate ['klaɪmət] *n* clima.

climb [klaɪm] *n* subida, escalada. ► *vt* **1** subir *(escalera)*. **2** trepar a *(árbol)*. **3** escalar.

clinic ['klɪnɪk] *n* clínica.

clip¹ [klɪp] *n* clip, fragmento *(de película)*. ► *vt* recortar *(barba)*.

clip² [klɪp] *n* **1** clip. **2** pasador.

clippers ['klɪpəz] *npl* cortaúñas.

cloak [kləʊk] *n* capa.

cloakroom ['kləʊkruːm] *n* **1** guardarropa. **2** GB servicios.

clock [klɒk] *n* reloj.

clod [klɒd] *n* terrón.

clog [klɒg] *n* zueco.

cloister ['klɔɪstəʳ] *n* claustro.

close¹ [kləʊs] *adj* **1** cercano,-a. **2** íntimo,-a *(amigo)*. **3** detenido,-a *(examen)*. ► *adv* cerca.

close² [kləʊz] *vt-vi* cerrar(se). ■ **close season** temporada de veda.

closet ['klɒzɪt] *n* US armario.

close-up ['kləʊsʌp] *n* primer plano.

closing ['kləʊzɪŋ] *n* cierre.

clot [klɒt] *n* coágulo.

cloth [klɒθ] *n* **1** tela. **2** trapo.

clothes [kləʊðz] *npl* ropa.

cloud [klaʊd] *n* nube.

cloudy ['klaʊdɪ] *adj* nublado,-a.

clove¹ [kləʊv] *n* clavo *(especie)*.

clove² [kləʊv] *n* diente *(de ajo)*.

clover ['kləʊvəʳ] *n* trébol.

clown [klaʊn] *n* payaso.

club [klʌb] *n* **1** club, sociedad. **2** palo *(de golf)*. **3** trébol *(cartas)*.

clue [kluː] *n* pista, indicio.

clumsy ['klʌmzɪ] *adj* torpe.

cluster ['klʌstəʳ] *n* grupo.

clutch [klʌtʃ] *n* embrague. ► *vt* agarrar.

coach [kəʊtʃ] *n* **1** autocar. **2** coche *(de tren, de caballos)*. **3** entrenador,-ra. ► *vt* entrenar. ■ **coach station** estación de autobuses.

coal [kəʊl] *n* carbón.

coalition [kəʊəˈlɪʃən] *n* coalición.

coarse [kɔːs] *adj* basto,-a.

coast [kəʊst] *n* costa, litoral.

coastguard ['kəʊstgɑːd] *n* guardacostas.

coastline ['kəʊstlaɪn] *n* litoral.

coat [kəʊt] *n* **1** abrigo *(prenda)*. **2** capa *(de pintura)*. **3** pelaje *(de animal)*. ► *vt* cubrir.

cob [kɒb] *n* mazorca.

cobble ['kɒbəl] *n* adoquín.

cobweb ['kɒbweb] *n* telaraña.

cock [kɒk] *n* gallo.

cockle ['kɒkəl] *n* berberecho.

cockpit ['kɒkpɪt] *n* cabina del piloto.

cockroach ['kɒkrəʊtʃ] *n* cucaracha.

cocktail ['kɒkteɪl] *n* cóctel.

cocoa ['kəʊkəʊ] *n* cacao.

coconut ['kəʊkənʌt] *n* coco.

cocoon [kə'ku:n] *n* capullo.

cod [kɒd] *n* bacalao.

code [kəʊd] *n* 1 código. 2 prefijo *(de teléfono)*. ► *vt* codificar.

coffee ['kɒfɪ] *n* café. ■ **coffee shop** cafetería.

coffeepot ['kɒfɪpɒt] *n* cafetera.

coffin ['kɒfɪn] *n* ataúd.

coherent [kəʊ'hɪərənt] *adj* coherente.

cohesion [kəʊ'hi:ʒən] *n* cohesión.

coin [kɔɪn] *n* moneda.

coincidence [kəʊ'ɪnsɪdəns] *n* coincidencia.

coke [kəʊk] *n* refesco de cola.

colander ['kʌləndə'] *n* colador.

cold [kəʊld] *adj* frío,-a. ► *n* 1 frío. 2 resfriado, catarro. ● **to catch a cold** resfriarse. ■ **cold sore** herpes.

collaboration [kəlæbə'reɪʃən] *n* colaboración.

collapse [kə'læps] *n* 1 derrumbamiento. 2 fracaso *(de plan)*. 3 colapso *(de persona)*. ► *vi* derrumbarse.

collapsible [kə'læpsəbəl] *adj* plegable.

collar ['kɒlə'] *n* 1 cuello *(de camisa)*. 2 collar *(de perro)*.

collarbone ['kɒləbəʊn] *n* clavícula.

colleague ['kɒli:g] *n* colega.

collect [kə'lekt] *vt* 1 reunir *(objetos)*. 2 coleccionar *(sellos)*. 3 recaudar *(impuestos)*. 4 ir a buscar *(persona)*. ► *vi* acumularse. ● **to call collect** US llamar a cobro revertido.

collection [kə'lekʃən] *n* 1 colección *(de sellos)*. 2 colecta *(de dinero)*. 3 recogida *(de correo)*. 4 recaudación *(de impuestos)*.

college ['kɒlɪdʒ] *n* centro de educación superior.

collide [kə'laɪd] *vi* chocar.

collision [kə'lɪʒən] *n* colisión.

colloquial [kə'ləʊkwɪəl] *adj* coloquial.

cologne [kə'ləʊn] *n* colonia.

colon¹ ['kəʊlən] *n* colon.

colon² ['kəʊlən] *n* dos puntos.

colonel ['kɜːnəl] *n* coronel.

colonial [kə'ləʊnɪəl] *adj* colonial.

colony ['kɒlənɪ] *n* colonia.

colour ['kʌlə'] (US **color**) *n* color. ► *vt* colorear, pintar.

colour-blind ['kʌləblaɪnd] (US **color-blind**) *adj* daltónico,-a.

colouring ['kʌlərɪŋ] (US **coloring**) *n* 1 colorante. 2 colorido.

colt [kəʊlt] *n* potro.

column ['kɒləm] *n* columna.

coma ['kəʊmə] *n* coma.

comb [kəʊm] *n* peine. ► *vt* peinar.

combat ['kɒmbæt] *n* combate.

combination [kɒmbɪˈneɪʃən] *n* combinación.

combine [kəmˈbaɪn] *vt-vi* combinar(se).

come [kʌm] *vi* **1** venir. **2** llegar.

to come apart *vi* romperse.

to come back *vi* volver.

to come from *vt* ser de.

to come in *vi* **1** entrar: *come in!*, ¡adelante! **2** llegar *(tren)*.

to come off *vi* **1** tener lugar. **2** desprenderse, caerse *(pieza)*. **3** quitarse *(mancha)*.

to come on *vi* progresar.

to come out *vi* salir.

to come round *vi* **1** volver en sí. **2** hacer una visita.

to come up *vi* **1** surgir *(tema)*. **2** acercarse. **3** salir *(sol)*.

comeback [ˈkʌmbæk] *n fam* reaparición.

comedy [ˈkɒmədɪ] *n* comedia.

comet [ˈkɒmɪt] *n* cometa.

comfort [ˈkʌmfət] *n* **1** comodidad. **2** consuelo.

comfortable [ˈkʌmfətəbəl] *adj* cómodo,-a. • **to make oneself comfortable** ponerse cómodo,-a.

comic [ˈkɒmɪk] *adj-n* cómico, -a. ▶ *n* tebeo, cómic.

comma [ˈkɒmə] *n* coma.

command [kəˈmɑːnd] *n* **1** orden. **2** mando. **3** comando, instrucción. **4** dominio. ▶ *vt-vi* mandar.

commander [kəˈmɑːndə*] *n* comandante.

commemorate [kəˈmeməreɪt] *vt* conmemorar.

comment [ˈkɒment] *n* comentario. ▶ *vi* comentar.

commerce [ˈkɒmɜːs] *n* comercio.

commercial [kəˈmɜːʃəl] *adj* comercial. ▶ *n* anuncio.

commission [kəˈmɪʃən] *n* comisión.

commissioner [kəˈmɪʃənə*] *n* comisario.

commit [kəˈmɪt] *vt* cometer. • **to commit oneself** comprometerse.

commitment [kəˈmɪtmənt] *n* compromiso.

committee [kəˈmɪtɪ] *n* comité, comisión.

commodity [kəˈmɒdɪtɪ] *n* producto, artículo.

common [ˈkɒmən] *adj* común.

communicate [kəˈmjuːnɪkeɪt] *vt-vi* comunicar(se).

communiqué [kəˈmjuːnɪkeɪ] *n* comunicado.

communism [ˈkɒmjənɪzəm] *n* comunismo.

community [kəˈmjuːnɪtɪ] *n* comunidad.

commute [kəˈmjuːt] *vi* desplazarse diariamente de casa al lugar de trabajo. ▶ *vt* conmutar.

compact [kəmˈpækt] *adj* compacto,-a. ■ **compact disc** disco compacto.

company [ˈkʌmpənɪ] *n* compañía.

compare [kəm'peəʳ] *vt-vi* comparar(se).

compartment [kəm'pɑːtmənt] *n* compartim(i)ento.

compass ['kʌmpəs] *n* 1 brújula. 2 compás.

compatible [kəm'pætɪbəl] *adj* compatible.

compel [kəm'pel] *vt* obligar.

compensate ['kɒmpənseɪt] *vt* compensar.

compere ['kɒmpeəʳ] *n* GB presentador,-ra.

compete [kəm'piːt] *vi* competir.

competence ['kɒmpɪtəns] *n* competencia.

competent ['kɒmpɪtənt] *adj* competente.

competition [kɒmpə'tɪʃən] *n* 1 competición. 2 competencia.

complain [kəm'pleɪn] *vt* quejarse.

complaint [kəm'pleɪnt] *n* 1 queja. 2 dolencia.

complement ['kɒmplɪmənt] *n* complemento.

complete [kəm'pliːt] *adj* completo,-a. ▶ *vt* completar.

complex ['kɒmpleks] *adj* complejo,-a. ▶ *n* complejo.

complexion [kəm'plekʃən] *n* cutis, tez.

complicate ['kɒmplɪkeɪt] *vt* complicar.

compliment [*(n)* 'kɒmplɪmənt, *(vb)* 'kɒmplɪment] *n* cumplido. ▶ *vt* felicitar.

component [kəm'pəʊnənt] *adj-n* componente.

composed [kəm'pəʊzd] *adj* sereno,-a.

composer [kəm'pəʊzəʳ] *n* compositor,-ra.

composition [kɒmpə'zɪʃən] *n* composición.

compost ['kɒmpɒst] *n* abono.

compound ['kɒmpaʊnd] *adj* compuesto,-a. ▶ *n* compuesto.

comprehensive [kɒmprɪ'hensɪv] *adj* 1 completo,-a. 2 amplio,-a. ▪ **comprehensive insurance** seguro a todo riesgo.

compress ['kɒmpres] *n* compresa. ▶ *vt* comprimir.

comprise [kəm'praɪz] *vt* constar de.

compromise ['kɒmprəmaɪz] *n* acuerdo. ▶ *vi* llegar a un acuerdo.

compulsory [kəm'pʌlsərɪ] *adj* obligatorio,-a.

computer [kəm'pjuːtəʳ] *n* ordenador. ▪ **computer science** informática.

computing [kəm'pjuːtɪŋ] *n* informática.

con [kɒn] *n fam* timo.

conceal [kən'siːl] *vt* ocultar.

conceit [kən'siːt] *n* vanidad.

conceive [kən'siːv] *vt-vi* concebir.

concentrate ['kɒnsəntreɪt] *vt-vi* concentrar(se).

concentration [kɒnsən'treɪʃən] *n* concentración.

concept ['kɒnsept] *n* concepto.
concern [kən'sɜːn] *n* **1** preocupación. **2** negocio, empresa. ► *vt* **1** afectar, concernir. **2** preocupar. **3** tener que ver con. ● **as far as I'm concerned** por lo que a mí se refiere; **to whom it may concern** a quien corresponda.
concerning [kən'sɜːnɪŋ] *prep* referente a, sobre, acerca de.
concert ['kɒnsət] *n* concierto. ■ **concert house** sala de conciertos.
concise [kən'saɪs] *adj* conciso,-a.
conclude [kən'kluːd] *vt-vi* concluir.
conclusion [kən'kluːʒən] *n* conclusión.
concrete ['kɒŋkriːt] *adj* concreto,-a. ► *n* hormigón. ■ **concrete mixer** hormigonera.
condemn [kən'dem] *vt* condenar.
condition [kən'dɪʃən] *n* **1** condición. **2** circunstancia. **3** afección *(médica)*. ► *vt* **1** condicionar. **2** acondicionar. ● **in bad/good condition** en mal/buen estado; **to be out of condition** no estar en forma.
conditioner [kən'dɪʃənə'] *n* suavizante.
condolences [kən'dəʊlənsɪz] *npl* pésame.
conduct [*(n)* 'kɒndəkt, *(vb)* kən'dʌkt] *n* **1** conducta. **2** dirección. ► *vt* **1** dirigir, llevar a cabo. **2** comportarse. ► *vt-vi* dirigir *(orquesta)*.
conductor [kən'dʌktə'] *n* **1** director,-ra *(de orquesta)*. **2** cobrador *(de autobús)*. **3** conductor *(de calor, electricidad)*.
cone [kəʊn] *n* cono.
confectionery [kən'fekʃənərɪ] *n* dulces.
conference ['kɒnfərəns] *n* congreso. ■ **conference call** teleconferencia.
confess [kən'fes] *vt-vi* confesar(se).
confidence ['kɒnfɪdəns] *n* **1** confianza. **2** confidencia *(secreto)*.
confirm [kən'fɜːm] *vt* confirmar.
conflict ['kɒnflɪkt] *n* conflicto.
conform [kən'fɔːm] *vi* **1** conformarse. **2** ajustarse.
confusion [kən'fjuːʒən] *n* confusión.
congenial [kən'dʒiːnɪəl] *adj* agradable.
congratulate [kən'grætjəleɪt] *vt* felicitar.
congratulations [kəngrætjə'leɪʃəns] *npl* felicidades.
congress ['kɒngres] *n* congreso.
conjunction [kən'dʒʌŋkʃən] *n* conjunción.
conjurer ['kʌndʒərə'] *n* mago,-a, prestidigitador,-ra.
conjuror ['kʌndʒərə'] *n* mago,-a, prestidigitador,-ra.

connect [kə'nekt] *vt* conectar.
► *vi* enlazar *(vuelos)*.
connection [kə'nekʃən] *n* conexión.
connoisseur [kɒnə'sɜːʳ] *n* entendido,-a.
conquer ['kɒŋkəʳ] *vt* conquistar.
conquest ['kɒŋkwest] *n* conquista.
conscience ['kɒnʃəns] *n* conciencia.
conscious ['kɒnʃəs] *adj* consciente.
consent [kən'sent] *n* consentimiento. ► *vi* consentir.
consequence ['kɒnsɪkwəns] *n* consecuencia.
conservation [kɒnsə'veɪʃən] *n* conservación.
conservative [kən'sɜːvətɪv] *adj-n* conservador,-ra.
conservatory [kən'sɜːvətrɪ] *n* 1 invernadero. 2 conservatorio.
consider [kən'sɪdəʳ] *vt* considerar.
considerable [kən'sɪdərəbəl] *adj* considerable.
consist [kən'sɪst] *vi* consistir.
consistent [kən'sɪstənt] *adj* 1 consecuente. 2 constante.
consolation [kɒnsə'leɪʃən] *n* consuelo.
console ['kɒnsəʊl] *n* consola.
consonant ['kɒnsənənt] *n* consonante.
conspicuous [kəns'pɪkjʊəs] *adj* llamativo,-a, visible.

conspiracy [kən'spɪrəsɪ] *n* conspiración.
constable ['kʌnstəbəl] *n* policía.
constant ['kɒnstənt] *adj* constante.
constipation [kɒnstɪ'peɪʃən] *n* estreñimiento.
constituency [kən'stɪtjʊənsɪ] *n* circunscripción.
constitution [kɒnstɪ'tjuːʃən] *n* constitución.
constraint [kən'streɪnt] *n* 1 coacción. 2 limitación.
construction [kən'strʌkʃən] *n* construcción.
consul ['kɒnsəl] *n* cónsul.
consulate ['kɒnsjələt] *n* consulado.
consult [kən'sʌlt] *vt-vi* consultar.
consume [kən'sjuːm] *vt* consumir.
consumer [kən'sjuːməʳ] *n* consumidor,-ra. ▪ **consumer goods** bienes de consumo.
contact ['kɒntækt] *n* contacto. ▪ **contact lens** lentilla.
contagious [kən'teɪdʒəs] *adj* contagioso,-a.
contain [kən'teɪn] *vt* contener.
container [kən'teɪnəʳ] *n* 1 recipiente. 2 contáiner.
contamination [kəntæmɪ'neɪʃən] *n* contaminación.
contemporary [kən'tempərərɪ] *adj-n* contemporáneo,-a.
contempt [kən'tempt] *n* desprecio, menosprecio. ▪ **con-**

tempt of court desacato a la autoridad.

contend [kən'tend] *vi* **1** luchar. **2** enfrentarse a.

content¹ [kən'tent] *adj* contento,-a.

content² ['kɒntent] *n* contenido.

contents ['kɒntents] *npl* contenido.

contest ['kɒntest] *n* **1** concurso. **2** contienda.

contestant [kən'testənt] *n* **1** concursante. **2** candidato,-a.

context ['kɒntekst] *n* contexto.

continent ['kɒntɪnənt] *n* continente.

continental [kɒntɪ'nentəl] *adj* **1** continental. **2** GB europeo,-a.

continuation [kəntɪnjʊ'eɪʃən] *n* continuación.

continue [kən'tɪnjuː] *vt-vi* continuar.

contraceptive [kɒntrə'septɪv] *adj* anticonceptivo,-a. ► *n* anticonceptivo.

contract [*(n)* 'kɒntrækt, *(vb)* kən'trækt] *n* contrato. ► *vi* contraerse. ► *vt* contraer *(enfermedad, matrimonio)*.

contradiction [kɒntrə'dɪkʃən] *n* contradicción.

contrary ['kɒntrərɪ] *adj* contrario,a. • **contrary to** en contra de, al contrario de; **on the contrary** al contrario.

contrast ['kɒntræst] *n* contraste.

contribute [kən'trɪbjuːt] *vt-vi* contribuir. ► *vi* colaborar *(en periódico)*.

contributor [kən'trɪbjətə'] *n* **1** contribuyente. **2** colaborador,-ra *(en periódico)*.

control [kən'trəʊl] *n* **1** control. **2** mando. ► *vt* **1** controlar. **2** dominar. ▪ **control tower** torre de control.

controller [kən'trəʊlə'] *n* **1** controlador,-ra. **2** director, -ra de programación.

convenience [kən'viːnɪəns] *n* conveniencia. ▪ **convenience food** plato precocinado.

convenient [kən'viːnɪənt] *adj* conveniente.

convent ['kɒnvənt] *n* convento.

convention [kən'venʃən] *n* convención.

conversation [kɒnvə'seɪʃən] *n* conversación.

convert [*(n)* 'kɒnvɜːt, *(vb)* kən'vɜːt] *n* converso,-a. ► *vt-vi* converti(se).

convertible [kən'vɜːtəbəl] *adj* convertible. ► *adj-n* descapotable *(coche)*.

convey [kən'veɪ] *vt* **1** transportar. **2** comunicar *(idea)*.

conveyor belt [kən'veɪəbelt] *n* cinta transportadora.

convict [*(n)* 'kɒnvɪkt, *(vb)* kə n'vɪkt] *n* preso,-a. ► *vt* declarar culpable.

conviction [kən'vɪkʃən] *n* **1** convicción. **2** condena.

convince [kən'vɪns] *vt* convencer.

convoy ['kɒnvɔɪ] *n* convoy.

cook [kʊk] *n* cocinero,-ra. ▶ *vt* cocinar.

cooker ['kʊkə'] *n* cocina *(aparato)*.

cookery ['kʊkərɪ] *n* cocina *(arte)*.

cookie ['kʊkɪ] *n* US galleta.

cool [kuːl] *adj* **1** fresco,-a *(bebida)*. **2** tranquilo,-a *(persona)*. **3** *sl* en la onda. ▶ *vt* refrescar. ▶ *vi* enfriarse.

coop [kuːp] *n* gallinero.

cooperation [kəʊɒpə'reɪʃən] *n* cooperación.

cooperative [kəʊ'ɒpərətɪv] *adj* dispuesto,-a a colaborar. ▶ *n* cooperativa.

coordinate [kəʊ'ɔːdɪneɪt] *vt* coordinar.

cop [kɒp] *n fam* poli.

cope [kəʊp] *vi* arreglárselas.

to cope with *vt* poder con, hacer frente a.

copper ['kɒpə'] *n* cobre.

copy ['kɒpɪ] *n* copia. ▶ *vt-vi* copiar.

coral ['kɒrəl] *n* coral.

cord [kɔːd] *n* cuerda, cordón.

corduroy ['kɔːdərɔɪ] *n* pana.

core [kɔː'] *n* **1** núcleo, centro. **2** corazón *(de manzana)*.

cork [kɔːk] *n* corcho. ■ **cork oak** alcornoque.

corkscrew ['kɔːkskruː] *n* sacacorchos.

corn¹ [kɔːn] *n* **1** maíz. **2** cereales. ■ **corn on the cob** mazorca, maíz tierno.

corn² [kɔːn] *n* callo *(dureza)*.

cornea ['kɔːnɪə] *n* córnea.

corner ['kɔːnə'] *n* esquina, rincón. ■ **corner kick** córner.

cornet ['kɔːnɪt] *n* **1** corneta. **2** GB cucurucho.

cornflakes ['kɔːnfleɪks] *npl* copos de maíz.

cornstarch ['kɔːnstɑːtʃ] *n* harina de maíz, maicena.

corporal ['kɔːpərəl] *n* cabo *(militar)*. ▶ *adj* corporal.

corporation [kɔːpə'reɪʃən] *n* corporación.

corpse [kɔːps] *n* cadáver.

corpuscle ['kɔːpəsəl] *n* glóbulo.

correct [kə'rekt] *adj* **1** correcto,-a. **2** exacto,-a. **3** formal. ▶ *vt* corregir.

correction [kə'rekʃən] *n* corrección.

correspond [kɒrɪs'pɒnd] *vi* **1** coincidir, corresponderse. **2** escribirse, cartearse.

correspondence [kɒrɪs'pɒndəns] *n* correspondencia.

corridor ['kɒrɪdɔː'] *n* pasillo.

corrosion [kə'rəʊʒən] *n* corrosión.

corruption [kə'rʌpʃən] *n* corrupción.

corset ['kɔːsɪt] *n* corsé.

cosmetic [kɒz'metɪk] *n* cosmético. ■ **cosmetic surgery** cirugía estética.

cost [kɒst] *n* coste, costo, precio. ▶ *vi* costar, valer. ● **at all costs** a toda costa; **at the cost of** a costa de; **whatever the cost** cueste lo que cueste.

costume ['kɒstjuːm] *n* traje, disfraz. ■ **costume jewellery** (US **jewelry**) bisutería.

cosy ['kəuzi] *adj* acogedor,-ra.

cot [kɒt] *n* cuna.

cottage ['kɒtɪdʒ] *n* casa de campo. ■ **cottage cheese** requesón.

cotton ['kɒtən] *n* algodón. ■ **cotton wool** algodón hidrófilo.

couch [kautʃ] *n* canapé, sofá.

couchette [kuːʃet] *n* litera.

cough [kɒf] *n* tos. ▶ *vi* toser. ■ **cough mixture** jarabe para la tos.

could [kud, kəd] *pt* → can.

council ['kaunsəl] *n* **1** ayuntamiento. **2** consejo.

count¹ [kaunt] *n* conde.

count² [kaunt] *n* cuenta, recuento. ▶ *vt-vi* contar.

to count on *vt* contar con.

countdown ['kauntdaun] *n* cuenta atrás.

counter ['kauntə'] *n* **1** mostrador *(de tienda)*. **2** ficha *(de juego)*.

counterfeit ['kauntəfɪt] *adj* falso,-a, falsificado,-a. ▶ *n* falsificación. ▶ *vt* falsificar.

counterpane ['kauntəpeɪn] *n* colcha, cubrecama.

counterpart ['kauntəpaːt] *n* homólogo,-a.

countess ['kauntəs] *n* condesa.

country ['kʌntri] *n* **1** país. **2** campo. **3** tierra, región.

countryside ['kʌntrɪsaɪd] *n* **1** campo. **2** paisaje.

county ['kaunti] *n* condado.

coup [kuː] *n* golpe de estado.

couple ['kʌpəl] *n* **1** par *(de cosas)*. **2** pareja *(de personas)*. ▶ *vt* enganchar, conectar.

coupon ['kuːpɒn] *n* cupón.

courage ['kʌrɪdʒ] *n* valor.

courgette [kuə'ʒet] *n* calabacín.

courier ['kuərɪə'] *n* **1** mensajero,-a. **2** guía turístico,-a.

course [kɔːs] *n* **1** rumbo *(de barco, avión)*. **2** curso *(de río)*. **3** curso. **4** plato. **5** campo *(de golf)*. ● **in due course** a su debido tiempo; **of course** desde luego, por supuesto. ■ **first course** primer plato; **main course** plato principal.

court [kɔːt] *n* **1** tribunal, juzgado. **2** pista *(de tenis)*. **3** patio. **4** corte *(de rey)*.

courteous ['kɜːtɪəs] *adj* cortés.

courtyard ['kɔːtjaːd] *n* patio.

cousin ['kʌzən] *n* primo,-a.

cove [kəuv] *n* cala, ensenada.

cover ['kʌvə'] *n* **1** cubierta, funda. **2** tapa *(de cazuela)*. **3** cubierta *(de libro)*, portada *(de revista)*. **4** cobertura *(de seguro)*. ▶ *vt* **1** cubrir. **2** tapar *(con*

tapa). **3** asegurar *(con seguro).* •
under cover of al amparo de,
al abrigo de. ■ **cover charge**
precio del cubierto.
to cover up *vt* tapar.
covet ['kʌvət] *vt* codiciar.
cow [kau] *n* vaca.
coward ['kauəd] *n* cobarde.
cowboy ['kaubɔɪ] *n* vaquero.
cowshed ['kauʃed] *n* establo.
crab [kræb] *n* cangrejo.
crack [kræk] *vt* **1** rajar, agrietar
(suelo). **2** forzar *(caja fuerte).* **3**
cascar *(huevo, nuez).* **4** soltar
(chiste). ► *vi* **1** rajarse, agri-
etarse. **2** quebrarse *(voz).* **3**
hundirse *(persona).* **4** crujir. ►
n **1** raja *(en taza).* **2** grieta *(en
pared).* **3** chasquido *(de látigo).*
cracker ['krækə'] *n* galleta salada.
cradle ['kreɪdəl] *n* cuna.
craft [krɑːft] *n* **1** arte, oficio. **2**
artesanía. **3** embarcación. ■ **a
pleasure craft** un barco de
recreo.
craftsman ['krɑːftsmən] *n* artesano.
crag [kræg] *n* risco, peñasco.
cramp [kræmp] *n* calambre. ►
cramps *npl* retortijones.
crane [kreɪn] *n* **1** grulla común. **2** grúa.
crash [kræʃ] *vi* estrellarse *(avión,
coche).* ► *n* **1** estallido, estrépito
(ruido). **2** accidente. ■ **crash
course** curso intensivo.
crate [kreɪt] *n* caja.

crawfish ['krɔːfɪʃ] *n* langosta.
crawl [krɔːl] *vi* arrastrarse
(adulto), gatear *(bebé).* ► *n* crol.
crayfish ['kreɪfɪʃ] *n* cangrejo de
río.
craze [kreɪz] *n* manía, moda.
crazy ['kreɪzɪ] *adj fam* loco,-a.
cream [kriːm] *n* crema, nata.
crease [kriːs] *n* arruga.
create [kriːˈeɪt] *vt* crear.
creature ['kriːtʃə'] *n* criatura.
crèche [kreʃ] *n* guardería.
credible ['kredɪbəl] *adj* creíble.
credit ['kredɪt] *n* **1** mérito,
reconocimiento. **2** crédito,
haber. ► *vt* **1** creer, dar crédito
a. **2** abonar, ingresar. ► *npl*
credits créditos *(de película).* •
on credit a crédito. ■ **credit
card** tarjeta de crédito.
creed [kriːd] *n* credo.
creek [kriːk] *n* **1** GB cala. **2** US
riachuelo.
creep [kriːp] *vi* arrastrarse *(insecto),* deslizarse *(animal).*
creeper ['kriːpə'] *n* enredadera.
crème caramel [kremkærə-
'mel] *n* flan.
crept [krept] *pt-pp* → creep.
crescent ['kresənt] *n* medialu-
na. ► creciente *(luna).*
crest [krest] *n* cresta.
crevice ['krevɪs] *n* raja, grieta.
crew [kruː] *n* **1** tripulación. **2**
equipo. ■ **crew cut** pelado al
cero.
crib [krɪb] *n* cuna. ► *vt fam* copiar, plagiar.

crick [krɪk] *n* tortícolis.

cricket[1] ['krɪkɪt] *n* grillo *(insecto)*.

cricket[2] ['krɪkɪt] *n* críquet.

crime [kraɪm] *n* **1** crimen. **2** delito.

criminal ['krɪmɪnəl] *adj-n* criminal. ▪ **criminal record** antecedentes penales.

crinkle ['krɪŋkəl] *vt-vi* arrugar(se).

cripple ['krɪpəl] *n* lisiado,-a, inválido,-a. ▸ *vt* paralizar.

crisis ['kraɪsɪs] *n* crisis.

crisp [krɪsp] *adj* **1** crujiente *(pan)*. **2** fresco,-a *(lechuga)*. **3** frío,-a y seco,-a *(tiempo)*. ▸ *n* GB patata frita *(de bolsa)*.

criterion [kraɪ'tɪərɪən] *n* criterio.

critic ['krɪtɪk] *n* crítico,-a.

critical ['krɪtɪkəl] *adj* crítico,-a.

criticize ['krɪtɪsaɪz] *vt-vi* criticar.

crockery ['krɒkərɪ] *n* loza.

crocodile ['krɒkədaɪl] *n* cocodrilo.

crocus ['krəʊkəs] *n* azafrán *(planta, flor)*.

crook [krʊk] *n* **1** gancho. **2** cayado. **3** *fam* delincuente.

crooked ['krʊkɪd] *adj* **1** torcido,-a. **2** tortuoso,-a *(camino)*.

crop [krɒp] *n* **1** cultivo, cosecha. **2** pelado corto.

cross [krɒs] *n* **1** cruz. **2** cruce; *vt* cruzar, atravesar. ▸ *vi* cruzar(se).

to cross off *vt* borrar, tachar.

to cross out *vt* borrar, tachar.

to cross over *vi* cruzar.

crossbar ['krɒsbɑːʳ] *n* travesaño.

crossbow ['krɒsbəʊ] *n* ballesta.

cross-country [krɒs'kʌntrɪ] *adj-adv* campo través. ▪ **cross-country race** cros.

cross-eyed ['krɒsaɪd] *adj* bizco,-a.

crossing ['krɒsɪŋ] *n* **1** cruce *(de carretera)*. **2** travesía *(en barco)*.

crossroads ['krɒsrəʊdz] *n* encrucijada, cruce.

crossword ['krɒswɜːd] *n* crucigrama.

crotch [krɒtʃ] *n* entrepierna.

crotchet ['krɒtʃɪt] *n* negra *(nota)*.

crouch [kraʊtʃ] *vi* agacharse, agazaparse.

crow [krəʊ] *n* cuervo.

crowbar ['krəʊbɑːʳ] *n* palanca.

crowd [kraʊd] *n* **1** multitud, gentío. **2** público. **3** gente.

crowded ['kraʊdɪd] *adj* abarrotado,-a.

crown [kraʊn] *n* **1** corona *(de monarca)*. **2** copa *(de árbol, sombrero)*. ▸ *vt* coronar.

crucifix ['kruːsɪfɪks] *n* crucifijo.

crude [kruːd] *n* **1** grosero,-a *(chiste)*. **2** crudo,-a *(petróleo)*.

cruel ['kruːəl] *adj* cruel.

cruet ['kruːɪt] *n* vinagreras.

cruise [kruːz] *vi* hacer un crucero. ▸ *n* crucero *(viaje)*.

cruiser ['kruːzəʳ] *n* crucero *(barco)*.

crumb [krʌm] *n* miga.

crumble ['krʌmbəl] *vt* desmigar. ► *vi* desmoronarse, deshacerse.

crumple ['krʌmpəl] *vt-vi* arrugar(se).

crunch [krʌntʃ] ► *vi* crujir. ► *n* crujido.

crusade [kruːˈseɪd] *n* cruzada.

crush [krʌʃ] *n* aglomeración, gentío. ► *vt* 1 aplastar. 2 triturar.

crust [krʌst] *n* corteza.

crutch [krʌtʃ] *n* muleta.

cry [kraɪ] *vt-vi* gritar. ► *vi* llorar. ► *n* 1 grito. 2 llanto.

to cry out *vi* gritar.

crypt [krɪpt] *n* cripta.

crystal ['krɪstəl] *n* cristal.

cub [kʌb] *n* cachorro,-a.

cube [kjuːb] *n* 1 cubo. 2 terrón *(de azúcar)*. ▪ **cube root** raíz cúbica.

cubic ['kjuːbɪk] *adj* cúbico,-a.

cuckoo ['kʊkuː] *n* cuco común.

cucumber ['kjuːkʌmbəʳ] *n* pepino.

cuddle ['kʌdəl] *vt-vi* abrazar(se). ► *n* abrazo.

cue¹ [kjuː] *n* 1 señal. 2 pie *(en teatro)*.

cue² [kjuː] *n* taco *(de billar)*.

cuff [kʌf] *n* puño. ▪ **cuff links** gemelos *(de camisa)*.

cul-de-sac ['kʌldəsæk] *n* calle sin salida.

culminate ['kʌlmɪneɪt] *vt* culminar.

culprit ['kʌlprɪt] *n* culpable.

cultivate ['kʌltɪveɪt] *vt* cultivar.

cultivated ['kʌltɪveɪtɪd] *adj* 1 culto,-a *(persona)*. 2 cultivado,-a *(tierra)*.

culture ['kʌltʃəʳ] *n* cultura.

cumbersome ['kʌmbəsəm] *adj* 1 voluminoso. 2 incómodo,-a.

cumin ['kʌmɪn] *n* comino.

cunning ['kʌnɪŋ] *adj* astuto,-a.

cup [kʌp] *n* 1 taza. 2 copa.

cupboard ['kʌbəd] *n* armario.

curb [kɜːb] *n* freno, restricción. ► *vt* refrenar, contener.

curd [kɜːd] *n* cuajada. ▪ **curd cheese** requesón.

cure [kjʊəʳ] *vt* curar. ► *n* cura.

curfew ['kɜːfjuː] *n* toque de queda.

curious ['kjʊərɪəs] *adj* 1 curioso,-a. 2 extraño.

curl [kɜːl] *vt-vi* rizar(se). ► *n* 1 rizo, bucle. 2 espiral.

currant ['kʌrənt] *n* pasa.

currency ['kʌrənsɪ] *n* moneda.

current ['kʌrənt] *adj* 1 actual *(precio)*. 2 en curso, corriente *(mes)*. 3 común *(idea)*. ► *n* corriente. ▪ **current account** cuenta corriente; **current affairs** temas de actualidad.

curriculum [kəˈrɪkjələm] *n* plan de estudios. ▪ **curriculum vitae** currículum.

curse [kɜːs] *n* 1 maldición, maleficio. 2 palabrota. ► *vt-vi* maldecir.

cursor ['kɜːsəʳ] *n* cursor.
curtail [kɜːˈteɪl] *vt* reducir.
curtain ['kɜːtən] *n* **1** cortina. **2** telón. • **to draw the curtains** correr las cortinas.
curve [kɜːv] *n* curva.
cushion ['kʊʃən] *n* cojín, almohadón. ▶ *vt fig* amortiguar.
custard ['kʌstəd] *n* natillas.
custom ['kʌstəm] *n* costumbre.
customer ['kʌstəməʳ] *n* cliente. ▪ **customer services** servicio de atención al cliente.
customs ['kʌstəmz] *n* aduana. ▪ **customs duties** derechos de aduana, aranceles.
cut [kʌt] *vt* **1** cortar. **2** tallar *(piedra, vidrio)*. **3** dividir. **4** recortar. ▶ *n* **1** corte, incisión. **2** parte *(ganancias)*. **3** rebaja, recorte. ▪ **cold cuts** fiambres.
to cut down *vt* **1** talar, cortar. **2** *fig* reducir: *to cut down on smoking*, fumar menos.
to cut in *vi* interrumpir.
to cut off *vt* **1** cortar *(electricidad)*. **2** aislar.
to cut out *vt* **1** recortar, cortar. **2** eliminar, suprimir.
cute [kjuːt] *adj* mono,-a, guapo,-a.
cutlery ['kʌtləri] *n* cubiertos, cubertería.
cutlet ['kʌtlət] *n* chuleta.
cuttlefish ['kʌtəlfɪʃ] *n* sepia.
cycle ['saɪkəl] *n* ciclo. ▶ *vi* ir en bicicleta.
cycling ['saɪklɪŋ] *n* ciclismo.

cyclist ['saɪklɪst] *n* ciclista.
cyclone ['saɪkləʊn] *n* ciclón.
cylinder ['sɪlɪndəʳ] *n* **1** cilindro. **2** bombona.
cynical ['sɪnɪkəl] *adj* cínico,-a.
cypress ['saɪprəs] *n* ciprés.
cyst [sɪst] *n* quiste.
czar [zɑːʳ] *n* zar.

D

dad [dæd] *n fam* papá.
daddy ['dædi] *n fam* papá.
daffodil ['dæfədɪl] *n* narciso.
daft [dɑːft] *adj fam* tonto,-a.
daily ['deɪli] *adj* diario,-a, cotidiano,-a. ▶ *adv* diariamente. ▶ *n* diario.
dairy ['deəri] *n* **1** vaquería. **2** lechería.
daisy ['deɪzi] *n* margarita.
dam [dæm] *n* **1** dique. **2** embalse, presa.
damage ['dæmɪdʒ] *vt* dañar. ▶ *n* daño.
damn [dæm] *interj fam* ¡maldito,-a sea! ▶ *adj fam* maldito,-a.
damp [dæmp] *adj* húmedo,-a. ▶ *n* humedad.
dance [dɑːns] *n* baile, danza. ▶ *vt-vi* bailar.
dancer ['dɑːnsəʳ] *n* bailarín,-ina.
dandelion ['dændɪlaɪən] *n* diente de león.

dandruff ['dændrʌf] *n* caspa.
danger ['deɪndʒəʳ] *n* peligro.
dare [deəʳ] *vi* atreverse. • **I dare say...** creo que; **don't you dare!** ¡ni se te ocurra!
dark [dɑːk] *adj* **1** oscuro,-a. **2** moreno,-a *(pelo, piel)*. ► *n* **1** oscuridad. **2** anochecer. • **to grow dark** anochecer.
darkness ['dɑːknəs] *n* oscuridad.
darling ['dɑːlɪŋ] *n* querido,-a, cariño.
darn [dɑːn] *n* zurcido. ► *vt* zurcir.
dart [dɑːt] *n* dardo.
dartboard ['dɑːtbɔːd] *n* diana.
dash [dæʃ] *n* **1** poco, pizca *(de sal)*. **2** chorro *(de líquido)*.
dashboard ['dæʃbɔːd] *n* salpicadero.
data ['deɪtə] *npl* datos, información. ■ **data base** base de datos; **data processing** procesamiento de datos.
date¹ [deɪt] *n* **1** fecha. **2** cita, compromiso. • **out of date** anticuado,-a.
date² [deɪt] *n* dátil.
dated ['deɪtɪd] *adj* anticuado,-a.
daughter ['dɔːtəʳ] *n* hija.
daughter-in-law ['dɔːtərɪnlɔː] *n* nuera.
daunt [dɔːnt] *vt* intimidar.
dawn [dɔːn] *n* amanecer.
day [deɪ] *n* **1** día. **2** jornada. **3** época, tiempo. • **by day** de día. ■ **day off** día libre.

daybreak ['deɪbreɪk] *n* alba.
daylight ['deɪlaɪt] *n* luz de día.
daytime *n* día.
dazzle ['dæzəl] *vt* deslumbrar.
dead [ded] *adj* **1** muerto,-a. **2** sordo,-a *(ruido)*. **3** total, absoluto,-a: *dead silence*, silencio total. ■ **dead end** callejón sin salida.
deadline ['dedlaɪn] *n* fecha límite, hora límite.
deadlock ['dedlɒk] *n* punto muerto.
deaf [def] *adj* sordo,-a.
deaf-and-dumb [defən'dʌm] *adj* sordomudo,-a.
deal [diːl] *n* **1** trato, pacto. **2** cantidad: *a great deal of noise*, mucho ruido. ► *vt* **1** dar, asestar *(golpe)*. **2** repartir *(cartas)*. ► *vi* comerciar.
to deal with *vt* **1** tratar con. **2** abordar, ocuparse de *(problema)*. **3** tratar de *(tema)*.
dealer ['diːləʳ] *n* **1** comerciante. **2** traficante *(de drogas)*.
dealt [delt] *pt-pp* → deal.
dear [dɪəʳ] *adj* **1** querido, a. **2** caro,-a *(precio)*. • **Dear Sir** Muy señor mío, Estimado señor.
death [deθ] *n* muerte. ■ **death penalty** pena de muerte.
debate [dɪ'beɪt] *n* debate. ► *vt-vi* debatir.
debit ['debɪt] *n* débito. ► *vt* cargar en cuenta.
debris ['deɪbriː] *n* escombros.
debt [det] *n* deuda.

debug [diːˈbʌg] *vt* depurar.
debut [ˈdeɪbjuː] *n* estreno.
decade [ˈdekeɪd] *n* década.
decadence [ˈdekədəns] *n* decadencia.
decaffeinated [dɪˈkæfɪneɪtɪd] *adj* descafeinado,-a.
decay [dɪˈkeɪ] *n* 1 descomposición *(de cuerpo)*. 2 caries *(de diente)*. 3 *fig* decadencia *(de sociedad)*. ▶ *vi* 1 descomponerse *(cuerpo)*. 2 deteriorarse *(edificio)*. 3 cariarse *(diente)*.
deceased [dɪˈsiːst] *adj-n* fallecido,-a.
deceive [dɪˈsiːv] *vt* engañar.
December [dɪˈsembəʳ] *n* diciembre.
decent [ˈdiːsənt] *adj* decente.
deception [dɪˈsepʃən] *n* engaño, mentira.
decide [dɪˈsaɪd] *vt-vi* decidir(se).
decimal [ˈdesɪməl] *adj-n* decimal.
decision [dɪˈsɪʒən] *n* decisión.
decisive [dɪˈsaɪsɪv] *adj* 1 decisivo,-a. 2 decidido,-a *(persona)*.
deck [dek] *n* 1 cubierta *(de barco)*. 2 piso *(de autobús)*. 3 US baraja.
deckchair [ˈdektʃeəʳ] *n* tumbona.
declare [dɪˈkleəʳ] *vt* declarar.
decorate [ˈdekəreɪt] *vt* decorar, adornar. ▶ *vt-vi* pintar, empapelar.
decoration [dekəˈreɪʃən] *n* 1 decoración. 2 condecoración.

decrease [dɪˈkriːs] *n* disminución. ▶ *vt-vi* disminuir.
decree [dɪˈkriː] *n* decreto.
dedicate [ˈdedɪkeɪt] *vt* dedicar.
deduce [dɪˈdjuːs] *vt* deducir.
deduct [dɪˈdʌkt] *vt* restar.
deed [diːd] *n* 1 acto. 2 hazaña. 3 escritura *(de propiedad)*.
deep [diːp] *adj* hondo,-a, profundo,-a.
deer [dɪəʳ] *n* ciervo.
default [dɪˈfɔːlt] *n* negligencia. ■ **default settings** valores por defecto.
defeat [dɪˈfiːt] *n* derrota. ▶ *vt* derrotar.
defect [(n) ˈdiːfekt, (vb) dɪˈfekt] *n* defecto. ▶ *vi* desertar.
defence [dɪˈfens] *n* defensa.
defend [dɪˈfend] *vt* defender.
defer [dɪˈfɜːʳ] *vt* aplazar.
deficient [dɪˈfɪʃənt] *adj* deficiente.
deficit [ˈdefɪsɪt] *n* déficit.
define [dɪˈfaɪn] *vt* definir.
definition [defɪˈnɪʃən] *n* definición.
definitive [dɪˈfɪnɪtɪv] *adj* definitivo,-a.
deflate [dɪˈfleɪt] *vt-vi* desinflar(se), deshinchar(se).
deflect [dɪˈflekt] *vt-vi* desviar(se).
defrost [diːˈfrɒst] *vt-vi* descongelar(se).
defy [dɪˈfaɪ] *vt* desafiar.
degree [dɪˈgriː] *n* 1 grado. 2 título, licenciatura. ● **to some**

degree hasta cierto punto. ■ **honorary degree** doctorado "honoris causa".

delay [dɪ'leɪ] *n* retraso. ► *vt* aplazar.

delegation [delɪ'geɪʃən] *n* delegación.

delete [dɪ'liːt] *vt* borrar.

deliberate [dɪ'lɪbəreɪt] *vt-vi* deliberar.

delicacy ['delɪkəsɪ] *n* **1** delicadeza. **2** manjar *(exquisito)*.

delicate ['delɪkət] *adj* delicado,-a.

delicatessen [delɪkə'tesən] *n* charcutería selecta.

delicious [dɪ'lɪʃəs] *adj* delicioso,-a.

delight [dɪ'laɪt] *n* placer, delicia.

delighted [dɪ'laɪtɪd] *adj* encantado,-a.

deliver [dɪ'lɪvəʳ] *vt* **1** entregar, *(mercancía).* **2** dar *(golpe, patada).* **3** pronunciar *(discurso).* **4** traer al mundo.

delivery [dɪ'lɪvərɪ] *n* **1** entrega. **2** parto. ■ **delivery man** repartidor.

delude [dɪ'luːd] *vt* engañar.

demand [dɪ'mɑːnd] *n* **1** reclamación, petición. **2** demanda. ► *vt* exigir, reclamar.

democracy [dɪ'mɒkrəsɪ] *n* democracia.

democrat ['deməkræt] *n* demócrata.

demolish [dɪ'mɒlɪʃ] *vt* derribar, demoler.

demon ['diːmən] *n* demonio.

demonstrate ['demənstreɪt] *vt* **1** demostrar. **2** mostrar. ► *vi* manifestarse.

demonstration [demən'streɪʃən] *n* **1** demostración. **2** manifestación.

denial [dɪ'naɪəl] *n* negativa.

denim ['denɪm] *n* tela vaquera.

denounce [dɪ'naʊns] *vt* denunciar.

dense [dens] *adj* denso,-a.

dent [dent] *n* abolladura. ► *vt* abollar.

dentist ['dentɪst] *n* dentista.

deny [dɪ'naɪ] *vt* negar.

deodorant [diː'əʊdərənt] *n* desodorante.

department [dɪ'pɑːtmənt] *n* **1** departamento, sección. **2** ministerio. ■ **department store** grandes almacenes.

departure [dɪ'pɑːtʃəʳ] *n* **1** partida, marcha *(de persona).* **2** salida *(de tren, avión).*

depend [dɪ'pend] *vi* depender.

to depend on *vt* confiar en.

deplore [dɪ'plɔːʳ] *vt* deplorar.

deploy [dɪ'plɔɪ] *vt fig* desplegar.

deport [dɪ'pɔːt] *vt* deportar.

deposit [dɪ'pɒzɪt] *n* **1** depósito. **2** yacimiento *(minerales).* **3** poso *(en vino).* ► *vt* **1** depositar. **2** ingresar. ■ **deposit account** cuenta de ahorros.

depot ['depəʊ] *n* **1** almacén. **2** depósito.

depress [dɪ'pres] *vt* deprimir.
depression [dɪ'preʃən] *n* depresión.
deprive [dɪ'praɪv] *vt* privar.
depth [depθ] *n* profundidad.
deputy ['depjətɪ] *n* **1** sustituto,-a, suplente. **2** diputado,-a.
derive [dɪ'raɪv] *vt-vi* derivar(se).
derogatory [dɪ'rɒgətərɪ] *adj* despectivo,-a.
descend [dɪ'send] *vt-vi* bajar.
descendant [dɪ'sendənt] *n* descendiente.
descent [dɪ'sent] *n* **1** descenso, bajada. **2** pendiente.
describe [dɪ'skraɪb] *vt* describir.
description [dɪ'skrɪpʃən] *n* descripción.
desert[1] ['dezət] *n* desierto.
desert[2] [dɪ'zɜːt] *vt* abandonar, dejar. ▸ *vi* desertar.
deserve [dɪ'zɜːv] *vt* merecerse.
design [dɪ'zaɪn] *n* diseño. ▸ *vt-vi* diseñar.
desire [dɪ'zaɪə'] *n* deseo. ▸ *vt* desear.
desk [desk] *n* **1** pupitre. **2** escritorio, mesa *(de trabajo)*.
desktop ['desktɒp] *n* escritorio. ▪ **desktop computer** ordenador de sobremesa; **desktop publishing** autoedición.
despair [dɪs'peə'] *n* desesperación. ▸ *vi* desesperarse.
despatch [dɪs'pætʃ] *vt-n* → dispatch.
desperate ['despərət] *adj* desesperado,-a.

desperation [despə'reɪʃən] *n* desesperación.
despicable [dɪ'spɪkəbəl] *adj* despreciable.
despise [dɪ'spaɪz] *vt* despreciar.
despite [dɪ'spaɪt] *prep* a pesar de.
dessert [dɪ'zɜːt] *n* postre.
destination [destɪ'neɪʃən] *n* destino.
destiny ['destɪnɪ] *n* destino.
destroy [dɪ'strɔɪ] *vt* destruir.
destruction [dɪ'strʌkʃən] *n* destrucción.
detach [dɪ'tætʃ] *vt* separar.
detail ['diːteɪl] *n* detalle.
detect [dɪ'tekt] *vt* detectar.
detective [dɪ'tektɪv] *n* detective.
detention [dɪ'tenʃən] *n* detención.
detergent [dɪ'tɜːdʒənt] *n* detergente.
determine [dɪ'tɜːmɪn] *vt* determinar.
deterrent [dɪ'terənt] *adj* disuasivo,-a. ▸ *n* fuerza disuasoria.
detest [dɪ'test] *vt* detestar.
detour ['diːtuə'] *n* desvío.
devaluation [diːvæljuː'eɪʃən] *n* devaluación.
develop [dɪ'veləp] *vt* **1** desarrollar. **2** revelar *(carrete)*. ▸ *vi* desarrollarse.
development [dɪ'veləpmənt] *n* **1** desarrollo. **2** revelado *(de carrete)*.
deviate ['diːvɪeɪt] *vi* desviarse.

device [dɪ'vaɪs] *n* mecanismo, dispositivo.
devil ['devəl] *n* diablo.
devise [dɪ'vaɪz] *vt* idear.
devoted [dɪ'vəʊtɪd] *adj* fiel.
devotion [dɪ'vəʊʃən] *n* dedicación.
dew [dju:] *n* rocío.
dexterity [dek'sterɪtɪ] *n* destreza, habilidad.
diabetes [daɪə'bi:ti:z] *n* diabetes.
diagnosis [daɪəg'nəʊsɪs] *n* diagnóstico.
diagonal [daɪ'ægənəl] *n* diagonal.
diagram ['daɪəgræm] *n* diagrama, esquema, gráfico.
dial ['daɪəl] *n* **1** esfera *(de reloj)*. **2** dial *(de radio)*. **2** teclado *(de teléfono)*. ▶ *vt* marcar. ■ **dialling code** prefijo telefónico; **dialling tone** señal de marcar.
dialect ['daɪəlekt] *n* dialecto.
dialogue ['daɪəlɒg] (US **dialog**) *n* diálogo.
diameter [daɪ'æmɪtə'] *n* diámetro.
diamond ['daɪəmənd] *n* diamante.
diaper ['daɪəpə'] *n* US pañal.
diarrhoea [daɪə'rɪə] *n* diarrea.
diary ['daɪərɪ] *n* **1** diario. **2** agenda.
dice [daɪs] *n* dado.
dictate [dɪk'teɪt] *vt* dictar. ▶ *vi* mandar.
dictation [dɪk'teɪʃən] *n* dictado.

dictator [dɪk'teɪtə'] *n* dictador, -ra.
dictionary ['dɪkʃənərɪ] *n* diccionario.
did [dɪd] *pt* → do.
die [daɪ] *vi* morir.
to die away *vi* desvanecerse.
diesel ['di:zəl] *n* gasoil, diesel.
diet ['daɪət] *n* dieta, régimen. ● **to go on a diet** ponerse a régimen.
differ ['dɪfə'] *vi* diferir.
difference ['dɪfərəns] *n* diferencia.
different ['dɪfərənt] *adj* diferente, distinto,-a.
difficult ['dɪfɪkəlt] *adj* difícil.
dig [dɪg] *vt* **1** cavar *(hoyo)*, excavar *(túnel)*. **2** clavar, hincar *(con uñas)*.
to dig out/up *vt* desenterrar.
digest ['daɪdʒest] *n* resumen.
digestion [dɪ'dʒestʃən] *n* digestión.
digestive [daɪ'dʒestɪv] *adj* digestivo,-a. ■ **digestive tract** aparato digestivo.
dignity ['dɪgnɪtɪ] *n* dignidad.
dike [daɪk] *n* US → dyke.
diligence ['dɪlɪdʒəns] *n* diligencia.
dilute [daɪ'lu:t] *vt* diluir.
dim [dɪm] *adj* **1** débil, difuso, -a, tenue. **2** oscuro,-a. **3** borroso,-a. **4** *fam* tonto,-a. ▶ *vt* **1** bajar, atenuar. **2** *fig* difuminar.
dime [daɪm] *n* US moneda de diez centavos.

dimension [dɪ'menʃən] *n* dimensión.

dimple ['dɪmpəl] *n* hoyuelo.

din [dɪn] *n* alboroto.

dine [daɪn] *vi* cenar.

diner ['daɪnəʳ] *n* **1** comensal. **2** US restaurante barato.

dinghy ['dɪŋɡɪ] *n* bote.

dingy ['dɪndʒɪ] *adj* **1** sucio,-a, sórdido,-a. **2** deslucido,-a, deslustrado,-a *(ropa)*.

dining car ['daɪnɪŋkɑːʳ] *n* coche restaurante.

dining room ['daɪnɪŋruːm] *n* comedor.

dinner ['dɪnəʳ] *n* comida, cena. ● **to have dinner** cenar. ■ **dinner jacket** esmoquin; **dinner table** mesa de comedor.

dinosaur ['daɪnəsɔːʳ] *n* dinosaurio.

dip [dɪp] *n vt* sumergir, bañar.

diploma [dɪ'pləʊmə] *n* diploma.

diplomacy [dɪ'pləʊməsɪ] *n* diplomacia.

direct [dɪ'rekt, daɪ'rekt] *adj* directo,-a. ► *vt* dirigir.

direction [dɪ'rekʃən, daɪ'rekʃən] *n* dirección. ► *npl* **directions** instrucciones de uso, modo de empleo.

director [dɪ'rektəʳ, daɪ'rektəʳ] *n* director,-ra.

directory [dɪ'rektərɪ, daɪ'rektərɪ] *n* **1** guía telefónica. **2** callejero.

dirt [dɜːt] *n* suciedad.

dirty ['dɜːtɪ] *adj* **1** sucio,-a. **2** verde *(chiste)*. ► *vt-vi* ensuciar(se). ■ **dirty trick** cochinada; **dirty word** palabrota.

disabled [dɪs'eɪbəld] *adj* minusválido,-a, incapacitado,-a.

disadvantage [dɪsəd'vɑːntɪdʒ] *n* desventaja.

disagree [dɪsə'griː] *vi* **1** discrepar. **2** sentar mal *(comida)*.

disappear [dɪsə'pɪəʳ] *vi* desaparecer.

disappoint [dɪsə'pɔɪnt] *vt* decepcionar, defraudar.

disaster [dɪ'zɑːstəʳ] *n* desastre.

disc [dɪsk] *n* disco. ■ **disc brake** freno de disco; **disc jockey** disc-jockey.

discard [dɪs'kɑːd] *vt* desechar.

discern [dɪ'sɜːn] *vt* discernir.

discharge [*(n)* 'dɪstʃɑːdʒ, *(vb)* dɪs'tʃɑːdʒ] *n* **1** descarga. **2** liberación *(de preso)*. **3** alta *(de paciente)*. ► *vt* **1** liberar *(preso)*. **2** dar de alta *(paciente)*. **3** licenciar *(soldado)*.

discipline ['dɪsɪplɪn] *n* disciplina.

disco ['dɪskəʊ] *n fam* discoteca.

discolour [dɪs'kʌləʳ] (US **discolor**) *vt-vi* desteñir(se).

disconnect [dɪskə'nekt] *vt* desconectar.

discotheque ['dɪskətek] *n* discoteca.

discount [*(n)* 'dɪskaʊnt, *(vb)* dɪs'kaʊnt] *n* descuento. ► *vt* descontar.

discourage [dɪs'kʌrɪdʒ] *vt* 1 desanimar. 2 disuadir.

discover [dɪ'skʌvəʳ] *vt* descubrir.

discovery [dɪ'skʌvərɪ] *n* descubrimiento.

discriminate [dɪ'skrɪmɪneɪt] *vi* discriminar.

discus ['dɪskəs] *n* disco.

discuss [dɪ'skʌs] *vt-vi* discutir.

discussion [dɪ'skʌʃən] *n* discusión.

disease [dɪ'ziːz] *n* enfermedad.

disembark [dɪsɪm'baːk] *vt-vi* desembarcar.

disgrace [dɪs'greɪs] *n* 1 desgracia. 2 escándalo, vergüenza.

disguise [dɪs'gaɪz] *n* disfraz. ► *vt* disfrazar.

disgusting [dɪs'gʌstɪŋ] *adj* asqueroso,-a, repugnante.

dish [dɪʃ] *n* plato, fuente *(para servir)*. ● **to do the dishes** lavar los platos.

dishcloth ['dɪʃklɒθ] *n* trapo de cocina.

dishevelled [dɪ'ʃevəld] *adj* 1 despeinado,-a *(pelo)*. 2 desarreglado,-a *(aspecto)*.

dishwasher ['dɪʃwɒʃəʳ] *n* lavavajillas.

disinfectant [dɪsɪn'fektənt] *n* desinfectante.

disk [dɪsk] *n* disco. ■ **disk drive** unidad de disco.

dislike [dɪs'laɪk] *n* aversión, antipatía. ► *vt* no gustar.

dislodge [dɪs'lɒdʒ] *vt* desalojar.

dismal ['dɪzməl] *adj* triste.

dismantle [dɪs'mæntəl] *vt-vi* desmontar(se), desarmar(se).

dismiss [dɪs'mɪs] *vt* 1 despedir *(empleado)*. 2 descartar, desechar.

disobey [dɪsə'beɪ] *vt-vi* desobedecer.

disorder [dɪs'ɔːdəʳ] *n* desorden.

dispatch [dɪ'spætʃ] *n* 1 despacho, parte. 2 reportaje *(de corresponsalía)*. 3 envío. ► *vt* enviar.

dispenser [dɪ'spensəʳ] *n* máquina expendedora.

display [dɪ'spleɪ] *n* 1 exposición *(de artículos)*. 2 exhibición *(de fuerzas)*. 3 visualización *(en pantalla)*. ► *vt* mostrar, exponer.

disposable [dɪ'spəʊzəbəl] *adj* desechable.

dispute [*(n)* 'dɪspjuːt, *(vb)* dɪ'spjuːt] *n* discusión, disputa. ► *vt* cuestionar.

disqualify [dɪs'kwɒlɪfaɪ] *vt* descalificar.

disrupt [dɪs'rʌpt] *vt* trastornar.

dissatisfied [dɪs'sætɪsfaɪd] *adj* descontento,-a.

dissident ['dɪsɪdənt] *adj-n* disidente.

dissolve [dɪ'zɒlv] *vt-vi* disolver(se).

dissuade [dɪ'sweɪd] *vt* disuadir.

distance ['dɪstəns] *n* distancia. ► *vt* distanciar. • **from a distance** desde lejos; **in the distance** a lo lejos.

distinction [dɪ'stɪŋkʃən] *n* distinción.

distinguish [dɪ'stɪŋgwɪʃ] *vt-vi* distinguir(se).

distort [dɪ'stɔːt] *vt* deformar.

distract [dɪ'strækt] *vt* distraer.

distraction [dɪ'strækʃən] *n* distracción.

distress [dɪ'stres] *n* angustia. ► *vt* afligir. ■ **distress call/signal** señal de socorro.

distribute [dɪ'strɪbjuːt] *vt* distribuir.

distribution [dɪstrɪ'bjuːʃən] *n* distribución.

district ['dɪstrɪkt] *n* distrito. ■ **district council** municipio.

disturb [dɪ'stɜːb] *vt* molestar.

ditch [dɪtʃ] *n* **1** zanja, cuneta. **2** acequia *(para agua)*.

dive [daɪv] *n* **1** zambullida. **2** buceo. **3** picado *(pájaro, avión)*. **4** *fam* antro. ► *vi* **1** tirarse de cabeza *(al agua)*. **2** bucear *(bajo el agua)*. **3** bajar en picado *(pájaro, avión)*.

diver ['daɪvəʳ] *n* **1** buceador,-ra. **2** saltador,-ra *(de trampolín)*.

diversion [daɪ'vɜːʃən] *n* **1** desvío, desviación. **2** distracción.

diversity [daɪ'vɜːsɪtɪ] *n* diversidad.

divert [daɪ'vɜːt] *vt* **1** desviar. **2** distraer.

divide [dɪ'vaɪd] *vt-vi* dividir(se).

diving ['daɪvɪŋ] *n* **1** submarinismo. **2** saltos de trampolín. ■ **diving board** trampolín.

division [dɪ'vɪʒən] *n* división.

divorce [dɪ'vɔːs] *n* divorcio. ► *vt-vi* divorciarse (de).

dizzy ['dɪzɪ] *adj* mareado,-a.

do [duː] *aux*: *do you smoke?*, ¿fumas?; *I don't want to dance*, no quiero bailar; *you don't smoke, do you?*, no fumas, ¿verdad? ► *vt* **1** hacer, realizar: *what are you doing?*, ¿qué haces? **2** ser suficiente: *ten packets will do us*, con diez paquetes tenemos suficiente. • **how do you do? 1** ¿cómo está usted? *(saludo)*. **2** mucho gusto, encantado,-a *(respuesta)*.

to do up *vt* **1** *fam* abrocharse, atar. **2** envolver. **3** arreglar, renovar.

dock¹ [dɒk] *n* **1** muelle *(en puerto)*. **2** banquillo *(de los acusados)*.

dockyard ['dɒkjɑːd] *n* astillero.

doctor ['dɒktəʳ] *n* médico,-a.

document ['dɒkjəmənt] *n* documento.

documentary [dɒkjə'mentərɪ] *adj-n* documental.

does [dʌz] *3rd pers sing pres* → do.

dog [dɒg] *n* perro,-a.

do-it-yourself [duːɪtjɔː'self] *n* bricolaje.

downward

dole [dəʊl] *n* GB *fam* subsidio de desempleo. • **to be on the dole** estar en el paro.

doll [dɒl] *n* muñeca.

dollar [ˈdɒləʳ] *n* dólar.

dolphin [ˈdɒlfɪn] *n* delfín.

domain [dəˈmeɪn] *n* dominio.

domestic [dəˈmestɪk] *adj* 1 doméstico,-a *(animal)*. 2 nacional *(vuelo)*.

dominate [ˈdɒmɪneɪt] *vt-vi* dominar.

domino [ˈdɒmɪnəʊ] *n* ficha de dominó. ► *npl* **dominoes** dominó.

donate [dəʊˈneɪt] *vt* donar, hacer un donativo de.

done [dʌn] *pp* → do.

donkey [ˈdɒŋkɪ] *n* burro,-a.

donor [ˈdəʊnəʳ] *n* donante.

don't [dəʊnt] *aux* contracción de *do + not*.

door [dɔːʳ] *n* puerta. • **to answer the door** abrir la puerta.

doorbell [ˈdɔːbel] *n* timbre.

doorman [ˈdɔːmən] *n* portero.

door-to-door [dɔːtəˈdɔː] *adj* a domicilio.

doorway [ˈdɔːweɪ] *n* entrada, portal.

dosage [ˈdəʊsɪdʒ] *n* posología.

dose [dəʊs] *n* dosis.

dot [dɒt] *n* punto.

double [ˈdʌbəl] *adj-adv* doble. ► *n* doble. ► *vt-vi* doblar(se). ► *npl* **doubles** dobles. ■ **double bass** contrabajo; **double bed** cama de matrimonio; **double chin** papada; **double room** habitación doble.

double-decker [dʌbəlˈdekəʳ] *n* GB autobús de dos pisos.

doubt [daʊt] *n* duda. ► *vt* dudar. • **no doubt** sin duda.

dough [dəʊ] *n* 1 masa *(de pan)*. 2 *fam* pasta *(dinero)*.

doughnut [ˈdəʊnʌt] *n* rosquilla, donut.

dove[1] [dʌv] *n* paloma.

dove[2] [dəʊv] *pt* US → dive.

down[1] [daʊn] *prep* abajo, hacia abajo. ► *adv* 1 abajo, hacia abajo, al suelo. 2 estropeado,-a: *the computer is down*, el ordenador está estropeado. ► *adj fam* deprimido. ■ **down payment** entrada.

down[2] [daʊn] *n* 1 plumón. 2 vello, pelusa, pelusilla.

downhill [daʊnˈhɪl] *adv* cuesta abajo. ► *adj* en pendiente.

download [ˈdaʊnˈləʊd] *vt* bajar, descargar.

downpour [ˈdaʊnpɔːʳ] *n* chaparrón.

downstairs [daʊnˈsteəz] *adv* abajo: *to go downstairs*, bajar la escalera. ► *adj* en la planta baja, de abajo.

downstream [daʊnˈstriːm] *adv* río abajo.

downtown [daʊnˈtaʊn] US *adv* al/en el centro de la ciudad. ► *adj* del centro de la ciudad.

downward [ˈdaʊnwəd] *adj* 1 descendente. 2 a la baja.

downwards ['daʊnwədz] *adv* hacia abajo.

doze [dəʊz] *n* cabezada.

dozen ['dʌzən] *n* docena.

draft [drɑːft] *n* 1 borrador. 2 letra de cambio, giro. 3 US → draught.

draftsman ['drɑːftsmən] *n* US → draughtsman.

drag [dræg] *n fam* calada. ▶ *vt* 1 arrastrar. 2 rastrear, dragar. • **in drag** vestido de mujer.

dragon ['drægən] *n* dragón.

drain [dreɪn] *n* desagüe, alcantarilla. ▶ *vt* 1 drenar *(pantano)*. 2 desecar *(lago)*. 3 apurar *(vaso)*. 4 vaciar *(depósito)*. 5 escurrir *(verduras)*. ▶ *vi* escurrirse.

drainpipe ['dreɪnpaɪp] *n* (tubería de) desagüe.

drama ['drɑːmə] *n* 1 drama. 2 teatro, arte dramático.

drank [dræŋk] *pt* → drink.

drastic ['dræstɪk] *adj* drástico,-a.

draught [drɑːft] *n* 1 corriente de aire. 2 trago. ▶ *npl* **draughts** GB damas. • **on draught** a presión, de barril.

draughtsman ['drɑːftsmən] *n* delineante.

draw [drɔː] *n* 1 sorteo. 2 empate. ▶ *vt* 1 dibujar *(línea, círculo)*. 2 tirar de. 3 correr *(cortinas)*. 4 cobrar *(sueldo)*. 5 extender *(talón)*. 6 sacar *(conclusión)*.

to draw apart separarse.

to draw back *vi* retroceder.

to draw in *vi* apartarse.

to draw on *vt* recurrir a.

drawback ['drɔːbæk] *n* inconveniente.

drawer ['drɔːəʳ] *n* cajón.

drawing ['drɔːɪŋ] *n* dibujo. ■ **drawing pin** GB chincheta; **drawing room** sala de estar.

drawn [drɔːn] *pp* → draw.

dreadful ['dredfʊl] *adj* espantoso,-a.

dream [driːm] *n* sueño. ▶ *vt-vi* soñar.

dreamt [dremt] *pt-pp* → dream.

dress [dres] *n* 1 vestido. 2 ropa. ▶ *vt* 1 vestir. 2 vendar *(herida)*. 3 aliñar *(ensalada)*. ▶ *vi* vestirse. ■ **dress rehearsal** ensayo general *(con trajes)*.

to dress up *vi* disfrazarse.

dresser ['dresəʳ] *n* 1 GB aparador. 2 US tocador.

dressing ['dresɪŋ] *n* 1 vendaje. 2 aliño *(de ensalada)*. ■ **dressing gown** bata; **dressing table** tocador.

drew [druː] *pt* → draw.

dribble ['drɪbəl] *n* 1 gotas. 2 baba. ▶ *vi* 1 gotear *(líquido)*. 2 babear *(bebé)*. ▶ *vt* driblar, regatear *(en fútbol)*.

drier ['draɪəʳ] *n* → dryer.

drift [drɪft] *n* 1 flujo. 2 ventisquero *(de nieve)*. 3 *fig* significado. ▶ *vi* ir a la deriva.

drill [drɪl] *n* 1 taladro. 2 broca. 3 ejercicio. 4 fresa *(de dentista)*. ▶ *vt* taladrar.

drink [drɪŋk] *n* bebida, copa. ► *vt-vi* beber.

drinking [ˈdrɪŋkɪŋ] *n*. ▪ **drinking water** agua potable.

drip [drɪp] *n* **1** goteo. **2** gota a gota *(de suero)*. ► *vi* gotear.

drive [draɪv] *n* **1** paseo en coche. **2** camino de entrada. **3** drive *(golf, tenis)*. **4** transmisión *(en motor)*. **5** tracción *(en coche)*. **6** unidad de disco. ► *vt* **1** conducir. **2** llevar, acompañar: *I'll drive you home*, te llevaré a casa. **3** volver: *you drive me mad*, me vuelves loco.

driven [ˈdrɪvən] *pp* → drive.

driver [ˈdraɪvəʳ] *n* conductor, -ra. ▪ **driver's license** US permiso de conducir.

driving [ˈdraɪvɪŋ] *adj*. ▪ **driving licence** GB permiso de conducir; **driving school** autoescuela.

drizzle [ˈdrɪzəl] *n* llovizna. ► *vi* lloviznar.

dromedary [ˈdrɒmədərɪ] *n* dromedario.

drop [drɒp] *n* **1** gota. **2** pastilla. **3** pendiente, desnivel. **4** caída. ► *vt* **1** dejar caer: *he dropped the glass*, se le cayó el vaso. **2** *fam* romper con. **3** abandonar *(hábito)*. **4** no seleccionar, excluir *(de equipo)*. ► *vi* **1** caerse *(persona)*. **2** bajar *(precios, voz)*. **3** amainar *(viento)*.

to drop off *vi* **1** *fam* quedarse dormido,-a. **2** disminuir.

to drop out *vi* **1** dejar los estudios. **2** retirarse *(de un partido)*.

dropper [ˈdrɒpəʳ] *n* cuentagotas.

drought [draʊt] *n* sequía.

drove [drəʊv] *pt* → drive.

drown [draʊn] *vt-vi* ahogar(se).

drug [drʌg] *n* **1** medicamento. **2** droga. ► *vt* drogar. ● **to be on/take drugs** drogarse. ▪ **drug addict** drogadicto,-a; **drug pusher** traficante de drogas.

drugstore [ˈdrʌgstɔːʳ] *n* US establecimiento donde se compran medicamentos, periódicos, comida etc.

drum [drʌm] *n* **1** tambor. **2** bidón *(contenedor)*. ► *vi* tocar el tambor. ► *npl* **drums** batería.

drumstick [ˈdrʌmstɪk] *n* **1** baqueta. **2** muslo *(de pollo)*.

drunk [drʌŋk] *pp* → drink. ► *adj-n* borracho,-a.

dry [draɪ] *adj* seco,-a. ► *vt-vi* secar(se).

dry-clean [draɪˈkliːn] *vt* limpiar en seco.

dry-cleaners [draɪˈkliːnəz] *n* tintorería.

dryer [ˈdraɪəʳ] *n* secadora.

dual [ˈdjuːəl] *adj* dual. ▪ **dual carriageway** autovía.

dub [dʌb] *vt* doblar *(película)*.

duchess [ˈdʌtʃəs] *n* duquesa.

duck [dʌk] *n* pato,-a.

duct [dʌkt] *n* conducto.
due [djuː] *adj* **1** debido,-a *(dinero)*. **2** pagadero,-a. **3** esperado,-a: *the train is due at five*, el tren debe llegar a las cinco. ► *npl* **dues** cuota. • **to be due to** deberse a. ■ **due date** vencimiento.
duel ['djuːəl] *n* duelo.
duet [djuːet] *n* dúo.
dug [dʌg] *pt-pp* → dig.
duke [djuːk] *n* duque.
dull [dʌl] *adj* **1** apagado,-a *(color)*. **2** gris *(día)*. **3** sordo,-a *(sonido)*. **4** torpe *(persona)*. **5** pesado,-a *(película)*.
dumb [dʌm] *adj* mudo,-a.
dummy ['dʌmɪ] *n* **1** imitación. **2** maniquí. **3** GB chupete.
dump [dʌmp] *n* vertedero, basurero. ► *vt* tirar: *"No dumping"*, "Prohibido tirar basuras".
dune [djuːn] *n* duna.
dungarees [dʌŋgə'riːz] *n* pantalones de peto, mono.
dungeon ['dʌndʒən] *n* mazmorra.
duo ['djuːəʊ] *n* dúo.
duplicate [*(adj-n)* 'djuːplɪkət, *(vb)* 'djuːplɪkeɪt] *adj* duplicado, -a. ► *n* duplicado. ► *vt* duplicar.
duration [djʊə'reɪʃən] *n* duración.
during ['djʊərɪŋ] *prep* durante.
dusk [dʌsk] *n* anochecer.
dust [dʌst] *n* polvo. ► *vt* quitar el polvo a.

dustbin ['dʌstbɪn] *n* GB cubo de la basura.
duster ['dʌstə'] *n* **1** paño, trapo. **2** borrador *(de pizarra)*.
dustman ['dʌstmən] *n* GB basurero.
dustpan ['dʌstpæn] *n* recogedor.
duty ['djuːtɪ] *n* **1** deber, obligación. **2** impuesto. **3** guardia. • **to be on/off duty** estar/no estar de servicio/ guardia.
duty-free ['djuːtɪfriː] *adj* libre de impuestos.
duvet ['duːveɪ] *n* edredón.
dwarf [dwɔːf] *n* enano,-a.
dwelling ['dwelɪŋ] *n* morada.
dye [daɪ] *n* tinte. ► *vt-vi* teñir(se).
dynamic [daɪ'næmɪk] *adj* dinámico,-a.
dynasty ['dɪnəstɪ] *n* dinastía.
dyslexia [dɪs'leksɪə] *n* dislexia.

E

each [iːtʃ] *adj* cada. ► *pron* cada uno,-a. • **each other** el/la uno,-a al/a la otro,-a: *we love each other*, nos queremos.
eager ['iːgə'] *adj* ansioso,-a, impaciente. • **to be eager for SB to do STH** estar deseando que ALGN haga algo.
eagle ['iːgəl] *n* águila.

ear¹ [ɪəʳ] *n* **1** oreja. **2** oído.

ear² [ɪəʳ] *n* espiga *(de trigo)*.

earache ['ɪəreɪk] *n* dolor de oídos.

eardrum ['ɪədrʌm] *n* tímpano.

early ['ɜːlɪ] *adj* temprano,-a. ▶ *adv* temprano.

earn [ɜːn] *vt* **1** ganar *(dinero)*. **2** merecer(se).

earnings ['ɜːnɪŋz] *npl* ingresos.

earphones ['ɪəfəʊnz] *npl* auriculares.

earplug ['ɪəplʌg] *n* tapón.

earring ['ɪərɪŋ] *n* pendiente.

earth [ɜːθ] *n* tierra. ■ **the Earth** la Tierra.

earthquake ['ɜːθkweɪk] *n* terremoto.

earthworm ['ɜːθwɜːm] *n* lombriz.

ease [iːz] *n* **1** facilidad. **2** tranquilidad. **3** comodidad. ▶ *vt* aliviar, calmar. ▶ *vi* disminuir. ● **at ease** relajado,-a.

to ease off *vi* disminuir.

easel ['iːzəl] *n* caballete.

easily ['iːzɪlɪ] *adv* **1** fácilmente. **2** con mucho.

east [iːst] *n* este, oriente. ▶ *adj* oriental, del este. ▶ *adv* hacia el este.

Easter ['iːstəʳ] *n* **1** Pascua. **2** Semana Santa.

eastern ['iːstən] *adj* oriental, del este.

easy ['iːzɪ] *adj* fácil. ● **take it easy!** ¡tranquilo,-a! ■ **easy chair** sillón.

easy-going [iːzɪ'gəʊɪŋ] *adj* tranquilo,-a.

eat [iːt] *vt-vi* comer.

to eat out *vi* comer fuera.

eaten ['iːtən] *pp* → eat.

ebb [eb] *n* reflujo.

ebony ['ebənɪ] *n* ébano.

echo ['ekəʊ] *n* eco.

ecology [ɪ'kɒlədʒɪ] *n* ecología.

economical [iːkə'nɒmɪkəl] *adj* barato,-a, económico,-a.

economize [ɪ'kɒnəmaɪz] *vi* ahorrar.

economy [ɪ'kɒnəmɪ] *n* economía.

ecosystem ['iːkəʊsɪstəm] *n* ecosistema.

eczema ['eksɪmə] *n* eccema.

edge [edʒ] *n* **1** borde. **2** canto *(de moneda)*. **3** filo *(de navaja)*. ● **on edge** nervioso,-a; **to have the edge on/over SB** llevar ventaja a ALGN.

edible ['edɪbəl] *adj* comestible.

edition [ɪ'dɪʃən] *n* edición.

editor ['edɪtəʳ] *n* **1** editor,-ra. **2** director,-ra *(de periódico)*.

editorial [edɪ'tɔːrɪəl] *adj-n* editorial.

educate ['edjukeɪt] *vt* educar.

education [edjʊ'keɪʃən] *n* educación.

eel [iːl] *n* anguila.

effect [ɪ'fekt] *n* efecto. ▶ *vt* efectuar. ● **to come into effect** entrar en vigor.

effective [ɪ'fektɪv] *adj* **1** eficaz *(medicamento)*. **2** efectivo,-a.

effervescent [efə'vesənt] *adj* efervescente.

efficiency [ɪ'fɪʃənsɪ] *n* **1** eficiencia *(de persona)*. **2** eficacia *(de producto)*. **3** rendimiento *(de máquina)*.

effort ['efət] *n* esfuerzo.

egg [eg] *n* huevo. ▪ **boiled egg** huevo pasado por agua; **egg cup** huevera; **fried egg** huevo frito; **hard-boiled egg** huevo duro.

eggplant ['egplɑːnt] *n* US berenjena.

egoist ['iːgəʊɪst] *n* egoísta.

eiderdown ['aɪdədaʊn] *n* edredón.

eight [eɪt] *num* ocho.

eighteen [eɪ'tiːn] *num* dieciocho.

eighteenth [eɪ'tiːnθ] *adj* decimoctavo,-a.

eighth [eɪtθ] *adj* octavo,-a.

eightieth ['eɪtɪɪθ] *adj* octogésimo,-a.

eighty ['eɪtɪ] *num* ochenta.

either ['aɪðəʳ, 'iːðəʳ] *adj* **1** cualquiera. **2** ni el uno/la una ni el otro/la otra, ninguno,-a: *I don't like either of them*, no me gusta ninguno de los dos. **3** cada, los/las dos, ambos, -as: *with a gun in either hand*, con una pistola en cada mano. ▶ *conj* o. ▶ *adv* tampoco. ▶ *pron* cualquiera de los dos.

eject [ɪ'dʒekt] *vt* expulsar.

elaborate [ɪ'læbərət] *adj* **1** detallado,-a. **2** complicado,-a.

elastic [ɪ'læstɪk] *adj* elástico,-a.

elbow ['elbəʊ] *n* codo.

elder ['eldəʳ] *adj-n* mayor.

elderly ['eldəlɪ] *adj* mayor, anciano,-a.

eldest ['eldɪst] *adj* mayor.

elect [ɪ'lekt] *vt* elegir.

election [ɪ'lekʃən] *n* elección.

electric [ɪ'lektrɪk] *adj* eléctrico, -a. ▪ **electric shock** descarga eléctrica.

electrical [ɪ'lektrɪkəl] *adj* eléctrico,-a. ▪ **electrical appliance** electrodoméstico.

electricity [ɪlek'trɪsɪtɪ] *n* electricidad.

electron [ɪ'lektrɒn] *n* electrón.

electronic [ɪlek'trɒnɪk] *adj* electrónico,-a. ▪ **electronic mail** correo electrónico.

elegant ['elɪgənt] *adj* elegante.

element ['elɪmənt] *n* elemento.

elephant ['elɪfənt] *n* elefante.

elevator ['elɪveɪtəʳ] *n* US ascensor.

eleven [ɪ'levən] *num* once.

eleventh [ɪ'levənθ] *adj* undécimo,-a.

eliminate [ɪ'lɪmɪneɪt] *vt* eliminar.

elk [elk] *n* alce.

elm [elm] *n* olmo.

else [els] *adv* otro, más. ● **or else** si no: *hurry up or else you'll be late*, date prisa o llegarás tarde.

endorse

elsewhere [els'weə'] *adv* en otro sitio.

e-mail ['i:meɪl] *n* correo electrónico. ► *vt* enviar un correo electrónico a.

embankment [ɪm'bæŋkmənt] *n* **1** terraplén. **2** dique *(de río)*.

embark [ɪm'bɑ:k] *vt-vi* embarcar(se).

embarrass [ɪm'bærəs] *vt* avergonzar. ● **to be embarrassed** sentir vergüenza.

embarrassing [ɪm'bærəsɪŋ] *adj* embarazoso,-a.

embassy ['embəsɪ] *n* embajada.

embrace [ɪm'breɪs] *n* abrazo. ► *vt* abrazar.

embroidery [ɪm'brɔɪdərɪ] *n* bordado.

embryo ['embrɪəʊ] *n* embrión.

emerald ['emərəld] *n* esmeralda.

emerge [ɪ'mɜ:dʒ] *vi* emerger.

emergency [ɪ'mɜ:dʒənsɪ] *n* **1** emergencia. **2** urgencia *(médica)*. ■ **emergency exit** salida de emergencia.

emery ['emərɪ] *n* esmeril. ■ **emery board** lima de uñas.

emigration [emɪ'greɪʃən] *n* emigración.

emission [ɪ'mɪʃən] *n* emisión.

emit [ɪ'mɪt] *vt* emitir.

emotion [ɪ'məʊʃən] *n* emoción.

emperor ['empərə'] *n* emperador.

emphasis ['emfəsɪs] *n* énfasis.

empire ['empaɪə'] *n* imperio.

employ [ɪm'plɔɪ] *vt* emplear.

employee [em'plɔɪi:, emplɔɪ'i:] *n* empleado,-a, trabajador,-ra.

employer [em'plɔɪə'] *n* patrón,-ona.

employment [em'plɔɪmənt] *n* empleo.

empress ['emprəs] *n* emperatriz.

empty ['emptɪ] *adj* **1** vacío,-a. **2** libre. ► *vt-vi* vaciar(se).

enable [ɪ'neɪbəl] *vt* permitir.

enamel [ɪ'næməl] *n* esmalte.

encircle [ɪn'sɜ:kəl] *vt* rodear.

enclose [ɪn'kləʊz] *vt* **1** cercar, rodear. **2** adjuntar.

encounter [ɪn'kaʊntə'] *n* encuentro. ► *vt* encontrarse con.

encourage [ɪn'kʌrɪdʒ] *vt* **1** animar. **2** fomentar.

encouraging [ɪn'kʌrɪdʒɪŋ] *adj* alentador,-ra.

encyclopedia [ensaɪklə'pi:dɪə] *n* enciclopedia.

end [end] *n* **1** fin, final. **2** extremo, punta. **3** objeto, objetivo. ► *vt-vi* acabar(se), terminar(se).

endanger [ɪn'deɪndʒə'] *vt* poner en peligro.

ending ['endɪŋ] *n* final.

endive ['endaɪv] *n* endibia.

endless ['endləs] *adj* interminable.

endorse [ɪn'dɔ:s] *vt* **1** endosar *(talón)*. **2** aprobar.

endurance [ɪn'djʊərəns] *n* resistencia.

enemy ['enəmɪ] *n* enemigo,-a.

energy ['enədʒɪ] *n* energía.

enforce [ɪn'fɔːs] *vt* hacer cumplir.

engaged [ɪn'geɪdʒd] *adj* 1 prometido,-a. 2 ocupado,-a *(servicio)*. 3 comunicando *(teléfono)*.

engagement [ɪn'geɪdʒmənt] *n* 1 petición de mano, noviazgo. 2 compromiso, cita.

engine ['endʒɪn] *n* 1 motor. 2 máquina, locomotora.

engineer [endʒɪ'nɪə'] *n* 1 ingeniero,-a. 2 US maquinista.

engrave [ɪn'greɪv] *vt* grabar.

enhance [ɪn'hɑːns] *vt* realzar.

enjoy [ɪn'dʒɔɪ] *vt* gozar de, disfrutar de. • **to enjoy oneself** divertirse, pasarlo bien.

enlargement [ɪn'lɑːdʒmənt] *n* ampliación.

enough [ɪ'nʌf] *adj* bastante, suficiente. ► *adv* bastante. ► *pron* suficiente. • **that's enough!** ¡ya basta!

enquire [ɪŋ'kwaɪə'] *vi* 1 preguntar. 2 investigar.

enquiry [ɪŋ'kwaɪərɪ] *n* 1 pregunta. 2 investigación.

enrol [ɪn'rəʊl] *vt-vi* matricular(se).

entail [ɪn'teɪl] *vt* implicar.

entangle [ɪn'tæŋgəl] *vt* enredar.

enter ['entə'] *vt* entrar en. ► *vi* entrar.

enterprise ['entəpraɪz] *n* empresa.

entertain [entə'teɪn] *vt* entretener, divertir.

entertainment [entə'teɪnmənt] *n* entretenimiento.

enthusiasm [ɪn'θjuːzɪæzəm] *n* entusiasmo.

entice [ɪn'taɪs] *vt* seducir.

entire [ɪn'taɪə'] *adj* entero,-a.

entrails ['entreɪlz] *npl* entrañas.

entrance ['entrəns] *n* entrada.

entrepreneur [ɒntrəprə'nɜː'] *n* empresario,-a.

entrust [ɪn'trʌst] *vt* confiar.

entry ['entrɪ] *n* entrada. • **"No entry"** "Prohibida la entrada".

envelope ['envələʊp] *n* sobre.

envious ['envɪəs] *adj* envidioso,-a.

environment [ɪn'vaɪrənmənt] *n* medio ambiente.

envy ['envɪ] *vt* envidiar.

epidemic [epɪ'demɪk] *n* epidemia.

epilepsy ['epɪlepsɪ] *n* epilepsia.

episode ['epɪsəʊd] *n* episodio.

equal ['iːkwəl] *adj* igual. ► *vt* 1 ser igual a, equivaler a. 2 igualar.

equation [ɪ'kweɪʒən] *n* ecuación.

equator [ɪ'kweɪtə'] *n* ecuador.

equip [ɪ'kwɪp] *vt* equipar.

equipment [ɪ'kwɪpmənt] *n* equipo.

equivalent [ɪ'kwɪvələnt] *adj-n* equivalente.

era ['ɪərə] n era.

erase [ɪ'reɪz] vt borrar.

eraser [ɪ'reɪzəʳ] n 1 US goma de borrar. 2 borrador (de pizarra).

erosion [ɪ'rəʊʒən] n erosión.

erotic [ɪ'rɒtɪk] adj erótico,-a.

errand ['erənd] n encargo, recado.

erratic [ɪ'rætɪk] adj inconstante.

error ['erəʳ] n error.

eruption [ɪ'rʌpʃən] n erupción.

escalator ['eskəleɪtəʳ] n escalera mecánica.

escape [ɪ'skeɪp] n fuga. ▶ vi escaparse. ▶ vt evitar.

escort [ɪ'skɔːt] vt 1 acompañar. 2 escoltar.

especial [ɪ'speʃəl] adj especial.

essay ['eseɪ] n 1 redacción, trabajo. 2 ensayo.

essence ['esəns] n esencia.

essential [ɪ'senʃəl] adj esencial.

establish [ɪ'stæblɪʃ] vt establecer.

estate [ɪ'steɪt] n 1 finca. 2 urbanización. ▪ **estate agent** GB agente inmobiliario,-a; **estate car** GB coche familiar.

estimate [(n) 'estɪmət, (vb) 'estɪmeɪt] n 1 cálculo. 2 presupuesto. ▶ vt calcular.

estuary ['estjʊərɪ] n estuario.

eternity [ɪ'tɜːnətɪ] n eternidad.

ethic ['eθɪk] n ética.

eucalyptus [juːkə'lɪptəs] n eucalipto.

euphemism ['juːfəmɪzəm] n eufemismo.

euro ['jʊərəʊ] n euro.

evade [ɪ'veɪd] vt evadir.

evaluate [ɪ'væljʊeɪt] vt evaluar.

evaporate [ɪ'væpəreɪt] vt-vi evaporar(se).

eve [iːv] n víspera, vigilia.

even ['iːvən] adj 1 llano,-a, liso,-a (superficie). 2 uniforme (color). 3 igualado,-a (puntuación). 4 par (número). ▶ adv 1 hasta, incluso. 2 siquiera: *not even John was there*, ni siquiera John estaba allí. 3 aún, todavía.• **even if** aunque; **even so** incluso; **even though** aunque.

evening ['iːvnɪŋ] n tarde, noche. •**good evening!** ¡buenas tardes!, ¡buenas noches!

event [ɪ'vent] n 1 suceso, acontecimiento. 2 prueba (deportiva). • **in any event** pase lo que pase; **in the event of** en caso de.

eventually [ɪ'ventʃʊəlɪ] adv finalmente.

ever ['evəʳ] adv 1 nunca, jamás. 2 alguna vez • **for ever** para siempre; **hardly ever** casi nunca.

evergreen ['evəgriːn] adj de hoja perenne. ▪ **evergreen oak** encina.

everlasting [evə'lɑːstɪŋ] adj eterno,-a.

every ['evrɪ] adj cada, todos,-as

everybody ['evrɪbɒdɪ] pron todos,-as, todo el mundo.

everyday ['evrɪdeɪ] *adj* diario,-a, de todos los días.

everyone ['evrɪwʌn] *pron* → everybody.

everything ['evrɪθɪŋ] *pron* todo.

everywhere ['evrɪweəʳ] *adv* 1 en/por todas partes. 2 a todas partes.

evidence ['evɪdəns] *n* pruebas. • **to give evidence** prestar declaración.

evident ['evɪdənt] *adj* evidente.

evil ['iːvəl] *adj* malo,-a. ▶ *n* mal.

evoke [ɪ'vəuk] *vt* evocar.

evolution [iːvə'luːʃən] *n* evolución.

exact [ɪg'zækt] *adj* exacto,-a.

exaggerate [ɪg'zædʒəreɪt] *vt-vi* exagerar.

exam [ɪg'zæm] *n fam* examen.

examination [ɪgzæmɪ'neɪʃən] *n* 1 examen. 2 reconocimiento, chequeo. 3 interrogatorio.

examine [ɪg'zæmɪn] *vt* examinar.

example [ɪg'zɑːmpəl] *n* ejemplo. • **for example** por ejemplo.

excellent ['eksələnt] *adj* excelente.

except [ɪk'sept] *prep* excepto.

excess [ɪk'ses] *n* exceso.

exchange [ɪks'tʃeɪndʒ] *n* 1 cambio. 2 intercambio. ▶ *vt* cambiar, intercambiar. ■ **exchange rate** tipo de cambio.

excite [ɪk'saɪt] *vt* 1 entusiasmar. 2 excitar *(sexualmente)*.

exclamation [eksklə'meɪʃən] *n* exclamación. ■ **exclamation mark** signo de admiración.

exclude [ɪk'skluːd] *vt* excluir.

exclusive [ɪk'skluːsɪv] *adj* 1 exclusivo,-a. 2 selecto,-a.

excursion [ɪk'skɜːʒən] *n* excursión.

excuse [*(n)* ɪk'skjuːs, *(vb)* ɪk'skjuːz] *n* disculpa, excusa. ▶ *vt* perdonar, disculpar. • **excuse me!** ¡perdone!, ¡por favor!

execute ['eksɪkjuːt] *vt* ejecutar.

executive [ɪg'zekjətɪv] *adj-n* ejecutivo,-a.

exempt [ɪg'zempt] *adj* exento,-a, libre. ▶ *vt* eximir.

exercise ['eksəsaɪz] *n* ejercicio. ■ **exercise book** cuaderno.

exhaust [ɪg'zɔːst] *vt* agotar. ■ **exhaust pipe** tubo de escape.

exhausted [ɪg'zɔːstɪd] *adj* agotado,-a.

exhibit [ɪg'zɪbɪt] *n* objeto en exposición. ▶ *vt* 1 exponer. 2 mostrar, dar muestras de, manifestar.

exhibition [eksɪ'bɪʃən] *n* exposición.

exile ['eksaɪl] *n* exilio. ▶ *vt* exiliar.

exist [ɪg'zɪst] *vi* existir.

exit ['egsɪt] *n* salida.

exotic [eg'zɒtɪk] *adj* exótico,-a.

expand [ɪk'spænd] *vt-vi* ampliar(se).

expansion [ɪk'spænʃən] *n* expansión.

expect [ɪk'spekt] *vt* esperar. • **to be expecting** *fam* estar embarazada.

expedition [ekspɪ'dɪʃən] *n* expedición.

expel [ɪk'spel] *vt* expulsar.

expenditure [ɪk'spendɪtʃəʳ] *n* gasto.

expense [ɪk'spens] *n* gasto.

expensive [ɪk'spensɪv] *adj* caro,-a.

experience [ɪk'spɪərɪəns] *n* experiencia. ► *vt* experimentar.

experiment [ɪk'sperɪmənt] *n* experimento.

expert ['ekspɜːt] *adj-n* experto,-a.

expire [ɪk'spaɪəʳ] *vi* **1** vencer *(contrato)*. **2** caducar *(pasaporte)*.

expiry [ɪk'spaɪərɪ] *n* vencimiento. ■ **expiry date** fecha de caducidad.

explain [ɪk'spleɪn] *vt-vi* explicar.

explanation [eksplə'neɪʃən] *n* explicación.

explode [ɪk'spləʊd] *vi* estallar.

explore [ɪk'splɔːʳ] *vt* explorar.

explosion [ɪk'spləʊʒən] *n* explosión.

explosive [ɪk'spləʊsɪv] *adj* explosivo,-a. ► *n* explosivo.

export [*(n)* 'ekspɔːt, *(vb)* ɪk'spɔːt] *n* exportación.► *vt* exportar.

expose [ɪk'spəʊz] *vt* exponer.

express [ɪk'spres] *adj* **1** expreso,-a *(tren)*. **2** urgente *(correo)*. ► *vt* expresar.

expression [ɪk'spreʃən] *n* expresión.

extend [ɪk'stend] *vt* extender.

extension [ɪk'stenʃən] *n* extensión.

extent [ɪk'stent] *n* extensión, alcance. • **to a certain extent** hasta cierto punto.

external [ek'stɜːnəl] *adj* externo,-a.

extinct [ɪk'stɪŋkt] *adj* **1** extinto,-a. **2** extinguido,-a.

extra ['ekstrə] *adj-n* extra. ■ **extra charge** suplemento; **extra time** prórroga.

extract [ɪk'strækt] *vt* extraer.

extraordinary [ɪk'strɔːdənrɪ] *adj* extraordinario,-a.

extravagant [ɪk'strævəgənt] *adj* **1** derrochador,-ra. **2** exagerado,-a, excesivo,-a.

extreme [ɪk'striːm] *adj* **1** extremo,-a. **2** excepcional *(caso)*. ► *n* extremo.

extremity [ɪk'stremɪtɪ] *n* extremidad.

eye [aɪ] *n* ojo.

eyebrow ['aɪbraʊ] *n* ceja.

eyelash ['aɪlæʃ] *n* pestaña.

eyelid ['aɪlɪd] *n* párpado.

eyeshadow ['aɪʃædəʊ] *n* sombra de ojos.

eyewitness ['aɪwɪtnəs] *n* testigo presencial.

F

fable ['feɪbəl] *n* fábula.

fabric ['fæbrɪk] *n* tela, tejido.

fabulous ['fæbjələs] *adj* fabuloso,-a.

facade [fə'sɑːd] *n* fachada.

façade [fə'sɑːd] *n* fachada.

face [feɪs] *n* **1** cara. **2** superficie. ► *vt* **1** dar a: *the house faces west*, la casa da al oeste. **2** afrontar, enfrentarse con/a. • **face down** boca abajo; **face up** boca arriba; **to lose face** desprestigiarse. ■ **face cream** crema facial; **face value** valor nominal.

to face up *vt* afrontar.

facelift ['feɪslɪft] *n* lifting.

facility [fə'sɪlɪti] *n* facilidad. ► *npl* **facilities** instalaciones, servicios.

fact [fækt] *n* hecho. • **in fact** de hecho.

factor ['fæktə'] *n* factor.

factory ['fæktəri] *n* fábrica.

faculty ['fækəlti] *n* facultad.

fade [feɪd] *vt* desteñir.

to fade away *vi* desvanecerse.

fag [fæg] *n* **1** *fam* lata, rollo. **2** GB *fam* pitillo.

fail [feɪl] *n* suspenso. ► *vt-vi* **1** fallar. **2** suspender. ► *vi* **1** fracasar. **2** quebrar, hacer bancarrota.

failing ['feɪlɪŋ] *n* defecto, fallo. ► *prep* a falta de.

failure ['feɪljə'] *n* **1** fracaso. **2** quiebra. **3** fallo, avería. **4** hecho de no hacer algo.

faint [feɪnt] *adj* **1** débil. **2** pálido,-a. **3** vago,-a.

fair[1] [feə'] *adj* **1** justo,-a. **2** considerable: *he has a fair chance of getting the job*, tiene bastantes posibilidades de conseguir el trabajo. **3** rubio,-a, blanco,-a: *fair hair*, pelo rubio. • **fair enough** de acuerdo, está bien. ■ **fair copy** copia en limpio; **fair play** juego limpio.

fair[2] [feə'] *n* feria, mercado.

fairground ['feəgraʊnd] *n* recinto ferial, parque de atracciones.

fairly ['feəli] *adv* **1** justamente. **2** bastante.

fairy ['feəri] *n* hada. ■ **fairy tale** cuento de hadas.

faith [feɪθ] *n* fe.

faithful ['feɪθfʊl] *adj* fiel.

faithfully ['feɪθfʊli] *adv*. • **yours faithfully** le saluda atentamente.

fake [feɪk] *n* falsificación. ► *adj* falso,-a, falsificado,-a. ► *vt* **1** falsificar. **2** fingir.

falcon ['fɔːlkən] *n* halcón.

fall [fɔːl] *n* **1** caída. **2** nevada. **3** US otoño. ► *vi* **1** caer, caerse. **2** bajar. ► *npl* **falls** cascada. • **to fall short** no alcanzar; **to fall flat** salir mal.

to fall back *vi* retroceder.

to fall down *vt-vi* caer, caerse.

to fall out *vi* reñir, enfadarse.

fallen ['fɔːlən] *pp* → fall.

false [fɔːls] *adj* falso,-a. ▪ **false alarm** falsa alarma; **false bottom** doble fondo; **false start** salida nula; **false teeth** dentadura postiza.

falsify ['fɔːlsɪfaɪ] *vt* falsificar.

fame [feɪm] *n* fama.

family ['fæmɪlɪ] *n* familia. ▪ **family film** película apta para todos los públicos; **family name** apellido.

famine ['fæmɪn] *n* hambre.

famous ['feɪməs] *adj* famoso,-a.

fan [fæn] *n* **1** abanico. **2** ventilador (*eléctrico*). **3** fan. ▶ *vt* abanicar, ventilar.

fanatic [fə'nætɪk] *adj-n* fanático,-a.

fancy ['fænsɪ] *n* **1** fantasía. **2** capricho. ▶ *adj* elegante. ▶ *vt* **1** imaginarse, figurarse. **2** apetecer: *I fancy an ice cream*, me apetece un helado. **3** gustar: *my friend fancies you*, le gustas a mi amigo. ▪ **fancy dress** disfraz.

fang [fæŋ] *n* colmillo.

fantastic [fæn'tæstɪk] *adj* fantástico,-a.

fantasy ['fæntəsɪ] *n* fantasía.

far [faːʳ] *adj* **1** lejano,-a. **2** opuesto,-a, extremo,-a: *at the far end of the stadium*, en el otro extremo del estadio.
▶ *adv* **1** lejos. **2** mucho: *far better*, mucho mejor. ● **as far as** hasta; **far away** lejos; **in so far as ...** en la medida en que ...; **so far 1** hasta ahora. **2** hasta cierto punto.

faraway ['faːrəweɪ] *adj* lejano,-a.

farce [faːs] *n* farsa.

fare [feəʳ] *n* tarifa, precio del billete/viaje.

farewell [feə'wel] *interj* ¡adiós! ▶ *n* despedida.

farm [faːm] *n* granja. ▪ **farm labourer** jornalero,-a agrícola.

farmer ['faːməʳ] *n* agricultor, -ra, granjero,-a.

farming ['faːmɪŋ] *n* agricultura, ganadería. ▪ **farming industry** industria agropecuaria.

farmyard ['faːmjaːd] *n* corral.

fascinate ['fæsɪneɪt] *vt* fascinar.

fashion ['fæʃən] *n* **1** moda. **2** modo. ● **in fashion** de moda; **out of fashion** pasado,-a de moda.

fashionable ['fæʃənəbəl] *adj* de moda.

fast¹ [faːst] *adj* **1** rápido,-a. **2** adelantado,-a: *my watch is fast*, mi reloj está adelantado. ▶ *adv* rápidamente, deprisa. ▪ **fast food** comida rápida.

fast² [faːst] *vi* ayunar.

fasten ['faːsən] *vt* **1** sujetar. **2** atar. **3** abrochar.

fastener ['faːsənəʳ] *n* cierre.

fat [fæt] *adj* gordo,-a. ► *n* grasa.

fatal ['feɪtəl] *adj* **1** fatídico. **2** mortal.

fate [feɪt] *n* destino.

father ['fɑːðəʳ] *n* padre. ► *vt* engendrar. ▪ **Father Christmas** Papá Noel.

father-in-law ['fɑːðərɪnlɔː] *n* suegro.

fatten ['fætən] *vt* **1** cebar. **2** engordar.

faucet ['fɔːsɪt] *n* US grifo.

fault [fɔːlt] *n* **1** defecto. **2** culpa. **3** error, falta. **4** falla *(geológica)*. **5** falta *(en deporte)*.

fauna ['fɔːnə] *n* fauna.

favour ['feɪvəʳ] (US **favor**) *n* favor. ► *vt* **1** favorecer. **2** estar a favor de.

favourite ['feɪvərɪt] (US **favorite**) *adj-n* preferido,-a.

fax [fæks] *n* fax. ► *vt* enviar por fax.

fear [fɪəʳ] *n* miedo, temor. ► *vt-vi* temer, tener miedo.

feast [fiːst] *n* **1** festín, banquete. **2** fiesta de guardar.

feat [fiːt] *n* proeza, hazaña.

feather ['feðəʳ] *n* pluma.

feature ['fiːtʃəʳ] *n* **1** rasgo, facción. **2** rasgo, característica. **3** artículo de fondo. ► *vt* **1** poner de relieve. **2** tener como protagonista. ▪ **feature film** largometraje.

February ['februərɪ] *n* febrero.

fed [fed] *pt-pp* → feed.

federal ['fedərəl] *adj* federal.

federation [fedə'reɪʃən] *n* federación.

fed up [fed'ʌp] *adj fam* harto,-a.

fee [fiː] *n* honorarios, cuota, tarifa.

feeble ['fiːbəl] *adj* débil.

feed [fiːd] *n* pienso. ► *vt* alimentar, dar de comer a. ► *vi* alimentarse.

feel [fiːl] *n* tacto, sensación. ► *vt* **1** tocar, palpar. **2** sentir, notar. **3** creer: *I feel I ought to tell her*, creo que debería decírselo. ► *vi* **1** sentir(se), encontrarse: *do you feel ill?*, ¿te encuentras mal? **2** parecer: *it feels like leather*, parece piel. ● **to feel like** apetecer: *I feel like an ice cream*, me apetece un helado.

feeling ['fiːlɪŋ] *n* **1** sentimiento. **2** sensación.

feet [fiːt] *npl* → foot.

feign [feɪn] *vt* fingir.

feline ['fiːlaɪn] *adj-n* felino,-a.

fell [fel] *pt* → fall.

fellow ['feləʊ] *n fam* tipo, tío.

felt¹ [felt] *pt-pp* → feel.

felt² [felt] *n* fieltro.

felt-tip pen ['felttɪp'pen] *n* rotulador.

female ['fiːmeɪl] *n* **1** hembra. **2** mujer, chica: *a white female*, una mujer blanca. ► *adj* **1** femenino,-a. **2** mujer: *a female singer*, una cantante. **3** hembra: *a female elephant*, un elefante hembra.

filling

feminine ['femɪnɪn] *adj* femenino,-a. ► *n* femenino.
fence [fens] *n* valla, cerca. ► *vi* practicar la esgrima. ► *vt* cercar.
fencing ['fensɪŋ] *n* esgrima.
fender ['fendəʳ] *n* 1 pantalla. 2 US parachoques.
fennel ['fenəl] *n* hinojo.
ferment [(*n*) 'fɜːmənt, (*vb*) fə'ment] *n* fermento. ► *vt-vi* fermentar.
fern [fɜːn] *n* helecho.
ferret ['ferɪt] *n* hurón.
ferry ['ferɪ] *n* transbordador, ferry. ► *vt-vi* transportar.
fertile ['fɜːtaɪl] *adj* fértil.
fervent ['fɜːvənt] *adj* ferviente.
festival ['festɪvəl] *n* 1 festival. 2 fiesta.
fetch [fetʃ] *vt* ir a buscar.
fetish ['fetɪʃ] *n* fetiche.
feudal ['fjuːdəl] *adj* feudal.
fever ['fiːvəʳ] *n* fiebre.
few [fjuː] *adj-pron* 1 pocos,-as. 2 **a few** unos, as cuantos,-as, algunos,-as. • **as few as** solamente; **no fewer than** no menos de.
fiancé [fɪ'ænseɪ] *n* prometido.
fiancée [fɪ'ænseɪ] *n* prometida.
fib [fɪb] *n fam* bola.
fibre ['faɪbəʳ] (US **fiber**) *n* fibra.
fibreglass ['faɪbəglɑːs] (US **fiberglass**) *n* fibra de vidrio.
fiction ['fɪkʃən] *n* 1 novela, narrativa. 2 ficción.
fictitious [fɪk'tɪʃəs] *adj* ficticio,-a.

fiddle ['fɪdəl] *n* 1 *fam* violín. 2 *fam* estafa, trampa. ► *vi fam* juguetear. ► *vt fam* falsificar.
fidelity [fɪ'delɪtɪ] *n* fidelidad.
field [fiːld] *n* 1 campo. 2 yacimiento.
fierce [fɪəs] *adj* feroz.
fifteen [fɪf'tiːn] *num* quince.
fifteenth [fɪf'tiːnθ] *adj* decimoquinto,-a.
fifth [fɪfθ] *adj* quinto,-a.
fifty ['fɪftɪ] *num* cincuenta.
fig [fɪg] *n* higo.
fight [faɪt] *n* lucha, pelea. ► *vt-vi* pelearse, luchar.
to fight back *vi* resistir.
to fight off *vt* rechazar.
figure ['fɪgəʳ] *n* 1 figura. 2 cifra, número. ► *vi* figurar. ► *vt* US suponer: *I figure she'll come*, supongo que vendrá. ■ **figure skating** patinaje artístico.
to figure out *vt fam* comprender, explicarse.
file [faɪl] *n* 1 lima. 2 carpeta. 3 archivo, expediente. 4 archivo, fichero. 5 fila. ► *vt* 1 limar. 2 archivar, fichar. ► *vi* desfilar. • **in single file** en fila india.
filing cabinet ['faɪlɪŋkæbɪnət] *n* archivador.
fill [fɪl] *vt* 1 llenar. 2 rellenar. 3 empastar.
to fill in *vt* rellenar.
fillet ['fɪlɪt] *n* filete.
filling ['fɪlɪŋ] *n* empaste. ■ **filling station** gasolinera.

film [fɪlm] *n* película. ► *vt* rodar, filmar. ■ **film star** estrella de cine.

filter ['fɪltə'] *n* filtro. ► *vt-vi* filtrar(se).

filth [fɪlθ] *n* suciedad.

fin [fɪn] *n* aleta.

final ['faɪnəl] *adj* **1** final, último,-a. **2** definitivo,-a. ► *n* final. ► *npl* **finals** exámenes finales.

finance ['faɪnæns] *vt* financiar. ► *n* finanzas.

find [faɪnd] *n* hallazgo. ► *vt* **1** encontrar. **2** declarar: *he was found guilty*, lo declararon culpable.

to find out *vt-vi* averiguar. ► *vi* enterarse.

fine¹ [faɪn] *adj* **1** bien: *how are you? –fine, thanks*, ¿cómo estás? –bien, gracias. **2** excelente, magnífico: *that's a fine building*, es un edificio magnífico. **3** bueno: *it's a fine day*, hace buen día. ► *adv fam* muy bien.

fine² [faɪn] *n* multa. ► *vt* multar, poner una multa a.

finger ['fɪŋgə'] *n* dedo.

fingerprint ['fɪŋgəprɪnt] *n* huella digital, huella dactilar.

fingertip ['fɪŋgətɪp] *n* punta del dedo, yema del dedo.

finish ['fɪnɪʃ] *n* **1** fin, final. **2** acabado. ► *vi-vt* acabar, terminar. ● **a close finish** un final muy reñido.

finishing ['fɪnɪʃɪŋ] *adj* final. ■ **finishing line** línea de meta.

fir [fɜː'] *n* abeto.

fire ['faɪə'] *n* **1** fuego. **2** incendio. **3** estufa. ► *vt* **1** disparar, lanzar. **2** *fam* despedir, echar. ► *vi* disparar. ► *interj* ¡fuego! ● **to be on fire** estar ardiendo, estar en llamas. ■ **fire engine** coche de bomberos; **fire escape** escalera de incendios; **fire extinguisher** extintor; **fire station** parque de bomberos; **fire hydrant** boca de incendios.

fireman ['faɪəmən] *n* bombero.

fireplace ['faɪəpleɪs] *n* chimenea, hogar.

fireproof ['faɪəpruːf] *adj* a prueba de fuego.

firewood ['faɪəwud] *n* leña.

fireworks ['faɪəwɜːks] *npl* fuegos artificiales.

firing ['faɪərɪŋ] *n* tiroteo. ■ **firing squad** pelotón de fusilamiento; **firing range** campo de tiro.

firm¹ [fɜːm] *n* empresa, firma.

firm² [fɜːm] *adj* firme.

first [fɜːst] *adj* primero,-a. ► *adv* **1** primero. **2** por primera vez. ► *n* **1** primero,-a. **2** sobresaliente. ● **at first** al principio; **first of all** en primer lugar. ■ **first aid** primeros auxilios; **first aid kit** botiquín de primeros auxilios; **first floor 1** GB primer piso. **2** US planta baja; **first name** nombre de pila; **first degree** licenciatura.

first-class ['fɜːstklɑːs] *adj* de primera clase.

first-rate ['fɜːstreɪt] *adj* excelente.

fiscal ['fɪskəl] *adj* fiscal.

fish [fɪʃ] *n* **1** pez. **2** pescado. ► *vi* pescar. ■ **fish and chips** pescado con patatas; **fish finger** varita de pescado; **fish shop** pescadería.

fisherman ['fɪʃəmən] *n* pescador.

fishing ['fɪʃɪŋ] *n* pesca. ■ **fishing rod** caña de pescar.

fishmonger ['fɪʃmʌŋgəʳ] *n* GB pescadero,-a.

fishmonger's ['fɪʃmʌŋgəz] *n* GB pescadería.

fist [fɪst] *n* puño.

fistful ['fɪstfʊl] *n* puñado.

fit[1] [fɪt] *n* ataque, acceso.

fit[2] [fɪt] *vt* **1** ir bien a: *these shoes don't fit me, they're too big*, estos zapatos no me van bien, me quedan grandes. **2** poner, colocar: *the spy fitted a microphone under the table*, el espía puso un micrófono debajo de la mesa. ► *vi* caber, entrar: *this box won't fit in the car*, esta caja no va a entrar en el coche. ► *adj* **1** apto,-a, adecuado,-a. **2** en forma.

to fit in *vi* encajar.

fitness ['fɪtnəs] *n* buena forma *(física)*.

fitting ['fɪtɪŋ] *adj fml* apropiado,-a. ► *n* prueba *(de traje, etc)*. ► *npl* **fittings** accesorios. ■ **fitting room** probador.

five [faɪv] *num* cinco.

fix [fɪks] *vt* **1** fijar. **2** arreglar. **3** US preparar: *let me fix you a drink*, te prepararé una copa.

fizzy ['fɪzɪ] *adj* gaseoso,-a, con gas, espumoso,-a.

flag [flæg] *n* bandera.

flagpole ['flægpəʊl] *n* asta, mástil.

flagstone ['flægstəʊn] *n* losa.

flair [fleəʳ] *n* talento, don.

flake [fleɪk] *n* **1** copo. **2** escama. ► *vi* descamarse.

flame [fleɪm] *n* llama.

flamingo [flə'mɪŋgəʊ] *n* flamenco *(ave)*.

flan [flæn] *n* tarta rellena.

flank [flæŋk] *n* flanco.

flannel ['flænəl] *n* franela.

flap [flæp] *n* **1** solapa. **2** faldón. ► *vt* batir. ► *vi* **1** agitarse. **2** ondear.

flare [fleəʳ] *n* **1** llamarada. **2** bengala. ► *vi* **1** llamear. **2** estallar.

flared [fleəd] *adj* acampanado,-a.

flash [flæʃ] *n* **1** destello. **2** flash *(de cámara, noticia)*. ► *vi* **1** brillar, destellar. **2** pasar como un rayo. ■ **flash of lightning** relámpago.

flashlight ['flæʃlaɪt] *n* linterna.
flask [flæsk] *n* termo.
flat¹ [flæt] *n* GB piso.
flat² [flæt] *adj* **1** llano,-a, plano,-a. **2** desinflado,-a, deshinchado,-a: *a flat tyre*, un neumático deshinchado. **3** descargado,-a: *a flat battery*, una batería descargada. **4** que ha perdido el gas: *this beer's flat!*, ¡esta cerveza no tiene gas! **5** rotundo,-a. ► *n* llanura. ► *adv*: *in ten seconds flat*, en diez segundos justos. ■ **flat rate** precio fijo; **flat roof** azotea.
flatten ['flætən] *vt* allanar.
flatter ['flætə'] *vt* adular, halagar.
flautist ['flɔːtɪst] *n* flautista.
flavour ['fleɪvə'] (US **flavor**) *n* sabor. ► *vt* condimentar.
flavouring ['fleɪvərɪŋ] (US **flavoring**) *n* condimento.
flea [fliː] *n* pulga.
fleck [flek] *n* mota, punto.
flee [fliː] *vt* huir de. ► *vi* huir.
fleet [fliːt] *n* **1** armada. **2** flota.
flesh [fleʃ] *n* carne.
flew [fluː] *pt* → fly.
flex [fleks] *n* GB cable *(eléctrico)*. ► *vt* doblar, flexionar.
flexible ['fleksəbəl] *adj* flexible.
flick [flɪk] *n* movimiento rápido, coletazo, latigazo. ► *vt* **1** dar. **2** sacudir.
flicker ['flɪkə'] *n* **1** parpadeo. **2** *fig* indicio. ► *vi* parpadear.

flight [flaɪt] *n* **1** vuelo. **2** bandada. **3** tramo: *flight of stairs*, tramo de escalera. **4** huida, fuga.
fling [flɪŋ] *n* **1** lanzamiento. **2** juerga. **3** lío *(amoroso)*. ► *vt* arrojar, tirar, lanzar.
flint [flɪnt] *n* **1** pedernal. **2** piedra.
flip [flɪp] *n* voltereta.
flipper ['flɪpə'] *n* aleta.
flirt [flɜːt] *n* coqueto,-a. ► *vi* flirtear, coquetear.
float [fləʊt] *n* **1** flotador. **2** corcho. **3** carroza. ► *vi* flotar.
flock [flɒk] *n* **1** rebaño, bandada. **2** *fam* tropel.
flood [flʌd] *n* inundación. ► *vt* inundar. ► *vi* desbordarse.
floodlight ['flʌdlaɪt] *n* foco.
floor [flɔː'] *n* **1** suelo. **2** piso, planta: *my flat is on the fourth floor*, mi casa está en el cuarto piso. ● **to give/ have the floor** dar/tener la palabra.
floppy ['flɒpɪ] *adj* blando,-a, flexible. ■ **floppy disk** disquete, disco flexible.
flora ['flɔːrə] *n* flora.
florist ['flɒrɪst] *n* florista. ■ **florist's** floristería.
flounce [flaʊns] *n* volante *(de vestido)*.
flour [flaʊə'] *n* harina.
flourish ['flʌrɪʃ] *n* ademán, gesto. ► *vt* ondear, agitar. ► *vi* florecer.

flourishing ['flʌrɪʃɪŋ] *adj* floreciente, próspero,-a.

flow [fləʊ] *n* 1 flujo. 2 corriente: *the flow of traffic*, la circulación del tráfico. ► *vi* 1 fluir, manar. 2 circular: *traffic is flowing*, el tráfico circula con fluidez. 3 correr, fluir. • **to flow into** desembocar en. ▪ **flow chart** diagrama de flujo, organigrama.

flower [flaʊəʳ] *n* flor. ► *vi* florecer. ▪ **flower bed** parterre.

flowerpot ['flaʊəpɒt] *n* maceta, tiesto.

flown [fləʊn] *pp* → fly.

flu [fluː] *n* gripe.

fluency ['fluːənsɪ] *n* fluidez.

fluent ['fluːənt] *adj* fluido,-a, suelto,-a: *she's fluent in French*, habla el francés con fluidez.

fluff [flʌf] *n* pelusa, lanilla.

fluffy ['flʌfɪ] *adj* mullido,-a.

fluid ['fluːɪd] *adj* fluido,-a. ► *n* fluido, líquido.

fluke [fluːk] *n fam* chiripa.

flung [flʌŋ] *pt-pp* → fling.

fluorescent [flʊə'resənt] *adj* fluorescente.

flurry ['flʌrɪ] *n* ráfaga: *a flurry of rain*, un chaparrón.

flush [flʌʃ] *n* rubor. ► *vt* 1 limpiar con agua. 2 *fig* hacer salir. ► *vi* ruborizarse. • **to flush the lavatory** tirar de la cadena *(del wáter)*.

flute [fluːt] *n* flauta.

flutter ['flʌtəʳ] *n* 1 agitación. 2 aleteo. 3 parpadeo. ► *vi* 1 ondear. 2 revolotear.

fly[1] [flaɪ] *vi* 1 volar. 2 ondear. 3 irse volando: *he flew down the stairs*, bajó la escalera volando. ► *vt* 1 pilotar *(avión)*. 2 izar. ► *npl* **flies** bragueta.

fly[2] [flaɪ] *n* mosca.

flying ['flaɪɪŋ] *n* 1 aviación. 2 vuelo. ► *adj* 1 volante. 2 rápido,-a. ▪ **flying saucer** platillo volante.

flyover ['flaɪəʊvəʳ] *n* GB paso elevado.

foal [fəʊl] *n* potro,-a.

foam [fəʊm] *n* espuma. ▪ **foam rubber** gomaespuma.

focus ['fəʊkəs] *n* foco. ► *vt* enfocar. ► *vi* centrarse. • **in focus** enfocado,-a; **out of focus** desenfocado,-a.

foetus ['fiːtəs] *n* feto.

fog [fɒg] *n* niebla. ► *vt-vi* empañar.

foggy ['fɒgɪ] *adj* de niebla.

foglamp ['fɒglæmp] *n* faro antiniebla.

foil [tɔɪl] *n* papel de aluminio.

fold[1] [fəʊld] *n* redil, aprisco.

fold[2] [fəʊld] *n* pliegue. ► *vt* doblar, plegar. ► *vi* doblarse, plegarse.

folder ['fəʊldəʳ] *n* carpeta.

folding ['fəʊldɪŋ] *adj* plegable: *a folding bed*, una cama plegable.

foliage ['fəʊlɪɪdʒ] *n fml* follaje.

folk [fəʊk] *adj* popular. ▶ *npl* **1** gente: *country folk*, gente del campo. **2 folks** *fam* familia. ▪ **folk music** música popular; **folk song** canción popular.

folklore ['fəʊklɔːʳ] *n* folclor.

follow ['fɒləʊ] *vt-vi* seguir. ▶ *vt* perseguir. ▶ *vi* deducirse: *it follows that he's innocent*, se deduce que es inocente.

follower ['fɒləʊəʳ] *n* seguidor,-ra, discípulo,-a.

following ['fɒləʊɪŋ] *adj* siguiente. ▶ *n* seguidores. ▶ *prep* tras.

fond [fɒnd] *adj* **1** cariñoso,-a. **2** ser aficionado,-a: *he's fond of photography*, le gusta mucho la fotografía. ● **to be fond of SB** tenerle cariño a ALGN.

fondle ['fɒndəl] *vt* acariciar.

font [fɒnt] *n* pila bautismal.

food [fuːd] *n* comida, alimento. ▪ **food poisoning** intoxicación alimenticia.

foodstuffs ['fuːdstʌfs] *npl* alimentos, comestibles, productos alimenticios.

fool [fuːl] *n* tonto,-a. ▶ *vt* engañar: *you can't fool me!*, ¡a mí no me engañas! ▶ *vi* bromear: *it wasn't true, I was just fooling*, no era verdad, solo bromeaba. ● **to make a fool of** poner en ridículo a; **to play the fool** hacer el tonto.

foolish ['fuːlɪʃ] *adj* estúpido,-a.

foot [fʊt] *n* **1** pie. **2** pata. ● **on foot** a pie.

football ['fʊtbɔːl] *n* fútbol. ▪ **football pools** quinielas.

footballer ['fʊtbɔːləʳ] *n* futbolista.

footnote ['fʊtnəʊt] *n* nota a pie de página.

footpath ['fʊtpɑːθ] *n* sendero, camino.

footprint ['fʊtprɪnt] *n* huella, pisada.

footstep ['fʊtstep] *n* paso, pisada.

footwear ['fʊtweəʳ] *n* calzado.

for [fɔːʳ] *prep* **1** para: *it's for you*, es para ti. **2** por: *do it for me*, hazlo por mí. **3** por, durante: *for two weeks*, durante dos semanas. **4** para, hacia: *her feelings for him*, sus sentimientos hacia él. **5** desde hace: *I have lived in Spain for twenty years*, vivo en España desde hace veinte años. **6** como: *what do they use for fuel?*, ¿qué utilizan como combustible? **7** de: *"T" for Tony*, "T" de Toni. **8 for + object + inf**: *it's time for you to go*, es hora de que te marches. ▶ *conj* ya que. ● **what for?** ¿para qué?

forbade [fɔːˈbeɪd] *pt* → forbid.

forbid [fəˈbɪd] *vt* prohibir.

forbidden [fəˈbɪdn] *pp* → forbid.

force [fɔːs] *n* fuerza. ► *vt* forzar. • **by force** a/por la fuerza; **to come into force** entrar en vigor.

forceps ['fɔːseps] *npl* fórceps.

ford [fɔːd] *n* vado. ► *vt* vadear.

forearm ['fɔːrɑːm] *n* antebrazo.

forecast ['fɔːkɑːst] *n* pronóstico, previsión. ► *vt* pronosticar.

forefinger ['fɔːfɪŋgəʳ] *n* dedo índice.

foreground ['fɔːgraʊnd] *n* primer plano.

forehead ['fɒrɪd, 'fɔːhed] *n* frente.

foreign ['fɒrɪn] *adj* **1** extranjero,-a. **2** exterior: *foreign policy*, política exterior. **3** ajeno, -a. ■ **foreign exchange** GB; **Foreign Office** GB Ministerio de Asuntos Exteriores; **foreign currency** divisa.

foreigner ['fɒrɪnəʳ] *n* extranjero,-a.

foreman ['fɔːmən] *n* capataz.

foremost ['fɔːməʊst] *adj* principal.

forerunner ['fɔːrʌnəʳ] *n* precursor,-ra.

foresee [fɔːˈsiː] *vt* prever.

foresight ['fɔːsaɪt] *n* previsión.

forest ['fɒrɪst] *n* bosque, selva.

foretell [fɔːˈtel] *vt* presagiar, pronosticar.

foretold [fɔːˈtəʊld] *pt-pp* → foretell.

forever [fəˈrevəʳ] *adv* **1** siempre. **2** para siempre.

foreword ['fɔːwɜːd] *n* prólogo.

forfeit ['fɔːfɪt] *n* **1** pena, multa. **2** prenda.

forgave [fəˈgeɪv] *pt* → forgive.

forge [fɔːdʒ] *n* fragua. ► *vt* **1** falsificar. **2** forjar, fraguar.

forgery ['fɔːdʒərɪ] *n* falsificación.

forget [fəˈget] *vt* olvidar, olvidarse de. • **forget it!** ¡olvídalo!, ¡déjalo!; **to forget oneself** perder el control.

forgive [fəˈgɪv] *vt* perdonar.

forgot [fəˈgɒt] *pt* → forget.

forgotten [fəˈgɒtən] *pp* → forget.

fork [fɔːk] *n* **1** tenedor. **2** horca, horquilla. **3** bifurcación.

form [fɔːm] *n* **1** forma. **2** impreso, formulario. **3** GB curso: *I'm in the third form*, hago tercero. ► *vt-vi* formar(se). • **off form** en baja forma; **on form** en forma. ■ **form of address** tratamiento.

formal ['fɔːməl] *adj* **1** formal. **2** de etiqueta.

format ['fɔːmæt] *n* formato. ► *vt* formatear.

former ['fɔːməʳ] *adj* **1** primer, -a: *the former case*, el primer caso. **2** antiguo,-a, ex-: *the former champion*, el excampeón. ► *pron* **the former** aquél, aquélla.

formula ['fɔ:mjələ] *n* fórmula.

forsake [fə'seɪk] *vt* **1** *fml* abandonar. **2** renunciar a.

fort [fɔ:t] *n* fuerte, fortaleza.

forth [fɔ:θ] *adv* en adelante. • **and so forth** y así sucesivamente.

forthcoming [fɔ:θ'kʌmɪŋ] *adj* próximo,-a.

fortieth ['fɔ:tɪəθ] *adj* cuadragésimo,-a.

fortify ['fɔ:tɪfaɪ] *vt* **1** fortificar. **2** *fig* fortalecer.

fortnight ['fɔ:tnaɪt] *n* GB quincena, dos semanas.

fortress ['fɔ:trəs] *n* fortaleza.

fortunate ['fɔ:tʃənət] *adj* afortunado,-a.

fortune ['fɔ:tʃən] *n* **1** fortuna. **2** suerte.

fortune-teller ['fɔ:tʃəntelə'] *n* adivino,-a.

forty ['fɔ:tɪ] *num* cuarenta.

forward ['fɔ:wəd] *adv* **1** hacia adelante. **2** en adelante. ► *adj* **1** hacia adelante. **2** delantero, -a, frontal: *a forward position*, una posición delantera. **3** adelantado,-a: *forward planning*, planificación anticipada. ► *n* delantero,-a. ► *vt* remitir: *please forward*, remítase al destinatario. • **to put the clock forward** adelantar el reloj.

forwards ['fɔ:wədz] *adv* → forward.

fossil ['fɒsəl] *n* fósil.

foster ['fɒstə'] *adj* adoptivo,-a. ■ **foster child** hijo,-a adoptivo,-a.

fought [fɔ:t] *pt-pp* → fight.

foul [faʊl] *adj* asqueroso,-a. ► *n* falta *(en deporte)*.

found[1] [faʊnd] *vt* fundar.

found[2] [faʊnd] *pt-pp* → find.

foundation [faʊn'deɪʃən] *n* **1** fundación. **2** fundamento, base. ► *npl* **foundations** cimientos.

foundry ['faʊndrɪ] *n* fundición.

fountain ['faʊntən] *n* fuente. ■ **fountain pen** pluma estilográfica.

four [fɔ:'] *num* cuatro. • **on all fours** a gatas.

fourteen [fɔ:'ti:n] *num* catorce.

fourteenth [fɔ:'ti:nθ] *adj* decimocuarto,-a.

fourth [fɔ:θ] *adj* cuarto,-a.

fowl [faʊl] *n* ave de corral.

fox [fɒks] *n* zorro,-a.

foxy ['fɒksɪ] *adj fam* astuto,-a.

foyer ['fɔɪeɪ, 'fɔɪə'] *n* vestíbulo.

fraction ['frækʃən] *n* fracción.

fracture ['fræktʃə'] *n* fractura. ► *vt-vi* fracturar(se).

fragile ['frædʒaɪl] *adj* frágil.

fragment ['frægmənt] *n* fragmento.

frame [freɪm] *n* **1** armazón, armadura. **2** cuadro *(de bici)*. **3** montura *(de gafas)*. **4** marco *(de ventana)*. **5** fotograma. ► *vt* **1** enmarcar. ■ **frame of mind** estado de ánimo.

framework ['freɪmwɜːk] *n* armazón, estructura.

franchise ['fræntʃaɪz] *n* franquicia.

frank [fræŋk] *adj* franco,-a.

frantic ['fræntɪk] *adj* frenético,-a.

fraud [frɔːd] *n* fraude.

fray [freɪ] *vi* deshilacharse, desgastarse.

freak [friːk] *n* **1** monstruo. **2** *sl* fanático,-a: *a film freak*, un fanático del cine. ► *adj* insólito,-a.

freckle ['frekəl] *n* peca.

free [friː] *adj* **1** libre. **2** gratuito,-a. ► *adv* **1** gratis. **2** suelto,-a. ► *vt* **1** poner en libertad. **2** soltar.

freedom ['friːdəm] *n* libertad.

freelance ['friːlɑːns] *adj* autónomo,-a, freelance.

freestyle ['friːstaɪl] *n* estilo libre.

freeway ['friːweɪ] *n* US autopista.

freeze [friːz] *n* **1** helada. **2** congelación *(de precios)*. ► *vt-vi* congelar(se).

freezer ['friːzə'] *n* congelador.

freight [freɪt] *n* **1** transporte. **2** carga, flete. ■ **freight train** tren de mercancías.

frenzy ['frenzɪ] *n* frenesí.

frequency ['friːkwənsɪ] *n* frecuencia.

frequent ['friːkwənt] *adj* frecuente.

fresco ['freskəʊ] *n* fresco.

fresh [freʃ] *adj* fresco,-a. ■ **fresh water** agua dulce.

freshen ['freʃən] *vt-vi* refrescar(se).

fret [fret] *vi* preocuparse.

friar [fraɪə'] *n* fraile.

friction ['frɪkʃən] *n* fricción.

Friday ['fraɪdɪ] *n* viernes.

fridge [frɪdʒ] *n* nevera, frigorífico.

fried [fraɪd] *adj* frito,-a.

friend [frend] *n* amigo,-a.

friendly ['frendlɪ] *adj* **1** simpático,-a. **2** acogedor,-ra. ■ **friendly game/match** partido amistoso.

friendship ['frendʃɪp] *n* amistad.

frieze [friːz] *n* friso.

frigate ['frɪgət] *n* fragata.

fright [fraɪt] *n* **1** susto. **2** miedo.

frighten ['fraɪtən] *vt* asustar.

frightened ['fraɪtənd] *adj* asustado,-a. • **to be frightened** tener miedo.

fringe [frɪndʒ] *n* **1** fleco. **2** flequillo.

frisk [frɪsk] *vt* registrar, cachear.

fritter ['frɪtə'] *n* buñuelo.

frivolous ['frɪvələs] *adj* frívolo,-a.

fro [frəʊ] *phr.* **to and fro** de un lado para otro.

frog [frɒg] *n* rana.

frogman ['frɒgmən] *n* hombre rana.

from [frɒm] *prep* **1** de: *the train from New York to Washington*, el tren de Nueva York a Washington. **2** de, desde: *from January to June*, desde enero hasta junio. **3** según, por: *from experience*, por experiencia. • **from now on** a partir de ahora.

front [frʌnt] *n* **1** parte delantera. **2** frente. **3** principio. **4** fachada. ► *adj* **1** delantero,-a, de delante. **2** primero. ► *vi* dar: *the window fronts onto the sea*, la ventana da al mar. • **in front of** delante de. ■ **front door** puerta principal, puerta de entrada.

frontier ['frʌntɪəʳ] *n* frontera.

frost [frɒst] *n* **1** escarcha. **2** helada. ► *vi* **to frost over** helarse, escarcharse.

froth [frɒθ] *n* espuma.

frown [fraʊn] *n* ceño. ► *vi* fruncir el ceño.

froze [frəʊz] *pt* → freeze.

frozen ['frəʊzən] *pp* → freeze.

fruit [fruːt] *n* **1** fruta. **2** fruto. ■ **fruit dish** frutero; **fruit machine** máquina tragaperras; **fruit salad** macedonia.

frustrate [frʌ'streɪt] *vt* frustrar.

fry [fraɪ] *vt-vi* freír, freírse.

frying pan ['fraɪɪŋpæn] *n* sartén.

fudge [fʌdʒ] *n* dulce hecho con azúcar, leche y mantequilla.

fuel [fjʊəl] *n* combustible, carburante.

fugitive ['fjuːdʒɪtɪv] *adj-n* fugitivo,-a.

fulfil [fʊl'fɪl] *vt* **1** cumplir. **2** realizar, efectuar. **3** satisfacer.

full [fʊl] *adj* **1** lleno,-a. **2** completo,-a. ► *adv* justo, de lleno. ■ **full moon** luna llena; **full stop** GB punto.

full-time [fʊl'taɪm] *adj* de jornada completa. ► *adv* a jornada completa.

fume [fjuːm] *vi* echar humo. ► *npl* **fumes** humos.

fumigate ['fjuːmɪgeɪt] *vt* fumigar.

fun [fʌn] *n* diversión. ► *adj* divertido,-a. • **in/for fun** en broma; **to have fun** divertirse, pasarlo bien; **to make fun of** reírse de.

function ['fʌŋkʃən] *n* **1** función. **2** acto, ceremonia. ► *vi* funcionar.

fund [fʌnd] *n* fondo. ► *vt* patrocinar.

fundamental [fʌndə'mentəl] *adj* fundamental.

funeral ['fjuːnərəl] *n* entierro, funerales. ■ **funeral procession** cortejo fúnebre; **funeral parlor** US funeraria.

funfair ['fʌnfeəʳ] *n* GB feria, parque de atracciones.

fungus ['fʌŋgəs] *n* hongo.

funnel ['fʌnəl] *n* **1** embudo. **2** chimenea *(de barco)*.

gander

G

funny ['fʌnɪ] adj 1 gracioso,-a, divertido,-a. 2 raro,-a, extraño,-a, curioso,-a.

fur [fɜː'] n 1 pelo, pelaje. 2 piel. ■ **fur coat** abrigo de pieles.

furious ['fjʊərəs] adj furioso,-a.

furnace ['fɜːnəs] n horno.

furnish ['fɜːnɪʃ] vt amueblar.

furnishings ['fɜːnɪʃɪŋz] npl 1 muebles, mobiliario. 2 accesorios.

furniture ['fɜːnɪtʃə'] n mobiliario, muebles. ● **a piece of furniture** un mueble. ■ **furniture van** camión de mudanzas.

further ['fɜːðə'] comp → far. ► adj 1 nuevo,-a: **until further notice**, hasta nuevo aviso. 2 adicional: **we need further information**, necesitamos más información. ► adv más.

furthermore [fɜːðə'mɔː'] adv fml además.

furthest ['fɜːðɪst] superl → far.

fury ['fjʊərɪ] n 1 furia. 2 frenesí.

fuse [fjuːz] n 1 fusible, plomo. 2 mecha, espoleta. ► vt-vi 1 fusionar(se). 2 fundir(se).

fusion ['fjuːʒən] n fusión.

fuss [fʌs] n alboroto, jaleo. ● **to make a fuss** quejarse.

fussy ['fʌsɪ] adj quisquilloso,-a.

future ['fjuːtʃə'] adj futuro,-a. ► n futuro.

fuzz [fʌz] n pelusa.

fuzzy ['fʌzɪ] adj 1 rizado,-a, crespo,-a. 2 borroso,-a.

gabardine ['gæbədiːn] n gabardina.

gadget ['gædʒɪt] n aparato, chisme.

gaffe [gæf] n metedura de pata.

gag [gæg] n 1 mordaza. 2 chiste, broma.

gage [geɪdʒ] n US → gauge.

gain [geɪn] n ganancia, beneficio. ► vt 1 lograr. 2 engordar. 3 aumentar. ► vi adelantarse (reloj).

gait [geɪt] n porte, andares.

gal [gæl] abbr (**gallon**) galón.

galaxy ['gæləksɪ] n galaxia.

gale [geɪl] n vendaval.

gallery ['gælərɪ] n 1 galería. 2 galería, gallinero (en teatro).

galley ['gælɪ] n galera.

gallon ['gælən] n galón.

gallop ['gæləp] n galope. ► vi galopar.

gallows ['gæləʊz] n horca.

gamble ['gæmbəl] vi jugar. ► vt apostar, jugarse.

gambling ['gæmblɪŋ] n juego. ■ **gambling den** casa de juego.

game [geɪm] n 1 juego. 2 partido (de tenis, fútbol, etc). 3 partida (de cartas, ajedrez). 4 caza. ■ **game reserve** coto de caza.

gammon ['gæmən] n jamón.

gander ['gændə'] n ganso.

gang [gæŋ] *n* **1** banda *(de delincuentes)*. **2** pandilla *(de amigos)*. **3** cuadrilla, brigada *(de obreros)*.

gangrene ['gæŋgriːn] *n* gangrena.

gangster ['gæŋstəʳ] *n* gángster.

gangway ['gæŋweɪ] *n* **1** pasillo. **2** pasarela *(en barco)*.

gaol [dʒeɪl] *n* GB cárcel.

gap [gæp] *n* **1** abertura, hueco. **2** espacio. **3** blanco. **4** intervalo.

garage ['gærɑːʒ, 'gærɪdʒ] *n* **1** garaje. **2** taller mecánico. **3** gasolinera.

garbage ['gɑːbɪdʒ] *n* basura.

garden ['gɑːdən] *n* jardín.

gardener ['gɑːdənəʳ] *n* jardinero,-a.

gardening ['gɑːdənɪŋ] *n* jardinería.

gargle ['gɑːgəl] *vi* hacer gárgaras.

garlic ['gɑːlɪk] *n* ajo.

garment ['gɑːmənt] *n* prenda de vestir.

garnish ['gɑːnɪʃ] *n* guarnición. ▶ *vt* guarnecer.

garrison ['gærɪsən] *n* guarnición *(militar)*.

garrulous ['gærələs] *adj* locuaz.

garter ['gɑːtəʳ] *n* liga.

gas [gæs] *n* **1** gas. **2** US gasolina. ▪ **gas chamber** cámara de gas; **gas mask** máscara antigás; **gas station** gasolinera.

gash [gæʃ] *n* raja, corte. ▶ *vt* rajar, cortar.

gasoline ['gæsəliːn] *n* US gasolina.

gastronomy [gæs'trɒnəmɪ] *n* gastronomía.

gate [geɪt] *n* **1** puerta, verja. **2** puerta de embarque.

gateau ['gætəʊ] *n* pastel.

gatecrash ['geɪtkræʃ] *vt-vi fam* colarse.

gateway ['geɪtweɪ] *n* puerta.

gather ['gæðəʳ] *vt* **1** juntar, reunir *(personas)*. **2** recoger, coger *(flores, fruta)*. **3** recaudar *(impuestos)*. ▶ *vi* **1** reunirse *(personas)*. **2** acumularse *(nubes)*.

gauge [geɪdʒ] *n* GB **1** indicador. **2** medida estándar. **3** calibre. ▶ *vt* **1** medir, calibrar. **2** *fig* juzgar.

gaunt [gɔːnt] *adj* demacrado,-a.

gauze [gɔːz] *n* gasa.

gave [geɪv] *pt* → give.

gay [geɪ] *adj* **1** alegre. **2** vistoso,-a *(aspecto)*. **3** gay, homosexual. ▶ *n* gay, homosexual.

gaze [geɪz] *vi* mirar fijamente.

gazelle [gə'zel] *n* gacela.

gazette [gə'zet] *n* gaceta.

gear [gɪəʳ] *n* **1** engranaje. **2** marcha, velocidad: *reverse gear*, marcha atrás. **3** *fam* efectos personales, ropa, cosas, equipo. ▪ **gear lever** palanca de cambio.

gearbox ['gɪəbɒks] *n* caja de cambios.

geese [giːs] *npl* → goose.

gem [dʒem] *n* gema.

gen [dʒen] *n fam* información.

gender ['dʒendə'] *n* género.

gene [dʒiːn] *n* gen.

general ['dʒenərəl] *adj-n* general. ● **in general** por lo general. ■ **general practitioner** médico,-a de cabecera; **the general public** el público.

generate ['dʒenəreɪt] *vt* generar.

generation [dʒenə'reɪʃən] *n* generación.

generous ['dʒenərəs] *adj* generoso,-a.

genetic [dʒə'netɪk] *adj* genético,-a.

genial ['dʒiːnɪəl] *adj* simpático,-a, afable.

genital ['dʒenɪtəl] *adj* genital.

genius ['dʒiːnɪəs] *n* genio.

genre ['ʒɒnrə] *n* género.

gent [dʒent] *n* **1** *fam* caballero. **2 gents** servicio de caballeros.

gentle ['dʒentəl] *adj* **1** amable *(persona)*. **2** suave *(brisa)*. **3** manso,-a *(animal)*.

gentleman ['dʒentəlmən] *n* caballero.

genuine ['dʒenjʊɪn] *adj* **1** genuino,-a. **2** sincero,-a *(sentimiento)*.

geography [dʒɪ'ɒgrəfɪ] *n* geografía.

geology [dʒɪ'ɒlədʒɪ] *n* geología.

geometry [dʒɪ'ɒmətrɪ] *n* geometría.

geranium [dʒə'reɪnɪəm] *n* geranio.

germ [dʒɜːm] *n* germen.

gerund ['dʒerənd] *n* gerundio.

gesture ['dʒestʃə'] *n* ademán, gesto. ► *vi* hacer gestos, hacer un ademán.

get [get] *vt* **1** obtener, conseguir. **2** recibir. **3** traer. **4** coger. **5** persuadir, convencer. **6** preparar, hacer. **7** *fam* entender. **8** comprar. **9** buscar, recoger. ► *vi* **1** ponerse, volverse: *to get better*, mejorar; *to get tired*, cansarse. **2** ir: *how do you get there?*, cómo se va hasta allí? **3** llegar: *we got to Seattle at six o'clock*, llegamos a Seattle a las seis. **4** llegar a: *I never got to see that film*, nunca llegué a ver esa película.

to get along *vi* arreglárselas.

to get along with *vt* llevarse (bien) con.

to get away *vi* escaparse.

to get back *vi* volver, regresar. ► *vt* recuperar.

to get down *vi* bajarse.

to get in *vi* **1** llegar. **2** entrar.

to get into *vt* **1** entrar en. **2** subir a *(coche)*.

to get off *vt* **1** quitar. **2** bajarse de *(coche)*. ► *vi* **1** bajarse *(de coche)*. **2** salir *(de viaje)*.

to get on vt 1 subir(se) a (vehículo). 2 montar (bicicleta). ▶ vi 1 llevarse bien. 2 seguir.

to get out vt 1 sacar (objeto). 2 quitar (mancha). ▶ vi salir: *get out of here!*, ¡sal de aquí!

to get over vt 1 recuperarse de. 2 salvar (obstáculo).

to get through vi conseguir hablar (por teléfono).

to get up vt-vi levantar(se).

getaway ['getəweɪ] n fuga.

gherkin ['gɜːkɪn] n pepinillo.

ghost [gəʊst] n fantasma.

giant ['dʒaɪənt] n gigante,-a.

gift [gɪft] n regalo, obsequio.

gild [gɪld] vt dorar.

gills [gɪlz] npl agallas.

gin [dʒɪn] n ginebra.

ginger ['dʒɪndʒəʳ] n jengibre.

gipsy ['dʒɪpsɪ] n gitano,-a.

giraffe [dʒɪ'rɑːf] n jirafa.

girdle ['gɜːdəl] n faja.

girl [gɜːl] n chica, muchacha, joven, niña.

girlfriend ['gɜːlfrend] n 1 novia. 2 US amiga, compañera.

giro ['dʒaɪrəʊ] n giro.

give [gɪv] vt dar. ▶ vi dar de sí, ceder. • **to give way** 1 ceder. 2 ceder el paso. ▪ **give and take** toma y daca.

to give back vt devolver.

to give in vi ceder, rendirse. ▶ vt entregar (deberes).

to give up vt dejar: *to give up smoking*, dejar de fumar. ▶ vi rendirse, entregarse.

glacier ['glæsɪəʳ, 'gleɪʃəʳ] n glaciar.

glad [glæd] adj feliz, contento, -a. • **to be glad** alegrarse; **to be glad to do STH** tener mucho gusto en hacer algo.

glamour ['glæməʳ] (US **glamor**) n 1 atractivo. 2 encanto.

glance [glɑːns] n vistazo, mirada. ▶ vi echar un vistazo. • **at first glance** a primera vista; **to take a glance** echar un vistazo.

gland [glænd] n glándula.

glass [glɑːs] n 1 vidrio, cristal. 2 vaso, copa. ▶ npl **glasses** gafas.

glaze [gleɪz] n vidriado (cerámica). ▶ vt vidriar, esmaltar (cerámica). ▪ **double glazing** doble acristalamiento.

gleam [gliːm] n destello. ▶ vi relucir, brillar.

glen [glen] n cañada.

glide [glaɪd] vi 1 planear. 2 deslizarse.

glider ['glaɪdəʳ] n planeador.

glimpse [glɪmps] n visión fugaz. ▶ vt vislumbrar.

global ['gləʊbəl] adj global.

globe [gləʊb] n 1 globo. 2 globo terrestre.

gloomy ['gluːmɪ] adj 1 lóbrego,-a, oscuro (lugar). 2 tristón,-ona, melancólico,-a (voz). 3 pesimista, poco prometedor,-ra (pronóstico).

glory ['glɔːrɪ] n gloria.

glossary ['glɒsərɪ] n glosario.

glossy ['glɒsɪ] adj brillante.

glove [glʌv] n guante.

glow [gləʊ] n 1 luz suave: *the red glow of the fire*, la suave luz roja del fuego. 2 rubor.

glucose ['glu:kəʊz] n glucosa.

glue [glu:] n cola, pegamento. ► vt encolar, pegar.

glutton ['glʌtən] n glotón,-ona.

glycerine ['glɪsərɪn] n glicerina.

gnat [næt] n mosquito.

gnaw [nɔ:] vt roer.

go [gəʊ] vi 1 ir. 2 marcharse, irse, salir. 3 desaparecer. 4 ir, funcionar. 5 volverse, ponerse, quedarse: *he's gone deaf*, se ha vuelto sordo. 6 terminarse, acabarse. 7 pasar. ► vt hacer: *it goes tick-tock*, hace tic-tac. ► n 1 energía, empuje. 2 turno: *it's my go now*, ahora me toca a mí. 3 intento. • **to be going to do STH** ir a hacer algo; **to have a go at SB** criticar a ALGN; **to make a go of STH** tener éxito en algo.

to go away vi marcharse.

to go back vi volver.

to go by vi pasar.

to go down vi 1 bajar. 2 deshincharse *(neumático)*.

to go in vi entrar.

to go off vi 1 irse, marcharse. 2 estallar *(bomba)*. 3 sonar *(alarma)*. 4 apagarse *(luz)*. 5 estropearse *(comida)*.

to go on vi 1 seguir. 2 pasar, suceder.

to go out vi 1 salir. 2 apagarse *(luz)*.

to go up vi 1 subir. 2 estallar.

goal [gəʊl] n 1 meta, portería. 2 gol, tanto. 3 fin, objeto.

goalkeeper ['gəʊlki:pəʳ] n portero, guardameta.

goat [gəʊt] n cabra.

goblet ['gɒblət] n copa.

god [gɒd] n dios.

godchild ['gɒdtʃaɪld] n ahijado,-a.

goddaughter ['gɒddɔ:təʳ] n ahijada.

goddess ['gɒdəs] n diosa.

godfather ['gɒdfɑ:ðəʳ] n padrino.

godmother ['gɒdmʌðəʳ] n madrina.

godparents ['gɒdpeərənts] npl padrinos.

godson ['gɒdsʌn] n ahijado.

goggles ['gɒgəls] npl gafas *(de esquí, buceo)*.

gold [gəʊld] n oro. ► adj 1 de oro. 2 dorado.

golden ['gəʊldən] adj 1 de oro. 2 dorado,-a.

goldfish ['gəʊldfɪʃ] n pez de colores.

goldsmith ['gəʊldsmɪθ] n orfebre.

golf [gɒlf] n golf. ■ **golf club 1** palo de golf. **2** club de golf; **golf course** campo de golf.

gone [gɒn] pp → go.

good [gʊd] *adj* bueno,-a. ► *interj* ¡bien! ► *n* bien. ► *npl* **goods 1** bienes. **2** género, artículos. • **as good as** prácticamente, como; **a good deal** bastante; **for good** para siempre; **to be good at STH** tener facilidad para algo, ser bueno en algo; **to do good** hacer bien.

goodbye [gʊd'baɪ] *n* adiós. ► *interj* ¡adiós! • **to say goodbye to** despedirse de.

good-for-nothing ['gʊdfə-nʌθɪŋ] *adj-n* inútil.

good-looking [gʊd'lʊkɪŋ] *adj* guapo,-a.

goodwill [gʊd'wɪl] *n* buena voluntad.

goose [guːs] *n* ganso, oca. ■ **goose pimples** carne de gallina.

gooseberry ['gʊzbrɪ, 'guːsbərɪ] *n* grosella espinosa.

gooseflesh ['guːsfleʃ] *n* carne de gallina.

gorge [gɔːdʒ] *n* desfiladero.

gorgeous ['gɔːdʒəs] *adj* espléndido,-a.

gorilla [gə'rɪlə] *n* gorila.

go-slow [gəʊ'sləʊ] *n* huelga de celo.

gospel ['gɒspəl] *n* evangelio.

gossip ['gɒsɪp] *n* **1** cotilleo. **2** cotilla. ► *vi* cotillear. ■ **gossip column** crónica de sociedad.

got [gɒt] *pt-pp* → get.

gout [gaʊt] *n* gota *(enfermedad)*.

govern ['gʌvən] *vt* gobernar.

government ['gʌvənmənt] *n* gobierno.

gown [gaʊn] *n* **1** vestido largo. **2** toga *(de juez)*. **3** bata *(de médico)*.

grab [græb] *vt* asir, coger.

grace [greɪs] *n* gracia.

graceful ['greɪsfʊl] *adj* elegante.

grade [greɪd] *n* **1** grado. **2** clase, categoría. **3** US pendiente, cuesta. **4** US nota, calificación. **5** US curso.

gradual ['grædjʊəl] *adj* gradual.

graduate [(*n*) 'grædjʊət, (*vb*) 'grædjʊeɪt] *n* graduado,-a, licenciado,-a. ► *vt* graduar. ► *vi* graduarse.

graffiti [grə'fiːtɪ] *npl* pintadas, grafiti.

graft [grɑːft] *n* injerto. ► *vt* injertar.

grain [greɪn] *n* **1** grano. **2** cereales. **3** veta *(en madera)*.

gram [græm] *n* gramo.

grammar ['græmə'] *n* gramática. ■ **grammar school** GB instituto de enseñanza secundaria.

gramme [græm] *n* gramo.

granary ['grænərɪ] *n* granero.

grand [grænd] *adj* **1** grandioso,-a, espléndido,-a. **2** *fam* fenomenal, estupendo,-a. ■ **grand piano** piano de cola; **grand total** total.

grandchild ['græntʃaɪld] *n* nieto,-a.

granddaughter ['grændɔːtəʳ] *n* nieta.

grandfather ['grændfɑːðəʳ] *n* abuelo.

grandmother ['grænmʌðəʳ] *n* abuela.

grandparents ['grændpeərənts] *npl* abuelos.

grandson ['grændsʌn] *n* nieto.

grandstand ['grændstænd] *n* tribuna.

granite ['grænɪt] *n* granito.

grant [grɑːnt] *n* **1** beca. **2** subvención. ► *vt* **1** conceder. **2** reconocer, admitir. ● **to take STH for granted** dar algo por sentado.

grape [greɪp] *n* uva.

grapefruit ['greɪpfruːt] *n* pomelo.

grapevine ['greɪpvaɪn] *n* vid.

graph [grɑːf] *n* diagrama. ■ **graph paper** papel cuadriculado.

graphic ['græfɪk] *adj* gráfico,-a.

graphite ['græfaɪt] *n* grafito.

grasp [grɑːsp] ► *vt* **1** asir, agarrar. **2** comprender. ● **to have a good grasp of** dominar.

grass [grɑːs] *n* hierba.

grasshopper ['grɑːshɒpəʳ] *n* saltamontes.

grate[1] [greɪt] *vt* rallar.

grate[2] [greɪt] *n* rejilla, parrilla.

grateful ['greɪtful] *adj* agradecido,-a.

grater ['greɪtəʳ] *n* rallador.

gratify ['grætɪfaɪ] *vt* complacer, satisfacer.

gratis ['grætɪs, 'grɑːtɪs] *adv* gratis.

gratitude ['grætɪtjuːd] *n* gratitud.

gratuity [grə'tjuːɪti] *n* propina.

grave[1] [greɪv] *n* tumba.

grave[2] [greɪv] *adj* grave.

gravel ['grævəl] *n* grava.

graveyard ['greɪvjɑːd] *n* cementerio.

gravity ['grævɪti] *n* gravedad.

gravy ['greɪvɪ] *n* salsa *(de carne)*.

gray [greɪ] *adj* US → grey.

graze [greɪz] *n* roce, rasguño. ► *vt* rozar. ► *vi* pacer, pastar.

grease [griːs] *n* grasa. ► *vt* engrasar.

great [greɪt] *adj* **1** grande, gran. **2** *fam* estupendo,-a, fantástico,-a.

greed [griːd] *n* **1** codicia, avaricia. **2** gula, glotonería.

green [griːn] *adj* **1** verde. **2** novato,-a. ► *n* **1** verde. **2** green *(en golf)*. ► *npl* **greens** verduras. ● **to be green with envy** morirse de envidia. ■ **green bean** judía verde.

greengrocer's ['griːngrəʊsəz] *n* verdulería.

greenhouse ['griːnhaʊs] *n* invernadero. ■ **greenhouse effect** efecto invernadero.

greet [griːt] *vt* **1** saludar, recibir *(persona)*. **2** acoger, recibir *(propuesta)*.

greeting ['gri:tɪŋ] n saludo.
■ **greetings card** tarjeta de felicitación; **greetings from...** recuerdos de...

gremlin ['gremlɪn] n duende.

grenade [grə'neɪd] n granada.

grew [gru:] pt → grow.

grey [greɪ] adj **1** gris. **2** cano,-a (pelo). ► n gris.

greyhound ['greɪhaʊnd] n galgo.

grid [grɪd] n reja, parrilla.

grief [gri:f] n dolor, pena.

grill [grɪl] n **1** parrilla. **2** parrillada: *mixed grill*, parrillada de carne. ► vt asar a la parrilla.

grille [grɪl] n rejilla.

grim [grɪm] adj **1** terrible. **2** lúgubre (lugar). **3** severo,-a, muy serio,-a (persona).

grimace ['grɪməs] n mueca. ► vi hacer una mueca.

grind [graɪnd] vt **1** moler. **2** afilar (cuchillo).

grinder ['graɪndə'] n molinillo.

grip [grɪp] vt asir, agarra. ► n **1** asimiento, apretón. **2** adherencia (sujección de neumático).

grizzly bear [grɪzlɪ'beə'] n oso pardo.

groan [grəʊn] n gemido, quejido (de dolor). ► vi **1** gemir, quejarse (de dolor). **2** crujir (puerta).

grocer ['grəʊsə'] n tendero,-a.

grocer's ['grəʊsəz] n tienda de comestibles.

groceries ['grəʊsərɪz] npl comestibles.

groin [grɔɪn] n ingle.

groom [gru:m] n novio.

groove [gru:v] n **1** ranura. **2** surco.

gross [grəʊs] adj bruto,-a (peso, cantidad).

ground¹ [graʊnd] n **1** tierra, suelo. **2** terreno. **3** campo (de fútbol, batalla). ► npl **grounds 1** razón, motivo. **2** posos.
■ **ground floor** planta baja.

ground² [graʊnd] pt-pp → grind.

group [gru:p] n grupo. ► vt agrupar.

grove [grəʊv] n arboleda.

grow [grəʊ] vi crecer. ► vt **1** cultivar (planta). **2** dejarse crecer (pelo, bigote).

to grow up vi criarse, crecer.

grown [grəʊn] pp → grow.

grown-up ['grəʊnʌp] adj-n adulto,-a.

growth [grəʊθ] n crecimiento.

grub [grʌb] n larva.

grudge [grʌdʒ] n resentimiento, rencor.

grumble ['grʌmbəl] n queja.

grunt [grʌnt] n gruñido. ► vi gruñir.

guarantee [gærən'ti:] n garantía. ► vt garantizar.

guard [gɑːd] n **1** guardia. **2** jefe de tren. ► vt **1** guardar, proteger. **2** vigilar. ● **on guard**

de guardia; **to stand guard** montar guardia. ▪ **guard dog** perro guardián.

guerrilla [gəˈrɪlə] n guerrillero,-a.

guess [ges] vt-vi **1** adivinar. **2** fam suponer. ► n conjetura: **have a guess!**, ¡a ver si lo adivinas!

guest [gest] n **1** invitado,-a. **2** cliente,-a, huésped,-a.

guesthouse [ˈgesthaʊs] n casa de huéspedes, pensión.

guide [gaɪd] n guía. ► vt guiar.

guidebook [ˈgaɪdbʊk] n guía.

guideline [ˈgaɪdlaɪn] n pauta, directriz.

guilty [ˈgɪltɪ] adj culpable.

guinea [ˈgɪnɪ] n. ▪ **guinea pig** conejillo de Indias.

guitar [gɪˈtaːʳ] n guitarra.

guitarist [gɪˈtaːrɪst] n guitarrista.

gulf [gʌlf] n golfo.

gull [gʌl] n gaviota.

gullible [ˈgʌlɪbəl] adj crédulo,-a.

gulp [gʌlp] n trago.

gum¹ [gʌm] n encía.

gum² [gʌm] n goma.

gun [gʌn] n arma de fuego.

gunman [ˈgʌnmən] n pistolero.

gunpoint [ˈgʌnpɔɪnt]. • **at gunpoint** a punta de pistola.

gunpowder [ˈgʌnpaʊdəʳ] n pólvora.

gunshot [ˈgʌnʃɒt] n disparo.

gust [gʌst] n ráfaga, racha.

gut [gʌt] n intestino, tripa. ► npl **guts 1** entrañas, vísceras. **2** fam agallas.

gutter [ˈgʌtəʳ] n **1** cuneta, alcantarilla (en calle). **2** canalón, desagüe (en tejado). ▪ **gutter press** prensa amarilla.

guy [gaɪ] n fam tipo, tío.

guzzle [ˈgʌzəl] vt zamparse.

gym [dʒɪm] n **1** fam gimnasio. **2** gimnasia. ▪ **gym shoes** zapatillas de deporte.

gymnastics [dʒɪmˈnæstɪks] n gimnasia.

gynaecology [gaɪnɪˈkɒlədʒɪ] (US **gynecology**) n ginecología.

gypsy [ˈdʒɪpsɪ] adj-n gitano,-a.

H

habit [ˈhæbɪt] n hábito.

habitat [ˈhæbɪtæt] n hábitat.

habitual [həˈbɪtjʊəl] adj habitual.

hack [hæk] vt COMPUT piratear.

had [hæd] pt-pp → have.

haemorrhage [ˈhemərɪdʒ] (US **hemorrhage**) n hemorragia.

haemorrhoids [ˈhemərɔɪdz] npl (US **hemorroids**) hemorroides.

hag [hæg] n bruja, arpía.

haggle ['hægəl] *vi* regatear.
hail[1] [heɪl] *vt* llamar.
hail[2] [heɪl] *n* granizo. ► *vi* granizar.
hair [heəʳ] *n* cabello, pelo.
haircut ['heəkʌt] *n* corte de pelo.
hairdresser ['heədresəʳ] *n* peluquero,-a. ■ **hairdresser's** peluquería.
hairdryer ['heədraɪəʳ] *n* secador de pelo.
hairpiece ['heəpiːs] *n* peluquín.
hairpin ['heəpɪn] *n* horquilla.
hairspray ['heəspreɪ] *n* laca.
hairstyle ['heəstaɪl] *n* peinado.
hake [heɪk] *n* merluza.
half [hɑːf] *n* 1 mitad: *the second half*, la segunda mitad. 2 medio: *a kilo and a half*, un kilo y medio. ► *adj* medio,-a. ► *adv* medio, a medias. ► *pron* mitad. **half past** y media: *it's half past two*, son las dos y media.
half-time [hɑːftaɪm] *n* descanso *(en partido)*.
halfway ['hɑːfweɪ] *adv* a mitad de camino.
hall [hɔːl] *n* 1 vestíbulo, entrada. 2 sala *(de conciertos)*. ■ **hall of residence** colegio mayor.
hallo [həˈləʊ] *interj* → hello.
hallucination [həluːsɪˈneɪʃən] *n* alucinación.
halo ['heɪləʊ] *n* halo, aureola.
halt [hɔːlt] *n* alto, parada. ► *vt-vi* parar(se), cesar.

ham [hæm] *n* jamón.
hamburger ['hæmbɜːgəʳ] *n* hamburguesa.
hammer ['hæməʳ] *n* martillo.
hammock ['hæmək] *n* hamaca.
hand [hænd] *n* 1 mano. 2 trabajador,-ra, operario,-a. 3 tripulante *(de barco)*. 4 manecilla *(de reloj)*. 5 letra, caligrafía. ► *vt* dar, entregar. ● **at first hand** de primera mano; **at hand** a mano; **by hand** a mano; **hands up!** ¡manos arriba!; **on the one hand** por una parte; **on the other hand** por otra parte; **to hold hands** estar cogidos,-as de la mano; **to lend a hand** echar una mano.
to hand in *vt* entregar.
to hand out *vt* repartir.
to hand over *vt* entregar.
handbag ['hændbæg] *n* bolso.
handball ['hændbɔːl] *n* balonmano.
handbook ['hændbʊk] *n* manual.
handbrake ['hændbreɪk] *n* freno de mano.
handcuff ['hændkʌf] *vt* esposar. ► *npl* **handcuffs** esposas.
handful ['hændfʊl] *n* puñado.
handicap ['hændɪkæp] *n* 1 discapacidad, minusvalía. 2 desventaja, obstáculo. 3 hándicap. ► *vt* obstaculizar.

handicapped ['hændɪkæpt] *adj* minusválido,-a.

handicraft ['hændɪkrɑːft] *n* artesanía.

handkerchief ['hæŋkətʃiːf] *n* pañuelo.

handle ['hændəl] *n* 1 pomo *(de puerta)*. 2 tirador *(de cajón)*. 3 asa *(de taza)*. 4 mango *(de cuchillo)*. ► *vt* 1 manejar. 2 tratar *(gente, problema)*.

handlebar ['hændəlbɑːʳ] *n* manillar.

handmade [hænd'meɪd] *adj* hecho,-a a mano.

handout ['hændaʊt] *n* 1 folleto. 2 nota de prensa. 3 limosna.

handshake ['hændʃeɪk] *n* apretón de manos.

handsome ['hænsəm] *adj* guapo,-a.

handwritten ['hænd'rɪtən] *adj* escrito,-a a mano.

handy ['hændɪ] *adj* 1 práctico,-a, útil. 2 a mano.

hang [hæŋ] *vt-vi* colgar.

to hang about/around *vi* 1 esperar. 2 perder el tiempo.

to hang out *vt* tender.

to hang up *vt-vi* colgar *(teléfono)*.

hangar ['hæŋəʳ] *n* hangar.

hanger ['hæŋəʳ] *n* percha.

hang-glider ['hæŋglaɪdəʳ] *n* ala delta.

hangover ['hæŋəʊvəʳ] *n* resaca.

happen ['hæpən] *vi* ocurrir.

happiness ['hæpɪnəs] *n* felicidad.

happy ['hæpɪ] *adj* 1 feliz, alegre. 2 contento,-a: *happy birthday!*, ¡feliz cumpleaños!

harass ['hærəs] *vt* acosar.

harbour ['hɑːbəʳ] (US **harbor**) *n* puerto.

hard [hɑːd] *adj* 1 duro,-a *(material)*. 2 difícil *(pregunta, tema)*. ► *adv* fuerte, duro. ▪ **hard court** pista rápida; **hard disk** disco duro; **hard shoulder** GB arcén.

hardly ['hɑːdlɪ] *adv* 1 apenas. 2 casi.

hardware ['hɑːdweəʳ] *n* 1 artículos de ferretería. 2 hardware, soporte físico. ▪ **hardware store** ferretería.

hare [heəʳ] *n* liebre.

haricot bean [hærɪkəʊ'biːn] *n* alubia.

harm [hɑːm] *n* mal, daño, perjuicio. ► *vt* dañar, perjudicar, hacer daño.

harmony ['hɑːmənɪ] *n* armonía.

harp [hɑːp] *n* arpa.

harpoon [hɑː'puːn] *n* arpón.

harvest ['hɑːvɪst] *n* cosecha. ► *vt* cosechar.

has [hæz] *3rd pers sing pres* → have.

hash [hæʃ] *n* picadillo.

haste [heɪst] *n* prisa.

hat [hæt] *n* sombrero.

hatch [hætʃ] *n* escotilla.

hate [heɪt] *n* odio. ▶ *vt* odiar.
haughty ['hɔːtɪ] *adj* arrogante.
haul [hɔːl] *n* **1** botín. **2** redada *(de peces)*. ▶ *vt* tirar de, arrastrar.
haulage ['hɔːlɪdʒ] *n* transporte.
haunted ['hɔːntɪd] *adj* encantado,-a.
have [hæv] *vt* **1** tener. **2** comer, beber, fumar: *to have lunch*, comer. **3** tomar: *to have a bath*, bañarse. **4** hacer, mandar: *he had the house painted*, hizo pintar la casa. ▶ *aux* haber. • **have got** GB tener; **to have just** acabar de.
to have on *vt* llevar puesto, -a *(prenda)*.
haversack ['hævəsæk] *n* mochila.
hawk [hɔːk] *n* halcón.
hay [heɪ] *n* heno.
hay-fever ['heɪfiːvəʳ] *n* fiebre del heno, alergia.
hazard ['hæzəd] *n* riesgo, peligro. ▶ *vt* aventurar.
haze [heɪz] *n* neblina.
hazelnut ['heɪzəlnʌt] *n* avellana.
he [hiː] *pron* él. ▶ *adj* macho: *a he bear*, un oso macho.
head [hed] *n* **1** cabeza. **2** cabecera *(de cama, mesa)*. ▶ *vt* **1** encabezar *(procesión)*. **2** cabecear. **3** dirigir *(organización)*. • **heads or tails?** ¿cara o cruz?

to head for *vt* dirigirse hacia.
headache ['hedeɪk] *n* dolor de cabeza.
header ['hedəʳ] *n* cabezazo.
headlamp ['hedlæmp] *n* faro.
headland ['hedlənd] *n* cabo.
headlight ['hedlaɪt] *n* faro.
headline ['hedlaɪn] *n* titular.
headphones ['hedfəʊnz] *npl* auriculares.
headquarters ['hedkwɔːtəz] *npl* **1** sede, oficina principal. **2** cuartel general.
heal [hiːl] *vt-vi* curar(se).
health [helθ] *n* salud.
healthy ['helθɪ] *adj* **1** sano,-a. **2** saludable.
heap [hiːp] *n* montón.
hear [hɪəʳ] *vt-vi* oír.
heart [hɑːt] *n* corazón. ▶ *npl* **hearts** corazones. • **by heart** de memoria; **to lose heart** desanimarse. ▪ **heart attack** ataque al corazón.
heartbeat ['hɑːtbiːt] *n* latido del corazón.
heartless ['hɑːtləs] *adj* cruel
heat [hiːt] *n* **1** calor. **2** calefacción. **3** eliminatoria *(en deporte)*. ▶ *vt-vi* calentar(se). • **on heat** en celo.
heater ['hiːtəʳ] *n* estufa, calefactor.
heather ['heðəʳ] *n* brezo.
heating ['hiːtɪŋ] *n* calefacción.
heaven ['hevən] *n* cielo.
heavy ['hevɪ] *adj* **1** pesado,-a. **2** fuerte *(lluvia, golpe)*. • **to be**

a heavy smoker fumar mucho.

heavyweight ['hevɪweɪt] *n* peso pesado.

hectare ['hektɑːʳ] *n* hectárea.

hedge [hedʒ] *n* seto.

hedgehog ['hedʒhɒg] *n* erizo.

heel [hiːl] *n* **1** talón. **2** tacón.

height [haɪt] *n* **1** altura. **2** altitud.

heir [eəʳ] *n* heredero.

heiress ['eəres] *n* heredera.

held [held] *pt-pp* → hold.

helicopter ['helɪkɒptəʳ] *n* helicóptero.

hell [hel] *n* infierno.

hello [he'ləʊ] *interj* **1** ¡hola! **2** ¡diga!, ¡dígame! *(por teléfono)*.

helm [helm] *n* timón.

helmet ['helmɪt] *n* casco.

help [help] *n* ayuda. ► *interj* ¡socorro! ► *vt* ayudar. • **help yourself** sírvete tú mismo, -a; **I can't help it** no lo puedo evitar.

helping ['helpɪŋ] *n* ración.

hem [hem] *n* dobladillo.

hemp [hemp] *n* cáñamo.

hen [hen] *n* gallina.

hence [hens] *adv* **1** por eso. **2** de aquí a, dentro de.

hepatitis [hepə'taɪtəs] *n* hepatitis.

her [hɜːʳ] *pron* **1** la *(complemento - directo)*; le, se *(- indirecto)*. **2** ella *(después de preposición)*. ► *adj* su, sus, de ella.

herb [hɜːb] *n* hierba.

herd [hɜːd] *n* **1** manada *(de ganado)*. **2** rebaño *(de cabras)*.

here [hɪəʳ] *adv* aquí. • **here you are** aquí tienes.

heritage ['herɪtɪdʒ] *n* herencia.

hero ['hɪərəʊ] *n* héroe.

heroin ['herəʊɪn] *n* heroína *(droga)*.

heroine ['herəʊɪn] *n* heroína.

herring ['herɪŋ] *n* arenque.

hers [hɜːz] *pron* (el) suyo, (la) suya, (los) suyos, (las) suyas.

herself [hɜːˈself] *pron* se, ella misma. • **by herself** sola.

hesitate ['hezɪteɪt] *vi* dudar.

hi [haɪ] *interj* ¡hola!

hiccough ['hɪkʌp] *n* hipo. ► *vi* tener hipo.

hiccup ['hɪkʌp] *n* hipo. ► *vi* tener hipo.

hid [hɪd] *pt-pp* → hide.

hidden ['hɪdən] *pp* → hide.

hide¹ [haɪd] *vt-vi* esconder(se).

hide² [haɪd] *n* piel, cuero.

hierarchy ['haɪərɑːkɪ] *n* jerarquía.

high [haɪ] *adj* **1** alto,-a. **2** agudo,-a *(voz)*. **3** fuerte *(viento)*. • **high court** tribunal supremo; **high jump** salto de altura; **high school** instituto de enseñanza secundaria; **high street** GB calle mayor; **high tide** pleamar.

high-heeled ['haɪˈhiːld] *adj* de tacón alto.

highlight ['haɪlaɪt] *vt* hacer resaltar, poner de relieve.

highly ['haɪlɪ] *adv* muy.
Highness ['haɪnəs] *n* Alteza.
highway ['haɪweɪ] *n* US autovía. ▪ **Highway Code** GB código de la circulación.
hijack ['haɪdʒæk] *n* secuestro. ▸ *vt* secuestrar.
hike [haɪk] *n* excursión. ▸ *vi* ir de excursión.
hill [hɪl] *n* colina.
hilt [hɪlt] *n* empuñadura.
him [hɪm] *pron* 1 lo *(complemento - directo)*; le, se *(- indirecto)*. 2 él *(después de preposición)*.
himself [hɪm'self] *pron* se, sí mismo. ● **by himself** solo.
hinder ['hɪndəʳ] *vt-vi* entorpecer, estorbar.
hinge [hɪndʒ] *n* bisagra.
hint [hɪnt] *n* 1 insinuación, indirecta. 2 consejo. 3 pista, indicio. ▸ *vt* insinuar. ▸ *vi* lanzar indirectas.
hip [hɪp] *n* cadera.
hippie ['hɪpɪ] *adj-n fam* hippie.
hippo(potamus) [hɪpə'pɒtəməs] *n* hipopótamo.
hippy ['hɪpɪ] *adj-n fam* hippie.
hire ['haɪəʳ] *n* alquiler. ▸ *vt* 1 alquilar. 2 contratar. ● **on hire purchase** compra a plazos.
his [hɪz] *adj* 1 su, sus. 2 de él. ▸ *pron* (el) suyo, (la) suya, (los) suyos, (las) suyas.
history ['hɪstərɪ] *n* historia.
hit [hɪt] *n* 1 golpe. 2 éxito. 3 visita *(a página web)*. ▸ *vt* golpear, pegar.

hitchhike ['hɪtʃhaɪk] *vi* hacer autoestop.
hive [haɪv] *n* colmena.
hoarding ['hɔːdɪŋ] *n* valla.
hoarse [hɔːs] *adj* ronco,-a.
hobby ['hɒbɪ] *n* afición, hobby.
hockey ['hɒkɪ] *n* hockey.
hog [hɒg] *n* cerdo.
hoist [hɔɪst] *n* 1 grúa. 2 montacargas. ▸ *vt* 1 levantar. 2 izar *(bandera)*.
hold [həʊld] *n* bodega *(de barco, avión)*. ▸ *vt* 1 aguantar, sostener, agarrar *(con la mano)*. 2 dar cabida a, tener capacidad para. 3 celebrar *(reunión)*. 4 mantener *(conversación)*.
to hold on *vi* esperar, no colgar *(por teléfono)*.
to hold up *vt* 1 atracar, asaltar. 2 levantar *(mano)*.
holder ['həʊldəʳ] *n* poseedor, -ra, titular *(de pasaporte)*.
hold-up ['həʊldʌp] *n* atraco.
hole [həʊl] *n* agujero, hoyo.
holiday ['hɒlɪdeɪ] *n* 1 fiesta. 2 vacaciones.
hollow ['hɒləʊ] *adj* hueco,-a. ▸ *n* hueco.
holly ['hɒlɪ] *n* acebo.
holy ['həʊlɪ] *adj* santo,-a, sagrado,-a.
home [həʊm] *n* hogar, casa. ▪ **home help** asistenta; **Home Office** Ministerio del Interior; **home page** página inicial.
homeland ['həʊmlænd] *n* patria.

homeless ['həʊmləs] *adj* sin techo, sin hogar.

home-made ['həʊm'meɪd] *adj* casero,-a.

homework ['həʊmwɜːk] *n* deberes.

honest ['ɒnɪst] *adj* honrado,-a.

honey ['hʌnɪ] *n* miel.

honeymoon ['hʌnɪmuːn] *n* luna de miel.

honour ['ɒnəʳ] (US **honor**) *n* honor.

hood [hʊd] *n* 1 capucha. 2 capota *(de coche)*. 3 US capó *(de coche)*.

hoof [huːf] *n* 1 pezuña. 2 casco *(de caballo)*.

hook [hʊk] *n* 1 gancho. 2 anzuelo *(para pescar)*. ► *vt* enganchar. ● **off the hook** 1 descolgado,-a *(teléfono)*. 2 a salvo *(persona)*.

hoop [huːp] *n* aro.

hoot [huːt] *n* bocinazo. ► *vi* tocar la bocina.

hooter ['huːtəʳ] *n* bocina.

hoover ['huːvəʳ] *n* aspiradora. ► *vt-vi* pasar la aspiradora (por).

hope [həʊp] *n* esperanza. ► *vt-vi* esperar.

hopeless ['həʊpləs] *adj* imposible, desesperado,-a, inútil.

horizon [hə'raɪzən] *n* horizonte.

horn [hɔːn] *n* 1 asta, cuerno. 2 bocina, cláxon.

horoscope ['hɒrəskəʊp] *n* horóscopo.

horror ['hɒrəʳ] *n* horror. ■ **horror film** película de terror.

hors d'oeuvre [ɔː'dɜːvʳ] *n* entremés.

horse [hɔːs] *n* caballo.

horsepower ['hɔːspaʊəʳ] *n* caballo *(de vapor)*.

horseshoe ['hɔːsʃuː] *n* herradura.

hose [həʊz] *n* manguera.

hospital ['hɒspɪtəl] *n* hospital.

host [həʊst] *n* 1 anfitrión, -ona. 2 presentador, -ra.

hostage ['hɒstɪdʒ] *n* rehén.

hostel ['hɒstəl] *n* 1 hostal, albergue. 2 residencia *(en universidad)*.

hostess ['həʊstəs] *n* 1 anfitriona. 2 azafata *(de avión, programa)*. 3 camarera.

hostile ['hɒstaɪl] *adj* hostil.

hot [hɒt] *adj* 1 caliente. 2 caluroso,-a *(día, tiempo)*. 3 picante *(comida)*. ● **to be hot** 1 tener calor. 2 estar caliente. ■ **hot dog** perrito caliente.

hotchpotch ['hɒtʃpɒtʃ] *n fam* batiburrillo.

hotel [həʊ'tel] *n* hotel.

hound [haʊnd] *n* perro de caza.

hour [aʊəʳ] *n* 1 hora. 2 horario. ● **on the hour** a la hora en punto.

house [haʊs] *n* casa.

housewife ['haʊswaɪf] *n* ama de casa.

housework ['haʊswɜːk] *n* tareas de la casa.

housing ['haʊzɪŋ] *n* vivienda.
■ **housing development/estate** urbanización.

how [haʊ] *adv* **1** cómo. **2** qué: *how beautiful you look!*, ¡qué guapa estás! ● **how about...?** ¿qué tal si...?; **how are you?** ¿cómo estás?; **how much** cuánto,-a; **how many** cuántos,-as.

however [haʊ'evə'] *conj* sin embargo, no obstante.

howl [haʊl] *n* aullido. ► *vi* aullar.

hub [hʌb] *n* cubo *(de rueda)*.

hug [hʌg] *n* abrazo. ► *vt* abrazar.

huge [hju:dʒ] *adj* enorme.

hull [hʌl] *n* casco *(de barco)*.

hullo [hʌ'ləʊ] *interj* → hello.

human ['hju:mən] *adj* humano,-a. ► *n* humano. ■ **human being** ser humano.

humanity [hju:'mænɪtɪ] *n* humanidad.

humble ['hʌmbəl] *adj* humilde. ► *vt* humillar.

humid ['hju:mɪd] *adj* húmedo,-a.

humiliate [hju:'mɪlɪeɪt] *vt* humillar.

humility [hju:'mɪlɪtɪ] *n* humildad.

hummingbird ['hʌmɪŋbɜ:d] *n* colibrí.

humour ['hju:mə'] (US **humor**) *n* humor.

hump [hʌmp] *n* giba, joroba.

hundred ['hʌndrəd] *num* cien, ciento.

hundredth ['hʌndrədθ] *adj-n* centésimo,-a.

hung [hʌŋ] *pt-pp* → hang.

hunger ['hʌŋgə'] *n* hambre.

hungry ['hʌŋgrɪ] *adj* hambriento,-a. ● **to be hungry** tener hambre.

hunt [hʌnt] *n* caza. ► *vt-vi* cazar. ● **to hunt for** buscar.

hunter ['hʌntə'] *n* cazador.

hunting ['hʌntɪŋ] *n* caza.

hurdle ['hɜ:dəl] *n* valla.

hurl [hɜ:l] *vt* lanzar, arrojar.

hurricane ['hʌrɪkən, 'hʌrɪkeɪn] *n* huracán.

hurry ['hʌrɪ] *n* prisa. ► *vt* meter prisa a. ► *vi* darse prisa. ● **to be in a hurry** tener prisa.

to hurry up *vi* darse prisa.

hurt [hɜ:t] *n* daño, dolor. ► *vt* herir, hacer daño. ► *vi* doler. ● **to get hurt** hacerse daño.

husband ['hʌzbənd] *n* marido, esposo.

hush [hʌʃ] *n* quietud.

husk [hʌsk] *n* cáscara.

hut [hʌt] *n* **1** cabaña. **2** cobertizo.

hutch [hʌtʃ] *n* conejera.

hyaena [haɪ'i:nə] *n* hiena.

hydrant ['haɪdrənt] *n* boca de riego.

hydraulic [haɪ'drɔ:lɪk] *adj* hidráulico,-a.

hydrofoil ['haɪdrəfɔɪl] *n* hidroala.

hydrogen ['haɪdrədʒən] *n* hidrógeno.

hydroplane ['haɪdrəpleɪn] *n* hidroavión.

hyena [haɪ'iːnə] *n* hiena.

hygiene ['haɪdʒiːn] *n* higiene.

hymn [hɪm] *n* himno.

hypermarket ['haɪpəmɑːkɪt] *n* hipermercado.

hyphen ['haɪfən] *n* guion.

hypnotize ['hɪpnətaɪz] *vt* hipnotizar.

hypocrite ['hɪpəkrɪt] *n* hipócrita.

hypothesis [haɪ'pʊθəsɪs] *n* hipótesis.

hysteria [hɪ'stɪərɪə] *n* histeria.

I

I [aɪ] *pron* yo.

ice [aɪs] *n* **1** hielo. **2** helado. ▪ **ice cube** cubito; **ice lolly** GB polo; **ice rink** pista de hielo.

iceberg ['aɪsbɜːg] *n* iceberg.

ice-cream ['aɪskriːm] *n* helado.

ice-skate ['aɪsskeɪt] *vi* patinar sobre hielo. ▶ *n* patín de hielo.

ice-skating ['aɪskeɪtɪn] *n* patinaje sobre hielo.

icicle ['aɪsɪkəl] *n* carámbano.

idea [aɪ'dɪə] *n* idea.

identify [aɪ'dentɪfaɪ] *vt* identificar.

identity [aɪ'dentɪtɪ] *n* identidad. ▪ **identity card** carnet de identidad.

ideology [aɪdɪ'ɒlədʒɪ] *n* ideología.

idiom ['ɪdɪəm] *n* locución.

idiot ['ɪdɪət] *n* idiota.

idle ['aɪdəl] *adj* perezoso,-a.

idol ['aɪdəl] *n* ídolo.

if [ɪf] *conj* **1** si: *if you want*, si quieres. **2** aunque: *a clever if rather talkative child*, un niño inteligente aunque demasiado hablador. ▪ **if only** ojalá, si.

igloo ['ɪgluː] *n* iglú.

ignition [ɪg'nɪʃən] *n* **1** ignición. **2** encendido *(de motor)*. ▪ **ignition key** llave de contacto.

ignorant ['ɪgnərənt] *adj* ignorante.

ignore [ɪg'nɔːʳ] *vt* ignorar.

ill [ɪl] *adj* enfermo,-a.

illegal [ɪ'liːgəl] *adj* ilegal.

illiterate [ɪ'lɪtərət] *adj-n* **1** analfabeto,-a. **2** inculto,-a.

illness ['ɪlnəs] *n* enfermedad.

illuminate [ɪ'luːmɪneɪt] *vt* iluminar.

illusion [ɪ'luːʒən] *n* ilusión.

illustration [ɪləs'treɪʃən] *n* **1** ilustración. **2** ejemplo.

image ['ɪmɪdʒ] *n* imagen.

imagination [ɪmædʒɪ'neɪʃən] *n* imaginación.

imagine [ɪ'mædʒɪn] *vt* imaginar.

imitate ['ɪmɪteɪt] *vt* imitar.

imitation [ɪmɪ'teɪʃən] *n* imitación.

immediate [ɪ'miːdɪət] *adj* inmediato,-a.

immense [ɪ'mens] *adj* inmenso,-a.

immerse [ɪ'mɜːs] *vt* sumergir.

immigrant ['ɪmɪgrənt] *adj* inmigrante. ► *n* inmigrante.

immobile [ɪ'məʊbaɪl] *adj* inmóvil.

immunity [ɪ'mjuːnɪtɪ] *n* inmunidad.

impact ['ɪmpækt] *n* impacto.

impassive [ɪm'pæsɪv] *adj* impasible, imperturbable.

imperative [ɪm'perətɪv] *adj* esencial, imprescindible. ► *n* imperativo.

imperfect [ɪm'pɜːfekt] *adj* defectuoso,-a. ► *n* imperfecto *(tiempo verbal)*.

imperial [ɪm'pɪərɪəl] *adj* imperial.

impersonal [ɪm'pɜːsənəl] *adj* impersonal.

impertinent [ɪm'pɜːtɪnənt] *adj* impertinente.

implant [ɪm'plɑːnt] *vt* implantar.

implausible [ɪm'plɔːzəbəl] *adj* inverosímil.

implement [*(n)* 'ɪmpləmənt, *(vb)* 'ɪmplɪment] *n* instrumento, utensilio. ► *vt* llevar a cabo, poner en práctica.

implicate ['ɪmplɪkeɪt] *vt* implicar.

implicit [ɪm'plɪsɪt] *adj* **1** implícito,-a. **2** absoluto,-a, incondicional.

implore [ɪm'plɔːʳ] *vt* implorar.

impolite [ɪmpə'laɪt] *adj* maleducado,-a.

import [*(n)* 'ɪmpɔːt; *(vb)* ɪm'pɔːt] *n* **1** artículo de importación. **2** importación. ► *vt* importar.

importance [ɪm'pɔːtəns] *n* importancia.

important [ɪm'pɔːtənt] *adj* importante.

impossible [ɪm'pɒsɪbəl] *adj* imposible.

impress [ɪm'pres] *vt* **1** impresionar. **2** subrayar, recalcar.

impression [ɪm'preʃən] *n* **1** impresión. **2** imitación.

impressive [ɪm'presɪv] *adj* impresionante.

imprisonment [ɪm'prɪzənmənt] *n* **1** encarcelamiento. **2** cárcel.

improve [ɪm'pruːv] *vt* mejorar. ► *vi* mejorar, mejorarse.

improvement [ɪm'pruːvmənt] *n* **1** mejora, mejoría. **2** reforma.

improvise ['ɪmprəvaɪz] *vt-vi* improvisar.

impulse ['ɪmpʌls] *n* impulso.

impulsive [ɪm'pʌlsɪv] *adj* impulsivo,-a.

in [ɪn] *prep* **1** en: *in May*, en mayo; *in the box*, en la caja. **2** en, vestido,-a de: *the man in black*, el hombre vestido de negro. **3** por: *in the after-noon*, por la tarde. **4** al: *in do-ing that*, al hacer eso. **5** de: *the biggest in the world*, el más grande del mundo. ► *adv* **1** dentro. **2** en casa: *is Judith in?*, ¿está Judith? **3** de moda: *short skirts are in*, las faldas cortas están de moda. ● **in so far as** en la medida en que; **in all** en total.

inaccurate [ɪn'ækjərət] *adj* inexacto,-a.

inadequate [ɪn'ædɪkwət] *adj* **1** insuficiente. **2** inepto,-a, incapaz *(persona)*.

inaugural [ɪ'nɔːgjʊrəl] *adj* inaugural.

inaugurate [ɪ'nɔːgjʊreɪt] *vt* **1** inaugurar *(edificio)*. **2** investir *(presidente)*.

incapacity [ɪnkə'pæsɪtɪ] *n* incapacidad.

incense ['ɪnsens] *n* incienso.

incentive [ɪn'sentɪv] *n* incentivo.

incessant [ɪn'sesənt] *adj* incesante.

inch [ɪntʃ] *n* pulgada.

incidence ['ɪnsɪdəns] *n* **1** índice *(frecuencia)*. **2** incidencia *(efecto)*.

incident ['ɪnsɪdənt] *n* incidente.

incidental [ɪnsɪ'dentəl] *adj* accesorio,-a, secundario,-a.

incinerate [ɪn'sɪnəreɪt] *vt* incinerar.

incision [ɪn'sɪʒən] *n* incisión.

incisive [ɪn'saɪsɪv] *adj* incisivo,-a.

incisor [ɪn'saɪzə'] *n* incisivo *(diente)*.

incite [ɪn'saɪt] *vt* incitar.

inclination [ɪnklɪ'neɪʃən] *n* inclinación.

incline [ɪn'klaɪn] *vt-vi* inclinar(se).

include [ɪn'kluːd] *vt* incluir.

including [ɪn'kluːdɪŋ] *prep* incluso, inclusive, incluido.

incoherent [ɪnkəʊ'hɪərənt] *adj* incoherente.

income ['ɪnkʌm] *n* ingresos, renta. ■ **income tax** impuesto sobre la renta; **income tax return** declaración de la renta.

incoming ['ɪnkʌmɪŋ] *adj* entrante.

incompetent [ɪn'kɒmpətənt] *adj* incompetente, inepto,-a.

inconclusive [ɪnkən'kluːsɪv] *adj* no concluyente.

incongruous [ɪn'kɒŋgrʊəs] *adj* incongruente.

inconsiderate [ɪnkən'sɪdərət] *adj* desconsiderado,-a.

inconsistent [ɪnkən'sɪstənt] *adj* incoherente.

inconspicuous [ɪnkən'spɪkjʊəs] *adj* que pasa inadvertido,-a.

inconvenient [ɪnkən'viːnɪənt] *adj* **1** mal situado,-a *(lugar)*. **2** inoportuno,-a *(momento)*.

incorporate [ɪn'kɔːpəreɪt] *vt* incorporar.

increase [(n) 'ɪnkriːs, (vb) ɪn-'kriːs] n aumento. ▸ vt-vi aumentar, subir.

incredible [ɪn'kredɪbəl] adj increíble.

incur [ɪn'kɜːʳ] vt 1 incurrir en (críticas). 2 contraer (deuda).

indeed [ɪn'diːd] adv 1 en efecto, efectivamente. 2 realmente, de veras: *thank you very much indeed*, muchísimas gracias.

indefinite [ɪn'defɪnət] adj indefinido,-a.

indemnity [ɪn'demnɪtɪ] n indemnización.

independence [ɪndɪ'pendəns] n independencia.

independent [ɪndɪ'pendənt] adj independiente.

in-depth [ɪn'depθ] adj exhaustivo,-a, a fondo.

index ['ɪndeks] n índice. ▸ vt poner un índice a, catalogar. ▪ **index finger** dedo índice.

indicate ['ɪndɪkeɪt] vt indicar.

indicative [ɪn'dɪkətɪv] adj indicativo,-a. ▸ n indicativo.

indicator ['ɪndɪkeɪtəʳ] n 1 indicador. 2 intermitente (de coche).

indigenous [ɪn'dɪdʒənəs] adj indígena.

indignant [ɪn'dɪgnənt] adj 1 indignado,-a (persona). 2 de indignación (mirada).

indistinct [ɪndɪ'stɪŋkt] adj 1 vago,-a (recuerdo). 2 borroso,-a, poco definido,-a (forma).

individual [ɪndɪ'vɪdjʊəl] adj 1 individual. 2 particular, personal (estilo). ▸ n individuo.

indoor ['ɪndɔːʳ] adj 1 interior, de estar por casa (ropa). 2 cubierto,-a (pista de tenis). ▪ **indoor football** fútbol sala; **indoor pool** piscina cubierta.

indoors [ɪn'dɔːz] adv dentro.

indulgent [ɪn'dʌldʒənt] adj indulgente.

industrial [ɪn'dʌstrɪəl] adj industrial. ▪ **industrial estate** polígono industrial.

industrious [ɪn'dʌstrɪəs] adj trabajador,-ra, aplicado,-a.

industry ['ɪndʌstrɪ] n industria.

inedible [ɪn'edɪbəl] adj no comestible.

inequality [ɪnɪ'kwɒlətɪ] n desigualdad.

inexpensive [ɪnɪk'spensɪv] adj barato,-a, económico,-a.

infantry ['ɪnfəntrɪ] n infantería.

infect [ɪn'fekt] vt 1 infectar. 2 contagiar.

infection [ɪn'fekʃən] n 1 infección. 2 contagio.

infectious [ɪn'fekʃəs] adj infeccioso,-a, contagioso,-a.

inferior [ɪn'fɪərɪəʳ] adj inferior. ▸ n inferior.

infertile [ɪn'fɜːtaɪl] adj estéril.

infest [ɪn'fest] vt infestar.

infiltrate ['ɪnfɪltreɪt] vt infiltrarse en.

infinite ['ɪnfɪnət] adj infinito,-a.

infinitive [ɪnˈfɪnɪtɪv] *n* infinitivo.

infirm [ɪnˈfɜːm] *adj* débil, enfermizo,-a.

infirmary [ɪnˈfɜːmərɪ] *n* **1** hospital. **2** enfermería.

inflammable [ɪnˈflæməbəl] *adj* inflamable.

inflammation [ɪnfləˈmeɪʃən] *n* inflamación.

inflation [ɪnˈfleɪʃən] *n* inflación.

influence [ˈɪnflʊəns] *n* influencia. ▶ *vt* influir en.

influenza [ɪnflʊˈenzə] *n* gripe.

inform [ɪnˈfɔːm] *vt* informar.

information [ɪnfəˈmeɪʃən] *n* información.

infuriate [ɪnˈfjʊərɪeɪt] *vt* enfurecer.

ingenious [ɪnˈdʒiːnɪəs] *adj* ingenioso,-a.

ingrained [ɪnˈɡreɪnd] *adj* **1** incrustado,-a *(suciedad)*. **2** arraigado,-a *(costumbre)*.

ingredient [ɪnˈɡriːdɪənt] *n* ingrediente.

inhabitant [ɪnˈhæbɪtənt] *n* habitante.

inherit [ɪnˈherɪt] *vt* heredar.

inheritance [ɪnˈherɪtəns] *n* herencia.

initial [ɪˈnɪʃəl] *adj-n* inicial.

initiate [ɪˈnɪʃɪeɪt] *vt* iniciar.

injection [ɪnˈdʒekʃən] *n* inyección.

injure [ˈɪndʒə^r] *vt* herir.

injury [ˈɪndʒərɪ] *n* herida, lesión. ▪ **injury time** tiempo de descuento *(en partido)*.

ink [ɪŋk] *n* tinta.

inkjet printer [ˈɪŋkdʒetˈprɪntə^r] *n* impresora de chorro de tinta.

inland [*(adj)* ˈɪnlənd, *(adv)* ɪnˈlænd] *adj* de tierra adentro. ▶ *adv* tierra adentro.

inlet [ˈɪnlet] *n* **1** cala, ensenada. **2** entrada.

inn [ɪn] *n* **1** posada, fonda, mesón. **2** taberna.

inner [ˈɪnə^r] *adj* interior.

innocent [ˈɪnəsənt] *adj-n* inocente.

innovation [ɪnəˈveɪʃən] *n* innovación.

inpatient [ˈɪnpeɪʃənt] *n* paciente hospitalizado,-a.

input [ˈɪnpʊt] *n* **1** entrada, inversión *(de dinero)*. **2** input, entrada *(de datos)*.

inquire [ɪnˈkwaɪə^r] *vt* preguntar. ● **"Inquire within"** "Razón aquí".

inquiry [ɪnˈkwaɪərɪ] *n* **1** pregunta. **2** investigación. ● **"Inquiries"** "Información".

inquisitive [ɪnˈkwɪzɪtɪv] *adj* curioso,-a.

insane [ɪnˈseɪn] *adj* demente, loco,-a.

insect [ˈɪnsekt] *n* insecto.

insert [ɪnˈsɜːt] *vt* insertar.

inside [ɪnˈsaɪd] *n* interior. ▶ *adj* interior, interno,-a. ▶ *adv* **1** dentro *(posición)*. **2** adentro *(movimiento)*. ▶ *prep* dentro de. ● **inside out** de dentro afuera, al revés, del revés.

insight ['ɪnsaɪt] n 1 perspicacia, penetración. 2 idea.

insinuate [ɪn'sɪnjʊeɪt] vt insinuar.

insist [ɪn'sɪst] vi insistir.

insomnia [ɪn'sɒmnɪə] n insomnio.

inspection [ɪn'spekʃən] n 1 inspección. 2 registro (a equipaje). 3 revista (a tropas).

inspector [ɪn'spektəʳ] n 1 inspector,-ra. 2 revisor,-ra (en tren).

inspiration [ɪnspɪ'reɪʃən] n inspiración.

install [ɪn'stɔːl] (US **instal**) vt instalar.

instalment [ɪn'stɔːlmənt] (US **installment**) n 1 plazo (de pago). 2 fascículo (de libro). 3 episodio (de serie).

instance ['ɪnstəns] n ejemplo. • **for instance** por ejemplo.

instant ['ɪnstənt] n instante. ▶ adj 1 inmediato,-a. 2 instantáneo,-a (café).

instead [ɪn'sted] adv en cambio. • **instead of** en vez de.

instinct ['ɪnstɪŋkt] n instinto.

institute ['ɪnstɪtjuːt] n instituto.

institution [ɪnstɪ'tjuːʃən] n institución.

instruction [ɪn'strʌkʃən] n instrucción.

instrument ['ɪnstrəmənt] n instrumento.

insulate ['ɪnsjəleɪt] vt aislar.

insult [(n) 'ɪnsʌlt, (vb) ɪn'sʌlt] n insulto. ▶ vt insultar.

insurance [ɪn'ʃʊərəns] n seguro. • **insurance policy** póliza de seguro.

insure [ɪn'ʃʊəʳ] vt asegurar.

intake ['ɪnteɪk] n consumo.

integral ['ɪntɪɡrəl] adj-n integral.

integrity [ɪn'teɡrətɪ] n integridad.

intellectual [ɪntə'lektjʊəl] adj-n intelectual.

intelligence [ɪn'telɪdʒəns] n inteligencia.

intelligent [ɪn'telɪʒənt] adj inteligente.

intend [ɪn'tend] vt tener la intención de, proponerse.

intense [ɪn'tens] adj 1 intenso,-a. 2 muy serio,-a (persona).

intensive [ɪn'tensɪv] adj intensivo,-a. • **intensive care** cuidados intensivos.

intention [ɪn'tenʃən] n intención.

interactive [ɪntər'æktɪv] adj interactivo,-a.

interchange ['ɪntətʃeɪndʒ] n 1 intercambio. 2 enlace.

intercom ['ɪntəkɒm] n interfono.

interest ['ɪntrəst] n interés. ▶ vt interesar. • **interest rate** tipo de interés.

interface ['ɪntəfeɪs] n interfaz.

interference [ɪntə'fɪərəns] n interferencia.

interior [ɪn'tɪərɪəʳ] adj-n interior.

interjection [ɪntəˈdʒekʃən] *n* 1 interjección. 2 comentario.

interlude [ˈɪntəluːd] *n* 1 intermedio, descanso. 2 interludio *(en música)*.

intermediate [ɪntəˈmiːdɪət] *adj* intermedio,-a.

intermission [ɪntəˈmɪʃən] *n* intermedio, descanso.

internal [ɪnˈtɜːnəl] *adj* interior, interno,-a. ▪ **internal flight** vuelo nacional.

international [ɪntəˈnæʃənəl] *adj* internacional.

Internet [ˈɪntənet] *n* Internet.

interplay [ˈɪntəpleɪ] *n* interacción.

interpret [ɪnˈtɜːprət] *vt* interpretar. ▶ *vi* hacer de intérprete.

interrogation [ɪntɛrəˈgeɪʃən] *n* interrogatorio.

interrogative [ɪntəˈrɒgətɪv] *adj* interrogativo,-a.

interrupt [ɪntəˈrʌpt] *vt-vi* interrumpir.

interval [ˈɪntəvəl] *n* 1 intervalo. 2 descanso, intermedio *(en teatro, etc)*.

intervention [ɪntəˈvenʃən] *n* intervención.

interview [ˈɪntəvjuː] *n* entrevista. ▶ *vt* entrevistar.

interviewer [ˈɪntəvjuːəʳ] *n* entrevistador,-ra.

intestine [ɪnˈtestɪn] *n* intestino.

intimacy [ˈɪntɪməsɪ] *n* intimidad.

intimate [ˈɪntɪmət] *adj* íntimo,-a.

into [ˈɪntʊ] *prep* 1 en, dentro de. 2 dividido entre.

intonation [ɪntəˈneɪʃən] *n* entonación.

intoxicated [ɪnˈtɒksɪkeɪtɪd] *adj* ebrio,-a.

intranet [ˈɪntrənet] *n* intranet.

intransitive [ɪnˈtrænsɪtɪv] *adj* intransitivo,-a.

intrigue [ɪnˈtriːg] *n* intriga.

introduce [ɪntrəˈdjuːs] *vt* 1 introducir. 2 presentar.

introduction [ɪntrəˈdʌkʃən] *n* 1 introducción. 2 presentación.

intruder [ɪnˈtruːdəʳ] *n* intruso,-a.

intuition [ɪntjuːˈɪʃən] *n* intuición.

invade [ɪnˈveɪd] *vt* invadir.

invaluable [ɪnˈvæljʊəbəl] *adj* inestimable.

invasion [ɪnˈveɪʒən] *n* invasión.

invent [ɪnˈvent] *vt* inventar.

invention [ɪnˈvenʃən] *n* 1 invento *(cosa)*. 2 invención *(acción)*.

inventor [ɪnˈventəʳ] *n* inventor,-ra.

inventory [ˈɪnvəntrɪ] *n* inventario.

inversion [ɪnˈvɜːʒən] *n* inversión.

invert [ɪnˈvɜːt] *vt* invertir.

inverted [ɪnˈvɜːtɪd] *adj* invertido,-a. ▪ **inverted commas** comillas.

invest [ɪnˈvest] *vt-vi* invertir.

investigation [ɪnvestɪ'geɪʃən] n investigación.

investment [ɪn'vestmənt] n inversión.

invitation [ɪnvɪ'teɪʃən] n invitación.

invite [ɪn'vaɪt] vt invitar.

inviting [ɪn'vaɪtɪŋ] adj tentador,-ra, atractivo,-a.

invoice ['ɪnvɔɪs] n factura. ▶ vt facturar.

involve [ɪn'vɒlv] vt 1 involucrar. 2 afectar a. 3 suponer.

inward ['ɪnwəd] adj interior. ▶ adv hacia adentro.

inwards ['ɪnwədz] adv hacia adentro.

iris ['aɪərɪs] n 1 iris (del ojo). 2 lirio.

iron ['aɪən] n 1 hierro. 2 plancha. ▶ vt planchar.

ironic [aɪ'rɒnɪk] adj irónico,-a.

ironmonger's ['aɪənmʌŋgəz] n ferretería.

irony ['aɪrənɪ] n ironía.

irrational [ɪ'ræʃənəl] adj irracional.

irregular [ɪ'regjələʳ] adj irregular.

irrelevant [ɪ'reləvənt] adj irrelevante.

irresistible [ɪrɪ'zɪstəbəl] adj irresistible.

irresponsible [ɪrɪ'spɒnsəbəl] adj irresponsable.

irrigate ['ɪrɪgeɪt] vt regar.

irritate ['ɪrɪteɪt] vt irritar.

irritating ['ɪrɪteɪtɪŋ] adj irritante, molesto,-a.

irritation [ɪrɪ'teɪʃən] n irritación.

is [ɪz] 3rd pers sing pres → be.

Islamic [ɪz'læmɪk] adj islámico,-a.

island ['aɪlənd] n isla.

isle [aɪl] n isla.

isolate ['aɪsəleɪt] vt aislar.

isolation [aɪsə'leɪʃən] n aislamiento.

issue ['ɪʃuː] n 1 asunto, tema. 2 edición (de libro). 3 número (de revista). 4 emisión (de sellos, acciones). 5 expedición (de pasaporte). ▶ vt 1 publicar (libro). 2 emitir (sellos, acciones). 3 expedir (pasaporte).

isthmus ['ɪsməs] n istmo.

it [ɪt] pron 1 él, ella, ello (sujeto). 2 lo, la (complemento - directo); le (- indirecto). 3 él, ella, ello (después de preposición).

italics [ɪ'tælɪks] npl cursiva.

itch [ɪtʃ] n picazón, picor. ▶ vi picar: **my leg itches**, me pica la pierna.

item ['aɪtəm] n 1 artículo, cosa. 2 asunto (en agenda). 3 partida (en factura). 4 noticia.

itinerary [aɪ'tɪnərərɪ] n itinerario.

its [ɪts] adj su, sus.

itself [ɪt'self] pron 1 se (reflexivo). 2 sí, sí mismo,-a (después de preposición). ● **by itself** solo.

ivory ['aɪvərɪ] n marfil.

ivy ['aɪvɪ] n hiedra.

J

jab [dʒæb] n pinchazo, inyección. ► vt pinchar, clavar.

jabber ['dʒæbə'] vi-vt farfullar.

jack [dʒæk] n **1** gato (para coche). **2** jota, sota.

jackal ['dʒækɔːl] n chacal.

jacket ['dʒækɪt] n **1** chaqueta, americana. **2** cazadora. **3** sobrecubierta (de libro).

jack-knife ['dʒæknaɪf] n navaja.

jackpot ['dʒækpɒt] n premio gordo.

jade [dʒeɪd] n jade.

jaguar ['dʒægjʊə'] n jaguar.

jail [dʒeɪl] n cárcel, prisión. ► vt encarcelar.

jam¹ [dʒæm] n mermelada.

jam² [dʒæm] n **1** aprieto, apuro. **2** atasco. ► vt **1** atestar, apiñar. **2** embutir, meter. ► vi atascarse, bloquearse.

janitor ['dʒænɪtə'] n portero.

January ['dʒænjʊərɪ] n enero.

jar [dʒɑː'] n tarro, pote.

jargon ['dʒɑːgən] n jerga.

jasmin ['dʒæzmɪn] n jazmín.

jaundice ['dʒɔːndɪs] n ictericia.

jaunt [dʒɔːnt] n excursión.

javelin ['dʒævəlɪn] n jabalina.

jaw [dʒɔː] n mandíbula.

jazz [dʒæz] n jazz.

jealous ['dʒeləs] adj celoso,-a.
● **to be jealous of** SB tener celos de ALGN.

jealousy ['dʒeləsɪ] n celos.

jeans [dʒiːnz] npl vaqueros.

jeep® [dʒiːp] n jeep®.

jeer [dʒɪə'] vi **1** burlarse. **2** abuchear. ► n **1** burla. **2** abucheo.

jelly ['dʒelɪ] n **1** jalea. **2** gelatina.

jellyfish ['dʒelɪfɪʃ] n medusa.

jerk [dʒɜːk] n **1** tirón, sacudida. **2** fam imbécil. ► vt sacudir, tirar de.

jersey ['dʒɜːzɪ] n jersey, suéter.

jet [dʒet] n **1** reactor, jet. **2** chorro.

jet-lag ['dʒetlæg] n jet-lag.

jetty ['dʒetɪ] n malecón.

Jew [dʒuː] n judío.

jewel ['dʒuːəl] n **1** joya, alhaja. **2** piedra preciosa.

jeweller ['dʒuːələ'] (US **jeweler**) n joyero,-a. ■ **jeweller's** joyería.

jewellery ['dʒuːəlrɪ] (US **jewelery**) n joyas.

Jewish ['dʒuːɪʃ] adj judío,-a.

jigsaw ['dʒɪgsɔː] n rompecabezas.

jingle ['dʒɪŋgəl] n **1** tintineo. **2** melodía (de anuncio). ► vi tintinear.

jinx [dʒɪŋks] n gafe.

job [dʒɒb] n trabajo.

jobless ['dʒɒbləs] adj parado,-a, sin trabajo.

jockey ['dʒɒkɪ] n jockey.

jog [dʒɒg] n trote. ► vt empujar, sacudir. ► vi hacer

footing, correr. • **to go for a jog** hacer footing.

jogging ['dʒɒgɪŋ] n footing.

join [dʒɔɪn] vt **1** juntar, unir. **2** reunirse con. **3** acompañar. **4** alistarse (en ejército); ingresar (en policía). **5** hacerse socio,-a (de un club). **6** afiliarse a (partido). ▶ vi confluir (ríos).

joiner ['dʒɔɪnəʳ] n carpintero.

joint [dʒɔɪnt] n **1** junta, juntura, unión. **2** articulación (de rodilla, cadera). ▶ adj conjunto,-a. ■ **joint venture** empresa conjunta.

joke [dʒəʊk] n **1** chiste. **2** broma. ▶ vi bromear.

joker ['dʒəʊkəʳ] n **1** bromista. **2** comodín.

jolly ['dʒɒlɪ] adj alegre.

jolt [dʒəʊlt] n **1** sacudida. **2** sorpresa, susto. ▶ vt sacudir. ▶ vi dar una sacudida.

jotter ['dʒɒtəʳ] n GB bloc.

journal ['dʒɜːnəl] n **1** revista, publicación (especializada). **2** diario.

journalism ['dʒɜːnəlɪzəm] n periodismo.

journalist ['dʒɜːnəlɪst] n periodista.

journey ['dʒɜːnɪ] n **1** viaje. **2** trayecto.

joy [dʒɔɪ] n gozo, alegría.

joyful ['dʒɔɪfʊl] adj alegre.

joystick ['dʒɔɪstɪk] n joystick.

judge [dʒʌdʒ] n juez, jueza. ▶ vt-vi juzgar.

judgement ['dʒʌdʒmənt] n juicio. fallo.

jug [dʒʌg] n jarro.

juggler ['dʒʌgləʳ] n malabarista.

juice [dʒuːs] n jugo; zumo.

jukebox ['dʒuːkbɒks] n máquina de discos.

July [dʒuˈlaɪ] n julio.

jump [dʒʌmp] n salto. ▶ vt-vi saltar. ▶ vi dar un salto.

jumper ['dʒʌmpəʳ] n **1** GB jersey. **2** US pichi.

jump-suit ['dʒʌmpsuːt] n mono.

junction ['dʒʌŋkʃən] n **1** salida, acceso (en autopista). **2** cruce.

June [dʒuːn] n junio.

jungle ['dʒʌŋgəl] n jungla.

juniper ['dʒuːnɪpəʳ] n enebro.

junk¹ [dʒʌnk] n trastos. ■ **junk food** comida basura; **junk mail** propaganda.

junk² [dʒʌnk] n junco (barco).

jury ['dʒʊərɪ] n jurado.

just¹ [dʒʌst] adj justo,-a.

just² [dʒʌst] adv **1** exactamente, justo. **2** solamente. **3** justo ahora. **4** justo. • **just now** ahora mismo.

justice ['dʒʌstɪs] n justicia.

justify ['dʒʌstɪfaɪ] vt justificar.

jute [dʒuːt] n yute.

juvenile ['dʒuːvɪnaɪl] adj **1** juvenil. **2** infantil. ▶ n menor.

juxtapose ['dʒʌkstəpəʊz] vt yuxtaponer.

K

kangaroo [kæŋgə'ruː] *n* canguro.

karate [kə'rɑːtɪ] *n* kárate.

kayak ['kaɪæk] *n* kayac.

keel [kiːl] *n* quilla.

keen [kiːn] *adj* **1** entusiasta, muy aficionado,-a. **2** agudo,-a *(mente)*. **3** penetrante *(mirada)*. **4** cortante *(viento)*. **5** fuerte *(competencia)*. • **keen on** aficionado,-a a.

keep [kiːp] *vt* **1** guardar. **2** retener, entretener. **3** tener *(tienda, negocio)*. **4** llevar *(cuentas, diario)*. **5** cumplir *(promesa)*. **6** acudir a, no faltar a *(cita)*. **7** mantener. **8** criar *(gallinas, cerdos)*. ► *vi* **1** seguir, continuar. **2** conservarse bien • **to keep** STH **to oneself** guardar algo para sí.

to keep on *vi* seguir, continuar.

keg [keg] *n* barril.

kennel ['kenəl] *n* perrera, caseta para perros.

kept [kept] *pt-pp* → keep.

kerb [kɜːb] *n* bordillo.

kernel ['kɜːnəl] *n* **1** semilla *(de nuez, fruta)*. **2** *fig* núcleo.

ketchup ['ketʃəp] *n* ketchup, catsup.

kettle ['ketəl] *n* hervidor.

key [kiː] *n* **1** llave *(de cerradura)*. **2** clave *(de misterio)*. **3** tecla *(de teclado)*. **4** soluciones, respuestas *(de ejercicios)*. ► *adj* clave. ► *vt* teclear. ▪ **key ring** llavero.

keyboard ['kiːbɔːd] *n* teclado.

keyhole ['kiːhəʊl] *n* ojo de la cerradura.

kick [kɪk] *n* **1** puntapié, patada. **2** coz. **3** emoción, sensación. ► *vt* **1** dar un puntapié a, dar una patada a. **2** dar coces a.

to kick out *vt* echar.

kick-off ['kɪkɒf] *n* saque inicial *(en fútbol, rugby)*.

kid[1] [kɪd] *n* **1** cabrito *(animal)*. **2** cabritilla *(piel)*. **3** *fam* niño,-a, chico,-a.

kid[2] [kɪd] *vt* tomar el pelo a. ► *vi* estar de broma: *you must be kidding!*, ¡debes de estar de broma!

kidnap ['kɪdnæp] *vt* secuestrar.

kidney ['kɪdnɪ] *n* riñón.

kill [kɪl] *vt* matar.

killer ['kɪlə'] *n* asesino,-a.

kilo ['kiːləʊ] *n* kilo.

kilogram ['kɪləgræm] *n* kilogramo.

kilometre [kɪ'lɒmɪtə'] (US **kilometer**) *n* kilómetro.

kilt [kɪlt] *n* falda escocesa.

kin [kɪn] *n* parientes, familia.

kind [kaɪnd] *adj* simpático,-a, amable. ► *n* tipo, género, clase. • **a kind of** una especie de; **to be so kind as to** tener la bondad de.

kindergarten ['kɪndəgæːtən] *n* jardín de infancia.

king [kɪŋ] *n* rey.

kingdom ['kɪŋdəm] *n* reino.

kiosk ['kiːɒsk] *n* **1** quiosco. **2** GB cabina telefónica.

kiss [kɪs] *n* beso. ► *vt-vi* besar(se).

kit [kɪt] *n* **1** equipo. **2** petate. **3** maqueta, kit.

kitchen ['kɪtʃɪn] *n* cocina.

kite [kaɪt] *n* cometa.

kitty ['kɪti] *n fam* bote *(de dinero)*.

kiwi ['kiːwiː] *n* kiwi.

knapsack ['næpsæk] *n* mochila.

knead [niːd] *vt* amasar.

knee [niː] *n* rodilla.

kneecap ['niːkæp] *n* rótula.

kneel [niːl] *vi* arrodillarse.

knelt [nelt] *pt-pp* → kneel.

knew [njuː] *pt* → know.

knickers ['nɪkəz] *npl* bragas.

knick-knack ['nɪknæk] *n* chuchería.

knife [naɪf] *n* cuchillo.

knight [naɪt] *n* **1** caballero. **2** caballo *(ajedrez)*.

knit [nɪt] *vt* tejer. ► *vi* hacer punto, tricotar.

knitting ['nɪtɪŋ] *n* punto.

knob [nɒb] *n* **1** pomo *(de puerta)*. **2** tirador *(de cajón)*. **3** botón *(de radio)*.

knock [nɒk] *n* golpe. ► *vt* golpear. ► *vi* llamar.

to knock down *vt* **1** derribar *(edificio)*. **2** atropellar.

to knock out *vt* **1** dejar sin conocimiento. **2** dejar fuera de combate *(en boxeo)*.

to knock over *vt* volcar *(vaso)*, atropellar *(persona)*.

knockout ['nɒkaʊt] *n* K.O., fuera de combate.

knot [nɒt] *n* nudo. ► *vt* anudar.

know [nəʊ] *vt-vi* **1** conocer. **2** saber. • **as far as I know** que yo sepa.

know-how ['nəʊhaʊ] *n* conocimientos prácticos.

knowledge ['nɒlɪdʒ] *n* conocimiento(s).

known [nəʊn] *pp* → know.

knuckle ['nʌkəl] *n* nudillo.

KO ['keɪ'əʊ] *abbr (knockout)* fuera de combate, KO.

koala [kəʊ'ɑːlə] *n* koala.

L

label ['leɪbəl] *n* etiqueta. ► *vt* etiquetar.

laboratory [ləˈbɒrətəri] *n* laboratorio.

labour ['leɪbəˈ] (US **labor**) *n* **1** trabajo. **2** mano de obra.

labourer ['leɪbərəˈ] (US **laborer**) *n* peón, obrero,-a.

lace [leɪs] *n* **1** cordón *(de zapato)*. **2** encaje.

lack [læk] *n* falta, carencia. ► *vt* faltar, carecer de.

lacquer ['lækə'] *n* laca.

lad [læd] *n* muchacho, chaval.

ladder ['lædə'] *n* **1** escalera de mano. **2** carrera *(en medias)*.

ladle ['leɪdəl] *n* cucharón.

lady ['leɪdɪ] *n* señora, dama.

ladybird ['leɪdɪbɜːd] (US **ladybug**) *n* mariquita *(insecto)*.

lager ['lɑːgə'] *n* cerveza rubia.

lagoon [lə'guːn] *n* laguna.

laid [leɪd] *pt-pp* → lay.

lain [leɪn] *pp* → lie.

lair [leə'] *n* guarida.

lake [leɪk] *n* lago.

lamb [læm] *n* cordero.

lame [leɪm] *adj* cojo,-a.

lamp [læmp] *n* lámpara.

lamp-post ['læmppəust] *n* farola.

lampshade ['læmpʃeɪd] *n* pantalla *(de lámpara)*.

lance [lɑːns] *n* lanza.

land [lænd] *n* tierra. ► *vi* aterrizar. ► *vt-vi* desembarcar.

landing ['lændɪŋ] *n* **1** aterrizaje *(de avión)*. **2** descansillo, rellano *(en escalera)*. **3** desembarco *(de personas)*.

landlady ['lændleɪdɪ] *n* **1** propietaria, casera *(de vivienda)*. **2** dueña *(de pensión)*.

landlord ['lændlɔːd] *n* **1** propietario, casero *(de vivienda)*. **2** dueño *(de pensión)*.

landscape ['lændskeɪp] *n* paisaje.

landslide ['lændslaɪd] *n* desprendimiento de tierras.

lane [leɪn] *n* **1** camino. **2** carril *(de autopista)*. **3** calle *(en atletismo, natación)*.

language ['læŋgwɪdʒ] *n* **1** lenguaje. **2** lengua, idioma.

lantern ['læntən] *n* linterna.

lap¹ [læp] *n* regazo, rodillas.

lap² [læp] *n* **1** vuelta *(de carrera)*. **2** etapa *(de viaje)*.

lapel [lə'pel] *n* solapa.

lapse [læps] *n* **1** lapso *(de tiempo)*. **2** lapsus.

laptop ['læptɒp] *n* ordenador portátil.

lard [lɑːd] *n* manteca de cerdo.

large [lɑːdʒ] *adj* grande, gran. ● **at large** suelto,-a.

lark [lɑːk] *n* alondra.

larynx ['lærɪŋks] *n* laringe.

lash [læʃ] *n* **1** latigazo, azote. **2** pestaña.

last [lɑːst] *adj* **1** último,-a. **2** pasado,-a: *last night*, anoche. ► *adv* **1** por última vez. **2** en último lugar. ► *n* el/la último,-a. ► *vt-vi* durar. ● **at last** al fin, por fin; **last but one** penúltimo,-a.

latch [lætʃ] *n* pestillo.

late [leɪt] *adj* **1**: *in the late afternoon*, a media tarde. **2** difunto,-a. ► *adv* tarde. ● **to be late** llegar tarde; **to get late** hacerse tarde.

later ['leɪtə'] *adj* posterior *(fecha, edición)*. ► *adv* **1** más tarde. **2** después, luego.

latest ['leɪtɪst] *adj* último,-a.

lather ['lɑːðəʳ] n espuma.

laugh [lɑːf] n risa. ► vi reír, reírse. • **to laugh at** reírse de

launch [lɔːntʃ] n lanzamiento. ► vt lanzar.

launder ['lɔːndəʳ] vt **1** lavar y planchar *(ropa)*. **2** blanquear *(dinero)*.

launderette [lɔːndəˈret] n lavandería automática.

laundry ['lɔːndrɪ] n **1** lavandería. **2** colada.

laurel ['lɒrəl] n laurel.

lavatory ['lævətərɪ] n servicios, aseo *(público)*.

lavender ['lævɪndəʳ] n lavanda.

lavish ['lævɪʃ] adj generoso,-a.

law [lɔː] n **1** ley. **2** derecho *(carrera)*.

lawn [lɔːn] n césped.

lawyer ['lɔːjəʳ] n abogado,-a.

lay[1] [leɪ] vt **1** poner, colocar. **2** poner *(huevos)*.

lay[2] [leɪ] pt → lie.

lay-by ['leɪbaɪ] n área de descanso.

layer ['leɪəʳ] n capa, estrato.

layout ['leɪaʊt] n diseño.

lazy ['leɪzɪ] adj perezoso,-a.

lead[1] [led] n **1** plomo *(metal)*. **2** mina *(de lápiz)*.

lead[2] [liːd] n **1** delantera, cabeza. **2** correa *(de perro)*. **3** papel principal. ► vt **1** llevar, conducir *(sendero, guía)*. **2** liderar. ► vi **1** ir primero,-a. **2** tener el mando. **3** conducir *(camino)*.

leader ['liːdəʳ] n líder.

leadership ['liːdəʃɪp] n liderazgo.

lead-free ['ledfriː] adj sin plomo.

leaf [liːf] n hoja.

leaflet ['liːflət] n folleto.

league [liːg] n liga.

leak [liːk] n **1** escape, fuga. **2** gotera.

lean [liːn] vi **1** apoyarse. **2** inclinarse *(curva, pendiente)*.

to lean out vt-vi asomar(se).

leant [lent] pt-pp → lean.

leap [liːp] n salto, brinco. ► vi saltar, brincar. ▪ **leap year** año bisiesto.

leapt [lept] pt-pp → leap.

learn [lɜːn] vt-vi aprender.

learner ['lɜːnəʳ] n estudiante.

learnt [lɜːnt] pt-pp → learn.

lease [liːs] n vt arrendar.

leash [liːʃ] n correa.

least [liːst] adj más mínimo, -a, menor. ► adv menos. • **at least** por lo menos.

leather ['leðəʳ] n piel, cuero.

leave[1] [liːv] vt **1** dejar *(gen)*. **2** salir de *(lugar)*. ► vi salir, marcharse, irse. • **to be left** quedar.

lecture ['lektʃəʳ] n **1** conferencia. **2** clase *(en universidad)*.

lecturer ['lektʃərəʳ] n **1** conferenciante. **2** profesor,-ra *(universitario)*.

led [led] pt-pp → lead.

leech [liːtʃ] n sanguijuela.

leek [liːk] *n* puerro.
left[1] [left] *adj* izquierdo,-a. ►
n izquierda. ► *adv* a la izquierda, hacia la izquierda.
left[2] [left] *pt-pp* → leave.
left-handed [left'hændɪd] *adj* zurdo,-a.
left-luggage office [left-'lʌgɪdʒ ɒfɪs] *n* consigna.
leftover *adj* sobrante.
leg [leg] *n* **1** pierna. **2** pata. **3** muslo *(de pollo)*.
legal [ˈliːgəl] *adj* legal.
legend [ˈledʒənd] *n* leyenda.
leggings [ˈlegɪnz] *npl* mallas.
legitimate [lɪˈdʒɪtɪmət] *adj* legítimo,-a.
leisure [ˈleʒəʳ] *n* ocio.
lemon [ˈlemən] *n* limón.
lemonade [leməˈneɪd] *n* limonada.
lend [lend] *vt* dejar, prestar.
length [lenθ] *n* **1** largo, longitud. **2** duración.
lens [lenz] *n* **1** lente *(de gafas)*. **2** objetivo *(de cámara)*.
lent [lent] *pt-pp* → lend.
Lent [lent] *n* Cuaresma.
lentil [ˈlentɪl] *n* lenteja.
leopard [ˈlepəd] *n* leopardo.
leotard [ˈliːətɑːd] *n* malla.
less [les] *adj-adv-prep* menos.
lesson [ˈlesən] *n* lección, clase.
let [let] *vt* **1** dejar. **2** arrendar, alquilar: *"To let"*, "Se alquila". ► *aux*: *let's go!*, ¡vamos!
to let in *vt* dejar entrar.

to let out *vt* **1** dejar salir, soltar. **2** alquilar.
letter [ˈletəʳ] *n* **1** letra. **2** carta. ■ **letter box** buzón.
lettuce [ˈletɪs] *n* lechuga.
level [ˈlevəl] *adj* **1** llano,-a. **2** nivelado,-a. **3** empatado,-a. ► *vt* nivelar. ■ **level crossing** GB paso a nivel.
lever [ˈliːvəʳ] *n* palanca.
levy [ˈlevɪ] *n* recaudación. ► *vt* recaudar.
liability [laɪəˈbɪlɪtɪ] *n* responsabilidad. ► *npl* **liabilities** COMM pasivo.
liar [ˈlaɪəʳ] *n* mentiroso,-a.
liberal [ˈlɪbərəl] *adj* liberal.
liberate [ˈlɪbəreɪt] *vt* liberar.
liberty [ˈlɪbətɪ] *n* libertad.
library [ˈlaɪbrərɪ] *n* biblioteca.
lice [laɪs] *npl* → louse.
licence [ˈlaɪsəns] *n* GB licencia, permiso.
license [ˈlaɪsəns] *vt* autorizar. ► *n* US licencia, permiso.
lick [lɪk] *n* lamedura, lametón. ► *vt* lamer.
licorice [ˈlɪkərɪs] *n* US regaliz.
lid [lɪd] *n* tapa, tapadera.
lie[1] [laɪ] *n* mentira: *to tell lies*, decir mentiras. ► *vi* mentir.
lie[2] [laɪ] *vi* **1** acostarse, tumbarse. **2** estar situado,-a, encontrarse.
to lie back *vi* recostarse.
to lie down *vi* acostarse.
lieutenant [lefˈtenənt] *n* teniente.

life [laɪf] n vida. • **for life** para toda la vida. ▪ **life belt** salvavidas; **life imprisonment** cadena perpetua; **life jacket** chaleco salvavidas; **life sentence** cadena perpetua.

life-boat ['laɪfbəʊt] n bote salvavidas.

lifeguard ['laɪfgɑːd] n socorrista.

lifestyle ['laɪfstaɪl] n estilo de vida.

lifetime ['laɪftaɪm] n vida.

lift [lɪft] n GB ascensor. ▶ vt-vi levantar.• **to give SB a lift** llevar a ALGN en coche.

light¹ [laɪt] n **1** luz. **2** fuego *(para cigarrillo)*. ▶ vt-vi encender(se). ▶ vt iluminar, alumbrar. ▶ adj claro,-a. ▪ **light bulb** bombilla.

light² [laɪt] adj ligero,-a.

lighter ['laɪtəʳ] n encendedor.

lighthouse ['laɪthaʊs] n faro.

lighting ['laɪtɪŋ] n **1** iluminación. **2** alumbrado.

lightning ['laɪtənɪŋ] n rayo, relámpago.

like¹ [laɪk] adj semejante, parecido,-a. ▶ prep como. • **like this** así.

like² [laɪk] vt gustar: *I like wine*, me gusta el vino. • **as you like** como quieras.

likeable ['laɪkəbəl] adj simpático,-a, agradable.

likelihood ['laɪklɪhʊd] n probabilidad.

likely ['laɪklɪ] adj probable.

lily ['lɪlɪ] n lirio, azucena.

limb [lɪm] n miembro.

lime¹ [laɪm] n cal.

lime² [laɪm] n lima *(fruto)*.

lime³ [laɪm] n tilo *(árbol)*.

limit ['lɪmɪt] n límite. ▶ vt limitar.

limited ['lɪmɪtɪd] adj limitado, -a. ▪ **limited company** sociedad anónima.

limp¹ [lɪmp] n cojera. ▶ vi cojear.

limp² [lɪmp] adj flojo,-a.

limpet ['lɪmpɪt] n lapa.

line¹ [laɪn] n **1** línea. **2** raya *(en papel)*. **3** cuerda, cordel. **4** sedal *(de pesca)*. **5** US cola. **6** tendedero. ▶ vt alinear.

line² [laɪn] vt forrar.

lined [laɪnd] adj forrado,-a.

linen ['lɪnɪn] n **1** lino. **2** ropa blanca.

liner ['laɪnəʳ] n transatlántico.

linesman ['laɪnzmən] n juez de línea.

lingerie ['lɑːnʒərɪː] n lencería.

lining ['laɪnɪŋ] n forro.

link [lɪŋk] vt unir, conectar. ▶ n **1** eslabón *(de cadena)*. **2** enlace, conexión. ▶ npl **links** campo de golf.

linkage ['lɪŋkɪdʒ] n conexión.

lion ['laɪən] n león.

lioness ['laɪənəs] n leona.

lip [lɪp] n labio.

lipstick ['lɪpstɪk] n pintalabios, lápiz de labios.

liqueur [lɪˈkjʊəʳ] *n* licor.

liquid [ˈlɪkwɪd] *adj* líquido,-a.
► *n* líquido.

liquor [ˈlɪkəʳ] *n* alcohol, bebida alcohólica.

liquorice [ˈlɪkərɪs] *n* GB regaliz.

list [lɪst] *n* lista. ► *vt* hacer una lista de.

listen [ˈlɪsən] *vi* escuchar.

listener [ˈlɪsənəʳ] *n* oyente.

lit [lɪt] *pt-pp* → light.

literal [ˈlɪtərəl] *adj* literal.

literature [ˈlɪtərɪtʃəʳ] *n* literatura.

litre [ˈliːtəʳ] (US **liter**) *n* litro.

litter [ˈlɪtəʳ] *n* 1 basura, papeles. 2 camada.

little [ˈlɪtəl] *adj* 1 pequeño,-a. 2 poco,-a. ► *pron* poco. ► *adv* poco.

live¹ [lɪv] *vt-vi* vivir.

live² [laɪv] *adj* 1 vivo,-a. 2 en directo *(programa, transmisión)*.

to live on *vt* vivir de, alimentarse de. ► *vi* sobrevivir.

lively [ˈlaɪvlɪ] *adj* animado,-a.

liven up [laɪvənˈʌp] *vt-vi* animar(se).

liver [ˈlɪvəʳ] *n* hígado.

livestock [ˈlaɪvstɒk] *n* ganado.

living [ˈlɪvɪŋ] *adj* vivo,-a. ► *n* medio de vida: *what do you do for a living?*, ¿cómo te ganas la vida? ■ **living room** sala de estar.

lizard [ˈlɪzəd] *n* lagarto *(grande)*, lagartija *(pequeño)*.

llama [ˈlɑːmə] *n* llama.

load [ləʊd] *n* carga. ► *vt-vi* cargar. ● **loads of...** montones de…

loaf [ləʊf] *n* pan, barra.

loan [ləʊn] *n* préstamo. ► *vt* prestar.

loathe [ləʊð] *vt* detestar.

lobby [ˈlɒbɪ] *n* 1 vestíbulo. 2 POL grupo de presión.

lobe [ləʊb] *n* lóbulo.

lobster [ˈlɒbstəʳ] *n* bogavante. ■ **spiny lobster** langosta.

local [ˈləʊkəl] *adj* local.

loch [lɒk] *n* lago.

lock¹ [lɒk] *n* 1 cerradura *(de puerta)*. 2 esclusa *(en canal)*. ► *vt* cerrar con llave.

lock² [lɒk] *n* mecha, mechón.

locker [ˈlɒkəʳ] *n* taquilla, armario.

locksmith [ˈlɒksmɪθ] *n* cerrajero.

locomotive [ləʊkəˈməʊtɪv] *n* locomotora.

locust [ˈləʊkəst] *n* langosta.

lodge [lɒdʒ] *vi* alojarse, hospedarse. ► *vt* presentar *(queja)*.

lodging [ˈlɒdʒɪŋ] *n* alojamiento.

loft [lɒft] *n* desván.

log [lɒg] *n* 1 tronco *(para fuego)*. 2 COMPUT registro. ► *vt* registrar, anotar.

to log in/log on *vi* COMPUT entrar *(en sistema)*.

to log off/log out *vi* COMPUT salir *(del sistema)*.

logical ['lɒdʒɪkəl] *adj* lógico,-a.

loin [lɔɪn] *n* **1** lomo *(de cerdo)*. **2** solomillo *(de ternera)*.

lollipop ['lɒlɪpɒp] *n* **1** piruleta, pirulí. **2** polo.

loneliness ['ləʊnlɪnəs] *n* soledad.

lonely ['ləʊnlɪ] *adj* solitario,-a.

long[1] [lɒŋ] *adj* largo,-a. ► *adv* **1** mucho, mucho tiempo. **2 no longer, not any longer:** *she doesn't work here any longer*, ya no trabaja aquí. ● **as long as** mientras, con tal de que; **so long** hasta la vista. ■ **long jump** salto de longitud.

long[2] [lɒŋ] *vi* **to long for** anhelar.

long-distance [lɒŋ'dɪstəns] *adj* **1** de larga distancia *(llamada)*. **2** de fondo *(corredor)*.

longing ['lɒŋɪŋ] *n* **1** ansia, anhelo. **2** nostalgia.

longitude ['lɒndʒɪtjuːd] *n* longitud.

long-playing [lɒŋ'pleɪɪŋ] *adj* de larga duración.

long-range [lɒŋ'reɪndʒ] *adj* **1** de largo alcance *(distancia)*. **2** a largo plazo *(tiempo)*.

long-sighted [lɒŋ'saɪtɪd] *adj* hipermétrope.

loo [luː] *n fam* wáter, servicio.

look [lʊk] *vi* **1** mirar. **2** parecer: *it looks easy*, parece fácil. ► *n* **1** mirada, vistazo. **2** aspecto, apariencia.

to look after *vt* **1** ocuparse de. **2** cuidar.

to look at *vt* mirar.

to look for *vt* buscar.

to look forward to *vt* esperar *(con ansia)*.

to look like *vt* **1** parecer: *what does Sarah look like?*, ¿cómo es Sarah? **2** parecerse a: *he looks like his father*, se parece a su padre.

lookalike ['lʊkəlaɪk] *n* doble.

lookout ['lʊkaʊt] *n* **1** vigía. **2** atalaya.

loop [luːp] *n* **1** lazo. **2** curva. **3** COMPUT bucle.

loose [luːs] *adj* **1** suelto,-a. **2** flojo,-a. ► *vt* soltar.

loosen ['luːsən] *vt-vi* soltar(se), aflojar(se).

loot [luːt] *n* botín.

lop [lɒp] *vt* podar.

lord [lɔːd] *n* **1** señor. **2** lord. ● **the Lord's Prayer** el padrenuestro.

lorry ['lɒrɪ] *n* camión.

lose [luːz] *vt-vi* **1** perder. **2** atrasarse *(reloj)*.

loser ['luːzəʳ] *n* perdedor,-a.

loss [lɒs] *n* pérdida.

lost [lɒst] *pt-pp* → lose. ► *adj* perdido,-a. ● **to get lost** perderse. ■ **lost property** objetos perdidos.

lot [lɒt] *n* **1** US solar, terreno. **2** lote *(en subasta)*. **3** cantidad: *a lot*, mucho, muchísimo.

lotion ['ləʊʃən] *n* loción.

macaroni

lottery ['lɒtərɪ] n lotería.
loud [laud] adj **1** fuerte (sonido). **2** alto,-a (voz). ► adv fuerte, alto.
loudspeaker [laud'spi:kəʳ] n altavoz.
lounge [laundʒ] n salón, sala de estar.
louse [laus] n piojo.
love [lʌv] n **1** amor. **2** cero (en tenis). ► vt **1** amar, querer. **2** gustar: *I love fish*, me encanta el pescado. • **to be in love with** estar enamorado,-a de.
lovely ['lʌvlɪ] adj encantador, -ra.
low [ləʊ] adj bajo,-a. ► adv bajo. ■ **low tide** bajamar.
lower ['ləʊəʳ] adj inferior. ► vt bajar.
low-necked [ləʊ'nekt] adj escotado,-a.
loyal ['lɔɪəl] adj leal, fiel.
lozenge ['lɒzɪndʒ] n **1** rombo. **2** pastilla para la tos.
lubricant ['lu:brɪkənt] n lubricante.
luck [lʌk] n suerte.
lucky ['lʌkɪ] adj afortunado, -a, con suerte. • **to be lucky** tener suerte. ■ **lucky charm** amuleto.
luggage ['lʌgɪdʒ] n equipaje. ■ **luggage rack** portaequipajes.
lull [lʌl] n momento de calma. ► vt adormecer, arrullar.
lullaby ['lʌləbaɪ] n canción de cuna, nana.

lumberjack ['lʌmbədʒæk] n leñador.
lump [lʌmp] n **1** pedazo, trozo. **2** terrón (de azúcar). **3** bulto (en cuerpo). **4** grumo (en salsa).
lunar ['lu:nəʳ] adj lunar.
lunch [lʌntʃ] n comida. ► vi comer.
luncheon ['lʌntʃən] n fml almuerzo.
lung [lʌŋ] n pulmón.
lurch [lɜːtʃ] n bandazo. ► vi **1** dar bandazos. **2** tambalearse.
lure [ljʊəʳ] n **1** señuelo. **2** fig atractivo. ► vt atraer.
lurid ['ljʊərɪd] adj **1** chillón, -ona (color). **2** horripilante, espeluznante (detalles).
lush [lʌʃ] adj exuberante.
lust [lʌst] n lujuria.
luxury ['lʌkʃərɪ] n lujo.
lynch [lɪntʃ] vt linchar.
lynx [lɪŋks] n lince.
lyric ['lɪrɪk] adj lírico,-a. ► npl **lyrics** letra (de canción).

M

mac [mæk] n impermeable.
macabre [mə'kɑːbrə] adj macabro,-a.
macaroni [mækə'rəʊnɪ] n macarrones.

machine [mə'ʃiːn] n máquina, aparato. ∎ **machine gun** ametralladora.

mackerel ['mækrəl] n caballa.

mackintosh ['mækɪntɒʃ] n impermeable.

mad [mæd] adj 1 loco,-a. 2 furioso,-a, muy enfadado,-a (persona).

madam ['mædəm] n fml señora.

madden ['mædən] vt enfurecer.

made [meɪd] pt-pp → make.

madness ['mædnəs] n locura.

magazine [mægə'ziːn] n revista.

maggot ['mægət] n larva.

magic ['mædʒɪk] n magia. ▶ adj mágico,-a.

magician [mə'dʒɪʃən] n mago,-a.

magnet ['mægnət] n imán.

magnetic [mæg'netɪk] adj magnético,-a. ∎ **magnetic tape** cinta magnética.

magnify ['mægnɪfaɪ] vt aumentar, ampliar.

magnifying glass ['mægnɪfaɪɪŋglɑːs] n lupa.

magnitude ['mægnɪtjuːd] n magnitud.

mahogany [mə'hɒgəni] n caoba.

maid [meɪd] n 1 criada, sirvienta. 2 camarera (en hotel). ∎ **maid of honour** dama de honor.

maiden ['meɪdən] ▶ adj 1 soltera. 2 inaugural. ∎ **maiden name** apellido de soltera.

mail [meɪl] n correo. ▶ vt US echar al buzón. ∎ **mail order** venta por correo.

mailbox ['meɪlbɒks] n US buzón.

mailman ['meɪlmæn] n US cartero.

main [meɪn] adj principal. ▶ n 1 tubería principa. 2 red eléctrica. ∎ **main beam** viga maestra; **main office** oficina central; **main street** calle mayor.

maintain [meɪn'teɪn] vt mantener.

maintenance ['meɪntənəns] n 1 mantenimiento. 2 pensión alimenticia.

maisonette [meɪzə'net] n dúplex.

maize [meɪz] n maíz.

majesty ['mædʒəsti] n majestad.

major ['meɪdʒər] adj principal. ▶ n comandante.

majority [mə'dʒɒrɪti] n mayoría.

make [meɪk] vt 1 hacer. 2 ganar: *how much do you make a year?*, ¿cuánto ganas al año? ▶ n marca.

to make up vt 1 inventar. 2 hacer, preparar (cama, paquete). 3 maquillar. ▶ vi maquillarse.

maker ['meɪkə'] n fabricante.
make-up ['meɪkʌp] n 1 maquillaje. 2 composición. ▪ **make-up remover** desmaquillador.
malaria [mə'leərɪə] n malaria.
male [meɪl] adj-n macho. ► adj 1 varón. 2 masculino,-a. ▪ **male chauvinism** machismo.
malfunction [mæl'fʌŋkʃən] n funcionamiento defectuoso.
malice ['mælɪs] n malicia.
malignant [mə'lɪgnənt] adj maligno,-a.
malt [mɔːlt] n malta.
mammal ['mæməl] n mamífero.
mammoth ['mæməθ] n mamut.
man [mæn] n hombre. ► vt 1 tripular (nave). 2 servir.
manage ['mænɪdʒ] vt 1 dirigir (negocio). 2 administrar (propiedad). ► vi 1 poder. 2 arreglárselas. 3 conseguir.
management ['mænɪdʒmənt] n dirección, administración, gestión.
manager ['mænɪdʒə'] n 1 director,-ra, gerente (de empresa). 2 administrador,-ra (de propiedad). 3 entrenador (de deportista).
manageress [mænɪdʒə'res] n directora, gerente.
mane [meɪn] n 1 crin (de caballo). 2 melena (de león).

mango ['mæŋgəʊ] n mango.
manhood ['mænhʊd] n 1 madurez. 2 hombría.
mania ['meɪnɪə] n manía.
manicure ['mænɪkjʊə'] n manicura.
manipulate [mə'nɪpjʊleɪt] vt manipular.
mankind [mæn'kaɪnd] n el género humano.
manly ['mænlɪ] adj viril.
man-made [mæn'meɪd] adj 1 artificial. 2 sintético,-a.
manner ['mænə'] n manera, modo. ► npl **manners** modales. ● **in this manner** de esta manera, así; **to be bad manners** ser de mala educación.
mannerism ['mænərɪzəm] n peculiaridad.
manoeuvre [mə'nuːvə'] (US **maneuver**) n maniobra. ► vt-vi maniobrar.
manor ['mænə'] n señorío. ▪ **manor house** casa solariega.
manpower ['mænpaʊə'] n mano de obra.
mansion ['mænʃən] n mansión.
manual ['mænjʊəl] adj-n manual.
manufacture [mænjʊ'fæktʃə'] n fabricación, manufactura. ► vt 1 fabricar, manufacturar.
manufacturer [mænjʊ'fæktʃərə'] n fabricante.
manure [mə'njʊə'] n abono, estiércol.

many ['menɪ] adj-pron mu-chos,-as. • **as many ... as** tan-tos,-as ... como; **how many?** ¿cuántos,-as?; **not many** po-cos,-as; **too many** demasia-dos,-as.

map [mæp] n **1** mapa (de país, región). **2** plano (de ciudad).

maple ['meɪpəl] n arce.

marathon ['mærəθən] n ma-ratón.

marble ['maːbəl] n **1** már-mol. **2** canica.

march [maːtʃ] n marcha. ► vi marchar, caminar.

to march past vi desfilar.

March [maːtʃ] n marzo.

mare [meəʳ] n yegua.

margarine [maːdʒəˈriːn] n margarina.

margin ['maːdʒɪn] n margen.

marginal ['maːdʒɪnəl] adj mar-ginal.

marine [məˈriːn] adj marino, -a, marítimo,-a. ► n soldado de infantería de marina.

marionette [mærɪəˈnet] n ma-rioneta.

marital ['mærɪtəl] adj matri-monial. ▪ **marital status** es-tado civil.

maritime ['mærɪtaɪm] adj ma-rítimo,-a.

mark [maːk] n **1** marca, señal. **2** mancha. **3** nota. ► vt **1** marcar. **2** corregir, puntuar. • **on your marks!** ¡prepara-dos!

marker ['maːkəʳ] n rotulador.

market ['maːkɪt] n mercado.

marketing ['maːkɪtɪŋ] n már-keting, mercadotecnia.

marmalade ['maːməleɪd] n mermelada (de cítricos).

marquee [maːˈkiː] n carpa.

marriage ['mærɪdʒ] n **1** ma-trimonio. **2** boda.

married ['mærɪd] adj casado,-a. • **to get married** casarse.

marrow ['mærəʊ] n **1** tué-tano, médula. **2** GB calabacín.

marry ['mærɪ] vt-vi casar(se).

marsh [maːʃ] n **1** pantano, ciénaga. **2** marisma.

marshal ['maːʃəl] n **1** maris-cal. **2** US jefe,-a de policía.

martial ['maːʃəl] adj marcial.

martyr ['maːtəʳ] n mártir.

marvellous ['maːvələs] adj maravilloso,-a.

mascara [mæˈskaːrə] n rímel.

mascot ['mæskɒt] n mascota.

masculine ['maːskjʊlɪn] adj masculino,-a. ► n masculino.

mash [mæʃ] vt triturar. ► n fam puré de patatas.

mask [maːsk] n **1** máscara. **2** mascarilla. ▪ **masked ball** baile de disfraces.

mason ['meɪsən] n albañil.

mass[1] [mæs] n masa. • **to mass produce** fabricar en serie. ▪ **mass media** medios de comunicación de masas; **mass production** fabrica-ción en serie.

mass² [mæs] *n* misa.

massacre ['mæsəkə'] *n* masacre.

massage ['mæsɑːʒ] *n* masaje. ► *vt* dar masajes a.

massive ['mæsɪv] *adj* **1** macizo,-a, sólido,-a. **2** enorme.

mast [mɑːst] *n* mástil.

master ['mɑːstə'] *n* **1** señor, amo, dueño. **2** maestro. ► *vt* dominar. ▪ **master key** llave maestra.

masterpiece ['mɑːstəpiːs] *n* obra maestra.

mat [mæt] *n* **1** alfombrilla, felpudo. **2** salvamanteles.

match¹ [mætʃ] *n* cerilla.

match² [mætʃ] *n* partido. ► *vt-vi* hacer juego (con).

matchbox ['mætʃbɒks] *n* caja de cerillas.

mate¹ [meɪt] *n* mate *(en ajedrez)*.

mate² [meɪt] *n* **1** compañero, -a, colega. **2** pareja *(persona)*. **3** macho, hembra *(animal)*. ► *vt-vi* aparear(se).

material [mə'tɪərɪəl] *adj-n* material.

maternity [mə'tɜːnɪtɪ] *n* maternidad. ▪ **maternity leave** baja por maternidad.

mathematics [mæθə'mætɪks] *n* matemáticas.

matt [mæt] *adj* mate.

matter ['mætə'] *n* **1** materia. **2** asunto, cuestión. ► *vi* importar. • **as a matter of fact** en realidad; **it's a matter of...** es cuestión de...; **no matter...**: *I never win, no matter what I do*, nunca gano, haga lo que haga; **the matter**: *what's the matter?*, ¿qué pasa?

mattress ['mætrəs] *n* colchón.

mature [mə'tʃʊə'] *adj* maduro,-a. ► *vt-vi* madurar.

maximum ['mæksɪməm] *adj* máximo,-a. ► *n* máximo.

may [meɪ] *aux* poder: *he may come*, es posible que venga, puede que venga; *may I go?*, ¿puedo irme?

May [meɪ] *n* mayo.

maybe ['meɪbiː] *adv* quizá, quizás, tal vez.

mayonnaise [meɪə'neɪz] *n* mayonesa, mahonesa.

mayor [meə'] *n* alcalde.

maze [meɪz] *n* laberinto.

me [miː] *pron* **1** me, mí. **2** yo: *it's me!*, ¡soy yo! • **with me** conmigo.

meadow ['medəʊ] *n* prado.

meagre ['miːgə'] (US **meager**) *adj* escaso,-a.

meal [miːl] *n* comida.

mean¹ [miːn] *adj* tacaño,-a.

mean² [miːn] *vt* **1** querer decir, significar. **2** querer, tener intención de: *I didn't mean to do it*, lo hice sin querer.

mean³ [miːn] *n* media.

meaning ['miːnɪŋ] *n* sentido, significado.

means [miːnz] *npl* medios, recursos económicos. • **by all means!** ¡naturalmente!; **by no means** de ninguna manera. ▪ **means of transport** medio de transporte.

meant [ment] *pt-pp* → mean.

meantime ['miːntaɪm] *phr.* **in the meantime** mientras tanto.

meanwhile ['miːnwaɪl] *adv* mientras tanto, entretanto.

measles ['miːzəlz] *n* sarampión. ▪ **German measles** rubeola.

measure ['meʒəʳ] *n* **1** medida. **2** MUS compás. ▶ *vt* medir.

measurement ['meʒəmənt] *n* **1** medición. **2** medida.

meat [miːt] *n* carne.

meatball ['miːtbɔːl] *n* albóndiga.

mechanic [mɪˈkænɪk] *n* mecánico,-a.

mechanism ['mekənɪzəm] *n* mecanismo.

medal ['medəl] *n* medalla.

meddle ['medəl] *vi* entrometerse.

media ['miːdɪə] *npl* medios de comunicación.

medical ['medɪkəl] *adj* médico,-a. ▶ *n fam* chequeo. ▪ **medical record** historial médico.

medicine ['medɪsɪn] *n* **1** medicina. **2** medicamento.

mediocre [miːdɪˈəʊkəʳ] *adj* mediocre.

medium ['miːdɪəm] *n* medio. ▶ *adj* mediano,-a.

meet [miːt] *vt* **1** encontrar, encontrarse con *(por casualidad)*. **2** reunirse con, verse con. **3** conocer. ▶ *vi* **1** encontrarse. **2** reunirse, verse. • **pleased to meet you!** ¡encantado,-a de conocerle!

meeting ['miːtɪŋ] *n* **1** reunión. **2** POL mítin. **3** encuentro. ▪ **meeting point** lugar de encuentro.

megaphone ['megəfəʊn] *n* megáfono.

mellow ['meləʊ] *adj* **1** maduro,-a *(fruta)*. **2** suave *(color, voz)*.

melody ['melədɪ] *n* melodía.

melon ['melən] *n* melón.

melt [melt] *vt-vi* **1** derretir(se) *(hielo, nieve)*. **2** fundir(se) *(metal)*.

member ['membəʳ] *n* **1** miembro. **2** socio,-a *(de club)*.

memorandum [meməˈrændəm] *n* memorándum.

memory ['memərɪ] *n* **1** memoria. **2** recuerdo. ▪ **memory card** tarjeta de memoria.

men [men] *npl* → man.

menace ['menəs] *n* amenaza.

mend [mend] *n* remiendo. ▶ *vt* **1** reparar, arreglar. **2** remendar *(ropa)*

menstruation [menstrʊˈeɪʃən] *n* menstruación.

menswear ['menzweəʳ] *n* ropa de caballero.

mental ['mentəl] *adj* mental.
mention ['menʃən] *n* mención. ▶ *vt* mencionar.
menu ['menjuː] *n* **1** carta *(en restaurante)*. **2** COMPUT menú.
merchandise ['mɜːtʃəndaɪz] *n* mercancías, géneros.
merchant ['mɜːtʃənt] *n* comerciante.
mercy ['mɜːsɪ] *n* misericordia, compasión. • **at the mercy of** a la merced de.
mere [mɪəʳ] *adj* mero,-a.
merge [mɜːdʒ] *vt* unir, empalmar *(carreteras)*. ▶ *vt-vi* fusionar(se) *(empresas)*.
merger ['mɜːdʒəʳ] *n* fusión.
meringue [məˈræŋ] *n* merengue.
merit ['merɪt] *n* mérito. ▶ *vt* merecer.
mermaid ['mɜːmeɪd] *n* sirena.
merry ['merɪ] *adj* alegre. • **Merry Christmas!** ¡Feliz Navidad!
merry-go-round ['merɪɡəʊraʊnd] *n* tiovivo, caballitos.
mesh [meʃ] *n* malla.
mess [mes] *n* desorden, lío.
to mess about/around *vi* gandulear.
to mess up *vt* **1** *fam* desordenar *(habitación)*. **2** estropear *(planes)*.
message ['mesɪdʒ] *n* mensaje.
messenger ['mesɪndʒəʳ] *n* mensajero,-a.
met [met] *pt-pp* → meet.

metabolism [meˈtæbəlɪzəm] *n* metabolismo.
metal ['metəl] *n* metal. ▶ *adj* metálico,-a, de metal.
meteorite ['miːtɪəraɪt] *n* meteorito.
meter[1] ['miːtəʳ] *n* US → metre.
meter[2] ['miːtəʳ] *n* contador.
method ['meθəd] *n* método.
metre ['miːtəʳ] (US **meter**) *n* metro.
mew [mjuː] *n* maullido.
mezzanine ['mezəniːn] *n* entresuelo.
miaow [mɪˈaʊ] *vi* maullar.
mice [maɪs] *npl* → mouse.
microbe ['maɪkrəʊb] *n* microbio.
microchip ['maɪkrəʊtʃɪp] *n* microchip.
microphone ['maɪkrəfəʊn] *n* micrófono.
microprocessor [maɪkrəʊˈprəʊsesəʳ] *n* microprocesador.
microscope ['maɪkrəskəʊp] *n* microscopio.
microwave ['maɪkrəʊweɪv] *n* microondas *(horno)*.
midday [mɪd'deɪ] *n* mediodía.
middle ['mɪdəl] *adj* del medio, central. ▶ *n* **1** medio, centro *(de habitación)*. **2** mitad. ▪ **middle age** mediana edad; **middle class** clase media.
middleman ['mɪdəlmən] *n* intermediario.
midnight ['mɪdnaɪt] *n* medianoche.

midway ['mɪdweɪ] *adv* a medio camino.

midwife ['mɪdwaɪf] *n* comadrona.

might [maɪt] *aux* → may.

migraine ['maɪgreɪn] *n* jaqueca, migraña.

migrate [mə'greɪt] *vi* emigrar.

mild [maɪld] *adj* **1** apacible *(persona)*. **2** suave *(clima)*.

mile [maɪl] *n* milla.

milestone ['maɪlstəʊn] *n* hito.

military ['mɪlɪtərɪ] *adj* militar.

milk [mɪlk] *n* leche. ■ **milk chocolate** chocolate con leche; **milk shake** batido.

mill [mɪl] *n* **1** molino. **2** molinillo *(de café)*. **3** fábrica. ▶ *vt* moler.

millimetre ['mɪlɪmiːtə'] (US **millimeter**) *n* milímetro.

million ['mɪljən] *n* millón.

mime [maɪm] *n* **1** mímica. **2** mimo *(persona)*.

mimic ['mɪmɪk] *vt* imitar.

mince [mɪns] *n* GB carne picada. ▶ *vt* picar.

mind [maɪnd] *n* mente. ▶ *vt* **1** hacer caso de. **2** cuidar. **3** tener cuidado con. ▶ *vt-vi* importar. ● **never mind** no importa, da igual; **to change one's mind** cambiar de opinión; **to have STH in mind** estar pensando en algo; **to make up one's mind** decidirse.

mine¹ [maɪn] *n* mina.

mine² [maɪn] *pron* (el) mío, (la) mía, (los) míos, (las) mías.

miner ['maɪnə'] *n* minero,-a.

mineral ['mɪnərəl] *adj* mineral. ▶ *n* mineral.

minimum ['mɪnɪməm] *adj* mínimo,-a. ▶ *n* mínimo.

minister ['mɪnɪstə'] *n* **1** ministro,-a. **2** pastor,-ra *(cura)*.

ministry ['mɪnɪstrɪ] *n* **1** ministerio. **2** sacerdocio.

mink [mɪŋk] *n* visón.

minor ['maɪnə'] *adj* de poca importancia. ▶ *n* menor de edad.

minority [maɪ'nɒrɪtɪ] *n* minoría. ▶ *adj* minoritario,-a.

mint¹ [mɪnt] *vt* acuñar.

mint² [mɪnt] *n* menta.

minus ['maɪnəs] *prep* menos: **minus five degrees**, cinco grados bajo cero.

minute¹ ['mɪnɪt] *adj* diminuto,-a.

minute² ['mɪnɪt] *n* minuto. ■ **minute hand** minutero.

miracle ['mɪrəkəl] *n* milagro.

mirage ['mɪrɑːʒ] *n* espejismo.

mirror ['mɪrə'] *n* espejo; retrovisor *(de coche)*.

miscarriage [mɪs'kærɪdʒ] *n* aborto *(espontáneo)*.

miscellaneous [mɪsɪ'leɪnɪəs] *adj* diverso,-a, variado,-a.

mischievous ['mɪstʃɪvəs] *adj* travieso,-a.

misdemeanour [mɪsdɪ'miːnə'] (US **misdemeanor**) *n* **1** fechoría. **2** delito menor.

miserable ['mɪzərəbəl] *adj* **1** triste. **2** desagradable *(tiempo)*. **3** miserable.

misery ['mɪzərɪ] *n* **1** tristeza, desdicha. **2** miseria.

misfire [mɪs'faɪə'] *vi* fallar.

misfortune [mɪs'fɔːtʃən] *n* infortunio, desgracia.

mishap ['mɪshæp] *n* percance.

misjudge [mɪs'dʒʌdʒ] *vt* juzgar mal.

mislaid [mɪs'leɪd] *pt-pp* → mislay.

mislay [mɪs'leɪ] *vt* extraviar.

mislead [mɪs'liːd] *vt* engañar.

misled [mɪs'led] *pt-pp* → mislead.

misprint ['mɪsprɪnt] *n* errata.

miss¹ [mɪs] *n* señorita.

miss² [mɪs] *n* fallo. ► *vt-vi* fallar. ► *vt* **1** perder: *he missed the train*, perdió el tren. **2** no oír, no entender, no ver. **3** echar de menos, añorar. **4** echar en falta. ► *vi* faltar.

missile ['mɪsaɪl] *n* misil. ■ **missile launcher** lanzamisiles.

missing ['mɪsɪŋ] *adj* **1** perdido,-a *(objeto)*. **2** desaparecido, -a *(persona)*.

mission ['mɪʃən] *n* misión.

missionary ['mɪʃənərɪ] *n* misionero,-a.

mistake [mɪs'teɪk] *n* error. ► *vt* **1** entender mal. **2** confundir. ● **by mistake** por error, por equivocación; **to make a mistake** equivocarse.

mister ['mɪstə'] *n* señor.

mistletoe ['mɪzəltəʊ] *n* muérdago.

mistook [mɪs'tʊk] *pt* → mistake.

mistreat [mɪs'triːt] *vt* maltratar.

mistress ['mɪstrəs] *n* **1** ama, señora. **2** profesora. **3** amante.

mistrust [mɪs'trʌst] *n* desconfianza, recelo. ► *vt* desconfiar de.

misunderstand [mɪsʌndə'stænd] *vt-vi* entender mal.

misunderstanding [mɪsʌndə'stændɪŋ] *n* malentendido.

misunderstood [mɪsʌndə'stʊd] *pt-pp* → misunderstand.

misuse [*(n)* mɪs'juːs, *(vb)* mɪs'juːz] *n* **1** mal uso. **2** abuso *(de poder)*. ► *vt* **1** emplear mal. **2** abusar de *(de poder)*.

mitten ['mɪtən] *n* manopla.

mix [mɪks] *n* mezcla. ► *vt-vi* mezclar(se).

mixed [mɪkst] *adj* **1** variado, -a. **2** mixto,-a *(de ambos sexos)*.

mixer ['mɪksə'] *n* batidora.

mixture ['mɪkstʃə'] *n* mezcla.

moan [məʊn] *n* gemido, quejido. ► *vi* gemir.

moat [məʊt] *n* foso.

mobile ['məʊbaɪl] *adj-n* móvil. ■ **mobile home** caravana, remolque; **mobile phone** móvil, teléfono móvil.

moccasin ['mɒkəsɪn] *n* mocasín.

mock [mɒk] *adj* **1** falso, de imitación. **2** de prueba, simulado,-a. ► *vt-vi* burlarse (de).

mockery ['mɒkərɪ] *n* burla.

model ['mɒdəl] *n* modelo. ∎ **model home** US casa piloto.

modem ['məʊdəm] *n* módem.

moderate ['mɒdərət] *adj* moderado,-a. ► *vt-vi* moderar(se).

modern ['mɒdən] *adj* **1** moderno,-a.

modest ['mɒdɪst] *adj* modesto,-a.

modify ['mɒdɪfaɪ] *vt* modificar.

module ['mɒdjuːl] *n* módulo.

moist [mɔɪst] *adj* húmedo,-a.

moisture ['mɔɪstʃəʳ] *n* humedad.

mold [məʊld] *n* US → mould.

mole¹ [məʊl] *n* lunar.

mole² [məʊl] *n* topo *(animal)*.

molecule ['mɒləkjuːl] *n* molécula.

molest [məˈlest] *vt* **1** hostigar, acosar. **2** agredir sexualmente.

moment ['məʊmənt] *n* momento. ∙ **just a moment** un momento.

monarchy ['mɒnəkɪ] *n* monarquía.

monastery ['mɒnəstərɪ] *n* monasterio.

Monday ['mʌndɪ] *n* lunes.

money ['mʌnɪ] *n* dinero. ∎ **money order** giro postal.

moneybox ['mʌnɪbɒks] *n* hucha.

monitor ['mɒnɪtəʳ] *n* monitor.

monk [mʌŋk] *n* monje.

monkey ['mʌŋkɪ] *n* mono. ∎ **monkey wrench** llave inglesa.

monopoly [məˈnɒpəlɪ] *n* monopolio.

monotonous [məˈnɒtənəs] *adj* monótono,-a.

monster ['mɒnstəʳ] *n* monstruo.

month [mʌnθ] *n* mes.

monthly ['mʌnθlɪ] *adj* mensual. ► *adv* mensualmente. ∎ **monthly instalment** mensualidad.

monument ['mɒnjʊmənt] *n* monumento.

moo [muː] *n* mugido.

mood [muːd] *n* humor. ∙ **to be in the mood for** tener ganas de.

moon [muːn] *n* luna. ∎ **moon landing** alunizaje.

moonlight ['muːnlaɪt] *n* luz de luna, claro de luna.

moor [mʊəʳ] *n* páramo.

Moor [mʊəʳ] *n* moro,-a.

mop [mɒp] *n* fregona.

moped ['məʊped] *n* ciclomotor.

moral ['mɒrəl] *adj* moral. ► *n* moraleja.

more [mɔːʳ] *adj-adv* más. ∙ **not any more** ya no ...; **more or less** más o menos.

moreover [mɔːˈrəʊvəˈ] *adv fml* además.

morgue [mɔːg] *n* depósito de cadáveres.

morning [ˈmɔːnɪŋ] *n* mañana. • **good morning!** ¡buenos días!; **tomorrow morning** mañana por la mañana.

morphine [ˈmɔːfiːn] *n* morfina.

morsel [ˈmɔːsəl] *n* bocado.

mortal [ˈmɔːtəl] *adj-n* mortal.

mortar [ˈmɔːtəˈ] *n* mortero.

mortgage [ˈmɔːgɪdʒ] *n* hipoteca. ► *vt* hipotecar. ■ **mortgage loan** préstamo hipotecario.

mosaic [məˈzeɪɪk] *adj* mosaico.

mosque [mɒsk] *n* mezquita.

mosquito [məsˈkiːtəʊ] *n* mosquito.

moss [mɒs] *n* musgo.

most [məʊst] *adj* **1** más. **2** la mayoría. ► *adv* más. ► *pron* **1** la mayor parte. **2** la mayoría.

mostly [ˈməʊstlɪ] *adv* principalmente.

motel [məʊˈtel] *n* motel.

moth [mɒθ] *n* **1** mariposa nocturna. **2** polilla.

mother [ˈmʌðəˈ] *n* madre. ■ **mother tongue** lengua materna.

motherhood [ˈmʌðəhʊd] *n* maternidad.

mother-in-law [ˈmʌðərɪnlɔː] *n* suegra.

motif [məʊˈtiːf] *n* motivo.

motion [ˈməʊʃən] *n* movimiento. • **in slow motion** a cámara lenta. ■ **motion picture** película.

motive [ˈməʊtɪv] *n* motivo.

motor [ˈməʊtəˈ] *n* motor. ■ **motor racing** carreras de coches.

motorbike [ˈməʊtəbaɪk] *n fam* moto.

motorboat [ˈməʊtəbəʊt] *n* lancha motora.

motorcycle [ˈməʊtəsaɪkəl] *n* motocicleta.

motorist [ˈməʊtərɪst] *n* automovilista.

motorway [ˈməʊtəweɪ] *n* GB autopista.

motto [ˈmɒtəʊ] *n* lema.

mould[1] [məʊld] *n* GB moho.

mould[2] [məʊld] *n* GB molde. ► *vt* GB moldear, modelar.

mount [maʊnt] *n* montura. ► *vt* **1** montar a *(caballo)*. **2** montar en *(bicicleta)*. **3** enmarcar *(foto)*.

mountain [ˈmaʊntən] *n* montaña. ■ **mountain bike** bicicleta de montaña; **mountain range** cordillera, sierra.

mourn [mɔːn] *vt* **1** llorar la muerte de. **2** echar de menos.

mourning [ˈmɔːnɪŋ] *n* luto.

mouse [maʊs] *n* ratón.

moustache [məsˈtɑːʃ] *n* bigote.

mouth [maʊθ] *n* **1** boca. **2** desembocadura *(de río)*.

mouthful ['maʊθfʊl] *n* bocado.
move [muːv] *n* movimiento.
► *vt-vi* mover(se).
movement ['muːvmənt] *n* movimiento.
movie ['muːvi] *n* US película.
mow [məʊ] *vt* segar, cortar.
mower ['məʊə'] *n* cortacésped.
much [mʌtʃ] *adj* mucho,-a.
► *adv-pron* mucho. • **how much?** ¿cuánto?
mud [mʌd] *n* barro, lodo.
muddle ['mʌdəl] *n* lío.
mudguard ['mʌdgɑːd] *n* guardabarros.
mug [mʌg] *n* **1** taza. **2** jarra.
mule [mjuːl] *n* mulo,-a.
multiple ['mʌltɪpəl] *adj* múltiple.
multiply ['mʌltɪplaɪ] *vt-vi* multiplicar(se).
mum [mʌm] *n* GB *fam* mamá.
mumps [mʌmps] *n* paperas.
murder ['mɜːdə'] *n* asesinato.
► *vt* asesinar.
murderer ['mɜːdərə'] *n* asesino,-a.
murmur ['mɜːmə'] *n* murmullo. ► *vt-vi* murmurar.
muscle ['mʌsəl] *n* músculo.
muse [mjuːz] *n* musa.
museum [mjuːˈzɪəm] *n* museo.
mushroom ['mʌʃrʊm] *n* seta, hongo, champiñón.
music ['mjuːzɪk] *n* música. ▪ **music hall** teatro de variedades; **music score** partitura; **music stand** atril.

musical ['mjuːzɪkəl] *adj-n* musical.
musician [mjuːˈzɪʃən] *n* músico,-a.
mussel ['mʌsəl] *n* mejillón.
must[1] [mʌst] *aux* **1** deber, tener que. **2** deber de. ► *n fam* cosa imprescindible.
must[2] [mʌst] *n* mosto.
mustard ['mʌstəd] *n* mostaza.
mute [mjuːt] *adj-n* mudo,-a.
mutiny ['mjuːtɪnɪ] *n* motín.
mutton ['mʌtən] *n* carne de oveja.
mutual ['mjuːtʃʊəl] *adj* mutuo,-a.
muzzle ['mʌzəl] *n* **1** hocico. **2** bozal.
my [maɪ] *adj* mi, mis.
myopia [maɪˈəʊpɪə] *n* miopía.
myself [maɪˈself] *pron* **1** me. **2** mí. • **by myself** yo mismo, -a, yo solo,-a.
mystery ['mɪstərɪ] *n* misterio.
myth [mɪθ] *n* mito.
mythology [mɪˈθɒlədʒɪ] *n* mitología.

N

nail [neɪl] *n* **1** uña. **2** clavo. ► *vt* clavar. ▪ **nail file** lima de uñas; **nail varnish** esmalte de uñas; **nail varnish remover** quitaesmaltes.

needless

naive [naɪ'iːv] *adj* ingenuo,-a.
naked ['neɪkɪd] *adj* desnudo,-a.
name [neɪm] *n* nombre.
nanny ['nænɪ] *n* niñera.
nap [næp] *n* siesta.
nape [neɪp] *n* nuca, cogote.
napkin ['næpkɪn] *n* servilleta.
nappy ['næpɪ] *n* GB pañal.
narcotic [naː'kʊtɪk] *adj* narcótico,-a. ► *n* narcótico.
narrate [nə'reɪt] *vt* narrar.
narrow ['nærəʊ] *adj* estrecho,-a. ► *vt-vi* estrechar(se).
narrow-minded [nærəʊ'maɪndɪd] *adj* estrecho,-a de miras.
nasal ['neɪzəl] *adj* nasal.
nasty ['naːstɪ] *adj* **1** desagradable, asqueroso,-a. **2** malo,-a.
nation ['neɪʃən] *n* nación.
national ['næʃnəl] *adj* nacional.
nationality [næʃə'nælɪtɪ] *n* nacionalidad.
nationalize [næʃnə'laɪz] *vt* nacionalizar.
nationwide ['neɪʃənwaɪd] *adj-adv* a escala nacional.
native ['neɪtɪv] *adj* **1** natal. **2** originario,-a. **3** materno. ► *n* nativo,-a.
natural ['nætʃərəl] *adj* natural.
nature ['neɪtʃəʳ] *n* naturaleza.
naught [nɔːt] *n* nada.
naughty ['nɔːtɪ] *adj* **1** travieso,-a. **2** atrevido,-a.
nausea ['nɔːzɪə] *n* náuseas.
nautical ['nɔːtɪkəl] *adj* náutico,-a.

naval ['neɪvəl] *adj* naval.
nave [neɪv] *n* nave central.
navel ['neɪvəl] *n* ombligo.
navigate ['nævɪgeɪt] *vt* navegar por.
navigation [nævɪ'geɪʃən] *n* navegación.
navy ['neɪvɪ] *n* armada. ■ **navy blue** azul marino.
near [nɪəʳ] *adj* **1** cercano,-a. **2** próximo,-a. ► *adv* **1** cerca. **2** a punto de. ► *prep* cerca de.
nearby ['nɪəbaɪ] *adj* cercano,-a. ► *adv* cerca.
nearly ['nɪəlɪ] *adv* casi.
neat [niːt] *adj* **1** ordenado,-a. **2** pulcro,-a. **3** claro,-a. **4** solo,-a.
necessary ['nesɪsərɪ] *adj* necesario,-a.
necessity [nɪ'sesɪtɪ] *n* necesidad.
neck [nek] *n* cuello.
necklace ['nekləs] *n* collar.
neckline ['neklaɪn] *n* escote.
nectar ['nektəʳ] *n* néctar.
née [neɪ] *adj* de soltera.
need [niːd] *n* necesidad. ► *vt* **1** necesitar. **2** tener que. ► *aux* tener que: *you needn't do it if you don't want to*, no tienes que hacerlo si no quieres. ● **in need** necesitado; **to be in need of** necesitar.
needle ['niːdəl] *n* aguja.
needless ['niːdləs] *adj* innecesario,-a. ● **needless to say** huelga decir.

negation [nɪ'geɪʃən] *n* negación.

negative ['negətɪv] *adj* negativo,-a. ► *n* **1** negativa. **2** negativo *(de foto)*.

neglect [nɪ'glekt] *n* descuido. ► *vt* descuidar.

neglectful [nɪ'glektfʊl] *adj* negligente, descuidado,-a.

negligée ['neglɪdʒeɪ] *n* salto de cama.

negligent ['neglɪdʒənt] *adj* negligente.

negotiate [nɪ'gəʊʃɪeɪt] *vt-vi* negociar.

negotiation [nɪgəʊʃɪ'eɪʃən] *n* negociación.

negro ['niːgrəʊ] *adj-n* negro,-a.

neighbour ['neɪbəʳ] (US **neighbor**) *n* vecino,-a.

neighbourhood ['neɪbəhʊd] (US **neighborhood**) *n* vecindad.

neither ['naɪðəʳ, 'niːðəʳ] *adj-pron* ninguno de los dos, ninguna de las dos. ► *adv-conj* **1** ni. **2** tampoco: *I can't swim. –Neither can I*, No sé nadar. –Yo tampoco. • **neither... nor...** ni... ni...

neon ['niːən] *n* neón.

nephew ['nevjuː] *n* sobrino.

nerve [nɜːv] *n* **1** nervio. **2** valor. **3** descaro: *you've got a nerve!*, ¡qué cara tienes!

nervous ['nɜːvəs] *adj* nervioso,-a. ■ **nervous breakdown** depresión nerviosa.

nest [nest] *n* nido. ► *vi* anidar.

nestle ['nesəl] *vi* acomodarse.

net¹ [net] *n* **1** red. **2 the Net** la Red. ► *vt* coger con red. ■ **Net user** internauta.

net² [net] *adj* neto,-a.

netball ['netbɔːl] *n* especie de baloncesto femenino.

netting ['netɪŋ] *n* malla.

nettle ['netəl] *n* ortiga. ► *vt* irritar.

network ['netwɜːk] *n* red.

neurotic [njʊ'rɒtɪk] *adj-n* neurótico,-a.

neuter ['njuːtəʳ] *adj* neutro,-a. ► *n* neutro.

neutral ['njuːtrəl] *adj* **1** neutro,-a. **2** POL neutral. ► *n* punto muerto.

never ['nevəʳ] *adv* nunca, jamás.

never-ending [nevə'rendɪŋ] *adj* interminable.

nevertheless [nevəðə'les] *adv* sin embargo.

new [njuː] *adj* nuevo,-a. • **as good as new** como nuevo; **new to STH** nuevo en algo. ■ **New Year** Año Nuevo; **New Year's Eve** Nochevieja.

newborn ['njuːbɔːn] *adj* recién nacido,-a.

newcomer ['njuːkʌməʳ] *n* recién llegado,-a.

newly ['njuːlɪ] *adv* recién, recientemente.

newlywed ['njuːlɪwed] *n* recién casado,-a.

nobody

news [njuːz] *n* noticias. • **to break the news to** SB dar la noticia a ALGN. ■ **a piece of news** una noticia; **news bulletin** boletín informativo.

newsagent ['njuːzeɪdʒənt] *n* vendedor,-ra de periódicos. ■ **newsagent's** quiosco de periódicos.

newsflash ['njuːzflæʃ] *n* noticia de última hora.

newsgroup ['njuːzgruːp] *n* grupo de noticias.

newsletter ['njuːzletəʳ] *n* hoja informativa.

newspaper ['njuːspeɪpəʳ] *n* diario, periódico.

newt [njuːt] *n* tritón.

next [nekst] *adj* **1** próximo,-a. **2** de al lado: *he lives next door*, vive en la casa de al lado. ▶ *adv* luego, después. • **next to** al lado de. ■ **next of kin** pariente(s) más cercano(s).

nibble ['nɪbəl] *n* **1** mordisco. **2** bocadito. ▶ *vt-vi* mordisquear.

nice [naɪs] *adj* **1** amable, simpático,-a. **2** agradable. **3** bonito,-a, guapo,-a.

niche [niːʃ] *n* nicho.

nick [nɪk] *n* mella, muesca.

nickel ['nɪkəl] *n* **1** níquel. **2** US moneda de cinco centavos.

nickname ['nɪkneɪm] *n* apodo. ▶ *vt* apodar.

niece [niːs] *n* sobrina.

night [naɪt] *n* noche. • **good night** buenas noches *(despedida)*; **last night** anoche.

nightclub ['naɪtklʌb] *n* discoteca.

nightdress ['naɪtdres] *n* camisón.

nightgown ['naɪtgaʊn] *n* camisón.

nightingale ['naɪtɪŋgeɪl] *n* ruiseñor.

nightmare ['naɪtmeəʳ] *n* pesadilla.

nil [nɪl] *n* nada, cero.

nimble ['nɪmbəl] *adj* ágil.

nine [naɪn] *num* nueve.

nineteen [naɪn'tiːn] *num* diecinueve.

nineteenth [naɪn'tiːnθ] *adj* decimonoveno,-a.

ninety ['naɪntɪ] *num* noventa.

ninth [naɪnθ] *adj* noveno,-a.

nip [nɪp] *n* **1** pellizco. **2** mordisco. ▶ *vt-vi* **1** pellizcar. **2** mordisquear.

nipple ['nɪpəl] *n* **1** pezón. **2** tetilla.

nit [nɪt] *n* liendre.

nite [naɪt] *n* US → night.

no [nəʊ] *adv* no. ▶ *adj* ninguno,-a, ningún: *I have no time*, no tengo tiempo; *he's no friend of mine*, no es amigo mío.

noble ['nəʊbəl] *adj* noble. ▶ *n* noble.

nobody ['nəʊbədɪ] *pron* nadie.

nod [nɒd] *n* **1** saludo *(con la cabeza)*. **2** señal de asentimiento. ► *vi* **1** saludar *(con la cabeza)*. **2** asentir *(con la cabeza)*.

noise [nɔɪz] *n* ruido, sonido.

noisy ['nɔɪzi] *adj* ruidoso,-a.

nomad ['nəʊmæd] *adj-n* nómada.

nominal ['nɒmɪnəl] *adj* **1** nominal. **2** simbólico,-a *(precio)*.

nominate ['nɒmɪneɪt] *vt* **1** nombrar. **2** proponer.

nonchalant ['nɒnʃələnt] *adj* **1** despreocupado. **2** impasible.

nonconformist [nɒnkən'fɔːmɪst] *adj-n* inconformista.

none [nʌn] *pron* **1** ninguno,-a. **2** nadie. **3** nada.

nonexistent [nɒnɪg'zɪstənt] *adj* inexistente.

nonplussed [nɒn'plʌst] *adj* perplejo,-a.

nonsense ['nɒnsəns] *n* tonterías.

nonsmoker [nɒn'sməʊkəʳ] *n* no fumador,-ra.

nonstick [nɒn'stɪk] *adj* antiadherente.

nonstop [nɒn'stɒp] *adj* directo,-a: *a nonstop flight*, un vuelo directo. ► *adv* sin parar.

noodle ['nuːdəl] *n* fideo.

noon [nuːn] *n* mediodía.

noone ['nəʊwʌn] *pron* nadie.

nor [nɔːʳ] *conj* **1** ni. **2** tampoco: *nor do I*, yo tampoco.

norm [nɔːm] *n* norma.

normal ['nɔːməl] *adj* normal.

north [nɔːθ] *n* norte. ► *adj* del norte. ► *adv* al norte.

northern ['nɔːðən] *adj* del norte, septentrional.

nose [nəʊz] *n* **1** nariz. **2** hocico, morro. **3** olfato.

nosey ['nəʊzi] *adj fam* curioso,-a.

nostalgia [nɒ'stældʒɪə] *n* nostalgia.

nostril ['nɒstrɪl] *n* fosa nasal.

not [nɒt] *adv* no.

notation [nəʊ'teɪʃən] *n* notación.

notch [nɒtʃ] *n* muesca. ► *vt* hacer muescas en.

note [nəʊt] *vt* **1** notar, observar. **2** apuntar, anotar. ► *n* **1** nota. **2** GB billete *(de banco)*. ● **to note down** apuntar, tomar nota.

notebook ['nəʊtbʊk] *n* **1** libreta, cuaderno. **2** ordenador portátil.

nothing ['nʌθɪŋ] *pron* nada. ● **for nothing 1** gratis, gratuitamente. **2** en vano, en balde; **if nothing else** al menos; **nothing but** tan solo.

notice ['nəʊtɪs] *n* **1** letrero. **2** anuncio. **3** aviso. ► *vt* notar, fijarse en, darse cuenta de. ● **to take no notice of** no hacer caso de; **until further notice** hasta nuevo aviso.

noticeboard ['nəʊtɪsbɔːd] *n* tablón de anuncios.

notify ['nəʊtɪfaɪ] *vt* notificar.

notion ['nəʊʃən] *n* noción.

notwithstanding [nɒtwɪθ-'stændɪŋ] *adv* no obstante. ► *prep* a pesar de.

nougat ['nuːgaː] *n* turrón blando.

nought [nɔːt] *n* cero.

noun [naʊn] *n* nombre.

nourish ['nʌrɪʃ] *vt* nutrir.

novel ['nɒvəl] *n* novela.

novelty ['nɒvəltɪ] *n* novedad.

November [nəʊ'vembəʳ] *n* noviembre.

now [naʊ] *adv* **1** ahora. **2** hoy en día. • **from now on** de ahora en adelante; **now and then** de vez en cuando.

nowadays ['naʊədeɪz] *adv* hoy día, hoy en día.

nowhere ['nəʊweəʳ] *adv* en/a ninguna parte.

noxious ['nɒkʃəs] *adj* nocivo,-a.

nozzle ['nɒzəl] *n* boquilla.

nuance [njuː'ɒns] *n* matiz.

nuclear ['njuːklɪəʳ] *adj* nuclear.

nucleus ['njuːklɪəs] *n* núcleo.

nude [njuːd] *adj* desnudo,-a. ► *n* desnudo.

nugget ['nʌgɪt] *n* pepita.

nuisance ['njuːsəns] *n* **1** molestia, fastidio, lata. **2** pesado,-a.

null [nʌl] *adj* nulo,-a.

numb [nʌm] *adj* entumecido,-a. ► *vt* entumecer.

number ['nʌmbəʳ] *n* número.

numberplate ['nʌmbəpleɪt] *n* GB placa de la matrícula.

nun [nʌn] *n* monja.

nunnery ['nʌnərɪ] *n* convento *(de monjas)*.

nurse [nɜːs] *n* **1** enfermero,-a. **2** niñera

nursery ['nɜːsrɪ] *n* **1** vivero. **2** guardería.

nut [nʌt] *n* **1** fruto seco. **2** tuerca. **3** *fam* chalado,-a.

nutcracker ['nʌtkrækəʳ] *n* cascanueces.

nutmeg ['nʌtmeg] *n* nuez moscada.

nutritious [njuː'trɪʃəs] *adj* nutritivo,-a.

nutshell ['nʌtʃel] *n* cáscara.

nylon ['naɪlɒn] *n* nilón, nailon.

O

O [əʊ] *n* cero.

oak [əʊk] *n* roble.

oar [ɔːʳ] *n* remo.

oarsman ['ɔːzmən] *n* remero.

oasis [əʊ'eɪsɪs] *n* oasis.

oath [əʊθ] *n* juramento.

oats [əʊts] *npl* avena.

obedient [ə'biːdɪənt] *adj* obediente.

obese [əʊ'biːs] *adj* obeso,-a.

obey [ə'beɪ] *vt* obedecer.

object ['ɒbdʒɪkt] *n* objeto.

objective [əb'dʒektɪv] *adj* objetivo,-a. ► *n* objetivo.

obligation [ɒblɪˈgeɪʃən] *n* obligación.

oblige [əˈblaɪdʒ] *vt* **1** obligar. **2** hacer un favor a.

oblivion [əˈblɪvɪən] *n* olvido.

obscene [ɒbˈsiːn] *adj* obsceno,-a.

obscure [əbsˈkjuəʳ] *adj* oscuro,-a.

observatory [əbˈzɜːvətrɪ] *n* observatorio.

observe [əbˈzɜːv] *vt* observar.

obsess [əbˈses] *vt* obsesionar.

obstacle [ˈɒbstəkəl] *n* obstáculo.

obstinate [ˈɒbstɪnət] *adj* obstinado,-a.

obstruct [əbˈstrʌkt] *vt* obstruir.

obtain [əbˈteɪn] *vt* obtener.

obvious [ˈɒbvɪəs] *adj* obvio,-a.

occasion [əˈkeɪʒən] *n* ocasión.

occult [ˈɒkʌlt] *adj* oculto,-a.

occupant [ˈɒkjʊpənt] *n* ocupante *(de silla, vehículo)*.

occupation [ɒkjʊˈpeɪʃən] *n* **1** ocupación. **2** pasatiempo.

occupy [ˈɒkjʊpaɪ] *vt* ocupar.

occur [əˈkɜːʳ] *vi* ocurrir.

ocean [ˈəʊʃən] *n* océano.

o'clock [əˈklɒk] *adv*: *it's one o'clock*, es la una.

October [ɒkˈtəʊbəʳ] *n* octubre.

octopus [ˈɒktəpəs] *n* pulpo.

odd [ɒd] *adj* **1** extraño,-a, raro,-a. **2** impar. **3**: *thirty odd*, treinta y pico, trenta y tantos.

odds [ɒdz] *npl* probabilidades.

odour [ˈəʊdəʳ] (US **odor**) *n* olor.

oesophagus [iːˈsɒfəgəs] (US **esophagus**) *n* esófago.

of [ɒf, unstressed əv] *prep* de.

off [ɒf] *prep* **1** de. **2** cerca. **3**: *there's a button off your coat*, a tu abrigo le falta un botón. ▶ *adv* **1**: *he ran off*, se fue corriendo. **2**: *two days off*, dos días libres. ▶ *adj* **1** ausente, de baja. **2** apagado,-a *(aparato)*. **3** malo,-a, pasado, -a, agrio,-a.

offence [əˈfens] *n* **1** ofensa. **2** infracción, delito.

offend [əˈfend] *vt* ofender.

offensive [əˈfensɪv] *adj* ofensivo,-a. ▶ *n* ofensiva.

offer [ˈɒfəʳ] *n* oferta. ▶ *vt* ofrecer. • **on offer** de oferta.

office [ˈɒfɪs] *n* **1** despacho, oficina. **2** cargo. • **in office** en el poder; **to take office** tomar posesión del cargo. ■ **office hours** horario de oficina; **office worker** oficinista.

officer [ˈɒfɪsəʳ] *n* **1** oficial *(militar)*. **2** agente, policía.

official [əˈfɪʃəl] *adj* oficial. ▶ *n* funcionario,-a.

off-key [ɒfˈkiː] *adj* desafinado,-a.

off-licence [ˈɒflaɪsəns] *n* GB tienda de bebidas alcohólicas.

off-line [ˈɒflaɪn] *adj* COMPUT desconectado,-a.

offshoot ['ɒfʃuːt] *n* vástago, retoño *(de planta, árbol).*

offside [ɒfˈsaɪd] *adj-adv* fuera de juego.

offspring ['ɔːfsprɪŋ] *n* descendiente.

often ['ɒfən] *adv* a menudo. • **how often…?** ¿cada cuánto…?

oil [ɔɪl] *n* **1** aceite. **2** petróleo. **3** óleo, pintura al óleo. ▪ **oil rig** plataforma petrolífera; **oil slick** marea negra; **oil tanker** petrolero; **oil well** pozo petrolífero.

oilcloth ['ɔɪlklɒθ] *n* hule.

oilfield ['ɔɪlfiːld] *n* yacimiento petrolífero.

ointment ['ɔɪntmənt] *n* ungüento.

okay [əʊˈkeɪ] *interj* ¡vale!, ¡de acuerdo! ▶ *adj-adv* bien. ▶ *n* visto bueno.

old [əʊld] *adj* viejo,-a. • **how old are you?** ¿cuántos años tienes?; **to be… years old** tener… años. ▪ **old age** vejez.

old-fashioned [əʊldˈfæʃənd] *adj* anticuado,-a.

olive ['ɒlɪv] *n* aceituna, oliva. ▪ **olive oil** aceite de oliva.

omelette ['ɒmlət] (US **omelet**) *n* tortilla.

omit [əʊˈmɪt] *vt* omitir.

on [ɒn] *prep* **1** en. **2** sobre. **3:** *on Sunday*, el domingo; *he got on the bus*, se subió al autobús; *he's on the phone*, está al teléfono. ▶ *adv* **1** conectado, -a, encendido,-a *(luz, aparato).* **2** abierto,-a *(grifo).* **3** puesto,-a. • **and so on** y así sucesivamente; **on and off** de vez en cuando; **on and on** sin parar.

once [wʌns] *adv* **1** una vez. **2** antes, anteriormente. ▶ *conj* una vez que. • **at once 1** enseguida. **2** a la vez. **3** de una vez; **once and for all** de una vez para siempre; **once upon a time** érase una vez.

one [wʌn] *adj* un, una. ▶ *num* uno. ▶ *pron* uno,-a. • **one another** el uno al otro.

oneself [wʌnˈself] *pron* uno,-a mismo,-a, sí mismo,-a. • **by oneself** solo.

one-way ['wʌnweɪ] *adj* **1** de sentido único *(calle).* **2** de ida *(billete).*

onion ['ʌnɪən] *n* cebolla.

on-line ['ɒnlaɪn] *adj* COMPUT en línea.

onlooker ['ɒnlʊkə'] *n* espectador,-ra.

only ['əʊnlɪ] *adj* único,-a. ▶ *adv* solo, solamente, únicamente. ▶ *conj* pero. • **if only** ojalá; **only just** apenas.

onto ['ɒntʊ] *prep* sobre.

onwards ['ɒnwədz] *adv* adelante, hacia adelante.

opaque [əʊˈpeɪk] *adj* opaco,-a.

open ['əʊpən] *adj* abierto,-a. ▶ *vt-vi* abrir(se). ▪ **open season** temporada de caza.

open-air ['əupəneə'] *adj* al aire libre.

opener ['əupənə'] *n* abridor.

opening ['əupənɪŋ] *n* abertura. ▪ **opening hours** horario de apertura; **opening night** noche de estreno.

open-minded [əupən'maɪndɪd] *adj* tolerante, abierto.

opera ['ɒpərə] *n* ópera. ▪ **opera house** ópera.

operate ['ɒpəreɪt] *vt* hacer funcionar. ▶ *vi* operar. ▪ **operating theatre** quirófano.

operation [ɒpə'reɪʃən] *n* operación.

operator ['ɒpəreɪtə'] *n* 1 operador,-a, telefonista. 2 operario,-a.

opinion [ə'pɪnɪən] *n* opinión.

opponent [ə'pəunənt] *n* adversario,-a.

opportunity [ɒpə'tjuːnɪtɪ] *n* oportunidad.

oppose [ə'pəuz] *vt* oponerse a.

opposite ['ɒpəzɪt] *adj* 1 de enfrente. 2 opuesto,-a, contrario,-a. ▶ *prep* enfrente de, frente a. ▶ *adv* enfrente.

opposition [ɒpə'zɪʃən] *n* oposición.

oppress [ə'pres] *vt* oprimir.

opt [ɒpt] *vi* optar.

optical ['ɒptɪkəl] *adj* óptico,-a.

optician [ɒp'tɪʃən] *n* óptico, -a. ● **optician's** óptica.

optimist ['ɒptɪmɪst] *n* optimista.

optimistic [ɒptɪ'mɪstɪk] *adj* optimista.

option ['ɒpʃən] *n* opción.

or [ɔː'] *conj* 1 o. 2 ni. ● **or else** de lo contrario, si no.

oral ['ɔːrəl] *adj* oral. ▶ *n* examen oral.

orange ['ɒrɪndʒ] *n* naranja. ▪ **orange blossom** azahar.

orbit ['ɔːbɪt] *n* órbita.

orchard ['ɔːtʃəd] *n* huerto.

orchestra ['ɔːkɪstrə] *n* orquesta.

orchid ['ɔːkɪd] *n* orquídea.

order ['ɔːdə'] *n* 1 orden. 2 pedido. ▶ *vt* 1 ordenar. 2 pedir. ● **in order to** para, a fin de; **"Out of order"** "No funciona".

ordinal ['ɔːdɪnəl] *adj* ordinal. ▶ *n* ordinal.

ordinary ['ɔːdɪnərɪ] *adj* normal, corriente.

oregano [ɒrɪ'gaːnəu] *n* orégano.

organ ['ɔːgən] *n* órgano.

organism ['ɔːgənɪzəm] *n* organismo.

organization [ɔːgənaɪ'zeɪʃən] *n* organización. ▪ **organization chart** organigrama.

organize ['ɔːgənaɪz] *vt-vi* organizar(se).

orientation [ɔːrɪen'teɪʃən] *n* orientación.

origin ['ɒrɪdʒɪn] *n* origen.

original [ə'rɪdʒɪnəl] *adj-n* original.

orphan ['ɔːfən] n huérfano,-a.
ostrich ['ɒstrɪtʃ] n avestruz.
other ['ʌðəʳ] adj-pron otro,-a.
• **other than** aparte de, salvo; **the others** los demás.
otherwise ['ʌðəwaɪz] adv 1 de otra manera. 2 por lo demás.
► conj si no, de lo contrario.
otter ['ɒtəʳ] n nutria.
ought [ɔːt] aux deber.
ounce [aʊns] n onza.
our ['aʊəʳ] adj nuestro,-a, nuestros,-as.
ours [aʊəz] pron (el) nuestro, (la) nuestra, (los) nuestros, (las) nuestras.
ourselves [aʊə'selvz] pron 1 nos. 2 nosotros,-as mismos, -as. • **by ourselves** solos.
out [aʊt] adv 1 fuera, afuera. 2 equivocado,-a. 3: *white socks are out*, los calcetines blancos ya no se llevan. 4 apagado,-a *(luz)*. 5 fuera, eliminado,-a *(jugador)*. 6 despedido,-a. ► prep **out of 1** fuera de. 2 de: *made out of wood*, hecho,-a de madera. 3 sin: *we're out of tea*, se nos ha acabado el té. 4 de cada: *eight women out of ten*, ocho de cada diez mujeres.
outboard ['aʊtbɔːd] adj fueraborda.
outbreak ['aʊtbreɪk] n 1 estallido *(de guerra)*. 2 comienzo *(de hostilidades)*. 3 brote *(de epidemia)*.

outburst ['aʊtbɜːst] n explosión.
outcast ['aʊtkɑːst] n marginado,-a.
outcome ['aʊtkʌm] n resultado.
outdated [aʊt'deɪtɪd] adj anticuado,-a.
outdoor [aʊt'dɔːʳ] adj al aire libre. ► adv **outdoors** fuera.
outer ['aʊtəʳ] adj exterior.
outfit ['aʊtfɪt] n 1 conjunto, traje. 2 equipo, grupo.
outgoing [aʊt'gəʊɪŋ] adj 1 saliente, cesante. 2 sociable.
outing ['aʊtɪŋ] n salida, excursión.
outlaw ['aʊtlɔː] n forajido,-a, proscrito,-a. ► vt prohibir.
outlay ['aʊtleɪ] n desembolso.
outlet ['aʊtlet] n 1 salida. 2 desagüe.
outline ['aʊtlaɪn] n 1 contorno. 2 resumen, esbozo. ► vt 1 perfilar. 2 resumir.
outlook ['aʊtlʊk] n 1 vista. 2 punto de vista.
outlying ['aʊtlaɪɪŋ] adj alejado,-a, remoto,-a.
outnumber [aʊt'nʌmbəʳ] vt exceder en número.
outpatient ['aʊtpeɪʃənt] n paciente externo,-a.
output ['aʊtpʊt] n 1 producción, rendimiento. 2 COMPUT salida.
outrage ['aʊtreɪdʒ] n indignación. ► vt ultrajar, atropellar.

outright ['aʊtraɪt] *adj* absoluto,-a.

outside [(n-prep-adv) aʊt'saɪd, (adj) 'aʊtsaɪd] *n* exterior. ► *prep* fuera de. ► *adv* fuera, afuera. ► *adj* exterior.

outsider [aʊt'saɪdə'] *n* forastero,-a.

outskirts ['aʊtskɜːts] *npl* afueras.

outstanding [aʊt'stændɪŋ] *adj* **1** destacado,-a. **2** pendiente.

outward ['aʊtwəd] *adj* **1** externo,-a. **2** de ida *(viaje)*. ► *adv* (**outward** o **outwards**) hacia fuera, hacia afuera.

oval ['əʊvəl] *adj* oval, ovalado,-a. ► *n* óvalo.

ovary ['əʊvəri] *n* ovario.

oven ['ʌvən] *n* horno.

over ['əʊvə'] *adv*: ***come over here***, ven aquí; ***over there***, allí; ***he fell over***, se cayó. ► *adj* acabado,-a. ► *prep* **1** encima de, por encima de. **2** más de. **3** al otro lado de. **5** durante. **6** por. • **over and over again** una y otra vez; **over here** aquí; **over there** allí.

overall [(adj) 'əʊvərɔːl, (adv) əʊvər'ɔːl] *adj* global, total. ► *adv* **1** en total. **2** en conjunto. ► *npl* **overalls** mono.

overboard ['əʊvəbɔːd] *adv* por la borda.

overcame [əʊvə'keɪm] *pt* → overcome.

overcast ['əʊvəkɑːst] *adj* cubierto,-a, nublado,-a.

overcoat ['əʊvəkəʊt] *n* abrigo.

overcome [əʊvə'kʌm] *vt* **1** vencer, superar. **2** abrumar.

overdose ['əʊvədəʊs] *n* sobredosis.

overexposed [əʊvərɪk'spəʊʒd] *adj* sobreexpuesto,-a.

overflow [əʊvə'fləʊ] *vi* desbordarse.

overhaul [(n) 'əʊvəhɔːl, (vb) əʊvə'hɔːl] *n* revisión general. ► *vt* repasar, revisar.

overheat [əʊvə'hiːt] *vi* recalentarse.

overjoyed [əʊvə'dʒɔɪd] *adj* encantadísimo,-a.

overland ['əʊvəlænd] *adj-adv* por tierra.

overlap [əʊvə'læp] *vi* superponerse.

overleaf [əʊvə'liːf] *adv* al dorso, a la vuelta.

overlook [əʊvə'lʊk] *vt* **1** pasar por alto, no notar. **2** hacer la vista gorda a, disculpar, dejar pasar. **3** dar a, tener vistas a.

overnight [əʊvə'naɪt] *adj* de una noche. ► *adv* por la noche. • **to stay overnight** pasar la noche.

overran [əʊvə'ræn] *pt* → overrun.

overrate [əʊvə'reɪt] *vt* sobrevalorar.

overrule [əʊvə'ruːl] *vt* **1** desautorizar. **2** denegar.

overrun [əʊvəˈrʌn] *vt* invadir. ► *vi* durar más de lo previsto.

overseas [əʊvəˈsiːz] *adj* de ultramar, del extranjero. ► *adv* en ultramar, en el extranjero.

oversee [əʊvəˈsiː] *vt* supervisar.

overshadow [əʊvəˈʃædəʊ] *vt* *fig* eclipsar, ensombrecer.

oversight [ˈəʊvəsaɪt] *n* descuido.

oversleep [əʊvəˈsliːp] *vi* dormirse, quedarse dormido.

overstep [əʊvəˈstep] *vt* sobrepasar, pasar de.

overt [ˈəʊvɜːt, əʊˈvɜːt] *adj* declarado,-a, abierto,-a.

overtake [əʊvəˈteɪk] *vt* adelantar.

overthrow [əʊvəˈθrəʊ] *vt* derribar, derrocar.

overtime [ˈəʊvətaɪm] *n* horas extraordinarias, horas extra.

overture [ˈəʊvətjʊəʳ] *n* obertura.

overturn [əʊvəˈtɜːn] *vt-vi* volcar.

overweight [əʊvəˈweɪt] *adj* demasiado gordo,-a. • **to be overweight** tener exceso de peso.

overwhelm [əʊvəˈwelm] *vt* **1** arrollar, aplastar. **2** *fig* abrumar.

overwhelming [əʊvəˈwelmɪŋ] *adj* aplastante, arrollador,-ra.

overwork [əʊvəˈwɜːk] *vi* trabajar demasiado. ► *vt* hacer trabajar demasiado.

overwrought [əʊvəˈrɔːt] *adj* muy nervioso,-a.

ovulation [ɒvjʊˈleɪʃən] *n* ovulación.

ovum [ˈəʊvəm] *n* óvulo.

owe [əʊ] *vt* deber.

owing [ˈəʊɪŋ] *adj* que se debe. • **owing to** debido a, a causa de.

owl [aʊl] *n* búho, mochuelo, lechuza.

own [əʊn] *adj* propio,-a: *he has his own car*, tiene su propio coche. ► *pron*: *my/your/ his own*, lo mío/ tuyo/ suyo; *a room of my own*, una habitación para mí solo. ► *vt* poseer, ser dueño,-a de, tener. • **on one's own** solo, sin ayuda: *can you do it on your own?*, ¿puedes hacerlo solo?

to own up *vi* confesar.

owner [ˈəʊnəʳ] *n* dueño,-a, propietario,-a, poseedor,-ra.

ownership [ˈəʊnəʃɪp] *n* propiedad, posesión.

ox [ɒks] *n* buey.

oxide [ˈɒksaɪd] *n* óxido.

oxidize [ˈɒksɪdaɪz] *vt-vi* oxidar(se).

oxygen [ˈɒksɪdʒən] *n* oxígeno. ▪ **oxygen mask** máscara de oxígeno.

oyster [ˈɔɪstəʳ] *n* ostra.

oz [aʊns, ˈaʊnsɪz] *abbr (ounce)* onza.

ozone [ˈəʊzəʊn] *n* ozono. ▪ **ozone layer** capa de ozono.

P

pace [peɪs] n **1** paso. **2** marcha, ritmo.

pacemaker ['peɪsmeɪkəʳ] n **1** liebre *(en carrera)*. **2** marcapasos.

pacific [pəˈsɪfɪk] adj pacífico,-a.

pacify ['pæsɪfaɪ] vt pacificar, apaciguar.

pack [pæk] n **1** paquete. **2** baraja. **3** banda *(de ladrones)*. ▶ vt **1** empaquetar. **2** hacer *(maleta)*. **3** apretar.

package ['pækɪdʒ] n paquete. ▪ **package tour** viaje organizado.

packaging ['pækɪdʒɪŋ] n embalaje.

packet ['pækɪt] n paquete.

pact [pækt] n pacto.

pad [pæd] n **1** almohadilla. **2** taco, bloc *(de papel)*.

paddle ['pædəl] n pala *(para remar)*. ▶ vt-vi remar con pala.

padlock ['pædlɒk] n candado. ▶ vt cerrar con candado.

pagan ['peɪgən] adj-n pagano,-a.

page [peɪdʒ] n página.

paid [peɪd] pt-pp → pay.

pain [peɪn] n dolor. • **on pain of** so pena de.

painful ['peɪnfʊl] adj doloroso,-a.

painkiller ['peɪnkɪləʳ] n calmante, analgésico.

painless ['peɪnləs] adj indoloro,-a.

paint [peɪnt] n pintura. ▶ vt-vi pintar.

paintbrush ['peɪntbrʌʃ] n **1** brocha. **2** pincel.

painter ['peɪntəʳ] n pintor,-ra.

painting ['peɪntɪŋ] n **1** pintura. **2** cuadro.

pair [peəʳ] n **1** par. **2** pareja.

pajamas [pəˈdʒæməz] npl US pijama.

pal [pæl] n fam camarada.

palace ['pæləs] n palacio.

palate ['pælət] n paladar.

pale [peɪl] adj pálido,-a.

palm[1] [pɑːm] n palma *(de la mano)*.

palm[2] [pɑːm] n palmera.

paltry ['pɔːltrɪ] adj mísero,-a, mezquino,-a.

pamper ['pæmpəʳ] vt mimar.

pamphlet ['pæmflət] n **1** folleto *(publicitario)*. **2** panfleto *(político)*.

pan [pæn] n cazo, olla.

pancake ['pænkeɪk] n crepe.

pancreas ['pæŋkrɪəs] n páncreas.

panda ['pændə] n oso panda, panda.

panel ['pænəl] n panel.

panic ['pænɪk] n pánico.

panther ['pænθəʳ] n pantera.

panties ['pæntɪz] npl bragas.

pantry ['pæntrɪ] n despensa.

pants [pænts] npl **1** calzoncillos. **2** bragas. **3** US pantalón.

paper ['peɪpəʳ] *n* papel. ▶ *vt* empapelar. • **on paper 1** por escrito. **2** sobre el papel.
paperclip ['peɪpəklɪp] *n* clip.
paperweight ['peɪpəweɪt] *n* pisapapeles.
paperwork ['peɪpəwɜːk] *n* papeleo.
par [pɑːʳ] *n* par *(en golf)*.
parachute ['pærəʃuːt] *n* paracaídas.
parade [pəˈreɪd] *n* desfile. ▶ *vi* desfilar.
paradise ['pærədaɪs] *n* paraíso.
paragraph ['pærəgrɑːf] *n* párrafo.
parakeet ['pærəkiːt] *n* periquito.
parallel ['pærəlel] *adj* paralelo,-a. ▶ *n* **1** paralelo. **2** paralela.
paralysis [pəˈrælɪsɪs] *n* parálisis.
parasite ['pærəsaɪt] *n* parásito,-a.
parasol [pærəˈsɒl] *n* sombrilla.
parcel ['pɑːsəl] *n* paquete.
parchment ['pɑːtʃmənt] *n* pergamino.
pardon ['pɑːdən] *n* perdón. ▶ *vt* perdonar. • **I beg your pardon** le ruego me disculpe, perdón; **pardon?** ¿perdón?, ¿cómo dice?
pare [peəʳ] *vt* **1** pelar *(fruta)*. **2** cortar *(uñas)*.
parent ['peərənt] *n* padre, madre. ▶ *npl* **parents** padres.

parenthesis [pəˈrenθəsɪs] *n* paréntesis.
parish ['pærɪʃ] *n* parroquia.
park [pɑːk] *n* parque. ▶ *vt-vi* aparcar.
parking ['pɑːkɪŋ] *n* aparcamiento. • **"No parking"** "Prohibido aparcar". ■ **parking lot** US aparcamiento; **parking meter** parquímetro; **parking place** sitio para aparcar.
parliament ['pɑːləmənt] *n* parlamento.
parlour ['pɑːləʳ] (US **parlor**) *n* salón.
parole [pəˈrəʊl] *n* libertad condicional. • **on parole** en libertad condicional.
parquet ['pɑːkeɪ] *n* parqué.
parrot ['pærət] *n* loro.
parsley ['pɑːslɪ] *n* perejil.
parson ['pɑːsən] *n* párroco.
part [pɑːt] *n* **1** parte. **2** pieza *(de máquina)*. **3** papel *(en obra, etc)*. ▶ *vt-vi* separar(se).
partial ['pɑːʃəl] *adj* parcial.
participate [pɑːˈtɪsɪpeɪt] *vi* participar.
participle ['pɑːtɪsɪpəl] *n* participio.
particle ['pɑːtɪkəl] *n* partícula.
particular [pəˈtɪkjʊləʳ] *adj* particular. ▶ *npl* **particulars** detalles, datos.
parting ['pɑːtɪŋ] *n* **1** despedida. **2** raya *(en pelo)*.
partition [pɑːˈtɪʃən] *n* **1** partición. **2** tabique.

partner ['pɑːtnə'] n **1** compañero,-a. **2** socio,-a *(en negocio)*. **3** compañero,-ra. **4** pareja.

part-time [pɑːt'taɪm] adj de media jornada. ► adv a tiempo parcial.

party ['pɑːtɪ] n **1** fiesta. **2** partido *(político)*. **3** parte *(en contrato, etc)*.

pass [pɑːs] n **1** pase. **2** aprobado. ► vt-vi **1** pasar. **2** aprobar.

to pass by vi pasar cerca.

to pass out vi desmayarse.

passage ['pæsɪdʒ] n **1** pasaje. **2** paso *(de vehículo, tiempo)*.

passenger ['pæsɪndʒə'] n pasajero,-a.

passer-by [pɑːsə'baɪ] n transeúnte.

passion ['pæʃən] n pasión.

passive ['pæsɪv] adj pasivo,-a. ► n voz pasiva.

passport ['pɑːspɔːt] n pasaporte.

password ['pɑːswɜːd] n contraseña.

past [pɑːst] adj **1** pasado,-a. **2** último,-a. ► adv por delante. ► n pasado. ► prep **1** más allá de. **2** por delante de. **3** y: *five past six*, las seis y cinco. ■ **past participle** participio pasado; **past tense** pasado.

pasta ['pæstə] n pasta.

paste [peɪst] n **1** pasta. **2** engrudo; cola. ► vt pegar.

pastel ['pæstəl] n pastel.

pastime ['pɑːstaɪm] n pasatiempo.

pastry ['peɪstrɪ] n **1** masa. **2** pastel, pasta.

pasture ['pɑːstʃə'] n pasto.

pasty ['pæstɪ] n empanada.

patch [pætʃ] n parche.

pâté ['pæteɪ] n paté.

patent ['peɪtənt] adj-n patente. ► vt patentar. ■ **patent leather** charol.

paternity [pə'tɜːnɪtɪ] n paternidad.

path [pɑːθ] n camino, sendero.

pathway ['pɑːθweɪ] n camino, sendero.

patience ['peɪʃəns] n paciencia.

patient ['peɪʃənt] adj paciente. ► n paciente.

patio ['pætɪəʊ] n patio.

patrimony ['pætrɪmənɪ] n patrimonio.

patriot ['peɪtrɪət] n patriota.

patrol [pə'trəʊl] n patrulla. ► vi-vt patrullar. ■ **patrol car** coche patrulla.

patron ['peɪtrən] adj. ■ **patron saint** patrón,-ona.

pattern ['pætən] n **1** modelo. **2** patrón *(en costura)*. **3** dibujo, diseño *(en tela)*.

pause [pɔːz] n pausa.

pavement ['peɪvmənt] n acera.

pavillion [pə'vɪlɪən] n pabellón.

paw [pɔː] n **1** pata *(de animal)*. **2** garra, zarpa *(de tigre)*.

pawn¹ [pɔːn] n peón.

pawn² [pɔːn] *vt* empeñar.
pay [peɪ] *n* paga, sueldo. ▶ *vt-vi* pagar. ■ **pay phone** teléfono público.
to pay back *vt* devolver.
payment ['peɪmənt] *n* pago.
payroll ['peɪrəʊl] *n* nómina.
payslip ['peɪslɪp] *n* nómina.
pea [piː] *n* guisante.
peace [piːs] *n* paz.
peach [piːtʃ] *n* melocotón.
peacock ['piːkɒk] *n* pavo real.
peak [piːk] *n* **1** cima, pico *(de montaña)*. **2** visera *(de gorra)*. ▶ *adj* máximo,-a. ■ **peak hour** hora punta; **peak period** período de tarifa máxima; **peak season** temporada alta.
peanut ['piːnʌt] *n* cacahuete.
pear [peəʳ] *n* pera.
pearl [pɜːl] *n* perla.
peasant ['pezənt] *n* campesino,-a.
pebble ['pebəl] *n* guijarro.
peck [pek] *vt* picotear.
pedagogy ['pedəɡɒdʒɪ] *n* pedagogía.
pedal ['pedəl] *n* pedal. ▶ *vi* pedalear.
peddler ['pedləʳ] *n* vendedor, -ra ambulante.
pedestrian [pɪ'destrɪən] *n* peatón. ■ **pedestrian crossing** paso de peatones; **pedestrian precinct** zona peatonal.
pediatrician [piːdɪə'trɪʃən] *n* pediatra.
peel [piːl] *n* piel. ▶ *vt* pelar.

peep [piːp] *n* ojeada, vistazo.
peep-hole ['piːphəʊl] *n* mirilla.
peg [peɡ] *n* **1** pinza *(de colgar ropa)*. **2** percha, colgador.
pelican ['pelɪkən] *n* pelícano.
pellet ['pelɪt] *n* perdigón.
pelvis ['pelvɪs] *n* pelvis.
pen¹ [pen] *n* **1** bolígrafo. **2** pluma.
pen² [pen] *n* corral.
penalty ['penəltɪ] *n* **1** pena. **2** penalti. ■ **penalty area** área de castigo.
pence [pens] *npl* → penny.
pencil ['pensəl] *n* lápiz. ■ **pencil case** plumier; **pencil sharpener** sacapuntas.
penetrate ['penɪtreɪt] *vt* penetrar.
penguin ['peŋgwɪn] *n* pingüino.
peninsula [pə'nɪnsjʊlə] *n* península.
penis ['piːnɪs] *n* pene.
penknife ['pennaɪf] *n* **1** cortaplumas. **2** navaja.
penny ['penɪ] *n* **1** GB penique. **2** US centavo.
pension ['penʃən] *n* pensión.
pensioner ['penʃənəʳ] *n* jubilado,-a, pensionista.
penthouse ['penthaʊs] *n* ático.
people ['piːpəl] *npl* gente, personas.
pepper ['pepəʳ] *n* **1** pimienta. **2** pimiento.
peppermint ['pepəmɪnt] *n* **1** menta. **2** hierbabuena.

per [pɜːʳ] *prep* por.

percentage [pəˈsentɪdʒ] *n* porcentaje.

perception [pəˈsepʃən] *n* percepción.

perch [pɜːtʃ] *n* perca.

percolator [ˈpɜːkəleɪtəʳ] *n* cafetera de filtro.

perfect [ˈpɜːfɪkt] *adj* perfecto,-a.

perfection [pəˈfekʃən] *n* perfección.

perform [pəˈfɔːm] *vt* 1 hacer, realizar. 2 interpretar *(música)*. 3 representar *(obra de teatro)*. ► *vi* actuar *(actor)*.

performance [pəˈfɔːməns] *n* 1 ejecución. 2 interpretación, actuación *(de cantante, actor)*. 3 representación *(de obra)*. 4 rendimiento *(de coche)*.

performer [pəˈfɔːməʳ] *n* intérprete.

perfume [ˈpɜːfjuːm] *n* perfume.

perhaps [pəˈhæps] *adv* quizá, quizás, tal vez.

period [ˈpɪərɪəd] *n* 1 período. 2 clase. 3 US punto final.

peripheral [pəˈrɪfərəl] *n* COMPUT unidad periférica.

perishable [ˈperɪʃəbəl] *adj* perecedero,-a.

permanent [ˈpɜːmənənt] *adj* permanente.

permission [pəˈmɪʃən] *n* permiso.

permit [ˈpɜːmɪt] *vt* permitir.

perpendicular [pɜːpənˈdɪkjʊləʳ] *adj-n* perpendicular.

persecution [pɜːsɪˈkjuːʃən] *n* persecución.

persist [pəˈsɪst] *vi* persistir.

person [ˈpɜːsən] *n* persona.

personal [ˈpɜːsənəl] *adj* personal. ▪ **personal computer** ordenador personal; **personal organizer** agenda personal.

personnel [pɜːsəˈnel] *n* personal.

perspective [pəˈspektɪv] *n* perspectiva.

perspiration [pɜːspɪˈreɪʃən] *n* transpiración, sudor.

persuade [pəˈsweɪd] *vt* persuadir, convencer.

perversion [pəˈvɜːʃən] *n* 1 perversión. 2 tergiversación.

pervert [pəˈvɜːt] *vt* 1 pervertir. 2 tergiversar *(verdad, etc)*.

pessimism [ˈpesɪmɪzəm] *n* pesimismo.

pessimist [ˈpesɪmɪst] *n* pesimista.

pest [pest] *n* 1 insecto nocivo, plaga. 2 *fam* pelma.

pester [ˈpestəʳ] *vt* molestar.

pet [pet] *n* animal doméstico.

petal [ˈpetəl] *n* pétalo.

petition [pəˈtɪʃən] *n* petición

petrol [ˈpetrəl] *n* gasolina. ▪ **petrol pump** surtidor de gasolina; **petrol station** gasolinera; **petrol tank** depósito de gasolina.

petticoat ['petɪkəʊt] *n* **1** enaguas. **2** combinación.

petty ['petɪ] *adj* **1** insignificante. **2** mezquino,-a. ▪ **petty cash** dinero para gastos menores.

phantom ['fæntəm] *n* fantasma.

pharmacy ['fɑːməsɪ] *n* farmacia.

phase [feɪz] *n* fase.

pheasant ['fezənt] *n* faisán.

phenomenon [fɪ'nɒmɪnən] *n* fenómeno.

philosopher [fɪ'lɒsəfə'] *n* filósofo,-a.

philosophy [fɪ'lɒsəfɪ] *n* filosofía.

phobia ['fəʊbɪə] *n* fobia.

phone [fəʊn] *n-vt-vi fam* → telephone. ▪ **phone book** listín telefónico; **phone box** cabina telefónica.

phonecard ['fəʊnkɑːd] *n* tarjeta telefónica.

phonetics [fə'netɪks] *n* fonética.

photo ['fəʊtəʊ] *n fam* foto.

photocopier ['fəʊtəʊkɒpɪə'] *n* fotocopiadora.

photocopy ['fəʊtəʊkɒpɪ] *n* fotocopia. ▶ *vt* fotocopiar.

photograph ['fəʊtəɡrɑːf] *n* fotografía. ▶ *vt-vi* fotografiar.

photographer [fə'tɒɡrəfə'] *n* fotógrafo,-a.

photography [fə'tɒɡrəfɪ] *n* fotografía.

phrasal verb [freɪzəl'vɜːb] *n* verbo con partícula.

phrase [freɪz] *n* frase.

physical ['fɪzɪkəl] *adj* físico,-a. ▪ **physical education** educación física.

physician [fɪ'zɪʃən] *n* médico,-a.

physicist ['fɪzɪsɪst] *n* físico,-a.

physics ['fɪzɪks] *n* física.

physiology [fɪzɪ'ɒlədʒɪ] *n* fisiología.

physiotherapy [fɪzɪəʊ'θerəpɪ] *n* fisioterapia.

pianist ['pɪənɪst] *n* pianista.

piano [pɪ'ænəʊ] *n* piano.

pick [pɪk] *vt* **1** escoger, elegir. **2** coger *(flores, fruta)*. **3** forzar *(cerradura)*.

to pick on *vt* meterse con.

to pick out *vt* **1** escoger. **2** distinguir.

to pick up *vt* **1** coger, recoger. **2** ir a buscar. **3** captar *(emisora de radio)*. **4** aprender *(lengua)*.

picket ['pɪkɪt] *n* piquete.

pickle ['pɪkəl] *n* **1** encurtido, escabeche. **2** aprieto. ▶ *vt* encurtir, escabechar.

pickpocket ['pɪkpɒkɪt] *n* carterista.

pick-up ['pɪkʌp] *n* **1** brazo del tocadiscos. **2** furgoneta.

picnic ['pɪknɪk] *n* merienda, picnic. ▶ *vi* ir de picnic.

picture ['pɪktʃə'] *n* **1** pintura, cuadro. **2** dibujo. **3** fotogra-

fía. **4** película. **5** imagen. ▶ *vt*
1 pintar, retratar. **2** imaginar,
imaginarse. • **to take a picture** hacer una foto.
picturesque [pɪktʃə'resk] *adj*
pintoresco,-a.
pie [paɪ] *n* **1** pastel, tarta
(dulce). **2** pastel, empanada
(salado).
piece [piːs] *n* **1** trozo, pedazo. **2** pieza. **3** moneda. • **to
take to pieces** desmontar;
in one piece 1 sano y salvo
(persona). **2** intacto,-a *(objeto)*.
pier [pɪəʳ] *n* muelle.
pierce [pɪəs] *vt* perforar.
pig [pɪg] *n* cerdo,-a.
pigeon ['pɪdʒɪn] *n* paloma.
pigeonhole ['pɪdʒɪnhəʊl] *n*
casilla.
piglet ['pɪglət] *n* cochinillo.
pigment ['pɪgmənt] *n* pigmento.
pigsty ['pɪgstaɪ] *n* pocilga.
pigtail ['pɪgteɪl] *n* trenza.
pile [paɪl] *n* montón, pila.
pile-up ['paɪlʌp] *n* choque en
cadena.
piles ['paɪlz] *npl* hemorroides.
pilgrim ['pɪlgrɪm] *n* peregrino,-a.
pill [pɪl] *n* píldora, pastilla.
pillar ['pɪləʳ] *n* pilar, columna.
pillow ['pɪləʊ] *n* almohada.
pilot ['paɪlət] *adj-n* piloto. ▶ *vt*
pilotar.
pimple ['pɪmpəl] *n* grano.
pin [pɪn] *n* **1** alfiler. **2** clavija.

pinafore ['pɪnəfɔːʳ] *n* delantal.
pincers ['pɪnsəz] *npl* **1** tenazas.
2 pinzas *(de cangrejo)*.
pinch [pɪntʃ] *n* **1** pellizco. **2**
pizca. ▶ *vt* **1** pellizcar. **2** apretar *(zapatos)*.
pine [paɪn] *n* pino. ▪ **pine
cone** piña; **pine nut** piñón.
pineapple ['paɪnæpəl] *n* piña.
ping-pong ['pɪŋpɒŋ] *n* tenis
de mesa, pimpón.
pink [pɪŋk] *adj-n* rosa. ▶ *n*
clavel.
pint [paɪnt] *n* pinta.
pioneer [paɪə'nɪəʳ] *n* pionero,-a.
pipe [paɪp] *n* **1** tubería, cañería
(de agua, gas). **2** pipa *(para fumar)*. ▶ *npl* **pipes** gaita.
pipeline ['paɪplaɪn] *n* **1** tubería. **2** gasoducto. **3** oleo-
ducto.
pirate ['paɪrət] *n* pirata.
pistol ['pɪstəl] *n* pistola.
piston ['pɪstən] *n* pistón.
pit¹ [pɪt] *n* **1** hoyo, foso. **2** mina.
pit² [pɪt] *n* US hueso *(de fruta)*.
pitch [pɪtʃ] *n* **1** MUS tono. **2**
campo, terreno *(de juego)*. ▶
vt **1** tirar, lanzar. **2** plantar,
armar *(tienda de campaña)*.
pitcher¹ ['pɪtʃəʳ] *n* **1** GB cán-
taro. **2** US jarro.
pitcher² ['pɪtʃəʳ] *n* US lanzador,-ra *(de béisbol)*.
pitchfork ['pɪtʃfɔːk] *n* horca.
pity ['pɪtɪ] *n* pena, lástima.
pivot ['pɪvət] *n* pivote, eje.
pizza ['piːtsə] *n* pizza.

placard ['plækɑːd] *n* pancarta.
placate [pləˈkeɪt] *vt* aplacar.
place [pleɪs] *n* **1** lugar, sitio. **2** asiento, sitio. **3** plaza *(en escuela, etc)*. ► *vt* colocar, poner, situar. • **in place of** en vez de.
placenta [pləˈsentə] *n* placenta.
plague [pleɪg] *n* plaga.
plain [pleɪn] *adj* **1** claro,-a. **2** sencillo,-a. **3** liso,-a *(tejido)*. **4** sin leche *(chocolate)*. ► *n* llanura. • **to make STH plain** dejar algo bien claro. ▪ **plain yoghurt** yogur natural.
plaintiff ['pleɪntɪf] *n* demandante.
plait [plæt] *n* trenza.
plan [plæn] *n* **1** plan. **2** plano. ► *vt* planear, planificar.
plane¹ [pleɪn] *n* **1** plano. **2** avión.
plane² [pleɪn] *n* cepillo.
plane³ [pleɪn] *n* plátano *(árbol)*.
planet ['plænət] *n* planeta.
plank [plæŋk] *n* tablón, tabla.
plant [plɑːnt] *n* planta. ► *vt* plantar. ▪ **plant pot** maceta, tiesto.
plaque [plæk] *n* placa.
plasma ['plæzmə] *n* plasma.
plaster ['plɑːstə'] *n* **1** yeso. **2** MED escayola. **3** esparadrapo, tirita®. ► *vt* enyesar. ▪ **plaster cast** escayola.
plastic ['plæstɪk] *adj* plástico,-a. ► *n* plástico.
plasticine® ['plæstɪsiːn] *n* plastilina®.

plate [pleɪt] *n* **1** plato. **2** placa.
plateau ['plætəʊ] *n* meseta.
platform ['plætfɔːm] *n* **1** plataforma. **2** andén.
platoon [pləˈtuːn] *n* pelotón.
play [pleɪ] *n* **1** juego. **2** obra de teatro. ► *vt-vi* **1** jugar. **2** tocar: *he plays the piano*, toca el piano. ► *vt* **1** interpretar. **2** jugar a: *she plays tennis*, juega al tenis. **3** jugar contra *(equipo, adversario)*. **4** poner *(disco)*. ▪ **play on words** juego de palabras.
player ['pleɪə'] *n* **1** jugador,-ra. **2** actor, actriz. **3** músico,-a: *a piano player*, un pianista.
playground ['pleɪgraʊnd] *n* patio de recreo.
playing field ['pleɪŋfiːld] *n* campo de juego.
playmate ['pleɪmeɪt] *n* compañero,-a de juego.
play-off ['pleɪɒf] *n* partido de desempate.
playtime ['pleɪtaɪm] *n* recreo.
plea [pliː] *n* petición, súplica.
plead [pliːd] *vi* suplicar. ► *vt* alegar. • **to plead guilty** declararse culpable; **to plead not guilty** declararse inocente.
pleasant ['plezənt] *adj* **1** agradable *(tiempo)*. **2** simpático,-a, amable *(persona)*.
please [pliːz] *vt-vi* agradar, gustar. ► *interj* por favor. • **as you please** como quieras.

pleased [pliːzd] *adj* contento, -a, satisfecho,-a. • **pleased to meet you!** ¡encantado,-a!, ¡mucho gusto!; **to be pleased to do STH** alegrarse de hacer algo.

pleasure ['pleʒəˀ] *n* placer. • **it's my pleasure** de nada, no hay de qué.

pleat [pliːt] *n* pliegue.

pledge [pledʒ] *n* 1 promesa. 2 prenda, señal.

plenty ['plentɪ] *n* abundancia. ► *pron* 1 muchos,-as. 2 de sobra.

pliers ['plaɪəz] *npl* alicates.

plot[1] [plɒt] *n* 1 complot. 2 trama, argumento.

plot[2] [plɒt] *n* parcela, terreno.

plough [plaʊ] *n* GB arado. ► *vt-vi* GB arar.

plow [plaʊ] *n-vt-vi* US → plough.

pluck [plʌk] *vt* 1 arrancar *(flor)*. 2 desplumar *(ave)*. • **to pluck one's eyebrows** depilarse las cejas.

plug [plʌg] *n* 1 tapón. 2 enchufe, clavija *(macho)*; toma *(hembra)*. 3 bujía.

to plug in *vt-vi* enchufar(se).

plughole ['plʌghəʊl] *n* desagüe.

plum [plʌm] *n* ciruela.

plumber ['plʌməˀ] *n* fontanero,-a.

plural ['plʊərəl] *adj-n* plural.

plus [plʌs] *prep* más. ► *conj* además de que. ► *n* ventaja.

plywood ['plaɪwʊd] *n* contrachapado.

pneumonia [njuːˈməʊnɪə] *n* neumonía, pulmonía.

poach [pəʊtʃ] *vt* 1 hervir. 2 escalfar *(huevos)*.

pocket ['pɒkɪt] *n* bolsillo. ■ **pocket money** 1 dinero para gastos personales. 2 paga.

pod [pɒd] *n* vaina.

poem ['pəʊəm] *n* poema.

poet ['pəʊət] *n* poeta.

poetry ['pəʊətrɪ] *n* poesía.

point [pɔɪnt] *n* 1 punta. 2 punto. 3 coma: *5 point 66*, cinco coma sesenta y seis. 4 sentido. ► *vi* indicar, señalar. ► *vt* apuntar. • **on the point of** a punto de; **there's no point in...** no vale la pena...

point-blank [pɔɪntˈblæŋk] *adj* a quemarropa.

poison ['pɔɪzən] *n* veneno. ► *vt* envenenar.

poker ['pəʊkəˀ] *n* póquer.

polar ['pəʊləˀ] *adj* polar. ■ **polar bear** oso polar.

pole[1] [pəʊl] *n* 1 palo, poste. 2 pértiga. ■ **pole vault** salto con pértiga.

pole[2] [pəʊl] *n* polo.

polemic [pəˈlemɪk] *adj* polémico,-a. ► *n* polémica.

police [pəˈliːs] *npl* policía. ■ **police station** GB comisaría de policía.

policeman [pəˈliːsmən] *n* policía, guardia.

policewoman [pəˈliːswʊmən] *n* mujer policía.

policy [ˈpɒlɪsɪ] *n* **1** política. **2** póliza *(de seguros)*.

polish [ˈpɒlɪʃ] *n* **1** cera *(para muebles)*. **2** betún *(para zapatos)*. **3** esmalte *(para uñas)*. ► *vt* **1** sacar brillo a. **2** pulir.

polite [pəˈlaɪt] *adj* cortés, educado,-a.

politician [pɒlɪˈtɪʃən] *n* político,-a.

politics [ˈpɒlɪtɪks] *n* política.

poll [pəʊl] *n* **1** votación. **2** encuesta, sondeo.

pollen [ˈpɒlən] *n* polen.

pollution [pəˈluːʃən] *n* contaminación.

polo [ˈpəʊləʊ] *n* polo. ■ **polo neck** cuello alto.

pomegranate [ˈpɒmɪɡrænət] *n* granada *(fruta)*.

pomp [pɒmp] *n* pompa.

pond [pɒnd] *n* estanque.

pony [ˈpəʊnɪ] *n* poni.

ponytail [ˈpəʊnɪteɪl] *n* cola de caballo.

pool[1] [puːl] *n* **1** charco. **2** estanque. **3** piscina.

pool[2] [puːl] *n* **1** fondo común. **2** billar americano. ► *npl* **the pools** las quinielas.

poor [pʊə] *adj* pobre.

popcorn [ˈpɒpkɔːn] *n* palomitas *(de maíz)*.

pope [pəʊp] *n* papa.

poplar [ˈpɒplə] *n* álamo.

poppy [ˈpɒpɪ] *n* amapola.

popular [ˈpɒpjʊlə] *adj* popular.

populate [ˈpɒpjʊleɪt] *vt* poblar.

population [pɒpjʊˈleɪʃən] *n* población.

porcelain [ˈpɔːsəlɪn] *n* porcelana.

porch [pɔːtʃ] *n* pórtico.

porcupine [ˈpɔːkjʊpaɪn] *n* puerco espín.

pore [pɔː] *n* poro.

pork [pɔːk] *n* carne de cerdo. ■ **pork chop** chuleta de cerdo.

porridge [ˈpɒrɪdʒ] *n* gachas de avena.

port[1] [pɔːt] *n* puerto *(de mar)*.

port[2] [pɔːt] *n* babor.

port[3] [pɔːt] *n* oporto *(vino)*.

portable [ˈpɔːtəbəl] *adj* portátil.

portal [ˈpɔːtəl] *n* COMPUT portal.

porter [ˈpɔːtə] *n* **1** portero,-a. **2** mozo.

portfolio [pɔːtˈfəʊlɪəʊ] *n* **1** carpeta. **2** POL cartera.

portion [ˈpɔːʃən] *n* porción, ración.

portrait [ˈpɔːtreɪt] *n* retrato.

pose [pəʊz] *n* pose. ► *vt* plantear *(problema)*. **2** representar *(amenaza)*. ► *vi* posar *(como modelo)*.

position [pəˈzɪʃən] *n* **1** sitio, posición. **2** postura, actitud. **3** puesto, empleo. ► *vt* colocar.

positive [ˈpɒzɪtɪv] *adj* **1** positivo,-a. **2** seguro,-a.

possess [pə'zes] *vt* poseer, tener.

possibility [pɒsɪ'bɪlɪtɪ] *n* posibilidad.

possible ['pɒsɪbəl] *adj* posible.

post¹ [pəʊst] *n* poste.

post² [pəʊst] *n* puesto. ▸ *vt* destinar.

post³ [pəʊst] *n* correo. ▸ *vt* **1** echar al correo *(carta)*. **2** poner *(anuncio)*. ▪ **post office** oficina de correos; **post office box** apartado de correos.

postage ['pəʊstɪdʒ] *n* franqueo, porte.

postal ['pəʊstəl] *adj* postal.

postbox ['pəʊstbɒks] *n* buzón.

postcard ['pəʊstkɑːd] *n* tarjeta postal, postal.

postcode ['pəʊstkəʊd] *n* código postal.

poster ['pəʊstə'] *n* póster.

posterior [pɒ'stɪərɪə'] *adj* posterior.

postman ['pəʊstmən] *n* cartero.

postmark ['pəʊstmɑːk] *n* matasellos.

postpone [pəs'pəʊn] *vt* posponer.

postscript ['pəʊstskrɪpt] *n* posdata.

posture ['pɒstʃə'] *n* postura.

postwoman ['pəʊstwʊmən] *n* cartera.

pot [pɒt] *n* **1** pote, tarro. **2** bote *(de pintura)*. **3** tetera. **4** cafetera. **5** olla. **6** maceta.

potato [pə'teɪtəʊ] *n* patata.

potent ['pəʊtənt] *adj* potente.

pothole ['pɒthəʊl] *n* **1** cueva. **2** bache *(de carretera)*.

pottery ['pɒtərɪ] *n* **1** alfarería. **2** cerámica.

potty ['pɒtɪ] *n* orinal *(de niño)*.

poultry ['pəʊltrɪ] *n* aves de corral.

pound¹ [paʊnd] *n* libra.

pound² [paʊnd] *n* **1** perrera. **2** depósito municipal *(de coches)*.

pour [pɔː'] *vt* verter, echar. ▸ *vi* llover a cántaros.

poverty ['pɒvətɪ] *n* pobreza.

powder ['paʊdə'] *n* polvo.

power ['paʊə'] *n* **1** fuerza. **2** poder, capacidad. **3** corriente *(eléctrica)*. **4** energía. **5** potencia. ▪ **power cut** apagón; **power station** central eléctrica.

powerful ['paʊəfʊl] *adj* poderoso,-a.

practical ['præktɪkəl] *adj* práctico,-a.

practice ['præktɪs] *n* **1** práctica. **2** consulta *(de médico)*. **3** bufete *(de abogados)*. ▸ *vt-vi* US → practise.

practise ['præktɪs] *vt-vi* GB **1** practicar. **2** ejercer *(profesión)*. ▸ *vi* entrenar *(deportes)*.

practitioner [præk'tɪʃənə'] *n* médico,-a.

prairie ['preərɪ] *n* pradera.

praise [preɪz] *n* alabanza, elogio. ▸ *vt* alabar.

pram [præm] *n* GB cochecito de niño.

prank [præŋk] *n* travesura, broma.

prawn [prɔːn] *n* gamba.

pray [preɪ] *vi* orar, rezar.

prayer [preəʳ] *n* oración, plegaria. ▪ **prayer book** misal.

preach [priːtʃ] *vt-vi* predicar.

precaution [prɪˈkɔːʃən] *n* precaución.

precede [prɪˈsiːd] *vt-vi* preceder.

precious [ˈpreʃəs] *adj* precioso,-a. ▪ **precious stone** piedra preciosa.

precipice [ˈpresɪpɪs] *n* precipicio.

precise [prɪˈsaɪs] *adj* preciso,-a.

precision [prɪˈsɪʒən] *n* precisión.

precocious [prɪˈkəʊʃəs] *adj* precoz.

precooked [priːˈkʊkt] *vt* precocinado,-a.

predator [ˈpredətəʳ] *n* depredador.

predicament [prɪˈdɪkəmənt] *n* apuro, aprieto.

predict [prɪˈdɪkt] *vt* predecir.

predictable [prɪˈdɪktəbəl] *adj* previsible.

prediction [prɪˈdɪkʃən] *n* predicción.

predominate [prɪˈdɒmɪneɪt] *vi* predominar.

pre-empt [priːˈempt] *vt* adelantarse a.

prefabricated [priːˈfæbrɪkeɪtɪd] *adj* prefabricado,-a.

preface [ˈprefəs] *n* prefacio.

prefer [prɪˈfɜːʳ] *vt* preferir.

preference [ˈprefərəns] *n* preferencia.

prefix [ˈpriːfɪks] *n* prefijo.

pregnancy [ˈpregnənsɪ] *n* embarazo. ▪ **pregnancy test** prueba del embarazo.

pregnant [ˈpregnənt] *adj-n* embarazada.

prehistoric [priːhɪˈstɒrɪk] *n* prehistórico,-a.

prejudice [ˈpredʒədɪs] *n* prejuicio.

prejudicial [predʒəˈdɪʃəl] *adj* perjudicial.

prelude [ˈpreljuːd] *n* preludio.

premature [ˈpremətjʊəʳ] *adj* prematuro,-a.

premier [ˈpremɪəʳ] *adj* primero,-a. ► *n* primer,-ra ministro,-a.

première [ˈpremɪeəʳ] *n* estreno.

premise [ˈpremɪs] *n* premisa. ► *npl* **premises** local.

premium [ˈpriːmɪəm] *n* prima.

preoccupy [priːˈɒkjʊpaɪ] *vt* preocupar.

prepaid [priːˈpeɪd] *adj* pagado,-a por adelantado.

preparation [prepəˈreɪʃən] *n* **1** preparación. **2** preparado. ► *npl* **preparations** preparativos.

prepare [prɪˈpeəʳ] *vt-vi* preparar(se).

preposition [prepə'zıʃən] *n* preposición.

prerogative [prɪ'rɒgətɪv] *n* prerrogativa.

preschool ['priːskuːl] *adj* preescolar.

prescribe [prɪs'kraɪb] *vt* **1** prescribir. **2** recetar.

prescription [prɪs'krɪpʃən] *n* receta médica. • **on prescription** con receta médica.

presence ['prezəns] *n* presencia.

present[1] ['prezənt] *adj* **1** presente. **2** actual. ► *n* presente. • **at present** actualmente; **for the present** por ahora.

present[2] [(*n*) 'prezənt, (*vb*) prɪ'zənt] *n* regalo. ► *vt* presentar.

presenter [prɪ'zentə'] *n* **1** locutor,-ra. **2** presentador,-ra.

presently ['prezəntlɪ] *adv* **1** GB pronto, dentro de poco. **2** US ahora.

preservation [prezə'veɪʃən] *n* conservación, preservación.

preservative [prɪ'zɜːvətɪv] *n* conservante.

preserve [prɪ'zɜːv] *n* **1** conserva *(de fruta, verdura)*. **2** confitura. **3** coto, vedado.

preside [prɪ'zaɪd] *vi* presidir.

president ['prezɪdənt] *n* presidente,-a.

press [pres] *n* **1** prensa. **2** imprenta. ► *vt* **1** pulsar, apretar *(botón)*. **2** prensar *(uvas, olivas)*. **3** planchar *(ropa)*. **4** presionar *(persona)*. ► *vi* apretar. ▪ **press briefing** rueda de prensa; **press release** comunicado de prensa.

pressing ['presɪŋ] *adj* urgente.

press-up ['presʌp] *n* flexión.

pressure ['preʃə'] *n* presión.

prestige [pres'tiːʒ] *n* prestigio.

presume [prɪ'zjuːm] *vt* suponer.

pretend [prɪ'tend] *vt-vi* **1** aparentar, fingir. **2** pretender. ► *adj* de mentira.

pretentious [prɪ'tenʃəs] *adj* pretencioso,-a.

pretext ['priːtekst] *n* pretexto.

pretty ['prɪtɪ] *adj* bonito,-a, mono,-a. ► *adv* bastante. • **pretty much** más o menos.

prevail [prɪ'veɪl] *vi* **1** predominar, imperar. **2** prevalecer.

prevent [prɪ'vent] *vt* impedir, evitar.

preview ['priːvjuː] *n* preestreno.

previous ['priːvɪəs] *adj* previo,-a.

prey [preɪ] *n* presa.

price [praɪs] *n* precio.

prick [prɪk] *n* pinchazo. ► *vt* pinchar.

prickle ['prɪkəl] *n* pincho, espina.

pride [praɪd] *n* orgullo.

priest [priːst] *n* sacerdote.

primary ['praɪmərɪ] *adj* **1** principal. **2** primario,-a.

prime [praɪm] *adj* **1** primero,-a. **2** selecto,-a, de primera. ▪ **Prime Minister** primer,-a ministro,-a; **prime time** franja de mayor audiencia.

primitive ['prɪmɪtɪv] *adj* primitivo,-a.

prince [prɪns] *n* príncipe.

princess ['prɪnses] *n* princesa.

principal ['prɪnsɪpəl] *adj* principal. ► *n* director,-ra *(de colegio)*; rector,-ra *(de universidad)*.

principle ['prɪnsɪpəl] *n* principio.

print [prɪnt] *n* **1** huella. **2** copia *(fotografía)*. **3** estampado *(de tela)*. ► *vt* **1** imprimir. **2** sacar una copia de *(fotografía)*. **3** estampar *(tela)*. ● **in print** en catálogo; **out of print** descatalogado,-a.

printer ['prɪntə'] *n* impresora.

print-out ['prɪntaʊt] *n* copia impresa.

prior ['praɪə'] *adj* anterior, previo,-a.

priority [praɪ'ɒrɪti] *n* prioridad.

prison ['prɪzən] *n* prisión.

prisoner ['prɪzənə'] *n* **1** preso,-a. **2** prisionero,-a.

privacy ['praɪvəsɪ] *n* intimidad.

private ['praɪvət] *adj* privado,-a. ► *n* soldado raso. ▪ **private eye** detective privado.

privilege ['prɪvɪlɪdʒ] *n* privilegio.

prize [praɪz] *n* premio.

probability [prɒbə'bɪlɪti] *n* probabilidad.

probation [prə'beɪʃən] *n* libertad condicional.

probe [prəʊb] *n* sonda.

problem ['prɒbləm] *n* problema.

procedure [prə'siːdʒə'] *n* procedimiento.

proceed [prə'siːd] *vi* **1** continuar, proseguir. **2** proceder.

process ['prəʊses] *n* proceso. ► *vt* **1** procesar. **2** revelar.

proclaim [prə'kleɪm] *vt* proclamar.

prodigious [prə'dɪdʒəs] *adj* prodigioso,-a.

produce [*(vb)* prə'djuːs, *(n)* 'prɒdjuːs] *vt* producir. ► *n* productos *(agrícolas)*.

product ['prɒdʌkt] *n* producto.

production [prə'dʌkʃən] *n* producción. ▪ **production line** cadena de producción.

profession [prə'feʃən] *n* profesión.

professional [prə'feʃənəl] *adj-n* profesional.

professor [prə'fesə'] *n* GB catedrático,-a de universidad.

proficiency [prə'fɪʃənsɪ] *n* competencia.

profile ['prəʊfaɪl] *n* perfil.

profit ['prɒfɪt] *n* ganancia, beneficio.

program ['prəʊɡræm] *n* US programa. ► *vt* US programar.

programme ['prəʊgræm] *n* GB programa. ▶ *vt* GB programar.

progress [(*n*) 'prəʊgres, (*vb*) prə'gres] *n* progreso. ▶ *vi* progresar. • **in progress** en curso.

prohibit [prə'hɪbɪt] *vt* prohibir.

prohibition [prəʊɪ'bɪʃən] *n* prohibición.

project [(*n*) 'prɒdʒekt, (*vb*) prə'dʒekt] *n* proyecto. ▶ *vt* proyectar.

projectile [prə'dʒektaɪl] *n* proyectil.

projector [prə'dʒektəʳ] *n* proyector.

prologue ['prəʊlɒg] (US **prolog**) *n* prólogo.

promenade [prɒmə'nɑːd] *n* paseo marítimo.

prominent ['prɒmɪnənt] *adj* prominente.

promise ['prɒmɪs] *n* promesa. ▶ *vt-vi* prometer.

promote [prə'məʊt] *vt* **1** promover. **2** promocionar.

promotion [prə'məʊʃən] *n* promoción.

prompt [prɒmpt] *adj* **1** inmediato, -a, rápido,-a *(servicio, acción)*. **2** puntual *(persona)*. ▶ *adv* en punto. ▶ *vt* **1** inducir, impulsar, incitar. **2** apuntar *(en teatro)*.

prompter ['prɒmptəʳ] *n* apuntador,-ra.

prone [prəʊn] *adj* boca abajo. • **prone to** propenso,-a a.

prong [prɒŋ] *n* diente, punta.

pronoun ['prəʊnaʊn] *n* pronombre.

pronounce [prə'naʊns] *vt* pronunciar.

pronunciation [prənʌnsɪ'eɪʃən] *n* pronunciación.

proof [pruːf] *n* **1** prueba. **2** graduación *(alcohólica)*.

prop [prɒp] *n* puntal *(objeto)*

propaganda [prɒpə'gændə] *n* propaganda.

propeller [prə'peləʳ] *n* hélice.

proper ['prɒpəʳ] *adj* **1** adecuado,-a *(procedimiento)*. **2** correcto,-a *(respuesta, conducta)*. ■ **proper noun** nombre propio.

property ['prɒpətɪ] *n* propiedad.

prophet ['prɒfɪt] *n* profeta.

proportion [prə'pɔːʃən] *n* proporción. • **out of proportion** desproporcionado,-a.

proposal [prə'pəʊzəl] *n* propuesta.

propose [prə'pəʊz] *vt* **1** proponer *(sugerencia)*. **2** pensar, tener la intención de. ▶ *vi* pedir la mano, declararse.

propriety [prə'praɪətɪ] *n* **1** corrección. **2** conveniencia.

propulsion [prə'pʌlʃən] *n* propulsión.

prose [prəʊz] *n* prosa.

prosecute ['prɒsɪkjuːt] *vt* procesar.

prosecution [prɒsɪ'kjuːʃən] *n* **1** proceso, juicio. **2** la acusación.

prosecutor ['prɒsɪkjuːtə'] *n* fiscal.

prospect ['prɒspekt] *n* **1** perspectiva. **2** probabilidad.

prospectus [prə'spektəs] *n* prospecto.

prosperous ['prɒspərəs] *adj* próspero,-a.

prostate ['prɒsteɪt] *n* próstata.

prostitute ['prɒstɪtjuːt] *n* prostituta.

protect [prə'tekt] *vt* proteger.

protection [prə'tekʃən] *n* protección.

protein ['prəʊtiːn] *n* proteína.

protest [*(n)* 'prəʊtest, *(vb)* prə'test] *n* protesta. ▶ *vt-vi* protestar.

protocol ['prəʊtəkɒl] *n* protocolo.

prototype ['prəʊtətaɪp] *n* prototipo.

protrude [prə'truːd] *vi* sobresalir.

proud [praʊd] *adj* orgulloso,-a.

prove [pruːv] *vt* probar, demostrar. ▶ *vi* resultar. • **to prove SB right** demostrar que ALGN tiene razón; **to prove SB wrong** demostrar que ALGN está equivocado,-a.

proverb ['prɒvɜːb] *n* proverbio.

provide [prə'vaɪd] *vt* proporcionar, suministrar.

provided [prə'vaɪdɪd] *conj.* **provided (that)** siempre que.

province ['prɒvɪns] *n* provincia.

provision [prə'vɪʒən] *n* **1** suministro, provisión. **2** disposición.

provisional [prə'vɪʒənəl] *adj* provisional.

provoke [prə'vəʊk] *vt* provocar.

prow [praʊ] *n* proa.

proxy ['prɒksɪ] *n* representante, apoderado,-a. • **by proxy** por poderes.

prudent ['pruːdənt] *adj* prudente.

prudish ['pruːdɪʃ] *adj* remilgado,-a.

prune[1] [pruːn] *n* ciruela pasa.

prune[2] [pruːn] *vt* podar.

psychiatry [saɪ'kaɪətrɪ] *n* psiquiatría.

psychology [saɪ'kɒledʒɪ] *n* psicología.

pub [pʌb] *n* bar, pub.

puberty ['pjuːbətɪ] *n* pubertad.

public ['pʌblɪk] *adj* público,-a. ▶ *n* público. ▪ **public holiday** fiesta nacional; **public school** colegio privado *(en GB)*, colegio público *(en EEUU)*; **public servant** funcionario,-a.

publicity [pʌ'blɪsɪtɪ] *n* publicidad.

publish ['pʌblɪʃ] *vt* publicar.

publisher ['pʌblɪʃə'] *n* **1** editor,-ra. **2** editorial.

pudding ['pʊdɪŋ] *n* **1** budín, pudín. **2** GB postre.

puddle ['pʌdəl] *n* charco.

pull [pʊl] *n* **1** tirón. **2** atracción. ▶ *vt* tirar de. ▶ *vi* tirar.

pulley ['pʊlɪ] *n* polea.

pullover ['pʊləʊvəʳ] *n* jersey.

pulp [pʌlp] *n* pulpa.

pulse [pʌls] *n* **1** pulsación. **2** pulso.

pumice stone ['pʌmɪsstəʊn] *n* piedra pómez.

pump [pʌmp] *n* **1** bomba *(de aire, líquido).* **2** surtidor *(de gasolina).* ▶ *vt* bombear.

pumpkin ['pʌmpkɪn] *n* calabaza.

pun [pʌn] *n* juego de palabras.

punch¹ [pʌntʃ] *n* puñetazo.

punch² [pʌntʃ] *n* ponche.

punch³ [pʌntʃ] *vt* **1** perforar. **2** picar *(billete).*

punctual ['pʌŋktjʊəl] *adj* puntual.

punctuation [pʌŋktjʊ'eɪʃən] *n* puntuación. ■ **punctuation mark** signo de puntuación.

puncture ['pʌŋktʃəʳ] *n* pinchazo. ▶ *vt-vi* pinchar(se).

punish ['pʌnɪʃ] *vt* castigar.

punishment ['pʌnɪʃmənt] *n* castigo.

pup [pʌp] *n* cría, cachorro,-a.

pupil¹ ['pjuːpɪl] *n* alumno,-a.

pupil² ['pjuːpɪl] *n* pupila.

puppet ['pʌpɪt] *n* títere.

puppy ['pʌpɪ] *n* cachorro,-a.

purchase ['pɜːtʃəs] *n* compra. ▶ *vt* comprar.

pure ['pjʊəʳ] *adj* puro,-a.

purée ['pjʊəreɪ] *n* puré.

purity ['pjʊərɪtɪ] *n* pureza.

purple ['pɜːpəl] *adj* púrpura.

purpose ['pɜːpəs] *n* propósito. ● **on purpose** a propósito.

purr [pɜːʳ] *n* ronroneo.

purse [pɜːs] *n* **1** GB monedero. **2** US bolso.

pursue [pə'sjuː] *vt* **1** perseguir. **2** proseguir.

pursuit [pə'sjuːt] *n* persecución.

purveyor [pɜːveɪəʳ] *n* proveedor,-ra.

pus [pʌs] *n* pus.

push [pʊʃ] *n* empujón. ▶ *vt-vi* empujar. ▶ *vt* pulsar, apretar *(botón).*

pushchair ['pʊʃtʃeəʳ] *n* cochecito de niño.

put [pʊt] *vt* poner, colocar.

to put aside *vt* **1** ahorrar, guardar *(dinero).* **2** dejar a un lado *(trabajo).*

to put away *vt* guardar.

to put forward *vt* **1** proponer *(plan).* **2** adelantar *(reloj).*

to put off *vt* aplazar.

to put on *vt* **1** encender *(luz, radio).* **2** ponerse *(ropa).* **3** ganar *(peso, velocidad).*

to put out *vt* apagar

to put up *vt* **1** levantar *(mano).* **2** armar *(tienda de campaña).* **4** construir.

puzzle ['pʌzəl] *n* rompecabezas.

pyjamas [pə'dʒɑːməz] *npl* GB pijama.

pylon ['paɪlən] *n* torre *(de tendido eléctrico)*.

pyramid ['pɪrəmɪd] *n* pirámide.

Q

quail [kweɪl] *n* codorniz.

quaint [kweɪnt] *adj* pintoresco,-a.

quake [kweɪk] *n fam* terremoto.

qualification [kwɒlɪfɪ'keɪʃən] *n* 1 requisito *(para empleo)*. 2 diploma, título.

qualified ['kwɒlɪfaɪd] *adj* cualificado,-a.

qualify ['kwɒlɪfaɪ] *vt* capacitar. ► *vi* 1 obtener el título. 2 clasificarse.

quality ['kwɒlɪtɪ] *n* 1 calidad. 2 cualidad.

quantity ['kwɒntɪtɪ] *n* cantidad.

quarantine ['kwɒrəntiːn] *n* cuarentena.

quarrel ['kwɒrəl] *n* riña, pelea. ► *vi* reñir, pelear.

quarter ['kwɔːtə'] *n* 1 cuarto, cuarta parte: *a quarter past five*, las cinco y cuarto.

quarterfinal [kwɔːtə'faɪnəl] *n* cuarto de final.

quartz [kwɔːts] *n* cuarzo.

quay [kiː] *n* muelle.

queen [kwiːn] *n* reina.

quench [kwentʃ] *vt* 1 saciar *(sed)*. 2 apagar *(fuego)*.

query ['kwɪərɪ] *n* pregunta.

quest [kwest] *n* búsqueda.

question ['kwestʃən] *n* 1 pregunta. 2 cuestión, problema. ► *vt* 1 hacer preguntas a, interrogar. 2 cuestionar. ■ **question mark** interrogante.

questionnaire [kwestʃə'neə'] *n* cuestionario.

queue [kjuː] *n* cola. ► *vi* hacer cola.

quick [kwɪk] *adj* rápido,-a. ► *adv* rápido, rápidamente.

quiet ['kwaɪət] *adj* 1 callado,-a: *be quiet!*, ¡cállate! 2 tranquilo,-a *(lugar)*.

quilt [kwɪlt] *n* edredón.

quince [kwɪns] *n* membrillo.

quirk [kwɜːk] *n* manía.

quit [kwɪt] *vt* dejar.

quite [kwaɪt] *adv* 1 bastante. 2 completamente.

quiver ['kwɪvə'] *n* temblor.

quiz [kwɪz] *n* concurso *(televisivo, etc)*.

quota ['kwəʊtə] *n* cuota.

quotation [kwəʊ'teɪʃən] *n* 1 cita *(de libro)*. 2 cotización. ■ **quotation marks** comillas.

quote [kwəʊt] *n* cita. ► *vt* 1 citar. 2 cotizar.

quotient ['kwəʊʃənt] *n* cociente.

R

rabbit ['ræbɪt] *n* conejo.
rabies ['reɪbiːz] *n* rabia.
raccoon [rə'kuːn] *n* mapache.
race[1] [reɪs] *n* raza.
race[2] [reɪs] *n* carrera.
racecourse ['reɪskɔːs] (US **racetrack**) *n* hipódromo.
racist ['reɪsɪst] *adj-n* racista.
rack [ræk] *n* **1** estante. **2** baca *(de coche)*. **3** rejilla *(en tren)*. **4** escurreplatos.
racket[1] ['rækɪt] *n* raqueta.
racket[2] ['rækɪt] *n* alboroto.
radar ['reɪdɑːʳ] *n* radar.
radiation [reɪdɪ'eɪʃən] *n* radiación.
radiator ['reɪdɪeɪtəʳ] *n* radiador.
radical ['rædɪkəl] *adj-n* radical.
radio ['reɪdɪəʊ] *n* radio.
radioactive [reɪdɪəʊ'æktɪv] *adj* radiactivo,-a.
radish ['rædɪʃ] *n* rábano.
radius ['reɪdɪəs] *n* radio.
raffle ['ræfəl] *n* rifa. ▶ *vt-vi* rifar, sortear.
raft [rɑːft] *n* balsa.
rafter ['rɑːftəʳ] *n* viga.
rag [ræg] *n* **1** harapo. **2** trapo.
rage [reɪdʒ] *n* rabia. ▶ *vi* **1** rabiar. • **to be all the rage** hacer furor.
raid [reɪd] *n* **1** incursión, razia. **2** redada. **3** atraco, asalto.

rail [reɪl] *n* **1** barra. **2** barandilla. **3** raíl, carril, riel. • **by rail** por ferrocarril.
railings ['reɪlɪŋz] *npl* verja.
railway ['reɪlweɪ] (US **railroad**) *n* ferrocarril. ▪ **railway line** vía férrea; **railway station** estación de ferrocarril.
rain [reɪn] *n* lluvia. ▶ *vi* llover. ▪ **rain forest** selva tropical.
rainbow ['reɪnbəʊ] *n* arco iris.
raincoat ['reɪnkəʊt] *n* impermeable.
raindrop ['reɪndrɒp] *n* gota de lluvia.
rainy ['reɪnɪ] *adj* lluvioso,-a.
raise [reɪz] *vt* **1** levantar. **2** subir, aumentar *(precios, temperatura)*. **3** criar, educar *(niños)*. **4** plantear *(asunto, problema)*. **5** recaudar, conseguir *(fondos)*.
raisin ['reɪzən] *n* pasa.
rake [reɪk] *n* rastrillo.
rally ['rælɪ] *n* **1** POL mitin. **2** rally.
ram [ræm] *n* carnero.
ramble ['ræmbəl] *n* excursión.
ramp [ræmp] *n* rampa.
ran [ræn] *pt* → run.
ranch [rɑːntʃ] *n* rancho.
rancid ['rænsɪd] *adj* rancio,-a.
random ['rændəm] *adj* fortuito,-a. • **at random** al azar.
rang [ræŋ] *pp* → ring.
range [reɪndʒ] *n* **1** gama, surtido. **2** alcance *(de misil, telescopio)*. **3** cordillera, sierra.

rank [ræŋk] n 1 fila. 2 grado (militar). 3 categoría

ranking ['ræŋkɪŋ] n ranking.

ransom ['rænsəm] n rescate. ► vt rescatar.

rap [ræp] n rap (música).

rape¹ [reɪp] n violación. ► vt violar.

rape² [reɪp] n colza.

rapid ['ræpɪd] adj rápido,-a.

rare [reər] adj 1 raro,-a. 2 poco hecho,-a (carne).

rascal ['rɑːskəl] n pillo.

rash¹ [ræʃ] n sarpullido.

rash² [ræʃ] adj imprudente.

rasher ['ræʃər] n loncha.

raspberry ['rɑːzbərɪ] n frambuesa.

rat [ræt] n rata.

rate [reɪt] n 1 tasa, índice, tipo. 2 velocidad, ritmo. 3 tarifa, precio. • **at any rate** de todos modos. ■ **rate of exchange** tipo de cambio.

rather ['rɑːðər] adv bastante. • **I would rather** preferiría; **rather than** en vez de, mejor que.

ratings ['reɪtɪŋs] npl índice de audiencia.

ratio ['reɪʃɪəu] n razón, relación.

ration ['ræʃən] n ración.

rational ['ræʃənəl] adj racional.

rattle ['rætəl] n 1 sonajero. 2 traqueteo.

rattlesnake ['rætəlsneɪk] n serpiente de cascabel.

rave [reɪv] n juerga.

raven ['reɪvən] n cuervo.

ravine [rəˈviːn] n barranco.

raw [rɔː] adj 1 crudo,-a. 2 bruto,-a. ■ **raw material** materia prima.

ray¹ [reɪ] n rayo (de luz).

ray² [reɪ] n raya (pez).

razor ['reɪzər] n 1 navaja de afeitar. 2 maquinilla de afeitar. ■ **razor blade** cuchilla de afeitar.

reach [riːtʃ] n alcance. ► vt 1 alcanzar, llegar a. 2 contactar. ► vi llegar. • **within reach of** al alcance de; **out of reach** fuera del alcance.

react [rɪˈækt] vi reaccionar.

reaction [rɪˈækʃən] n reacción.

read [riːd] vt 1 leer. 2 estudiar (en universidad). ► vi 1 poner (cartel, anuncio). • **to read back** volver a leer, releer; **to read out** leer en voz alta.

reader ['riːdər] n lector,-ra.

reading ['riːdɪŋ] n lectura.

ready ['redɪ] adj preparado,-a.

ready-made [redɪˈmeɪd] adj hecho,-a, confeccionado,-a.

real [rɪəl] adj real. ► adv fam muy. ■ **real estate** bienes inmuebles.

reality [rɪˈælɪtɪ] n realidad.

realize ['rɪəlaɪz] vt 1 darse cuenta de. 2 realizar.

reap [riːp] vt cosechar.

rear [rɪər] adj trasero,-a, de atrás. ► n parte de atrás.

rearrange [riːəˈreɪndʒ] *vt* **1** colocar de otra manera. **2** volver a concertar *(reunión)*.

rear-view [ˈrɪəvjuː] *adj.* ▪ **rear-view mirror** retrovisor.

reason [ˈriːzən] *n* razón. ► *vi* razonar.

reasonable [ˈriːzənəbəl] *adj* razonable.

reassure [riːəˈʃʊəʳ] *vt* tranquilizar.

rebate [ˈriːbeɪt] *n* devolución, reembolso.

rebel [*(adj-n)* ˈrebəl, *(vb)* rɪˈbel] *adj-n* rebelde. ► *vi* rebelarse.

rebellion [rɪˈbeliən] *n* rebelión.

reboot [riːˈbuːt] *vt* reiniciar.

rebound [*(n)* ˈriːbaʊnd, *(vb)* rɪˈbaʊnd] *n* rebote. ► *vi* rebotar.

rebuild [riːˈbɪld] *vt* reconstruir.

rebuke [rɪˈbjuːk] *vt* reprender.

recall [rɪˈkɔːl] *vt* recordar.

receipt [rɪˈsiːt] *n* recibo. ► *npl* **receipts** recaudación *(en taquilla)*.

receive [rɪˈsiːv] *vt* recibir.

receiver [rɪˈsiːvəʳ] *n* **1** receptor. **2** auricular *(de teléfono)*.

recent [ˈriːsənt] *adj* reciente.

reception [rɪˈsepʃən] *n* recepción. ▪ **reception desk** recepción.

receptionist [rɪˈsepʃənɪst] *n* recepcionista.

recess [ˈriːses] *n* **1** hueco. **2** descanso.

recession [rɪˈseʃən] *n* recesión.

rechargeable [riːˈtʃɑːdʒəbəl] *adj* recargable.

recipe [ˈresəpɪ] *n* receta.

reciprocal [rɪˈsɪprəkəl] *adj* recíproco,-a.

recital [rɪˈsaɪtəl] *n* recital.

reckless [ˈrekləs] *adj* **1** precipitado,-a. **2** temerario,-a.

reckon [ˈrekən] *vt-vi* **1** considerar. **2** calcular. **3** *fam* creer. ► *vt* creer, considerar.

reclaim [rɪˈkleɪm] *vt* reclamar.

recline [rɪˈklaɪn] *vt-vi* reclinar(se).

recognize [ˈrekəgnaɪz] *vt* reconocer.

recollect [rekəˈlekt] *vt* recordar.

recommend [rekəˈmend] *vt* recomendar.

reconsider [riːkənˈsɪdəʳ] *vt* reconsiderar.

reconstruct [riːkənsˈtrʌkt] *vt* reconstruir.

record [*(n)* ˈrekɔːd, *(vb)* rɪˈkɔːd] *n* **1** registro, documento. **2** historial, expediente. **3** disco *(música)*. **4** récord, marca. ► *vt* **1** hacer constar. **2** anotar. **3** grabar. ● **off the record** confidencialmente; **to beat the record** batir el récord. ▪ **record player** tocadiscos.

recorder [rɪˈkɔːdəʳ] *n* flauta dulce.

recount [ˈriːkaʊnt] *n* recuento.

recover [rɪˈkʌvəʳ] *vt-vi* recuperar(se).

recovery [rɪˈkʌvərɪ] *n* recuperación.

recruit [rɪ'kruːt] *n* recluta. ► *vt* reclutar.

rectangle ['rektæŋgəl] *n* rectángulo.

rectify ['rektɪfaɪ] *vt* rectificar.

recycle [riː'saɪkəl] *vt* reciclar.

red [red] *adj* **1** rojo,-a. **2** pelirrojo,-a *(pelo)*. ► *n* rojo. • **to be in the red** estar en números rojos. ■ **red tape** papeleo burocrático; **red wine** vino tinto.

redeem [rɪ'diːm] *vt* rescatar.

reduce [rɪ'djuːs] *vt-vi* reducir(se).

redundancy [rɪ'dʌndənsɪ] *n* despido.

redundant [rɪ'dʌndənt] *adj* **1** redundante. **2** despedido,-a. • **to be made redundant** ser despedido,-a.

reed [riːd] *n* **1** caña, junco. **2** lengüeta *(de instrumento)*.

reef [riːf] *n* arrecife.

reek [riːk] *vi* apestar.

reel [riːl] *n* carrete.

refer [rɪ'fɜː'] *vi* **1** referirse. **2** consultar.

referee [refə'riː] *n* árbitro.

reference ['refərəns] *n* referencia. ■ **reference book** libro de consulta.

referendum [refə'rendəm] *n* referéndum.

refill [*(n)* 'riːfɪl, *(vb)* riː'fɪl] *n* recambio. ► *vt* rellenar.

refine [rɪ'faɪn] *vt* refinar.

refinery [rɪ'faɪnərɪ] *n* refinería.

reflect [rɪ'flekt] *vt* reflejar. ► *vi* reflexionar.

reflection [rɪ'flekʃən] *n* **1** reflejo. **2** reflexión.

reflex ['riːfleks] *adj* reflejo,-a.

reflexive [rɪ'fleksɪv] *adj* reflexivo,-a.

reform [rɪ'fɔːm] *n* reforma. ► *vt* reformar.

refrain [rɪ'freɪn] *n* estribillo.

refresh [rɪ'freʃ] *vt* refrescar.

refreshment [rɪ'freʃmənt] *n* refresco, refrigerio.

refrigerator [rɪ'frɪdʒəreɪtə'] *n* frigorífico, nevera.

refuge ['refjuːdʒ] *n* refugio.

refugee [refjuː'dʒiː] *n* refugiado,-a.

refund [*(n)* 'riːfʌnd, *(vb)* riː'fʌnd] *n* reembolso. ► *vt* reembolsar.

refusal [rɪ'fjuːzəl] *n* negativa.

refuse[1] ['refjuːs] *n* basura.

refuse[2] [rɪ'fjuːz] *vi* negarse.

regain [rɪ'geɪn] *vt* recobrar.

regard [rɪ'gɑːd] *vt* considerar. ► *n* respeto. ► *npl* **regards** recuerdos. • **as regards...** en lo que se refiere a...; **with regard to** con respecto a.

regarding [rɪ'gɑːdɪŋ] *prep* respecto a, en relación con.

regime [reɪ'ʒiːm] *n* régimen.

regiment ['redʒɪmənt] *n* regimiento.

region ['riːdʒən] *n* región.

register ['redʒɪstə'] *n* registro, lista. ► *vi* **1** registrarse *(en ho-*

tel). **2** matricularse *(para clases).* **3** inscribirse. ► *vt* **1** certificar *(carta).* **2** inscribir en el registro *(boda, nacimiento).* ▪ **registered post** (US **mail**) correo certificado.

registration [redʒɪsˈtreɪʃən] *n* **1** registro. **2** matriculación. ▪ **registration number** matrícula.

regret [rɪˈgret] *n* pesar. ► *vt* **1** lamentar. **2** arrepentirse de.

regular [ˈregjʊləʳ] *adj* **1** regular. **2** habitual *(cliente).* **3** normal.

regulate [ˈregjʊleɪt] *vt* regular.

rehearsal [rɪˈhɜːsəl] *n* ensayo.

rehearse [rɪˈhɜːs] *vt* ensayar.

reign [reɪn] *n* reinado. ► *vi* reinar.

reimburse [riːɪmˈbɜːs] *vt* reembolsar.

rein [reɪn] *n* rienda.

reindeer [ˈreɪndɪəʳ] *n* reno.

reinforce [riːɪnˈfɔːs] *vt* reforzar. ▪ **reinforced concrete** hormigón armado.

reinstate [riːɪnˈsteɪt] *vt* readmitir.

reject [rɪˈdʒekt] *vt* rechazar.

relapse [rɪˈlæps] *n* **1** recaída. **2** reincidencia. ► *vi* **1** recaer. **2** reincidir.

relate [rɪˈleɪt] *vt* **1** relatar, contar. **2** relacionar. ► *vi* **1** estar relacionado,-a. **2** identificarse, entenderse.

relation [rɪˈleɪʃən] *n* **1** relación. **2** pariente,-a.

relationship [rɪˈleɪʃənʃɪp] *n* relación.

relative [ˈrelətɪv] *adj* relativo, -a. ► *n* pariente,-a.

relax [rɪˈlæks] *vt-vi* relajar(se).

relay [ˈriːleɪ] *n* **1** relevo. **2** relé.

release [rɪˈliːs] *n* **1** liberación. **2** estreno *(de película).* **3** disco recién salido. ► *vt* **1** poner en libertad. **2** estrenar *(película).* **3** sacar *(disco).*

relevant [ˈreləvənt] *adj* pertinente.

reliable [rɪˈlaɪəbəl] *adj* **1** de fiar *(persona).* **2** fidedigno,-a *(noticia).* **3** seguro,-a *(máquina).*

relieve [rɪˈliːv] *vt* aliviar.

religion [rɪˈlɪdʒən] *n* religión.

reluctant [rɪˈlʌktənt] *adj* reacio,-a.

rely [rɪˈlaɪ] *vi* **rely on** confiar en, contar con.

remain [rɪˈmeɪn] *vi* quedar(se). ► *npl* **remains** restos.

remark [rɪˈmɑːk] *n* comentario. ► *vt* comentar.

remarkable [rɪˈmɑːkəbəl] *adj* notable, extraordinario,-a.

remedy [ˈremədɪ] *n* remedio. ► *vt* remediar.

remember [rɪˈmembəʳ] *vt* recordar, acordarse de.

remind [rɪˈmaɪnd] *vt* recordar.

remit [rɪˈmɪt] *vt* remitir.

remittance [rɪˈmɪtəns] *n* giro.

remorse [rɪˈmɔːs] *n* remordimiento.

remote [rɪˈməʊt] *adj* remoto,-a.

■ **remote control** mando a distancia.

remove [rɪ'muːv] *vt* quitar. ► *vi* trasladarse, mudarse.

renew [rɪ'njuː] *vt* renovar.

renovate ['renəveɪt] *vt* reformar.

renown [rɪ'naʊn] *n* fama.

rent[1] [rent] *n* alquiler. ► *vt* alquilar.

rental ['rentəl] *n* alquiler.

repair [rɪ'peəʳ] *n* reparación. ► *vt* reparar, arreglar.

repayment [riː'peɪmənt] *n* devolución, reembolso.

repeat [rɪ'piːt] *n* repetición. ► *vt* repetir.

repetition [repə'tɪʃən] *n* repetición.

replace [rɪ'pleɪs] *vt* **1** devolver a su sitio. **2** reemplazar.

replay [(*n*) 'riːpleɪ, (*vb*) riː'pleɪ] *n* **1** repetición. **2** partido de desempate. ► *vt* repetir.

reply [rɪ'plaɪ] *n* respuesta. ► *vi* responder.

report [rɪ'pɔːt] *n* informe. ► *vt* informar sobre. ► *vi* presentarse.

reporter [rɪ'pɔːtəʳ] *n* reportero,-a, periodista.

represent [reprɪ'zent] *vt* representar.

repression [rɪ'preʃən] *n* represión.

repressive [rɪ'presɪv] *adj* represivo,-a.

reprieve [rɪ'priːv] *n* indulto. ► *vt* indultar.

reprimand ['reprɪmɑːnd] *vt* reprender.

reprisal [rɪ'praɪzəl] *n* represalia.

reproach [rɪ'prəʊtʃ] *n* reproche. ► *vt* reprochar.

reproduce [riːprə'djuːs] *vt-vi* reproducir(se).

reproduction [riːprə'dʌkʃən] *n* reproducción.

reptile ['reptaɪl] *n* reptil.

republic [rɪ'pʌblɪk] *n* república.

reputable ['repjʊtəbəl] *adj* **1** acreditado,-a. **2** de confianza.

reputation [repjʊ'teɪʃən] *n* reputación.

request [rɪ'kwest] *n* solicitud, petición. ► *vt* pedir, solicitar.

require [rɪ'kwaɪəʳ] *vt* requerir.

requirement [rɪ'kwaɪəmənt] *n* requisito.

rescue ['reskjuː] *n* rescate. ► *vt* rescatar.

research [rɪ'sɜːtʃ] *n* investigación. ► *vt-vi* investigar.

resemble [rɪ'zembəl] *vt* parecerse a.

resent [rɪ'zent] *vt* **1** tener celos de. **2** molestar: *I resent that*, eso me molesta.

reservation [rezə'veɪʃən] *n* reserva.

reserve [rɪ'zɜːv] *n* reserva. ► *vt* reservar.

reservoir ['rezəvwɑːʳ] *n* embalse.

residence ['rezɪdəns] *n* residencia.

resident ['rezɪdənt] *adj-n* residente.

residential [resɪ'denʃəl] *adj* residencial.

residue ['rezɪdjuː] *n* residuo.

resign [rɪ'zaɪn] *vt-vi* dimitir. • **to resign oneself to** STH resignarse a algo.

resignation [rezɪg'neɪʃən] *n* **1** dimisión. **2** resignación.

resin ['rezɪn] *n* resina.

resist [rɪ'zɪst] *vt* resistir.

resistance [rɪ'zɪstəns] *n* resistencia.

resistant [rɪ'zɪstənt] *adj* resistente.

resolution [rezə'luːʃən] *n* resolución.

resolve [rɪ'zɒlv] *vt* resolver.

resort [rɪ'zɔːt] *n* lugar de vacaciones.

resource [rɪ'zɔːs] *n* recurso.

respect [rɪ'spekt] *n* respeto. ▶ *vt* respetar.

respective [rɪ'spektɪv] *adj* respectivo,-a.

respond [rɪ'spɒnd] *vi* responder.

response [rɪ'spɒns] *n* respuesta.

responsibility [rɪspɒnsɪ'bɪlɪtɪ] *n* responsabilidad.

rest[1] [rest] *n* descanso. ▶ *vt-vi* **1** descansar. **2** apoyar(se).

rest[2] [rest] *n* resto.

restaurant ['restərɒnt] *n* restaurante.

restore [rɪ'stɔːʳ] *vt* restaurar.

restrain [rɪ'streɪn] *vt* contener.

restrict [rɪ'strɪkt] *vt* restringir.

restriction [rɪ'strɪkʃən] *n* restricción.

result [rɪ'zʌlt] *n* resultado.

to result in *vt* tener como resultado.

resume [rɪ'zjuːm] *vt-vi* reanudar(se).

résumé ['rezjuːmeɪ] *n* **1** resumen. **2** US currículum.

retail ['riːteɪl] *n* venta al por menor. ▪ **retail price** precio de venta al público.

retailer ['riːteɪləʳ] *n* detallista.

retain [rɪ'teɪn] *vt* retener.

retaliation [rɪtælɪ'eɪʃən] *n* represalias.

retch [retʃ] *vi* tener arcadas.

retina ['retɪnə] *n* retina.

retire [rɪ'taɪəʳ] *vt* jubilar. ▶ *vi* **1** jubilarse. **2** retirarse.

retired [rɪ'taɪəd] *adj* jubilado,-a.

retirement [rɪ'taɪəmənt] *n* jubilación.

retort [rɪ'tɔːt] *n* réplica.

retreat [rɪ'triːt] *n* retirada. ▶ *vi* retirarse.

retrieve [rɪ'triːv] *vt* recuperar.

return [rɪ'tɜːn] *n* **1** vuelta, regreso. **2** devolución. ▶ *vi* volver, regresar. ▶ *vt* devolver. • **in return for** a cambio de. ▪ **return ticket** GB billete de ida y vuelta.

reunite [riːjuː'naɪt] *vt-vi* reunir(se).

reveal [rɪ'viːl] *vt* revelar.

revenge [rɪ'vendʒ] *n* venganza. ► *vt* vengar.
revenue ['revənjuː] *n* ingresos.
reverence ['revərəns] *n* reverencia.
reverse [rɪ'vɜːs] *adj* inverso,-a. ►
n **1** reverso *(de moneda)*. **2** revés.
3 marcha atrás. ► *vt* **1** invertir. **2**
volver al revés. **3** revocar *(decisión)*. ► *vi* dar marcha atrás. ■
reverse gear marcha atrás.
review [rɪ'vjuː] *n* **1** revista. **2**
examen. **3** crítica. ► *vt* **1**
pasar revista a *(tropas)*. **2** examinar. **3** hacer una crítica de
(libro, película).
reviewer [rɪ'vjuːə'] *n* crítico,-a.
revise [rɪ'vaɪz] *vt* **1** revisar. **2**
corregir. ► *vt-vi* repasar.
revision [rɪ'vɪʒən] *n* **1** revisión.
2 repaso *(para examen)*.
revival [rɪ'vaɪvəl] *n* reestreno,
reposición.
revolt [rɪ'vəʊlt] *n* revuelta. ►
vi sublevarse. ► *vt* repugnar.
revolting [rɪ'vəʊltɪŋ] *adj* repugnante.
revolution [revə'luːʃən] *n* revolución.
reward [rɪ'wɔːd] *n* recompensa. ► *vt* recompensar.
rewind [riː'waɪnd] *vt* rebobinar.
rheumatism ['ruːmətɪzəm] *n*
reumatismo, reuma.
rhinoceros [raɪ'nɒsərəs] *n*
rinoceronte.
rhyme [raɪm] *n* rima.

rhythm ['rɪðəm] *n* ritmo.
rib [rɪb] *n* costilla.
ribbon ['rɪbən] *n* cinta.
rice [raɪs] *n* arroz. ■ **rice pudding** arroz con leche.
rich [rɪtʃ] *adj* **1** rico,-a. **2** fuerte, pesado,-a *(comida)*.
ricochet ['rɪkəʃeɪ] *n* rebote. ►
vi rebotar.
rid [rɪd] *vt* librar. ● **to get rid
of** deshacerse de.
ridden ['rɪdən] *pp* → ride.
riddle ['rɪdəl] *n* **1** acertijo, adivinanza. **2** enigma.
ride [raɪd] *n* paseo, vuelta. ► *vi*
montar a caballo. ► *vt* montar
(a caballo, en moto, bicicleta).
rider ['raɪdə'] *n* **1** jinete, amazona. **2** ciclista. **3** motorista.
ridiculous [rɪ'dɪkjʊləs] *adj* ridículo,-a.
riding ['raɪdɪŋ] *n* equitación.
rife [raɪf] *adj* extendido.
rifle ['raɪfəl] *n* rifle, fusil.
rig [rɪg] *n* plataforma petrolífera.
right [raɪt] *adj* **1** derecho,-a
(mano). **2** correcto,-a. **3** justo,-
a. ► *adv* **1** a la derecha, hacia la
derecha. **2** bien: *he spelt her
name right*, escribió bien su
nombre. **3** inmediatamente.
► *n* **1** derecha. **2** derecho. **3**
bien.. ● **all right!** ¡bien!, ¡vale!;
right away enseguida; **right
now** ahora mismo; **to be
right** tener razón. ■ **right angle** ángulo recto.

right-hand ['raɪthænd] *adj* derecho,-a.

rigid ['rɪdʒɪd] *adj* rígido,-a.

rigour ['rɪgə'] (US **rigor**) *n* rigor.

rim [rɪm] *n* **1** borde, canto. **2** llanta.

rind [raɪnd] *n* corteza.

ring[1] [rɪŋ] *n* **1** anillo. **2** anilla. **3** círculo *(de personas)*. **4** pista. **5** ring, cuadrilátero. ■ **ring road** carretera de circunvalación.

ring[2] [rɪŋ] *n* **1** tañido; toque *(de campana)*. **2** llamada *(de teléfono, al timbre)*. ▶ *vi* **1** tañer, repicar *(campana)*. **2** sonar *(teléfono, timbre)*. ▶ *vt* **1** llamar *(por teléfono)*. **2** tocar *(timbre)*.

rink [rɪŋk] *n* pista de patinaje.

rinse [rɪns] *vt* aclarar.

riot ['raɪət] *n* **1** disturbio. **2** motín. ▶ *vi* amotinarse.

rip [rɪp] *n* rasgadura. ▶ *vt-vi* rasgar(se).

ripe [raɪp] *adj* maduro,-a.

rip-off ['rɪpɒf] *n fam* timo.

rise [raɪz] *n* **1** ascenso, subida. **2** aumento *(de sueldo)*. **3** subida, cuesta *(en montaña)*. ▶ *vi* **1** ascender, subir. **2** aumentar *(precios)*. **3** levantarse *(de la cama)*. **4** salir *(sol, luna)*. **5** alzarse *(voz)*. ● **to give rise to** dar origen a.

risen ['rɪzən] *pp* → rise.

risk [rɪsk] *n* riesgo, peligro. ▶ *vt* arriesgar.

risky ['rɪskɪ] *adj* arriesgado,-a.

rite [raɪt] *n* rito.

ritual ['rɪtjʊəl] *adj-n* ritual.

rival ['raɪvəl] *adj-n* competidor,-ra, rival. ▶ *vt* competir con, rivalizar con.

rivalry ['raɪvəlrɪ] *n* rivalidad.

river ['rɪvə'] *n* río.

riverside ['rɪvəsaɪd] *n* ribera.

rivet ['rɪvɪt] *n* remache. ▶ *vt* remachar.

road [rəʊd] *n* **1** carretera. **2** camino. ■ **road sign** señal de tráfico.

roadway ['rəʊdweɪ] *n* calzada.

roam [rəʊm] *vi* vagar.

roar [rɔː'] *n* **1** bramido. **2** rugido *(de león)*. **3** estruendo *(de tráfico)*. ▶ *vi* rugir, bramar.

roast [rəʊst] *adj* asado,-a. ▶ *n* asado. ▶ *vt* **1** asar *(carne)*. **2** tostar *(café, cacahuetes)*.

rob [rɒb] *vt* **1** robar. **2** atracar *(banco)*.

robber ['rɒbə'] *n* **1** ladrón,-ona. **2** atracador,-ra *(de banco)*.

robbery ['rɒbərɪ] *n* **1** robo. **2** atraco *(de banco)*.

robe [rəʊb] *n* bata.

robot ['rəʊbɒt] *n* robot.

rock [rɒk] *n* **1** roca. **2** rock *(música)*. ▶ *vt-vi* mecer(se). ● **on the rocks** con hielo *(bebida)*.

rocker ['rɒkə'] *n* balancín.

rocket ['rɒkɪt] *n* cohete.

rocking-chair ['rɒkɪntʃeə'] *n* mecedora.

rod [rɒd] *n* **1** vara. **2** barra.

rub out

rode [rəʊd] *pt* → ride.
role [rəʊl] *n* papel.
roll [rəʊl] *n* **1** rollo. **2** lista. **3** bollo, panecillo. ► *vt* **1** hacer rodar. **2** enroscar. **3** liar *(cigarrillo)*. ► *vi* **1** rodar. **2** enroscarse.
roller ['rəʊləʳ] *n* **1** rodillo. **2** rulo. ■ **roller coaster** montaña rusa; **roller skating** patinaje sobre ruedas.
roller-skate ['rəʊləskeɪt] *vi* patinar sobre ruedas.
romance [rəʊ'mæns] *n* **1** romanticismo. **2** romance.
romantic [rəʊ'mæntɪk] *adj* romántico,-a.
roof [ruːf] *n* **1** tejado. **2** cielo *(de boca)*. **3** techo *(de coche)*.
roof-rack ['ruːfræk] *n* baca.
rook [rʊk] *n* **1** grajo. **2** torre *(en ajedrez)*.
room [ruːm] *n* **1** cuarto, habitación. **2** espacio, sitio. ● **to take up room** ocupar sitio.
roomy ['ruːmɪ] *adj* espacioso,-a, amplio,-a.
rooster ['ruːstəʳ] *n* gallo.
root [ruːt] *n* raíz.
rope [rəʊp] *n* cuerda.
rosary ['rəʊzərɪ] *n* rosario.
rose¹ [rəʊz] *n* rosa.
rose² [rəʊz] *pt* → rise.
rosé ['rəʊzeɪ] *n* vino rosado.
rosemary ['rəʊzmərɪ] *n* romero.
rot [rɒt] *vt-vi* pudrir(se).
rotate [rəʊ'teɪt] *vi* girar. ► *vt-vi* *fig* alternar.

rotten ['rɒtən] *adj* podrido,-a.
rouge [ruːʒ] *n* colorete.
rough [rʌf] *adj* **1** áspero,-a, basto,-a *(superficie)*. **2** desigual *(suelo)*. **3** agitado,-a *(mar)*. **4** rudo,-a, tosco,-a *(persona, modales)*. **5** aproximado,-a *(presupuesto)*. ■ **rough copy** borrador; **rough sea** marejada; **rough version** borrador.
roughly ['rʌflɪ] *adv* aproximadamente.
roulette [ruː'let] *n* ruleta.
round [raʊnd] *adj* redondo,-a. ► *n* **1** círculo. **2** ronda. **3** asalto *(de boxeo)*. ► *adv* por ahí. ► *prep* **1** alrededor de. **2** a la vuelta de.
roundabout ['raʊndəbaʊt] *adj* indirecto,-a. ► *n* **1** tiovivo. **2** GB rotonda.
rouse [raʊz] *vt-vi* despertar(se). ► *vt* provocar.
route [ruːt, US raʊt] *n* ruta.
routine [ruː'tiːn] *n* rutina.
row¹ [raʊ] *n* **1** riña, pelea. **2** jaleo, ruido.
row² [rəʊ] *n* fila, hilera. ● **in a row** en fila.
row³ [rəʊ] *vt-vi* remar.
rowing ['rəʊɪŋ] *n* remo.
royal ['rɔɪəl] *adj* real.
royalty ['rɔɪəltɪ] *n* realeza. ► *npl* **royalties** derechos.
rub [rʌb] *vt* frotar, restregar. ► *vi* rozar.
to rub out *vt* borrar.

rubber ['rʌbəʳ] *n* **1** caucho, goma. **2** goma de borrar. ■ **rubber ring** flotador.

rubbish ['rʌbɪʃ] *n* basura.

rubble ['rʌbəl] *n* escombros.

rubella [ruːˈbelə] *n* rubeola, rubéola.

ruby ['ruːbɪ] *n* rubí.

rucksack ['rʌksæk] *n* mochila.

rudder ['rʌdəʳ] *n* timón.

rude [ruːd] *adj* maleducado,-a.

rug [rʌg] *n* alfombrilla.

rugby ['rʌgbɪ] *n* rugby.

ruin [ruːɪn] *n* ruina. ► *vt* **1** arruinar. **2** estropear.

rule [ruːl] *n* **1** regla, norma. **2** gobierno. **3** reinado. ► *vt-vi* **1** gobernar. **2** reinar.

ruler ['ruːləʳ] *n* **1** gobernante. **2** regla.

rum [rʌm] *n* ron.

ruminant ['ruːmɪnənt] *adj-n* rumiante.

rumour ['ruːməʳ] (US **rumor**) *n* rumor. ► *vt* rumorear.

rump [rʌmp] *n* ancas.

rumpus ['rʌmpəs] *n fam* jaleo, escándalo.

run [rʌn] *vi* **1** correr. **2** funcionar *(aparato, organización)*. **3** presentarse *(a elecciones)*. **4** durar. **5** circular *(autobús, tren)*. **6** desteñirse *(color)*. ► *vt* **1** correr en. **2** llevar *(en coche, moto)*. **3** dirigir *(organización)*. **4** hacer funcionar *(aparato)*. **5** ejecutar *(macro, programa)*. ► *n* **1** carrera. **2** viaje, paseo.

3 racha. **4** pista *(de esquí)*. **5** carrera *(en media)*. ● **in the long run** a la larga.

to run after *vt* perseguir.

to run away *vi* escaparse.

to run into *vt* **1** chocar con *(coche)*. **2** tropezar con *(persona)*.

to run out *vi* acabarse.

runaway ['rʌnəweɪ] *adj-n* fugitivo,-a.

rung [rʌŋ] *n* escalón. ► *pp* → ring.

runner ['rʌnəʳ] *n* corredor,-ra.

runner-up [rʌnərˈʌp] *n* subcampeón,-ona.

running ['rʌnɪŋ] *n* **1** atletismo. **2** gestión, dirección. ► *adj* **1** corriente *(agua)*. **2** continuo, -a. ■ **running costs** gastos de mantenimiento.

runny ['rʌnɪ] *adj* blando,-a, líquido,-a.

run-of-the-mill [rʌnəvðəˈmɪl] *adj* corriente y moliente.

runway ['rʌnweɪ] *n* pista de aterrizaje.

rupture ['rʌptʃəʳ] *n* ruptura.

rural ['rʊərəl] *adj* rural.

rush [rʌʃ] *n* prisa. ► *vt* **1** apresurar, dar prisa a. **2** llevar rápidamente. ► *vi* apresurarse. ■ **rush hour** hora punta.

rust [rʌst] *n* óxido. ► *vt-vi* oxidar(se).

rustic ['rʌstɪk] *adj* rústico,-a.

rut [rʌt] *n* surco.

rye [raɪ] *n* centeno.

S

sabotage ['sæbətɑːʒ] *n* sabotaje. ► *vt* sabotear.

sack [sæk] *n* saco. ► *vt fam* despedir. • **to get the sack** *fam* ser despedido,-a.

sacred ['seɪkrəd] *adj* sagrado,-a.

sacrifice ['sækrɪfaɪs] *n* sacrificio. ► *vt* sacrificar.

sad [sæd] *adj* triste.

saddle ['sædəl] *n* **1** silla *(de montar)*. **2** sillín *(de bicicleta)*.

sadness ['sædnəs] *n* tristeza.

safe [seɪf] *adj* **1** a salvo. **2** seguro,-a. ► *n* caja fuerte.

safety ['seɪftɪ] *n* seguridad. ■ **safety belt** cinturón de seguridad; **safety pin** imperdible.

said [sed] *pt-pp* → say.

sail [seɪl] *n* vela. ► *vi* navegar. • **to set sail** zarpar.

sailing ['seɪlɪŋ] *n* vela *(deporte)*. ■ **sailing boat** velero.

sailor ['seɪləʳ] *n* marinero.

saint [seɪnt] *n* san, santo,-a.

sake [seɪk] *n* bien. • **for the sake of** por, por el bien de.

salad ['sæləd] *n* ensalada. ■ **salad bowl** ensaladera; **salad dressing** aliño, aderezo.

salary ['sælərɪ] *n* salario.

sale [seɪl] *n* **1** venta. **2** liquidación, rebajas. **3** subasta. • **for sale** en venta; **on sale 1** a la venta. **2** rebajado,-a.

salesclerk ['seɪlzklɑːk] *n* dependiente,-a.

salesman ['seɪlzmən] *n* **1** vendedor. **2** dependiente. **3** representante, viajante.

saleswoman ['seɪlzwumən] *n* **1** vendedora. **2** dependienta. **3** representante, viajante.

saliva [sə'laɪvə] *n* saliva.

salmon ['sæmən] *n* salmón.

salon ['sælɒn] *n* salón.

salt [sɔːlt] *n* sal. ■ **salt beef** cecina; **salt pork** tocino.

salty ['sɔːltɪ] *adj* salado,-a.

salute [sə'luːt] *n* saludo.

same [seɪm] *adj* mismo,-a. ► *pron* **the same** lo mismo. ► *adv* igual, del mismo modo. • **all the same** a pesar de todo.

sample ['sɑːmpəl] *n* muestra. ► *vt* probar, catar *(vino)*.

sanction ['sæŋkʃən] *n* sanción. ► *vt* sancionar.

sanctuary ['sæŋktjʊərɪ] *n* santuario.

sand [sænd] *n* arena. ■ **sand dune** duna.

sandal ['sændəl] *n* sandalia.

sandpaper ['sændpeɪpəʳ] *n* papel de lija. ► *vt* lijar.

sandwich ['sænwɪdʒ] *n* sandwich, emparedado.

sang [sæŋ] *pt* → sing.

sanitary ['sænɪtərɪ] *adj* **1** sanitario,-a. **2** higiénico,-a. ■ **sanitary towel** compresa.

sank [sæŋk] *pt* → sink.

sap [sæp] *n* savia.

sapphire ['sæfaɪə'] *n* zafiro.

sardine [sɑːˈdiːn] *n* sardina.

sash [sæʃ] *n* faja.

sat [sæt] *pt-pp* → sit.

satchel ['sætʃəl] *n* cartera.

satellite ['sætəlaɪt] *n* satélite. ▪ **satellite dish aerial** antena parabólica.

satisfaction [sætɪsˈfækʃən] *n* satisfacción.

satisfy ['sætɪsfaɪ] *vt* satisfacer.

Saturday ['sætədɪ] *n* sábado.

sauce [sɔːs] *n* salsa. ▪ **sauce boat** salsera.

saucepan ['sɔːspən] *n* 1 cazo, cacerola. 2 olla.

saucer ['sɔːsə'] *n* platillo.

sauna ['sɔːnə] *n* sauna.

sausage ['sɒsɪdʒ] *n* salchicha.

savage ['sævɪdʒ] *adj-n* salvaje.

save [seɪv] *vt* 1 salvar *(vida)*. 2 guardar *(comida, fuerzas)*. 3 ahorrar *(dinero)*. 4 archivar *(en ordenador)*. 5 evitar. 6 parar *(pelota)*. ▶ *vi* ahorrar.

saving ['seɪvɪŋ] *n* ahorro. ▶ *npl* **savings** ahorros. ▪ **savings account** cuenta de ahorros; **savings bank** caja de ahorros.

savour ['seɪvə'] (US **savor**) *n* sabor. ▶ *vt* saborear.

savoury ['seɪvərɪ] (US **savory**) *adj* salado,-a. ▶ *n* canapé, entremés.

saw[1] [sɔː] *n* sierra. ▶ *vt-vi* serrar.

saw[2] [sɔː] *pt* → see.

sawdust ['sɔːdʌst] *n* serrín.

sawn [sɔːn] *pp* → saw.

saxophone ['sæksəfəʊn] *n* saxofón.

say [seɪ] *vt* decir. ● **it is said that ...** dicen que ..., se dice que ...; **that is to say** es decir.

saying ['seɪɪŋ] *n* dicho, decir.

scab [skæb] *n* costra.

scaffold ['skæfəʊld] *n* 1 andamio. 2 patíbulo.

scald [skɔːld] *vt* escaldar.

scale[1] [skeɪl] *n* escama.

scale[2] [skeɪl] *n* balanza.

scale[3] [skeɪl] *n* escala. ▪ **scale model** maqueta.

scalp [skælp] *n* cuero cabelludo.

scalpel ['skælpəl] *n* bisturí.

scampi ['skæmpɪ] *n* gambas a la gabardina.

scan [skæn] *vt* examinar. ▶ *n* ecografía.

scandal ['skændəl] *n* escándalo.

scar [skɑː'] *n* cicatriz.

scarce [skeəs] *adj* escaso,-a.

scarcely ['skeəslɪ] *adv* apenas.

scare [skeə'] *vt-vi* asustar(se).

scarecrow ['skeəkrəʊ] *n* espantapájaros.

scarf [skɑːf] *n* 1 pañuelo. 2 bufanda.

scarlet ['skɑːlət] *adj-n* escarlata. ▪ **scarlet fever** escarlatina.

scary ['skeərɪ] *adj* espeluznante.

scatter ['skætə^r] *vt-vi* **1** dispersar(se). **2** esparcir(se).

scenario [sɪ'nɑːrɪəʊ] *n* **1** guion. **2** perspectiva, panorama.

scene [siːn] *n* **1** escena. **2** escenario. **3** vista, panorama. • **behind the scenes** entre bastidores.

scent [sent] *n* **1** olor, fragancia. **2** perfume. **3** pista, rastro.

schedule ['ʃedjuːl, 'skedjuːl] *n* **1** programa. **2** lista. **3** US horario. ▶ *vt* programar, fijar. • **on schedule** a la hora prevista. ▪ **scheduled flight** vuelo regular.

scheme [skiːm] *n* **1** plan, programa. **2** intriga, ardid.

scholarship ['skɒləʃɪp] *n* beca.

school [skuːl] *n* escuela, colegio, instituto. ▪ **school book** libro de texto.

science ['saɪəns] *n* ciencia. ▪ **science fiction** ciencia ficción.

scientific [saɪən'tɪfɪk] *adj* científico,-a.

scientist ['saɪəntɪst] *n* científico,-a.

scissors ['sɪzəz] *npl* tijeras.

scoff¹ [skɒf] *vi* mofarse.

scoff² [skɒf] *vt fam* zamparse.

scold [skəʊld] *vt* reñir.

scoop [skuːp] *n* exclusiva.

scooter ['skuːtə^r] *n* Vespa®.

scope [skəʊp] *n* **1** alcance. **2** posibilidades.

scorch [skɔːtʃ] *vt* chamuscar.

score [skɔː^r] *n* **1** tanteo, puntuación *(en golf, naipes)*. **2** resultado. **3** partitura, música *(de película)*. ▶ *vt-vi* marcar *(gol, etc)*. ▶ *vi* obtener una puntuación. ▶ *vt* lograr, conseguir.

scoreboard ['skɔːbɔːd] *n* marcador.

scorn [skɔːn] *n* desprecio. ▶ *vt* despreciar.

scorpion ['skɔːpɪən] *n* escorpión.

scoundrel ['skaʊndrəl] *n* canalla.

scout [skaʊt] *n* explorador,-ra.

scowl [skaʊl] *n* ceño fruncido. ▶ *vi* fruncir el ceño.

scramble ['skræmbəl] *n* lucha. ▶ *vi* **1** trepar. **2** pelearse. ▶ *vt* revolver, mezclar. ▪ **scrambled eggs** huevos revueltos.

scrap [skræp] *vt* desechar. ▶ *n* trozo, pedazo. ▶ *npl* **scraps** restos, sobras *(de comida)*. ▪ **scrap metal** chatarra; **scrap paper** papel usado.

scrape [skreɪp] *vt* **1** rascar. **2** rasparse.

scratch [skrætʃ] *n* rasguño, arañazo. ▶ *vt* **1** arañar. **2** rascar.

scream [skriːm] *n* grito. ▶ *vt-vi* gritar, chillar.

screen [skriːn] *n* **1** biombo. **2** pantalla *(de cine, televisión)*. ▶ *vt* **1** proteger. **2** examinar. **3** proyectar *(película)*. ▪ **screen saver** protector de pantalla.

screw [skruː] *n* tornillo. ▶ *vt* atornillar.

screwdriver ['skruːdraɪvəʳ] *n* destornillador.

scribble ['skrɪbəl] *n* garabatos. ▶ *vt-vi* garabatear.

script [skrɪpt] *n* guion.

scrounge [skraʊndʒ] *vi* gorronear. ▶ *vt* gorronear.

scrub [skrʌb] *n* 1 maleza. 2 fregado. ▶ *vt* fregar.

scruff [skrʌf] *n* cogote.

scruffy ['skrʌfɪ] *adj* desaliñado,-a.

scrupulous ['skruːpjʊləs] *adj* escrupuloso,-a.

scrutinize ['skruːtɪnaɪz] *vt* escudriñar.

scuba diving ['skuːbədaɪvɪŋ] *n* submarinismo.

sculptor ['skʌlptəʳ] *n* escultor,-ra.

sculptress ['skʌlptrəs] *n* escultora.

sculpture ['skʌlptʃəʳ] *n* escultura.

scum [skʌm] *n* espuma.

sea [siː] *n* mar. ■ **sea lion** león marino; **sea trout** trucha de mar, reo.

seafood ['siːfuːd] *n* marisco.

seafront ['siːfrʌnt] *n* paseo marítimo.

seagull ['siːgʌl] *n* gaviota.

sea-horse ['siːhɔːs] *n* caballito de mar.

seal¹ [siːl] *n* foca.

seal² [siːl] *n* sello. ▶ *vt* sellar.

seam [siːm] *n* 1 costura. 2 juntura, junta.

search [sɜːtʃ] *n* 1 búsqueda. 2 registro *(de edificio, persona)*. ▶ *vi* buscar. ▶ *vt* registrar. ■ **search engine** buscador; **search warrant** orden de registro.

seasick ['siːsɪk] *adj* mareado,-a.

seaside ['siːsaɪd] *n* playa, costa. ■ **seaside resort** centro turístico en la costa.

season ['siːzən] *n* 1 estación *(del año)*. 2 temporada *(para deporte, etc)*. ▶ *vt* sazonar. ● **in season 1** en sazón *(fruta)*. 2 en celo *(animal)*. 3 en temporada alta *(turismo)*; **out of season 1** fuera de temporada *(fruta)*. 2 en temporada baja *(turismo)*. ■ **season ticket** abono.

seat [siːt] *n* 1 asiento. 2 localidad *(en teatro, etc)*. 3 escaño. ▶ *vt* sentar(se). ● **to take a seat** sentarse. ■ **seat belt** cinturón de seguridad.

seaweed ['siːwiːd] *n* alga.

second¹ ['sekənd] *adj-n* segundo,-a. ▶ *adv* segundo. ▶ *vt* secundar. ▶ *npl* **seconds** artículos defectuosos. ■ **second name** apellido.

second² [sekənd] *n* segundo.

secondary ['sekəndərɪ] *adj* secundario,-a. ■ **secondary school** escuela de enseñanza secundaria.

second-hand ['sekəndhænd] *adj* de segunda mano.

secret ['si:krət] *adj* secreto,-a. ▶ *n* secreto.

secretary ['sekrətərɪ] *n* secretario,-a. ■ **Secretary of State** 1 ministro,-a con cartera *(en GB)*. 2 ministro,-a de Estado *(en EEUU)*.

secrete [sɪ'kri:t] *vt* secretar.

sect [sekt] *n* secta.

section ['sekʃən] *n* sección.

sector ['sektə'] *n* sector.

secure [sɪ'kjʊə'] *adj* seguro,-a.

security [sɪ'kjʊərɪtɪ] *n* seguridad. ▶ *npl* **securities** COMM valores.

sedative ['sedətɪv] *adj-n* sedante.

seduce [sɪ'dju:s] *vt* seducir.

see[1] [si:] *vt-vi* 1 ver. 2 procurar. 3 acompañar. 4 entender. ● **let's see** a ver, vamos a ver; **see you later!** ¡hasta luego!

to see off *vt* despedirse de.

to see out *vt* acompañar hasta la puerta.

seed [si:d] *n* 1 semilla *(de planta)*. 2 pepita *(de fruta)*. 3 cabeza de serie *(tenis)*.

seek [si:k] *vt* 1 buscar. 2 solicitar.

seem [si:m] *vi* parecer.

seen [si:n] *pp* → see.

seesaw ['si:sɔ:] *n* balancín.

see-through ['si:θru:] *adj* transparente.

segment ['segmənt] *n* segmento.

seize [si:z] *vt* 1 agarrar, coger. 2 incautar, embargar. 3 tomar, apoderarse de.

seldom ['seldəm] *adv* rara vez.

select [sɪ'lekt] *vt* seleccionar. ▶ *adj* selecto,-a.

selection [sɪ'lekʃən] *n* selección.

self [self] *n* yo.

self-conscious [self'kɒnʃəs] *adj* cohibido,-a, tímido,-a.

self-defence [selfdɪ'fens] *n* autodefensa. ● **in self-defence** en defensa propia.

self-employed [selfɪm'plɔɪd] *adj* autónomo,-a.

selfish ['selfɪʃ] *adj* egoísta.

self-portrait [self'pɔ:treɪt] *n* autorretrato.

self-service [self'sɜ:vɪs] *n* autoservicio.

sell [sel] *vt-vi* vender.

to sell off *vt* liquidar.

to sell out *vt* agotarse.

sell-by date ['selbaɪdeɪt] *n* fecha de caducidad.

seller ['selə'] *n* vendedor,-ra.

Sellotape® ['seləteɪp] *n* Celo®, cinta adhesiva.

semester [sɪ'mestə'] *n* semestre.

semicolon [semɪ'kəʊlən] *n* punto y coma.

semidetached [semɪdɪ'tætʃt] *adj* adosado,-a. ▶ *n* casa adosada.

semifinal [semɪˈfaɪnəl] *n* semifinal.

senate [ˈsenət] *n* senado.

senator [ˈsenətəʳ] *n* senador,-ra.

send [send] *vt* enviar, mandar.

sender [ˈsendəʳ] *n* remitente.

senior [ˈsiːnɪəʳ] *adj* 1 mayor *(por edad)*. 2 superior *(por rango)*. ► *n* 1 mayor *(por edad)*. 2 superior *(por rango)*. ■ **senior citizen** persona de la tercera edad.

sensation [senˈseɪʃən] *n* sensación.

sense [sens] *n* sentido. ► *vt* sentir, percibir. • **to make sense** tener sentido, ser sensato,-a.

sensibility [sensɪˈbɪlɪti] *n* sensibilidad.

sensible [ˈsensɪbəl] *adj* sensato,-a.

sensitive [ˈsensɪtɪv] *adj* 1 sensible. 2 confidencial.

sent [sent] *pt-pp* → send.

sentence [ˈsentəns] *n* 1 frase. 2 sentencia, fallo. ► *vt* condenar.

sentry [ˈsentrɪ] *n* centinela.

separate [*(vb)* ˈsepəreɪt, *(adj)* ˈsepərət] *vt-vi* separar(se). ► *adj* 1 separado,-a. 2 distinto,-a.

September [sepˈtembəʳ] *n* septiembre, setiembre.

sequence [ˈsiːkwəns] *n* 1 secuencia. 2 sucesión, serie.

serene [səˈriːn] *adj* sereno,-a.

sergeant [ˈsɑːdʒənt] *n* sargento.

serial [ˈsɪərɪəl] *n* serial. ■ **serial number** número de serie.

series [ˈsɪəriːz] *n* serie.

serious [ˈsɪərɪəs] *adj* 1 serio,-a. 2 grave *(accidente)*.

servant [ˈsɜːvənt] *n* criado,-a.

serve [sɜːv] *vt-vi* servir. ► *vt* cumplir *(condena)*. ► *n* saque *(en tenis)*.

service [ˈsɜːvɪs] *n* 1 servicio. 2 revisión, puesta a punto *(de coche)*. 3 oficio *(religioso)*. • **in service** en funcionamiento; **out of service** fuera de servicio. ■ **service station** estación de servicio.

serviette [sɜːvɪˈet] *n* GB servilleta.

session [ˈseʃən] *n* sesión.

set¹ [set] *n* 1 juego. 2 conjunto. 3 set *(tenis)*. 4 aparato *(televisor, radio)*.

set² [set] *n* plató *(de televisión)*. ► *adj* 1 fijo,-a *(cantidad)*. 2 listo,-a. ► *vt* 1 poner, colocar,. 2 fijar *(fecha)*. 3 marcar *(pelo)*. ► *vi* 1 ponerse *(sol)*. 2 cuajar *(líquido)*. 3 endurecerse *(cemento)*. • **to set (oneself) up** establecerse. ■ **set lunch** menú del día.

to set back *vt* 1 atrasar, retrasar. 2 *fam* costar.

to set off *vi* salir, ponerse en camino. ► *vt* 1 hacer estallar *(bomba)*. **2** hacer saltar *(alarma)*.

to set out *vi* **1** partir, salir. **2** proponerse, pretender. ► *vt* disponer, exponer.

to set up *vt* **1** levantar *(monumento)*. **2** montar *(tienda de campaña, negocio)*. **3** planear, convocar.

setback ['setbæk] *n* revés.

settee [se'tiː] *n* sofá.

setting ['setɪŋ] *n* **1** escenario *(de película)*. **2** ajuste *(de máquina)*.

settle ['setəl] *vt* **1** acordar *(precio)*. **2** resolver *(disputa)*. ► *vi* **1** posarse *(pájaro)*; depositarse *(polvo)*. **2** afincarse, establecerse. **3** calmarse.

to settle down *vi* **1** instalarse, afincarse. **2** sentar la cabeza. **3** tranquilizarse.

settlement ['setəlmənt] *n* **1** poblado, colonia. **2** acuerdo. **3** pago.

seven ['sevən] *num* siete.

seventeen [sevən'tiːn] *num* diecisiete.

seventeenth [sevən'tiːnθ] *adj* decimoséptimo,-a.

seventh ['sevənθ] *adj-n* séptimo,-a.

seventy ['sevəntɪ] *num* setenta.

several ['sevərəl] *adj-pron* varios,-as.

severe [sɪ'vɪəʳ] *adj* **1** severo, -a. **2** grave *(enfermedad)*.

sew [səʊ] *vt-vi* coser.

sewage ['sjuːɪdʒ] *n* aguas residuales.

sewer [sjʊəʳ] *n* alcantarilla.

sewing ['səʊɪŋ] *n* costura. ■ **sewing machine** máquina de coser.

sewn [səʊn] *pp* → sew.

sex [seks] *n* sexo.

shabby ['ʃæbɪ] *adj* raído,-a.

shack [ʃæk] *n* choza.

shade [ʃeɪd] *n* **1** sombra. **2** pantalla *(de lámpara)*. **3** tono *(de color)*. ► *vt* dar sombra.

shadow ['ʃædəʊ] *n* sombra.

shady ['ʃeɪdɪ] *adj* **1** a la sombra *(lugar)*. **2** *fam* sospechoso,-a *(persona)*.

shaft [ʃɑːft] *n* **1** mango. **2** eje.

shake [ʃeɪk] *n* **1** sacudida. **2** batido *(bebida)*. ► *vt* sacudir. ► *vi* temblar.

shall [ʃæl, unstressed ʃəl] *aux* **1** *indica un tiempo futuro:* **I shall go tomorrow**, iré mañana. **2** *indica ofrecimiento:* **shall I close the window?**, ¿cierro la ventana? **3** *indica una sugerencia:* **shall we go to the cinema?**, ¿vamos al cine? **4** *indica una promesa:* **you shall have everything you want, my dear**, tendrás todo lo que desees, cariño. **5** *uso enfático, una orden:* **you shall stop work immediately**, debes parar de trabajar enseguida.

shallow ['ʃæləʊ] *adj* poco profundo,-a.

shame [ʃeɪm] *n* **1** vergüenza. **2** lástima, pena.

shampoo [ʃæm'puː] *n* champú.

shandy ['ʃændɪ] *n* GB clara.

shape [ʃeɪp] *n* forma, figura. ▶ *vt* modelar.• **out of shape** en baja forma.

share [ʃeəʳ] *n* **1** parte. **2** acción *(en bolsa)*. ▶ *vt-vi* compartir. ▶ *vt* repartir.

shareholder ['ʃeəhəʊldəʳ] *n* accionista.

shark [ʃɑːk] *n* tiburón.

sharp [ʃɑːp] *adj* **1** afilado,-a *(cuchillo)*. **2** puntiagudo,-a *(palo)*. **3** agudo,-a *(dolor, persona)*. **4** cerrado,-a *(curva)*. ▶ *adv* en punto.

sharpen ['ʃɑːpən] *vt* **1** afilar *(cuchillo)*. **2** sacar punta a *(lápiz)*.

sharpener ['ʃɑːpənəʳ] *n* sacapuntas.

shatter ['ʃætəʳ] *vi* romperse, hacerse añicos.

shave [ʃeɪv] *n* afeitado. ▶ *vt-vi* afeitar(se).

shaver ['ʃeɪvəʳ] *n* máquina de afeitar.

shaving ['ʃeɪvɪŋ] *n* afeitado. ■ **shaving brush** brocha de afeitar; **shaving foam** espuma de afeitar.

shawl [ʃɔːl] *n* chal.

she [ʃiː] *pron* ella.

shear [ʃɪəʳ] *vt* esquilar.

shed¹ [ʃed] *n* cobertizo.

shed² [ʃed] *vt* **1** derramar *(lágrimas)*. **2** quitarse *(ropa)*.

sheep [ʃiːp] *n* oveja.

sheet [ʃiːt] *n* **1** sábana. **2** hoja *(de papel)*. **3** lámina *(de metal)*.

shelf [ʃelf] *n* estante. ▶ *npl* **shelves** estantería.

shell [ʃel] *n* **1** cáscara *(de huevo, nuez)*. **2** vaina *(de guisante)*. **3** caparazón *(de tortuga)*. **4** concha *(de caracola)*. **5** obús, proyectil.

shellfish ['ʃelfɪʃ] *n* marisco.

shelter ['ʃeltəʳ] *n* refugio. ▶ *vt* proteger.

shepherd ['ʃepəd] *n* pastor.

sherry ['ʃerɪ] *n* jerez.

shield [ʃiːld] *n* escudo.

shift [ʃɪft] *n* **1** cambio. **2** turno *(de trabajo)*. ▶ *vt-vi* cambiar(se) de sitio.

shilling ['ʃɪlɪŋ] *n* chelín.

shin [ʃɪn] *n* espinilla.

shine [ʃaɪn] *n* brillo, lustre. ▶ *vi* brillar.

shingles ['ʃɪŋɡəlz] *npl* herpes.

shiny ['ʃaɪnɪ] *adj* brillante.

ship [ʃɪp] *n* barco, buque.

shipwreck ['ʃɪprek] *n* naufragio.

shipyard ['ʃɪpjɑːd] *n* astillero.

shirt [ʃɜːt] *n* camisa.

shit [ʃɪt] *n* *vulg* mierda.

shiver ['ʃɪvəʳ] *n* escalofrío. ▶ *vi* **1** tiritar. **2** temblar.

shock [ʃɒk] *n* **1** choque. **2** golpe, conmoción. **3** susto. **4** shock. ▶ *vt* escandalizar.

shocking [ˈʃɒkɪŋ] *adj* escandaloso,-a, chocante.

shoe [ʃuː] *n* **1** zapato. **2** herradura. ■ **shoe polish** betún; **shoe shop** zapatería.

shoehorn [ˈʃuːhɔːn] *n* calzador.

shoelace [ˈʃuːleɪs] *n* cordón.

shoemaker [ˈʃuːmeɪkəʳ] *n* zapatero,-a.

shone [ʃɒn] *pt-pp* → shine.

shook [ʃʊk] *pt* → shake.

shoot [ʃuːt] *n* **1** brote, retoño. **2** rodaje *(de película)*. ► *vt* **1** pegar un tiro a. **2** disparar. **3** rodar *(película)*. **4** chutar *(pelota)*. ► *vi* disparar. ■ **shooting star** estrella fugaz.

to shoot down *vt* **1** derribar. **2** matar a tiros.

shop [ʃɒp] *n* tienda. ► *vi* hacer compras, ir de compras. ■ **shop assistant** dependiente,-a; **shop window** escaparate.

shoplifting [ˈʃɒplɪftɪŋ] *n* hurto *(en tiendas)*.

shopping [ˈʃɒpɪŋ] *n* compras. ■ **shopping arcade** galerías comerciales; **shopping centre** GB centro comercial.

shore [ʃɔːʳ] *n* orilla, costa.

shorn [ʃɔːn] *pp* → shear.

short [ʃɔːt] *adj* **1** corto,-a. **2** bajo,-a *(estatura, persona)*. **3** seco,-a, brusco,-a *(modales)*. ► *n* cortometraje. ► *npl* **shorts** pantalón corto. • **in short** en pocas palabras; **for short** para abreviar; **to be short of** andar mal de. ■ **short circuit** cortocircuito; **short cut** atajo; **short story** cuento, relato.

shortage [ˈʃɔːtɪdʒ] *n* escasez.

shorten [ˈʃɔːtən] *vt-vi* acortar(se).

shortly [ˈʃɔːtlɪ] *adv* en breve. • **shortly after** poco después; **shortly before** poco antes.

short-sighted [ʃɔːtˈsaɪtɪd] *adj* miope.

shot[1] [ʃɒt] *n* **1** tiro, disparo. **2** intento. **3** trago. **4** foto. **5** toma *(en cine)*.

shot[2] [ʃɒt] *pt-pp* → shoot.

shotgun [ˈʃɒtɡʌn] *n* escopeta.

should [ʃʊd] *aux* **1** debe. **2** deber de.

shoulder [ˈʃəʊldəʳ] *n* **1** hombro *(de persona)*. **2** espalda *(de carne)*. ■ **shoulder blade** omoplato, omóplato.

shout [ʃaʊt] *n* grito. ► *vt-vi* gritar.

shove [ʃʌv] *n* empujón. ► *vt-vi* empujar.

shovel [ˈʃʌvəl] *n* pala.

show [ʃəʊ] *n* **1** espectáculo, función. **2** programa *(televisivo, de radio)*. **3** exposición, feria. **4** demostración, muestra. ► *vt* **1** mostrar. **2** exponer. **3** indicar, marcar, señalar. **4** demostrar. ► *vt-vi* poner *(película)*. ■ **show business** el mundo del espectáculo.

to show off *vi* presumir.

to show up *vi fam* presentarse, aparecer.

shower ['ʃauə'] *n* **1** ducha. **2** chaparrón. ▶ *vi* ducharse.

shown [ʃəun] *pp* → show.

showroom ['ʃəurum] *n* sala de exposición.

shrank [ʃræŋk] *pt* → shrink.

shrapnel ['ʃræpnəl] *n* metralla.

shred [ʃred] *n* jirón.

shrimp [ʃrimp] *n* GB camarón; US gamba.

shrink [ʃrɪŋk] *vt-vi* encoger(se).

shrivel ['ʃrɪvəl] *vi* marchitarse.

shroud [ʃraud] *n* mortaja.

shrub [ʃrʌb] *n* arbusto.

shrug [ʃrʌg] *vi* encogerse de hombros.

shrunk [ʃrʌŋk] *pp* → shrink.

shuffle ['ʃʌfəl] *vt* barajar. ▶ *vi* andar arrastrando los pies.

shut [ʃʌt] *vt-vi* cerrar(se).

to shut down *vt-vi* cerrar(se).

to shut up *vi fam* callar(se).

shutdown ['ʃʌtdaun] *n* cierre.

shutter ['ʃʌtə'] *n* **1** postigo, contraventana. **2** obturador.

shuttle ['ʃʌtəl] *n* **1** puente aéreo *(de avión)*. **2** servicio regular *(de bus, tren)*. **3** transbordador espacial.

shy [ʃai] *adj* tímido,-a.

shyness ['ʃainəs] *n* timidez.

sick [sik] *adj* **1** enfermo,-a. **2** mareado,-a. ■ **sick leave** baja por enfermedad.

sickness ['siknəs] *n* **1** enfermedad. **2** náusea, mareo.

side [said] *n* **1** lado. **2** costado *(de persona)*. ● **side by side** juntos,-as. ■ **side effect** efecto secundario; **side street** calle lateral, travesía.

sideboard ['saidbɔːd] *n* aparador.

sideburns ['saidbɜːnz] *npl* patillas.

sidelight ['saidlait] *n* luz de posición.

sideline ['saidlain] *n* línea de banda.

sidewalk ['saidwɔːk] *n* US acera.

sideways ['saidweiz] *adj* **1** lateral *(movimiento)*. **2** de soslayo *(mirada)*. ▶ *adv* **1** de lado *(movimiento)*. **2** de soslayo *(mirada)*.

siege [siːdʒ] *n* sitio.

sieve [siv] *n* **1** tamiz *(para harina)*. **2** criba *(para granos)*. **3** colador *(para líquidos)*.

sigh [sai] *n* suspiro. ▶ *vi* suspirar.

sight [sait] *n* **1** vista. **2** mira *(de escopeta)*. ▶ *npl* **sights** atracciones. ● **at first sight** a primera vista.

sightseeing ['saitsiːɪŋ] *n* visita turística, turismo.

sign [sain] *n* **1** signo. **2** señal, gesto. **3** letrero. ▶ *vt-vi* firmar.

to sign in *vi* firmar el registro.

signal ['sɪgnəl] *n* señal.
signature ['sɪgnɪtʃəʳ] *n* firma.
significant [sɪg'nɪfɪkənt] *adj* significativo,-a.
signpost ['saɪnpəʊst] *n* señal indicadora, poste indicador.
silence ['saɪləns] *n* silencio.
silent ['saɪlənt] *adj* silencioso,-a.
silhouette [sɪluː'et] *n* silueta.
silk [sɪlk] *n* seda.
silkworm ['sɪlkwɜːm] *n* gusano de la seda.
sill [sɪl] *n* alféizar, antepecho.
silly ['sɪlɪ] *adj* tonto,-a.
silver ['sɪlvəʳ] *n* plata. ■ **silver foil** papel de plata.
similar ['sɪmɪləʳ] *adj* similar.
simmer ['sɪməʳ] *vt-vi* cocer(se) a fuego lento.
simple ['sɪmpəl] *adj* simple.
simplify ['sɪmplɪfaɪ] *vt* simplificar.
sin [sɪn] *n* pecado. ► *vi* pecar.
since [sɪns] *adv* desde entonces. ► *prep* desde. ► *conj* **1** desde que. **2** ya que, puesto que.
sincere [sɪn'sɪəʳ] *adj* sincero,-a.
sincerely [sɪn'sɪəlɪ] *adv* sinceramente. ● **yours sincerely** atentamente *(en carta)*.
sing [sɪŋ] *vt-vi* cantar..
singer ['sɪŋəʳ] *n* cantante.
single ['sɪŋgəl] *adj* **1** solo,-a. **2** único,-a. **3** individual *(cama)*. **4** soltero,-a. ► *n* **1** GB billete de ida. **2** single *(disco)*. ► *npl*

singles individuales. ■ **single bed** cama individual; **single parent** madre soltera, padre soltero; **single room** habitación individual.
singular ['sɪŋgjʊləʳ] *adj-n* singular.
sinister ['sɪnɪstəʳ] *adj* siniestro,-a.
sink [sɪŋk] *n* **1** fregadero. **2** US lavabo. ► *vt* hundir. ► *vi* **1** hundirse *(barco)*. **2** ponerse *(sol, luna)*. **3** bajar, descender.
sinner ['sɪnəʳ] *n* pecador,-ra.
sip [sɪp] *n* sorbo.
sir [sɜːʳ] *n* **1** *fml* señor. **2** sir. ● **Dear Sir** muy señor mío.
siren ['saɪərən] *n* sirena.
sirloin ['sɜːlɔɪn] *n* solomillo.
sister ['sɪstəʳ] *n* hermana.
sister-in-law ['sɪstərɪnlɔː] *n* cuñada.
sit [sɪt] *vi* sentarse.
to sit down *vi* sentarse.
site [saɪt] *n* emplazamiento.
situation [sɪtjʊ'eɪʃən] *n* situación. ■ **"Situations vacant"** "Ofertas de trabajo".
six [sɪks] *num* seis.
sixteen [sɪks'tiːn] *num* dieciséis.
sixteenth [sɪks'tiːnθ] *adj-n* decimosexto,-a.
sixth [sɪksθ] *adj-n* sexto,-a.
sixty ['sɪkstɪ] *num* sesenta.
size [saɪz] *n* **1** tamaño. **2** talla *(de prenda)*. **3** número *(de zapatos)*.

skate [skeɪt] *n* patín. ► *vi* patinar.

skateboard ['skeɪtbɔːd] *n* monopatín.

skating ['skeɪtɪŋ] *n* patinaje. ■ **skating rink** pista de patinaje.

skeleton ['skelɪtən] *n* esqueleto. ■ **skeleton key** llave maestra.

sketch [sketʃ] *n* **1** boceto. **2** esquema. **3** sketch. ► *vt* bosquejar.

ski [skiː] *n* esquí. ► *vi* esquiar. ■ **ski lift** telesquí, telesilla; **ski resort** estación de esquí.

skid [skɪd] *n* patinazo. ► *vi* patinar.

skier ['skɪəʳ] *n* esquiador,-ra.

skiing ['skɪɪŋ] *n* esquí.

skill [skɪl] *n* habilidad.

skilled [skɪld] *adj* **1** especializado,-a. **2** hábil.

skim [skɪm] *vt* desnatar.

skin [skɪn] *n* piel. ► *vt* **1** pelar. **2** despellejar.

skip¹ [skɪp] *n* salto. ► *vi* saltar. ■ **skipping rope** comba.

skip² [skɪp] *n* contenedor.

skirt [skɜːt] *n* falda. ■ **skirting board** GB zócalo, rodapié.

skittle ['skɪtəl] *n* bolo. ► *npl* **skittles** bolos.

skull [skʌl] *n* cráneo.

sky [skaɪ] *n* cielo.

skylight ['skaɪlaɪt] *n* tragaluz.

skyscraper ['skaɪskreɪpəʳ] *n* rascacielos.

slack [slæk] *adj* flojo,-a.

slacken ['slækən] *vi* **1** aflojarse. **2** reducirse, disminuir.

slam [slæm] *n* portazo. ► *vt* cerrar de golpe.

slang [slæŋ] *n* argot, jerga.

slap [slæp] *n* **1** palmadita *(en la espalda)*. **2** bofetada.

slash [slæʃ] *n* **1** tajo. **2** cuchillada, navajazo. **3** barra oblicua.

slate [sleɪt] *n* pizarra.

slaughter ['slɔːtəʳ] *n* matanza. ► *vt* masacrar.

slave [sleɪv] *n* esclavo,-a.

sledge [sledʒ] *n* trineo.

sleep [sliːp] *n* sueño. ► *vt-vi* dormir.● **to go to sleep** irse a dormir.

sleeping ['sliːpɪŋ] *adj.* ■ **sleeping bag** saco de dormir; **sleeping car** coche-cama.

sleepwalker ['sliːpwɔːkəʳ] *n* sonámbulo,-a.

sleet [sliːt] *n* aguanieve. ► *vi* caer aguanieve.

sleeve [sliːv] *n* **1** manga. **2** funda *(de disco)*.

sleigh [sleɪ] *n* trineo.

slice [slaɪs] *n* **1** rebanada *(de pan)*. **2** loncha *(de jamón)*. **3** tajada *(de carne)*. **4** rodaja *(de limón)*. **5** porción *(de pastel)*. ► *vt* cortar a rebanadas/lonchas *etc.*

slide [slaɪd] *n* **1** resbalón. **2** tobogán. **3** diapositiva. **4** portaobjetos *(de microscopio)*. ► *vi* **1** deslizarse. **2** resbalar.

slight [slaɪt] *adj* ligero,-a.
slightly ['slaɪtlɪ] *adv* un poco.
slim [slɪm] *adj* **1** delgado,-a. ► *vi* adelgazar.
sling [slɪŋ] *n* cabestrillo.
slip[1] [slɪp] *n* **1** resbalón. **2** combinación *(prenda femenina).* ► *vi* esbalar.
slip[2] [slɪp] *n* **1** papelito. **2** ficha.
slipper ['slɪpə'] *n* zapatilla.
slippery ['slɪpərɪ] *adj* resbaladizo,-a
slit [slɪt] *n* abertura.
slogan ['sləʊgən] *n* eslogan.
slope [sləʊp] *n* cuesta *(de montaña).* ► *vi* inclinarse.
slot [slɒt] *n* **1** abertura. **2** ranura. **3** muesca. ▪ **slot machine 1** máquina expendedora. **2** tragaperras.
slow [sləʊ] *adj* **1** lento,-a. **2** atrasado,-a *(reloj).*
to slow down *vi* reducir la velocidad.
slug [slʌg] *n* babosa.
slum [slʌm] *n* **1** barrio bajo. **2** chabola, tugurio.
slump [slʌmp] *n* crisis económica.
sly [slaɪ] *adj* **1** astuto,-a,. **2** furtivo,-a *(mirada).*
smack [smæk] *n* bofetada, cachete. ► *vt* dar una bofetada a.
small [smɔːl] *adj* pequeño,-a. ▪ **small ads** anuncios por palabras; **small change** cambio, suelto.

smallpox ['smɔːlpɒks] *n* viruela.
smart [smɑːt] *adj* **1** elegante. **2** listo,-a.
smash [smæʃ] *n* smash, mate *(en tenis).* ► *vt* romper. ▪ **smash hit** gran éxito, exitazo.
smashing ['smæʃɪŋ] *adj* GB *fam* fenomenal.
smear [smɪə'] *n* mancha. ► *vt* **1** untar. **2** manchar.
smell [smel] *n* **1** olfato. **2** olor. ► *vt-vi* oler.
smelt[1] [smelt] *vt* fundir.
smelt[2] [smelt] *pt-pp* → smell.
smile [smaɪl] *n* sonrisa. ► *vi* sonreír.
smog [smɒg] *n* smog.
smoke [sməʊk] *n* humo. ► *vt-vi* fumar. ► *vt* ahumar. • **"No smoking"** "Prohibido fumar".
smoked [sməʊkt] *adj* ahumado,-a.
smoker ['sməʊkə'] *n* fumador,-ra.
smooth [smuːð] *adj* **1** liso,-a, llano,-a. **2** sin grumos *(líquido).* **3** suave *(vino).* ► *vt* alisar.
snack [snæk] *n* tentempié. • **to have a snack** picar algo. ▪ **snack bar** cafetería, bar.
snail [sneɪl] *n* caracol.
snake [sneɪk] *n* serpiente.
snap [snæp] *n* foto. ► *vt* **1** partir *(en dos).* **2** chasquear *(los dedos).*

snapshot ['snæpʃɒt] *n* foto instantánea.

sneakers ['sniːkrz] *npl* US zapatillas de deporte.

sneeze [sniːz] *n* estornudo. ► *vi* estornudar.

sniff [snɪf] *vt-vi* oler, olfatear.

snip [snɪp] *vt* cortar.

sniper ['snaɪpəʳ] *n* francotirador,-ra.

snob [snɒb] *n* esnob, snob.

snore [snɔːʳ] *n* ronquido. ► *vi* roncar.

snorkel ['snɔːkəl] *n* tubo de bucear.

snout [snaʊt] *n* hocico.

snow [snəʊ] *n* nieve. ► *vi* nevar.

snowfall ['snəʊfɔːl] *n* nevada.

snowflake ['snəʊfleɪk] *n* copo de nieve.

snowman ['snəʊmæn] *n* muñeco de nieve.

so [səʊ] *adv* 1 tan, tanto,-a: *she's so tired that...*, está tan cansada que... 2 mucho: *I miss you so*, te echo mucho de menos. 3 así: *It's Mary –So it is*, Es Mary –Así es. 4 que sí, que no: *I guess so*, supongo que sí; *I don't think so*, creo que no. 5 también: *I went to the demonstration and so did David*, fui a la manifestación y David también. ► *conj* 1 así que, por lo tanto. 2 para. • **and so on** y así sucesivamente; **if so** en ese caso; **not so... as...** no tan... como...; **or so** más o menos; **so that...** para que...; **so what?** *fam* ¿y qué?

soak [səʊk] *vt* 1 poner en remojo. 2 empapar.

soap [səʊp] *n* jabón. ► *vt* enjabonar. ▪ **soap opera** telenovela, culebrón.

sob [sɒb] *n* sollozo. ► *vi* sollozar.

sober ['səʊbəʳ] *adj* sobrio,-a.

so-called ['səʊkɔːld] *adj* llamado,-a.

soccer ['sɒkəʳ] *n* fútbol.

sociable ['səʊʃəbəl] *adj* sociable.

social ['səʊʃəl] *adj* social. ▪ **social security** seguridad social; **social worker** asistente,-a social.

socialism ['səʊʃəlɪzəm] *n* socialismo.

socialize ['səʊʃəlaɪz] *vi* relacionarse, alternar.

society [sə'saɪətɪ] *n* sociedad.

sociology [səʊsɪ'blɒdʒɪ] *n* sociología.

sock [sɒk] *n* calcetín.

socket ['sɒkɪt] *n* 1 cuenca *(del ojo)*. 2 enchufe.

soda ['səʊdə] *n* soda. ▪ **soda water** soda, sifón.

sofa ['səʊfə] *n* sofá.

soft [sɒft] *adj* 1 blando,-a *(cojín)*. 2 suave *(música)*. ▪ **soft drink** refresco.

soften ['sɒfən] *vt-vi* **1** ablandar(se). **2** suavizar(se).

software ['sɒftweəʳ] *n* software.

soil [sɔɪl] *n* tierra. ► *vt* ensuciar, manchar.

solar ['səʊləʳ] *adj* solar.

sold [səʊld] *pt-pp* → sell.

solder ['sɒldəʳ] *n* soldadura. ► *vt* soldar.

soldier ['səʊldʒəʳ] *n* soldado.

sole¹ [səʊl] *n* **1** planta *(del pie)*. **2** suela *(de zapato)*.

sole² [səʊl] *n* lenguado.

sole³ [səʊl] *adj* único,-a.

solicitor [səˈlɪsɪtəʳ] *n* **1** abogado,-a. **2** notario,-a.

solid ['sɒlɪd] *adj* **1** sólido,-a. **2** macizo,-a. ► *n* sólido.

solidarity [sɒlɪˈdærɪtɪ] *n* solidaridad.

solitary ['sɒlɪtərɪ] *adj* **1** solitario,-a. **2** solo,-a.

solitude ['sɒlɪtjuːd] *n* soledad.

solo ['səʊləʊ] *n* solo.

solution [səˈluːʃən] *n* solución.

solve [sɒlv] *vt* resolver.

some [sʌm] *adj* **1** unos,-as, algunos,-as *(con sust pl)*. **2** un poco *(de) (con sust sing)*. **3** cierto,-a, alguno,-a. **4** bastante. ► *pron* **1** algunos,-as, unos, -as. **2** algo, un poco.

somebody ['sʌmbədɪ] *pron* alguien.

somehow ['sʌmhaʊ] *adv* **1** de algún modo. **2** por alguna razón.

someone ['sʌmwʌn] *pron* → somebody.

something ['sʌmθɪŋ] *n* algo.

sometime ['sʌmtaɪm] *adv* un día, algún día. ► *adj* antiguo, -a, ex-.

sometimes ['sʌmtaɪmz] *adv* a veces, de vez en cuando.

somewhat ['sʌmwɒt] *adv* algo, un tanto.

somewhere ['sʌmweəʳ] *adv* en alguna parte, a alguna parte. ► *pron* un lugar, un sitio.

son [sʌn] *n* hijo.

song [sɒŋ] *n* canción.

son-in-law ['sʌnɪnlɔː] *n* yerno.

soon [suːn] *adv* pronto. • **as soon as** en cuanto; **soon afterwards** poco después.

sooner ['suːnəʳ] *adv* más temprano. • **no sooner...** nada más...; **sooner or later** tarde o temprano; **the sooner the better** cuanto antes mejor.

soot [sʊt] *n* hollín.

soothe [suːð] *vt* **1** calmar *(nervios)*. **2** aliviar *(dolor)*.

soprano [səˈprɑːnəʊ] *n* soprano.

sore [sɔːʳ] *adj* **1** dolorido,-a. **2** *fam* enfadado,-a. ► *n* llaga.

sorrow ['sɒrəʊ] *n* pena, pesar.

sorry ['sɒrɪ] *interj* ¡perdón!, ¡disculpe! • **to be sorry** sentirlo.

sort [sɔːt] *n* clase, tipo. ► *vt* clasificar. • **all sorts of** todo tipo de.

so-so ['səʊsəʊ] *adv fam* así así.

sought [sɔ:t] *pt-pp* → seek.

soul [səʊl] *n* alma.

sound[1] [saʊnd] *n* sonido. ▶ *vi* sonar.

sound[2] [saʊnd] *adj* **1** sano,-a. **2** en buen estado. **3** razonable. **4** robusto,-a.

soundproof ['saʊndpru:f] *adj* insonorizado,-a.

soundtrack ['saʊndtræk] *n* banda sonora.

soup [su:p] *n* **1** sopa, caldo. ▪ **soup plate** plato hondo, plato sopero; **soup spoon** cuchara sopera.

sour ['saʊə'] *adj* ácido,-a, agrio,-a.

source [sɔ:s] *n* fuente.

south [saʊθ] *n* sur. ▶ *adj* del sur. ▶ *adv* hacia el sur, al sur.

southern ['sʌðən] *adj* del sur.

souvenir [su:və'nɪə'] *n* recuerdo.

sovereign ['sɒvrɪn] *adj-n* soberano,-a.

sow[1] [saʊ] *n* cerda, puerca.

sow[2] [səʊ] *vt* sembrar.

space [speɪs] *n* espacio. ▪ **space shuttle** transbordador espacial.

spacecraft ['speɪskrɑ:ft] *n* nave espacial.

spaceship ['speɪsʃɪp] *n* nave espacial.

spacious ['speɪʃəs] *adj* espacioso,-a, amplio,-a.

spade[1] [speɪd] *n* pala.

spade[2] [speɪd] *n* pica *(naipes)*.

span [spæn] *n* **1** lapso *(de tiempo)*. **2** envergadura *(de alas)*. **3** luz *(de arco)*.

spank [spæŋk] *vt* zurrar.

spanner ['spænə'] *n* llave de tuerca.

spare [speə'] *adj* **1** de sobra, libre. **2** de recambio, de repuesto. ▶ *n* recambio. ▪ **spare room** habitación de invitados; **spare time** tiempo libre.

spark [spɑ:k] *n* chispa. ▪ **spark plug** bujía.

sparrow ['spærəʊ] *n* gorrión.

spasm ['spæzəm] *n* espasmo.

spat [spæt] *pt-pp* → spit.

speak [spi:k] *vi-vt* hablar. ▶ *vt* decir. ▪ **so to speak** por así decirlo.

to speak out *vi* hablar claro.

speaker ['spi:kə'] *n* **1** persona que habla. **2** interlocutor,-ra. **3** conferenciante. **4** altavoz.

spear [spɪə'] *n* **1** lanza. **2** arpón.

special ['speʃəl] *adj* especial. ▪ **special delivery** correo urgente.

specialist ['speʃəlɪst] *n* especialista.

species ['spi:ʃi:z] *n* especie.

specific [spə'sɪfɪk] *adj* específico,-a.

specify ['spesɪfaɪ] *vt* especificar.

specimen ['spesɪmən] *n* espécimen, muestra, ejemplar.

speck [spek] *n* **1** mota *(de polvo)*. **2** pizca.

spectacle ['spektəkəl] *n* espectáculo. ► *npl* **spectacles** gafas.

spectacular [spek'tækjʊləʳ] *adj* espectacular.

spectator [spek'teɪtəʳ] *n* espectador,-ra.

speculate ['spekjʊleɪt] *vi* especular.

sped [sped] *pt-pp* → speed.

speech [spiːtʃ] *n* **1** habla. **2** pronunciación. **3** discurso

speed [spiːd] *n* velocidad. ► *vi* **1** ir corriendo. **2** exceder el límite de velocidad. ▪ **speed limit** límite de velocidad.

to speed up *vt-vi* acelerar.

speedometer [spɪ'dɒmɪtəʳ] *n* velocímetro.

spell[1] [spel] *n* hechizo.

spell[2] [spel] *n* período, temporada.

spell[3] [spel] *vt-vi* deletrear. ► *vt fig* significar.

spelling ['spelɪŋ] *n* ortografía. ▪ **spelling mistake** falta de ortografía.

spelt [spelt] *pt-pp* → spell.

spend [spend] *vt* **1** gastar *(dinero)*. **2** pasar.

spent [spent] *pt-pp* → spend.

sperm [spɜːm] *n* esperma.

sphere [sfɪəʳ] *n* esfera.

spice [spaɪs] *n* especia. ► *vt* sazonar, condimentar.

spicy ['spaɪsɪ] *adj* picante.

spider ['spaɪdəʳ] *n* araña. ▪ **spider's web** telaraña.

spike [spaɪk] *n* **1** punta. **2** pincho. **3** clavo.

spill [spɪl] *n* derrame. ► *vt-vi* derramar(se), verter(se).

spin [spɪn] *n* **1** vuelta. **2** centrifugado *(de lavadora)*. **3** efecto *(de pelota)*. ► *vt* **1** dar vueltas (a). **2** centrifugar.

spinach ['spɪnɪdʒ] *n* espinacas.

spin-dryer [spɪn'draɪəʳ] *n* secadora.

spine [spaɪn] *n* **1** espina dorsal. **2** lomo *(de libro)*.

spiral ['spaɪərəl] *n* espiral. ▪ **spiral staircase** escalera de caracol.

spire ['spaɪəʳ] *n* aguja.

spirit[1] ['spɪrɪt] *n* alcohol. ► *npl* **spirits** licores.

spirit[2] ['spɪrɪt] *n* espíritu. ► *npl* **spirits** humor, moral. ● **to be in high spirits** estar animado,-a; **to be in low spirits** estar desanimado,-a.

spit[1] [spɪt] *n* asador, espetón.

spit[2] [spɪt] *n* esputo. ► *vt-vi* escupir.

spite [spaɪt] *n* despecho. ● **in spite of** a pesar de.

splash [splæʃ] *n* **1** chapoteo. **2** salpicadura. ► *vt* salpicar, rociar. ► *vi* chapotear.

splendid ['splendɪd] *adj* espléndido.

splinter ['splɪntəʳ] *n* astilla.

split [splɪt] *n* **1** grieta *(en madera)*. **2** desgarrón *(en tela)*. **3** división. ► *adj* **1** partido,-a. **2** dividido,-a. ► *vt-vi* **1** agrietar(se). **2** partir(se). **3** rajar(se), rasgar(se).

to split up *vt* partir, dividir. ► *vi* separarse *(pareja)*.

spoil [spɔɪl] *vt* **1** echar a perder. **2** malcriar.

spoke¹ [spəʊk] *pt* → speak.

spoke² [spəʊk] *n* radio *(de rueda)*.

spoken ['spəʊkən] *pp* → speak.

spokesman ['spəʊksmən] *n* portavoz.

sponge [spʌndʒ] *n* esponja. ■ **sponge cake** bizcocho.

sponsor ['spɒnsəʳ] *n* patrocinador,-ra. ► *vt* patrocinar.

spontaneous [spɒn'teɪnɪəs] *adj* espontáneo,-a.

spool [spuːl] *n* carrete, bobina.

spoon [spuːn] *n* cuchara.

spoonful ['spuːnfʊl] *n* cucharada.

sport [spɔːt] *n* deporte.

sportsman ['spɔːtsmən] *n* deportista.

sportswear ['spɔːtsweəʳ] *n* ropa deportiva.

sportswoman ['spɔːtswʊmən] *n* deportista.

spot [spɒt] *n* **1** lunar. **2** mancha. **3** grano *(en cara)*. **4** sitio, lugar. **5** aprieto, apuro. **6** spot *(publicitario)*. ► *vt* **1** darse cuenta de. **2** notar.

spotlight ['spɒtlaɪt] *n* foco.

spouse [spaʊz] *n* cónyuge.

spout [spaʊt] *n* **1** pico *(de jarra)*. **2** surtidor *(de fuente)*.

sprain [spreɪn] *n* torcedura. ► *vt* torcerse.

sprang [spræŋ] *pt* → spring.

spray [spreɪ] *n* **1** espuma *(del mar)*. **2** spray. ■ **spray can** aerosol.

spread [spred] ► *vt-vi* **1** extender(se). **2** desplegar(se) *(alas)*. **3** propagar(se). ► *vt* untar *(mantequilla)*.

spreadsheet ['spredʃiːt] *n* hoja de cálculo.

spree [spriː] *n* juerga.

spring [sprɪŋ] *n* **1** primavera. **2** manantial, fuente. **3** muelle. **4** ballesta *(de coche)*. ► *vi* saltar. ■ **spring onion** cebolleta; **spring roll** rollito de primavera.

springboard ['sprɪŋbɔːd] *n* trampolín.

sprinkle ['sprɪŋkəl] *vt* rociar.

sprinkler ['sprɪŋkələʳ] *n* aspersor.

sprint [sprɪnt] *n* esprin. ► *vi* esprintar.

sprout [spraʊt] *n* brote. ► *vi* brotar.

sprung [sprʌŋ] *pp* → spring.

spun [spʌn] *pt-pp* → spin.

spur [spɜːʳ] *n* espuela.

spurt [spɜːt] *n* chorro.

spy [spaɪ] *n* espía. ► *vi* espiar.

squad [skwɒd] *n* brigada.

squadron ['skwɒdrən] *n* escuadrón.

square [skweəˡ] *n* **1** cuadrado. **2** cuadro *(en tela)*. **3** casilla *(en tablero)*. **4** plaza. ▶ *adj* cuadrado,-a. ▶ *vt-vi* cuadrar. ▶ *vt* elevar al cuadrado. ■ **square brackets** corchetes.

squash[1] [skwɒʃ] *n* **1** zumo. **2** squash. ▶ *vt* aplastar.

squash[2] [skwɒʃ] *n* calabaza.

squat [skwɒt] *adj* rechoncho,-a. ▶ *vi* **1** agacharse. **2** ocupar ilegalmente.

squatter ['skwɒtəˡ] *n* okupa.

squeak [skwiːk] *n* **1** chillido *(de animal)*. **2** chirrido *(de neumático)*. ▶ *vi* **1** chillar *(animal)*. **2** chirriar *(neumático)*.

squeeze [skwiːz] *n* **1** apretón *(de manos)*. **2** aprieto. ▶ *vt* **1** apretar. **2** exprimir *(limón)*.

squid [skwɪd] *n* calamar.

squint [skwɪnt] *n* bizquera.

squirrel ['skwɪrəl] *n* ardilla.

stab [stæb] *n* puñalada. ▶ *vt-vi* apuñalar. ■ **stab of pain** punzada de dolor.

stability [stəˡbɪlɪtɪ] *n* estabilidad.

stable[1] ['steɪbəl] *adj* estable.

stable[2] ['steɪbəl] *n* cuadra, establo.

stack [stæk] *n* montón, pila.

stadium ['steɪdɪəm] *n* estadio.

staff [stɑːf] *n* personal.

stage [steɪdʒ] *n* **1** etapa. **2** escenario. ● **on stage** en escena.

stagger ['stægəˡ] *vi* tambalearse.

stain [steɪn] *n* mancha. ▶ *vt-vi* manchar(se). ■ **stain remover** quitamanchas.

stainless ['steɪnləs] *adj* inoxidable. ■ **stainless steel** acero inoxidable.

stair [steəˡ] *n* escalón, peldaño. ▶ *npl* **stairs** escalera.

staircase ['steəkeɪs] *n* escalera.

stake[1] [steɪk] *n* **1** apuesta. **2** intereses. ▶ *vt* apostar.

stake[2] [steɪk] *n* estaca, palo.

stalemate ['steɪlmeɪt] *n* tablas *(en ajedrez)*.

stalk[1] [stɔːk] *n* **1** tallo *(de planta)*. **2** rabillo *(de fruta)*.

stalk[2] [stɔːk] *vt* acechar.

stall [stɔːl] *n* **1** puesto *(de mercado)*. **2** caseta *(de feria)*. ▶ *npl* **stalls** platea.

stammer ['stæməˡ] *n* tartamudeo. ▶ *vi* tartamudear.

stamp [stæmp] *n* **1** sello, timbre. **2** tampón. ▶ *vt* sellar.

stand [stænd] *n* **1** postura. **2** pie *(de lámpara)*. **3** puesto *(de mercado)*. **4** stand *(de feria)*. **5** plataforma. **6** tribuna. ▶ *vi* **1** estar de pie, ponerse de pie. **2** estar, encontrarse. **3** seguir en pie *(oferta)*. **4** estar. ▶ *vt fam* aguantar: *I can't stand him*, no lo aguanto.

to stand for *vt* **1** significar. **2** defender, representar.

to stand out vi destacar.

to stand up vi ponerse de pie.

standard ['stændəd] n **1** nivel. **2** criterio. **3** norma. **4** patrón. ► adj normal, estándar.

standby ['stændbaɪ] n sustituto,-a. • **to be on standby** estar en lista de espera.

stank [stæŋk] pt → stink.

staple¹ ['steɪpəl] n producto básico.

staple² ['steɪpəl] n grapa.

stapler ['steɪpələ'] n grapadora.

star [stɑː'] n estrella. ► adj estelar. ► vi protagonizar.

starboard ['stɑːbəd] n estribor.

starch [stɑːtʃ] n almidón, fécula.

stare [steə'] n mirada fija. ► vi mirar fijamente.

starfish ['stɑːfɪʃ] n estrella de mar.

start [stɑːt] n **1** principio. **2** salida (de carrera). ► vt-vi **1** empezar. **2** arrancar (coche).

to start up vt-vi arrancar.

starter ['stɑːtə'] n **1** juez de salida. **2** motor de arranque. • **for starters 1** para empezar. **2** como primer plato.

starvation [stɑːˈveɪʃən] n hambre, inanición.

starve [stɑːv] vi **1** pasar hambre. **2** tener mucha hambre.

state [steɪt] n estado. ► vt exponer.

statement ['steɪtmənt] n declaración, afirmación.

statesman ['steɪtsmən] n estadista, hombre de Estado.

station ['steɪʃən] n **1** estación (de autobuses; tren). **2** emisora (de radio). **3** canal (de TV).

stationery ['steɪʃənərɪ] n artículos de escritorio.

statistics [stəˈtɪstɪks] n estadística.

statue ['stætjuː] n estatua.

status ['steɪtəs] n **1** estado. **2** estatus.

stave [steɪv] n pentagrama.

stay [steɪ] n estancia. ► vi **1** quedarse, permanecer. **2** alojarse (en hotel).

to stay in vi quedarse en casa.

to stay on vi quedarse.

to stay up vi no acostarse.

steady ['stedɪ] adj **1** firme, estable. **2** constante (movimiento).

steak [steɪk] n bistec, filete.

steal [stiːl] vt-vi robar.

steam [stiːm] n vapor. ► vt cocer al vapor. ▪ **steam engine** máquina de vapor; **steam iron** plancha de vapor.

steamer ['stiːmə'] n → steamship.

steamroller ['stiːmrəʊlə'] n apisonadora.

steamship ['stiːmʃɪp] n buque de vapo.

steel [stiːl] n acero. ▪ **steel wool** estropajo de aluminio.

steep¹ [stiːp] adj **1** empinado,-a, escarpado,-a (colina). **2** fig excesivo,-a (precio).

steep² [sti:p] vt remojar.

steeple ['sti:pəl] n aguja.

steer [stɪəʳ] vt conducir.

steering ['stɪərɪŋ] n dirección.
■ **steering wheel** volante.

stem [stem] n 1 tallo (de planta). 2 pie (de vaso).

step [step] n 1 paso. 2 escalón, peldaño. ▶ vi dar un paso, andar.

to step aside vi apartarse.

stepbrother ['stepbrʌðəʳ] n hermanastro.

stepchild ['steptʃaɪld] n hijastro,-a.

stepdaughter ['stepdɔ:təʳ] n hijastra.

stepfather ['stepfɑ:ðəʳ] n padrastro.

stepladder ['steplædəʳ] n escalera de mano.

stepmother ['stepmʌðəʳ] n madrastra.

stepsister ['stepsɪstəʳ] n hermanastra.

stepson ['stepsʌn] n hijastro.

stereo ['steriəu] adj estereofónico,-a.

sterile ['steraɪl] adj estéril, esterilizado,-a.

sterling ['stɜ:lɪŋ] n libra esterlina.

stern [stɜ:n] n popa.

stew [stju:] n estofado, guisado. ▶ vt estofar, guisar.

steward ['stju:əd] n 1 camarero (de barco). 2 auxiliar de vuelo (de avión).

stewardess ['stju:ədes] n 1 camarera (de barco). 2 azafata (de avión).

stick¹ [stɪk] n 1 palo. 2 bastón (para caminar).

stick² [stɪk] vt 1 clavar, hincar (punta). 2 pegar (con pegamento). ▶ vi atrancarse.

sticker ['stɪkəʳ] n 1 etiqueta adhesiva. 2 pegatina.

stiff [stɪf] adj rígido,-a, tieso,-a.
● **to feel stiff** tener agujetas.

still [stɪl] adj 1 quieto,-a. 2 tranquilo,-a (lago). 3 sin gas (agua). ▶ adv 1 todavía, aún. 2 aun así. 3 sin embargo.
■ **still life** ART naturaleza muerta, bodegón.

stimulate ['stɪmjuleɪt] vt estimular.

stimulus ['stɪmjuləs] n estímulo.

sting [stɪŋ] n 1 aguijón (de avispa). 2 picadura (herida). ▶ vt-vi picar.

stingy ['stɪndʒɪ] adj tacaño,-a.

stink [stɪŋk] n peste, hedor. ▶ vi apestar, heder.

stipulate ['stɪpjuleɪt] vt estipular.

stir [stɜ:ʳ] vt remover .

stirrup ['stɪrəp] n estribo.

stitch [stɪtʃ] n 1 puntada (al coser). 2 punto. ▶ vt 1 coser. 2 suturar.

stock [stɒk] n 1 reserva. 2 COMM existencias. 3 capital social. 4 ganado. 5 caldo. ●**to**

be out of stock estar agotado,-a. ■ **stock exchange** bolsa; **stock market** bolsa de valores.

stockbroker ['stɒkbrəʊkə'] n corredor,-ra de bolsa.

stocking ['stɒkɪŋ] n media.

stole¹ [stəʊl] pt → steal.

stole² [stəʊl] n estola.

stolen ['stəʊlən] pp → steal.

stomach ['stʌmək] n estómago.

stone [stəʊn] n 1 piedra. 2 GB hueso (de cereza, aceituna).

stood [stʊd] pt-pp → stand.

stool [stuːl] n taburete.

stop [stɒp] n 1 parada, alto. 2 punto (signo de puntuación). ► vt 1 parar. 2 impedir, evitar. 3 poner fin a (injusticia). 4 dejar de: *stop smoking!*, ¡deja de fumar! ► vi 1 pararse. 2 terminar. ► interj ¡pare!, ¡alto! ■ **stop sign** señal de stop.

stopover ['stɒpəʊvə'] n escala (de avión).

stopper ['stɒpə'] n tapón.

stopwatch ['stɒpwɒtʃ] n cronómetro.

storage ['stɔːrɪdʒ] n almacenamiento.

store [stɔː'] n tienda, almacén. ► vt almacenar.

storey ['stɔːrɪ] n piso, planta.

stork [stɔːk] n cigüeña.

storm [stɔːm] n tormenta.

story ['stɔːrɪ] n historia, cuento.

stout [staʊt] n cerveza negra.

stove [stəʊv] n 1 estufa. 2 cocina, hornillo.

straight [streɪt] adj 1 recto,-a. 2 liso,-a (pelo). 3 seguido,-a. 4 solo,-a (bebida). ► adv 1 en línea recta. 2 directamente.► n recta (en carrera). ● **straight ahead** todo recto.

straightaway [streɪtə'weɪ] adv en seguida.

straightforward [streɪt'fɔːwəd] adj 1 franco,-a. 2 sencillo,-a.

strain [streɪn] n 1 presión, tensión. 2 torcedura. ► vt 1 estirar (cuerda). 2 torcerse (músculo). 3 forzar (vista, voz).

strait [streɪt] n GEOG estrecho.

strand [strænd] n 1 hebra, hilo. 2 mechón.

strange [streɪndʒ] adj extraño,-a.

stranger ['streɪndʒə'] n extraño,-a.

strangle ['stræŋgəl] vt estrangular.

strap [stræp] n 1 correa (de reloj). 2 tirante (de vestido).

strategy ['strætədʒɪ] n estrategia.

straw [strɔː] n paja.

strawberry ['strɔːbərɪ] n fresa.

stray [streɪ] vi perderse.

streak ['striːk] n 1 raya, lista. 2 fig racha (de suerte).

stream [striːm] n 1 arroyo. 2 corriente. ► vi 1 manar. 2 fig desfilar (gente).

streamer ['stri:mə^r] *n* serpentina.

street [stri:t] *n* calle.

streetlamp ['stri:tlæmp] *n* farola.

strength [streŋθ] *n* fuerza. ■ **strength of will** fuerza de voluntad.

strengthen ['streŋθən] *vt-vi* fortalecer(se).

stress [stres] *n* 1 estrés. 2 acento. ► *vt* 1 recalcar, subrayar. 2 acentuar.

stretch [stretʃ] *n* 1 extensión. 2 tramo *(de terreno)*. 3 intervalo *(de tiempo)*. ► *vt-vi* 1 extender(se) *(terreno)*. 2 estirar(se).

to stretch out *vt* 1 estirar *(piernas)*. 2 alargar *(mano)*. ► *vi* 1 estirarse. 2 alargarse.

stretcher ['stretʃə^r] *n* camilla.

strict [strɪkt] *adj* estricto,-a.

stride [straɪd] *n* zancada.

strike [straɪk] *n* huelga. ► *vt* 1 pegar, golpear. 2 chocar contra. ► *vi* 1 atacar. 2 hacer huelga. 3 dar la hora. • **to be on strike** estar en huelga.

striker ['straɪkə^r] *n* 1 huelguista. 2 delantero,-a *(en fútbol)*.

string [strɪŋ] *n* 1 cuerda, cordón. 2 ristra *(de ajos, mentiras)*. 3 serie *(de acontecimientos)*.

strip[1] [strɪp] *n* 1 tira. 2 franja *(de tierra)*.

strip[2] [strɪp] *vi* desnudarse.

stripe [straɪp] *n* raya.

stroke [strəuk] *n* 1 golpe. 2 brazada *(en natación)*. 3 campanada. ► *vt* acariciar.

stroll [strəul] *n* paseo. ► *vi* pasear, dar un paseo.

strong [strɒŋ] *adj* fuerte. ► *adv* fuerte.

struck [strʌk] *pt-pp* → strike.

structure ['strʌktʃə^r] *n* estructura. ► *vt* estructurar.

struggle ['strʌgəl] *n* lucha. ► *vi* luchar.

stub [stʌb] *n* 1 colilla *(de cigarrillo)*. 2 resguardo.

stubble ['stʌbəl] *n* 1 rastrojo. 2 barba *(incipiente)*.

stubborn ['stʌbən] *adj* terco,-a.

stuck [stʌk] *pt-pp* → stick.

stud[1] [stʌd] *n* tachuela.

stud[2] [stʌd] *n* semental.

student ['stju:dənt] *n* estudiante.

studio ['stju:dɪəu] *n* estudio. ■ **studio flat** estudio.

study ['stʌdɪ] *n* estudio. ► *vt-vi-vt* estudiar.

stuff [stʌf] *n* 1 *fam* cosas, trastos. 2 cosa. ► *vt* rellenar. 1 disecar. 2 atiborrar. • **to stuff oneself** *fam* hartarse de comida.

stuffing ['stʌfɪŋ] *n* relleno.

stuffy ['stʌfɪ] *adj* cargado,-a, mal ventilado,-a.

stumble ['stʌmbəl] *vi* tropezar.

stun [stʌn] *vt* aturdir.

stung [stʌŋ] *pt-pp* → sting.

stunk [stʌŋk] *pt-pp* → stink.
stunning ['stʌnɪŋ] *adj* **1** pasmoso. **2** estupendo,-a.
stuntman ['stʌntmæn] *n* doble, especialista.
stuntwoman ['stʌntwumən] *n* doble, especialista.
stupid ['stjuːpɪd] *adj-n* tonto,-a.
stutter ['stʌtəʳ] *n* tartamudeo. ▶ *vi* tartamudear.
style [staɪl] *n* estilo.
stylish ['staɪlɪʃ] *adj* elegante.
subdue [səb'djuː] *vt* someter, dominar.
subject [(*n-adj*) 'sʌbdʒekt, (*vb*) səb'dʒekt] *n* **1** tema. **2** asignatura. **3** súbdito. **4** sujeto. ▶ *adj* sujeto,-a. ▶ *vt* someter.
subjunctive [səb'dʒʌŋktɪv] *adj* subjuntivo,-a. ▶ *n* subjuntivo.
sublet [sʌb'let] *vt-vi* realquilar.
submarine [sʌbmə'riːn] *n* submarino.
submerge [səb'mɜːdʒ] *vt-vi* sumergir(se).
submit [səb'mɪt] *vt* someter. ▶ *vi* someterse.
subordinate [(*adj-n*) sə'bɔːdɪnət, (*vb*) sə'bɔːdɪneɪt] *adj-n* subordinado,-a. ▶ *vt* subordinar.
subscribe [səb'skraɪb] *vi* **1** subscribirse (*a revista*). **2** suscribir (*opinión*).
subscriber [səb'skraɪbəʳ] *n* **1** subscriptor,-ra (*de revista*). **2** abonado,-a (*de servicio*).

subscription [səb'skrɪpʃən] *n* **1** subscripción (*de revista*). **2** abono (*de servicio*).
subsidize ['sʌbsɪdaɪz] *vt* subvencionar.
subsidy ['sʌbsɪdɪ] *n* subsidio.
substance ['sʌbstəns] *n* sustancia.
substitute ['sʌbstɪtjuːt] *n* substituto,-a. ▶ *vt* sustituir.
subtle ['sʌtəl] *adj* sutil.
subtract [səb'trækt] *vt* restar.
suburb ['sʌbɜːb] *n* barrio periférico, barrio residencial. ■ **the suburbs** las afueras.
subway ['sʌbweɪ] *n* **1** GB paso subterráneo. **2** US metro.
succeed [sək'siːd] *vi* tener éxito.
success [sək'ses] *n* éxito.
successful [sək'sesful] *adj* que tiene éxito.
successive [sək'sesɪv] *adj* sucesivo,-a.
such [sʌtʃ] *adj* **1** tal, semejante. **2** tan… como, tanto, -a… que. ▶ *adv* muy, mucho,-a, tan, tanto,-a.
suck [sʌk] *n vt-vi* chupar.
sudden ['sʌdən] *adj* repentino,-a.
suddenly ['sʌdənlɪ] *adv* de repente, de pronto.
sue [suː] *vt-vi* demandar.
suede [sweɪd] *n* ante, gamuza.
suffer ['sʌfəʳ] *vt-vi* sufrir.
sufficient [sə'fɪʃənt] *adj* suficiente.

suffix ['sʌfɪks] *n* sufijo.
suffocate ['sʌfəkeɪt] *vt-vi* asfixiar(se).
sugar ['ʃʊgəʳ] *n* azúcar. ■ **sugar bowl** azucarero.
sugarbeet ['ʃʊgəbiːt] *n* remolacha azucarera.
suggest [sə'dʒest] *vt* **1** sugerir. **2** implicar.
suggestion [sə'dʒestʃən] *n* sugerencia.
suicide ['sjuːɪsaɪd] *n* suicidio. • **to commit suicide** suicidarse.
suit [sjuːt] *n* **1** traje. **2** pleito. **3** palo *(de naipes)*. ► *vt* **1** convenir a. **2** sentar bien.
suitable ['sjuːtəbəl] *adj* **1** apropiado,-a. **2** conveniente.
suitcase ['suːtkeɪs] *n* maleta.
suite [swiːt] *n* suite.
sultry ['sʌltrɪ] *adj* bochornoso,-a.
sum [sʌm] *n* suma.
summarize ['sʌməraɪz] *vt* resumir.
summary ['sʌmərɪ] *n* resumen.
summer ['sʌməʳ] *n* verano.
summit ['sʌmɪt] *n* cumbre.
sun [sʌn] *n* sol.
sunbathe ['sʌnbeɪð] *vi* tomar el sol.
Sunday ['sʌndeɪ] *n* domingo.
sunflower ['sʌnflaʊəʳ] *n* girasol.
sung [sʌŋ] *pp* → sing.
sunglasses ['sʌnglaːsɪz] *npl* gafas de sol.

sunk [sʌŋk] *pp* → sink.
sunlight ['sʌnlaɪt] *n* luz del sol.
sunny ['sʌnɪ] *adj* soleado,-a.
sunrise ['sʌnraɪz] *n* salida del sol, amanecer.
sunset ['sʌnset] *n* puesta del sol.
sunshine ['sʌnʃaɪn] *n* luz del sol.
sunstroke ['sʌnstrəʊk] *n* insolación.
suntan ['sʌntæn] *n* bronceado.
superb [suː'pɜːb] *adj* estupendo,-a.
superficial [suːpə'fɪʃəl] *adj* superficial.
superintendent [suːpərɪn'tendənt] *n* inspector,-ra.
superior [suː'pɪərɪəʳ] *adj* superior. ► *n* superior,-ra.
superlative [suː'pɜːlətɪv] *adj* superlativo,-a. ► *n* superlativo.
supermarket [suːpə'maːkɪt] *n* supermercado.
supernatural [suːpə'nætʃərəl] *adj* sobrenatural.
superstitious [sjuːpə'stɪʃəs] *adj* supersticioso,-a.
supervise ['suːpəvaɪz] *vt* supervisar.
supper ['sʌpəʳ] *n* cena.
supplement ['sʌplɪmənt] *n* suplemento.
supplier [sə'plaɪəʳ] *n* proveedor,-ra.
supply [sə'plaɪ] *vt* **1** suministrar, abastecer. ► *n* suministro.

► *npl* **supplies** provisiones. • **supply and demand** la oferta y la demanda.

support [sə'pɔːt] *n* apoyo. ► *vt* **1** sostener *(peso)*. **2** apoyar *(causa)*.

supporter [sə'pɔːtə^r] *n* **1** POL partidiario,-a. **2** seguidor,-ra.

suppose [sə'pəʊz] *vt* suponer. • **I suppose so/not** supongo que sí/no.

suppository [sə'pɒzɪtərɪ] *n* supositorio.

suppress [sə'pres] *vt* **1** suprimir *(texto)*. **2** reprimir *(sentimientos, revuelta)*.

supreme [suː'priːm] *adj* supremo,-a.

surcharge ['sɜːtʃɑːdʒ] *n* recargo.

sure [ʃʊə^r] *adj* seguro,-a. ► *adv* **1** claro. **2** seguro. **3** de verdad.

surf [sɜːf] *n* **1** oleaje. **2** espuma. ► *vi* hacer surf. • **to surf the Net** navegar por Internet.

surface ['sɜːfəs] *n* superficie.

surgeon ['sɜːdʒən] *n* cirujano,-a.

surgery ['sɜːdʒərɪ] *n* **1** cirugía. **2** GB consultorio, consulta.

surname ['sɜːneɪm] *n* apellido.

surplus ['sɜːpləs] ► *n* **1** excedente. **2** superávit.

surprise [sə'praɪz] *n* sorpresa. ► *vt* sorprender.

surprising [sə'praɪzɪŋ] *adj* sorprendente.

surrender [sə'rendə^r] *n* rendición. ► *vt-vi* rendir(se).

surround [sə'raʊnd] *vt* rodear.

surroundings [sə'raʊndɪŋs] *npl* alrededores.

survey ['sɜːveɪ] *n* **1** sondeo *(de opinión)*. **2** encuesta, estudio *(de tendencias)*.

survive [sə'vaɪv] *vt-vi* sobrevivir (a).

survivor [sə'vaɪvə^r] *n* superviviente.

suspect [*(adj-n)* 'sʌspekt, *(vb)* sə'spekt] *adj-n* sospechoso,-a. ► *vt* sospechar.

suspend [sə'spend] *vt* suspender *(partido)*.

suspender [sə'spendə^r] *n* liga. ► *npl* **suspenders** tirantes.

suspense [səs'spens] *n* suspense.

suspension [sə'spenʃən] *n* suspensión *(de partido)*, expulsión *(de alumno)*.

suspicion [sə'spɪʃən] *n* sospecha.

suspicious [sə'spɪʃəs] *adj* **1** sospechoso,-a. **2** desconfiado,-a.

sustain [sə'steɪn] *vt* sostener.

swallow¹ ['swɒləʊ] *n* **1** trago *(de bebida)*. **2** bocado *(de comida)*. ► *vt-vi* tragar(se).

swallow² ['swɒləʊ] *n* golondrina *(ave)*.

swam [swæm] *pt* → swim.

swamp [swɒmp] *n* pantano, ciénaga.

swan [swɒn] *n* cisne.
swap [swɒp] *vt-vi fam* intercambiar, cambiar.
swarm [swɔːm] *n* enjambre.
swear [sweəʳ] *vt-vi* jurar. ► *vi* decir palabrotas.
swearword ['sweəwɜːd] *n* palabrota, taco.
sweat [swet] *n* sudor. ► *vt-vi* sudar.
sweater ['swetəʳ] *n* suéter.
sweep [swiːp] *n* **1** barrido. **2** redada *(de policía)*. ► *vt-vi* barrer.
sweeper ['swiːpəʳ] *n* barrendero,-a.
sweet [swiːt] *adj* dulce. ► *n* **1** caramelo, golosina. **2** postre.
  ▪ **sweet potato** boniato.
sweeten ['swiːtən] *vt* endulzar.
swelling ['swelɪŋ] *n* hinchazón.
swept [swept] *pt-pp* → sweep.
swim [swɪm] *n* baño. ► *vi* nadar.
swimmer ['swɪməʳ] *n* nadador,-ra.
swimming ['swɪmɪŋ] *n* natación. ▪ **swimming baths** piscina *(pública)*; **swimming costume** bañador; **swimming pool** piscina; **swimming trunks** bañador.
swimsuit ['swɪmsuːt] *n* bañador, traje de baño.
swindle ['swɪndəl] *n* estafa, timo. ► *vt* estafar, timar.

swing [swɪŋ] *n* columpio. ► *vt-vi* **1** balancear(se). **2** columpiar(se).
switch [swɪtʃ] *n* interruptor. ► *vt* cambiar, intercambiar.
to switch off *vt* apagar.
to switch on *vt* encender.
sword [sɔːd] *n* espada.
swordfish ['sɔːdfɪʃ] *n* pez espada.
swore [swɔːʳ] *pt* → swear.
sworn [swɔːn] *pp* → swear.
swum [swʌm] *pp* → swim.
swung [swʌŋ] *pt-pp* → swing.
syllable ['sɪləbəl] *n* sílaba.
syllabus ['sɪləbəs] *n* plan de estudios.
symbol ['sɪmbəl] *n* símbolo.
sympathize ['sɪmpəθaɪz] *vi* **1** compadecerse. **2** comprender.
sympathy ['sɪmpəθɪ] *n* **1** compasión. **2** pésame. **3** comprensión.
symphony ['sɪmfənɪ] *n* sinfonía.
symptom ['sɪmptəm] *n* síntoma.
synonym ['sɪnənɪm] *n* sinónimo.
syntax ['sɪntæks] *n* sintaxis.
synthesis ['sɪnθəsɪs] *n* síntesis.
synthetic [sɪn'θetɪk] *adj* sintético,-a.
syringe [sɪ'rɪndʒ] *n* jeringuilla.
syrup ['sɪrəp] *n* **1** jarabe. **2** almíbar.
system ['sɪstəm] *n* sistema.

tab 194

T

tab [tæb] *n* **1** lengüeta. **2** etiqueta *(en ropa)*.

table ['teɪbəl] *n* **1** mesa. **2** tabla, cuadro. ▪ **table football** futbolín; **table tennis** tenis de mesa.

tablecloth ['teɪbəlklɒθ] *n* mantel.

tablespoon ['teɪbəlspuːn] *n* cuchara de servir.

tablet ['tæblət] *n* pastilla.

tabloid ['tæblɔɪd] *n* periódico.

tact [tækt] *n* tacto.

tactics ['tæktɪks] *npl* táctica.

tadpole ['tædpəʊl] *n* renacuajo.

tag [tæg] *n* etiqueta.

tail [teɪl] *vt* seguir. ▶ *n* cola. ▶ *npl* **tails** cruz *(de moneda)*.

tailor ['teɪləʳ] *n* sastre,-a.

take [teɪk] *vt* **1** tomar, coger. **2** llevar. **3** requerir, necesitar. **4** apuntar, anotar. **5** ocupar. **6** llevar, tardar.

to take away *vt* **1** llevarse. **2** quitar, sacar. **3** restar.

to take back *vt* **1** devolver. **2** retractarse.

to take down *vt* apuntar.

to take off *vt* quitarse *(ropa)*. ▶ *vi* despegar *(avión)*.

to take out *vt* invitar a salir.

takeaway ['teɪkəweɪ] *n* establecimiento que vende comida para llevar.

taken ['teɪkən] *pp* → take.

takeoff ['teɪkɒf] *n* despegue.

talcum powder ['tælkəm-paʊdəʳ] *n* polvos de talco.

tale [teɪl] *n* cuento.

talent ['tælənt] *n* talento. ▪ **talent scout** cazatalentos.

talk [tɔːk] *vt-vi* hablar. ▶ *n* conversación. ▪ **talk show** programa de entrevistas.

talkative ['tɔːkətɪv] *adj* hablador,-ra.

tall [tɔːl] *adj* alto,-a.

tambourine [tæmbə'riːn] *n* pandereta.

tame [teɪm] *vt* domar.

tampon ['tæmpɒn] *n* tampón.

tan [tæn] *n* bronceado. ▶ *vi* ponerse moreno,-a.

tangent ['tændʒənt] *n* tangente.

tangerine [tændʒəriːn] *n* mandarina.

tank [tæŋk] *n* **1** depósito. **2** tanque.

tanker ['tæŋkəʳ] *n* **1** buque cisterna. **2** petrolero. **3** camión cisterna.

tantrum ['tæntrəm] *n* rabieta.

tap[1] [tæp] *n* grifo.

tap[2] [tæp] *n* golpecito.

tape [teɪp] *n* cinta. ▶ *vt* grabar. ▪ **tape measure** cinta métrica; **tape recorder** magnetófono, grabadora.

tapestry ['tæpəstrɪ] *n* tapiz.

tar [tɑːʳ] *n* alquitrán.

target ['tɑːgɪt] *n* blanco, objetivo.

tariff ['tærɪf] n tarifa.
tarmac ['tɑːmæk] n asfalto.
tart [tɑːt] n tarta, pastel.
task [tɑːsk] n tarea, labor.
taste [teɪst] n sabor, gusto. ▶
vt 1 probar (comida). 2 catar
(vino). ▶ vi saber.
tasteless ['teɪstləs] adj 1 de mal
gusto. 2 insípido,-a, soso,-a.
tattoo [tə'tuː] n tatuaje. ▶ vt ta-
tuar.
taught [tɔːt] pt-pp → teach.
tavern ['tævən] n taberna.
tax [tæks] n impuesto. ▶ vt
gravar. ▪ **tax free** libre de
impuestos; **tax return** declaración de la renta.
taxi ['tæksɪ] n taxi. ▪ **taxi driver** taxista.
taxpayer ['tækspeɪəʳ] n contribuyente.
tea [tiː] n 1 té. 2 merienda. 3
cena.
teach [tiːtʃ] vt 1 enseñar. 2
dar clases de (asignatura).
teacher ['tiːtʃəʳ] n maestro,-a,
profesor,-ra.
teaching ['tiːtʃɪn] n enseñanza.
teacup ['tiːkʌp] n taza de té.
team [tiːm] n equipo.
teapot ['tiːpɒt] n tetera.
tear¹ [tɪəʳ] n lágrima. ▪ **tear
gas** gas lacrimógeno.
tear² [teəʳ] n rotura, siete. ▶ vt
rasgar.
tease [tiːz] vt burlarse de.
teaspoon ['tiːspuːn] n cucharilla.

teat [tiːt] n 1 teta. 2 tetina (de
botella).
technical ['teknɪkəl] adj técnico,-a.
technique [tek'niːk] n técnica.
technology [tek'nɒlədʒɪ] n tecnología.
teddy bear ['tedɪbeəʳ] n osito
de peluche.
teenager ['tiːneɪdʒəʳ] n adolescente (de 13 a 19 años).
tee-shirt ['tiːʃɜːt] n camiseta.
teeth [tiːθ] npl → tooth.
teetotaller [tiː'təʊtləʳ] n abstemio,-a.
telegram ['telɪgræm] n telegrama.
telegraph ['telɪgrɑːf] n telé-
grafo.
telephone ['telɪfəʊn] n teléfono. ▶ vt-vi llamar por teléfono.
▪ **telephone box** cabina telefónica; **telephone directory**
guía telefónica; **telephone
operator** telefonista.
telephoto lens [telɪfəʊtəʊ'-
lenz] n teleobjetivo.
telescope ['telɪskəʊp] n telescopio.
television ['telɪvɪʒən] n televisión. ▪ **television set** televisor.
telex ['teleks] n télex.
tell [tel] vt 1 decir. 2 contar
(historia). ▶ vi saber.
to tell off vt echar una bronca a, reñir.
teller ['teləʳ] n cajero,-a.

telling-off [telɪŋ'ɒf] *n fam* bronca.

telly ['telɪ] *n fam* tele.

temper ['tempə'] *n* temperamento. ► *vt* templar. • **to lose one's temper** enfadarse.

temperature ['tempərətʃə'] *n* temperatura. • **to have a temperature** tener fiebre.

tempest ['tempəst] *n* tempestad.

temple ['tempəl] *n* **1** templo. **2** sien.

temporary ['tempərərɪ] *adj* temporal.

tempt [tempt] *vt* tentar.

temptation [temp'teɪʃən] *n* tentación.

ten [ten] *num* diez.

tenacity [tə'næsɪtɪ] *n* tenacidad.

tenant ['tenənt] *n* inquilino,-a.

tend [tend] *vi* tender a, tener tendencia a. ► *vt* cuidar.

tendency ['tendənsɪ] *n* tendencia.

tender[1] ['tendə'] *adj* tierno,-a.

tender[2] ['tendə'] *n* oferta.

tendon ['tendən] *n* tendón.

tenement ['tenəmənt] *n* bloque de pisos.

tennis ['tenɪs] *n* tenis. ▪ **tennis court** pista de tenis.

tenor ['tenə'] *n* tenor.

tense [tens] *adj* tenso,-a. ► *n* tiempo *(de verbo)*.

tension ['tenʃən] *n* tensión.

tent [tent] *n* tienda de campaña.

tentacle ['tentəkəl] *n* tentáculo.

tenth [tenθ] *adj-n* décimo,-a.

tepid ['tepɪd] *adj* tibio,-a.

term [tɜːm] *vt* calificar de. ► *n* **1** trimestre. **2** período, plazo. **3** término. ► *npl* **terms 1** condiciones. **2** relaciones.

terminal ['tɜːmɪnəl] *adj-n* terminal.

terminate ['tɜːmɪneɪt] *vt-vi* terminar.

terminus ['tɜːmɪnəs] *n* terminal.

termite ['tɜːmaɪt] *n* termita.

terrace ['terəs] *n* terraza.

terrain [tə'reɪn] *n* terreno.

terrible ['terɪbəl] *adj* terrible.

terrific [tə'rɪfɪk] *adj* fabuloso,-a.

terrify ['terɪfaɪ] *vt* aterrar.

territory ['terɪtərɪ] *n* territorio.

terror ['terə'] *n* terror.

terrorism ['terərɪzəm] *n* terrorismo.

test [test] *n* **1** prueba. **2** examen, test. ► *vt* probar, poner a prueba. ▪ **test tube** tubo de ensayo.

testament ['testəmənt] *n* testamento.

testicle ['testɪkəl] *n* testículo.

testify ['testɪfaɪ] *vt-vi* testificar.

testimony ['testɪmənɪ] *n* testimonio.

tetanus ['tetənəs] *n* tétanos.

text [tekst] *n* texto.

textbook ['tekstbʊk] *n* libro de texto.

textile ['tekstaɪl] *adj* textil. ► *n* textil, tejido.

thirst

texture ['tekstʃəʳ] *n* textura.
than [ðæn] *conj* **1** que. **2** de.
thank [θæŋk] *vt* agradecer. ►
npl **thanks** gracias. • **thanks
to** gracias a; **thank you** gracias.
thankful ['θæŋkful] *adj* agradecido,-a.
that [ðæt] *adj* ese, esa, aquel,
aquella. ► *pron* **1** ése, ésa,
aquél, aquélla. **2** eso, aquello. **3** que *(relativo)*. ► *conj*
que. • **that is** es decir.
thaw [θɔː] *n* deshielo. ► *vt-vi*
deshelar(se).
the [ðə] *det* el, la, los, las.
theatre ['θɪətəʳ] (US **theater**)
n **1** teatro. **2** quirófano.
theft [θeft] *n* robo, hurto.
their [ðeəʳ] *adj* su, sus.
theirs [ðeəz] *pron* (el) suyo, (la)
suya, (los) suyos, (las) suyas.
them [ðem, *unstressed* ðəm]
pron **1** los, las *(comp directo)*. **2**
les *(comp indirecto)*. **3** ellos,
ellas *(con preposisición)*.
theme [θiːm] *n* tema. ▪ **theme
park** parque temático.
themselves [ðəm'selvz] *pron*
1 ellos mismos, ellas mismas. **2** se.
then [ðen] *adv* **1** entonces. **2**
luego, después. **3** en ese caso. • **then again** también.
theology [θɪ'bləʤɪ] *n* teología.
theory ['θɪərɪ] *n* teoría.
therapy ['θerəpɪ] *n* terapia.

there [ðeəʳ] *adv* allí, allá, ahí.
• **there is/are** hay; **there
was/were** había; **there you
are** ahí tienes.
thereabouts [ðeərə'bauts] *adv*
por ahí.
thereafter [ðeə'ræftəʳ] *adv* a
partir de entonces.
thereby ['ðeəbaɪ] *adv* de ese
modo.
therefore ['ðeəfɔːʳ] *adv* por lo
tanto.
thermal ['θɜːməl] *adj* termal.
thermometer [θe'mɒmɪtəʳ]
n termómetro.
thermos® ['θɜːmɒs] *n* termo.
También **thermos flask**.
these [ðiːz] *adj* estos,-as. ►
pron éstos,-as.
thesis ['θiːsɪs] *n* tesis.
they [ðeɪ] *pron* ellos,-as.
thick [θɪk] *adj* **1** grueso,-a. **2**
espeso,-a. **3** poblado,-a *(barba)*.
thief [θiːf] *n* ladrón,-ona.
thigh [θaɪ] *n* muslo.
thimble ['θɪmbəl] *n* dedal.
thin [θɪn] *adj* **1** delgado,-a,
flaco,-a *(persona)*. **2** fino,-a
(rebanada, material). **3** ralo,-a
(pelo, vegetación). **4** claro,-a,
poco espeso,-a *(líquido)*.
thing [θɪŋ] *n* cosa. • **the
thing is…** el caso es que…
think [θɪŋk] *vt - vi* pensar.
third [θɜːd] *adj* tercero,-a. ▪
Third World Tercer Mundo.
thirst [θɜːst] *n* sed.

thirsty ['θɜːstɪ] *adj* sediento,-a.
• **to be thirsty** tener sed.
thirteen [θɜː'tiːn] *num* trece.
thirteenth [θɜː'tiːnθ] *adj - n*
decimotercero,-a.
thirty ['θɜːtɪ] *num* treinta.
this [ðɪs] *adj* este, esta. ▶ *pron*
éste, ésta, esto.
thistle ['θɪsəl] *n* cardo.
thong [θɒŋ] *n* correa.
thorn [θɔːn] *n* espina, pincho.
thorough ['θʌrə] *adj* **1** a fondo
(investigación). **2** cuidadoso,-a,
minucioso,-a *(persona)*.
those [ðəʊz] *adj* esos,-as, aque-
llos,-as. ▶ *pron* ésos,-as, aqué-
llos,-as.
though [ðəʊ] *conj* **1** aunque,
si bien. **2** pero. ▶ *adv* sin embargo.
thought [θɔːt] *ptpp* → think.
▶ *n* **1** pensamiento. **2** idea.
thoughtful ['θɔːtful] *adj* **1** pen-
sativo,-a. **2** considerado,-a.
thousand ['θaʊzənd] *num*
mil.
thrash [θræʃ] *vt* dar una paliza a.
thread [θred] *n* **1** hilo. **2** rosca
(de tornillo). ▶ *vt* **1** enhebrar
(aguja). **2** ensartar *(cuentas)*.
threat [θret] *n* amenaza.
threaten ['θretən] *vt - vi* amenazar.
three [θriː] *num* tres.
threshold ['θreʃəʊld] *n* umbral.
threw [θruː] *pt* → throw.
thrifty ['θrɪftɪ] *adj* frugal.

thrill [θrɪl] *n* emoción.
thriller ['θrɪlə'] *n* novela de suspense, película de suspense.
thrive [θraɪv] *vi* **1** crecer *(planta)*. **2** prosperar *(industria)*.
throat [θrəʊt] *n* garganta.
throb [θrɒb] *n* latido, palpitación. ▶ *vi* latir, palpitar.
throne [θrəʊn] *n* trono.
through [θruː] *prep* **1** por. **2**
durante todo,-a. **3** hasta el final de. ▶ *adv* **1** de un lado a
otro. **2** hasta el final. ▶ *adj*
directo,-a. • **to be through
with** haber acabado con.
throughout [θruː'aʊt] *prep* **1**
por, en todo,-a. **2** durante todo,-a, a lo largo de. ▶ *adv* **1**
por todas partes, en todas
partes. **2** completamente. **3**
todo el tiempo.
throve [θrəʊv] *pt* → thrive.
throw [θrəʊ] *n* lanzamiento.
▶ *vt* tirar, lanzar.
to throw away *vt* **1** tirar *(basura)*. **2** desaprovechar *(oportunidad)*
to throw up *vi* vomitar.
thru [θruː] *prep-adv* US →
through.
thrush [θrʌʃ] *n* tordo.
thrust [θrʌst] *n* **1** empuje. **2**
estocada *(de espada)*.
thumb [θʌm] *n* pulgar.
thumbtack ['θʌmtæk] *n* US
chincheta.
thump [θʌmp] *n* golpe. ▶ *vt*
golpear.

thunder ['θʌndər] *n* trueno. ▶ *vi* tronar.

thunderstorm ['θʌndəstɔːm] *n* tormenta.

Thursday ['θɜːzdɪ] *n* jueves.

thus [ðʌs] *adv* así.

thyme [taɪm] *n* tomillo.

tic [tɪk] *n* tic.

tick[1] [tɪk] *n* garrapata.

tick[2] [tɪk] *n* **1** tictac *(ruido)*. **2** marca, señal.

to tick off *vt* marcar.

ticket ['tɪkɪt] *n* **1** billete *(de bus, etc)*. **2** entrada *(de cine, etc)*. **3** etiqueta, resguardo. **4** *fam* multa. ■ **ticket collector** revisor, -ra; **ticket machine** máquina expendedora de billetes; **ticket office** taquilla.

tickle ['tɪkəl] *vt* hacer cosquillas a. ▶ *vi* tener cosquillas.

tide [taɪd] *n* marea.

tidy ['taɪdɪ] *adj* **1** ordenado,-a *(habitación, persona)*. **2** arreglado,-a *(aspecto)*.

to tidy up *vt* **1** ordenar, arreglar *(habitación)*. **2** arreglar, acicalar *(persona.*

tie [taɪ] *n* **1** corbata. **2** lazo, vínculo. **3** empate. ▶ *vt* atar, hacer *(nudo)*. ▶ *vi* empatar.

tier [tɪər] *n* **1** grada, fila *(de asientos)*. **2** piso *(de pastel)*.

tiger ['taɪgər] *n* tigre.

tight [taɪt] *adj* **1** apretado,-a. **2** tenso,-a *(cuerda)*. **3** ajustado,-a, ceñido,-a *(ropa)*. ▶ *adv* con fuerza.

tighten ['taɪtən] *vt* **1** apretar. **2** tensar *(cuerda)*.

tightrope ['taɪtrəʊp] *n* cuerda floja.

tights [taɪts] *npl* **1** panties, medias. **2** leotardos.

tile [taɪl] *n* **1** azulejo *(de pared)*. **2** baldosa *(de suelo)*. **3** teja *(de tejado)*.

till [tɪl] *prep* hasta. ▶ *conj* hasta que. ▶ *n* caja registradora.

tilt [tɪlt] *n* inclinación, ladeo. ▶ *vt-vi* inclinar(se).

timber ['tɪmbər] *n* **1** madera *(de construcción)*. **2** viga.

time [taɪm] *n* **1** tiempo. **2** rato. **3** hora: *what time is it?*, ¿qué hora es? **4** vez: *two at a time*, de dos en dos. ▶ *vt* **1** cronometrar. **2** fijar la hora de. ▶ *prep* **times** por, multiplicado por. ● **at any time** en cualquier momento; **at times** a veces; **for the time being** de momento; **from time to time** de vez en cuando; **it's about time** ya va siendo hora; **on time** puntualmente; **to have a good time** divertirse, pasarlo bien; **to tell the time** decir la hora.

timetable ['taɪmteɪbəl] *n* horario.

timid ['tɪmɪd] *adj* tímido,-a.

tin [tɪn] *n* **1** estaño. **2** lata, bote. ■ **tin opener** abrelatas.

tinkle ['tɪŋkəl] *n* tintineo.

tiny ['taɪnɪ] *adj* diminuto,-a.

tip¹ [tɪp] *n* extremo, punta.

tip² [tɪp] *n* **1** propina. **2** consejo. ► *vt* dar una propina a.

tiptoe ['tɪptəu] *vi* ir de puntillas. • **on tiptoe** de puntillas.

tire¹ ['taɪəʳ] *vt-vi* cansar(se).

tire² ['taɪəʳ] *n* US neumático.

tired ['taɪəd] *adj* cansado,-a.

tireless ['taɪələs] *adj* incansable.

tissue ['tɪʃuː] *n* pañuelo de papel.

title ['taɪtəl] *n* título.

to [tʊ, unstressed tə] *prep* **1** a. **2** hacia, a. **3** a, hasta. **4** menos. **5** para, a fin de.

toad [təud] *n* sapo.

toadstool ['təudstuːl] *n* seta venenosa.

toast [təust] *n* **1** pan tostado: *a piece of toast*, una tostada. **2** brindis. ► *vt* **1** tostar *(pan)*. **2** brindar por. • **to drink a toast to** hacer un brindis por, brindar por.

toaster ['təustəʳ] *n* tostador.

tobacco [tə'bækəu] *n* tabaco.

tobacconist [tə'bækənɪst] *n* estanquero,-a. ■ **tobacconist's** estanco.

today [tə'deɪ] *n* hoy. ► *adv* **1** hoy. **2** hoy en día.

toe [təu] *n* dedo del pie.

together [tə'geðəʳ] *adv* junto, juntos,-as. • **all together** todos,-as juntos,-as; **together with** junto con.

toilet ['tɔɪlət] *n* **1** váter, lavabo *(en casa)*. **2** servicios *(públicos)*. **3** aseo, arreglo personal. ■ **toilet bag** neceser; **toilet paper** papel higiénico.

token ['təukən] *n* ficha.

told [təuld] *pt-pp* → tell.

tolerate ['tɒləreɪt] *vt* tolerar.

toll [təul] *n* **1** peaje. **2** número.

tomato [tə'mɑːtəu, US tə'meɪtəu] *n* tomate.

tomb [tuːm] *n* tumba.

tombstone ['tuːmstəun] *n* lápida.

tomorrow [tə'mɒrəu] *adv-n* mañana.

ton [tʌn] *n* tonelada.

tone [təun] *n* tono.

tongs [tɒŋz] *npl* pinzas.

tongue [tʌŋ] *n* lengua. ■ **tongue twister** trabalenguas.

tonic ['tɒnɪk] *adj* tónico,-a.

tonight [tə'naɪt] *adv-n* esta noche.

tonne [tʌn] *n* tonelada.

tonsil ['tɒnsəl] *n* amígdala.

too [tuː] *adv* **1** demasiado, mucho. **2** también. • **too many** demasiados,-as; **too much** demasiado,-a.

took [tʊk] *pt* → take.

tool [tuːl] *n* herramienta.

tooth [tuːθ] *n* diente, muela.

toothache ['tuːθeɪk] *n* dolor de muelas.

toothbrush ['tuːθbrʌʃ] *n* cepillo de dientes.

toothpaste ['tuːθpeɪst] *n* pasta de dientes.

top [tɒp] n **1** parte superior, parte de arriba. **2** tapón (de botella). **3** top, blusa. ► adj de arriba, superior, más alto,-a.

topic ['tɒpɪk] n tema, asunto.

topical ['tɒpɪkəl] adj de actualidad.

torch [tɔːtʃ] n **1** antorcha. **2** linterna.

tore [tɔːʳ] pt → tear.

torn [tɔːn] pp → tear.

tornado [tɔː'neɪdəʊ] n tornado.

torpedo [tɔː'piːdəʊ] n torpedo.

tortoise ['tɔːtəs] n tortuga.

torture ['tɔːtʃə] n tortura. ► vt torturar.

total ['təʊtəl] adj - n total. ► vt-vi sumar.

touch [tʌtʃ] n **1** toque. **2** tacto. ► vt-vi tocar(se). ► vt conmover. • **to get in touch with** ponerse en contacto con; **to keep in touch** mantenerse en contacto.

touchdown ['tʌtʃdaʊn] n **1** aterrizaje. **2** amerizaje. **3** ensayo (en rugby).

tough [tʌf] adj **1** fuerte (persona). **2** duro,-a. ▪ **tough luck** mala suerte.

toupee ['tuːpeɪ] n peluquín.

tour [tʊəʳ] n **1** viaje. **2** visita (de edificio). **3** gira. ► vt **1** recorrer (país). **2** visitar (edificio).

tourism ['tʊərɪzəm] n turismo.

tourist ['tʊərɪst] n turista. ▪ **tourist office** oficina de turismo.

tournament ['tʊənəmənt] n torneo.

tow [təʊ] vt remolcar.

towards [tə'wɔːdz] prep **1** hacia. **2** para con (actitud, responsabilidad). **3** para. También **toward**.

towel ['taʊəl] n toalla.

tower ['taʊəʳ] n torre.

town [taʊn] n **1** ciudad. **2** pueblo. ▪ **town council** ayuntamiento; **town hall** ayuntamiento.

toxic ['tɒksɪk] n tóxico,-a.

toy [tɔɪ] n juguete.

toyshop ['tɔɪʃɒp] n juguetería.

trace [treɪs] n indicio, rastro.

track [træk] n **1** pista, huellas. **2** camino, senda. **3** pista, calle (atletismo). **4** circuito (de carreras). **5** vía (de ferrocarril). ► vt seguir la pista de.

tracksuit ['træksuːt] n chándal.

tractor ['træktəʳ] n tractor.

trade [treɪd] n **1** oficio. **2** negocio. **3** comercio. ► vi comerciar. ► vt cambiar. ▪ **trade union** sindicato obrero.

trademark ['treɪdmɑːk] n marca registrada.

trading ['treɪdɪŋ] n comercio. ▪ **trading estate** polígono comercial.

tradition [trə'dɪʃən] n tradición.

traffic ['træfɪk] n tráfico. ► vi traficar. ▪ **traffic jam** embotellamiento, atasco; **traffic light** semáforo.

tragedy ['trædʒədɪ] *n* tragedia.
tragic ['trædʒɪk] *adj* trágico,-a.
trail [treɪl] *n* **1** rastro, pista. **2** camino, sendero. **3** estela.
trailer ['treɪlə'] *n* **1** remolque. **2** tráiler, avance *(película)*.
train [treɪn] *n* **1** tren. **2** cola *(de vestido)*. ► *vt-vi* **1** entrenar(se). **2** formar(se). ■ **train station** estación de tren.
trainee [treɪ'niː] *n* aprendiz,-za.
trainer ['treɪnə'] *n* **1** entrenador,-ra. **2** zapatilla *(de deporte)*.
training ['treɪnɪŋ] *n* **1** formación. **2** entrenamiento.
traitor ['treɪtə'] *n* traidor,-ra.
tram [træm] *n* tranvía.
tramp [træmp] *n* vagabundo,-a.
trampoline ['træmpəliːn] *n* cama elástica.
trance [trɑːns] *n* trance.
transatlantic [trænzət'læntɪk] *adj* transatlántico,-a.
transcript ['trænskrɪpt] *n* transcripción.
transfer [*(n)* 'trænsfɜː', *(vb)* træns'fɜː'] *n* **1** transferencia *(de dinero)*. **2** traslado *(de empleado)*. **3** traspaso *(de bienes, poderes)*. ► *vt* **1** transferir *(dinero)*. **2** traspasar *(bienes, poderes)*. ► *vi* hacer trasbordo.
transform [træns'fɔːm] *vt-vi* transformar(se).
transfusion [træns'fjuːʒən] *n* transfusión.
transitive ['trænsɪtɪv] *adj* transitivo,-a.

translate [træns'leɪt] *vt* traducir.
translation [træns'leɪʃən] *n* traducción.
translator [træns'leɪtə'] *n* traductor,-ra.
transmit [trænz'mɪt] *vt* transmitir.
transparent [træns'peərənt] *adj* transparente.
transplant ['trænsplɑːnt] *n* trasplante.
transport [*(n)* 'trænspɔːt, *(vb)* træns'pɔːt] *n* transporte. ► *vt* transportar.
trap [træp] *n* trampa. ► *vt* atrapar.
trash [træʃ] *n* US basura.
travel ['trævəl] *n* viajes. ► *vi* **1** viajar. **2** ir, circular. ■ **travel agency** agencia de viajes.
traveller ['trævələ'] *n* **1** viajero,-a. **2** viajante. ■ **traveller's cheque** cheque de viaje.
travel-sick ['trævəlsɪk] *adj* mareado,-a.
tray [treɪ] *n* bandeja.
treacherous ['tretʃərəs] *adj* **1** traidor,-ra, traicionero,-a. **2** muy peligroso,-a.
treason ['triːzən] *n* traición.
treasure ['treʒə'] *n* tesoro.
treat [triːt] *vt* **1** tratar. **2** convidar, invitar. **3** darse el gusto, permitirse el lujo.
treatment ['triːtmənt] *n* **1** tratamiento. **2** trato, conducta.
treaty ['triːtɪ] *n* tratado.
tree [triː] *n* árbol.

trek [trek] *n* **1** viaje. **2** caminata *(a pie)*. ► *vi* caminar.

tremble ['trembəl] *vi* temblar, estremecerse.

trench [trentʃ] *n* **1** zanja. **2** trinchera.

trend [trend] *n* tendencia.

trespass ['trespəs] *vi* entrar ilegalmente. • **"No trespassing"** "Prohibido el paso".

trestle ['tresəl] *n* caballete.

trial ['traɪəl] *n* **1** proceso, juicio. **2** prueba. • **on trial** a prueba. ▪ **trial run** ensayo.

triangle ['traɪæŋgəl] *n* triángulo.

tribe [traɪb] *n* tribu.

tribunal [traɪ'bjuːnəl] *n* tribunal.

tributary ['trɪbjʊtərɪ] *n* afluente.

trick [trɪk] *n* truco. ► *vt* engañar.

trill [trɪl] *n* trino. ► *vt* - *vi* trinar.

trim [trɪm] *adj* bien arreglado, -a. ► *n* recorte *(de pelo)*. ► *vt* **1** recortar *(pelo, bigote)*. **2** decorar.

trinket ['trɪŋkɪt] *n* baratija.

trip [trɪp] *n* **1** viaje. **2** excursión. ► *vi* tropezar.

tripe [traɪp] *n* callos *(plato)*.

triple ['trɪpəl] *adj* triple.

tripod ['traɪpɒd] *n* trípode.

triumph ['traɪəmf] *n* triunfo. ► *vi* triunfar.

trivial ['trɪvɪəl] *adj* trivial.

trolley ['trɒlɪ] *n* carro, carrito.

trombone [trɒm'bəʊn] *n* trombón.

troop [truːp] *n* grupo, banda *(de gente)*. ► *npl* **troops** tropas.

trophy ['trəʊfɪ] *n* trofeo.

tropic ['trɒpɪk] *n* trópico.

tropical ['trɒpɪkəl] *adj* tropical.

trot [trɒt] *n* trote. ► *vi* trotar.

trotter ['trɒtər] *n* manita *(de cerdo)*.

trouble ['trʌbəl] *n* **1** problema. **2** preocupación. **3** molestia. ► *vt* **1** preocupar. **2** molestar. ► *vi* molestarse.

trough [trɒf] *n* abrevadero.

trousers ['traʊzəz] *npl* pantalón.

trousseau ['truːsəʊ] *n* ajuar.

trout [traʊt] *n* trucha.

truant ['truːənt] *phr.* • **to play truant** hacer novillos.

truce [truːs] *n* tregua.

truck [trʌk] *n* **1** GB vagón. **2** US camión.

true [truː] *adj* verdadero,-a. • **it's true** es verdad.

truffle ['trʌfəl] *n* trufa.

truly ['truːlɪ] *adv* verdaderamente. • **yours truly** atentamente.

trumpet ['trʌmpɪt] *n* trompeta.

truncheon ['trʌntʃən] *n* porra.

trunk [trʌŋk] *n* **1** tronco. **2** baúl. **3** trompa. **4** US maletero. ► *npl* **trunks** bañador. ▪ **trunk call** llamada interurbana.

trust [trʌst] *n* confianza, fe. ► *vt* confiar en, fiarse de.

truth [truːθ] n verdad.

try [traɪ] n 1 intento. 2 ensayo *(en rugby)*. ► vt - vi intentar. ► vt probar *(comida)*.

T-shirt ['tiːʃɜːt] n camiseta.

tub [tʌb] n 1 tina. 2 bañera, baño. 3 tarrina.

tube [tjuːb] n 1 tubo. 2 GB metro.

Tuesday ['tjuːzdɪ] n martes.

tuft [tʌft] n 1 mechón. 2 mata.

tug [tʌg] vt tirar de.

tuition [tjuˈɪʃən] n enseñanza.

tulip ['tjuːlɪp] n tulipán.

tumble ['tʌmbəl] n. ▪ **tumble dryer** secadora.

tumbler ['tʌmbələ'] n vaso.

tumour ['tjuːmə'] (US **tumor**) n tumor.

tuna ['tjuːnə] n atún, bonito.

tundra ['tʌndrə] n tundra.

tune [tjuːn] n melodía. ► vt 1 afinar *(piano, etc)*. 2 poner a punto *(motor)*. 3 sintonizar *(radio, etc)*. • **in tune** afinado,-a; **out of tune** desafinado,-a.

tunnel ['tʌnəl] n túnel.

turbot ['tɜːbət] n rodaballo.

tureen [tjʊˈriːn] n sopera.

turf [tɜːf] n césped.

turkey ['tɜːkɪ] n pavo.

turn [tɜːn] n 1 vuelta. 2 curva. 3 turno. ► vt 1 girar, dar la vuelta a. 2 doblar *(esquina)*. 3 pasar *(página)*. ► vi 1 girar, dar vueltas. 2 volverse, dar la vuelta *(persona)*. 3 torcer. 4 hacerse, ponerse, volverse.

to turn back vi volver(se).

to turn down vt bajar *(radio, etc)*.

to turn into vt convertir.

to turn off vt 1 desconectar *(electricidad)*. 2 apagar *(luz, gas)*. 3 cerrar *(agua)*. 4 parar *(máquina)*.

to turn on vt 1 conectar *(electricidad)*. 2 encender *(luz)*. 3 abrir *(gas, grifo)*. 4 poner en marcha *(máquina)*.

to turn up vi aparecer.

turnip ['tɜːnɪp] n nabo.

turnover ['tɜːnəʊvə'] n volumen de negocio.

turnpike ['tɜːnpaɪk] n US autopista de peaje.

turpentine ['tɜːpəntaɪn] n trementina, aguarrás.

turtle ['tɜːtəl] n tortuga.

tusk [tʌsk] n colmillo.

tutor ['tjuːtə'] n 1 profesor,-ra particular. 2 tutor,-ra.

tuxedo [tʌkˈsiːdəʊ] n US esmoquin.

twelfth [twelfθ] adj - n duodécimo,-a.

twelve [twelv] num doce.

twentieth ['twentɪəθ] adj - n vigésimo,-a.

twenty ['twentɪ] num veinte.

twice [twaɪs] adv dos veces.

twilight ['twaɪlaɪt] n crepúsculo.

twin [twɪn] n gemelo,-a. ▪ **twin room** habitación con dos camas.

twist [twɪst] n 1 recodo, vuelta *(de carretera)*. 2 torcedura. 3 twist *(baile)*. ► vt 1 torcer. 2 girar *(tapa)*. ► vi torcerse *(tobillo)*.

two [tuː] num dos.

type [taɪp] n 1 tipo, clase. 2 letra, carácter.

typewriter ['taɪpraɪtə'] n máquina de escribir.

typhoon [taɪ'fuːn] n tifón.

typical ['tɪpɪkəl] adj típico,-a.

typist ['taɪpɪst] n mecanógrafo,-a.

tyranny ['tɪrənɪ] n tiranía.

tyrant ['taɪərənt] n tirano,-a.

tyre ['taɪə'] (US **tire**) n neumático, llanta.

U

udder ['ʌdə'] n ubre.

ugly ['ʌglɪ] adj feo,-a.

ulcer ['ʌlsə'] n úlcera.

umbrella [ʌm'brelə] n paraguas.

umpire ['ʌmpaɪə'] n árbitro. ► vt arbitrar.

unable [ʌn'eɪbəl] adj incapaz.

unanimous [juː'nænɪməs] adj unánime.

unavailable [ʌnə'veɪləbəl] adj no disponible.

unaware [ʌnə'weə'] adj inconsciente.

unbalanced [ʌn'bælənst] adj desequilibrado,-a.

unbeatable [ʌn'biːtəbəl] adj 1 invencible, insuperable *(rival)*. 2 inmejorable *(precio)*.

unbelievable [ʌnbɪ'liːvəbəl] adj increíble.

unbiassed [ʌn'baɪəst] adj imparcial.

unbutton [ʌn'bʌtən] vt desabrochar, desbotonar.

uncertain [ʌn'sɜːtən] adj 1 incierto,-a, dudoso,-a *(futuro)*. 2 indeciso,-a *(persona)*.

uncle ['ʌnkəl] n tío.

uncommon [ʌn'kɒmən] adj 1 poco común. 2 insólito,-a.

unconscious [ʌn'kɒnʃəs] adj inconsciente.

uncouth [ʌn'kuːθ] adj tosco,-a.

uncover [ʌn'kʌvə'] vt 1 destapar, descubrir. 2 revelar.

under ['ʌndə'] prep 1 bajo, debajo de. 2 menos de. ► adv abajo, debajo.

underclothes ['ʌndəkləʊðz] npl ropa interior.

undercoat ['ʌndəkəʊt] n primera mano *(de pintura)*.

undercover [ʌndə'kʌvə'] adj clandestino,-a, secreto,-a.

underdeveloped [ʌndədɪ'veləpt] adj subdesarrollado,-a.

underdone [ʌndə'dʌn] adj poco hecho,-a.

underestimate [ʌndər'estɪmeɪt] vt subestimar, infravalorar.

undergo [ʌndə'gəʊ] *vt* **1** experimentar, sufrir *(cambio, dificultades)*. **2** someterse a *(operación)*.

undergraduate [ʌndə'grædjʊət] *n* estudiante universitario,-a no licenciado,-a.

underground [*(adj-n)* 'ʌndəgraʊnd, *(adv)* ʌndə'graʊnd] *adj* **1** subterráneo. **2** *fig* clandestino, -a. ► *n* **1** metro. **2** resistencia, movimiento clandestino. ► *adv* **1** bajo tierra. **2** en secreto.

undergrowth ['ʌndəgrəʊθ] *n* maleza.

underline [ʌndə'laɪn] *vt* subrayar.

underneath [ʌndə'niːθ] *prep* debajo de. ► *adv* debajo. ► *n* parte inferior.

underpants ['ʌndəpænts] *npl* calzoncillos, eslip.

underpass ['ʌndəpæs] *n* paso subterráneo.

underskirt ['ʌndəskɜːt] *n* enaguas.

understand [ʌndə'stænd] *vt* entender, comprender.

understanding [ʌndə'stændɪŋ] *n* **1** entendimiento, comprensión. **2** acuerdo, arreglo.

understood [ʌndə'stʊd] *pt-pp* → understand.

undertake [ʌndə'teɪk] *vt* **1** emprender. **2** asumir. **3** comprometerse.

undertook [ʌndə'tʊk] *pt* → undertake.

underwater [ʌndə'wɔːtəʳ] *adj* submarino,-a.

underwear ['ʌndəwɜːəʳ] *n* ropa interior.

underwent [ʌndə'went] *pt* → undergo.

undid [ʌn'dɪd] *pt* → undo.

undo [ʌn'duː] *vt* **1** deshacer *(nudo)*. **2** desabrochar *(botón)*. **3** abrir *(paquete)*.

undress [ʌn'dres] *vt-vi* desnudar(se), desvestir(se).

uneasy [ʌn'iːzɪ] *adj* intranquilo,-a, inquieto,-a.

unemployed [ʌnɪm'plɔɪd] *adj* desempleado,-a.

unemployment [ʌnɪm'plɔɪmənt] *n* paro, desempleo. ▪ **unemployment benefit** subsidio de desempleo.

unequal [ʌn'iːkwəl] *adj* desigual.

uneven [ʌn'iːvən] *adj* **1** desigual. **2** irregular *(superficie)*. **3** lleno,-a de baches *(carretera)*.

unexpected [ʌnɪk'spektɪd] *adj* inesperado,-a.

unfamiliar [ʌnfə'mɪlɪəʳ] *adj* desconocido,-a.

unfasten [ʌn'fɑːsən] *vt* **1** desabrochar *(botón)*. **2** desatar *(nudo)*. **3** abrir *(puerta)*.

unfit [ʌn'fɪt] *adj* **1** inadecuado,-a. **2** desentrenado,-a.

unfold [ʌn'fəʊld] *vt-vi* desplegar(se), abrir(se).

unforeseen [ʌnfɔː'siːn] *adj* imprevisto,-a.

unhappy [ʌn'hæpɪ] *adj* infeliz, triste.

unhurt [ʌn'hɜːt] *adj* ileso,-a.

unidentified [ʌnaɪ'dentɪfaɪd] *adj* no identificado,-a.

unification [juːnɪfɪ'keɪʃən] *n* unificación.

uniform ['juːnɪfɔːm] *adj-n* uniforme.

unify ['juːnɪfaɪ] *vt* unificar.

union ['juːnɪən] *n* **1** unión. **2** sindicato.

unique [juː'niːk] *adj* único,-a.

unisex ['juːnɪseks] *adj* unisex.

unit ['juːnɪt] *n* unidad.

unite [juː'naɪt] *vt-vi* unir(se).

universe ['juːnɪvɜːs] *n* universo.

university [juːnɪ'vɜːsɪtɪ] *n* universidad.

unjust [ʌn'dʒʌst] *adj* injusto,-a.

unkind [ʌn'kaɪnd] *adj* **1** poco amable *(persona)*. **2** cruel.

unknown [ʌn'nəʊn] *adj* desconocido,-a.

unless [ən'les] *conj* a menos que, a no ser que, si no.

unlike [ʌn'laɪk] *adj* diferente.
▶ *prep* a diferencia de.

unlikely [ʌn'laɪklɪ] *adj* improbable, poco probable.

unload [ʌn'ləʊd] *vt* descargar.

unlock [ʌn'lɒk] *vt* abrir.

unmanned [ʌn'mænd] *adj* no tripulado,-a.

unnoticed [ʌn'nəʊtɪst] *adj* inadvertido,-a, desapercibido,-a.

unoccupied [ʌn'ɒkjʊpaɪd] *adj* **1** deshabitado,-a *(casa)*. **2** desocupado,-a *(persona)*. **3** vacante *(empleo)*.

unofficial [ʌnə'fɪʃəl] *adj* extraoficial, oficioso,-a.

unpack [ʌn'pæk] *vt* **1** desempaquetar, desembalar. **2** deshacer *(maleta)*.

unpleasant [ʌn'plezənt] *adj* desagradable.

unplug [ʌn'plʌg] *vt* desenchufar.

unpublished [ʌn'pʌblɪʃt] *adj* inédito,-a.

unreadable [ʌn'riːdəbəl] *adj* **1** ilegible. **2** imposible de leer.

unreal [ʌn'rɪəl] *adj* irreal.

unreasonable [ʌn'riːzənəbəl] *adj* **1** poco razonable. **2** desmesurado,-a, excesivo,-a.

unreliable [ʌnrɪ'laɪəbəl] *adj* **1** de poca confianza *(persona)*. **2** poco fiable *(máquina)*.

unrest [ʌn'rest] *n* **1** malestar, intranquilidad. **2** disturbios.

unripe [ʌn'raɪp] *adj* verde *(fruta)*.

unroll [ʌn'rəʊl] *vt-vi* desenrollar(se).

unsafe [ʌn'seɪf] *adj* inseguro,-a.

unscrew [ʌn'skruː] *vt* **1** desatornillar. **2** desenroscar.

unskilled [ʌn'skɪld] *adj* **1** no cualificado,-a *(obrero)*. **2** no especializado,-a *(trabajo)*.

unspeakable [ʌn'spiːkəbəl] *adj* indecible.

unstable [ʌn'steɪbəl] *adj* inestable.

unsteady [ʌn'stedɪ] *adj* inseguro,-a, inestable.

unsuccessful [ʌnsək'sesfʊl] *adj* fracasado,-a, sin éxito.

unsuitable [ʌn'suːtəbəl] *adj* **1** poco apropiado,-a *(persona)*. **2** inoportuno, inconveniente.

untidy [ʌn'taɪdɪ] *adj* **1** desordenado,-a *(habitación)*. **2** desaliñado,-a *(persona)*.

untie [ʌn'taɪ] *vt* desatar.

until [ən'tɪl] *prep* hasta. ► *conj* hasta que.

untrue [ʌn'truː] *adj* **1** falso,-a. **2** infiel.

unveil [ʌn'veɪl] *vt* revelar.

unwell [ʌn'wel] *adj* indispuesto,-a.

unwilling [ʌn'wɪlɪŋ] *adj* reacio,-a, poco dispuesto,-a.

unwind [ʌn'waɪnd] *vt* desenrollar(se).

unwise [ʌn'waɪz] *adj* imprudente, poco aconsejable.

unworthy [ʌn'wɜːðɪ] *adj* indigno,-a.

unwound [ʌn'waʊnd] *pt-pp* → unwind.

unwrap [ʌn'ræp] *vt* desenvolver, abrir.

up [ʌp] *adv* **1** arriba, hacia arriba. **2** levantado,-a. **3** hacia. **4** más alto,-a. **5** acabado,-a.► *prep* **1** *to go up the stairs*, subir la escalera. **2** en lo alto de: *up a tree*, en lo alto de un árbol. ► *vt fam* subir, aumentar. • **up to** hasta; **it's up**

to you *fam* es cosa tuya; **up and down** de arriba a abajo, de un lado al otro. ▪ **ups and downs** altibajos.

update [(n) 'ʌpdeɪt, (vb) ʌp-'deɪt] *n* actualización. ► *vt* actualizar.

upgrade [ʌp'greɪd] *vt* **1** ascender *(persona)*. **2** mejorar. **3** actualizar. ► *n* actualización.

uphill [ʌp'hɪl] *adv* cuesta arriba.

upholstery [ʌp'həʊlstərɪ] *n* tapicería, tapizado.

upkeep ['ʌpkiːp] *n* mantenimiento.

upon [ə'pɒn] *prep* → on.

upper ['ʌpə'] *adj* superior, de arriba. ▪ **upper case** mayúsculas, caja alta; **upper class** clase alta.

uppermost ['ʌpəməʊst] *adj* **1** más alto,-a. **2** *fig* principal.

upright ['ʌpraɪt] *adj* derecho, -a, vertical.

uprising [ʌp'raɪzɪŋ] *n* sublevación, rebelión.

upset [ʌp'set] *adj* disgustado,-a, ofendido,-a. ► *vt* **1** disgustar. **2** desbaratar *(planes)*. **3** volcar *(barco)*. **4** derramar *(recipiente)*. ► *n* revés.

upside down [ʌpsaɪd'daʊn] *adv* al revés.

upstairs [(adv) ʌp'steəz, (n) 'ʌpsteəz] *adv* **1** en el piso de arriba *(situación)*. **2** al piso de arriba *(movimiento)*. ► *n* piso de arriba. ► *adj* de arriba.

up-to-date [ˌʌptəˈdeɪt] *adj* al día, actualizado,-a.

upward [ˈʌpwəd] *adj* hacia arriba, ascendente. ▶ *adv* hacia arriba.

upwards [ˈʌpwədz] *adv* hacia arriba.

urban [ˈɜːbən] *adj* urbano,-a.

urge [ɜːdʒ] ▶ *vt* encarecer.

urgency [ˈɜːdʒənsɪ] *n* urgencia.

urgent [ˈɜːdʒənt] *adj* urgente.

urn [ɜːn] *n* urna.

us [ʌs, unstressed əz] *pron* nos, nosotros,-as.

usage [ˈjuːzɪdʒ] *n* uso.

use [(n) juːs, (vb) juːz] *n* uso. ▶ *vt* usar, utilizar. • **used to** soler, acostumbrar *(se refiere solo al pasado)*: **he used to get up early**, solía levantarse temprano. • **"Not in use"** "No funciona"; **out of use** en desuso; **what's the use of...?** ¿de qué sirve...?

used [juːst] *adj* usado,-a. • **to be used to STH** estar acostumbrado,-a a algo; **to get used to STH** acostumbrarse a algo.

useful [ˈjuːsfʊl] *adj* útil.

useless [ˈjuːsləs] *adj* inútil.

user [ˈjuːzəʳ] *n* usuario,-a.

usher [ˈʌʃəʳ] *n* **1** ujier. **2** acomodador,-ra.

usual [ˈjuːʒʊəl] *adj* usual, habitual, normal. • **as usual** como de costumbre, como siempre.

usually [ˈjuːʒʊəlɪ] *adv* normalmente.

utensil [juːˈtensəl] *n* utensilio. • **kitchen utensils** batería de cocina.

utility [juːˈtɪlɪtɪ] *n* **1** utilidad. **2** empresa de servicio público.

utilize [ˈjuːtɪlaɪz] *vt* utilizar.

utmost [ˈʌtməʊst] *adj* sumo,-a.

utopia [juːˈtəʊpɪə] *n* utopía.

utter [ˈʌtəʳ] *adj* absoluto,-a, total. ▶ *vt* pronunciar, articular.

U-turn [ˈjuːtɜːn] *n* cambio de sentido, giro de 180 grados.

V

vacancy [ˈveɪkənsɪ] *n* **1** vacante *(puesto de trabajo)*. **2** habitación libre. • **"No vacancies"** "Completo".

vacant [ˈveɪkənt] *adj* **1** vacío. **2** vacante. **3** libre.

vacate [vəˈkeɪt] *vt* **1** dejar vacante. **2** desocupar.

vacation [vəˈkeɪʃən] *n* vacaciones.

vaccinate [ˈvæksɪneɪt] *vt* vacunar.

vaccine [ˈvæksiːn] *n* vacuna.

vacuum [ˈvækjʊəm] *n* vacío. ▶ *vt* pasar la aspiradora por. ■ **vacuum cleaner** aspiradora; **vacuum flask** termo.

vacuum-packed ['vækjʊəmpækt] *adj* envasado,-a al vacío.

vagina [və'dʒaɪnə] *n* vagina.

vague [veɪg] *adj* vago,-a, indefinido,-a.

valid ['vælɪd] *adj* 1 válido,-a.

valley ['vælɪ] *n* valle.

valuable ['væljʊəbəl] *adj* valioso,-a. ► *npl* **valuables** objetos de valor.

value ['væljuː] *n* valor. ► *vt* 1 valorar.

valve [vælv] *n* válvula.

vampire ['væmpaɪəʳ] *n* vampiro.

van [væn] *n* 1 camioneta, furgoneta. 2 GB furgón.

vandalism ['vændəlɪzəm] *n* vandalismo.

vanguard ['vængɑːd] *n* vanguardia.

vanish ['vænɪʃ] *vi* desaparecer.

vanity ['vænɪtɪ] *n* vanidad.

vapour ['veɪpəʳ] (US **vapor**) *n* vapor, vaho.

variable ['veərɪəbəl] *adj-n* variable.

variation [veərɪ'eɪʃən] *n* variación.

varied ['veərɪd] *adj* variado,-a.

variety [və'raɪətɪ] *n* variedad. ■ **variety show** espectáculo de variedades.

various ['veərɪəs] *adj* varios, -as.

varnish ['vɑːnɪʃ] *n* barniz. ► *vt* barnizar.

vary ['veərɪ] *vt-vi* variar.

vase [vɑːz] *n* jarrón, florero.

vast [vɑːst] *adj* vasto,-a, inmenso,-a.

vat [væt] *n* tina, cuba.

VAT [væt, 'viː'eɪ'tiː] *abbr* (**value added tax**) IVA.

vault [vɔːlt] *n* 1 bóveda. 2 cámara acorazada (*de banco*). 3 panteón, cripta (*de iglesia*).

veal [viːl] *n* ternera.

vegetable ['vedʒɪtəbəl] *adj* vegetal. ► *n* hortaliza, verdura, legumbre.

vegetarian [vedʒɪ'teərɪən] *adj-n* vegetariano,-a.

vegetation [vedʒɪ'teɪʃən] *n* vegetación.

vehicle ['viːəkəl] *n* vehículo.

veil [veɪl] *n* velo.

vein [veɪn] *n* vena.

velocity [və'lɒsɪtɪ] *n* velocidad.

velvet ['velvɪt] *n* terciopelo.

vending machine ['vendɪŋməʃiːn] *n* máquina expendedora.

vengeance ['vendʒəns] *n* venganza.

vent [vent] *n* abertura, respiradero.

ventilate ['ventɪleɪt] *vt* ventilar.

ventilator ['ventɪleɪtəʳ] *n* ventilador.

venture ['ventʃəʳ] *n* empresa arriesgada, aventura. ► *vt-vi* arriesgar(se).

venue ['venjuː] *n* lugar.

veranda [və'rændə] *n* veranda, terraza.

verb [vɜːb] n verbo.

verge [vɜːdʒ] n borde, margen.

verify ['verɪfaɪ] vt verificar.

vermin ['vɜːmɪn] n 1 alimaña. 2 bichos, sabandijas.

verruca [vəˈruːkə] n verruga.

versatile ['vɜːsətaɪl] adj versátil.

verse [vɜːs] n 1 estrofa, versículo. 2 verso, poesía.

version ['vɜːʒən] n versión.

versus ['vɜːsəs] prep contra.

vertebra ['vɜːtɪbrə] n vértebra.

vertical ['vɜːtɪkəl] adj vertical.

vertigo ['vɜːtɪɡəʊ] n vértigo.

very ['verɪ] adv 1 muy. 2 mucho.

vessel ['vesəl] n nave.

vest [vest] n 1 camiseta (interior). 2 US chaleco.

vet [vet] n fam veterinario,-a. ▶ vt GB investigar, examinar.

veteran ['vetərən] adj-n veterano,-a.

veterinarian [vetərɪˈneərɪən] n US veterinario,-a.

veterinary ['vetərɪnərɪ] adj veterinario,-a.

veto ['viːtəʊ] n veto. ▶ vt vetar.

via ['vaɪə] prep vía, por vía de, por.

viaduct ['vaɪədʌkt] n viaducto.

vibrate [vaɪˈbreɪt] vi vibrar.

vice [vaɪs] n vicio.

vice versa [vaɪsˈvɜːsə] adv viceversa.

vicinity [vɪˈsɪnɪtɪ] n cercanías.

vicious ['vɪʃəs] adj 1 cruel. 2 violento,-a, brutal.

victim ['vɪktɪm] n víctima.

victory ['vɪktərɪ] n victoria.

video ['vɪdɪəʊ] n vídeo. ■ **video camera** videocámara; **video cassette** videocasete; **video game** videojuego; **video shop** videoclub; **video recorder** vídeo.

videotape ['vɪdɪəʊteɪp] vt grabar en vídeo. ▶ n cinta de vídeo.

view [vjuː] n 1 vista, panorama. 2 parecer, opinión. ▶ vt mirar, ver. ● **in my view** en mi opinión; **in view of** en vista de.

viewer ['vjuːəʳ] n telespectador,-ra.

viewpoint ['vjuːpɔɪnt] n punto de vista.

vigour ['vɪɡəʳ] (US **vigor**) n vigor.

villa ['vɪlə] n chalet.

village ['vɪlɪdʒ] n pueblo.

villain ['vɪlən] n malo,-a.

vinaigrette [vɪnəˈɡret] n vinagreta.

vindicate ['vɪndɪkeɪt] vt reivindicar.

vine [vaɪn] n vid, parra.

vinegar ['vɪnɪɡəʳ] n vinagre.

vineyard ['vɪnjɑːd] n viña, viñedo.

vintage ['vɪntɪdʒ] n cosecha. ■ **vintage car** coche antiguo.

vinyl ['vaɪnəl] n vinilo.

violate ['vaɪəleɪt] *vt* violar.
violence ['vaɪələns] *n* violencia.
violent ['vaɪələnt] *adj* violento,-a.
violet ['vaɪələt] *n* violeta.
violin [vaɪə'lɪn] *n* violín.
viper ['vaɪpəʳ] *n* víbora.
virgin ['vɜːdʒɪn] *adj-n* virgen.
virtual ['vɜːtjuəl] *adj* virtual. ■ **virtual reality** realidad virtual.
virtue ['vɜːtjuː] *n* virtud.
virus ['vaɪərəs] *n* virus. ■ **virus checker** antivirus.
visa ['viːzə] *n* visado.
visible ['vɪzɪbəl] *adj* visible.
vision ['vɪʒən] *n* visión, vista.
visit ['vɪzɪt] *n* visita. ► *vt* visitar. • **to pay a visit** visitar.
visitor ['vɪzɪtəʳ] *n* **1** visita. **2** visitante.
visor ['vaɪzəʳ] *n* visera.
visual ['vɪzjuəl] *adj* visual. ■ **visual display unit** pantalla.
vital ['vaɪtəl] *adj* vital.
vitality [vaɪ'tælɪtɪ] *n* vitalidad.
vitamin ['vɪtəmɪn] *n* vitamina.
vivid ['vɪvɪd] *adj* **1** vivo,-a, intenso,-a. **2** gráfico,-a.
vixen ['vɪksən] *n* zorra.
vocabulary [və'kæbjʊlərɪ] *n* vocabulario.
vocal ['vəʊkəl] *adj* vocal.
vocation [vəʊ'keɪʃən] *n* vocación.
vodka ['vɒdkə] *n* vodka.
vogue [vəʊg] *n* boga, moda. •

to be in vogue estar de moda.
voice [vɔɪs] *n* voz. ■ **voice mail** buzón de voz.
volcano [vɒl'keɪnəʊ] *n* volcán.
volley ['vɒlɪ] *n* volea. ► *vi* volear.
volleyball ['vɒlɪbɔːl] *n* balonvolea, voleibol.
volt [vəʊlt] *n* voltio.
voltage ['vəʊltɪdʒ] *n* voltaje.
voluble ['vɒljʊbəl] *adj* locuaz, hablador,-ra.
volume ['vɒljuːm] *n* volumen.
voluntary ['vɒləntərɪ] *adj* voluntario,-a. ■ **voluntary organization** organización benéfica.
volunteer [vɒlən'tɪəʳ] *n* **1** voluntario,-a. **2** cooperante. ► *vt-vi* ofrecerse *(voluntario)* para hacer algo.
vomit ['vɒmɪt] *n* vómito. ► *vt-vi* vomitar.
vote [vəʊt] *n* **1** voto. **2** votación. ► *vt-vi* votar.
voter ['vəʊtəʳ] *n* votante.
voucher ['vaʊtʃəʳ] *n* vale, bono.
vow [vaʊ] *n* promesa solemne, voto.
vowel ['vaʊəl] *n* vocal.
voyage ['vɔɪɪdʒ] *n* viaje.
voyager ['vɔɪədʒəʳ] *n* viajero,-a.
vulgar ['vʌlgəʳ] *adj* vulgar.
vulnerable ['vʌlnərəbəl] *adj* vulnerable.
vulture ['vʌltʃəʳ] *n* buitre.
vulva ['vʌlvə] *n* vulva.

W

wafer ['weɪfə'] *n* **1** barquillo, galleta, oblea. **2** hostia.

waffle ['wɒfəl] *n* gofre.

wag [wæg] *n* meneo. ► *vt-vi* menear(se).

wage [weɪdʒ] *n* sueldo.

wager ['weɪdʒə'] *n* apuesta.

wagon ['wægən] *n* **1** carro, carromato. **2** vagón *(de tren)*.

waist [weɪst] *n* cintura, talle.

waistcoat ['weɪskəʊt] *n* chaleco.

wait [weɪt] *n* espera. ► *vi* esperar.

waiter ['weɪtə'] *n* camarero.

waiting ['weɪtɪŋ] *n* espera. ■ **waiting list** lista de espera; **waiting room** sala de espera.

waitress ['weɪtrəs] *n* camarera.

wake [weɪk] *n* velatorio. ► *vt* despertar.

to wake up *vt-vi* despertar(se).

waken ['weɪkən] *vt-vi* despertar(se).

walk [wɔːk] *n* paseo, caminata. ► *vi* andar, caminar. ► *vt* **1** pasear *(perro)*. **2** acompañar *(persona)*. • **to go for a walk** dar un paseo.

to walk out *vi* **1** marcharse. **2** ir a la huelga.

walkie-talkie [wɔːkɪ'tɔːkɪ] *n* walkie-talkie.

walking stick ['wɔːkɪŋstɪk] *n* bastón.

Walkman® ['wɔːkmən] *n* Walkman®.

wall [wɔːl] *n* **1** muro *(exterior)*. **2** pared *(interior)*.

wallet ['wɒlɪt] *n* cartera.

wallpaper ['wɔːlpeɪpə'] *n* papel pintado. ► *vt* empapelar.

wally ['wɒlɪ] *n fam* inútil, imbécil.

walnut ['wɔːlnʌt] *n* nuez. ■ **walnut tree** nogal.

walrus ['wɔːlrəs] *n* morsa.

waltz [wɔːls] *n* vals.

wand [wɒnd] *n* varita.

wander ['wɒndə'] *vi* vagar.

want [wɒnt] *vt* **1** querer. **2** *fam* necesitar.

wanted ['wɒntɪd] *adj* **1** necesario,-a: *"Boy wanted"*, "Se necesita chico". **2** buscado,-a: *"Wanted"*, "Se busca".

war [wɔː'] *n* guerra.

ward [wɔːd] *n* **1** sala *(de hospital)*. **2** GB distrito electoral.

warden ['wɔːdən] *n* vigilante, guardián,-ana.

wardrobe ['wɔːdrəʊb] *n* **1** armario *(ropero)*, guardarropa. **2** vestuario.

warehouse ['wɛəhaʊs] *n* almacén.

warfare ['wɔːfɛə'] *n* guerra.

warm [wɔːm] *adj* **1** caliente. **2** tibio,-a, templado,-a. **3** cálido,-a *(clima)*. **4** de abrigo *(ropa)*. ► *vt* calentar.

to warm up *vt* calentar. ▶ *vi*
1 calentarse. 2 hacer ejercicios de calentamiento.
warmth [wɔːmθ] *n* calor.
warn [wɔːn] *vt* avisar, advertir, prevenir.
warning [ˈwɔːnɪŋ] *n* aviso, advertencia.
warrant [ˈwɒrənt] *n* orden judicial. ▶ *vt* justificar.
warranty [ˈwɒrəntɪ] *n* garantía.
warrior [ˈwɒrɪəʳ] *n* guerrero,-a.
wart [wɔːt] *n* verruga.
was [wɒz] *pt* → be.
wash [wɒʃ] *vt-vi* lavar(se).
to wash up *vt-vi* fregar *(platos)*.
washbasin [ˈwɒʃbeɪsən] *n* lavabo.
washer [ˈwɒʃəʳ] *n* 1 arandela,
junta. 2 lavadora.
washing [ˈwɒʃɪŋ] *n* 1 lavado.
2 colada. • **to do the washing** hacer la colada. ▪ **washing machine** lavadora.
washing-up [wɒʃɪŋˈʌp] *n* 1
fregado. 2 platos. • **to do the
washing up** fregar los platos,
lavar los platos. ▪ **washing-
up liquid** lavavajillas.
washroom [ˈwɒʃruːm] *n* US
servicios, lavabo.
wasp [wɒsp] *n* avispa.
waste [weɪst] *n* 1 desperdi-
cio. 2 derroche *(de dinero)*. 3
desechos. ▶ *vt* 1 desperdiciar,
malgastar *(comida, oportunidad)*. 2 despilfarrar, derrochar *(dinero)*.

watch [wɒtʃ] *n* reloj *(de
pulsera)*. ▶ *vt* 1 mirar, ver *(televisión, película)*. 2 observar. 3
vigilar. 4 tener cuidado con. •
watch out! ¡ojo!, ¡cuidado!
watchdog [ˈwɒtʃdɒg] *n* perro
guardián.
watchman [ˈwɒtʃmən] *n* vigilante.
water [ˈwɔːtəʳ] *n* agua. ▶ *vt*
regar. ▶ *vi* 1 llorar *(ojos)*. 2 hacerse agua *(boca)*. ▪ **water bottle** cantimplora; **water lily**
nenúfar; **water polo** waterpolo.
to water down *vt* aguar.
watercolour [ˈwɔːtəkʌləʳ] (US
watercolor) *n* acuarela.
watercress [ˈwɔːtəkres] *n* be-
rros.
waterfall [ˈwɔːtəfɔːl] *n* cascada.
watermelon [ˈwɔːtəmelən] *n*
sandía.
watermill [ˈwɔːtəmɪl] *n* molino de agua.
waterproof [ˈwɔːtəpruːf] *adj*
impermeable.
water-skiing [ˈwɔːtəskiːɪŋ] *n*
esquí acuático.
watertight [ˈwɔːtətaɪt] *adj* hermético,-a.
wave [weɪv] *n* 1 ola *(de mar)*.
2 onda. ▶ *vt* 1 agitar. 2 marcar, ondular *(pelo)*.
wavelength [ˈweɪvleŋθ] *n*
longitud de onda.
wavy [ˈweɪvɪ] *adj* ondulado,-a.

well

wax [wæks] *n* cera. ► *vt* encerar.

way [weɪ] *n* **1** camino. **2** dirección. **3** manera, modo. • **by the way** a propósito; **on the way** por el camino; **the right way round** bien puesto; **the wrong way round** al revés; **to get out of the way** apartarse del camino, quitarse de en medio; **to give way** ceder el paso; **to lose one's way** perderse; **to stand in the way of** obstruir el paso de.

we [wiː, unstressed wɪ] *pron* nosotros,-as.

weak [wiːk] *adj* débil.

weakness [ˈwiːknəs] *n* debilidad.

wealth [welθ] *n* riqueza.

wealthy [ˈwelθɪ] *adj* rico,-a.

weapon [ˈwepən] *n* arma.

wear [weəʳ] *n* **1** uso. **2** desgaste, deterioro. **3** ropa. ► *vt* **1** llevar puesto,-a. **2** vestir, ponerse *(ropa)*. **3** calzar *(zapatos)*. **4** desgastar.

weary [ˈwɪərɪ] *adj* cansado,-a.

weasel [ˈwiːzəl] *n* comadreja.

weather [ˈweðəʳ] *n* tiempo. ■ **weather forecast** pronóstico del tiempo.

weathercock [ˈweðəkɒk] *n* veleta.

weave [wiːv] *n* tejido. ► *vt-vi* tejer.

web [web] *n* **1** telaraña. **2** *fig* red. **3** Internet. ■ **web page** página web.

website [ˈwebsaɪt] *n* sitio web.

wedding [ˈwedɪŋ] *n* boda. ■ **wedding dress** vestido de novia; **wedding ring** alianza.

wedge [wedʒ] *n* cuña, calce.

Wednesday [ˈwenzdɪ] *n* miércoles.

week [wiːk] *n* semana.

weekday [ˈwiːkdeɪ] *n* día laborable.

weekend [ˈwiːkend] *n* fin de semana.

weekly [ˈwiːklɪ] *adj* semanal. ► *adv* semanalmente. ► *n* semanario.

weep [wiːp] *vi* llorar.

weigh [weɪ] *vt* pesar.

weight [weɪt] *n* **1** peso. **2** pesa. • **to lose weight** perder peso; **to put on weight** engordar.

weightlifting [ˈweɪtlɪftɪŋ] *n* halterofilia.

weir [wɪəʳ] *n* presa *(de río)*.

weird [wɪəd] *adj* raro,-a.

welcome [ˈwelkəm] *adj* bienvenido,-a. ► *n* bienvenida. ► *vt* dar la bienvenida a. • **you're welcome** de nada, no hay de qué.

weld [weld] *n* soldadura. ► *vt* soldar.

welfare [ˈwelfeəʳ] *n* bienestar.

well[1] [wel] *adj-adv* bien. ► *interj* bueno • **as well** también; **as well as** además de; **just as well** menos mal; **pretty well 1** bastante bien. **2** casi.

well[2] [wel] *n* pozo.

well-being [wel'biːɪŋ] *n* bienestar.

well-built [wel'bɪlt] *adj* fornido,-a.

wellington ['welɪŋtən] *n* bota de goma.

well-known [wel'nəʊn] *adj* conocido,-a, famoso,-a.

well-meaning [wel'miːnɪŋ] *adj* bien intencionado,-a.

well-off [wel'ɒf] *adj* rico,-a.

well-timed [wel'taɪmd] *adj* oportuno,-a.

well-to-do [weltə'duː] *adj* acomodado,-a.

went [went] *pt* → go.

wept [wept] *pt-pp* → weep.

were [wɜːʳ] *pt* → be.

west [west] *n* oeste, occidente. ► *adj* del oeste, occidental. ► *adv* al oeste, hacia el oeste.

western ['westən] *adj* del oeste. ► *n* western,.

wet [wet] *adj* **1** mojado,-a. **2** húmedo,-a. **3** lluvioso,-a *(tiempo)*. ► *vt* humedecer. • **"Wet paint"** "Recién pintado".

whale [weɪl] *n* ballena.

wharf [wɔːf] *n* muelle.

what [wɒt] *adj* **1** qué *(preguntas)*. **2** qué, menudo *(exclamaciones)*. ► *pron* **1** qué *(preguntas)*. **2** lo que *(subordinadas)*: *that's what he said*, eso es lo que dijo.

whatever [wɒt'evəʳ] *adj* **1** cualquiera que. **2** en absoluto. ► *pron* (todo) lo que.

whatsoever [wɒtsəʊ'evəʳ] *adj* → whatever.

wheat [wiːt] *n* trigo.

wheel [wiːl] *n* **1** rueda. **2** volante.■ **wheel clamp** cepo.

wheelbarrow ['wiːlbærəʊ] *n* carretilla de mano.

wheelchair ['wiːltʃeəʳ] *n* silla de ruedas.

when [wen] *adv* cuándo. ► *conj* cuando.

whenever [wen'evəʳ] *conj* cuando quiera que, siempre que. ► *adv* **1** cuando sea. **2** cuándo.

where [weəʳ] *adv* dónde, adónde. ► *conj* **1** donde. **2** mientras que.

whereabouts [(*n*) 'weərəbaʊts, (*adv*) weərə'baʊts] *n* paradero. ► *adv* dónde, adónde.

whereas [weər'æz] *conj* mientras que.

whereby [weə'baɪ] *adv* por el/la/lo cual.

wherever [weər'evəʳ] *adv* dónde, adónde. ► *conj* dondequiera que.

whether ['weðəʳ] *conj* si.

which [wɪtʃ] *adj* qué. ► *pron* **1** cuál, cuáles *(en interrogativas)*. **2** que *(en subordinadas)*. **3** el/la/lo que, el/la/lo cual *(con preposición)*, los/las que, los/las cuales. **4** el/la cual, los/las cuales. **5** lo que/cual.

whichever [wɪtʃ'evər] *adj* (no importa) el/la/los/las que. ►

pron cualquiera, el/la/los/las que.

while [waɪl] *n* rato, tiempo. ▶ *conj* **1** mientras. **2** aunque. **3** mientras que. • **for a while** un rato; **once in a while** de vez en cuando.

whilst [waɪlst] *conj* → while.

whim [wɪm] *n* antojo.

whip [wɪp] *n* látigo, fusta. ▶ *vt* **1** azotar. **2** batir, montar *(nata, etc)*. ▪ **whipped cream** nata montada.

whirlpool [ˈwɜːlpuːl] *n* remolino.

whisk [wɪsk] *n* **1** batidor. **2** batidora *(eléctrica)*. ▶ *vt* montar *(nata, claras)*.

whisker [ˈwɪskəʳ] *n* pelo *(de bigote)*. ▶ *npl* **whiskers 1** patillas *(de persona)*. **2** bigotes *(de gato)*.

whiskey [ˈwɪskɪ] *n* whisky, güisqui *(irlandés)*.

whisky [ˈwɪskɪ] *n* whisky, güisqui.

whisper [ˈwɪspəʳ] *n* susurro. ▶ *vt-vi* susurrar.

whistle [ˈwɪsəl] *n* **1** silbato. **2** silbido, pitido. ▶ *vt-vi* silbar.

white [waɪt] *adj* blanco,-a. ▶ *n* **1** blanco *(color)*. **2** clara *(de huevo)*. ▪ **white coffee** café con leche.

white-collar [waɪtˈkɒləʳ] *adj* administrativo,-a.

whitewash [ˈwaɪtwɒʃ] *n* cal. ▶ *vt* encalar.

who [huː] *pron* **1** quién, quiénes *(en interrogativas directas e indirectas)*. **2** que *(en subordinadas-objeto)*.

whoever [huːˈevəʳ] *pron* **1** quien. **2** quienquiera que, cualquiera que.

whole [həʊl] *adj* **1** entero,-a. **2** intacto,-a. ▶ *n* conjunto, todo. • **as a whole** en conjunto.

wholemeal [ˈhəʊlmiːl] *adj* integral.

wholesale [ˈhəʊlseɪl] *adj-adv* COMM al por mayor.

whom [huːm] *pron* **1** *fml* a quién, a quiénes *(en interrogativas)*. **2** a quien, a quienes *(en subordinadas)*.

whose [huːz] *pron* de quién, de quiénes. ▶ *adj* **1** de quién, de quiénes. **2** cuyo,-a, cuyos,-as.

why [waɪ] *adv* por qué.

wick [wɪk] *n* pábilo.

wicked [ˈwɪkɪd] *adj* malo,-a.

wicker [ˈwɪkəʳ] *n* mimbre.

wide [waɪd] *adj* **1** ancho,-a. **2** amplio,-a. • **wide open** abierto,-a de par en par.

widow [ˈwɪdəʊ] *n* viuda.

widower [ˈwɪdəʊəʳ] *n* viudo.

width [wɪdθ] *n* ancho.

wife [waɪf] *n* esposa, mujer.

wig [wɪg] *n* peluca.

wild [waɪld] *adj* **1** salvaje. **2** silvestre, campestre *(planta)*.

wildcat [ˈwaɪldkæt] *n* gato montés.

wildlife ['waɪldlaɪf] n fauna.

will¹ [wɪl] aux **1** se usa para formar el futuro de los verbos: **she will be here tomorrow**, estará aquí mañana. **2** indica voluntad: **the car won't start**, el coche no arranca. **3** indica insistencia: **he will leave the door open**, es que no hay manera de que cierre la puerta. **4** poder: **this phone will accept credit cards**, este teléfono acepta tarjetas de crédito. **5** indica una suposición: **that will be the postman**, debe de ser el cartero.

will² [wɪl] n **1** voluntad. **2** testamento.

willing ['wɪlɪŋ] adj complaciente. • **willing to do STH** dispuesto,-a a hacer algo.

willow ['wɪləʊ] n sauce.

willpower ['wɪlpaʊəʳ] n fuerza de voluntad.

win [wɪn] n victoria, triunfo. ► vt-vi ganar.

wind¹ [wɪnd] n **1** viento, aire. **2** gases, flato. ▪ **wind instrument** instrumento de viento; **wind power** energía eólica.

wind² [waɪnd] vt **1** envolver. **2** arrollar, enrollar. **3** dar cuerda a (reloj). **4** dar vueltas a (palanca). ► vi serpentear.

to wind up ['waɪnd'ʌp] vt dar cuerda a (reloj).

windmill ['wɪndmɪl] n molino de viento.

window ['wɪndəʊ] n **1** ventana. **2** ventanilla (de vehículo). **3** escaparate (de tienda).

windpipe ['wɪndpaɪp] n tráquea.

windscreen ['wɪndskriːn] n GB parabrisas.

wind-shield ['wɪndʃiːld] n US parabrisas.

wine [waɪn] n vino.

wing [wɪŋ] n **1** ala. **2** aleta (de coche). **3** banda (fútbol). ► npl **wings** bastidores.

wink [wɪŋk] n guiño.

winner ['wɪnəʳ] n ganador,-ra.

winning ['wɪnɪŋ] adj ganador, -ra. ► npl **winnings** ganancias.

winter ['wɪntəʳ] n invierno.

wipe [waɪp] vt **1** limpiar, pasar un trapo a. **2** secar.

to wipe out vt borrar.

wiper ['waɪpəʳ] n limpiaparabrisas.

wire ['waɪəʳ] n **1** alambre. **2** cable. **3** US telegrama.

wisdom ['wɪzdəm] n **1** sabiduría. **2** prudencia, juicio. ▪ **wisdom tooth** muela del juicio.

wise [waɪz] adj **1** sabio,-a. **2** prudente.

wish [wɪʃ] n deseo. ► vt-vi desear. • **I wish to...** quisiera...; **(with) best wishes** muchos recuerdos.

wit [wɪt] n agudeza, ingenio.

witch [wɪtʃ] n bruja. ▪ **witch doctor** hechicero.

with [wɪð] *prep* con.

withdraw [wɪðˈdrɔː] *vt-vi* retirar(se).

withdrawal [wɪðˈdrɔːəl] *n* **1** retirada. **2** reintegro.

withdrawn [wɪðˈdrɔːn] *pp* → withdraw.

withdrew [wɪðˈdruː] *pt* → withdraw.

wither [ˈwɪðəʳ] *vt-vi* marchitar(se).

within [wɪˈðɪn] *prep* **1** dentro de. **2** al alcance de. **3** a menos de. **4** antes de. ► *adv* dentro.

without [wɪˈðaʊt] *prep* sin.

withstand [wɪðˈstænd] *vt* resistir, aguantar.

witness [ˈwɪtnəs] *n* testigo. ► *vt* presenciar.

witty [ˈwɪtɪ] *adj* ingenioso,-a.

wizard [ˈwɪzəd] *n* brujo.

woke [wəʊk] *pt* → wake.

woken [ˈwəʊkən] *pp* → wake.

wolf [wʊlf] *n* lobo.

woman [ˈwʊmən] *n* mujer.

womb [wuːm] *n* útero.

won [wʌn] *pt-pp* → win.

wonder [ˈwʌndəʳ] *n* **1** maravilla. **2** admiración, asombro. ► *vi* preguntarse.

wonderful [ˈwʌndəfʊl] *adj* maravilloso,-a.

wood [wʊd] *n* **1** madera. **2** bosque.

wooden [ˈwʊdən] *adj* de madera.

woodpecker [ˈwʊdpekəʳ] *n* pájaro carpintero.

woodwork [ˈwʊdwɜːk] *n* carpintería.

wool [wʊl] *n* lana.

woollen [ˈwʊlən] *adj* de lana.

word [wɜːd] *n* palabra. • **in a word** en pocas palabras; **in other words** en otras palabras, o sea; **to have words with SB** discutir con ALGN. ■ **word processor** procesador de textos.

wore [wɔːʳ] *pt* → wear.

work [wɜːk] *vt-vi* trabajar. ► *vi* **1** funcionar *(máquina, plan)*. **2** surtir efecto *(medicamento)*. ► *n* **1** trabajo. **2** obra. • **out of work** parado,-a. ■ **work of art** obra de arte.

to work out *vt* **1** calcular. **2** planear *(plan)*. **3** solucionar *(problema)*. ► *vi* salir bien.

worker [ˈwɜːkəʳ] *n* trabajador,-ra.

workforce [ˈwɜːkfɔːs] *n* mano de obra.

working [ˈwɜːkɪŋ] *adj* de trabajo, laboral.

workout [ˈwɜːkaʊt] *n* entrenamiento.

works [wɜːks] *n* fábrica.

workshop [ˈwɜːkʃɒp] *n* taller.

worktop [ˈwɜːktɒp] *n* encimera.

world [wɜːld] *n* mundo.

worldwide [ˈwɜːldwaɪd] *adj* mundial, universal.

worm [wɜːm] *n* gusano, lombriz.

worn [wɔːn] *pp* → wear.

worn-out [wɔːn'aʊt] *adj* **1** gastado,-a *(ropa, neumático)*. **2** rendido,-a *(persona)*.

worried ['wʌrɪd] *adj* preocupado,-a.

worry ['wʌrɪ] *n* preocupación. ► *vt-vi* preocupar(se).

worse [wɜːs] *adj-adv* peor. ► *n* lo peor. • **to get worse** empeorar.

worst [wɜːst] *adj-adv* peor. ► *n* lo peor.

worth [wɜːθ] *n* valor. ► *adj* que vale. • **to be worth** valer.

worthless ['wɜːθləs] *adj* **1** sin valor *(objeto)*. **2** despreciable *(persona)*.

worthwhile [wɜːθ'waɪl] *adj* que vale la pena.

worthy ['wɜːðɪ] *adj* digno,-a.

would [wʊd] *aux* **1** *(condicional)*: *she would tell you if she knew*, te lo diría si lo supiese. **2** *(disponibilidad)*: *he wouldn't help me*, se negó a ayudarme. **3** *(suposición)*: *that would have been Jim*, ese debió de ser Jim. **4** soler: *we would often go out together*, solíamos salir juntos. • **would like** querer.

wound¹ [wuːnd] *n* herida. ► *vt* herir.

wound² [waʊnd] *pt-pp* → wind.

wounded ['wuːndɪd] *adj* herido,-a.

wove [wəʊv] *pt* → weave.

woven ['wəʊvən] *pp* → weave.

wrap [ræp] *vt* envolver.

wrapping ['ræpɪŋ] *n* envoltorio. ▪ **wrapping paper** papel de envolver.

wreath [riːθ] *n* corona.

wreck [rek] *n* **1** naufragio. **2** barco naufragado. **3** restos *(de coche)*.

wrench [rentʃ] *n* llave inglesa.

wrestle ['resəl] *vi* luchar.

wrestler ['resələʳ] *n* luchador,-ra.

wrestling ['reslɪŋ] *n* lucha.

wretched ['retʃɪd] *adj* **1** desgraciado,-a. **2** *fam* horrible.

wrinkle ['rɪŋkəl] *n* arruga. ► *vt-vi* arrugar(se).

wrist [rɪst] *n* muñeca.

wristwatch ['rɪstwɒtʃ] *n* reloj de pulsera.

write [raɪt] *vt-vi* escribir. ► *vt* extender *(cheque)*.

to write back *vi* contestar.

to write down *vt* anotar.

writer ['raɪtəʳ] *n* escritor,-ra.

writing ['raɪtɪŋ] *n* **1** escritura. **2** letra. ► *npl* **writings** obras. ▪ **writing desk** escritorio; **writing paper** papel de cartas.

written ['rɪtən] *pp* → write. ► *adj* escrito,-a.

wrong [rɒŋ] *adj* **1** equivocado,-a. **2** malo,-a. ► *adv* mal. • **to be in the wrong** no tener razón, tener la culpa; **to be wrong** estar equivocado,-a,

equivocarse; **to go wrong**
1 equivocarse *(persona)*. **2** estropearse *(máquina)*.
wrote [rəʊt] *pt* → write.
wrought [rɔːt] *adj* forjado,-a.

X

xenophobia [zenəˈfəʊbɪə] *n* xenofobia.
X-ray [ˈeksreɪ] *n* **1** rayo X. **2** radiografía. ► *vt* radiografiar.
xylophone [ˈzaɪləfəʊn] *n* xilófono.

Y

yacht [jɒt] *n* yate.
yard [jɑːd] *n* **1** patio. **2** US jardín. **3** yarda.
yarn [jɑːn] *n* hilo.
yawn [jɔːn] *n* bostezo. ► *vi* bostezar.
yeah [jeə] *adv fam* sí.
year [jɪəʳ] *n* **1** año. **2** curso.
yeast [jiːst] *n* levadura.
yell [jel] *n* grito, alarido. ► *vi* gritar, dar alaridos.
yellow [ˈjeləʊ] *adj* amarillo,-a. ► *n* amarillo. ▪ **yellow press** prensa amarilla.

yes [jes] *adv* sí. ► *n* sí.
yesterday [ˈjestədɪ] *adv* ayer.
yet [jet] *adv* **1** todavía, aún: *the taxi hasn't arrived yet*, aún no ha llegado el taxi. **2** ya: *has the taxi arrived yet?*, ¿ya ha llegado el taxi? ► *conj* no obstante, sin embargo.
yew [juː] *n* tejo.
yield [jiːld] *n* **1** rendimiento. **2** cosecha. ► *vt* **1** producir, dar. **2** rendir. ► *vi* rendirse, ceder.
yoga [ˈjəʊgə] *n* yoga.
yoghurt [ˈjɒgət] *n* yogur.
yoke [jəʊk] *n* yugo. ► *vt* uncir.
yolk [jəʊk] *n* yema.
you [juː] *pron* **1** tú, vosotros, -as. **2** usted, ustedes. **3** se *(sujeto - impersonal)*. **4** ti *(complemento)*. **5** te *(antes del verbo)*. **6** vosotros,-as *(plural)*. **7** os *(antes del verbo)*. **8** usted *(complemento)*. **9** le *(antes del verbo)*. **10** ustedes *(plural)*. **11** les *(antes del verbo)*. **12** *(complemento - impersonal)*: *you never know*, nunca se sabe.
young [jʌŋ] *adj* joven.
your [jɔːʳ] *adj* **1** tu, tus, vuestro,-a, vuestros,-as. **2** su, sus.
yours [jɔːz] *pron* **1** (el) tuyo, (la) tuya, (los) tuyos, (las) tuyas, (el) vuestro, (la) vuestra, (los) vuestros, (las) vuestras. **2** (el) suyo, (la) suya, (los) suyos, (las) suyas.

yourself [jɔː'self] *pron* **1** te, tú mismo,-a. **2** se, usted mismo,-a.

yourselves [jɔː'selvz] *pron* **1** os, vosotros,-as mismos,-as. **2** se, ustedes mismos,-as.

youth [juːθ] *n* **1** juventud. **2** joven. ▪ **youth hostel** albergue de juventud.

yo-yo® ['jəυjəυ] *n* yoyo, yoyó.

Z

zeal [ziːl] *n* celo, entusiasmo.

zealous ['zeləs] *adj* celoso,-a, entusiasta.

zebra ['ziːbrə, 'zebrə] *n* cebra. ▪ **zebra crossing** paso de peatones, paso de cebra.

zenith ['zenɪθ] *n* cenit.

zeppelin ['zepəlɪn] *n* zepelín.

zero ['zɪərəυ] *n* cero.

zest [zest] *n* entusiasmo.

zigzag ['zɪgzæg] *n* zigzag. ▶ *vt* zigzaguear.

zip [zɪp] *n* cremallera. ▶ *vi* ir como un rayo. ▪ **zip code** US código postal.

to zip up *vt* cerrar con cremallera.

zipper ['zɪpr] *n* US cremallera.

zodiac ['zəυdɪæk] *n* zodiaco, zodíaco.

zombie ['zɒmbɪ] *n* zombi.

zone [zəυn] *n* zona.

zoo [zuː] *n* zoo, zoológico.

zoological [zυə'lɒdʒɪkəl] *adj* zoológico,-a.

zoology [zυ'blədʒɪ] *n* zoología.

zoom [zuːm] *n* **1** zumbido. **2** zoom, teleobjetivo. ▶ *vt-vi* pasar zumbando. ▪ **zoom lens** teleobjetivo.

Español-Inglés

ABBREVIATIONS USED
IN THIS DICTIONARY

a.	adjective	ECCL.	ecclesiastic
adv.	adverb	EDUC.	education
AER.	aeronautics	ELEC.	electricity
AGR.	agriculture	ENG.	engineering
ALG.	algebra	ENTOM.	entomology
Am.	Spanish America		
ANAT.	anatomy	*f.*	feminine; feminine
ARCH.	architecture		noun
ARCHEOL.	archeology	F. ARTS.	fine arts
Arg.	Argentina	FENC.	fencing
ARITH.	arithmetic	fig.	figuratively
art.	article	FISH.	fishing
ARTILL.	artillery	Fut.	Future
ASTR.	astronomy		
aug.	augmentative	GEOG.	geography
AUTO.	automobile	GEOL.	geology
aux.	auxiliary verb	GEOM.	geometry
		GER.	Gerund
BACT.	bacteriology	GRAM.	grammar
BIB.	Bible; Biblical	GYM.	gymnastics
BILL.	billiards		
BIOL.	biology	HIST.	history
BOOKBIND.	bookbinding		
BOOKKEEP.	bookkeeping	*i.*	intransitive
BOT.	botany	ICHTH.	ichthyology
BULL.	bullfighting	*imper.*	imperative
		IMPERF.	imperfect
CARP.	carpentry	*impers.*	impersonal verb
CHEM.	chemistry	*indef.*	indefinite
coll.	colloquial	INDIC.	Indicative
COM.	commerce	IND.	industry
comp.	comparative	INF.	Infinitive
COND.	Conditional	INSUR.	insurance
conj.	conjunction	*interj.*	interjection
CONJUG.	Conjugation	*interrog.*	interrogative
COOK.	cooking	iron.	ironic
cop.	copulative verb	*irr., irreg.*	irregular
def.	defective; definite		
dim.	diminutive	JEW.	jewelry

LIT.	literature	Pres.	Present
LITURG.	liturgy	*pres. p.*	present participle
LOG.	logic	Pret.	preterit
		PRINT.	printing
m.	masculine;	*pr. n.*	proper noun
	masculine noun	*pron.*	pronoun
MACH.	machinery		
MATH.	mathematics	RADIO.	radio;
MECH.	mechanics		broadcasting
MED.	medicine	*ref.*	reflexive verb
METAL.	metallurgy	*reg.*	regular
Mex.	Mexico	REL.	religion
MIL.	military	RLY.	railway; railroad
MIN.	mining		
MINER.	mineralogy	SUBJ.	Subjunctive
MUS.	music	*superl.*	superlative
MYTH.	mythology	SURG.	surgery
		SURV.	surveying
n.	noun; masculine		
	and feminine	*t.*	transitive verb
	noun	TELEV.	television
NAUT.	nautical	THEAT.	theater
NAV.	naval; navy	THEOL.	theology
neut.	neuter		
not cap.	not capitalized	usu.	usually
obs.	obsolete	V.	Vide; See
OPT.	optics	vul.	vulgar
ORN.	ornithology		
		WEAV.	weaving
PAINT.	painting		
pers., pers.	person; personal	ZOOL.	zoology
PHIL.	philosophy		
PHOT.	photography		
PHYS.	physics		
pl.	plural		
POET.	poetry		
POL.	politics		
poss.	possessive		
p. p.	past participle		
prep.	preposition		

KEY TO PRONUNCIATION
IN SPANISH

VOWELS

Letter	Approximate sound
a	Like *a* in English *far*, *father*, e.g., **casa**, **mano**.
e	When stressed, like *a* in English *pay*, e.g., **dedo**. When unstressed, it has a shorter sound like in English *bet*, *net*, e.g., **estado**, **decidir**.
i	Like *i* in English *machine* or *ee* in *feet*, e.g., **fin**.
o	Like *o* in English *obey*, e.g., **mona**, **poner**.
u	Like *u* in English *rule* or *oo* in *boot*, e.g., **atún**. It is silent in **gue** and **gui**, e.g., **guerra**, **guisado**. If it carries a diaeresis (**ü**), it is pronounced (see Diphthongs), e.g., **bilingüe**. It is also silent in **que** and **qui**, e.g., **querer**, **quinto**.
y	When used as a vowel, it sounds like the Spanish i, e.g., **y**, **rey**.

DIPHTHONGS

Diph.	Approximate sound
ai, ay	Like *i* in English *light*, e.g., **caigo**, **hay**.
au	Like *ou* in English *sound*, e.g., **cauto**, **paular**.
ei, ey	Like *ey* in English *they* or *a* in *ale*, e.g., **reina**, **ley**.
eu	Like the *a* in English *pay* combined with the sound of *ew* in English *knew*, e.g., **deuda**, **feudal**.
oi, oy	Like *oy* in English *toy*, e.g., **oiga**, **soy**.
ia, ya	Like *ya* in English *yarn*, e.g., **rabia**, **raya**.
ua	Like *wa* in English *wand*, e.g., **cuatro**, **cual**.
ie, ye	Like *ye* in English *yet*, e.g., **bien**, **yeso**.
ue	Like *wa* in English *wake*, e.g., **buena**, **fue**.
io, yo	Like *yo* in English *yoke*, without the following sound of *w* in this word, e.g., **región**, **yodo**.

Diph.	Approximate sound
uo	Like *uo* in English *quote*, e.g., **cuota**, **oblicuo**.
iu, yu	Like *yu* in English *Yule*, e.g., **ciudad**, **triunfo**.
ui	Like *wee* in English *week*, e.g., **ruido**.

TRIPHTHONGS

Triph.	Approximate sound
iai	Like *ya* in English *yard* combined with the *i* in *fight*, e.g., **estudiáis**.
iei	Like the English word *yea*, e.g., **estudiéis**.
uai, uay	Like *wi* in English *wide*, e.g., **averiguáis**, **guay**.
uei, uey	Like *wei* in English *weigh*, e.g., **amortigüéis**.

CONSONANTS

Letter	Approximate sound
b	Generally like the English *b* in *boat*, *bring*, *obsolete*, when it is at the beginning of a word or preceded by *m*, e.g., **baile**, **bomba**. Between two vowels and when followed by *l* or *r*, it has a softer sound, almost like the English *v* but formed by pressing both lips together, e.g., **acaba**, **haber**, **cable**.
c	Before *a*, *o*, *u*, or a consonant, it sounds like the English *c* in *coal*, e.g., **casa**, **saco**. Before *e* or *i*, it is pronounced like the English *s* in *six* in American Spanish and like the English *th* in *thin* in Castillian Spanish, e.g., **cerdo**, **cine**. If a word contains two *c*s, the first is pronounced like *c* in *coal*, and the second like *s* or *th* accordingly, e.g., **acción**.
ch	Like *ch* in English *cheese* or *such*, e.g., **chato**.
d	Generally like *d* in English *dog* or *th* in English *this*, e.g., **dedo**, **digo**. When ending a syllable, it is pronounced like the English *th*, e.g., **usted**.
f	Like *f* in English *fine*, *life*, e.g., **final**.

Letter	Approximate sound
g	Before *a, o,* and *u;* the groups *ue* and *ui;* or a consonant, it sounds like *g* in English *gain,* e.g., **gato, guitar, digno.** Before *e* or *i,* like a strongly aspirated English *h,* e.g., **general.**
h	Always silent, e.g., **hoyo, historia.**
j	Like *h* in English *hat,* e.g., **joven, reja.**
k	Like *c* in English *coal,* e.g., **kilo.** It is found only in words of foreign origin.
l	Like *l* in English *lion,* e.g., **libro, límite.**
ll	In some parts of Spain and Spanish America, like the English *y* in *yet;* generally in Castillian Spanish, like the *lli* in English *million;* e.g., **castillo, silla.**
m	Like *m* in English *map,* e.g., **moneda, tomo.**
n	Like *n* in English *nine,* e.g., **nuevo, canto.**
ñ	Like *ni* in English *onion* or *ny* in English *canyon,* e.g., **cañón, paño.**
p	Like *p* in English *parent,* e.g., **pipa, pollo.**
q	Like *c* in English *coal.* This letter is only used in the combinations *que* and *qui* in which the *u* is silent, e.g., **queso, aquí.**
r	At the beginning of a word and when preceded by *l, n,* or *s,* it is strongly trilled, e.g., **roca.** In all other positions, it is pronounced with a single tap of the tongue, e.g., **era, padre.**
rr	Strongly trilled, e.g., **carro, arriba.**
s	Like *s* in English *so,* e.g., **cosa, das.**
t	Like *t* in English *tip* but generally softer, e.g., **toma.**
v	Like *v* in English *mauve,* but in many parts of Spain and the Americas, like the Spanish **b,** e.g., **variar.**
x	Generally like *x* in English *expand,* e.g., **examen.** Before a consonant, it is sometimes pronounced like *s* in English *so,* e.g., **excepción, extensión.** In the word **México,** and in other place names of that country, it is pronounced like the Spanish **j.**

Letter	Approximate sound
y	When used as a consonant between vowels or at the beginning of a word, like the *y* in English *yet*, e.g., **yate, yeso, hoyo.**
z	Like Spanish c when it precedes **e** or **i**, e.g., **azul.**

Español - Inglés

A

a *prep* **1** *(dirección)* to: *girar a la derecha*, to turn (to the) right. **2** *(destino)* to, towards. **3** *(distancia)* away. **4** *(lugar)* at, on. **5** *(tiempo)* at: *a los tres días*, three days later; *estamos a 30 de mayo*, it's the thirtieth of May. **6** *(modo, manera)*: *a ciegas*, blindly; *a pie*, on foot. **7** *(instrumento)*: *escrito a mano*, handwritten; *escrito a máquina*, typewritten. **8** *(precio)* a: *a 3 euros el kilo*, three euros a kilo. **9** *(medida)* at. **10** *(complemento directo, no se traduce)*: *vi a Juana*, I saw Juana. **11** *(complemento indirecto)* to: *te lo di a ti*, I gave it to you. **12** *verbo* + *a* + *inf*: *aprender a nadar*, to learn (how) to swim.

abadía *nf (edificio)* abbey.

abajo *adv* **1** *(situación)* below, down. **2** *(en una casa)* downstairs. **3** *(dirección)* down, downwards. • **hacia abajo** downwards.

abandonar *vt* **1** *(desamparar)* to abandon. **2** *(lugar)* to leave.

abanico *nm* fan.

abarrotado,-a *adj* packed.

abastecer *vt* to supply.

abastecimiento *nm* supply.

abatir *vt* **1** *(derribar)* to bring down. **2** *(matar)* to shoot.

abdomen *nm* abdomen.

abecedario *nm* alphabet.

abedul *nm* birch tree.

abeja *nf* bee.

abeto *nm* fir tree.

abierto,-a *adj* **1** *(puerta, boca, ojos)* open. **2** *(grifo)* on, running. **3** *(sincero)* frank.

abismo *nm* abyss.

abogado,-a *nm,f* lawyer.

abollar *vt* to dent.

abonado,-a *nm,f (a teléfono, revista)* subscriber; *(a teatro etc)* season-ticket holder.

abonar *vt* **1** *(pagar)* to pay. **2** *(tierra)* to fertilize. ▶ *vpr* **abonarse** *(a revista)* to subscribe; *(a teatro)* to buy a season ticket.

abono *nm* **1** *(pago)* payment. **2** *(para tierra)* fertilizer. **3** *(a revista)* subscription; *(a teatro, tren, etc)* season ticket.

aborrecer *vt* to abhor, hate.

aborto *nm (voluntario)* abortion; *(espontáneo)* miscarriage.

abrasar *vt (quemar)* to burn. ▶ *vi (comida, etc)* to be boiling hot.

abrazar *vt* to embrace.

abrazo *nm* hug, embrace.

abrebotellas *nm* bottle opener.

abrelatas *nm* GB tin opener; US can opener.

abreviatura nf abbreviation.
abridor nm opener.
abrigarse vpr to wrap oneself up.
abrigo nm coat, overcoat.
abril nm April.
abrir vt 1 (gen) to open. 2 (luz) to switch on, turn on. 3 (grifo, gas) to turn on.
abrochar(se) vt-vpr to do up, fasten: **abróchense los cinturones**, please fasten your seatbelts.
ábside nm apse.
absoluto,-a adj absolute. • **en absoluto** not at all.
absolver vt to acquit.
absorber vt to absorb.
abstemio,-a nm,f teetotaller.
abstenerse vpr 1 (en votación) to abstain. 2 (de hacer algo) to refrain (de, from).
abstracto,-a adj abstract.
absurdo,-a adj absurd.
abuchear vt to boo.
abuela nf grandmother.
abuelo nm grandfather. ► nm pl **abuelos** grandparents.
abultar vi to be bulky.
abundancia nf abundance, plenty.
abundante adj abundant, plentiful.
aburrido,-a adj 1 (con ser) boring, tedious: **es un libro muy aburrido**, it's a very boring book. 2 (con estar) bored: **estoy aburrido**, I'm bored.

aburrir vt to bore. ► vpr **aburrirse** to get bored.
abusar vi **abusar de 1** (persona) to take advantage of; (autoridad, paciencia) to abuse. 2 (sexualmente) to sexually abuse.
abuso nm 1 (uso excesivo) abuse, misuse. 2 (injusticia) injustice.
acá adv (lugar) here, over here: **de acá para allá**, to and fro, up and down.
acabar vt 1 (gen) to finish. 2 (consumir) to use up, run out of. ► vi **acabar por** + inf **acabar** + ger to end up: **acabarás comprando el vestido**, you'll end up buying the dress. ► vpr **acabarse** (terminarse) to end, finish; (no quedar) to run out. • **acabar con** to destroy, put an end to; **acabar de** to have just.
acacia nf acacia.
academia nf 1 (institución) academy. 2 (escuela) school.
acampada nf camping.
acampar vi to camp.
acantilado nm cliff.
acariciar vt (persona) to caress, fondle; (animal) to stroke.
acaso adv 1 (en preguntas): **¿acaso no me crees?**, don't you believe me? 2 fml (quizá) perhaps, maybe: **acaso necesite tu ayuda**, I might need your help. • **por si acaso** just in case.

acatarrarse *vpr* to catch a cold.

acceder *vi* 1 *(consentir)* to consent, agree. 2 *(tener entrada)* to enter. 3 INFORM to access.

acceso *nm* 1 *(entrada)* access, entry. 2 *(carretera)* approach road.

accesorio *nm* accessory.

accidentado,-a *nm,f* casualty, accident victim.

accidente *nm* 1 *(percance)* accident. 2 *(geográfico)* feature. ■ **accidente aéreo** plane crash; **accidente de coche** car crash.

acción *nf* 1 *(gen)* action. 2 *(acto)* act, deed. 3 *(en bolsa)* share.

accionar *vt* 1 *(manivela)* to pull. 2 *(pieza mecánica)* to operate; *(alarma etc)* to set off.

accionista *nmf* shareholder, stockholder.

acecho • **al acecho** in wait.

aceite *nm* oil. ■ **aceite de oliva** olive oil.

aceitera *nf* oil bottle.

aceituna *nf* olive. ■ **aceituna rellena** stuffed olive.

acelerador *nm* accelerator.

acelerar *vt* to accelerate.

acelga *nf* chard.

acento *nm* 1 *(gráfico)* accent, written accent; *(tónico)* stress. 2 *(regional, etc)* accent.

acentuar *vt* 1 *(palabra, letra)* to accent. 2 *(resaltar)* to emphasize, stress.

aceptable *adj* acceptable.

aceptar *vt* to accept, receive.

acequia *nf* irrigation ditch.

acera *nf* GB pavement; US sidewalk.

acerca de *prep* about, concerning.

acercar *vt* to bring closer. ► *vpr* **acercarse** to come closer.

acero *nm* steel.

acertante *nmf* winner.

acertar *vt* 1 *(repuesta)* to get right. 2 *(adivinanza)* to guess.

achaque *nm* ailment.

acidez *nf* *(de fruta, vinagre)* sourness; *(en química)* acidity. ■ **acidez de estómago** heartburn.

ácido,-a *adj* 1 *(sabor)* sharp, tart. 2 acidic. ► *nm* **ácido** acid.

acierto *nm* 1 *(solución correcta)* right answer. 2 *(decisión adecuada)* wise decision.

aclaración *nf* explanation.

aclarar *vt* 1 *(cabello, color)* to lighten. 2 *(enjuagar)* to rinse. 3 *(explicar)* to explain.

acogedor,-ra *adj* *(lugar)* cosy, warm.

acoger *vt* *(recibir)* to receive; *(invitado)* to welcome.

acomodador,-ra *nm,f* *(hombre)* usher; *(mujer)* usherette.

acomodarse *vpr* to make oneself comfortable.

acompañamiento *nm* *(guarnición)* accompaniment.

acompañante *nmf* companion.

acompañar *vt* *(ir con)* to go with, come with. • **le acompaño en el sentimiento** please accept my condolences.

aconsejar *vt* to advise.

acontecimiento *nm* event, happening.

acordar *vt* to agree. ▶ *vpr* **acordarse** to remember.

acordeón *nm* accordion.

acortar *vt* to shorten.

acostar *vpr* to go to bed.

acostumbrado,-a *adj* **1** *(persona)* accustomed, used to. **2** *(hecho)* usual, customary.

acostumbrar(se) *vi-vpr.* • **acostumbrar a hacer algo** to be in the habit of doing STH. • **acostumbrarse a algo** to get used to STH.

acreedor,-ra *nm,f* creditor.

acrílico,-a *adj* acrylic.

acróbata *nmf* acrobat.

acta *nf* **1** *(de reunión)* minutes. **2** *(certificado)* certificate.

actitud *nf* attitude.

activar *vt* to activate.

actividad *nf* activity.

activo,-a *adj* active. ▶ *nm* **activo** assets.

acto *nm* **1** *(acción)* act. **2** *(ceremonia)* ceremony. **3** *(de obra teatral)* act. • **acto seguido** immediately afterwards; **en el acto** at once.

actor *nm* actor.

actriz *nf* actress.

actuación *nf* **1** *(interpretación)* performance. **2** *(comportamiento)* GB behaviour; US behavior.

actual *adj* **1** *(de este momento)* present, current. **2** *(moderno)* up-to-date.

actualidad *nf* **1** *(momento presente)* present time, present. **2** *(hechos)* current affairs.

actualizar *vt* **1** *(poner al día)* to bring up to date. **2** *(programa)* to upgrade; *(página de Internet)* to refresh.

actualmente *adv* *(hoy en día)* nowadays; *(ahora)* at present.

actuar *vi* *(gen)* to act; *(cantante, bailarín)* to perform.

acuarela *nf* GB watercolour; US watercolor.

acuario *nm* aquarium.

acuático,-a *adj* aquatic, water.

acudir *vi* *(ir)* to go; *(venir)* to come.

acueducto *nm* aqueduct.

acuerdo *nm* agreement. • **¡de acuerdo!** all right!, O.K.!; **estar de acuerdo** to agree.

acusación *nf* *(inculpación)* accusation; *(en derecho)* charge.

acusar *vt* *(culpar)* to accuse; *(en derecho)* to charge.

acústico,-a *adj* acoustic.

adaptación *nf* adaptation.

adaptar(se) *vt-vpr* to adapt.

adecuado,-a *adj* adequate, suitable.

adelantado,-a adj 1 *(desarrollado)* developed. 2 *(reloj)* fast. • **por adelantado** in advance.

adelantamiento nm overtaking.

adelantar vt 1 *(mover adelante)* to move forward. 2 *(reloj)* to put forward. 3 *(pasar adelante)* to pass; *(vehículo)* to overtake. 4 *(dinero)* to pay in advance. ▶ vi *(reloj)* to be fast. ▶ vpr **adelantarse** 1 *(llegar temprano)* to be early. 2 *(reloj)* to gain, be fast.

adelante adv forward. ▶ interj come in! • **en adelante** from now on; **hacia adelante** forwards; **más adelante** later on.

adelanto nm 1 *(avance)* advance. 2 advance.

adelgazar vi *(perder peso)* to lose weight; *(con régimen)* to slim.

además adv 1 *(por añadidura)* besides. 2 *(también)* also. • **además de** besides.

adentro adv inside.

aderezar vt *(condimentar)* to season; *(ensalada)* to dress.

adicto,-a nm,f addict.

adiós nm goodbye.

adivinanza nf riddle.

adivinar vt to guess.

adjetivo nm adjective.

adjudicar vt to award. ▶ vpr **adjudicarse** *(victoria)* to win.

administración nf 1 *(de empresa)* administration, management. 2 *(de medicamento)* administering. ▪ **administración de lotería** lottery office.

administrar vt 1 *(organizar)* to manage. 2 *(proporcionar)* to give.

administrativo,-a nm,f *(funcionario)* official; *(de empresa, banco)* office worker.

admirable adj admirable.

admiración nf 1 *(estima)* admiration. 2 *(signo)* exclamation mark.

admirar vt 1 *(estimar)* to admire. 2 *(sorprender)* to amaze, surprise.

admisión nf admission. • **"Reservado el derecho de admisión"** "The management reserves the right to refuse admission".

admitir vt 1 *(dar entrada a, reconocer)* to admit. 2 *(aceptar)* to accept.

adobar vt to marinate.

adolescente adj-nmf adolescent.

adonde adv where.

adónde adv where.

adoptar vt to adopt.

adoquín nm *(piedra redonda)* cobble; *(piedra cuadrada)* paving stone.

adorar vt to adore, worship.

adornar vt to decorate.

adorno *nm* decoration. • **de adorno** decorative.

adosado,-a *adj*: *casas adosadas*, semidetached houses.

adquirir *vt (comprar)* to buy, get.

adrede *adv* on purpose.

aduana *nf* customs *pl*.

aduanero,-a *nm,f* customs officer.

adulto,-a *adj-nm,f* adult.

adverbio *nm* adverb.

adversario,-a *nm,f* adversary, opponent.

advertencia *nf* 1 *(aviso)* warning. 2 *(consejo)* piece of advice.

advertir *vt* 1 *(avisar)* to warn. 2 *(aconsejar)* to advise.

aéreo,-a *adj* 1 *(vista, fotografía)* aerial. 2 *(tráfico)* air.

aeropuerto *nm* airport.

aerosol *nm* aerosol, spray.

afán *nm* 1 *(anhelo)* eagerness. 2 *(esfuerzo)* hard work.

afección *nf (enfermedad)* complaint, illness.

afectar *vt* 1 *(concernir)* to affect. 2 *(impresionar)* to move.

afecto *nm* affection.

afeitado *nm* shave, shaving.

afeitar(se) *vt-vpr* to shave.

afición *nf* 1 *(inclinación)* liking. 2 *(pasatiempo)* hobby.

aficionado,-a *adj* 1 *(entusiasta)* keen, fond. 2 *(no profesional)* amateur. ▶ *nm,f* 1 *(entusiasta)*, fan, enthusiast. 2 *(no profesional)* amateur.

aficionarse *vpr* to become fond *(de, of)*.

afilar *vt* to sharpen.

afinar *vt* 1 *(piano, etc)* to tune. 2 *(puntería)* to sharpen.

afirmación *nf* statement, assertion.

afirmar *vt (aseverar)* to state, say.

aflojar *vt (soltar)* to loosen.

afluente *nm* tributary.

afonía *nf* loss of voice.

afónico,-a *adj* hoarse. • **estar afónico,-a** to have lost one's voice.

afortunado,-a *adj* lucky, fortunate.

África *nf* Africa.

africano,-a *adj-nm,f* African.

afrontar *vt* to face up to.

afuera *adv* outside. ▶ *nf pl* **afueras** outskirts.

agacharse *vpr* 1 *(acuclillarse)* to crouch down; *(inclinarse)* to bend down.

agallas *nf (de pez)* gills.

agarrado,-a *adj* stingy. • **bailar agarrado** to dance cheek to cheek.

agarrar *vt (coger fuerte)* to grab; *(sujetar)* to hold. ▶ *vpr* **agarrarse** to hold on, cling *(a, to)*.

agencia *nf* agency. ▪ **agencia de viajes** travel agency; **agencia inmobiliaria** estate agent's.

agenda *nf* 1 *(libro)* diary. 2 *(de direcciones)* address book.

agente *nmf* agent. ▪ **agente de policía** police officer.

ágil *adj* agile.

agitar *vt (líquido)* to shake.

aglomeración *nf (acumulación)* agglomeration; *(de gente)* crowd.

agobiar *vt* to overwhelm. ▶ *vpr* **agobiarse** to get worked up.

agonía *nf (sufrimiento)* agony, grief; *(de moribundo)* death throes.

agosto *nm* August.

agotado,-a *adj* **1** *(cansado)* exhausted. **2** *(libro)* out of print; *(mercancía)* sold out.

agotar *vt* to exhaust. ▶ *vpr* **agotarse** **1** *(cansarse)* to become exhausted. **2** *(acabarse)* to run out; *(existencias)* to be sold out.

agradable *adj* nice, pleasant.

agradar *vi* to please.

agradecer *vt* to thank.

agradecimiento *nm* gratitude, thankfulness.

agrandar *vt* to enlarge.

agravante *nm & nf* **1** *(gen)* added difficulty. **2** JUR aggravating circumstance.

agravarse *vpr* to get worse.

agredir *vt* to attack.

agregar *vt* to add.

agresión *nf* aggression.

agresivo,-a *adj* aggressive.

agresor,-ra *nm,f* aggressor.

agrícola *adj* agricultural.

agricultor,-ra *nm,f* farmer.

agricultura *nf* agriculture, farming.

agridulce *adj* **1** *(gen)* bittersweet. **2** *(salsa)* sweet and sour.

agrio,-a *adj* sour.

agruparse *vpr* **1** *(congregarse)* to group together. **2** *(asociarse)* to associate.

agua *nf* water. ▪ **agua con gas** sparkling water; **agua dulce** fresh water; **agua mineral** mineral water; **agua oxigenada** hydrogen peroxide; **agua potable** drinking water; **agua salada** salt water; **agua sin gas** still water; **aguas termales** thermal waters.

aguacate *nm* avocado, avocado pear.

aguacero *nm* downpour.

aguantar *vt* **1** *(sostener)* to hold; *(peso)* to support, bear. **2** *(sufrir - frases afirmativas)* to put up with; *(- frases negativas)* to stand: *no sé cómo aguanta a su marido*, I don't know how she puts up with her husband; *no aguanto a gente como él*, I can't stand people like him. **3** *(contener - respiración)* to hold; *(- risa, lágrimas)* to hold back. ▶ *vpr* **aguantarse** *(resignarse)*: *tendrás que aguantarte*, you'll have to put up with it.

aguardar *vt-vi* to wait *(for)*, await.

aguardiente *nm* liquor, brandy.

aguarrás *nm* turpentine.

agudo,-a *adj* 1 *(afilado)* sharp. 2 *(dolor, acento, ángulo)* acute. 3 *(ingenioso)* witty. 4 *(voz)* high-pitched.

aguijón *nm* 1 *(de animal)* sting. 2 *(de planta)* thorn, prickle.

águila *nf* eagle.

aguja *nf* 1 *(de coser, jeringuilla)* needle. 2 *(de reloj)* hand. 3 *(de tocadiscos)* stylus. 4 *(de torre, iglesia)* spire, steeple. 5 *(de tren)* GB point; US switch.

agujero *nm* hole.

agujetas *nf pl* stiffness.

ahí *adv* there. • **por ahí** 1 *(lugar)* round there. 2 *(aproximadamente)* more or less.

ahogar *vt* to drown. ▶ *vpr* **ahogarse** 1 *(en agua)* to be drowned. 2 *(asfixiarse)* to choke.

ahora *adv* 1 *(en este momento)* now. 2 *(hace un momento)* a moment ago. 3 *(dentro de un momento)* in a minute, shortly. • **ahora bien** however; **ahora mismo** 1 *(en este momento)* right now. 2 *(enseguida)* right away; **de ahora en adelante** from now on; **hasta ahora** until now, so far; **por ahora** for the time being.

ahorcar *vt* to hang.

ahorrar *vt* to save.

ahorros *nm pl* savings.

ahumado,-a *adj* smoked; *(bacon)* smoky.

aire *nm* 1 *(fluido)* air. 2 *(viento)* wind. 3 *(aspecto)* air, appearance. • **al aire libre** in the open air, outdoors; **tomar el aire** to get some fresh air. ▪ **aire acondicionado** air conditioning.

aislamiento *nm* 1 *(acción, estado)* isolation. 2 *(eléctrica)* insulation.

aislante *adj* insulating. ▶ *nm* insulator.

aislar *vt* 1 *(apartar)* to isolate. 2 *(eléctricamente)* to insulate.

ajedrez *nm* *(juego)* chess; *(tablero y piezas)* chess set.

ajeno,-a *adj* *(de otro)* another's.

ajillo • **al ajillo** with garlic.

ajo *nm* garlic.

ajustado,-a *adj* 1 *(ropa)* tight, close-fitting. 2 *(resultado, victoria)* close.

ajustar *vt* *(adaptar)* to adjust; *(uso técnico)* to fit.

al *contr* → a.

ala *nf* wing. ▪ **ala delta** hang glider.

alabar *vt* to praise.

alacrán *nm* scorpion.

alambre *nm* wire.

alameda *nf* 1 *(bosque)* poplar grove. 2 *(paseo)* avenue.

álamo *nm* poplar.

alargar *vt* 1 *(prenda)* to lengthen; *(cuerda)* to stretch. **2** *(prolongar)* to prolong, extend. **3** *(brazo, mano)* to stretch out.

alarma *nf* alarm. ■ **alarma antirrobo 1** *(para casa)* burglar alarm. **2** *(para coche)* car alarm; **alarma contra incendios** fire alarm.

alba *nf* dawn, daybreak.

albañil *nm* bricklayer.

albaricoque *nm* apricot.

albergar *vt* **1** *(alojar)* to put up. **2** *(esperanzas)* to cherish. **3** *(duda)* GB to harbour; US to harbour.

albergue *nm* hostel. ■ **albergue juvenil** youth hostel.

albóndiga *nf* meatball.

albornoz *nm* bathrobe.

alborotar *vt* **1** *(agitar)* to agitate, excite. **2** *(sublevar)* to incite to rebel.

albufera *nf* lagoon.

álbum *nm* album.

alcachofa *nf* artichoke.

alcalde *nm* mayor.

alcaldesa *nf* mayoress.

alcaldía *nf* **1** *(cargo)* mayorship. **2** *(oficina)* mayor's office.

alcance *nm* **1** *(de persona)* reach: *fuera del alcance de los niños*, out of children's reach. **2** *(de arma, emisora)* range. **3** *(trascendencia)* scope, importance.

alcantarilla *nf (cloaca)* sewer; *(boca)* drain.

alcanzar *vt* **1** *(lugar, edad, temperatura)* to reach; *(persona)* to catch up with. **2** *(conseguir)* to attain, achieve.

alcaparra *nf* caper.

alcázar *nm* fortress.

alcoba *nf* bedroom.

alcohol *nm* alcohol. • **sin alcohol** non-alcoholic.

alcohólico,-a *adj-nm,f* alcoholic.

alcornoque *nm* cork oak.

aldaba *nf* **1** *(llamador)* knocker. **2** *(pestillo)* latch.

aldea *nf* hamlet, small village.

aleación *nf* alloy.

alegrar *vt* to make happy. ► *vpr* **alegrarse** to be happy, be pleased.

alegre *adj* **1** *(persona - contenta)* happy; *(- borracha)* tipsy. **2** *(color)* bright.

alegría *nf* happiness.

alejar *vt* to move away. ► *vpr* **alejarse** to go away, move away.

alemán,-ana *adj-nm,f* German. ► *nm* **alemán** *(idioma)* German.

Alemania *nf* Germany.

alergia *nf* allergy.

alérgico,-a *adj* allergic.

alero *nm* **1** *(del tejado)* eaves. **2** *(de baloncesto)* forward.

alerta *adv* on the alert. ► *nf* alert.

aleta *nf* fin.

alfabeto *nm* alphabet.
alfalfa *nf* alfalfa, lucerne.
alfarería *nf* pottery.
alfil *nm* bishop.
alfiler *nm* 1 *(en costura)* pin. 2 *(joya)* brooch.
alfombra *nf* *(grande)* carpet; *(pequeña)* rug.
alga *nf* alga; *(marina)* seaweed; *(de agua dulce)* weed.
álgebra *nf* algebra.
algo *pron (en frases afirmativas)* something; *(en frases interrogativas)* anything: ***vamos a tomar algo***, let's have something to drink; ***¿hay algo que no entiendas?***, is there anything you don't understand? ► *adv (un poco)* a bit, a little. • **algo es algo** something is better than nothing.
algodón *nm* cotton. ▪ **algodón hidrófilo** cotton wool.
alguien *pron (en frases afirmativas)* somebody, someone; *(en frases interrogativas y negativas)* anybody, anyone: ***alguien se lo habrá olvidado***, somebody must have left it behind; ***¿conoces alguien que hable japonés?***, do you know anyone who speaks Japanese?
algún *adj* → alguno,-a.
alguno,-a *adj (en frases afirmativas)* some; *(en frases interrogativas)* any; *(en frases negativas)* no, not … any: ***me he comprado algunos libros***, I've bought some books; ***¿tienes alguna idea mejor?***, do you have any better idea?; ***sin éxito alguno***, with no success at all; ***no vino persona alguna***, nobody came. ► *pron (en frases afirmativas)* someone, somebody; *(en frases interrogativas)* anybody: ***hubo alguno que se quejó***, there was somebody who complained; ***puedes quedarte con alguna de estas fotos***, you can keep some of those pictures; ***¿alguno sabe la respuesta?***, does anyone know the answer?
alhaja *nf* jewel.
aliado,-a *nm,f* ally.
alianza *nf* 1 *(pacto)* alliance. 2 *(anillo)* wedding ring.
aliarse *vpr* to form an alliance.
alicates *nm pl* pliers.
aliciente *nm* incentive, inducement.
aliento *nm* breath. • **sin aliento** breathless.
alimentación *nf* 1 *(acción)* feeding. 2 *(comida)* food; *(dieta)* diet.
alimentar *vt* to feed. ► *vi (servir de alimento)* to be nutritious, be nourishing. ► *vpr* **alimentarse de** to live on.
alimento *nm* food.
aliñar *vt (ensalada)* to dress; *(guiso)* to season.

aliño *nm (de ensalada)* dressing; *(de guiso)* seasoning.

alisar *vt* to smooth.

alistarse *vpr* to enlist.

aliviar *vt* **1** *(enfermedad, dolor)* to relieve. **2** *(consolar)* to comfort.

alivio *nm* relief.

allá *adv* there.

allí *adv* there. • **por allí** that way.

alma *nf* soul.

almacén *nm* warehouse. ► *nm pl* **(grandes) almacenes** department store.

almacenar *vt* to store.

almeja *nf* clam.

almendra *nf* almond. ▪ **almendra garapiñada** sugared almond.

almendro *nm* almond tree.

almíbar *nm* syrup.

almidón *nm* starch.

almirante *nm* admiral.

almohada *nf* pillow.

almohadón *nm* cushion.

almorzar *vi* to have lunch.

almuerzo *nm* lunch.

alojamiento *nm* lodging, accommodation.

alojarse *vpr* to stay.

alpargata *nf* rope-soled sandal, espadrille.

alpinismo *nm* mountaineering.

alpinista *nmf* mountaineer, mountain climber.

alpiste *nm* birdseed.

alquilar *vt* **1** *(dar en alquiler - casa)* to rent out, GB let; *(- coche, bicicleta)* to hire, rent; *(- aparato)* to rent. **2** *(tomar en alquiler - casa)* to rent; *(- coche, bicicleta)* to hire, rent.

alquiler *nm* **1** *(cesión - de casa)* renting, GB letting; *(- de coche etc.)* hire, rental; *(- de aparato)* rental. **2** *(cuota - de casa)* rent; *(- de coche etc.)* hire charge; *(- de aparato)* rental.

alquitrán *nm* tar.

alrededor *adv (gen)* around; *(cantidad)* around, about: *alrededor de veinte*, about twenty. ► *nm pl* **alrededores** surrounding area *sing*.

alta *nf (a un enfermo)* discharge.

altar *nm* altar.

altavoz *nm* loudspeaker.

alterar *vt* to alter, change. ► *vpr* **alterarse** *(enfadarse)* to lose one's temper.

altercado *nm* **1** *(discusión)* argument. **2** *(disturbio)* disturbance.

alternar *vt-vi (sucederse)* to alternate. ► *vi (relacionarse)* to socialize, mix.

alternativo,-a *adj* alternative.

alteza *nf* Highness.

altibajos *nm pl* ups and downs.

altillo *nm (armario)* cupboard.

altitud *nf* height, altitude.

alto,-a *adj* **1** *(gen)* high. **2** *(persona, edificio, árbol)* tall. **3** *(so-*

nido, voz) loud ► *nm* **alto 1**
(altura): ***Pepe mide dos metros
de alto***, Pepe's two metres tall.
2 *(elevación)* height, hillock.
3 *(parada)* halt, stop. ► *adv* **1**
(volar, subir) high. **2** *(hablar)*
loud, loudly.

altura *nf* **1** *(gen)* height. **2**
(persona) tall: ***mide dos metros de altura***, he's two metres tall. **3** *(cosa)* high: ***mide
dos metros de altura***, it's two
metres high. **4** *(altitud)* altitude. • **a la altura de** next to: *a
la altura de la catedral*, next
to the cathedral.

alubia *nf* bean.

alud *nm* avalanche.

alumbrado *nm* lighting.

alumbrar *vt (iluminar - calles,
habitación)* to light; *(- monumento, estadio)* to light up, illuminate.

aluminio *nm* GB aluminium;
US aluminum.

alumno,-a *nm,f (de colegio)*
pupil; *(de universidad)* student.

alza *nf* rise, increase.

alzar *vt (levantar - mano, cabeza)* to raise, lift; *(voz)* to raise.

ama *nf*. ▪ **ama de casa** housewife.

amabilidad *nf* kindness.

amable *adj* kind, nice.

amainar *vi* to die down.

amanecer *vi* **1** *(hacerse de día)*
to dawn. **2** *(clarear)* to get
light. ► *nm* dawn, daybreak.

amante *nmf* lover.

amapola *nf* poppy.

amar *vt* to love.

amargo,-a *adj* bitter.

amarillo,-a *adj* yellow. ► *nm*
amarillo yellow.

amarra *nf* mooring cable. •
soltar amarras to cast off.

amasar *vt* **1** *(masa)* to knead;
(cemento) to mix. **2** *(dinero)* to
amass.

amazona *nf* horsewoman.

ámbar *nm* amber.

ambición *nf* ambition.

ambicioso,-a *adj* ambitious.

ambiental *adj* **1** *(contaminación, impacto)* environmental.
2 *(música)* background.

ambiente *nm* **1** *(aire)* air,
atmosphere. **2** *(entorno)* environment; *(de casa, ciudad, época)* atmosphere. **3** *(animación)*
life, atmosphere.

ambiguo,-a *adj* ambiguous.

ambos,-as *adj-pron* both.

ambulancia *nf* ambulance.

ambulante *adj* itinerant, travelling.

ambulatorio *nm* surgery,
clinic.

amenaza *nf* threat. ▪ **amenaza de bomba** bomb scare.

amenazar *vt-vi* to threaten.

ameno,-a *adj (agradable)*
pleasant; *(entretenido)* entertaining.

América *nf* America.

americana *nf* jacket.

americano,-a *adj-nm,f* American.

ametralladora *nf* machine gun.

amígdala *nf* tonsil.

amigo,-a *nm,f* friend.

amistad *nf* friendship.

amnesia *nf* amnesia.

amo *nm* **1** *(señor)* master. **2** *(dueño)* owner.

amoniaco *nm* ammonia.

amontonar *vt* to pile up.

amor *nm* love. • **hacer el amor** to make love. ▪ **amor propio** self-esteem.

amortiguador *nm* shock absorber.

amparar *vt* to protect, shelter. ► *vpr* **ampararse en** *(una ley)* to seek protection in.

ampliación *nf* **1** *(de edificio, plazo)* extension. **2** *(de negocio, mercado)* expansion. **3** *(de fotografía)* enlargement.

ampliar *vt* **1** *(edificio, plazo)* to extend. **2** *(negocio, mercado)* to expand. **3** *(fotografía)* to enlarge, blow up.

amplio,-a *adj* **1** *(espacioso)* roomy, spacious. **2** *(margen, gama)* wide; *(mayoría)* large.

ampolla *nf* *(en la piel)* blister.

amueblar *vt* to furnish.

amuleto *nm* charm, amulet.

analfabeto,-a *adj-nm,f* illiterate.

analgésico,-a *adj* analgesic. ► *nm* **analgésico** analgesic.

análisis *nm* analysis. ▪ **análisis de sangre** blood test.

analizar *vt* GB to analyse; US analyze.

anarquía *nf* anarchy.

anatomía *nf* anatomy.

anca *nf* haunch.

ancho,-a *adj* **1** *(calle, cama, habitación)* wide; *(espalda, cara)* broad. **2** *(prenda)* loose, loose-fitting. ► *nm* **ancho** breadth, width. • **de ancho**: *tres metros de ancho*, three metres wide.

anchoa *nf* anchovy.

anchura *nf* breadth, width.

anciano,-a *nm,f* *(hombre)* elderly man; *(mujer)* elderly woman.

ancla *nf* anchor.

anclar *vi* to anchor.

andamio *nm* scaffolding.

andar *vi* **1** *(caminar)* to walk. **2** *(funcionar)* to work, go.

andén *nm* platform.

anécdota *nf* anecdote.

anemia *nf* GB anaemia; US anemia.

anestesia *nf* GB anaesthesia; US anesthesia.

anfibio *nm* amphibian.

anfitrión,-ona *nm,f* *(hombre)* host; *(mujer)* hostess.

ángel *nm* angel.

angina *nf* angina. • **tener anginas** to have a sore throat. ▪ **angina de pecho** angina pectoris.

anguila *nf* eel.

angula *nf* elver.

ángulo *nm* **1** *(geometría)* angle. **2** *(rincón)* corner.

angustia *nf* anguish, distress.

anilla *nf* ring.

anillo *nm* ring.

animación *nf* liveliness.

animado,-a *adj* **1** *(persona)* cheerful. **2** *(situación)* animated, lively. **3** *(calle)* full of people.

animal *adj* animal. ► *nm* **1** *(ser vivo)* animal. **2** *(persona bruta)* blockhead. ▪ **animal doméstico 1** *(de granja)* domestic animal. **2** *(de compañía)* pet.

animar *vt* **1** *(alentar)* to encourage. **2** *(alegrar - persona)* to cheer up; *(- fiesta, reunión)* to liven up. ► *vpr* **animarse 1** *(alegrarse - persona)* to cheer up; *(- fiesta, reunión)* to liven up. **2** *(decidirse)* to make up one's mind.

ánimo *nm* **1** *(estado emocional)* spirits. **2** *(aliento)* encouragement.

anís *nm* **1** *(planta)* anise. **2** *(bebida)* anisette.

aniversario *nm* anniversary.

ano *nm* anus.

anoche *adv* last night.

anochecer *vi* to get dark. ► *nm* nightfall, dusk.

anónimo,-a *adj* anonymous.

anorak *nm* anorak.

anormal *adj* abnormal.

anotar *vt* *(apuntar)* to make a note of, take down.

ansia *nf* *(deseo)* longing.

ansiedad *nf* anxiety.

ante¹ *prep* **1** *(delante de)* before. **2** *(frente a)* in the face of. • **ante todo 1** *(primero)* first of all. **2** *(por encima de)* above all.

ante² *nm* *(piel)* suede.

anteayer *adv* the day before yesterday.

antebrazo *nm* forearm.

antelación *nf*. • **con antelación** in advance.

antemano *adv*. • **de antemano** beforehand, in advance.

antena *nf* **1** *(de aparato)* aerial. **2** *(de animal)* antenna. ▪ **antena parabólica** satellite dish.

antepasado *nm* ancestor.

anterior *adj* previous.

antes *adv* **1** *(en el tiempo - previamente)* before; *(- más temprano)* earlier: *te lo he dicho antes*, I told you earlier. **2** *(en el espacio)* before. • **antes de** before.

antibiótico *nm* antibiotic.

anticiclón *nm* anticyclone, high pressure area.

anticiparse *vpr* **1** *(suceder antes)* to be early. **2** *(adelantarse)* to beat to it.

anticipo *nm* advance.

anticonceptivo *nm* contraceptive.

anticongelante *adj-nm* antifreeze.

anticuario *nm* antiquary, antiques dealer.

antídoto *nm* antidote.

antigüedad *nf* 1 *(período)* antiquity. 2 *(edad)*: *una ciudad de tres mil años de antigüedad*, a city which is three thousand years old. ► *nf pl* **antigüedades** antiques.

antiguo,-a *adj* 1 *(muy viejo)* ancient. 2 *(viejo)* old. 3 *(anterior)* old, former: *mi antiguo jefe*, my former boss.

antipatía *nf* antipathy, dislike.

antipático,-a *adj* unpleasant.

antirrobo *adj* antitheft.

antivirus *nm* antivirus system.

antojo *nm* 1 *(capricho)* whim; *(de embarazada)* craving. 2 *(en la piel)* birthmark.

antorcha *nf* torch.

anual *adj* annual, yearly.

anular¹ *nm* ring finger.

anular² *vt* to annul, cancel.

anunciar *vt* 1 *(notificar)* to announce. 2 *(hacer publicidad de)* to advertise.

anuncio *nm* 1 *(en periódico)* advertisement, advert, ad; *(en televisión, radio)* advertisement, advert, commercial. 2 *(notificación)* announcement.

anzuelo *nm* hook.

añadir *vt* to add.

añejo,-a *adj (vino)* mature.

año *nm* year. • **tener… años** to be… years old: *¿cuántos años tienes?*, how old are you? ■ **Año Nuevo** New Year.

aorta *nf* aorta.

apagar *vt* 1 *(fuego)* to extinguish, put out. 2 *(luz)* to turn off. 3 *(aparato)* to turn off, switch off. ► *vpr* **apagarse** *(luz)* to go out.

apagón *nm* power cut, blackout.

aparato *nm* 1 *(máquina)* machine; *(dispositivo)* device. 2 *(electrodoméstico)* appliance; *(televisor, radio)* set. 3 *(de gimnasio)* piece of apparatus. 4 *(para los dientes)* brace; *(audífono)* hearing aid. 5 *(conjunto de órganos)* system.

aparcamiento *nm* 1 *(acción)* parking. 2 *(lugar)* GB car park; US parking lot; *(en la calle)* place to park.

aparcar *vt-vi* to park.

aparecer *vi* 1 *(gen)* to appear; *(objeto perdido)* to turn up. 2 *(dejarse ver)* to show up, turn up.

apariencia *nf* appearance.

apartado,-a *adj* 1 *(lejano)* distant. 2 *(aislado)* isolated, remote. ► *nm* **apartado** section. ■ **apartado de correos** post office box.

apartamento *nm* apartment.

apartar vt 1 (alejar) to move away. 2 (poner a un lado) to set aside. ▶ vpr **apartarse** (de un lugar) to move away.

aparte adv 1 (a un lado) aside, to one side; (por separado) apart, separately. 2 (además) besides.

apasionante adj exciting, fascinating.

apasionar vt to excite, fascinate.

apeadero nm (de trenes) halt.

apearse vpr (de caballo) to dismount; (de vehículo) to get off.

apellidarse vpr to be called: ¿cómo se apellida usted?, what's your surname?

apellido nm surname, family name.

apenas adv 1 (casi no) hardly, scarcely. 2 (casi nunca) hardly ever.

apéndice nm appendix.

apendicitis nf appendicitis.

aperitivo nm 1 (bebida) aperitif. 2 (comida) appetizer.

apertura nf (gen) opening; (de temporada, curso académico) start, beginning.

apetecer vi: me apetece un café, I feel like a coffee, I fancy a coffee; ¿te apetece ir a la playa?, do you fancy going to the beach?

apetito nm appetite.

apetitoso,-a adj appetizing.

apio nm celery.

apisonadora nf steamroller.

aplanar vt to level, make even.

aplastar vt to squash, flatten.

aplaudir vt to clap, applaud.

aplauso nm applause.

aplazar vt (reunión, acto) to postpone, put off; (pago) to defer.

aplicación nf application.

aplicado,-a adj 1 (ciencia) applied. 2 (estudiante) studious, diligent.

aplicar vt 1 (extender) to apply. 2 (poner en práctica) to put into practice.

apoderarse vpr to take possession.

apodo nm nickname.

aportar vt to contribute.

aposento nm 1 (cuarto) room. 2 (hospedaje) lodgings.

aposta adv on purpose.

apostar vt-vi to bet.

apóstol nm apostle.

apoyar vt 1 (reclinar) to rest, lean. 2 (basar) to base, found. 3 (defender) to back, support. ▶ vpr **apoyarse** (basarse) to be based.

apoyo nm support.

apreciar vt 1 (sentir aprecio por) to regard highly. 2 (valorar) to appreciate.

aprecio nm esteem, regard.

aprender vt-vi to learn.

aprendizaje nm learning.

apresurar(se) *vt-vpr* to hurry.

apretar *vt* **1** *(estrechar)* to squeeze. **2** *(tornillo, nudo)* to tighten. **3** *(pulsar - botón)* to press; *(- gatillo)* to pull.

aprieto *nm* fix, awkward situation.

aprisa *adv* quickly.

aprobación *nf (gen)* approval; *(de ley)* passing.

aprobado *nm* pass.

aprobar *vt* **1** *(decisión, plan, préstamo)* to approve. **2** *(comportamiento)* to approve of. **3** *(examen, ley)* to pass.

aprovechar *vt* **1** *(sacar provecho de)* to make good use of. **2** *(emplear)* to use. ▶ *vpr* **aprovecharse** to take advantage. • **¡que aproveche!** enjoy your meal!

aproximarse *vpr* to approach, draw near.

apto,-a *adj* **1** *(apropiado)* suitable. **2** *(capaz)* capable, able. • **apta para todos los públicos** GB U-certificate; US rated G; **no apta** for adults only.

apuesta *nf* bet.

apuesto,-a *adj* good-looking.

apuntar *vt* **1** *(señalar)* to point at. **2** *(arma)* to aim. **3** *(anotar)* to note down, make a note of. ▶ *vt-vpr* **apuntar(se)** *(inscribir - en curso)* GB to enrol; US to enroll; *(- en lista)* to put down.

apuntes *nm pl (de clase)* notes.

apuñalar *vt* to stab.

apurar *vt (terminar)* to finish up. ▶ *vpr* **apurarse** to worry.

apuro *nm* tight spot.

aquel,-lla *adj* that.

aquél,-lla *pron* that one.

aquello *pron*: **aquello fue lo que más me gustó**, that was what I liked the most; **¿te acuerdas de aquello que me dijiste?**, do you remember what you told me?

aquí *adv* **1** *(lugar)* here. **2** *(tiempo)* now. • **por aquí por favor** this way please.

árabe *adj (gen)* Arab; *(de Arabia)* Arabian; *(alfabeto, número)* Arabic. ▶ *nmf (persona)* Arab; *(de Arabia)* Arabian. ▶ *nm (idioma)* Arabic.

arado *nm* GB plough; US plow.

araña *nf (animal)* spider.

arañar(se) *vt-vpr* to scratch.

arañazo *nm* scratch.

arar *vt* GB to plough; US to plow.

arbitrar *vt (fútbol, rugby, boxeo)* to referee; *(tenis)* to umpire.

árbitro *nm (en fútbol, rugby, boxeo)* referee; *(en tenis)* umpire.

árbol *nm* tree.

arbusto *nm* shrub, bush.

arca *nf* chest.

arcada *nf* **1** *(de puente)* arcade. **2** *(al vomitar)*: **me dieron arcadas**, I retched.

arcaico,-a *adj* archaic.

archipiélago *nm* archipelago.

archivar *vt* **1** *(ordenar)* to file.
2 INFORM to save.

archivo *nm* **1** *(documento)* file.
2 *(lugar)* archive. ▪ **archivo
adjunto** INFORM attachment.

arcilla *nf* clay.

arco *nm* **1** ARQ arch. **2** MAT arc.
3 *(de violín, flecha)* bow. ▪ **arco
iris** rainbow.

arder *vi* **1** *(quemarse)* to burn.
2 *(estar muy caliente)* to be
boiling hot.

ardilla *nf* squirrel.

ardor *nm* GB ardour; US ardor.
▪ **ardor de estómago** heartburn.

área *nf* **1** *(zona, medida)* area.
2 *(en fútbol)* penalty area.

arena *nf* sand. ▪ **arenas mo-
vedizas** quicksand.

arenque *nm* herring.

Argentina *nf* Argentina, the
Argentine.

argentino,-a *adj-nm,f* Argen-
tinian.

argot *nm* **1** *(popular)* slang. **2**
(técnico) jargon.

argumento *nm* **1** *(razón)* argument. **2** *(de novela, obra,
etc)* plot.

árido,-a *adj* **1** *(tierra)* arid, dry.
2 *(texto, tema)* dry.

arista *nf* edge.

aristócrata *nmf* aristocrat.

aritmética *nf* arithmetic.

arma *nf* weapon, arm. ▪ **arma
blanca** knife; **arma de fuego**
firearm.

armada *nf* navy.

armadura *nf* **1** *(defensa)* GB armour; US armor. **2** *(armazón)*
framework.

armamento *nm* armament.

armar *vt* *(proveer de armas)*
to arm. **2** *(ruido, alboroto)* to
make.

armario *nm* *(de cocina)* cupboard; *(de ropa)* GB wardrobe;
US closet.

armonía *nf* harmony.

armónica *nf* harmonica,
mouth organ.

aro *nm* hoop, ring.

aroma *nm* aroma; *(del vino)*
bouquet.

arpa *nf* harp.

arpón *nm* harpoon.

arqueología *nf* GB archaeology; US archeology.

arquitecto,-a *nm,f* architect.

arquitectura *nf* architecture.

arrancar *vt* **1** *(planta)* to up-
root, pull up. **2** *(página)* to tear
out. ▶ *vi* **1** *(coche)* to start. **2**
(ordenador) to boot.

arranque *nm* **1** *(de motor)* starting mechanism: *el motor de
arranque*, the starter motor. **2**
(arrebato) fit.

arrasar *vt* to raze, demolish.
▶ *vi* to sweep the board.

arrastrar *vt* *(llevar por el suelo)*
to drag (along), pull (along).
▶ *vpr* **arrastrarse** *(reptar)* to
crawl.

arrebato *nm* fit, outburst.

arrecife *nm* reef.

arreglar *vt* 1 *(resolver - conflicto)* to settle; *(- asunto)* to sort out. 2 *(ordenar)* to tidy, tidy up. 3 *(reparar)* to mend, fix up. ▶ *vpr* **arreglarse** *(componerse)* to get ready; *(cabello)* to do.

arreglo *nm* 1 *(reparación)* repair. 2 *(acuerdo)* agreement. • **con arreglo a** according to.

arrepentirse *vpr* to regret, be sorry.

arrestar *vt* to arrest.

arresto *nm* arrest.

arriar *vt* 1 *(velas)* to lower. 2 *(bandera)* to strike.

arriba *adv* 1 *(dirección)* up; *(encima)* on (the) top. 2 *(situación)* above. 3 *(piso)* upstairs. ▶ *interj* up! • **hacia arriba** upwards.

arriesgado,-a *adj* risky, dangerous.

arriesgar(se) *vt-vpr* to risk.

arrimarse *vpr* to come closer, come nearer.

arrodillarse *vpr* to kneelz-down.

arrojar *vt* 1 *(tirar)* to throw. 2 *(resultado)* to show.

arroyo *nm* *(río)* stream.

arroz *nm* rice. ▪ **arroz con leche** rice pudding; **arroz integral** brown rice.

arruga *nf* *(en la piel)* wrinkle; *(en la ropa)* crease.

arrugar(se) *vt-vpr* 1 *(piel)* to wrinkle. 2 *(ropa)* to crease. 3 *(papel)* to crumple.

arruinar *vt* to bankrupt, ruin. ▶ *vpr* **arruinarse** to be bankrupt, be ruined.

arsenal *nm* arsenal.

arte *nm* 1 *(gen)* art: *bellas artes*, fine arts. 2 *(habilidad)* craft, skill. ▪ **arte dramático** drama.

artefacto *nm* device.

arteria *nf* artery.

artesanía *nf* 1 *(actividad)* craftsmanship. 2 *(productos)* handicrafts.

artesano,-a *nm,f* craftsman, artisan.

articulación *nf* joint.

artículo *nm* article.

artificial *adj* artificial.

artillería *nf* artillery.

artista *nmf* artist.

artístico,-a *adj* artistic.

artritis *nf* arthritis.

as *nm* ace.

asa *nf* handle.

asado,-a *adj* *(carne)* roast; *(pescado, patata)* baked. ▶ *nm* **asado** roast.

asaltante *nmf* attacker.

asaltar *vt* 1 *(atacar)* to assault, attack. 2 *(robar - banco)* to rob, raid; *(- persona)* to mug.

asalto *nm* 1 *(ataque)* assault, attack. 2 *(robo - de banco)* raid, robbery; *(- a persona)* mugging. 3 *(en boxeo)* round.

asamblea *nf* 1 *(en parlamento)* assembly. 2 *(reunión)* meeting.

asar *vt (carne)* to roast; *(pescado, patata)* to bake.

ascender *vi* **1** *(subir)* to climb. **2** *(sumar)* to amount.

ascenso *nm* **1** *(subida - de temperatura, precio)* rise; *(- de montaña)* ascent. **2** *(- de empleado, equipo)* promotion.

ascensor *nm* GB lift; US elevator.

asco *nm* disgust. • **dar asco** to be disgusting.

asearse *vpr* to wash.

asegurado,-a *nm,f* policy holder.

aseguradora *nf* insurance company.

asegurar *vt* **1** *(coche, casa)* to insure. **2** *(garantizar)* to ensure, guarantee. **4** *(afirmar)* to assure. ▶ *vpr* **asegurarse 1** *(cerciorarse)* to make sure. **2** *(tomar un seguro)* to insure oneself.

aseo *nm* **1** *(limpieza)* cleanliness, tidying up. **2** *(cuarto)* bathroom, toilet.

asequible *adj* accessible: *a un precio asequible*, at a reasonable price.

asesinar *vt* to kill, murder.

asesinato *nm* killing, murder.

asesino,-a *nm,f* killer.

asesorar *vt* to advise, give advice.

asesor,-ra *nm,f* adviser, consultant.

asfalto *nm* asphalt.

asfixia *nf* asphyxia, suffocation.

asfixiarse *vpr* to suffocate.

así *adv* **1** *(de esta manera)* like that, like this, in this way. **2** *(de esa manera)* that way. ▶ *adj* such: *un hombre así*, a man like that, such a man. • **así así** so-so; **así que 1** *(de manera que)* so, therefore. **2** *(tan pronto como)* as soon as; **aun así 1** even so. **2** *(por así decirlo)* so to speak.

Asia *nf* Asia.

asiático,-a *adj-nm,f* Asian.

asiento *nm (silla etc)* seat; *(de bicicleta)* saddle.

asignatura *nf* subject.

asilo *nm (amparo)* asylum; *(residencia)* home.

asimilar *vt* to assimilate.

asimismo *adv* **1** *(también)* also. **2** *(de esta manera)* likewise.

asistencia *nf* **1** *(presencia)* attendance. **2** *(público)* audience, public. **3** *(ayuda)* assistance. ■ **asistencia médica** medical care.

asistente *adj* attending. ▶ *nmf* assistant.

asistir *vi* to attend, be present. ▶ *vt* **1** *(ayudar)* to assist, help. **2** *(cuidar)* to treat.

asma *nf* asthma.

asmático,-a *adj-nm,f* asthmatic.

asno *nm* ass, donkey.
asociación *nf* association.
asociar *vt* to associate. ▶ *vpr* **asociarse** to form a partnership.
asomar *vi* to appear, show. ▶ *vpr* **asomarse** *(a ventana)* to lean out; *(a balcón)* to come out. • **"Prohibido asomarse por la ventanilla"** "Do not lean out of the window".
asombrar *vt* to amaze, astonish. ▶ *vpr* **asombrarse** to be amazed, be astonished.
asombroso,-a *adj* amazing, astonishing.
aspa *nf* **1** *(cruz)* X-shaped cross. **2** *(de molino)* arm; *(de ventilador)* blade.
aspecto *nm* **1** *(apariencia)* look, appearance. **2** *(faceta)* aspect.
áspero,-a *adj* rough, coarse.
aspiración *nf* **1** *(al respirar)* inhalation. **2** *(ambición)* aspiration, ambition.
aspiradora *nf* vacuum cleaner, GB hoover.
aspirante *nmf* candidate.
aspirar *vt* to inhale, breathe in. ▶ *vi* to aspire to.
aspirina® *nf* aspirin®.
asqueroso,-a *adj* **1** *(sucio)* dirty, filthy. **2** *(desagradable)* disgusting.
asta *nf* **1** *(de bandera)* flagpole. **2** *(cuerno)* horn.
asterisco *nm* asterisk.
astilla *nf* splinter.

astillero *nm* shipyard, dockyard.
astro *nm* star.
astrología *nf* astrology.
astronauta *nmf* astronaut.
astronomía *nf* astronomy.
astucia *nf* *(sagacidad)* astuteness, shrewdness; *(malicia)* cunning.
astuto,-a *adj* *(sagaz)* astute, shrewd; *(malicioso)* cunning.
asumir *vt* **1** *(gen)* to assume, take part on. **2** *(aceptar)* to come to term with, accept.
asunto *nm* **1** *(cuestión)* matter, subject. **2** *(ocupación)* affair, business.
asustar *vt* to frighten. ▶ *vpr* **asustarse** to be frightened.
atacar *vt* to attack.
atajo *nm* short cut.
atalaya *nf* watchtower.
ataque *nm* **1** *(gen)* attack. **2** *(acceso)* fit. ■ **ataque cardíaco** heart attack; **ataque de nervios** nervous breakdown.
atar *vt* to tie, fasten. ▶ *vpr* **atarse** to tie up, do up.
atardecer *vi* to get dark, grow dark. ▶ *nm* evening, dusk.
atascar *vt* to block, obstruct. ▶ *vpr* **atascarse 1** *(obstruirse)* to get blocked. **2** *(mecanismo)* to jam.
atasco *nm* traffic jam.
ataúd *nm* coffin.
ateísmo *nm* atheism.

atención *nf* attention. • **prestar atención** to pay attention. ■ **atención al cliente** customer service.

atender *vt* 1 *(cliente)* to attend to; *(bar, tienda)* to serve: *¿ya la atienden?*, are you being served? 2 *(enfermo)* to take care of, look after. 3 *(llamada)* to answer. ► *vi* to pay attention.

atentado *nm* attack, assault.

atentamente *adv (en carta)* sincerely, faithfully.

atentar *vi.* • **atentar contra AL-GN** to make an attempt on SB's life.

atento,-a *adj* 1 *(pendiente)* attentive. 2 *(amable)* polite, courteous.

ateo,-a *adj-nm,f* atheist.

aterrizaje *nm* landing.

aterrizar *vt* to land.

ático *nm (buhardilla)* attic; *(piso - último)* top floor; *(- lujoso)* penthouse.

atlántico,-a *adj* Atlantic. • **el (océano) Atlántico** the Atlantic *(Ocean)*.

atlas *nm* atlas.

atleta *nmf* athlete.

atletismo *nm* athletics.

atmósfera *nf* atmosphere.

atmosférico,-a *adj* atmospheric.

atómico,-a *adj* atomic.

átomo *nm* atom.

atracador,-ra *nm,f (de banco)* bank robber; *(en la calle)* mugger.

atracar *vt (robar - banco)* to hold up, rob; *(- persona)* to mug. ► *vi (amarrar)* to tie up.

atracción *nf* attraction.

atraco *nm (de banco)* hold-up, robbery; *(de persona)* mugging.

atractivo,-a *adj* attractive. ► *nm* **atractivo** *(de persona)* attractiveness, charm; *(de cosa)* attraction.

atraer *vt* to attract.

atragantarse *vpr* to choke.

atrapar *vt* to capture, catch.

atrás *adv* 1 *(posición)* back. 2 *(tiempo)* ago. • **hacia atrás** backwards.

atrasar *vt* 1 *(salida)* to delay. 2 *(reloj)* to put back. ► *vi (reloj)* to be slow. ► *vpr* **atrasarse** 1 *(tren etc)* to be late. 2 *(quedarse atrás)* to stay behind.

atraso *nm* 1 *(retraso)* delay. 2 *(de reloj)* slowness. 3 *(de país)* backwardness.

atravesar *vt* 1 *(cruzar)* to cross. 2 *(crisis, situación)* to go through.

atreverse *vpr* to dare.

atrevido,-a *adj* 1 *(osado)* daring, bold. 2 *(indecoroso)* risqué.

atribuir *vt* to attribute, ascribe.

atributo *nm* attribute, quality.

atril *nm* lectern.

atrio *nm* **1** *(patio)* atrium. **2** *(vestíbulo)* vestibule.

atropellar *vt* to knock down, run over.

atropello *nm* **1** *(accidente)*: **ha habido un atropello**, someone has been run over. **2** *(abuso)* outrage, abuse.

ATS *abr* **(ayudante técnico sanitario)** medical auxiliary.

atún *nm* tuna.

audaz *adj* audacious, bold.

audición *nf* **1** *(acción)* hearing. **2** *(para obra etc)* audition.

audiencia *nf* **1** *(recepción, público)* audience. **2** *(tribunal)* court.

audífono *nm* hearing aid.

audiovisual *adj* audio-visual.

auditorio *nm* **1** *(público)* audience. **2** *(lugar)* auditorium.

auge *nm* **1** *(del mercado)* boom. **2** *(subida)* rise. **3** *(crecimiento)* growth.

aula *nf* *(en escuela)* classroom; *(en universidad)* lecture hall.

aullido *nm* howl.

aumentar *vt* **1** *(incrementar)* to increase, raise. **2** *(fotos)* to enlarge.

aumento *nm* **1** *(incremento)* rise, increase. **2** *(de foto)* enlargement.

aun *adv* even. • **aun así** even so; **aun cuando** although.

aún *adv* **1** *(en afirmativas, interrogativas)* still: **aún la estoy esperando**, I'm still waiting for her. **2** *(en negativas)* yet: **aún no ha llegado**, he hasn't arrived yet. **3** *(en comparaciones)* even: **dicen que aún hará más frío**, they say it's going to get even colder.

aunque *conj* **1** *(a pesar de que)* although, even though. **2** *(incluso)* even if. **3** *(pero)* although, though.

auricular *nm* *(de teléfono)* receiver, earpiece. ► *nm pl* **auriculares** headphones.

aurora *nf* dawn.

auscultar *vt* to sound.

ausencia *nf* absence.

ausente *adj* absent.

austero,-a *adj* austere.

Australia *nf* Australia.

australiano,-a *adj-nm,f* Australian.

Austria *nf* Austria.

austríaco,-a *adj-nm,f* Austrian.

auténtico,-a *adj* *(cuadro)* authentic, genuine; *(persona, afecto)* genuine; *(piel, joya)* real.

auto *nm* *(coche)* car.

autobús *nm* bus.

autocar *nm* coach.

autoescuela *nf* driving school.

autógrafo *nm* autograph.

automático,-a *adj* automatic.

automóvil *nm* car; US automobile.

automovilismo *nm* motoring.

automovilista *nmf* motorist.

autonomía *nf* 1 *(independencia)* autonomy. 2 *(comunidad)* autonomous region.

autónomo,-a *adj* 1 POL autonomous, self-governing. 2 *(trabajador)* self-employed; *(traductor etc)* freelance.

autopista *nf* GB motorway; US expressway; US freeway.

autor, -ra *nm,f* 1 *(de libro)* author, writer; *(de canción)* writer. 3 *(de crimen)* perpetrator.

autoridad *nf* authority.

autorización *nf* authorization.

autorizar *vt* to authorize.

autoservicio *nm* self-service restaurant.

autostop *nm* hitch-hiking. • **hacer autostop** to hitch-hike.

autovía *nf* GB dual-carriageway; US highway.

auxiliar *vt* to help, assist. ► *nmf* assistant. ■ **auxiliar de vuelo** flight attendant.

auxilio *nm* help, assistance.

avalancha *nf* avalanche.

avance *nm* 1 *(progreso, movimiento)* advance. 2 *(pago)* advance payment.

avanzar *vt* to advance, move forward. ► *vi* 1 *(ir hacia adelante)* to advance, to move forward. 2 *(progresar)* to make progress.

avaro,-a *nm,f* miser.

ave *nf* bird.

AVE *abr (Alta Velocidad Española)* Spanish high-speed train.

avellana *nf* hazelnut.

avena *nf* oats.

avenida *nf* avenue.

aventura *nf* 1 *(suceso)* adventure. 2 *(riesgo)* venture. 3 *(relación amorosa)* affair, love affair.

avergonzarse *vpr* 1 *(por mala acción)* to be ashamed. 2 *(por situación bochornosa)* to be embarrassed.

avería *nf* 1 *(en coche)* breakdown. 2 *(en máquina)* fault.

averiado,-a *adj* 1 *(aparato)* faulty, not working. 2 *(coche)* broken down. • **"Averiado"** "Out of order".

averiarse *vpr* 1 *(coche)* to break down. 2 *(máquina)* to malfunction.

averiguar *vt* to find out.

avestruz *nm* ostrich.

avión *nm* plane; GB aeroplane; US airplane.

avioneta *nf* light aircraft.

avisar *vt* 1 *(informar)* to tell. 2 *(advertir)* to warn. 3 *(mandar llamar)* to call for.

aviso *nm* 1 *(información)* notice. 2 *(advertencia)* warning.

avispa *nf* wasp.

axila *nf* armpit.

ayer *adv* yesterday.

ayuda *nf* help, assistance.

ayudante *nmf* assistant.

ayudar *vt* to help, aid, assist.

ayunas *nm pl.* • **en ayunas** without having eaten breakfast.

ayuntamiento *nm* **1** *(corporación)* GB town council; US city council. **2** *(edificio)* GB town hall; US city hall.

azada *nf* hoe.

azafata *nf* **1** *(de avión)* flight attendant. **2** *(de congresos)* hostess.

azafrán *nm* saffron.

azar *nm* chance. • **al azar** at random; **por azar** by chance.

azotar *vt* **1** *(con látigo)* to whip. **2** *(golpear)* to beat.

azotea *nf* flat roof.

azúcar *nm & nf* sugar.

azucarero *nm* sugar bowl.

azul *adj-nm* blue.

azulejo *nm* tile.

B

baba *nf (de adulto)* spittle; *(de niño)* dribble.

babero *nm* bib.

babor *nm* port, port side.

bacalao *nm* cod.

bache *nm* **1** *(en carretera)* pothole. **2** *(en el aire)* air pocket. **3** *fig (mal momento)* bad patch.

bacon *nm* bacon.

bacteria *nf* bacterium.

bahía *nf* bay.

bailar *vt-vi* to dance. • **sacar a ALGN a bailar** to ask SB to dance.

bailarín,-ina *nm,f* dancer.

baile *nm* **1** *(danza, fiesta)* dance. **2** *(de etiqueta)* ball.

baja *nf* **1** *(descenso)* fall, drop. **2** *(en guerra)* casualty. **3** *(por enfermedad)* sick leave: **está de baja**, he's off sick. • **darse de baja 1** *(de un club)* to resign. **2** *(en una suscripción)* to cancel one's subscription.

bajada *nf* **1** *(acción)* descent. **2** *(en carretera etc)* slope. **3** *(de temperatura)* fall, drop.

bajamar *nf* low tide.

bajar *vt* **1** *(de un lugar alto)* to bring down, take down. **2** *(mover abajo)* to lower. **3** *(recorrer de arriba abajo)* to come down, go down. **4** *(voz, radio, volumen)* to lower. **5** *(precios)* to reduce. **6** INFORM *(de la red)* to download. ► *vi* **1** *(ir abajo - acercándose)* to come down; *(- alejándose)* to go down. **2** *(apearse - de coche)* to get out; *(- de bicicleta, caballo, avión, tren)* to get off. **3** *(reducirse)* to fall, drop, come down. ► *vpr* **bajarse 1** *(ir abajo - acercándose)* to come down; *(- alejándose)* to go down. **2** *(apearse - de coche)* to get out; *(- de bicicleta, caballo, avión, tren)* to get off. **3** *(pantalones, falda)* to pull down.

bajo,-a *adj* **1** *(de poca altura)* low. **2** *(persona)* short. **3** *(inferior)* poor, low: *la clase baja*, the lower classes; *los bajos fondos*, the underworld. ► *adv* **bajo 1** *(volar)* low. **2** *(hablar)* softly, quietly. ► *prep (gen)* under; *(con temperaturas)* below. ► *nm* **bajo 1** *(piso)* GB ground floor; US first floor. **2** *(instrumento)* bass. ► *nm pl* **bajos** GB ground floor; US first floor. • **por lo bajo 1** *(disimuladamente)* on the sly. **2** *(en voz baja)* in a low voice.

bala *nf* bullet: *un disparo de bala*, a gunshot. • **como una bala** *fam* like a shot.

balance *nm* **1** balance, balance sheet. **2** *(resultado)* result.

balancear(se) *vi-vpr (mecerse)* to rock; *(en columpio)* to swing; *(barco)* to roll.

balanza *nf* **1** *(para pesar)* scales. **2** balance.

balar *vi* to bleat.

balcón *nm* balcony.

balda *nf* shelf.

balde *nm (cubo)* bucket, pail. • **de balde** free, for nothing; **en balde** in vain.

baldosa *nf* floor tile.

balear *adj* ▪ **Islas Baleares** Balearic Islands.

ballena *nf* whale.

ballet *nm* ballet.

balneario *nm* spa, health resort.

balón *nm* ball.

baloncesto *nm* basketball.

balonmano *nm* handball.

balonvolea *nf* volleyball.

balsa *nf (barca)* raft.

bálsamo *nm* balsam, balm.

bambú *nm* bamboo.

banana *nf* banana.

banca *nf (sector)* banking; *(los bancos)* the banks.

bancarrota *nf* bankruptcy.

banco *nm* **1** *(institución financiera)* bank. **2** *(asiento)* bench. ▪ **banco de datos** data bank.

banda¹ *nf* **1** *(de gala)* sash. **2** *(lado)* side. ▪ **banda magnética** magnetic srip; **banda sonora** sound track.

banda² *nf* **1** *(de ladrones)* gang. **2** *(musical)* band.

bandeja *nf* tray.

bandera *nf* flag.

bandido,-a *nm,f* bandit.

bando *nm (facción)* faction, party.

banqueta *nf (taburete)* stool, footstool.

banquete *nm* banquet, feast. ▪ **banquete de boda** wedding reception.

banquillo *nm* **1** *(de acusados)* dock. **2** *(en deporte)* bench.

bañador *nm (de mujer)* bathing costume, swimming costume; *(de hombre)* swimming trunks.

bañar *vt* **1** *(en bañera)* to bath. **2** *(con salsa)* to coat. **3** *(con* *licor)* to soak. ► *vpr* **bañarse** *(en bañera)* to have a bath, take a bath; *(en el mar, piscina)* to swim • **"Prohibido bañarse"** "No swimming".

bañera *nf* bath, bathtub.

baño *nm* 1 *(acción)* bath. 2 *(bañera)* bath, bathtub. 3 *(capa)* coat, coating. 4 *(sala de baño)* bathroom. 5 *(wáter)* toilet. ► *nm pl* **baños** *(balneario)* spa *sing*. ■ **baño María** bain-marie.

bar *nm (cafetería)* café, snack bar; *(de bebidas alcohólicas)* bar.

baraja *nf* pack, deck.

barajar *vt (naipes)* to shuffle.

barandilla *nf* handrail, banister.

barato,-a *adj* cheap. ► *adv* **barato** cheaply, cheap.

barba *nf* beard. • **dejarse la barba** to grow a beard; **por barba** each, a head.

barbaridad *nf* 1 *(crueldad)* cruelty. 2 *(disparate)* piece of nonsense: *cuesta una barbaridad*, it costs a fortune.

bárbaro,-a *adj* 1 HIST barbarian. 2 *(cruel)* cruel. 3 *fam (grande)* enormous. 4 *fam (espléndido)* tremendous, terrific.

barbería *nf* barber's.

barbilla *nf* chin.

barca *nf* boat.

barco *nm* boat, vessel, ship. ■ **barco de vela** GB sailing boat; US sailboat.

barómetro *nm* barometer.

barón *nm* baron.

barquero,-a *nm,f (hombre)* boatman; *(mujer)* boatwoman.

barquillo *nm* wafer.

barra *nf* 1 *(de hierro)* bar. 2 *(de pan)* loaf. 3 *(de bar, cafetería)* bar. ■ **barra de labios** lipstick; **barra libre** free bar.

barraca *nf* 1 *(chabola)* shanty. 2 *(de feria)* stall.

barranco *nm* 1 *(precipicio)* precipice. 2 *(entre montañas)* gully.

barrendero,-a *nm,f* street sweeper.

barrer *vt* to sweep.

barrera *nf* barrier. ■ **barrera de coral** coral reef.

barricada *nf* barricade.

barriga *nf* belly.

barril *nm* barrel, keg.

barrio *nm* GB district, area; US neighborhood. ■ **barrio bajo** seedy area; **barrio residencial** residential area.

barro *nm* 1 *(lodo)* mud. 2 *(arcilla)* clay.

barroco,-a *adj* baroque. ► *nm* **barroco** baroque.

barrote *nm* 1 *(de celda)* bar. 2 *(de escalera, silla)* rung.

basar *vt* to base. ► *vpr* **basarse** to be based.

báscula *nf* scales.

base *nf* 1 *(superficie)* base. 2 *(fundamento)* basis. 3 *(componente principal)*: *la base de su* *dieta es la carne*, his diet is meat-based; *la base del éxito*, the key to success. ● **a base de**: *un postre hecho a base de leche y huevos*, a pudding made of milk and eggs; *a base de mucho trabajo*, by working hard. ■ **base de datos** database.

básico,-a *adj* basic.

basílica *nf* basilica.

bastante *adj-pron* **1** *(suficiente)* enough, sufficient. **2** *(abundante)* quite a lot. ► *adv* **1** enough. **2** *(un poco)* fairly, quite.

bastar *vi* to be sufficient, be enough.

basto,-a *adj* **1** *(grosero)* coarse, rough. **2** *(sin pulimentar)* rough, unpolished.

bastón *nm* stick, walking stick.

basura *nf* GB rubbish; US garbage. ● **tirar algo a la basura** to throw STH away, throw STH in the bin; **sacar la basura** to take out the rubbish (US garbage).

bata *nf* **1** *(de casa)* dressing gown. **2** *(de trabajo)* overall; *(de médicos etc)* white coat. **3** *(de colegial)* child's overall.

batalla *nf* battle. ● **de batalla** *fam* ordinary, everyday: *zapatos de batalla*, everyday shoes.

bate *nm* bat.

batería *nf* **1** *(de coche)* battery. **2** *(cañones)* battery. **3** *(de conjunto)* drums. ► *nmf* drummer. ● **en batería** *(coches)* at an angle to the kerb (US curb). ■ **batería de cocina** set of pots and pans.

batido *nm* milk shake.

batir *vt* **1** *(huevos)* to beat; *(nata, claras)* to whip. **2** *(alas)* to flap. **5** *(vencer)* to beat, defeat. **6** *(récord)* to break. ► *vpr* **batirse** to fight.

batuta *nf* baton.

baúl *nm* trunk.

bautismo *nm* baptism, christening.

bautizar *vt* **1** to baptize, christen. **2** *(poner nombre a)* to name.

bautizo *nm* **1** *(sacramento)* baptism, christening. **2** *(fiesta)* christening party.

baya *nf* berry.

bayeta *nf* cloth.

bazar *nm* bazaar.

bazo *nm* spleen.

bebé *nm* baby.

beber *vt* to drink.

bebida *nf* drink, beverage. ■ **bebida alcohólica** alcoholic drink.

beca *nf* **1** *(ayuda)* grant. **2** *(por méritos)* scholarship.

becerro *nm* calf.

béchamel *nf* béchamel sauce.

béisbol *nm* baseball.

belén *nm* nativity scene, crib.

belga *adj-nmf* Belgian.
Bélgica *nf* Belgium.
belleza *nf* beauty.
bello,-a *adj* beautiful.
bellota *nf* acorn.
bendecir *vt* to bless.
bendición *nf* blessing.
beneficiar *vt* to benefit. ▶
vpr **beneficiarse** to benefit
from.
beneficio *nm* profit.
beneficioso,-a *adj* beneficial,
useful.
benéfico,-a *adj* charitable:
función benéfica, charity performance.
bengala *nf* flare.
benigno,-a *adj* 1 *(tumor)* benign. 2 *(clima)* mild.
berberecho *nm* cockle.
berenjena *nf* GB aubergine;
US eggplant.
bermudas *nf pl* Bermuda
shorts.
berro *nm* watercress, cress.
berza *nf* cabbage.
besamel *nf* bechamel sauce.
besar *vt* to kiss. ▶ *vpr* **be-
sarse** to kiss one another.
beso *nm* kiss.
bestia *nf (animal)* beast. ▶ *nmf*
(persona) brute.
besugo *nm* 1 *(pez)* sea bream.
2 *(persona)* idiot.
betún *nm* shoe polish.
biberón *nm* baby bottle.
Biblia *nf* Bible.
bíblico,-a *adj* biblical.

bibliografía *nf* 1 *(en libro)* bibli-
ography. 2 *(de curso)* reading
list.
biblioteca *nf* 1 *(edificio)* library. 2 *(mueble)* bookcase,
bookshelf.
bicarbonato *nm* bicarbonate.
bíceps *nm* biceps.
bicho *nm* 1 *(insecto)* bug. 2
(persona) nasty character: *es
un bicho raro*, he's a weirdo.
bici *nf fam* bike.
bicicleta *nf* bicycle: *ir en bicicleta*, to cycle. ▪ **bicicleta de
carreras** racing bicycle; **bicicleta de montaña** mountain
bike; **bicicleta estática** exercise bike.
bidé *nm* bidet.
bidón *nm* 1 *(pequeño)* can. 2
(grande) drum.
bien *adv* 1 *(de manera satisfac-
toria)* well. 2 *(correctamente)*
right, correctly. 3 *(debida-
mente)* properly: *¡pórtate bi-
en!*, behave yourself! 4 *(de
acuerdo)*: *¡muy bien!*, O.K.,
all right. 5 *(mucho)* very, *(bastante)* quite: *es bien sencillo*,
it's very simple; *bien tarde*,
pretty late. ▶ *nm* good: *el
bien y el mal*, good and
evil. ▶ *adj* well-to-do: *gente
bien*, the upper classes. ▶
nm pl **bienes** property, pos-
sessions. ▪ **bien que** althoug;
más bien rather; **si bien** although.

bienestar *nm* well-being, comfort.

bienvenida *nf* welcome. • **dar la bienvenida a** ALGN to welcome SB.

bigote *nm* **1** *(de persona)* GB moustache; US mustache. **2** *(de gato)* whiskers.

bikini *nm* bikini.

bilingüe *adj* bilingual.

bilis *nf* bile.

billar *nm* **1** *(juego)* billiards. *(mesa)* billiard table.

billete *nm* **1** *(de banco)* GB note; US bill. **2** *(de tren, autobús, sorteo, etc)* ticket: *sacar un billete*, to buy a ticket. ▪ **billete de ida** one-way ticket; **billete de ida y vuelta** GB return ticket; US round-trip ticket.

billetero *nm* wallet.

billón *nm* trillion; GB *(antiguamente)* billion; .

bingo *nm* **1** *(juego)* bingo. **2** *(sala)* bingo hall.

biografía *nf* biography.

biología *nf* biology.

biológico,-a *adj* **1** *(ciclo, madre)* biological. **2** *(alimento)* organic.

biombo *nm* folding screen.

biquini *nm* bikini.

bisagra *nf* hinge.

bisiesto *adj*: *año bisiesto*, leap year.

bisté *nm* steak.

bistec *nm* steak.

bisturí *nm* scalpel.

bisutería *nf* GB imitation jewellery; US imitation jewelry.

bit *nm* bit.

bizco,-a *adj* cross-eyed.

bizcocho *nm* sponge cake.

blanco,-a *adj* white. ▶ *nm* **blanco 1** *(color)* white. **2** *(objetivo físico)* target. **3** *(hueco)* blank, gap. • **dar en el blanco 1** *(diana)* to hit the mark. **2** *(acertar)* to hit the nail on the head; **quedarse en blanco** *(olvidar)* to forget everything.

blando,-a *adj* **1** *(superficie, madera, queso)* soft; *(carne)* tender. **2** *(persona)* soft.

blanquear *vt* **1** *(poner blanco)* to whiten. **2** *(con cal)* to whitewash. **3** *fam (dinero)* to launder.

bloc *nm* pad, notepad.

bloque *nm* **1** *(de piedra)* block. **2** *(de papel)* pad, notepad. **3** POL bloc. ▪ **bloque de pisos** block of flats.

bloquear *vt* **1** *(camino, entrada)* to block. **2** *(puerto, país)* to blockade. ▶ *vpr* **bloquearse 1** *(quedarse paralizado)* to freeze. **2** *(quedarse en blanco)* to have a blank. **3** *(mecanismo)* to jam.

blusa *nf* blouse.

boa *nf* boa.

bobina *nf* **1** *(carrete)* reel, bobbin. **2** *(eléctrica)* coil.

bobo,-a *adj* silly, foolish. ▶ *nm,f* fool, dunce.

boca *nf* 1 mouth. 2 *(abertura)* entrance, opening. • **boca abajo** face down; **boca arriba** face up. ▪ **boca a boca** mouth to mouth resuscitation; **boca del estómago** pit of the stomach.

bocacalle *nf* side street: *la primera bocacalle a la izquierda*, the first turn to the left.

bocadillo *nm* 1 *(de pan de molde)* sandwich. 2 *(en barra)* roll. 3 *(en cómics)* speech balloon.

bocata *nm* 1 *fam (de pan de molde)* sandwich. 2 *(en barra)* roll.

bochorno *nm* 1 *(calor)* sultry weather, close weather. 2 *(vergüenza)* embarrassment, shame.

bocina *nf* horn.

boda *nf* 1 *(ceremonia)* marriage, wedding. 2 *(fiesta)* reception.

bodega *nf* 1 *(de vinos)* cellar, wine cellar. 2 *(tienda)* wine shop. 3 *(de barco, avión)* hold.

bodegón *nm* still-life painting.

bofetada *nf* slap in the face.

boicot *nm* boycott.

boina *nf* beret.

bol *nm* bowl.

bola *nf* 1 *(cuerpo esférico)* ball. 2 *(de helado)* scoop. 3 *fam (mentira)* fib, lie.

bolera *nf* bowling alley.

boleto *nm* *(de lotería)* ticket; *(de quiniela)* coupon.

boli *nm* *fam* ballpen, Biro®.

bolígrafo *nm* ballpoint pen, Biro®.

Bolivia *nf* Bolivia.

boliviano,-a *adj-nm,f* Bolivian.

bollo *nm* 1 *(dulce)* bun. 2 *(de pan)* roll.

bolo *nm* skittle, ninepin: *jugar a los bolos*, to go bowling.

bolsa[1] *nf* bag. ▪ **bolsa de basura** bin liner; **bolsa de viaje** travel bag.

bolsa[2] *nf* stock exchange.

bolsillo *nm* pocket.

bolso *nm* GB handbag; US purse.

bomba[1] *nf* *(explosivo)* bomb. • **pasarlo bomba** to have a ball.

bomba[2] *nf* *(para bombear)* pump.

bombero,-a *nm,f (hombre)* firefighter, fireman; *(mujer)* firefighter, firewoman.

bombilla *nf* light bulb, bulb.

bombo *nm* 1 bass drum. 2 *(para sorteo)* drum.

bombón *nm* chocolate.

bombona *nf* cylinder, bottle. ▪ **bombona de butano** butane cylinder.

bondad *nf* 1 *(cualidad)* goodness. 2 *(afabilidad)* kindness: *tenga la bondad de contestar*, be so good as to reply.

bonito,-a *adj* nice, pretty. ►
nm **bonito** *(pez)* tuna, bonito.
bono *nm* **1** bond. **2** *(vale)*
voucher. **3** *(para transporte)*
pass.
bonobús *nm* bus pass.
boquerón *nm* anchovy.
borda *nf* gunwale. • **arrojar
por la borda** to throw overboard.
bordado *nm* embroidering,
embroidery.
bordar *vt* to embroider.
borde¹ *adj fam* nasty.
borde² *nm (extremo)* edge; *(de
prenda)* hem; *(de camino)* side;
(de vaso, taza) rim: *al borde
del mar*, beside the sea.
bordillo *nm* kerb.
bordo *nm* board. • **a bordo** on
board.
borrachera *nf* • **pillar una borrachera** to ger drunk.
borracho,-a *adj* drunk. ► *nm,f*
drunkard.
borrador *nm* **1** *(de texto)* rough
copy, first draft. **2** *(de pizarra)*
duster.
borrar *vt* **1** *(con goma etc.)* to
erase, rub out. **2** INFORM to
delete.
borrasca *nf* area of low pressure.
borrego,-a *nm,f (animal)* lamb.
borroso,-a *adj* blurred, hazy.
bosque *nm* wood; *(grande)*
forest.
bostezar *vi* to yawn.

bostezo *nm* yawn.
bota¹ *nf (calzado)* boot. • **ponerse las botas** *(al comer)* to
stuff oneself.
bota² *nf (de vino)* wineskin.
botánico,-a *adj* botanical.
botar *vt* **1** *(pelota)* to bounce. **2**
(barco) to launch. ► *vi (saltar)*
to jump.
bote¹ *nm* small boat. ■ **bote
salvavidas** lifeboat.
bote² *nm (salto)* bounce.
bote³ *nm* **1** *(recipiente)* tin, can;
(para propinas) box for tips. **2**
(de lotería) jackpot.
bote⁴ • **estar de bote en bote**
to be jam-packed.
botella *nf* bottle.
botellín *nm* small bottle.
botijo *nm* drinking jug.
botín *nm* **1** *(de guerra)* booty.
2 *(de ladrones)* loot.
botiquín *nm* **1** *(de medicinas)*
first-aid kit. **2** *(enfermería)* sick
bag.
botón *nm* **1** *(de camisa)* button. **2** *(tecla)* button. ■ **botón
de arranque** starter; **botón
de muestra** sample.
botones *nm (de hotel)* GB bellboy; US bellhop.
bóveda *nf* vault.
boxeador,-a *nm* boxer.
boxear *vi* to box.
boxeo *nm* boxing.
boya *nf* **1** buoy. **2** *(corcho de
pesca)* float.
bragas *nf pl* panties, knickers.

bragueta *nf* fly, flies.

brasa *nf* live coal. • **a la brasa** barbecued.

Brasil *nm* Brazil.

brasileño,-a *adj-nm,f* Brazilian.

bravo,-a *adj* **1** *(valiente)* brave, courageous. **2** *(fiero)* fierce, ferocious. ▶ *interj* well done!, bravo!

braza *nf* *(en natación)* breast stroke.

brazo *nm* **1** *(de persona, sillón)* arm. **2** *(de animal)* foreleg.

brecha *nf* **1** *(abertura)* break, opening. **2** *(herida)* gash.

Bretaña *nf* Brittany. ■ **Gran Bretaña** Great Britain.

breve *adj* short, brief. • **en breve** soon, shortly.

bricolaje *nm* do-it-youself, DIY.

brida *nf* bridle.

brillante *adj* **1** *(luz, color)* bright; *(pelo, calzado)* shiny. **2** *(destacado)* brilliant. ▶ *nm* *(diamante)* diamond.

brillar *vi* **1** *(sol, luz, ojos, oro)* to shine. **2** *(sobresalir)* to shine, be outstanding.

brillo *nm* **1** *(resplandor)* shine. **2** *(de estrella)* brightness, brilliance.

brincar *vi* to jump, leap.

brindar *vi* to toast. ▶ *vt* *(proporcionar)* to offer: *me brindó su apoyo*, she gave me her support.

brindis *nm* toast.

brisa *nf* breeze.

británico,-a *adj* British. ▶ *nm,f* *(hombre)* British man, Briton; *(mujer)* British woman, Briton.

brocha *nf* paintbrush. ■ **brocha de afeitar** shaving brush.

broche *nm* **1** *(cierre)* fastener. **2** *(joya)* brooch.

broma *nf* joke. • **gastar una broma a ALGN** to play a joke on SB. ■ **broma pesada** practical joke.

bronca *nf* row, quarrel. • **armar una bronca** to kick up a fuss; **echar una bronca a ALGN** to come down on SB.

bronce *nm* bronze.

bronceado *nm* tan, suntan.

bronceador *nm* suntan lotion.

bronquios *nm pl* bronchial tubes.

bronquitis *nf* bronchitis.

brotar *vi* **1** *(planta)* to sprout, bud. **2** *(hoja)* to sprout, come out. **3** *(agua)* to spring.

brote *nm* **1** *(de planta)* bud, sprout. **2** *(de conflicto, epidemia)* outbreak.

bruja *nf* **1** *(hechicera)* witch, sorceress. **2** *fam (harpía)* old hag.

brujo *nm* wizard, sorcerer.

brújula *nf* compass.

bruma *nf* mist, fog.

brusco,-a *adj* **1** *(persona)* brusque, abrupt. **2** *(movimiento)* sudden.

bruto,-a *adj* **1** *(necio)* stupid, ignorant. **2** *(tosco)* rough, coarse. **3** *(montante, peso)* gross. **4** *(petróleo)* crude.

bucear *vi* to swim under water.

budista *adj-nmf* Buddhist.

buen *adj* → bueno,-a.

bueno,-a *adj* **1** *(gen)* good. **2** *(persona - amable)* kind; *(- agradable)* nice, polite. **3** *(apropiado)* right, suitable. **4** *(grande)* big; *(considerable)* considerable: *un buen número de participantes*, quite a few participants. • **de buenas a primeras** *fam* from the very start; **por las buenas** willingly.

buey *nm* ox.

búfalo *nm* buffalo.

bufanda *nf* scarf.

bufé *nm* buffet. ▪ **bufé libre** self-service buffet.

bufete *nm* **1** *(mesa)* writing desk. **2** *(de abogado)* lawyer's office.

buhardilla *nf* attic.

búho *nm* owl.

buitre *nm* vulture.

bujía *nf* spark plug.

bulevar *nm* boulevard.

bulto *nm* **1** *(tamaño)* size, bulk. **2** *(hinchazón)* swelling, lump. **3** *(fardo)* bundle, pack: *¿cuántos bultos lleva?*, how many pieces of luggage do you have?

buñuelo *nm* **1** *(dulce)* doughnut. **2** *(de bacalao etc)* fritter.

buque *nm* ship, vessel.

burbuja *nf* bubble.

burla *nf* mockery, gibe.

burlar *vt* **1** *(engañar)* to deceive, trick. **2** *(eludir)* to dodge, evade. ▶ *vpr* **burlarse** to mock. • **burlarse de ALGN** to make fun of SB, laugh at SB.

burocracia *nf* bureaucracy.

burro,-a *nm,f* **1** *(asno)* donkey. **2** *(ignorante)* idiot. **3** *(bruto)* brute.

busca *nf* search.

buscador *nm* INFORM search engine.

buscar *vt* *(gen)* to look for, search for; *(en diccionario)* to look up: *ir a buscar algo*, to go and get STH; *vinieron a buscarme a la estación*, they came to pick me up from the station.

búsqueda *nf* search.

busto *nm* bust.

butaca *nf* **1** *(sillón)* armchair. **2** *(en teatro)* seat.

butano *nm* butane.

butifarra *nf* pork sausage.

buzo *nm* diver.

buzón *nm* **1** *(en casa)* GB letterbox; US mailbox. **2** *(en calle)* GB post box; US mailbox. **3** INFORM mailbox. • **echar una carta al buzón** to post a letter. ▪ **buzón de voz** voicemail.

byte *nm* byte.

C

caballa *nf* mackerel.

caballero *nm* **1** *(señor)* gentleman. **2** HIST knight.

caballo *nm* **1** horse. **2** *(en ajedrez)* knight. • **a caballo** on horseback; **montar a caballo** to ride.

cabaña *nf* cabin, hut.

cabecera *nf* **1** *(de periódico)* headline. **2** *(de cama)* bedhead.

cabello *nm* hair. ▪ **cabello de ángel** sweet pumpkin preserve.

caber *vi* to fit: *en esta lata caben diez litros*, this can holds ten litres; *no caben más*, there is no room for any more. • **dentro de lo que cabe** all things considered; **no cabe duda** there is no doubt.

cabestrillo *nm*. • **en cabestrillo** in a sling.

cabeza *nf* head. • **cabeza abajo** upside down; **cabeza arriba** the right way up; **por cabeza** a head, per person. ▪ **cabeza de ajo** head of garlic; **cabeza rapada** skinhead.

cabida *nf* capacity, room.

cabina *nf* cabin, booth. ▪ **cabina telefónica** phone box.

cable *nm* cable.

cabo *nm* **1** *(gen)* end: *al cabo de un mes*, in a month. **2** *(cuerda)* strand. **3** GEOG cape.

4 *(militar)* corporal. • **de cabo a rabo** from head to tail; **llevar a cabo** to carry out.

cabra *nf* goat.

cabrito *nm* kid.

caca *nf* **1** *fam* poo; US poop. **2** *(cosa sucia)* dirty thing. **3** *(basura)* load of rubbish.

cacahuete *nm* peanut.

cacao *nm* **1** *(planta)* cacao. **2** *(polvo, bebida)* cocoa.

cacarear *vi* **1** *(gallina)* to cluck. **2** *(gallo)* to crow.

cacerola *nf* saucepan.

cachalote *nm* cachalot, sperm whale.

cacharro *nm* **1** *(de cocina)* pot. **2** *fam (cosa)* thing, piece of junk.

caché *nm* cache memory.

cachear *vt* to search, frisk.

cacho *nm fam* bit, piece.

cachorro,-a *nm,f (de perro)* puppy; *(de león, tigre)* cub.

cacto *nm* cactus.

cactus *nm* cactus.

cada *adj* **1** *(para individualizar)* each: *tres caramelos para cada uno*, three sweets for each; *cada cual, cada uno*, each one, every one. **2** *(con números, tiempo)* every: *cada cuatro años hay un año bisiesto*, there's a leap year every four years. **3** *(uso enfático)*: *¡dice cada tontería!*, he says such stupid things! • **cada vez más** more and more;

cada vez que whenever, every time that.

cadáver *nm* corpse, body.

cadena *nf* 1 *(de eslabones, establecimientos)* chain. 2 *(industrial)* line. 3 *(montañosa)* range. 4 *(musical)* music centre. 5 *(de televisión)* channel. 6 *(de radio)* station. ▶ *nf pl* **cadenas** *(de nieve)* tyre (US tire) chains. • **tirar de la cadena del wáter** to flush the toilet.

cadera *nf* hip.

caducar *vi* to expire: *¿cuándo caduca la leche?*, what's the sell-by date on the milk?

caducidad *nf* 1 *(de documento)* expiration, loss of validity. 2 *(de alimento)* best before date.

caer *vi* 1 *(gen)* to fall. 2 *(coincidir fechas)* to be: *el día cuatro cae en jueves*, the fourth is a Thursday. ▶ *vpr* **caerse** to fall. • **caer bien**: *me cae bien*, I like her; **caer mal**: *me cae mal*, I don't like him; **caer enfermo,-a** to fall ill; **dejar caer** to drop; **estar al caer** to be about to arrive.

café *nm* 1 *(bebida)* coffee. 2 *(cafetería)* café. ■ **café con leche** white coffee; **café descafeinado** decaffeinated coffee; **café exprés** expresso; **café solo** black coffee.

cafeína *nf* caffeine.

cafetera *nf* coffeepot.

cafetería *nf* cafeteria, café.

caída *nf* 1 *(gen)* fall. 2 *(de tejidos)* body, hang.

caimán *nm* alligator.

caja *nf* 1 *(gen)* box; *(de madera)* chest; *(grande)* crate. 2 *(de bebidas)* case. 3 *(en tienda, bar)* cash desk; *(en supermercado)* checkout; *(en banco)* cashier's desk. ■ **caja de ahorros** savings bank; **caja de cambios** gearbox; **caja fuerte** safe; **caja negra** black box; **caja registradora** cash register.

cajero,-a *nm,f* cashier. ■ **cajero automático** cash dispenser.

cajetilla *nf* packet *(of cigarettes)*.

cajón *nm* drawer.

cal *nf* lime.

cala *nf* cove.

calabacín *nm* GB courgette; US zucchini.

calabaza *nf* pumpkin.

calabozo *nm* 1 *(prisión)* jail. 2 *(celda)* cell.

calado,-a *adj fam* soaked.

calamar *nm* squid. ■ **calamares a la romana** squid fried in batter.

calambre *nm* 1 *(muscular)* cramp. 2 *(eléctrico)* shock, electric shock.

calamidad *nf* calamity, disaster.

calar *vt* 1 *(mojar)* to soak, drench. 2 *fam (intención)* to rumble. ▶ *vpr* **calarse** 1 *(con* *agua)* to get soaked. **2** *(motor)* to stop, stall.

calavera *nf* skull.

calcetín *nm* sock.

calcio *nm* calcium.

calculadora *nf* calculator.

calcular *vt* to calculate, work out.

cálculo *nm* **1** *(de cantidad, presupuesto)* calculation. **2** *(del riñón, etc)* stone.

caldera *nf* boiler.

calderilla *nf* small change.

caldero *nm* cauldron.

caldo *nm* **1** *(sopa)* broth. **2** *(para cocinar)* stock. ▪ **caldo de cultivo** culture medium.

calefacción *nf* heating. ▪ **calefacción central** central heating.

calendario *nm* calendar.

calentador *nm* heater.

calentar *vt-vi (gen)* to warm up; *(agua, horno, etc)* to heat, heat up.

calidad *nf* quality. ● **en calidad de** as.

cálido,-a *adj* warm.

caliente *adj (ardiendo)* hot; *(templado)* warm.

calificar *vt* **1** *(etiquetar)* to describe. **2** *(dar nota)* to mark, grade.

callado,-a *adj* silent, quiet.

callar(se) *vi-vpr (dejar de hablar)* to stop talking; *(no hablar)* to say nothing, remain silent: *¡cállate!*, shut up!

calle *nf* **1** street, road. **2** *(en atletismo)* lane. ▪ **calle mayor** high street, main street; **calle peatonal** pedestrian street.

callejero *nm* street directory.

callejón *nm.* ▪ **callejón sin salida** cul-de-sac, dead end.

callo *nm (en mano, planta del pie)* callus; *(en dedo del pie)* corn. ▶ *nm pl* **callos** tripe.

calma *nf* calm.

calmante *adj* soothing. ▶ *nm* painkiller.

calmar *vt* **1** *(nervios)* to calm; *(persona)* to calm down. **2** *(dolor)* to relieve, soothe. ▶ *vt-vpr* **calmar(se)** to calm down.

calor *nm (sensación)* heat: *hace calor*, it is hot; *tengo calor*, I feel warm, I feel hot.

caloría *nf* calorie.

caluroso,-a *adj (tiempo)* hot, warm.

calva *nf* bald patch.

calvo,-a *adj (persona)* bald. ▶ *nm,f* bald person.

calzada *nf* road, roadway.

calzado *nm* footwear, shoes.

calzador *nm* shoehorn.

calzarse *vpr* to put one's shoes on. ● *¿qué número calzas?* what size shoes do you take?

calzoncillos *nm pl* underpants, pants.

cama *nf* bed. ▪ **cama de matrimonio** double bed; **cama individual** single bed.

camaleón *nm* chameleon.

cámara *nf* **1** *(fotográfica)* camera. **2** *(del parlamento)* house. **3** *(de rueda)* inner tube. • **a cámara lenta** in slow motion.

camarada *nmf* **1** *(colega)* colleague; *(de colegio)* schoolmate. **2** POL comrade.

camarero,-a *nm,f* **1** *(en bar - hombre)* waiter; *(- mujer)* waitress. **2** *(en barco, - hombre)* steward; *(- mujer)* stewardess.

camarón *nm* shrimp.

camarote *nm* cabin.

cambiar *vt* **1** *(gen)* to change. **2** *(intercambiar)* to exchange, swap. ▶ *vi* to change. ▶ *vpr* **cambiarse** to change: *cambiarse de ropa*, to get changed. • **cambiar de** to change: *cambiar de trabajo*, to change jobs.

cambio *nm* **1** *(gen)* change. **2** *(canje)* exchange. **3** *(de divisas)* exchange rate. **4** *(de tren)* switch. **5** *(de marchas)* gear change. • **a cambio de** in exchange for; **en cambio 1** *(por otro lado)* on the other hand. **2** *(en lugar de)* instead. ▪ **cambio automático** *(de coche)* automatic transmission; **cambio de marchas** gearshift.

camello *nm* camel.

camerino *nm* dressing room.

camilla *nf* stretcher.

caminar *vt-vi* to walk.

camino *nm* **1** *(sendero)* path, track. **2** *(ruta)* way.

camión *nm* GB lorry; US truck.

camioneta *nf* van.

camisa *nf* shirt.

camiseta *nf* **1** *(interior)* vest. **2** *(exterior)* T-shirt. **3** *(de deportes)* shirt.

camisón *nm* nightdress, nightgown, nightie.

campamento *nm* camp.

campana *nf* bell. ▪ **campana extractora** cooker hood.

campanario *nm* belfry, bell tower.

campanilla *nf* *(úvula)* uvula.

campaña *nf* campaign.

campeonato *nm* championship.

campeón,-ona *nm,f* champion.

campesino,-a *nm,f* *(que vive en el campo)* country person; *(que trabaja en el campo)* farm worker.

camping *nm* camping site. • **ir de camping** to go camping.

campo *nm* **1** *(gen)* field. **2** *(campiña)* country, countryside; *(paisaje)* countryside. • **ir campo a través** to cut across the fields. ▪ **campo de concentración** concentration camp; **campo de fútbol** football pitch; US soccerfield; **campo de golf** golf course.

cana *nf* grey hair; US gray hair.
canal *nm* **1** *(artificial)* canal. **2** *(natural, de televisión)* channel.
canapé *nm* *(comida)* canapé.
Canarias *nf pl.* ▪ **islas Canarias** Canary Islands.
canario *nm* *(pájaro)* canary.
canasta *nf* basket.
cancelar *vt* **1** *(anular)* to cancel. **2** *(deuda)* to pay off, settle.
cáncer *nm* **1** *(tumor)* cancer. **2** *(signo)* Cancer.
cancha *nf* court.
canción *nf* song.
candado *nm* padlock.
candidato,-a *nm,f* candidate.
canela *nf* cinnamon.
canelones *nm pl* cannelloni.
cangrejo *nm* crab. ▪ **cangrejo (de río)** crayfish.
canguro *nm* kangaroo. ▶ *nmf* baby-sitter.
canoa *nf* canoe.
cansado,-a *adj* **1** *(fatigado, harto)* tired. **2** *(trabajo, viaje)* tiring, boring.
cansancio *nm* tiredness.
cansar *vt* **1** *(fatigar)* to tire, tire out. **2** *(molestar)* to annoy: *me cansan sus discursos*, I'm fed up with his speeches. ▶ *vi* to be tiring. ▶ *vpr* **cansarse** to get tired.
cantante *nmf* singer.
cantar *vt-vi* *(gen)* to sing; *(gallo)* to crow.
cante *nm.* ▪ **cante hondo** flamenco.

cantidad *nf* **1** *(volumen)* quantity, amount. **2** *(de dinero)* sum, amount. ▶ *adv fam* a lot: *me gusta cantidad*, I love it.
cantimplora *nf* water bottle.
cantina *nf* **1** *(en fábrica, colegio)* canteen. **2** *(en estación)* buffet, cafetería.
canto[1] *nm* *(arte)* singing.
canto[2] *nm* **1** *(borde)* edge. **2** *(piedra)* stone. • **de canto** sideways.
caña *nf* **1** *(planta)* reed. **2** *(tallo)* cane. **3** *(de pescar)* fishing rod. **4** *(de cerveza)* beer, glass of beer. ▪ **caña de azúcar** sugar cane.
cañería *nf* pipe.
cañón *nm* **1** *(de artillería)* cannon. **2** *(de arma)* barrel. **3** GEOG canyon.
caoba *nf* mahogany.
caos *nm* chaos.
capa *nf* **1** *(prenda)* cloak, cape. **2** *(baño)* coat. **3** *(estrato)* layer.
capacidad *nf* **1** *(cabida)* capacity. **2** *(habilidad)* capability, ability.
capaz *adj* capable, able.
capilla *nf* *(de iglesia)* chapel. ▪ **capilla ardiente** funeral chapel.
capital *nm* *(dinero)* capital. ▶ *nf* *(ciudad)* capital.
capitán,-ana *nm,f* captain.
capitel *nm* capital.
capítulo *nm* *(de libro)* chapter; *(de serie televisiva)* episode.

capó *nm* GB bonnet; US hood.

capote *nm (de torero)* cape.

capricho *nm* whim, caprice.

capricornio *nm* Capricorn.

cápsula *nf* capsule.

captar *vt* 1 *(atraer interés, atención)* to capture; *(adeptos)* to attract. 2 *(comprender)* to understand.

capturar *vt (persona, animal)* to capture; *(alijo)* to seize.

capucha *nf* hood.

capullo *nm* 1 *(de insectos)* cocoon. 2 *(de flor)* bud.

caqui *nm (fruta)* persimmon.

cara *nf* 1 face. 2 *(lado)* side. 3 *(descaro)* cheek, nerve. • **cara a cara** face to face; **cara o cruz** heads or tails; **dar la cara** to take responsibility; **de cara a** opposite, facing; **tener buena cara** to look well; **tener cara de + adj** to look + *adj*; **tener mala cara** to look ill.

caracol *nm* 1 *(de tierra)* snail; *(de mar)* winkle. 2 *(del oído)* cochlea.

caracola *nf* conch.

carácter *nm* 1 *(personalidad, genio)* character: *tiene mucho carácter*, he's got a strong personality. 2 *(condición)* nature: *el proyecto tiene carácter científico*, this project is of a scientific nature. 3 *(de imprenta)* letter. • **tener buen carácter** to be good-natured;

tener mal carácter to be bad-tempered.

característico,-a *adj* characteristic.

carambola *nf (billar)* GB cannon; US carom.

caramelo *nm* 1 *(golosina)* GB sweet; US candy. 2 *(azúcar quemado)* caramel.

caravana *nf* 1 *(vehículo)* caravan. 2 *(atasco)* GB tailback; US backup.

carbón *nm (mineral)* coal. ▪ **carbón vegetal** charcoal.

carbono *nm* carbon.

carburador *nm* GB carburettor; US carburetor.

carburante *nm* fuel.

carcajada *nf* burst of laughter, guffaw.

cárcel *nf* prison, jail.

cardenal¹ *nm (de la iglesia)* cardinal.

cardenal² *nm (hematoma)* bruise.

cardíaco,-a *adj* cardiac, heart.

cardo *nm (planta)* thistle

carecer *vi.* • **carecer de algo** to lack STH.

carga *nf* 1 *(mercancías)* load. 2 *(peso)* burden. 3 *(flete)* cargo, freight. 4 *(obligación)* duty. 5 *(explosiva, eléctrica, militar)* charge. 6 *(de pluma, bolígrafo)* refill.

cargamento *nm (de tren, camión)* load; *(de avión, barco)* cargo.

cargar vt 1 (vehículo, arma, mercancías) to load. 2 (pluma, encendedor) to fill. 3 (pila) to charge. ► vpr **cargarse** fam (destrozar) to smash, ruin. • **cargar con 1** (peso) to carry. 2 (responsabilidad) to take.

cargo nm 1 (puesto) post, position. 2 (gobierno, custodia) charge, responsibility. 3 JUR charge, accusation. • **hacerse cargo de 1** (responsabilizarse de) to take charge of. 2 (entender) to take into consideration, realize.

caricatura nf caricature.

caricia nf 1 (a persona) caress, stroke. 2 (a animal) stroke.

caridad nf charity.

caries nf tooth decay, caries.

cariño nm 1 (afecto) love, affection, fondness. 2 (apelativo) darling.

carnaval nm carnival.

carne nf 1 meat. 2 (de persona, fruta) flesh. • **en carne viva** raw; **ser de carne y hueso** to be only human. ▪ **carne asada** roasted meat; **carne de buey** beef; **carne de gallina** goose flesh, goose bumps; **carne picada** GB mincemeat; US ground beef.

carné nm card. ▪ **carné de conducir** GB driving licence; US driver's license; **carné de identidad** identity card.

carnet nm → carné.

carnicería nf (tienda) butcher's.

caro,-a adj expensive, dear. ► adv **caro** at a high price.

carpa¹ nf (pez) carp.

carpa² nf (toldo) marquee; (de circo) big top.

carpeta nf folder, file.

carpintería nf 1 (labor) carpentry. 2 (taller) carpenter's shop.

carrera nf 1 (competición) race. 2 (estudios) university education. 3 (profesión) career. 4 (trayecto) route. 5 (en las medias) ladder.

carreta nf cart.

carrete nm 1 (de película) roll of film, film. 2 (de hilo, pesca) reel.

carretera nf road. ▪ **carretera nacional** GB A road, main road; US state highway.

carril nm lane. ▪ **carril bici** GB cycle lane; US bikeway.

carro nm 1 (carreta) cart. 2 (militar) tank. 3 (en supermercado, aeropuerto) GB trolley; US cart.

carrocería nf bodywork.

carroza nf 1 (de caballos) coach, carriage. 2 (de carnaval) float.

carruaje nm carriage, coach.

carta nf 1 (documento) letter. 2 (naipe) card. 3 (en restaurante) menu. ▪ **carta certificada** registered letter.

cartel nm poster.

cartelera nf 1 (para carteles) GB hoarding; US billboard. 2

(en periódicos) entertainment guide.

cartera *nf* **1** *(monedero)* wallet. **2** *(de colegial)* satchel, schoolbag. **3** *(de ejecutivo)* briefcase; *(sin asa)* portfolio.

carterista *nmf* pickpocket.

cartero,-a *nm,f* *(hombre)* GB postman; US mailman; *(mujer)* GB postwoman; US mailwoman.

cartilla *nf*. ▪ **cartilla de ahorros** savings book; **cartilla del seguro** social security card.

cartón *nm* **1** *(material)* cardboard. **2** *(de cigarrillos, leche)* carton.

casa *nf* **1** *(edificio)* house. **2** *(hogar)* home. ▪ **casa adosada** terraced house; **casa de campo** country house; **casa de huéspedes** guesthouse, boarding house; **casa de socorro** first aid post; **casa pareada** semi-detached house.

casarse *vpr* to get married.

cascada *nf* waterfall, cascade.

cascanueces *nm* nutcracker.

cáscara *nf* **1** *(de huevo, nuez)* shell. **2** *(de plátano)* skin. **3** *(de naranja, limón)* peel, rind. **4** *(de grano)* husk.

casco *nm* **1** *(protector)* helmet. **2** *(envase)* empty bottle. **3** *(de barco)* hull. **4** *(de caballo)* hoof. ▶ *nm pl* **cascos** *(auriculares)* headphones. ▪ **casco antiguo** old town; **casco azul** blue beret; **casco urbano** city centre; US downtown area.

caserío *nm* country house.

casero,-a *adj* *(productos)* homemade. ▶ *nm,f* *(dueño - hombre)* landlord; *(- mujer)* landlady.

caseta *nf* **1** *(de feria)* stall. **2** *(de bañistas)* GB bathing hut; US bath house. **3** *(de perro)* kennel.

casete *nm* *(aparato)* cassette player, cassette recorder. ▶ *nf* *(cinta)* cassette *(tape)*.

casi *adv* **1** *(gen)* almost, nearly. **2** *(en frases negativas)* hardly: *casi nunca*, hardly ever.

casilla *nf* **1** *(de casillero)* pigeonhole. **2** *(cuadrícula)* square. **3** *(de formulario)* box.

casino *nm* casino.

caso *nm* case. • **en caso de que** if; **en ese caso** in that case; **en todo caso** anyhow, at any rate.

caspa *nf* dandruff.

castaña *nf* *(fruto)* chestnut.

castaño,-a *adj* chestnut-coloured; *(pelo)* brown. ▶ *nm* **castaño** *(árbol)* chestnut tree.

castañuela *nf* castanet.

castellano,-a *adj-nm,f* Castilian. ▶ *nm* **castellano** *(idioma)* Castilian, Spanish.

castigar *vt* to punish.

castigo *nm* punishment.

castillo *nm* castle.

castor *nm* beaver.

casualidad *nf* chance, coincidence. • **por casualidad** by chance.

catalán,-ana *adj-nm,f* Catalan, Catalonian. ► *nm* **catalán** *(idioma)* Catalan.

catálogo *nm* catalogue.

catarata *nf* 1 *(de agua)* waterfall. 2 *(en ojo)* cataract.

catarro *nm* cold.

catástrofe *nf* catastrophe.

catedral *nf* cathedral.

catedrático,-a *nm,f (de universidad)* professor; *(de instituto)* head of department.

categoría *nf* 1 *(rango)* category. 2 *(nivel)* level.

católico,-a *adj-nm,f* Catholic.

catorce *num* fourteen; *(en fechas)* fourteenth.

cauce *nm* 1 *(de río)* river bed. 2 *(canal)* channel.

caucho *nm* rubber.

caudal *nm* 1 *(de río)* volume of water. 2 *(riqueza)* fortune, wealth.

causa *nf* 1 *(motivo, ideal)* cause. 2 *(proceso)* lawsuit. • **a causa de** because of, on account of.

causar *vt* to cause, bring about.

cautiverio *nm* captivity.

cauto,-a *adj* cautious.

cava *nm (bebida)* cava. ► *nf (bodega)* wine cellar.

cavar *vt* to dig.

caverna *nf* cavern, cave.

caviar *nm* caviar.

cavidad *nf* cavity.

caza *nf* 1 *(acción)* hunting. 2 *(animales)* game. ► *nm (avión)* fighter.

cazadora *nf (chaqueta)* jacket.

cazador,-ra *nm,f* hunter.

cazar *vt* to hunt.

cazo *nm* 1 *(cucharón)* ladle. 2 *(cacerola)* saucepan.

cazuela *nf* casserole.

CD-ROM *nm* CD-ROM.

cebada *nf* barley.

cebo *nm* 1 *(para animales)* food. 2 *(para pescar)* bait.

cebolla *nf* onion.

cebolleta *nf* 1 *(hierba)* chive. 2 *(cebolla)* spring onion.

cebra *nf* zebra.

ceder *vt (dar)* to give. ► *vi* 1 *(rendirse)* to give in yield: *cedió a mis peticiones*, she gave in to my requests. 2 *(caerse)* to fall, give way: *las paredes cedieron*, the walls caved in. • **ceder el paso** GB to give way; US to yield.

cedro *nm* cedar.

ceguera *nf* blindness.

ceja *nf* eyebrow.

celda *nf* cell.

celebración *nf* 1 *(fiesta)* celebration. 2 *(de reunión, congreso, etc)* holding.

celebrar *vt* 1 *(festejar)* to celebrate. 2 *(reunión, congreso, etc)* to hold. 3 *(misa)* to say. ► *vpr* **celebrarse** to take place, be held.

célebre *adj* well-known, famous.

celo¹ *nm* **1** *(entusiasmo)* zeal. **2** *(cuidado)* care. ► *nm pl* **celos** jealousy. • **estar en celo** to be on heat, be in season; **tener celos** to be jealous.

celo®² *nm* GB Sellotape®; US Scotch tape®.

celofán *nm* Cellophane®.

célula *nf* cell.

cementerio *nm* cemetery.

cemento *nm* cement. ▪ **cemento armado** reinforced concrete.

cena *nf* dinner, supper.

cenar *vi* to have dinner, have supper. ► *vt* to have for dinner, have for supper.

cenicero *nm* ashtray.

ceniza *nf* ash.

censo *nm* census. ▪ **censo electoral** electoral roll.

centeno *nm* rye.

centígrado,-a *adj* centigrade.

centímetro *nm* GB centimetre; US centimeter.

céntimo *nm* cent, centime.

centollo *nm* spider crab.

central *adj* central. ► *nf* **1** *(oficina principal)* head office, headquarters. **2** *(eléctrica)* power station.

centralita *nf* switchboard.

céntrico,-a *adj* central: *una calle céntrica*, a street in the centre (US center) of town.

centro *nm* **1** *(gen)* GB centre; US center. **2** *(de la ciudad)* town centre; US downtown. ▪ **centro comercial** GB shopping centre; US mall.

cepa *nf* *(de vid)* vine.

cepillar(se) *vt-vpr* *(pelo, zapato, etc)* to brush.

cepillo *nm* brush. ▪ **cepillo de dientes** toothbrush.

cera *nf* *(gen)* wax; *(de abeja)* beeswax; *(de oreja)* earwax.

cerámica *nf* ceramics, pottery.

cerca¹ *nf* *(valla)* fence.

cerca² *adv* near, close. • **cerca de 1** *(cercano a)* near. **2** *(casi)* nearly; **de cerca** close up.

cercano,-a *adj* **1** *(lugar)* nearby. **2** *(tiempo)* near. **3** *(pariente, amigo)* close.

cerda *nf* *(animal)* sow.

cerdo *nm* **1** *(animal)* pig. **2** *(carne)* pork.

cereal *adj-nm* cereal.

cerebro *nm* brain.

ceremonia *nf* ceremony.

cereza *nf* cherry.

cerilla *nf* match.

cero *nm* **1** zero, nought. **2** nil: *ganamos tres a cero*, we won three-nil. • **bajo cero** below zero.

cerrado,-a *adj* **1** *(gen)* shut, closed. **2** *(con llave)* locked. **3** *(acento)* broad. **4** *(curva)* sharp.

cerradura *nf* lock.

cerrajero *nm* locksmith.

cerrar vt **1** to close, shut. **2** (con llave) to lock. **3** (grifo, gas) to turn off. **4** (luz) to switch off. **5** (cremallera) to zip (up).

cerrojo nm bolt.

certamen nm competition, contest.

certeza nf certainty.

certificado,-a adj **1** (documento) certified. **2** (envío) registered. ▶ nm **certificado** (documento) certificate.

cerveza nf beer. ▪ **cerveza de barril** GB draught beer; US draft beer.

cesar vi (parar) to cease, stop. ● **sin cesar** nonstop.

césped nm lawn, grass. ● "**Prohibido pisar el césped**" "Keep off the grass".

cesta nf basket.

cesto nm basket.

chabola nf shack.

chacal nm jackal.

chal nm shawl.

chalé nm **1** (gen) house. **2** (en campo, playa) villa.

chaleco nm GB waistcoat; US vest. ▪ **chaleco salvavidas** life jacket.

chalet nm chalé.

champán nm champagne.

champiñón nm mushroom.

champú nm shampoo.

chancleta nf GB flip-flop; US thong.

chándal nm tracksuit, jogging suit.

chantaje nm blackmail.

chapa nf **1** (de metal) sheet. **2** (de madera) board. **3** (tapón) bottle top. **4** (de coche) bodywork.

chaparrón nm downpour, heavy shower.

chapuzón nm dip.

chaqué nm morning coat.

chaqueta nf jacket.

chaquetón nm short coat.

charanga nf brass band.

charca nf pool, pond.

charco nm (de lluvia) puddle; (de sangre, etc.) pool.

charcutería nf pork butcher's shop, delicatessen.

charlar vi to chat, talk.

chárter adj-nm charter.

chasis nm chassis.

chatarra nf **1** (metal) scrap metal. **2** fam (monedas) small change.

chatear vi to chat.

chato,-a adj **1** (nariz) snub. **2** (persona) snub-nosed. **3** (objeto) flat. ▶ nm **chato** (vaso) small glass.

chaval,-la nm,f kid, youngster; (chico) lad; (chica) lass.

cheque nm GB cheque; US check. ● **extender un cheque** to issue a cheque. ▪ **cheque al portador** cheque payable to bearer; **cheque de viaje** traveller's cheque; **cheque en blanco** blank cheque; **cheque sin fondos** dud cheque.

chequeo *nm* checkup.
chichón *nm* bump, lump.
chicle *nm* chewing gum.
chico,-a *nm,f* **1** *(niño)* kid; *(niña)* girl. **2** *(muchacho)* boy, guy; *(muchacha)* girl.
Chile *nm* Chile.
chileno,-a *adj-nm,f* Chilean.
chillar *vi* *(persona)* to scream, yell; *(gritar)* to shout.
chillido *nm* **1** *(de persona)* scream, yell.
chimenea *nf* **1** *(exterior)* chimney. **2** *(hogar)* fireplace. **3** *(de barco)* funnel.
chimpancé *nm* chimpanzee.
chincheta *nf* GB drawing pin; US thumbtack.
chino,-a *adj* Chinese.
chip *nm* INFORM chip.
chipirón *nm* baby squid.
chiquito,-a *adj* tiny, very small. ► *nm* **chiquito** small glass of wine.
chiringuito *nm* *fam* *(en playa)* bar, restaurant; *(en carretera)* roadside snack bar.
chispa *nf* **1** *(de fuego)* spark. **2** *fig (ingenio)* wit.
chiste *nm* joke. ▪ **chiste verde** blue joke, dirty joke.
chistera *nf* top hat.
chivato,-a *nm,f fam (delator)* informer, GB grass; *(acusica)* GB telltale; US tattletale. ► *nm* **chivato** *(piloto)* warning light.
chocar *vi* **1** *(colisionar)* to collide, crash. **2** *fig (sorprender)* to surprise. **4** *(escandalizar)* to shock. ► *vt (manos)* to shake.
chocolate *nm* chocolate. ▪ **chocolate a la taza** drinking chocolate; **chocolate con leche** milk chocolate.
chocolatina *nf* chocolate bar.
chófer *nm* *(particular)* chauffeur; *(de autocar etc)* driver.
chopo *nm* poplar.
choque *nm* collision, crash.
chorizo *nm* spicy pork sausage.
chorro *nm* **1** *(de líquido)* stream, jet. **2** *(de vapor)* jet.
choza *nf* hut.
christmas *nm* Christmas card.
chubasco *nm* heavy shower.
chubasquero *nm* raincoat.
chufa *nf* tiger nut.
chuleta *nf (de carne)* chop.
chulo,-a *adj* **1** *(engreído)* cocky. **2** *fam (bonito)* nice. ► *nm,f (presuntuoso)* show-off.
chupar *vt* **1** *(succionar)* to suck. **2** *(lamer)* to lick. **3** *(absorber)* to absorb, soak up.
chupete *nm* GB dummy; US pacifier.
churrería *nf* fritter shop.
churro *nm* **1** *(comida)* fritter. **2** *fam (chapuza)* botch.
chutar *vi* to shoot.
cibercafé *nm* Internet café, cybercafé.
ciberespacio *nm* cyberspace.
cibernética *nf* cybernetics.
cicatriz *nf* scar.

cicatrizar(se) *vt-vpr* to heal.

ciclismo *nm* cycling.

ciclista *nmf* cyclist.

ciclo *nm* **1** *(gen)* cycle. **2** *(de conferencias)* series. **3** *(de películas)* season.

ciclón *nm* cyclone.

ciego,-a *adj (persona)* blind. ► *nm,f (persona)* blind person.

cielo *nm* **1** *(gen)* sky. **2** REL heaven. **3** *(apelativo)* darling.

ciempiés *nm* centipede.

cien *num* a hundred, one hundred. • **cien por cien** a hundred per cent.

ciencia *nf* science. • **a ciencia cierta** with certainty. ▪ **ciencia ficción** science fiction.

científico,-a *adj* scientific. ► *nm,f* scientist.

ciento *num* a hundred, one hundred. • **por ciento** per cent.

cierre *nm* **1** *(de prenda)* fastener. **2** *(de collar, pulsera)* clasp. **3** *(de fábrica)* closure; *(de tienda)* closing-down. ▪ **cierre centralizado** central locking.

cierto,-a *adj* **1** *(seguro)* certain, sure. **2** *(verdadero)* true. **3** *(algún)* (a) certain, some: *cierto día,* one day. ► *adv* **cierto** certainly. • **estar en lo cierto** to be right; **por cierto** by the way.

ciervo *nm* deer.

cifra *nf* figure.

cigala *nf* Dublin Bay prawn.

cigarrillo *nm* cigarette.

cigarro *nm* **1** *(cigarrillo)* cigarette. **2** *(puro)* cigar.

cigüeña *nf (ave)* stork.

cilindro *nm* cylinder.

cima *nf* summit, peak.

cimiento *nf* foundation.

cinc *nm* zinc.

cinco *num* five; *(en fechas)* fifth.

cincuenta *num* fifty.

cine *nm* **1** *(lugar)* GB cinema; US movie theater. **2** *(arte)* cinema. ▪ **cine mudo** silent films; **cine negro** film noir.

cinta *nf* **1** *(casete, vídeo)* tape. **2** *(tira)* tape, band; *(decorativa)* ribbon. ▪ **cinta adhesiva** sticky tape; **cinta aislante** insulating tape; **cinta métrica** tape measure; **cinta transportadora** conveyor belt; **cinta virgen** blank tape.

cintura *nf* waist.

cinturón *nm* belt. ▪ **cinturón de seguridad** seat belt, safety belt.

ciprés *nm* cypress.

circo *nm* circus.

circuito *nm* circuit.

circulación *nf* **1** *(de sangre, dinero)* circulation. **2** *(de vehículos)* traffic.

circular *adj* circular. ► *nf (carta)* circular letter. ► *vi* **1** *(sangre)* to circulate. **2** *(trenes, autobuses)* to run; *(coches)* to drive; *(peatones)* to walk.

círculo *nm* circle.

circunferencia *nf* circumference.

circunstancia *nf* circumstance.

ciruela *nf* plum. ▪ **ciruela claudia** greengage; **ciruela pasa** prune.

cirugía *nf* surgery.

cirujano,-a *nm,f* surgeon.

cisne *nm* swan.

cisterna *nf* cistern, tank.

cita *nf* 1 *(para negocios, médico, etc)* appointment. 2 *(con novio, novia)* date. 3 *(mención)* quotation.

citar *vt* 1 *(convocar)* to arrange to meet. 2 *(mencionar)* to quote.

cítricos *nm pl* citrus fruits.

ciudad *nf (grande)* city; *(más pequeña)* town.

ciudadano,-a *nm,f* citizen.

civil *adj* civil.

civilización *nf* civilization.

clandestino,-a *adj* 1 *(actividad, reunión)* clandestine, secret. 2 *(periódico, asociación)* underground.

clara *nf* 1 *(de huevo)* egg white. 2 *(bebida)* shandy.

claridad *nf* clarity, clearness.

clarinete *nm* clarinet. ▶ *nmf* clarinettist.

claro,-a *adj* 1 *(gen)* clear. 2 *(color)* light. 3 *(salsa)* thin. ▶ *adv* **claro** clearly. ▶ *nm (de bosque)* clearing. ▶ *interj* ¡**cla-**

ro! of course! ● **claro que no** of course not; **claro que sí** of course; **estar claro** to be clear.

clase *nf* 1 *(alumnos)* class. 2 *(lección)* lesson, class. 3 *(aula)* classroom. 4 *(tipo)* type, sort. ● **dar clase** to teach. ▪ **clase alta** upper class; **clase baja** lower class; **clase media** middle class; **clase obrera** working class; **clase particular** private class.

clásico,-a *adj* classical.

clasificación *nf* 1 *(ordenación)* classification, sorting. 2 *(deportiva)* league, table.

clasificar *vt* 1 *(ordenar)* to class, classify. 2 *(documentos, cartas)* to sort. ▶ *vpr* **clasificarse** *(deportista)* to qualify.

claustro *nm (de iglesia)* cloister.

cláusula *nf* clause.

clavar *vt* 1 *(sujetar)* to nail. 2 *(a golpes)* to hammer. 3 *(aguja, cuchillo)* to stick.

clave *nf* 1 *(gen)* key. 2 *(de signos)* code.

clavel *nm* carnation.

clavícula *nf* collarbone, clavicle.

clavija *nf (enchufe macho)* plug; *(pata de enchufe)* pin.

clavo *nm* 1 *(de metal)* nail. 2 *(especia)* clove.

claxon *nm* horn, hooter.

cliente *nmf* 1 *(de empresa)* client. 2 *(de tienda)* customer.

clientela *nf* **1** *(de empresa)* clients. **2** *(de tienda)* customers. **3** *(de restaurante)* clientele.

clima *nm* climate.

climatizado,-a *adj* air-conditioned.

clínica *nf* clinic, private hospital.

clip *nm (para papel)* paper clip.

clon *nm* clone.

cloro *nm* chlorine.

club *nm* club.

coartada *nf* alibi.

cobarde *nmf* coward.

cobra *nf* cobra.

cobrador,-ra *nm,f (de autobús - hombre)* conductor; *(- mujer)* conductress.

cobrar *vt (fijar precio por)* to charge; *(cheques)* to cash; *(salario)* to earn. ► *vi* to be paid.

cobre *nm* copper.

cobro *nm* cashing, collection. ▪ **cobro revertido** reverse charge.

cocción *nf (acción de guisar)* cooking; *(en agua)* boiling; *(en horno)* baking.

cocer(se) *vt-vpr (guisar)* to cook; *(hervir)* to boil; *(hornear)* to bake.

coche *nm* **1** *(automóvil)* GB car; US car, automobile. **2** *(de tren, de caballos)* carriage, coach. ▪ **coche cama** sleeping car; **coche de alquiler** hire car.

cochinillo *nm* sucking pig.

cochino,-a *adj (sucio)* filthy. ► *nm,f* **1** *(animal)* pig. **2** *fam (persona)* dirty person.

cocido,-a *adj* cooked; *(en agua)* boiled. ► *nm* **cocido** *(plato)* stew.

cocina *nf* **1** *(lugar)* kitchen. **2** *(gastronomía)* cooking, cuisine. **3** *(aparato)* GB cooker; US stove. ▪ **cocina casera** home cooking; **cocina de mercado** food in season.

cocinar *vt* to cook.

cocinero,-a *nm,f* cook.

coco *nm* coconut.

cocodrilo *nm* crocodile.

cocotero *nm* coconut palm.

cóctel *nm* **1** *(bebida)* cocktail. **2** *(fiesta)* cocktail party.

código *nm* code. ▪ **código de barras** bar code; **código de circulación** highway code; **código postal** GB postcode; US zipcode.

codo *nm* elbow.

codorniz *nf* quail.

cofre *nm* trunk, chest.

coger *vt* **1** *(gen)* to catch. **2** *(tomar)* to take. **3** *(fruta, flor)* to pick.

cogollo *nm* **1** *(de lechuga etc)* heart. **2** *(brote)* shoot.

coherente *adj* coherent.

cohete *nm* rocket.

coincidencia *nf* coincidence.

coincidir *vi* **1** *(fechas, resultados)* to coincide. **2** *(estar de* *acuerdo)* to agree. **3** *(encontrarse)* to meet.

cojear *vi* to limp, hobble.

cojo,-a *adj* lame.

col *nf* cabbage. ■ **col de Bruselas** Brussels sprout.

cola¹ *nf* **1** *(de animal)* tail. **2** *(fila)* GB queue; US line. • **hacer cola** GB to queue up; US to stand in line.

cola² *nf (pegamento)* glue.

colaborar *vi* **1** *(en tarea)* to collaborate. **2** *(en prensa)* to contribute.

colada *nf* washing.

colador *nm* **1** *(de té, café)* strainer. **2** *(de alimentos)* colander.

colar *vt (filtrar)* to strain, filter. ► *vpr* **colarse 1** *(en un lugar)* to sneak in. **2** *(en una cola)* to push in.

colcha *nf* bedspread.

colchón *nm* mattress.

colchoneta *nf* **1** *(de gimnasio)* mat. **2** *(de playa)* air bed.

colección *nf* collection.

colectivo,-a *adj* collective.

colega *nmf* **1** *(de trabajo)* colleague. **2** *fam (amigo)* GB mate; US buddy.

colegio *nm (escuela)* school. ■ **colegio electoral** polling station; **colegio mayor** hall of residence; **colegio privado** private school; **colegio público** state school.

cólera¹ *nf (furia)* anger, rage.

cólera² *nm (enfermedad)* cholera.

coleta *nf* pigtail.

colgador *nm* hanger.

colgar *vt* **1** *(cuadro)* to hang, put up; *(colada)* to hang out; *(abrigo)* to hang up. **2** *(teléfono)* to put down.

colibrí *nm* humming bird.

cólico *nm* colic.

coliflor *nf* cauliflower.

colilla *nf* cigarette end, cigarette butt.

colina *nf* hill.

colirio *nm* eyewash.

collar *nm* **1** *(joya)* necklace. **2** *(de animal)* collar.

colmena *nf* beehive.

colmillo *nm* **1** *(de persona)* eye tooth, canine tooth. **2** *(de elefante)* tusk.

colocación *nf* **1** *(acto)* placing. **2** *(situación)* situation. **3** *(empleo)* employment.

colocar *vt* **1** *(situar)* to place, put. **2** *(emplear)* to give a job to.

Colombia *nf* Colombia.

colombiano,-a *adj-nm,f* Colombian.

colon *nm* colon.

colonia¹ *nf (grupo, territorio)* colony. ► *nf pl* summer camp.

colonia² *nf (perfume)* cologne.

color *nm* GB colour; US color.

colorete *nm* rouge.

columna *nf* column. ■ **columna vertebral** spine, spinal column.

columpio *nm* swing.

coma[1] *nf (signo)* comma.

coma[2] *nm* MED coma.

comandante *nm* **1** *(oficial)* commander, commanding officer. **2** *(graduación)* major.

comando *nm* **1** *(de combate)* commando. **2** INFORM command.

comarca *nf* area, region.

combate *nm* **1** *(lucha)* combat, battle. **2** *(en boxeo)* fight.

combinar *vt (ingredientes, esfuerzos)* to combine. ▶ *vi (colores)* to match, go with.

combustible *adj* combustible. ▶ *nm* fuel.

comedia *nf* comedy.

comedor *nm* **1** *(de casa)* dining room. **2** *(de fábrica)* canteen. **3** *(de colegio)* dining hall.

comentar *vt* **1** *(por escrito)* to comment on; *(oralmente)* to talk about, discuss. **2** *(decir)* to tell.

comentario *nm* remark, comment. • **sin comentarios** no comment.

comenzar *vt-vi* to begin, start.

comer *vt* to eat. ▶ *vi* **1** *(alimentarse)* to eat. **2** *(al mediodía)* to have lunch.

comercial *adj* commercial.

comerciante *nmf* **1** *(tendero)* GB shop-keeper; US store-keeper. **2** *(negociante)* trader, dealer.

comerciar *vi* to trade, deal.

comercio *nm* **1** *(ocupación)* commerce, trade. **2** *(tienda)* GB shop; US store. ■ **comercio electrónico** e-commerce.

comestible *adj* edible. ▶ *nm pl* **comestibles** groceries, food.

cometa *nm (astro)* comet. ▶ *nf (juguete)* kite.

cometer *vt (crimen)* to commit; *(falta, error)* to make.

cómic *nm* comic.

cómico,-a *adj* comic.

comida *nf* **1** *(comestibles)* food. **2** *(a cualquier hora)* meal. **3** *(a mediodía)* lunch.

comienzo *nm* start, beginning.

comillas *nf pl* inverted commas.

comino *nm* cumin.

comisaría *nf* police station.

comisario *nm* GB superintendent; US captain.

comisión *nf* **1** *(retribución)* commission. **2** *(comité)* committee.

comité *nm* committee.

como *adv* **1** *(lo mismo que)* as: **negro como el tizón**, as dark as night. **2** *(de tal modo)* like: **hablas como un político**, you talk like a politician. **3** *(según)* as: **como dice tu amigo**, as your friend says. **4** *(en calidad de)* as: **como invitado**, as a guest. ▶ *conj* **1** *(así que)* as soon as. **2** *(si)* if: **como lo**

vuelvas a hacer ..., if you do it again ... **3** *(porque)* as, since: *como llegamos tarde no pudimos entrar*, since we arrived late we couldn't get in. • **como quiera que** since, as, given that; **como sea** whatever happens, no matter what.

cómo *adv* **1** *(de qué modo)* how: *¿cómo se hace?*, how do you do it? **2** *(por qué)* why: *¿cómo no viniste?*, why didn't you come? • **¿cómo está usted? 1** *(al conocerse)* how do you do? **2** *(de salud)* how are you?; **¡cómo no!** but of course!, certainly!

comodidad *nf* **1** *(confort)* comfort. **2** *(facilidad)* convenience.

comodín *nm* joker.

cómodo,-a *adj* comfortable, cosy.

compact disc *nm* compact disc.

compacto *adj* compact. ▶ *nm* compact disc.

compañero,-a *nm,f* **1** *(de trabajo)* colleague. **2** *(pareja)* partner.

compañía *nf* company.

comparación *nf* comparison.

comparar *vt* to compare.

compartimento *nm* compartment.

compartir *vt* to share.

compás *nm* **1** *(instrumento)* compass, a pair of compasses. **2** *(ritmo)* beat.

compatible *adj* compatible.

compatriota *nmf* compatriot.

competencia *nf* **1** *(rivalidad)* competition. **2** *(competidores)* competitors. **3** *(habilidad)* competence, ability.

competente *adj* competent, capable.

competición *nf* competition.

competir *vi* to compete.

complejo,-a *adj* complex. ▶ *nm* **complejo** complex.

complemento *nm* complement. ▶ *nm pl* **complementos** accessories.

completar *vt* to complete, finish.

completo,-a *adj* **1** *(entero, total)* complete. **2** *(lleno)* full. • **al completo 1** *(lleno)* full up, filled to capacity. **2** *(la totalidad de)* the whole, all of; **por completo** completely.

complicado,-a *adj* complicated, complex.

complicar *vt* to complicate.

cómplice *nmf* accomplice.

componente *adj-nm* component.

componer *vt* **1** *(formar)* to make up. **2** *(música)* to compose; *(poema)* to write, compose.

comportamiento *nm* GB behaviour; US behavior.

comportarse *vpr* to behave.

composición *nf* composition.

compositor,-ra *nm,f* composer.

compota *nf* compote.

compra *nf* purchase, buy. • **hacer la compra** to do the shopping; **ir de compras** to go shopping.

comprador,-ra *nm,f* buyer.

comprar *vt* to buy.

comprender *vt* **1** *(entender)* to understand. **2** *(contener)* to comprise, include.

compresa *nf* **1** *(higiénica)* sanitary towel. **2** *(venda)* compress.

comprimido *nm* tablet.

comprobante *nm* receipt, voucher.

comprobar *vt* to check.

comprometerse *vpr* **1** *(prometer)* to commit oneself. **2** *(novios)* to get engaged.

compromiso *nm* **1** *(obligación)* commitment. **2** *(acuerdo)* agreement. **3** *(cita)* engagement.

compuesto,-a *adj* compound.

computadora *nf* computer.

comulgar *vi* to receive Holy Communion.

común *adj* common. • **por lo común** generally.

comunicación *nf* **1** *(relación)* communication. **2** *(telefónica)* connection.

comunicado *nm* communiqué. ▪ **comunicado de prensa** press release.

comunicar *vi* *(teléfono)* GB to be engaged; US to be busy. ► *vt* **1** *(hacer saber)* to inform. **2** *(unir)* to connect, link.

comunidad *nf* community.

comunión *nf* communion.

comunismo *nm* communism.

comunista *adj-nmf* communist.

con *prep* **1** *(compañía, instrumento, medio)* with: *hay que comerlo con una cuchara*, you have to eat it with a spoon. **2** *(modo, circunstancia)* in, with: *¿vas a salir con ese frío?*, are you going out in this cold? **3** *(relación)* to: *sé amable con ella*, be kind to her.

conceder *vt* *(dar - préstamo, deseo)* to grant; *(- premio)* to award.

concentración *nf* concentration.

concentrar(se) *vt-vpr* to concentrate.

concepto *nm* concept. • **bajo ningún concepto** under no circumstances; **en concepto de** by way of.

concertar *vt* *(entrevista, cita)* to arrange.

concesión *nf* **1** *(en negociación)* concession. **2** *(de premio)* awarding.

concesionario *nm* dealer.

concha *nf* shell.

conciencia *nf* **1** *(moral)* conscience. **2** *(conocimiento)* awareness. • **a conciencia** conscientiously.

concierto *nm (espectáculo)* concert; *(obra)* concerto.

conclusión *nf* conclusion.

concretar *vt (precisar)* to specify: *concretar una hora*, to fix a time, set a time.

concreto,-a *adj* **1** *(real)* concrete. **2** *(particular)* specific, definite. • **en concreto 1** *(en particular)* in particular. **2** *(para ser exacto)* to be precise.

concurrido,-a *adj* busy, crowded.

concursante *nmf* contestant, participant.

concursar *vi* to compete.

concurso *nm (competición - gen)* competition; *(- de belleza, deportivo)* contest; *(- en televisión)* quiz show.

conde *nm* count.

condecoración *nf* decoration, medal.

condena *nf* sentence.

condenar *vt* **1** *(declarar culpable)* to convict. **2** *(sentenciar)* to sentence.

condesa *nf* countess.

condición *nf* condition. • **a condición de que** on condition that, provided (that).

condimentar *vt* to season, GB flavour; US flavor.

condimento *nm* seasoning, GB flavouring; US flavoring.

conducir *vt (guiar)* to lead; *(coche, animales)* to drive; *(moto)* to ride. ► *vi* **1** *(dirigir un vehículo)* to drive. **2** *(llevar)* to lead: *esta carretera conduce a Teruel*, this road leads to Teruel.

conducta *nf* conduct.

conducto *nm* **1** *(tubería)* pipe, conduit. **2** *(del cuerpo)* duct.

conductor,-ra *nm,f* driver.

conectar *vt* **1** *(unir)* to connect. **2** *(aparato, luz, etc.)* to switch on, turn on.

conejo *nm* rabbit.

conexión *nf* connection.

confección *nf* **1** *(de prendas)* dressmaking. **2** *(elaboración)* making.

conferencia *nf* **1** *(charla)* talk, lecture. **2** *(congreso)* conference. **3** *(llamada telefónica)* long-distance call.

conferenciante *nmf* lecturer.

confesar(se) *vt-vpr* to confess.

confesión *nf* confession.

confianza *nf* **1** *(seguridad)* confidence. **2** *(fe)* trust. **3** *(familiaridad)* familiarity.

confiar *vi* **1** confiar en ALGN/algo *(tener fe)* to trust SB/STH. **2** **confiar en** + *inf (estar seguro)* to be confident that, be sure that: *confío en aprobar el examen*, I'm confident that I'll pass the exam.

configuración *nf* INFORM configuration. ▪ **configuración por defecto** default settings.

confirmar *vt* to confirm.

confitería *nf (bombonería)* GB sweet shop; US candy shop; *(pastelería)* cake shop.

conflicto *nm* conflict.

conformarse *vpr* to resign oneself, be content.

conforme *adj* 1 *(de acuerdo)*: **estar conforme**, to agree. 2 *(satisfecho)* satisfied, happy.

confortable *adj* comfortable.

confundir *vt* 1 *(mezclar)* to mix up. 2 *(desconcertar)* to confuse. 3 *(no reconocer)* to mistake. ▶ *vpr* **confundirse** *(equivocarse)* to be mistaken, make a mistake.

confusión *nf* 1 *(desorden)* confusion. 2 *(equivocación)* mistake.

congelado,-a *adj* frozen.

congelador *nm* freezer.

congelar(se) *vt-vpr* to freeze.

congestión *nf* congestion.

congreso *nm* conference, congress.

congrio *nm* conger eel.

conífera *nf* conifer.

conjugación *nf* conjugation.

conjunción *nf* conjunction.

conjuntivitis *nf* conjunctivitis.

conjunto *nm* 1 *(grupo)* group, collection. 2 *(todo)* whole. 3 *(de música - pop)* band, group; *(- clásica)* ensemble. 4 *(prenda)* outfit.

conmigo *pron* with me.

conmoción *nf (cerebral)* concussion.

cono *nm* cone.

conocer *vt* 1 *(gen)* to know; *(persona por primera vez)* to meet. 2 *(país, lugar)* to have been to.

conocido,-a *adj* 1 *(reconocible)* familiar. 2 *(famoso)* well-known. ▶ *nm,f* acquaintance.

conocimiento *nm* 1 *(saber)* knowledge. 2 *(conciencia)* consciousness.

conquista *nf* conquest.

conquistador,-ra *nm,f* conqueror.

conquistar *vt* 1 *(con armas)* to conquer. 2 *(victoria, título)* to win. 3 *(ligar con)* to win over.

consciente *adj* conscious.

consecuencia *nf* consequence, result.

conseguir *vt (cosa)* to obtain, get; *(objetivo)* to attain, get. • **conseguir + *inf*** to manage to + *inf*.

consejero,-a *nm,f* 1 *(asesor)* adviser. 2 POL counsellor.

consejo *nm (recomendación)* advice: **te daré un consejo**, I'll give you a piece of advice. ▪ **consejo de administración** board of directors; **consejo de ministros** cabinet.

consentir *vt* **1** *(permitir)* to allow, permit, tolerate. **2** *(a un niño)* to spoil.

conserje *nmf* **1** *(de hotel, oficina)* porter. **2** *(de escuela)* caretaker.

conservas *nf pl* tinned food, canned food.

conservación *nf* **1** *(de naturaleza, especie)* conservation. **2** *(de alimentos)* preservation.

conservante *nm* preservative.

conservar *vt* **1** *(alimentos)* to preserve. **2** *(calor)* retain. **3** *(guardar)* to keep.

consideración *nf* **1** *(deliberación, atención)* consideration. **2** *(respeto)* regard.

considerar *vt* **1** *(reflexionar)* to consider, think over. **2** *(juzgar)* to consider.

consigna *nf (en estación etc)* GB left-luggage office; US checkroom.

consigo *pron (con él)* with him; *(con ella)* with her; *(con usted, ustedes, vosotros,-as)* with you; *(con ellos,-as)* with them; *(con uno mismo)* with oneself.

consiguiente *adj* consequent. • **por consiguiente** therefore, consequently.

consistir *vi* to consist *(en,* of).

consola *nf* INFORM console.

consolar *vt* to console, comfort.

consomé *nm* consommé, clear soup.

consonante *adj-nf* consonant.

conspiración *nf* conspiracy, plot.

constante *adj* **1** *(invariable)* constant. **2** *(persona)* persevering. • **constantes vitales** vital signs.

constar *vi* **1** *(consistir en)* to consist (**de,** of). **2** *(ser cierto)*: *me consta que ha llegado*, I am absolutely certain that he has arrived.

constipado *nm* cold.

constitución *nf* constitution.

constituir *vt* to constitute.

construcción *nf* **1** *(acción)* construction, building. **2** *(edificio)* building.

construir *vt* to build, construct.

consuelo *nm* consolation, comfort.

cónsul *nmf* consul.

consulado *nm* **1** *(oficina)* consulate. **2** *(cargo)* consulship.

consulta *nf* **1** *(pregunta)* consultation. **2** *(de médico)* GB surgery; US office.

consultar *vt (persona)* to consult; *(libro)* to look it up in.

consumición *nf* *(bebida)* drink.

consumidor,-ra *nm,f* consumer.

consumir *vt* to consume.

control

contabilidad *nf* **1** *(profesión)* accountancy. **2** *(ciencia)* accountancy, book-keeping.

contacto *nm* **1** *(entre personas, cosas)* contact. **2** *(de coche)* ignition.

contagiar *vt* **1** *(enfermedad)* to transmit, pass on. **2** *(persona)* to infect.

contagioso,-a *adj* contagious.

contaminación *nf* *(de agua, radiactiva)* contamination; *(atmosférica)* pollution.

contar *vt* **1** *(calcular)* to count. **2** *(explicar)* to tell. ► *vi* to count. • **contar con ALGN** *(confiar)* to count on SB, rely on SB; **contar con algo** *(esperar)* to expect STH.

contemplar *vt-vi* to contemplate.

contener *vt* **1** *(tener dentro)* to contain, hold. **2** *(reprimir)* to contain, hold back.

contenido *nm* content, contents.

contento,-a *adj* happy.

contestación *nf* *(respuesta)* answer, reply.

contestador *nm*. • **contestador automático** answering machine.

contestar *vt* to answer.

contigo *pron* with you.

contiguo,-a *adj* contiguous, adjoining.

continental *adj* continental.

continente *nm* continent.

continuación *nf* continuation. • **a continuación** next.

continuar *vt-vi* to continue, carry on.

contra *prep* against. • **en contra** against.

contrabando *nm* **1** *(actividad)* smuggling. **2** *(mercancía)* contraband.

contraer *vt* **1** *(gen)* to contract. **2** *(enfermedad)* to catch.

contrario,-a *adj* **1** *(dirección, sentido)* contrary, opposite. **2** *(opinión)* contrary. **3** *(rival)* opposing. ► *nm,f* opponent. • **al contrario** on the contrary.

contrarreloj *adj* against the clock. ► *nf* time trial.

contraseña *nf* password.

contratar *vt* **1** *(servicio etc)* to sign a contract for. **2** *(empleado)* to hire, take on.

contrato *nm* contract. ▪ **contrato de alquiler** lease, leasing agreement.

contraventana *nf* shutter.

contribución *nf* **1** *(aportación)* contribution. **2** *(impuesto)* tax.

contribuir *vt-vi* to contribute.

contrincante *nm* opponent.

control *nm* **1** *(dominio)* control. **2** *(verificación)* examination, inspection. ▪ **control remoto** remote control; **control de pasaportes** passport control; **control de policía** police checkpoint.

controlador,-ra *nm,f.* • **controlador,-ra aéreo,-a** air traffic controller.

controlar *vt* to control.

convencer *vt* to convince.

conveniente *adj* **1** *(cómodo)* convenient. **2** *(ventajoso)* advantageous. **3** *(aconsejable)* advisable.

convenio *nm* agreement.

convenir *vi* **1** *(ser oportuno)* to suit. **2** *(ser aconsejable)*: *te conviene descansar*, you should get some rest.

convento *nm (de monjas)* convent; *(de monjes)* monastery.

conversación *nf* conversation.

conversar *vi* to talk.

convertir *vt* to turn into.

convivir *vi* to live together.

convocar *vt* to call.

convocatoria *nf* **1** *(llamamiento)* call. **2** *(examen)* examination, sitting.

coñac *nm* cognac, brandy.

cooperación *nf* cooperation.

cooperar *vi* to cooperate.

coordinación *nf* coordination.

coordinar *vt* to coordinate.

copa *nf* **1** *(recipiente)* glass. **2** *(bebida)* drink. **3** *(de árbol)* top. • **ir de copas** to go (out) drinking; **tomar una copa** to have a drink.

copia *nf* copy. ■ **copia de seguridad** backup.

copiar *vt* to copy.

copo *nm (de cereal)* flake; *(de nieve)* snowflake.

coral¹ *adj* choral. ► *nf* choir.

coral² *nm* coral.

corazón *nm* heart.

corbata *nf* tie.

corcho *nm* cork.

cordero,-a *nm,f* lamb.

cordial *adj* cordial, friendly.

cordillera *nf* mountain range.

cordón *nm (cuerda)* cord, string; *(de zapatos)* lace, shoelace. ■ **cordón policial** police cordon; **cordón umbilical** umbilical cord.

coreografía *nf* choreography.

córnea *nf* cornea.

córner *nm* corner.

corneta *nf* bugle.

coro *nm (grupo)* choir.

corona *nf* **1** *(de rey)* crown. **2** *(de flores etc)* wreath.

coronel *nm* colonel.

corporación *nf* corporation.

corral *nm (de aves)* yard.

correa *nf* **1** *(de piel)* strap. **2** *(cinturón)* belt. **3** *(de perro)* lead. **4** *(de máquina)* belt.

correcto,-a *adj* **1** *(exacto, adecuado)* correct. **2** *(educado)* polite, courteous.

corredor,-ra *nm,f* **1** *(atleta)* runner. **2** *(ciclista)* cyclist. ► *nm* **corredor** corridor.

corregir *vt* to correct.

correo *nm* GB post; US mail. ► *nm pl* **correos** *(oficina)* post office. • **echar al correo** GB to post; US to mail; **mandar por correo** GB to post; US to mail. ▪ **correo certificado** GB registered post; US registered mail; **correo electrónico** e-mail, electronic mail: *envíamelo por correo electrónico*, e-mail it to me; **correo urgente** express mail.

correr *vi* **1** *(persona, animal)* to run. **2** *(agua)* to flow. **3** *(tiempo)* to pass. **4** *(darse prisa)* to hurry. ► *vt* **1** *(carrera)* to run. **2** *(deslizar)* to close; *(cortina)* to draw.

correspondencia *nf* **1** *(relación)* correspondence. **2** *(cartas)* GB post; US mail. **3** *(de trenes etc)* connection.

corresponder *vi* **1** *(equivaler)* to correspond. **2** *(pertenecer)* to belong, pertain. **3** *(devolver)* to return.

correspondiente *adj* **1** *(perteneciente)* corresponding. **2** *(respectivo)* respective.

corrida *nf*. ▪ **corrida de toros** bullfight.

corriente *adj* **1** *(frecuente)* common. **2** *(no especial)* ordinary. **3** *(agua)* running. ► *nf* **1** *(masa de agua)* current, stream. **2** *(de aire)* GB draught; US draft. **3** *(eléctrica)* current. **4** *(de arte etc)* current, trend. • **al corriente** up to date; **estar al corriente de algo** to know about STH.

corrupción *nf* corruption.

cortado *nm* coffee with a dash of milk.

cortar *vt* **1** *(gen)* to cut. **2** *(interrumpir)* to cut off, interrupt. **3** *(calle, carretera)* to close. ► *vpr* **cortarse 1** *(herirse)* to cut. **2** *(pelo - por otro)* to have one's hair cut; *(- uno mismo)* to cut one's hair. **3** *(leche)* to curdle.

cortaúñas *nm* nail clippers.

corte¹ *nf* court.

corte² *nm* *(herida, interrupción)* cut. ▪ **corte de pelo** haircut.

cortés *adj* courteous, polite.

cortesía *nf* courtesy.

corteza *nf* **1** *(de árbol)* bark. **2** *(de pan)* crust. **3** *(de queso)* rind. ▪ **corteza terrestre** earth's crust.

cortina *nf* curtain.

corto,-a *adj* short.

cortocircuito *nm* short circuit.

cortometraje *nm* short (film).

cosa *nf* thing. • **¿alguna cosa más?** anything else?

cosecha *nf* **1** *(acción)* harvest. **2** *(producto)* crop. **3** *(año del vino)* vintage.

cosechar *vt-vi (recoger cosecha)* to harvest, gather; *(- éxitos etc)* to reap.

coser *vt* **1** *(gen)* to sew. **2** *(herida)* to stitch up.

cosmético,-a *adj* cosmetic. ► *nm* **cosmético** cosmetic.

cosquillas *nf pl* • **tener cosquillas** to be ticklish.

cosquilleo *nm* tickling.

costa¹ *nf* coast.

costa². • **a costa de** at the expense of; **a toda costa** at all costs.

costado *nm* side.

costar *vt* 1 *(valer)* to cost. 2 *(esfuerzo, tiempo)* to take. ▶ *vi* 1 *(al comprar)* to cost. 2 *(ser difícil)* to be difficult.

coste *nm* cost.

costero,-a *adj* coastal.

costilla *nf* 1 *(de persona, animal)* rib. 2 *(como comida)* chop.

costo *nm (precio)* cost.

costumbre *nf* 1 *(hábito)* habit. 2 *(tradición)* custom.

costura *nf* 1 *(cosido)* sewing. 2 *(línea de puntadas)* seam.

cotidiano,-a *adj* daily, everyday.

coto *nm*. ▪ **coto de caza** game preserve.

cotorra *nf (animal)* parrot.

coyote *nm* coyote.

coz *nf* kick.

cráneo *nm* skull, cranium.

cráter *nm* crater.

creación *nf* creation.

crear *vt* 1 *(producir)* to create. 2 *(fundar)* to found, establish.

crecer *vi* 1 *(gen)* to grow. 2 *(corriente, marea)* to rise.

creciente *adj (luna)* crescent.

crecimiento *nm* growth, increase.

crédito *nm* 1 *(al comprar)* credit. 2 *(préstamo)* loan.

creencia *nf* belief.

creer *vi* 1 *(tener fe)* to believe (**en**, in). 2 *(pensar)* to think. ▶ *vt* 1 *(gen)* to believe. 2 *(pensar)* to think, suppose. • **creo que sí** I think so; **creo que no** I don't think so.

crema *nf* 1 *(nata)* cream. 2 *(natillas)* custard.

cremallera *nf* 1 *(de vestido)* GB zip; US zipper. 2 *(de máquina)* rack.

cremoso,-a *adj* creamy.

cresta *nf* 1 *(de ola)* crest. 2 *(de gallo)* comb.

cría *nf (cachorro)* baby.

criar *vt* 1 *(educar)* to bring up. 2 *(dar el pecho)* to nurse. 3 *(animales)* to breed; *(plantas)* to grow.

crimen *nm* 1 *(delito)* crime. 2 *(asesinato)* murder.

criminal *adj-nmf* criminal.

crin *nf* mane.

crisis *nf* 1 *(mal momento)* crisis. 2 *(ataque)* fit, attack.

cristal *nm* glass.

cristalino *nm* crystalline lens.

cristiano,-a *adj-nm,f* Christian.

criterio *nm* 1 *(norma)* criterion. 2 *(juicio)* judgement. 3 *(opinión)* opinion.

crítica *nf* 1 *(juicio, censura)* criticism. 2 *(reseña)* review.

criticar *vt* to criticize.
crítico,-a *adj* critical. ► *nm,f* critic.
croar *vi* to croak.
croissant *nm* croissant.
crol *nm* crawl.
cromo *nm* 1 *(metal)* chromium. 2 *(estampa)* picture card.
crónica *nf (en periódico)* article.
crónico,-a *adj* chronic.
cronómetro *nm* stopwatch.
croqueta *nf* croquette.
cross *nm* cross-country race.
cruce *nm* 1 *(acción)* crossing. 2 *(de calles)* crossroads. 3 *(de carreteras)* junction.
crucero *nm* 1 *(buque)* cruiser. 2 *(viaje)* cruise. 3 *(de templo)* transept.
crucifijo *nm* crucifix.
crucigrama *nm* crossword.
crudo,-a *adj* 1 *(sin cocer)* raw; *(poco hecho)* underdone. 2 *(color)* off-white. ► *nm* **crudo** *(petróleo)* crude.
cruel *adj* cruel.
crujiente *adj* crunchy.
crujir *vi (puerta)* to creak.
crustáceo *nm* crustacean.
cruz *nf* 1 *(figura)* cross. 2 *(de moneda)* tails.
cruzar *vt* 1 *(río, piernas, animales)* to cross. 2 *(miradas, palabras)* to exchange. ► *vpr* **cruzarse** to pass each other.
cuaderno *nm* 1 *(de notas)* notebook. 2 *(escolar)* exercise book.
cuadra *nf* stable.

cuadrado,-a *adj* square: *diez metros cuadrados*, ten square meters. ► *nm* **cuadrado** square.
cuadrilátero *nm* ring.
cuadro *nm* 1 *(pintura)* painting. 2 *(cuadrado)* square. 3 *(diagrama)* chart. • **a cuadros** 1 *(estampado)* checkered. 2 *(camisa)* checked, check.
cual *pron (precedido de artículo - persona)* who, whom; *(- cosa)* which: *la gente a la cual preguntamos dijo que...*, the people whom we asked said that... • **cada cual** everyone, everybody; **con lo cual** with the result that.
cuál *pron* which one, what.
cualidad *nf* quality.
cualificado,-a *adj* qualified, skilled.
cualquier *adj* → cualquiera.
cualquiera *adj* any. ► *pron (persona indeterminada)* anybody, anyone; *(cosa indeterminada)* any, any one: *cualquiera te lo puede decir* anyone can tell you. • **cualquier cosa** anything; **cualquier otro** anyone else; **cualquiera que** whatever, whichever.
cuando *adv* when. ► *conj* 1 *(temporal)* when: *cuando deje de llover*, when it stops raining. 2 *(condicional)* if: *cuando ella lo dice...*, if she says so... • **de (vez en) cuando** now and then.

cuándo *adv* when.

cuanto,-a *adj (singular)* as much as; *(plural)* as many as. ▶ *pron (singular)* everything, all; *(plural)* all who, everybody who. • **cuanto antes** as soon as possible; **en cuanto** as soon as; **en cuanto a** as far as; **unos,-as cuantos,-as** some, a few.

cuánto,-a *adj* 1 *(interrogativo - singular)* how much; *(- plural)* how many. 2 *(exclamativo)* what a lot of. ▶ *pron (singular)* how much; *(plural)* how many. ▶ *adv* how, how much: *¡cuánto me alegro!*, I'm so glad!

cuarenta *num* forty.

cuartel *nm* barracks. ▪ **cuartel general** headquarters.

cuarto,-a *num* fourth. ▶ *nm* **cuarto** 1 *(parte)* quarter. 2 *(habitación)* room. ▪ **cuarto creciente** first quarter; **cuarto menguante** last quarter; **cuarto de baño** bathroom; **cuarto de estar** living room.

cuarzo *nm* quartz.

cuatro *num* four; *(en fechas)* fourth. ▪ **cuatro por cuatro** four-wheel drive.

cuatrocientos,-as *num* four hundred.

cuba *nf* cask, barrel.

cubalibre *nm (de ron)* rum and coke; *(de ginebra)* gin and coke.

cubano,-a *adj-nm,f* Cuban.

cúbico,-a *adj* cubic.

cubierta *nf* 1 *(tapa)* covering. 2 *(de libro)* jacket. 3 *(de neumático)* GB tyre; US tire. 5 *(de barco)* deck.

cubierto,-a *adj* 1 covered. 2 *(cielo)* overcast. ▶ *nm* **cubierto** 1 *(en la mesa)* place setting. 2 *(menú)* set menu.

cubito *nm*. ▪ **cubito (de hielo)** ice cube.

cubo¹ *nm* 1 *(recipiente)* bucket. 2 *(de rueda)* hub. ▪ **cubo de la basura** GB dustbin; US garbage can.

cubo² *nm (figura)* cube.

cubrir *vt* 1 *(tapar)* to cover. 2 *(puesto, vacante)* to fill.

cucaracha *nf* cockroach.

cuchara *nf* spoon.

cucharilla *nf* teaspoon.

cuchilla *nf* blade. ▪ **cuchilla de afeitar** razor blade.

cuchillo *nm* knife.

cucurucho *nm* 1 *(de papel)* cone. 2 *(helado)* cornet, cone.

cuello *nm* 1 *(de persona, animal)* neck. 2 *(de prenda)* collar. 3 *(de botella)* neck. ▪ **cuello alto** GB polo neck; US turtleneck; **cuello de pico** V-neck.

cuenta *nf* 1 *(bancaria)* account. 2 *(factura)* GB bill; US check. • **darse cuenta de algo** to realize STH; **tener en cuenta** to take into account. ▪ **cuenta atrás** countdown.

cuentagotas *nm* dropper.

cuentakilómetros *nm* GB mileometer; US odometer.

cuento *nm* short story, tale.

cuerda *nf* 1 (*soga*) rope; (*cordel, de guitarra*) string. 2 (*de reloj*) spring. • **dar cuerda a un reloj** to wind up a watch.

cuerno *nm* (*de toro*) horn; (*de ciervo*) antler.

cuero *nm* 1 (*de animal*) skin, hide. 2 (*curtido*) leather.

cuerpo *nm* body. • **a cuerpo** without a coat.

cuervo *nm* raven.

cuesta *nf* slope. • **a cuestas** on one's back, on one's shoulders; **cuesta abajo** downhill; **cuesta arriba** uphill.

cuestión *nf* question.

cuestionario *nm* questionnaire.

cueva *nf* cave.

cuidado *nm* 1 (*atención*) care. 2 (*recelo*) worry. ▶ *interj* ¡**cuidado!** look out!, watch out! • "**Cuidado con el perro**" "Beware of the dog"; **tener cuidado** to be careful. ▪ **cuidados intensivos** intensive care.

cuidar *vt-vi* to look after, take care of.

culebra *nf* snake.

culinario,-a *adj* culinary.

culo *nm* 1 (*trasero*) bottom, backside, GB bum; US butt. 2 (*de recipiente*) bottom.

culpa *nf* 1 (*culpabilidad*) guilt, blame. 2 (*falta*) fault.

culpabilidad *nf* guilt, culpability.

culpable *adj* guilty. ▶ *nmf* offender, culprit.

cultivar *vt* 1 (*terreno*) to cultivate, farm. 2 (*plantas*) to grow.

culto,-a *adj* 1 (*con cultura*) cultured, educated. 2 (*estilo*) refined. ▶ *nm* **culto** worship.

cultura *nf* culture.

cumbre *nf* (*de montaña*) summit, top. 2 (*reunión*) summit.

cumpleaños *nm* birthday.

cumplir *vt* 1 (*orden*) to carry out. 2 (*compromiso, obligación*) to fulfil. 3 (*promesa*) to keep. 4 (*condena*) to serve. 5 (*años*): *mañana cumplo veinte años*, I'll be twenty tomorrow.

cuna *nf* GB cot; US crib, cradle.

cuneta *nf* ditch.

cuñado,-a *nm,f* (*hombre*) brother-in-law; (*mujer*) sister-in-law.

cuota *nf* 1 (*pago*) membership fee, dues. 2 (*porción*) quota, share.

cúpula *nf* cupola, dome.

cura *nm* (*párroco*) priest. ▶ *nf* (*curación*) cure.

curación *nf* cure, healing.

curar *vt* 1 (*sanar*) to cure. 2 (*herida*) to dress; (*enfermedad*) to treat. ▶ *vpr* **curarse** (*recuperarse*) to recover, get well.

curiosidad *nf* curiosity.

curioso,-a *adj* **1** *(interesado)* curious, inquisitive. **2** *(indiscreto)* nosy. **3** *(extraño)* strange: *¡qué curioso!*, how strange!

currículum *nm* curriculum (vitae), CV.

curso *nm* **1** *(gen)* course. **2** *(académico)* year. • **en curso** current.

cursor *nm* cursor.

curva *nf* **1** curve. **2** *(de carretera)* bend.

cutis *nm* skin, complexion.

cuyo,-a *pron* whose, of which. • **en cuyo caso** in which case.

D

dado *nm* die.

dama *nf* **1** *(señora)* lady. **2** *(en ajedrez)* queen; *(en damas)* king. ▶ *nf pl* **damas** GB draughts; US checkers. ▪ **dama de honor** bridesmaid.

danza *nf* dance.

dañar *vt (cosa)* to damage; *(persona)* to harm.

daño *nm* **1** *(en cosas)* damage. **2** *(en personas)* harm. • **hacer daño 1** *(doler)* to hurt. **2** *(perjudicar)* to do harm; **hacerse daño** to hurt oneself. ▪ **daños y perjuicios** damages.

dar *vt* **1** *(gen)* to give. **2** *(las horas)* to strike. **3** *(película)* to show; *(obra de teatro)* to perform. ▶ *vi (mirar a)* to look out.

dardo *nm* dart.

dátil *nm* date.

dato *nm* piece of information. ▶ *nm pl* **datos** *(información)* information; *(informáticos)* data. ▪ **datos personales** personal details.

de *prep* **1** *(gen)* of. **2** *(posesión)* 's, s': *el coche de María*, María's car; *los libros de los chicos*, the boys' books. **3** *(materia, tema)*: *una profesora de inglés*, an English teacher. **4** *(origen, procedencia)* from: *es de Navarra*, he's from Navarre. **5** *(descripción)* with, in: *la chica del pelo largo*, the girl with long hair; *el hombre de negro*, the man in black. **6** *(agente)* by: *un libro de Dickens*, a book by Dickens. **7** **de** + *inf* if: *de seguir así, acabarás en la cárcel*, if you continue like this, you'll end up in prison.

debajo *adv* underneath, below. • **debajo de** under.

debate *nm* debate.

deber *nm (obligación)* duty. ▶ *vt (dinero)* to owe. ▶ *aux* **1 deber** + *inf (obligación)* must, to have to; *(recomendación)* should: *debo irme*, I must go; *de-*

berías ir al médico, you should see the doctor. **2 deber de** *(conjetura)* must: **deben de ser las seis**, it must be six o'clock. ► *nm pl* **deberes** homework.

debido,-a *adj.* • **como es debido** properly; **debido,-a** due to, owing to.

débil *adj* **1** *(persona)* weak. **2** *(ruido)* faint. **3** *(luz)* dim.

década *nf* decade.

decadencia *nf* decadence.

decente *adj* **1** *(decoroso)* decent. **2** *(honesto)* honest.

decepcionar *vt* to disappoint.

decidir *vt-vi* to decide. ► *vpr* **decidirse** to make up one's mind.

décima *nf* tenth.

decimal *adj-nm* decimal.

décimo,-a *num* tenth. ► *nm* **décimo** lottery ticket.

decir *vt* **1** *(gen)* to say: *dijo que vendría mañana*, he said he'd come tomorrow. **2** *(a alguien)* to tell: *dime lo que piensas*, tell me what you think. • **es decir** that is to say; **querer decir** to mean.

decisión *nf* decision.

declaración *nf* **1** *(afirmación)* statement. **2** *(de guerra, amor)* declaration. • **prestar declaración** *(en juicio)* to give evidence. ▪ **declaración de la renta** income tax return.

declarar *vt* **1** *(gen)* to declare: *¿no tiene nada que declarar?*, do you have anything to declare? **2** *(considerar)* to find. ► *vi (dar testimonio)* to testify. ► *vpr* **declararse** *(fuego, guerra)* to start, break out.

decoración *nf* decoration.

decorado *nm* scenery, set.

decorar *vt* to decorate.

decreto *nm* decree.

dedal *nm* thimble.

dedicar *vt* to dedicate. ► *vpr* **dedicarse** to devote oneself: *¿a qué te dedicas?*, what do you do?

dedo *nm (de la mano)* finger; *(del pie)* toe. • **hacer dedo** hitchhike. ▪ **dedo del corazón** middle finger; **dedo gordo** thumb.

deducir *vt* **1** *(inferir)* to deduce. **2** *(descontar)* to deduct.

defecto *nm* defect, fault.

defectuoso,-a *adj* defective, faulty.

defender *vt* to defend.

defensa *nf* GB defence; US defense. ► *nmf (jugador)* defender.

defensor,-ra *adj* defending. ► *nm,f* defender.

déficit *nm* deficit.

definición *nf* definition.

definir *vt* to define.

definitivo,-a *adj* definitive, final.

deformar *vt* to deform.

defraudar vt 1 (decepcionar) to disappoint. 2 (estafar) to defraud; (robar) to steal.

dejar vt 1 (gen) to leave. 2 (permitir) to let: *déjame entrar*, let me in. 3 (prestar) to lend: *¿me dejas tu bici?*, will you lend me your bike?, can I borrow your bike? ► aux 1 **dejar de** + inf to stop: *deja de gritar*, stop shouting. 2 **no dejar de** + inf: *no dejaron de bailar*, they went on dancing. ► vpr **dejarse** (olvidar) to forget.

delantal nm apron.

delante adv in front. ► prep **delante de** in front of. • **de delante** front; **hacia delante** forward; **por delante** ahead.

delantero,-a adj (rueda) front; (pata) fore. ► nm **delantero** (deportista) forward. ▪ **delantero centro** centre forward.

delegación nf 1 (personas) delegation. 2 (sucursal) branch.

delegar vt to delegate.

deletrear vt to spell.

delfín nm (animal) dolphin.

delgado,-a adj thin.

delicado,-a adj 1 (gen) delicate. 2 (sensible) sensitive; (tiquismiquis) hard to please.

delicioso,-a adj delicious.

delincuente adj-nmf delinquent.

delito nm offence, crime.

demanda nf 1 (de producto) demand. 2 (legal) lawsuit.

demandar vt JUR to sue.

demás adj other. ► pron the others, the rest. • **por lo demás** otherwise.

demasiado,-a adj (singular) too much; (plural) too many. ► adv **demasiado** (después de verbo) too much; (delante de adjetivo) too.

democracia nf democracy.

democrático,-a adj democratic.

demonio nm demon, devil.

demostración nf 1 (muestra) demonstration. 2 (prueba) proof.

demostrar vt 1 (mostrar) to demonstrate. 2 (probar) to prove.

denegar vt to refuse.

denominación nf denomination.

denominar vt to denominate, name.

denso,-a adj dense.

dentadura nf teeth. ▪ **dentadura postiza** false teeth.

dentífrico nm toothpaste.

dentista nmf dentist.

dentro adv (gen) inside; (de edificio) indoors. ► prep **dentro de** in. • **por dentro** inside.

denuncia nf report, complaint. • **presentar una denuncia** to lodge a complaint.

denunciar vt *(situación)* to condemn; *(delito)* to report.

departamento nm department.

dependencia nf 1 *(de persona, drogas)* dependence, dependency. 2 *(en edificio)* outbuilding.

depender vi to depend.

dependiente,-a nm,f sales assistant.

depilar vt *(con cera)* to wax.

deporte nm sport.

deportista nmf *(hombre)* sportsman; *(mujer)* sportswoman.

depositar vt to deposit.

depósito nm 1 *(gen)* deposit. 2 *(almacén)* store. 3 *(receptáculo)* tank. ▪ **depósito de gasolina** GB petrol tank; US gas tank.

depresión nf depression.

deprisa adv quickly.

derecha nf 1 *(dirección)* right. 2 *(mano)* right hand; *(pierna)* right leg. 3 POL right wing. • **a la derecha** to the right: *girar a la derecha*, to turn right.

derecho,-a adj 1 *(diestro)* right. 2 *(recto)* straight. ▶ nm **derecho** 1 *(poder, oportunidad)* right. 2 *(ley)* law. ▪ **derechos de autor** copyright.

derramar vt 1 *(leche, vino)* to spill. 2 *(sangre, lágrimas)* to shed.

derrapar vi to skid.

derretir(se) vt-vpr to melt.

derribar vt 1 *(edificio)* to demolish. 2 *(avión)* to shoot down.

derrochar vt to squander.

derrota nf defeat.

derrotar vt to defeat.

derrumbarse vpr *(edificio, techo)* to collapse.

desabrochar vt to undo, unfasten.

desacuerdo nm disagreement.

desafiar vt to defy.

desafinar vi to be out of tune.

desafío nm 1 *(reto)* challenge. 2 *(duelo)* duel.

desagradable adj unpleasant.

desagüe nm drain.

desalojar vt 1 *(persona)* to remove. 2 *(inquilino)* to evict. 3 *(ciudad)* to evacuate. 4 *(edificio)* to clear.

desangrarse vpr to bleed to death.

desanimado,-a adj despondent.

desapacible adj unpleasant.

desaparecer vi to disappear.

desaparición nf disappearance.

desaprovechar vt to waste.

desarmar vt 1 *(quitar armas)* to disarm. 2 *(desmontar)* to dismantle.

desarrollar vt 1 *(gen)* to develop. 2 *(realizar)* to carry

out. ► *vpr* **desarrollarse 1**
(crecer) to develop. **2** *(ocurrir)*
to take place.

desarrollo *nm* development.
• **en vías de desarrollo** developing.

desastre *nm* disaster.

desatar *vt* to untie.

desatascar *vt* to unblock.

desatornillar *vt* to unscrew.

desayunar *vt* to have for
breakfast. ► *vi* to have breakfast.

desayuno *nm* breakfast.

desbordar *vt* *(sobrepasar)* to
surpass. ► *vpr* **desbordarse**
(río) to overflow.

descafeinado,-a *adj* *(café)*
decaffeinated.

descalificar *vt* **1** *(de un concurso)* to disqualify. **2** *(desprestigiar)* to dismiss.

descalzo,-a *adj* barefoot.

descampado *nm* piece of open
ground.

descansar *vi* **1** *(reposar)* to
have a rest. **2** *(apoyarse)* to
rest.

descansillo *nm* landing.

descanso *nm* **1** *(reposo)* rest;
(en el trabajo) break. **2** *(en encuentro deportivo)* half time.

descapotable *adj-nm* convertible.

descarga *nf* **1** *(de electricidad)*
discharge. **2** *(de fuego)* discharge, volley. **3** *(en ordenador)*
download.

descargar *vt* **1** *(mercancías)* to
unload. **2** *(en ordenador)* to
download. ► *vpr* **descargarse** *(batería)* to go flat.

descarrilar *vi* to be derailed.

descartar *vt* to rule out.

descendencia *nf* offspring,
children.

descender *vi* **1** *(ir abajo)* to go
down, come down. **2** *(temperatura, índice)* to drop, fall.

descendiente *nmf* descendant.

descenso *nm* **1** *(de escalera,
cumbre)* descent. **2** *(de temperatura, índice)* fall.

descolgar *vt* **1** *(cuadro, cortina)* to take down. **2** *(teléfono)*
to pick up.

descomposición *nf* **1** *(putrefacción)* decomposition, decay. **2** *(diarrea)* GB diarrhoea;
US diarrhea.

desconectar *vt* to disconnect.

desconfiar *vi* to be distrustful.

descongelar *vt* **1** *(comida)* to
thaw. **2** *(nevera)* to defrost.

desconocido,-a *adj* **1** *(no
conocido)* unknown. **2** *(extraño)* strange, unfamiliar. ►
nm,f stranger.

descontento *nm* dissatisfaction.

descorchar *vt* to uncork.

descosido *nm* split seam.

descremado,-a *adj* skimmed.

describir *vt* to describe.

descripción *nf* description.

descubierto,-a *adj* **1** *(sin cubrir)* uncovered; *(sin sombrero)* bareheaded. **2** *(piscina)* outdoor.

descubrimiento *nm* discovery.

descubrir *vt* **1** *(encontrar)* to discover. **2** *(revelar)* to make known. **3** *(averiguar)* to find out.

descuento *nm* discount.

descuido *nm* **1** *(negligencia)* carelessness. **2** *(desliz)* slip, error.

desde *prep* **1** *(lugar)* from: *desde aquí no se ve*, you can't see it from here. **2** *(tiempo)* since: *salen juntos desde junio*, they've been going out together since June. • **desde ahora** from now on; **desde entonces** since then; **desde hace** for: *vivo aquí desde hace cinco años*, I've lived here for five years; **desde luego** of course; **desde que** ever since.

desdoblar *vt* to unfold.

desear *vt* to want.

desechable *adj* disposable.

desechos *nm pl* **1** *(basura)* waste *sing*. **2** *(sobras)* leftovers.

desembarcar *vi* to land.

desembocadura *nf* mouth.

desembocar *vi* **1** *(río)* to flow. **2** *(calle, acontecimiento)* to lead.

desempate *nm* breakthrough.

desempeñar *vt* **1** *(obligación)* to discharge. **2** *(cargo)* to hold.

desempleo *nm* unemployment.

desencadenar *vt* *(crisis, debate)* to spark off. ► *vpr* **desencadenarse** *(tormenta, guerra)* to break out

desenchufar *vt* to unplug.

desenfocado,-a *adj* out of focus.

desengaño *nm* disappointment.

desenlace *nm* **1** *(de aventura)* outcome. **2** *(de libro, película)* ending.

desenterrar *vt* **1** *(objeto escondido)* to unearth. **2** *(cadáver)* to dig up.

desenvolver *vt* to unwrap. ► *vpr* **desenvolverse** **1** *(transcurrir)* to develop. **2** *(espabilarse)* to manage.

deseo *nm* **1** *(anhelo)* wish. **2** *(apetito sexual)* desire.

desequilibrio *nm* imbalance.

desertar *vi* *(soldado)* to desert.

desértico,-a *adj* *(clima, zona)* desert.

desesperación *nf* **1** *(irritación)* exasperation. **2** *(angustia)* desperation.

desesperar *vt* **1** *(irritar)* to exasperate. **2** *(angustiar)* to drive to despair. ► *vi-vpr* **desesperar(se)** **1** *(irritarse)* to be exasperated. **2** *(angustiarse)* to despair.

desfallecer *vi* to faint.

desfiladero *nm* **1** *(barranco)* gorge. **2** *(paso)* narrow pass.

desfile *nm* parade.

desgracia *nf (mala suerte)* misfortune. **2** *(accidente)* mishap. • **por desgracia** unfortunately.

deshacer *vt* **1** *(gen)* to undo. **2** *(disolver)* to dissolve; *(fundir)* to melt. ► *vpr* **deshacerse 1** *(costura, nudo)* to come undone. **2** *(disolverse)* to dissolve; *(fundirse)* to melt.

deshidratarse *vpr* to get dehydrated.

deshielo *nm* thaw.

deshinchar *vt* to deflate.

desierto *nm* desert.

designar *vt* **1** *(nombrar)* to appoint. **2** *(fijar)* to designate.

desigualdad *nf* **1** *(diferencia)* inequality. **2** *(irregularidad)* unevenness.

desilusión *nf* disappointment.

desinfectante *adj-nm* disinfectant.

desinflar(se) *vt-vpr* to deflate.

desinterés *nm* lack of interest.

deslizar *vt-vi* to slide. ► *vpr* **deslizarse** *(resbalar)* to slip; *(sobre agua)* to glide.

desmayarse *vpr* to faint.

desmayo *nm* fainting fit.

desmontar *vt (mueble)* to dismantle. ► *vi (del caballo)* to dismount.

desnatado,-a *adj (leche)* skimmed; *(yogur)* low-fat.

desnivel *nm* **1** *(desigualdad)* unevenness. **2** *(distancia vertical)* drop.

desnudarse *vpr* to get undressed.

desnudo,-a *adj* naked.

desobedecer *vt* to disobey.

desocupado,-a *adj* **1** *(libre)* free. **2** *(ocioso)* unoccupied. **3** *(desempleado)* unemployed.

desodorante *adj-nm* deodorant.

desorden *nm* disorder.

despachar *vt* **1** *(enviar)* to dispatch. **2** *(despedir)* to sack. **3** *(en tienda)* to serve; *(vender)* to sell.

despacho *nm (en oficina)* office; *(en casa)* study.

despacio *adv* slowly.

despedida *nf* goodbye.

despedir *vt* **1** *(lanzar)* to throw. **2** *(del trabajo)* to dismiss. **3** *(decir adiós a)* to say goodbye to. ► *vpr* **despedirse** to say goodbye.

despegar *vt (desenganchar)* to detach. ► *vi (avión)* to take off.

despegue *nm* takeoff.

despejado,-a *adj* clear.

despejar *vt (habitación, calle)* to clear. ► *vi* to clear up. ► *vpr* **despejarse 1** *(tiempo, cielo)* to clear up. **2** *(persona)* to clear one's head.

despensa *nf* pantry.

desperdiciar *vt* to waste.
desperdicios *nm pl* scraps.
desperfecto *nm* slight damage.
despertador *nm* alarm clock.
despertar(se) *vt-vpr* to wake up.
despido *nm* dismissal.
despierto,-a *adj* **1** *(no dormido)* awake. **2** *(espabilado)* sharp.
despistado,-a *adj* absentminded.
despistar *vt* *(desorientar)* to confuse. ▶ *vpr* **despistarse 1** *(perderse)* to get lost. **2** *(distraerse)* to get distracted.
desplazar *vt* to move. ▶ *vpr* **desplazarse** to travel.
desplegar *vt* **1** *(mapa)* to unfold. **2** *(alas)* to spread. **3** *(actividad, cualidad)* to display. **4** *(tropas, armas)* to deploy.
despreciar *vt* **1** *(menospreciar)* to despise. **2** *(rechazar)* to reject.
desprecio *nm* contempt.
desprenderse *vpr* **1** *(soltarse)* to come off. **2** *(deducirse)* to emerge.
desprevenido,-a *adj* unprepared.
después *adv* **1** *(más tarde)* afterwards, later. **2** *(entonces)* then: *y después dijo que sí*, and then he said yes. ▶ *prep* **después de** *(tras)* after. • **después de todo** after all; **poco después** soon after.

destacar *vt* **1** *(tropas)* to detach. **2** *(resaltar)* to emphasize.
destapar *vt* **1** *(olla, caja)* to take the lid off. **2** *(botella)* to open.
destierro *nm* exile.
destinar *vt* **1** *(asignar)* to allocate. **2** *(a un puesto)* to post.
destinatario,-a *nm,f* **1** *(de carta)* addressee. **2** *(de mercancías)* consignee.
destino *nm* **1** *(sino)* destiny, fate. **2** *(lugar)* destination. **3** *(empleo)* post. • **con destino a** bound for: *el tren con destino a Bilbao*, the train to Bilbao.
destituir *vt* to dismiss.
destornillador *nm* screwdriver.
destreza *nf* skill.
destrozar *vt* *(edificio, enemigo)* to destroy; *(mueble, cristalera)* to smash; *(planes, vida)* to ruin; *(corazón)* to break.
destrucción *nf* destruction.
destruir *vt* to destroy.
desván *nm* loft, attic.
desventaja *nf* disadvantage.
desvestirse *vpr* to undress.
desviar *vt* **1** *(trayectoria)* to deviate. **2** *(carretera)* to divert. ▶ *vpr* **desviarse** *(de un camino)* to go off course; *(coche)* to take a detour.
desvío *nm* diversion.
detalle *nm* **1** *(pormenor)* detail. **2** *(delicadeza)* gesture.
detectar *vt* to detect.

detective *nmf* detective.

detener *vt* 1 *(parar)* to stop. 2 *(arrestar)* to arrest. ▶ *vpr* **detenerse** to stop.

detenido,-a *nm,f* prisoner.

detergente *adj-nm* detergent.

deteriorar *vt* to damage. ▶ *vpr* **deteriorarse** to deteriorate.

determinación *nf* 1 *(valor)* determination. 2 *(decisión)* decision. 3 *(firmeza)* firmness.

determinar *vt* 1 *(decidir)* to decide. 2 *(fijar)* to determine.

detestar *vt* to detest.

detrás *adv (gen)* behind. ▶ *prep* **detrás de** behind.

deuda *nf* debt.

devolución *nf* 1 *(de dinero pagado)* refund. 2 *(de artículo comprado)* return.

devolver *vt* 1 to give back. 2 *(vomitar)* to vomit.

día *nm* 1 *(gen)* day. 2 *(horas de luz)* daylight. • **¡buenos días!** good morning!; **hoy en día** today, now, nowadays. ▪ **día festivo** holiday; **día laborable** working day; **día libre** day off.

diabetes *nf* diabetes.

diabético,-a *adj-nm,f* diabetic.

diablo *nm* devil.

diagnosticar *vt* to diagnose.

diagnóstico *nm* diagnosis.

diagonal *adj-nf* diagonal.

diagrama *nm* diagram.

diálogo *nm* dialogue.

diamante *nm* diamond.

diámetro *nm* diameter.

diana *nf (blanco de tiro)* target; *(para dardos)* dartboard.

diapositiva *nf* slide.

diario,-a *adj* daily. ▶ *nm* **diario** 1 *(prensa)* newspaper. 2 *(íntimo)* diary, journal. • **a diario** every day.

diarrea *nf* GB diarrhoea; US diarrhea.

dibujar *vt* to draw.

dibujo *nm* 1 *(gen)* drawing. 2 *(estampado)* pattern. ▪ **dibujos animados** cartoons.

diccionario *nm* dictionary.

dicho,-a *adj* said. • **mejor dicho** or rather.

diciembre *nm* December.

dictado *nm* dictation.

dictador *nm* dictator.

dictadura *nf* dictatorship.

dictar *vt* to dictate.

diecinueve *num* nineteen; *(en fechas)* nineteenth.

dieciocho *num* eighteen; *(en fechas)* eighteenth.

dieciséis *num* sixteen; *(en fechas)* sixteenth.

diecisiete *num* seventeen; *(en fechas)* seventeenth.

diente *nm* 1 *(de la boca)* tooth. 2 *(de ajo)* clove.

diestro,-a *adj (mano)* right; *(persona)* right-handed. ▶ *nm* **diestro** bullfighter.

dieta *nf (régimen)* diet.

dietas *nf pl* expense allowance.

diez *num* ten; *(en fechas)* tenth.

diferencia *nf* difference.

diferente *adj* different.

diferido,-a *adj* recorded.

difícil *adj* **1** *(costoso)* difficult. **2** *(improbable)* unlikely.

dificultad *nf* difficulty.

difunto,-a *nm,f* deceased.

difusión *nf* **1** *(de luz)* diffusion. **2** *(de noticia)* spreading. **3** *(por radio, televisión)* broadcast.

digerir *vt* to digest.

digestión *nf* digestion.

digital *adj* digital.

digno,-a *adj* **1** *(merecedor)* worthy. **2** *(adecuado)* fitting. **3** *(respetable)* respectable.

diluvio *nm* flood.

dimensión *nf* **1** *(magnitud física)* dimension. **2** *(tamaño)* size.

diminuto,-a *adj* tiny.

dimisión *nf* resignation.

dimitir *vt* to resign.

Dinamarca *nf* Denmark.

dinero *nm* money. ▪ **dinero en efectivo** cash.

dinosaurio *nm* dinosaur.

dintel *nm* lintel.

dioptría *nf* GB dioptre; US diopter.

dios *nm* god.

diosa *nf* goddess.

dióxido *nm* dioxide.

diploma *nm* diploma.

diplomático,-a *adj* diplomatic. ▶ *nm,f* diplomat.

diputado,-a *nm,f* deputy.

dirección *nf* **1** *(rumbo)* direction; *(sentido)* way. **2** *(en empresa)* management. **3** *(domicilio)* address. **4** *(de coche)* steering. ▪ **dirección electrónica** e-mail address.

directo,-a *adj* direct. • **en directo** *(transmisión)* live.

director,-ra *nm,f* *(gerente)* manager; *(de orquesta)* conductor.

dirigente *adj* *(clase, élite)* ruling. ▶ *nm,f* leader.

dirigir *vt* **1** *(orientar)* to direct. **2** *(negocio)* to manage. **3** *(orquesta)* to conduct. ▶ *vpr* **dirigirse 1** *(ir)* to go. **2** *(hablar)* to address, speak to.

disciplina *nf* discipline.

disco *nm* **1** *(de música)* record. **2** *(en deporte)* discus. **3** *(de ordenador)* disk. ▪ **disco compacto** compact disc; **disco duro** hard disk.

discoteca *nf* nightclub.

discreto,-a *adj* **1** *(callado)* discreet. **2** *(sobrio)* sober.

discriminación *nf* discrimination.

disculpa *nf* apology.

discurso *nm* speech.

discusión *nf* **1** *(disputa)* argument. **2** *(debate)* discussion.

discutir *vt-vi* **1** *(debatir)* to discuss. **2** *(disputar)* to argue.

diseño *nm* design.

disfraz *nm* **1** *(para engañar)* disguise. **2** *(para fiesta)* costume.

disfrutar *vt* to enjoy.

disgusto *nm* upset. • **a disgusto** unwillingly.

disimular *vt (ocultar)* to hide. ► *vi (fingir)* to pretend.

disminuir *vt* to reduce. ► *vi* to decrease, fall.

disparar *vt* 1 *(arma)* to fire. 2 *(balón)* to drive.

disparo *nm* shot.

disponer *vt-vi (colocar)* to arrange. ► *vt (ordenar)* to order. ► *vi (poseer)* to have. ► *vpr* **disponerse** *(prepararse)* to get ready to.

disposición *nf* 1 *(actitud)* disposition. 2 *(colocación)* arrangement. • **a su disposición** at your disposal.

dispositivo *nm* device.

disputar *vt* 1 *(discutir)* to dispute. 2 *(partido)* to play.

disquete *nm* diskette.

disquetera *nf* disk drive.

distancia *nf* distance.

distinguir *vt* 1 *(diferenciar)* to distinguish. 2 *(ver)* to see.

distinto,-a *adj* different.

distracción *nf* 1 *(divertimiento)* amusement. 2 *(despiste)* distraction.

distraer *vt* 1 *(divertir)* to keep amused. 2 *(atención)* to distract. ► *vpr* **distraerse** 1 *(divertirse)* to amuse oneself . 2 *(despistarse)* to get distracted.

distribución *nf* 1 *(reparto)* distribution. 2 *(colocación)* arrangement.

distribuir *vt* 1 *(repartir)* to distribute. 2 *(colocar)* to arrange.

diurno,-a *adj* 1 *(curso, autobús)* daytime. 2 *(animal)* diurnal.

diversidad *nf* diversity.

diversión *nf (gozo)* fun; *(pasatiempo)* pastime.

diversos,-as *adj pl* several, various.

divertir *vt* to amuse. ► *vpr* **divertirse** to enjoy oneself.

dividir *vt* to divide.

divino,-a *adj* divine.

divisa *nf* currency.

divisar *vt* make out.

división *nf* division.

divorcio *nm* divorce.

divulgar *vt* 1 *(dar a conocer)* to make public. 2 *(propagar)* to spread.

doblar *vt* 1 *(duplicar)* to double. 2 *(plegar)* to fold. 3 *(esquina)* to turn. 4 *(película)* to dub.

doble *adj-nm* double.

doce *num* twelve; *(en fechas)* twelfth.

docena *nf* dozen.

doctor,-ra *nm,f* doctor.

documentación *nf* documentation.

documento *nm* document.

dólar *nm* dollar.

doler *vi* to hurt: *me duele la cabeza*, I've got a headache.

dolor *nm (físico, moral)* pain; *(sordo)* ache. ▪ **dolor de cabeza** headache; **dolor de es-**

tómago stomachache; **dolor de garganta** sore throat; **dolor de muelas** toothache.

doméstico,-a *adj* domestic.

domicilio *nm* address.

dominar *vt* **1** *(gen)* to dominate. **2** *(tema)* to master.

domingo *nm* Sunday.

dominical *nm* Sunday newspaper.

dominio *nm* **1** *(poder)* control. **2** *(de tema)* mastery. **3** INFORM domain.

dominó *nm* *(ficha)* domino; *(juego)* dominoes *pl*.

don *nm* *(título)* don.

donante *nmf* donor.

donde *conj* where.

dónde *adv* where.

dondequiera *adv* wherever.

dorado,-a *adj* *(gen)* gold; *(color)* golden.

dormir *vi* to sleep. ▶ *vpr* **dormirse** to go to sleep. • **dormir la siesta** to have a nap.

dormitorio *nm* bedroom.

dorso *nm* back.

dos *num* two; *(en fechas)* second. • **de dos en dos** in twos; **dos puntos** colon.

doscientos,-as *num* two hundred.

dosis *nf* dose.

drama *nm* drama.

dramático,-a *adj* dramatic.

droga *nf* drug. • **droga blanda** soft drug; **droga dura** hard drug.

drogadicto,-a *nm,f* drug addict.

droguería *nf* hardware and household goods shop.

dromedario *nm* dromedary.

ducha *nf* shower. • **darse una ducha** to have a shower.

ducharse *vpr* to have a shower.

duda *nf* doubt. • **sin duda** undoubtedly.

dudar *vi* to hesitate. ▶ *vt* to doubt.

duelo *nm* duel.

duende *nm* elf.

dueño,-a *nm,f* **1** *(propietario)* owner. **2** *(de casa alquilada - hombre)* landlord; *(- mujer)* landlady.

dulce *adj* *(comida, bebida)* sweet.▶ *nm* *(caramelo)* sweet.

duna *nf* dune.

dúo *nm* **1** *(pareja)* duo. **2** *(composición)* duet.

duodécimo,-a *num* twelfth.

dúplex *adj-nm* duplex.

duque *nm* duke.

duquesa *nf* duchess.

duración *nf* duration.

durante *adv* **1** *(a lo largo de un periodo)* for: ***durante todo el día***, all day long. **2** *(dentro de un periodo)* during, in: ***durante la noche***, during the night, in the night.

durar *vi* to last.

duro,-a *adj* *(gen)* hard; *(carne)* tough.

E

ébano *nm* ebony.

ebrio,-a *adj* drunk.

eccema *nm* eczema.

echar *vt* 1 *(lanzar)* to throw. 2 *(del trabajo)* to sack. 3 *(correo)* GB to post; US to mail. ► *vi-vpr* **echar(se) a** + *inf* to begin to: *echar a correr*, to run off. ► *vpr* **echarse** *(tenderse)* to lie down. ● **echar algo a perder** to spoil STH; **echar de menos** to miss; **echarse atrás** 1 *(inclinarse)* to lean back. 2 *(desdecirse)* to back out.

eclipse *nm* eclipse.

eco *nm* echo.

ecología *nf* ecology.

ecológico,-a *adj* 1 *(gen)* ecological. 2 *(cultivo)* organic.

ecologista *nmf* environmentalist.

economía *nf* 1 *(de un país)* economy. 2 *(ciencia)* economics.

económico,-a *adj* 1 *(de la economía)* economic. 2 *(barato)* economical.

ecosistema *nm* ecosystem.

ecuación *nf* equation.

ecuador *nm* equator.

ecuatorial *adj* equatorial.

edad *nf* age: *¿qué edad tiene usted?*, how old are you? ■ **la tercera edad** 1 *(etapa de la vida)* old age. 2 *(gente mayor)* senior citizens.

edición *nf* 1 *(tirada)* edition. 2 *(publicación)* publication. ■ **edición electrónica** electronic publishing.

edificio *nm* building.

editor,-ra *nm,f* 1 *(que publica)* publisher. 2 *(que prepara)* editor. ■ **editor de texto** text editor.

editorial *nm* *(artículo)* editorial, leading article. ► *nf* publishing house, publisher.

edredón *nm* quilt. ■ **edredón nórdico** duvet.

educación *nf* 1 *(enseñanza)* education. 2 *(crianza)* upbringing. 3 *(cortesía)* manners.

educado,-a *adj* polite.

educar *vt* *(enseñar)* to educate.

efectivo,-a *adj* *(eficaz)* effective. ► *nm* **efectivo** cash. ► *nm pl* **efectivos** forces.

efecto *nm* 1 *(gen)* effect. 2 *(impresión)* impression. 3 *(pelota)* spin. ● **en efecto** indeed; **hacer efecto** to take effect. ■ **efecto invernadero** greenhouse effect; **efectos especiales** special effects; **efectos personales** personal belongings.

efectuar *vt* 1 *(maniobra, investigación, etc.)* to carry out. 2 *(pago, viaje, etc.)* to make.

efervescente *adj* 1 *(pastilla)* effervescent. 2 *(bebida)* fizzy.

eficaz *adj* 1 *(que surte efecto)* effective. 2 *(eficiente)* efficient.

eficiente *adj* efficient.
egoísta *adj* selfish, egoistic.
► *nmf* egoist.
eje *nm* **1** *(en geometría, astronomía)* axis. **2** *(de motor)* shaft. **3** *(de ruedas)* axle.
ejecución *nf* execution.
ejecutar *vt* **1** *(orden)* to carry out. **2** *(programa informático)* to run. **3** *(ajusticiar)* to execute.
ejecutivo,-a *adj-nm,f* executive.
ejemplar *nm* **1** *(obra)* copy. **2** *(espécimen)* specimen.
ejemplo *nm* example. • **por ejemplo** for example, for instance.
ejercer *vt* **1** *(profesión etc)* to practise. **2** *(derecho, poder)* to exercise. **3** *(influencia)* to exert.
ejercicio *nm* **1** *(gen)* exercise. **2** *(financiero)* year. • **hacer ejercicio** to exercise.
ejército *nm* army.
el *det* **1** the: *el coche*, the car. **2** **el +** *de* the one: *el de tu amigo*, your friend's. **3 el +** *que* the one: *el que vino ayer*, the one who came yesterday.
él *pron* **1** *(sujeto - persona)* he; *(- cosa, animal)* it. **2** *(después de preposición - persona)* him; *(- cosa, animal)* it. • **de él** *(posesivo)* his: *es de él*, it's his; **él mismo** himself.
elaborar *vt* to make, manufacture.
elástico,-a *adj* elastic.

elección *nf* **1** *(nombramiento)* election. **2** *(opción)* choice. ► *nf pl* **elecciones** elections.
electricidad *nf* electricity.
eléctrico,-a *adj* electric.
electrocutarse *vpr* to be electrocuted.
electrodoméstico *nm* electrical appliance.
electrónico,-a *adj* electronic.
elefante *nm* elephant.
elegante *adj* elegant.
elegir *vt* **1** *(escoger)* to chose. **2** *(por votación)* to elect.
elemental *adj* elementary.
elemento *nm* element.
elevado,-a *adj* *(edificio)* tall; *(montaña, número)* high.
elevar *vt* to raise. ► *vpr* **elevarse** *(ascender - avión)* to climb; *(- globo)* to rise.
eliminación *nf* elimination.
eliminar *vt* **1** *(gen)* to eliminate. **2** *(obstáculo, mancha)* to remove.
ella *pron* **1** *(sujeto - persona)* she; *(- cosa, animal)* it. **2** *(después de preposición - persona)* her; *(- cosa, animal)* it. • **de ella** hers.
ello *pron* it.
ellos,-as *pron* **1** *(sujeto)* they. **2** *(complemento)* them. • **de ellos** theirs: *es de ellas*, it's theirs.
elogio *nm* praise.
embajada *nf* embassy.
embajador,-ra *nm,f* ambassador.

embalaje *nm* packing.
embalar *vt* to pack.
embalse *nm* reservoir.
embarazada *nf* pregnant woman.
embarazo *nm* *(preñez)* pregnancy.
embarcación *nf* boat.
embarcadero *nm* jetty.
embarcar(se) *vt-vpr* to embark.
embargo *nm* **1** *(incautación de bienes)* seizure. **2** *(prohibición de comercio)* embargo. • **sin embargo** however.
embarque *nm* *(de personas)* boarding.
emblema *nm* emblem.
emborrachar *vt* to make drunk. ▶ *vpr* **emborracharse** to get drunk.
emboscada *nf* ambush.
embotellamiento *nm* *(de tráfico)* traffic jam.
embrague *nm* clutch.
embrión *nm* embryo.
embudo *nm* funnel.
embustero,-a *nm,f* liar.
embutido *nm* cold meat.
emergencia *nf* emergency.
emigración *nf* emigration.
emigrante *adj-nmf* emigrant.
emisión *nf* **1** *(de energía, gas)* emission. **2** *(de bonos, acciones)* issue. **3** *(en radio, TV)* broadcast.
emisor *nm* radio transmitter.
emisora *nf* radio station.

emitir *vt* **1** *(sonido, luz, calor)* to emit. **2** *(bonos, acciones)* to issue. **3** *(programa de radio, TV)* to broadcast.
emoción *nf* **1** *(sentimiento)* emotion. **2** *(excitación)* excitement.
emocionante *adj* **1** *(conmovedor)* moving. **2** *(excitante)* exciting.
emocionar *vt* **1** *(conmover)* to move. **2** *(excitar)* to excite. ▶ *vpr* **emocionarse** *(conmoverse)* to be moved.
empacho *nm* indigestion.
empalagoso,-a *adj* *(dulces)* sickly.
empalme *nm* **1** *(de tuberías, cables)* connection. **2** *(de carreteras, vías)* junction.
empanada *nf* pasty.
empanadilla *nf* pasty.
empañarse *vpr* *(cristal)* to steam up.
empapar *vt* to soak.
empaquetar *vt* to pack.
emparedado *nm* sandwich.
empaste *nm* filling.
empatar *vi* *(acabar igualados)* to draw; *(igualar)* to equalize.
empate *nm* tie, draw.
empeine *nm* instep.
empeñar *vt* *(objeto)* to pawn. ▶ *vpr* **empeñarse** *(insistir)* to insist.
empeño *nm* *(insistencia)* determination. •

emperador *nm* emperor.

emperatriz *nf* empress.

empezar *vt-vi* to begin, start.

empinado,-a *adj* steep.

empleado,-a *nm,f (gen)* employee; *(oficinista)* clerk. ▪
empleada de hogar maid.

emplear *vt* to employ.

empleo *nm* **1** *(puesto)* job. **2** *(trabajo)* employment.

empotrado,-a *adj* built-in.

emprender *vt* to undertake.

empresa *nf (compañía)* firm, company.

empresario,-a *nm,f* **1** *(hombre)* businessman; *(mujer)* businesswoman. **2** *(patrón)* employer.

empujar *vt* to push.

empujón *nm* push, shove.

en *prep* **1** *(lugar - gen)* in, at; *(- en el interior)* in, inside; *(- sobre)* on: **en casa**, at home; **en Valencia**, in Valencia; **en el cajón**, in the drawer; **en la mesa**, on the table. **2** *(tiempo - año, mes, estación)* in; *(- día)* on: **en 2004**, in 2004; **en viernes**, on Friday. **3** *(dirección)* into: **entró en su casa**, he went into his house. **4** *(transporte)* by, in: **ir en coche**, to go by car. **5** *(tema, materia)* at, in: **es experto en política**, he's an expert in politics. **6** *(modo)* in: **en voz baja**, in a low voice. ● **en seguida** at once, straight away.

enamorado,-a *adj* in love. ▶
nm,f lover.

enamorarse *vpr* to fall in love.

enano,-a *adj-nm,f* dwarf.

encabezar *vt* **1** *(en escrito)* to head. **2** *(ser líder)* to lead.

encadenar *vt* **1** *(poner cadenas a)* to chain. **2** *(enlazar)* to link.

encajar *vt-vi* to fit.

encaje *nm (tejido)* lace.

encallar *vi* to run aground

encaminarse *vpr* to head.

encantado,-a *adj (contento)* delighted. ● **encantado,-a de conocerle** *fml* pleased to meet you.

encantador,-ra *adj* charming.

encantar *vi*: **me encanta la natación**, I love swimming.

encanto *nm (atractivo)* charm.

encarcelar *vt* to imprison.

encargado,-a *nm,f (responsable)* person in charge; *(de negocio - hombre)* manager; *(- mujer)* manageress.

encargar *vt* **1** *(encomendar)* to entrust. **2** *(solicitar)* to order. ▶ *vpr* **encargarse** to take charge.

encargo *nm* **1** *(recado)* errand; *(tarea)* job. **2** *(de productos)* order. ● **por encargo** to order.

encendedor *nm* lighter.

encender *vt* **1** *(fuego, vela, cigarro)* to light; *(cerilla)* to strike.

2 *(luz, radio, tele)* to turn on, switch on.

encerrar *vt* **1** *(persona - en habitación)* to shut in; *(- en cárcel)* to lock up. **2** *fig (contener)* to contain.

encestar *vi* to score (a basket).

enchufar *vt* *(aparato)* to plug in.

enchufe *nm* *(de aparato - hembra)* socket; *(- macho)* plug.

encía *nf* gum.

encierro *nm* **1** *(protesta)* sit-in. **2** *(de toros)* bullpen.

encima *adv* **1** *(más arriba)* above; *(sobre)* on top. **2** *(consigo)* on me/you/him *etc*: *¿llevas cambio encima?*, do you have any change on you? **3** *(además)* in addition. • **encima de** on; **por encima 1** *(a más altura)* above. **2** *(de pasada)* superficially; **por encima de** above.

encina *nf* evergreen oak.

encoger(se) *vt-vi-vpr* to shrink.

encontrar *vt* **1** *(hallar)* to find. **2** *(creer)* to think. ► *vpr* **encontrarse 1** *(hallarse)* to be. **2** *(personas)* to meet. **3** *(sentirse)* to feel: *me encuentro bien,* I feel fine; *me encuentro mal*, I feel ill.

encubrir *vt* *(delito)* to cover up.

encuentro *nm* **1** *(coincidencia)* encounter. **2** *(reunión)* meeting. **3** *(en deporte)* match.

encuesta *nf* survey.

endibia *nf* endive.

endulzar *vt* *(hacer dulce)* to sweeten.

endurecer(se) *vt-vpr* to harden.

enemigo,-a *adj-nm,f* enemy.

energía *nf* energy. ■ **energía atómica** atomic power; **energía eléctrica** electric power; **energía nuclear** nuclear power; **energía solar** solar power, solar energy.

enero *nm* January.

enfadado,-a *adj* angry.

enfadarse *vpr* to get angry.

enfado *nm* anger.

enfermedad *nf* *(estado de enfermo)* illness; *(patología específica)* disease.

enfermería *nf* **1** *(profesión)* nursing. **2** *(lugar)* infirmary.

enfermero,-a *nm,f* *(hombre)* (male) nurse; *(mujer)* nurse.

enfermo,-a *adj* ill, sick. ► *nm,f* sick person.

enfocar *vt* **1** *(con cámara)* to focus on. **2** *(problema etc)* to approach.

enfrentarse *vpr* **1** *(encararse)* to face up. **2** *(pelearse)* to have a confrontation.

enfrente *adv* opposite. • **enfrente de** opposite.

enfriarse *vpr* **1** *(algo caliente)* to cool down. **2** *(acatarrarse)* catch a cold.

enfurecerse *vpr* to get furious.

enganchar vt (gen) to hook; (animales) to hitch; (vagones) to couple.

engañar vt 1 (gen) to deceive. 2 (mentir) to lie to. 3 (a la pareja) to be unfaithful to.

engaño nm deceit.

engordar vi 1 (persona) to put on weight: *he engordado cinco kilos*, I've put on five kilos. 2 (alimento) to be fattening.

engrasar vt (gen) to lubricate; (con grasa) to grease; (con aceite) to oil.

enhorabuena nf congratulations. • **dar la enhorabuena a** ALGN to congratulate SB.

enigma nm enigma, puzzle.

enjabonar vt to soap.

enjuagar(se) vt-vpr to rinse.

enlace nm 1 (conexión) link. 2 (boda) marriage. 3 (en internet) link.

enlazar vi to connect.

enmienda nf 1 (de error) correction; (de daño) repair. 2 (de texto, ley) amendment.

enojado,-a adj (enfadado) angry; (molesto) annoyed.

enojarse vpr (enfadarse) to get angry; (molestarse) to get annoyed.

enorgullecerse vpr to be proud, feel proud.

enorme adj enormous, huge.

enredadera nf creeper, climbing plant.

enredar vt 1 (enmarañar) to tangle. 2 (dificultar) to complicate. ▶ vi (hacer travesuras) to get up to mischief. ▶ vpr **enredarse** (cuerda, pelo) to get tangled.

enriquecerse vpr to get rich.

enrollado,-a adj fam (persona) cool.

enrollar vt to roll up. ▶ vpr **enrollarse** fam (hablar) to go on and on. • **enrollarse con** ALGN to get off with SB.

ensalada nf salad.

ensaladera nf salad bowl.

ensaladilla nf. ■ **ensaladilla rusa** Russian salad.

ensanchar vt (agrandar) to widen; (prenda) to let out.

ensanche nm 1 (de carretera) widening. 2 (de ciudad) new development.

ensayar vt (obra de teatro) to rehearse; (música) to practise.

ensayo nm 1 (de obra de teatro) rehearsal; (de música) practice. 2 (prueba) test, trial. 3 (literario) essay. ■ **ensayo general** dress rehearsal.

enseguida adv at once, straight away.

enseñanza nf 1 (educación) education. 2 (docencia) teaching.

enseñar vt 1 (en escuela etc) to teach. 2 (mostrar) to show.

ensuciar(se) vt-vpr to get dirty.

entablar *vt (conversación)* to start; *(amistad)* to strike up.

entender *vt* 1 *(comprender)* to understand. 2 *(opinar)* to consider. ► *vi* to know: *¿tú entiendes de motores?*, do you know anything about engines? ► *vpr* **entenderse** *fam (llevarse bien)* to get along well together. • **dar a entender que…** to imply that…

entendido,-a *nm,f* expert.

enterarse *vpr* 1 *(averiguar)* to find out. 2 *(darse cuenta)* to notice. 3 *(comprender)* to understand.

entero,-a *adj (completo)* whole.

enterrar *vt* to bury.

entidad *nf* 1 *(organismo)* body. 2 *(ente, ser)* entity. ▪ **entidad bancaria** bank.

entierro *nm* 1 *(acto)* burial. 2 *(ceremonia)* funeral.

entonación *nf* intonation.

entonces *adv* then.

entorno *nm* environment.

entorpecer *vt (dificultar)* to obstruct, hinder.

entrada *nf* 1 *(acción)* entrance, entry. 2 *(lugar)* entrance. 3 *(en espectáculo - billete)* ticket; *(admisión)* admission. 4 *(pago inicial)* down payment. ► *nf pl* **entradas** receding hairline. • **"Prohibida la entrada"** "No admittance".

entrañable *adj* beloved.

entrañas *nf pl* entrails.

entrar *vi* 1 *(ir adentro)* to come in, go in. 2 *(en una sociedad etc.)* to join. 3 *(encajar)* to fit. 4 *(en fase, etapa)* to enter. 5 *(venir)*: *me entraron ganas de llorar*, I felt like crying.

entre *prep* 1 *(dos términos)* between; *(más de dos términos)* among. 2 *(sumando)* counting: *entre niños y adultos somos doce*, counting children and adults, there are twelve of us. • **entre tanto** meanwhile.

entreacto *nm* interval.

entrecot *nm* entrecôte.

entrega *nf (acción)* handing over; *(de mercancía)* delivery.

entregar *vt* 1 *(dar)* to hand over; *(deberes, solicitud)* to hand in. 2 *(mercancía)* to deliver.

entremés *nm* hors d'oeuvre.

entrenador,-ra *nm,f* trainer, coach.

entrenamiento *nm (acción)* training; *(sesión)* training session.

entrenar(se) *vt-vpr* to train.

entresuelo *nm* mezzanine.

entretanto *adv* meanwhile.

entretener *vt* 1 *(divertir)* to entertain. 2 *(distraer)* to distract. ► *vpr* **entretenerse** 1 *(retrasarse)* to be late. 2 *(divertirse)* keep oneself amused.

entretenido,-a *adj* 1 *(divertido)* entertaining. 2 *(complicado)* timeconsuming.

entretenimiento *nm* entertainment.

entrevista *nf* interview.

entusiasmar *vt* to excite: *me entusiasma la ópera*, I love opera. ► *vpr* **entusiasmarse** to get enthusiastic.

entusiasmo *nm* enthusiasm.

enumerar *vt* to enumerate.

enunciado *nm* statement.

envasar *vt* *(en paquete)* to pack; *(en botella)* to bottle; *(en lata)* to can, tin. • **envasado,-a al vacío** vacuum-packed.

envase *nm* *(recipiente)* container; *(botella)* bottle.

envejecer *vt* *(dar aspecto viejo)* to make look older. ► *vi* *(hacerse viejo)* to grow old.

envenenamiento *nm* poisoning.

envenenarse *vpr* to poison oneself.

enviado,-a *nm,f.* ■ **enviado,-a especial** special correspondent.

enviar *vt* to send.

envidia *nf* envy.

envío *nm* **1** *(acción)* sending. **2** *(remesa)* consignment; *(de mercancía)* dispatch, shipment. ■ **envío contra reembolso** cash on delivery.

envolver *vt* **1** *(cubrir)* to wrap. **2** *(rodear)* to surround. **3** *(implicar)* to involve.

enyesar *vt* *(pierna, brazo)* to put in plaster.

epidemia *nf* epidemic.

episodio *nm* episode.

época *nf* **1** *(período)* time, period. **2** *(del año)* season.

equilibrio *nm* balance. • **mantener el equilibrio** to keep one's balance; **perder el equilibrio** to lose one's balance.

equipaje *nm* luggage, baggage. • **hacer el equipaje** to pack, do the packing. ■ **equipaje de mano** hand luggage.

equipo *nm* **1** *(de personas, jugadores)* team. **2** *(equipamiento)* equipment. **3** *(ordenador)* machine.

equivalente *adj-nm* equivalent.

equivaler *vi* **1** *(ser igual)* to be equivalent. **2** *(significar)* to be tantamount.

equivocación *nf* mistake, error.

equivocarse *vpr* **1** *(no tener razón)* to be mistaken, be wrong. **2** *(cometer un error)* to make a mistake.

era *nf* *(período)* era, age.

erguirse *vpr* to straighten up.

erigir *vt* to erect. ► *vpr* **erigirse** to set oneself up.

erizo *nm* hedgehog. ■ **erizo de mar** sea urchin.

ermita *nf* *(capilla)* chapel.

erosión *nf* erosion.

erótico,-a *adj* erotic.

errar *vt* *(objetivo, disparo)* to miss; *(pronóstico)* to get wrong.

error *nm* mistake, error. • **por error** by mistake.

eructo *nm* belch.

erupción *nf* 1 (*volcánica*) eruption. 2 (*cutánea*) rash.

esbozo *nm* (*dibujo*) sketch.

escabeche *nm* pickle.

escafandra *nf* diving suit.

escala *nf* scale. • **a escala** scale; **hacer escala 1** (*avión*) to stop over. **2** (*barco*) to put in.

escalador,-ra *nm,f* climber.

escalar *vt* to climb.

escalera *nf* 1 (*de edificio*) stairs. 2 (*portátil*) ladder. 3 (*naipes*) run. ▪ **escalera de caracol** spiral staircase; **escalera mecánica** escalator.

escalerilla *nf* (*de barco*) gangway; (*de avión*) steps.

escalofrío *nm* shiver.

escalón *nm* (*peldaño*) step.

escalope *nm* escalope.

escama *nf* scale.

escándalo *nm* 1 (*acto inmoral*) scandal. 2 (*alboroto*) racket.

escanear *vt* to scan.

escáner *nm* scanner.

escapada *nf* 1 *fam* (*viaje*) quick trip. 2 (*en ciclismo*) breakaway.

escapar(se) *vi-vpr* (*lograr salir*) to escape; (*irse corriendo*) to run away. ▶ *vpr* **escaparse 1** (*gas etc*) to leak out. 2 (*autobús etc.*) to miss.

escaparate *nm* shop window.

escape *nm* 1 (*huida*) escape. 2 (*de gas etc*) leak. 3 (*de coche*) exhaust.

escarabajo *nm* beetle.

escarcha *nf* frost.

escarola *nf* GB curly endive; US escarole.

escaso,-a *adj* scarce, scant.

escayola *nf* plaster.

escayolar *vt* to put in plaster.

escena *nf* 1 (*gen*) scene. 2 (*escenario*) stage.

escenario *nm* 1 (*en teatro*) stage. 2 (*de suceso*) scene.

escéptico,-a *adj* GB sceptical; US skeptical.

esclavo,-a *nm,f* slave.

esclusa *nf* (*de canal*) lock; (*compuerta*) sluice gate.

escoba *nf* broom.

escobilla *nf* 1 (*gen*) brush. 2 (*de coche*) windscreen (US windshield) wiper blade.

escocer *vi* (*herida*) to smart.

escocés,-a *adj* Scottish. ▶ *nm,f* (*persona*) Scot.

Escocia *nf* Scotland.

escoger *vt* to choose.

escolar *adj* school.

escolta *nmf* escort.

escombros *nm pl* rubble.

esconder(se) *vt-vpr* to hide.

escopeta *nf* shotgun.

escorpión *nm* scorpion.

escote[1] *nm* (*de vestido*) neckline.

escote[2]. • **pagar a escote** to share the expenses.

escotilla *nf* hatchway.

escozor *nm (picor)* irritation, smarting.

escribir *vt-vi* to write. ► *vpr* **escribirse 1** *(dos personas)* to write to each other. **2** *(palabra)* to spell: *se escribe con "j"*, it's spelt with a "j".

escrito,-a *adj* written.• **por escrito** in writing.

escritor,-ra *nm,f* writer.

escritorio *nm* **1** *(mueble)* writing desk. **2** INFORM desktop.

escrupuloso,-a *adj* **1** *(cuidadoso)* scrupulous. **2** *(aprensivo)* finicky, fussy.

escuadra *nf* **1** *(instrumento)* square. **2** *(de soldados)* squad.

escuchar *vt* **1** *(atender)* to listen to. **2** *(oír)* to hear.

escudo *nm* shield.

escuela *nf* school.

escultor,-ra *nm,f (hombre)* sculptor; *(mujer)* sculptress.

escultura *nf* sculpture.

escupir *vi* to spit.

escurridor *nm* **1** *(colador)* colander. **2** *(de platos)* dish rack.

escurrir *vt (platos)* to drain; *(ropa)* to wring out. ► *vpr* **escurrirse** *(resbalarse)* to slip.

ese,-a *adj* that.

ése,-a *pron* that one.

esencial *adj* essential.

esfera *nf* **1** *(figura)* sphere. **2** *(de reloj)* face.

esforzarse *vpr* to try hard.

esfuerzo *nm* effort.

esgrima *nf* fencing.

esguince *nm* sprain.

eslabón *nm* link.

eslip *nm* briefs, underpants.

eslogan *nm* slogan.

esmalte *nm* enamel. ▪ **esmalte de uñas** nail polish, nail varnish.

esmeralda *nf* emerald.

esmerarse *vpr* to do one's best.

esmoquin *nf* GB dinner jacket; US tuxedo.

eso *pron* that.

esófago *nm* GB oesophagus; US esophagus.

espacial *adj (cohete etc)* space; *(en física)* spatial.

espacio *nm* **1** *(sitio)* space. **2** *(de tiempo)* period. **3** *(en radio, televisión)* programme. ▪ **espacio aéreo** air space.

espada *nf* sword.

espaguetis *nm pl* spaghetti.

espalda *nf* **1** *(parte del cuerpo)* back. **2** *(en natación)* backstroke.

espantapájaros *nm* scarecrow.

espantar *vt* **1** *(asustar)* to frighten, scare. **2** *(ahuyentar)* to frighten away.

espantoso,-a *adj* **1** *(terrible)* frightful, dreadful. **2** *(muy feo)* hideous, frightful.

español,-la *adj* Spanish. ► *nm,f (persona)* Spaniard. ► *nm* **español** *(idioma)* Spanish.

esparadrapo *nm* GB sticking plaster; US Band-Aid®.

espárrago *nm* asparagus.

esparto *nm* esparto grass.

especia *nf* spice.

especial *adj* special.

especialidad *nf* GB speciality; US specialty.

especie *nf* 1 *(de animales, plantas)* species. 2 *(tipo)* kind, sort.

específico,-a *adj* specific.

espectáculo *nm* 1 *(escena)* spectacle, sight. 2 *(de TV, radio etc)* show.

espectador,-ra *nm,f* 1 *(en un estadio)* spectator. 2 *(en teatro, cine)* member of the audience; *(de televisión)* viewer.

espejo *nm* mirror. ▪ **espejo retrovisor** rear-view mirror.

espera *nf* wait.

esperanza *nf* hope. • **perder la esperanza** to lose hope. ▪ **esperanza de vida** life expectancy.

esperar *vt* 1 *(aguardar)* to wait for, await. 2 *(confiar)* to hope for, expect: *espero que sí*, I hope so. 3 *(bebé)* to expect. ▶ *vi* to wait.

esperma *nm* sperm.

espeso,-a *adj* thick.

espía *nmf* spy.

espiga *nf* *(de trigo)* ear; *(de flor)* spike.

espina *nf* 1 *(de planta)* thorn. 2 *(de pez)* fishbone. ▪ **espina dorsal** spine, backbone.

espinacas *nf pl* spinach *sing.*

espinilla *nf* 1 *(tibia)* shinbone. 2 *(grano)* blackhead.

espiral *adj-nf* spiral.

espíritu *nm* spirit.

espléndido,-a *adj* 1 *(magnífico)* splendid, magnificent. 2 *(generoso)* lavish.

esponja *nf* sponge.

espontáneo,-a *adj* spontaneous.

esposas *nf pl* handcuffs.

esposo,-a *nm,f* spouse; *(hombre)* husband; *(mujer)* wife.

espuela *nf* spur.

espuma *nf* *(de mar)* foam; *(de olas)* surf; *(de jabón)* lather; *(de cerveza)* froth. ▪ **espuma de afeitar** shaving foam.

espumadera *nf* skimmer.

espumoso,-a *adj* *(vino)* sparkling.

esquela *nf* death notice.

esqueleto *nm* skeleton.

esquema *nm* *(plan)* outline; *(gráfica)* diagram.

esquí *nm* 1 *(tabla)* ski. 2 *(deporte)* skiing. ▪ **esquí acuático** water-skiing.

esquiar *vi* to ski.

esquimal *adj-nmf* Eskimo.

esquina *nf* corner. • **a la vuelta de la esquina** just around the corner; **doblar la esquina** to turn the corner.

esquivar *vt* 1 *(persona)* to avoid. 2 *(golpe)* to dodge.

estable *adj* stable, steady.

establecer vt to establish. ►
vpr **establecerse** to settle.
establecimiento nm (local)
establishment; (tienda) shop.
establo nm stable.
estación nf 1 (del año)
season. 2 (de tren) station. ■
estación de esquí ski resort; **estación de servicio**
service station.
estacionarse vt-vpr to park.
estadio nm stadium.
estadística nf statistics.
estado nm 1 (gen) state. 2
(médico) condition. ● **estar
en mal estado 1** (alimento)
to be off. 2 (carretera) to be in
poor condition; **estar en estado** to be pregnant. ■ **estado civil** marital status.
estafar vt 1 (timar) to swindle. 2 (defraudar) to defraud.
estalactita nf stalactite.
estalagmita nf stalagmite.
estallar vi 1 (bomba) to explode. 2 (neumático, globo)
to burst. 3 (rebelión, guerra) to
break out.
estancarse vpr 1 (líquido) to
stagnate. 2 (proceso) to come
to a standstill.
estancia nf 1 (permanencia)
stay. 2 (aposento) room.
estanco nm tobacconist's.
estándar adj-nm standard.
estanque nm pool, pond.
estante nm (gen) shelf; (para
libros) bookcase.

estantería nf shelves.
estaño nm tin.
estar vi to be. ► aux **estar +
inf** to be: **estar comiendo**, to
be eating.
estatua nf statue.
estatura nf height.
este adj-nm east.
este,-a adj this.
éste,-a pron this one.
estela nf (de barco) wake; (de
avión) GB vapour trail; US vapor trail.
estelar adj 1 (sideral) stellar.
2 (actuación, elenco) star.
estepa nf steppe.
estéreo adj stereo.
estéril adj sterile.
esternón nm sternum.
esteticista nmf beautician.
estético,-a adj GB aesthetic;
US esthetic.
estetoscopio nm stethoscope.
estilo nm 1 (gen) style. 2 (en
natación) stroke. ● **estilo de
vida** way of life, lifestyle.
estilográfica nf fountain pen.
estimado,-a adj 1 (aprecia-
do) esteemed. 2 (valorado)
valued. ● **estimada señora**
(en carta) Dear Madam; **estimado señor** (en carta) Dear
Sir.
estimar vt 1 (apreciar) to esteem; (objeto) to value. 2 (juzgar) to consider.
estímulo nm 1 stimulus. 2
(aliciente) encouragement.

estirar(se) *vt-vpr* to stretch.

estival *adj* summer.

esto *pron* this.

estofado *nm* stew.

estómago *nm* stomach.

estorbar *vt* **1** *(dificultar)* to hinder. **2** *(molestar)* to annoy. ▶ *vi* to get in the way.

estornudo *nm* sneeze.

estos,-as *adj pl* these.

éstos,-as *pron* these.

estragón *nm* tarragon.

estrangular *vt* to strangle.

estrategia *nf* strategy.

estrechar *vt* **1** *(calle)* to narrow; *(vestido)* to take in. **2** *(abrazar)* to embrace. • **estrechar la mano** to shake hands.

estrecho,-a *adj* **1** *(gen)* narrow; *(vestido, zapatos)* tight. **2** *(amistad etc)* close. ▶ *nm* **estrecho** straits, strait.

estrella *nf* star. ■ **estrella de mar** starfish.

estrellarse *vpr* to crash, smash.

estrenar *vt* **1** *(gen)* to use for the first time; *(ropa)* to wear for the first time. **2** *(obra de teatro)* to open; *(película)* to release.

estreno *nm* **1** *(de cosa)* first use. **2** *(de obra de teatro)* first night, opening night; *(de película)* premiere.

estreñimiento *nm* constipation.

estrés *nm* stress.

estribillo *nm* *(de canción)* chorus.

estribo *nm* stirrup. • **perder los estribos** to lose one's head.

estribor *nm* starboard.

estricto,-a *adj* strict.

estrofa *nf* stanza.

estropajo *nm* scourer.

estropear *vt* **1** *(máquina)* to damage, break. **2** *(plan etc)* to spoil, ruin. ▶ *vpr* **estropearse** **1** *(máquina)* to break down. **2** *(comida)* to go off.

estructura *nf* structure.

estruendo *nm* great noise, din.

estuario *nm* estuary.

estuche *nm* case, box.

estudiante *nmf* student.

estudiar *vt-vi* to study.

estudio *nm* **1** *(gen)* study. **2** *(apartamento, oficina; de cine, televisión)* studio. ▶ *nm pl* **estudios** studies, education.

estufa *nf* heater

estupendo,-a *adj* wonderful.

estúpido,-a *adj* stupid. ▶ *nm,f* idiot.

etapa *nf* **1** *(gen)* stage. **2** *(en competición)* leg, stage.

eterno,-a *adj* eternal, everlasting.

ético,-a *adj* ethical.

etiqueta *nf* **1** *(rótulo)* label. **2** *(formalidad)* etiquette.

eucalipto *nm* eucalyptus.
euforia *nf* euphoria, elation.
euro *nm* euro.
Europa *nf* Europe.
europeo,-a *adj-nm,f* European.
evacuar *vt* to evacuate.
evadir *vt* (*capital*) to evade. ▶ *vpr* **evadirse** (*escaparse*) to escape.
evaluar *vt* to evaluate, assess.
evaporar(se) *vt-vpr* to evaporate.
evasión *nf* escape.
eventual *nmf* casual worker, temporary worker.
evidencia *nf* obviousness.
evidente *adj* evident, obvious.
evitar *vt* to avoid.
evolución *nf* (*gen*) evolution; (*de enfermedad*) development; (*de enfermo*) progress.
evolucionar *vi* (*gen*) to evolve; (*enfermedad*) to develop; (*enfermo*) progress.
exacto,-a *adj* exact, accurate
exagerar *vt-vi* to exaggerate.
examen *nm* exam, examination. ■ **examen de conducir** driving test; **examen médico** check-up, medical.
examinar *vt* **1** (*estudiante*) to examine. **2** (*considerar*) to look into, consider.
excavar *vt* (*gen*) to dig; (*en arqueología*) to excavate.

excelente *adj* excellent.
excepción *nf* exception.
excepcional *adj* exceptional.
excepto *adv* except, apart from.
exceso *nm* (*demasía*) excess; (*de mercancía*) surplus. ■ **exceso de equipaje** excess baggage; **exceso de velocidad** speeding.
excitar *vt* **1** (*gen*) to excite. **2** (*emociones*) to stir up.
exclamación *nf* exclamation.
exclusivo,-a *adj* exclusive.
excursión *nf* excursion, outing.
excursionista *nmf* (*turista*) tripper; (*a pie*) hiker.
excusa *nf* excuse.
exhaustivo,-a *adj* exhaustive, thorough.
exhibición *nf* **1** (*exposición*) exhibition. **2** (*de película*) showing.
exhibir *vt* (*mostrar*) to exhibit, put on, show.
exigente *adj* demanding.
exigir *vt* (*pedir*) to demand; (*necesitar*) to require, demand.
exilio *nm* exile.
existencia *nf* existence. ▶ *nf pl* **existencias** inventory, stocks. ● **en existencia** in stock.
existir *vi* **1** (*ser real*) to exist. **2** (*haber*) to be.
éxito *nm* success. ● **tener éxito** to be successful.

exótico,-a *adj* exotic.
expedición *nf* **1** *(viaje, grupo)* expedition. **2** *(envío)* shipping.
expedir *vt* **1** *(documento)* to issue. **2** *(carta, paquete)* to dispatch.
experiencia *nf* experience.
experimentar *vt* **1** *(probar)* to test. **2** *(sentir)* to experience; *(cambio)* to undergo.
experimento *nm* experiment.
experto,-a *adj-nm,f* expert.
explicación *nf* explanation.
explicar *vt* to explain.
explorador,-ra *nm,f* explorer.
explorar *vt* to explore.
explosión *nf* explosion.
explosivo *nm* explosive.
explotación *nf* exploitation.
explotar *vt* *(sacar provecho de)* to exploit; *(mina)* to work; *(tierra)* to cultivate. ► *vi (explosionar)* to explode.
exponer *vt* **1** *(explicar)* to explain. **2** *(mostrar)* to show.
exportación *nf* export.
exportar *vt* to export.
exposición *nf* **1** *(de arte)* exhibition. **2** *(de fotografía)* exposure.
expresar(se) *vt-vpr* to express (oneself).
expresión *nf* expression.
expreso *nm* *(tren)* express train, express.
exprimir *vt* to squeeze.
expulsar *vt* **1** *(gen)* to expel. **2** *(jugador)* to send off.

expulsión *nf* **1** *(gen)* expulsion. **2** *(de jugador)* sending off.
exquisito,-a *adj* delicious.
extender *vt* **1** *(gen)* to extend. **2** *(cheque)* to make out. **3** *(mantequilla, pintura)* to spread.
extensión *nf* **1** *(gen)* extension. **2** *(dimensión)* extent.
exterior *adj* **1** *(de fuera)* exterior, outer. **2** *(extranjero)* foreign. ► *nm* exterior, outside.
externo,-a *adj* external, outward. • **"Para uso externo"** "External use only".
extinción *nf* extinction.
extintor *nm* fire extinguisher.
extra *adj* **1** *(adicional)* extra. **2** *(superior)* top. ► *nmf (actor)* extra. ► *nm* **1** *(gasto)* extra expense. **2** *(plus)* bonus.
extracto *nm* **1** *(substancia)* extract. **2** *(resumen)* summary. ■ **extracto de cuenta** statement of account.
extraer *vt* to extract.
extranjero,-a *adj* foreign. ► *nm,f* foreigner. • **vivir en el extranjero** to live abroad.
extraño,-a *adj* **1** *(raro)* strange. **2** *(desconocido)* alien, foreign.
extraordinario,-a *adj* extraordinary.
extraviado,-a *adj* missing, lost.
extremo,-a *adj* extreme. ► *nm* **extremo** **1** *(límite)* extreme; *(punta)* end. **2** *(en deporte)* wing.

F

fa *nf (nota)* F.
fábrica *nf* factory.
fabricar *vt (crear)* to make; *(en fábrica)* to manufacture.
fabuloso,-a *adj* fabulous.
fachada *nf* façade, front.
fácil *adj* easy.
facilitar *vt* 1 *(simplificar)* to make easy. 2 *(proporcionar)* to provide.
factor *nm* factor.
factura *nf* bill.
facturar *vt* 1 *(cobrar)* to invoice; *(vender)* to have a turnover of. 2 *(equipaje)* to check in.
facultad *nf* 1 *(capacidad)* faculty. 2 *(de universidad)* faculty.
faena *nf* 1 *(tarea)* job. 2 *fam (mala pasada)* dirty trick.
faisán *nm* pheasant.
faja *nf (de mujer)* girdle.
fajo *nm (de billetes)* wad.
falda *nf* 1 *(prenda)* skirt. 2 *(regazo)* lap. 3 *(ladera)* slope. ▪ **falda pantalón** culottes.
fallar[1] *vt (tiro, penalty)* to miss. ▶ *vi (no funcionar)* to fail
fallar[2] *vt (premio)* to award.
fallecimiento *nm* death.
fallo[1] *nm* 1 *(error)* mistake; *(fracaso)* failure. 2 *(defecto)* fault.
fallo[2] *nm* 1 *(de tribunal)* judgement. 2 *(premio)* awarding.

falsedad *nf* 1 *(hipocresía)* falseness. 2 *(mentira)* falsehood.
falsificar *vt* to forge.
falso,-a *adj* false, untrue.
falta *nf* 1 *(carencia)* lack, shortage. 2 *(ausencia)* absence. 3 *(error)* mistake: **falta de ortografía**, spelling mistake. 4 *(delito menor)* GB misdemeanour; US misdemeanor. 5 *(en fútbol)* foul; *(en tenis)* fault. ● **hacer falta** to be necessary: *no hace falta preguntar*, there is no need to ask; **sin falta** without fail. ▪ **falta de educación** bad manners.
faltar *vi* 1 *(cosa)* to be missing; *(persona)* to be absent. 2 *(haber poco)* to be needed: *me falta azúcar*, I haven't got enough sugar. 3 *(no acudir)* to miss. 4 *(quedar)* to be left: **faltan dos semanas para el examen**, there are two weeks to go till the exam. ● **¡no faltaba más!** *(por supuesto)* of course!
fama *nf (renombre)* fame, renown. ● **tener buena fama** to have a good name; **tener mala fama** to have a bad name.
familia *nf* 1 *(parientes)* family. 2 *(prole)* children.
famoso,-a *adj* famous.
fan *nmf* fan.
fanático,-a *adj-nm,f* fanatic.
fango *nm (barro)* mud.
fantasía *nf* fantasy.

fantasma *nm (espectro)* ghost.
fantástico,-a *adj* fantastic.
faringe *nf* pharynx.
farmacéutico,-a *adj* pharmaceutical. ▶ *nm,f (de farmacia)* GB chemist; US druggist, pharmacist.
farmacia *nf (tienda)* GB chemist's; US drugstore, pharmacy.
faro *nm* 1 *(torre)* lighthouse. 2 *(en coche)* headlight.
farol *nm (de luz)* lantern; *(farola)* streetlamp, streetlight.
farola *nf* streetlight, streetlamp.
fascículo *nm* part, GB instalment; US installment.
fascinante *adj* fascinating.
fase *nf* 1 *(etapa)* stage. 2 *(en física)* phase.
fastidiar *vt* 1 *(molestar)* to annoy, bother. 2 *(dañar)* to hurt. ▶ *vpr* **fastidiarse** *(aguantarse)* to put up with: *si no le gusta que se fastidie*, if he doesn't like it that's tough.
fatal *adj* 1 *(inexorable)* fateful. 2 *(mortal)* deadly, fatal. 3 *fam (muy malo)* awful, terrible. ▶ *adv fam* badly, terribly: *me siento fatal*, I feel awful.
fatiga *nf (cansancio)* fatigue.
fauna *nf* fauna.
favor *nm* GB favour; US favor. • **por favor** please;
favorable *adj* GB favourable; US favorable; *(condiciones)* suitable.

favorecer *vt* 1 *(ayudar)* GB to favour; US to favor. 2 *(agraciar)* to suit.
favorito,-a *adj-nm,f* GB favourite; US favorite.
fax *nm* fax. • **enviar por fax** to fax.
fe *nf* faith. • **de buena fe** in good faith.
febrero *nm* February.
fecha *nf* 1 *(día, mes, etc)* date. 2 *(día)* day. • **hasta la fecha** to date. ▪ **fecha de caducidad** best before date: *"Fecha de caducidad..."*, "Best before...".
fecundación *nf* fertilization. ▪ **fecundación in vitro** in vitro fertilization.
federación *nf* federation.
felicidad *nf* happiness. • **¡felicidades!** congratulations!
felicitación *nf (tarjeta)* greetings card.
felicitar *vt* to congratulate.
feliz *adj* 1 *(contento)* happy. 2 *(acertado)* fortunate.
felpa *nf* felt.
felpudo *nm* doormat.
femenino,-a *adj (gen)* feminine; *(sexo)* female.
fenomenal *adj* 1 *(extraordinario)* phenomenal. 2 *fam (fantástico)* fantastic, terrific.
fenómeno *nm* 1 *(hecho)* phenomenon. 2 *(prodigio)* genius.
feo,-a *adj* ugly.
féretro *nm* coffin.

feria *nf* 1 *(exhibición)* fair. 2 *(fiesta)* fair, festival. ■ **feria de muestras** trade fair.

fermentar *vi* to ferment.

feroz *adj* fierce, ferocious.

ferretería *nf (tienda)* GB ironmonger's; US hardware store.

ferrocarril *nm* GB railway; US railroad.

fértil *adj* fertile.

fertilizante *nm* fertilizer.

festejo *nm (celebración)* celebration.

festival *nm* festival.

festivo,-a *adj* 1 *(alegre)* festive. 2 *(agudo)* witty.

fiable *adj* reliable.

fiambre *nm* cold meat.

fiambrera *nf* lunch box.

fianza *nf* 1 *(depósito)* deposit, security. 2 *(para acusado)* bail. • **bajo fianza** on bail.

fiar *vt* to sell on credit. ► *vpr* **fiarse** to trust.

fibra *nf* GB fibre; US fiber.

ficción *nf* fiction.

ficha *nf* 1 *(tarjeta)* index card; *(datos)* file. 2 *(de máquina)* token. 3 *(en juegos)* counter; *(de ajedrez)* piece, man; *(de dominó)* domino.

fichar *vt* 1 *(anotar)* to put on an index card, put on a file. 2 *(futbolista etc)* to sign up. ► *vi (al entrar)* to clock in; *(al salir)* to clock out. • **estar fichado,-a por la policía** to have a police record.

fichero *nm* 1 *(de ordenador)* file. 2 *(archivo)* card index.

fidelidad *nf* 1 *(lealtad)* fidelity. 2 *(exactitud)* accuracy.

fideo *nm* noodle.

fiebre *nf* fever. • **tener fiebre** GB to have a temperature; US to have a fever.

fiel *adj* 1 *(leal)* faithful. 2 *(exacto)* accurate.

fieltro *nm* felt.

fiera *nf* 1 *(animal)* wild animal. 2 *(persona)* beast, brute. 3 *(genio)* wizard.

fiesta *nf* 1 *(día festivo)* holiday. 2 *(celebración)* party. ■ **la fiesta nacional** bullfighting.

figura *nf* figure.

figurarse *vpr (imaginarse)* to imagine.

fijador *nm (laca)* hair-spray; *(gomina)* hair gel.

fijar *vt* 1 *(sujetar)* to fix, fasten. 2 *(pegar)* to stick. 3 *(establecer)* to set. ► *vpr* **fijarse** 1 *(darse cuenta)* to notice. 2 *(poner atención)* to pay attention.

fijo,-a *adj* 1 *(sujeto)* fixed, fastened. 2 *(permanente)* fixed, permanent.

fila *nf* 1 *(línea)* line. 2 *(en cine, clase)* row. • **en fila india** in single file.

filete *nm (de carne, pescado)* fillet; *(solomillo)* sirloin.

filial *adj-nf (empresa)* subsidiary.

filmar *vt (gen)* to film; *(escena, película)* to shoot.

filo nm edge.
filosofía nf philosophy.
filósofo,-a nm,f philosopher.
filtro nm filter.
fin nm 1 *(final)* end. 2 *(objetivo)* purpose, aim. • **a fin de** in order to; **a fin de que** so that; **al fin y al cabo** when all's said and done; **en fin** anyway; **¡por fin!** at last! ▪ **fin de año** New Year's Eve; **fin de semana** weekend.
final adj final. ► nm *(conclusión)* end. ► nf *(en competición)* final.
finalizar vt-vi to end, finish.
financiar vt to finance.
finanzas nm pl finances.
finca nf property, estate. ▪ **finca urbana** building.
fingir vt to feign.
fino,-a adj 1 *(gen)* fine. 2 *(alimento)* fine, choice. 3 *(educado)* refined, polite. ► nm **fino** *(vino)* dry sherry. • **no estar fino** *(de salud)* 1 not to be feeling well. 2 *(agudo, centrado)* not to be on the ball.
firma nf 1 *(autógrafo)* signature. 2 *(acto)* signing. 3 *(empresa)* firm.
firmar vt to sign.
firme adj firm, steady.
fiscal adj fiscal. ► nmf GB public prosecutor; US district attorney.
física nf physics.
físico,-a adj physical.

flaco,-a adj skinny.
flan nm caramel custard, crème caramel.
flash nm flash.
flato nm stitch.
flauta nf flute. ▪ **flauta dulce** recorder.
flecha nf arrow.
flemón nm gumboil, abscess.
flequillo nm GB fringe; US bangs pl.
flexible adj flexible.
flexo nm desk lamp.
flojo,-a adj 1 *(suelto)* loose. 2 *(débil)* weak.
flor nf flower.
floreciente adj flourishing.
florero nm vase.
floristería nf florist's.
flota nf fleet.
flotador nm 1 *(para pescar)* float. 2 *(de niño)* rubber ring.
flotar vi to float.
flote nm. • **salir a flote** 1 *(recuperarse)* to get back on one's feet. 2 *(descubrirse)* to emerge.
fluido,-a adj 1 *(sustancia)* fluid. 2 *(lenguaje)* fluent. ► nm **fluido** fluid. ▪ **fluido eléctrico** current.
flúor nm fluorine.
fluorescente adj fluorescent. ► nm fluorescent light.
foca nf *(animal)* seal.
foco nm 1 *(centro)* centre, focal point. 2 *(en fotografía, física)* focus. 3 *(en teatro)* spotlight; *(en estadio)* floodlight.

folleto *nm (prospecto)* leaflet; *(explicativo)* instruction leaflet; *(turístico)* brochure.

fomentar *vt (industria, turismo)* to promote; *(desarrollo, ahorro)* to encourage.

fonda *nf* **1** *(para comer)* restaurant. **2** *(para alojarse)* guest house.

fondo *nm* **1** *(parte más baja)* bottom. **2** *(parte más lejana)* end, back. **3** *(segundo término)* background. ► *nm pl* **fondos** *(dinero)* funds. • **a fondo** thoroughly; **en el fondo** deep down, at heart. ■ **fondo del mar** sea bed.

fontanero,-a *nm,f* plumber.

footing *nm* jogging.

forestal *adj* forest.

forma *nf* **1** *(figura)* form, shape. **2** *(manera)* way. **3** *(condiciones físicas)* form. • **de forma que** so that; **de todas formas** anyway; **estar en forma** to be fit. ■ **forma de pago** method of payment; **forma física** physical fitness.

formación *nf* **1** *(gen)* formation. **2** *(educación)* training.

formal *adj* **1** *(serio)* serious. **2** *(cumplidor)* reliable, dependable.

formalidad *nf (trámite)* formality.

formar *vt* **1** *(gen)* to form. **2** *(educar)* to educate; *(en técnicas)* to train.

formatear *vt* to format.

formidable *adj (maravilloso)* wonderful.

fórmula *nf* formula.

formulario *nm (documento)* form.

forofo,-a *nm,f* fan.

forrar *vt* **1** *(por dentro)* to line. **2** *(por fuera)* to cover. ► *vpr* **forrarse** *fam (de dinero)* to make a packet.

forro *nm* **1** *(interior)* lining. **2** *(funda)* cover.

fortaleza *nf* **1** *(vigor)* strength. **2** *(castillo)* fortress.

fortuna *nf* **1** *(suerte)* luck. **2** *(capital)* fortune.

forzar *vt* to force.

fosa *nf* **1** *(sepultura)* grave. **2** *(hoyo)* pit. ■ **fosas nasales** nostrils.

fósforo *nm* **1** *(elemento)* phosphorus. **2** *(cerilla)* match.

fósil *nm* fossil.

foso *nm (gen)* pit; *(de castillo etc.)* moat.

foto *nf fam* photo. • **hacer una foto** to take a photo.

fotocopia *nf* photocopy.

fotografía *nf* **1** *(proceso)* photography. **2** *(retrato)* photograph.

fotógrafo,-a *nm,f* photographer.

fracaso *nm* failure.

fractura *nf* fracture.

frágil *adj* **1** *(delicado)* fragile. **2** *(débil)* frail.

fragmento *nm* **1** *(pedazo)* fragment. **2** *(literario)* passage.

fraile *nm* friar.

frambuesa *nf* raspberry.

francés,-esa *adj* French. ► *nm,f (persona)* French person. ► *nm* **francés** *(idioma)* French.

Francia *nf* France.

franela *nf* flannel.

franja *nf* band, strip.

franquear *vt (carta)* to frank. • **a franquear en destino** postage paid.

franqueo *nm* postage.

frasco *nm* flask.

frase *nf* **1** *(oración)* sentence. **2** *(expresión)* phrase.

fraterno,-a *adj* fraternal, brotherly.

fraude *nm* fraud. ▪ **fraude fiscal** tax evasion.

frecuencia *nf* frequency.

frecuente *adj* **1** *(repetido)* frequent. **2** *(usual)* common.

fregadero *nm* kitchen sink.

fregar *vt* **1** *(lavar)* to wash. **2** *(frotar)* to scrub. **3** *(suelo)* to mop. • **fregar los platos** to do the washing up.

fregona *nf (utensilio)* mop.

freidora *nf* fryer.

freír *vt* to fry.

frenar *vt-vi* to brake.

freno *nm* **1** *(de vehículo)* brake. **2** *(de caballería)* bit.

frente *nm* front. ► *nf* forehead. ► *adv* **frente a** in front of, opposite. • **al frente de** at the head of; **frente a frente** face to face.

fresa *nf* strawberry.

fresco,-a *adj* **1** *(gen)* cool. **2** *(comida)* fresh. **3** *(desvergonzado)* cheeky, shameless. ► *nm* **fresco** **1** *(frescor)* fresh air. **2** *(pintura)* fresco. • **hacer fresco** to be chilly.

fresno *nm* ash tree.

fresón *nm* large strawberry.

frialdad *nf* coldness.

fricción *nf* **1** *(gen)* friction. **2** *(friega)* rubbing.

frigorífico *nm* refrigerator, fridge.

frío,-a *adj* cold. ► *nm* **frío** cold. • **hacer frío** to be cold; **tener frío, pasar frío** to be cold.

frito,-a *adj (comida)* fried. ► *nm pl* **fritos** fried food *sing*.

frontal *adj* **1** *(choque)* head-on. **2** *(oposición)* direct.

frontera *nf (geográfica)* frontier; *(entre países)* border.

frotar *vt* to rub.

frustración *nf* frustration.

fruta *nf* fruit. ▪ **fruta del tiempo** seasonal fruit.

frutal *nm* fruit tree.

frutería *nf* fruit shop.

frutero *nm* fruit bowl.

fruto *nm* fruit. ▪ **frutos secos** **1** *(almendras etc)* nuts. **2** *(pasas etc)* dried fruit.

fuego *nm* **1** *(gen)* fire. **2** *(lumbre)* light. **3** *(fogón de cocina)*

futuro

burner, ring. • **a fuego lento 1** *(cocinar)* on a low flame. **2** *(al horno)* in a slow oven. • **¿me da fuego?** have you got a light? ▪ **fuegos artificiales** fireworks.

fuente *nf* **1** *(manantial)* spring. **2** *(artificial)* fountain. **3** *(recipiente)* serving dish. **4** *(de información)* source.

fuera *adv* **1** *(gen)* out, outside. **2** *(en otro lugar)* away; *(en el extranjero)* abroad. • **fuera de combate** knocked out. ▪ **fuera de juego** offside.

fuerte *adj* **1** *(gen)* strong. **2** *(intenso)* severe. **3** *(sonido)* loud. **4** *(golpe)* heavy. ► *nm (fortificación)* fort.

fuerza *nf* strength. • **a la fuerza** by force. ▪ **fuerza de voluntad** willpower **fuerzas del orden** police force.

fuga *nf* **1** *(escapada)* escape. **2** *(de gas, líquido)* leak.

fugarse *vpr* to flee, escape.

fumador,-ra *adj* smoking. ► *nm,f* smoker.

fumar(se) *vt-vi-vpr* to smoke. • **"No fumar"** "No smoking".

función *nf* **1** *(gen)* function. **2** *(espectáculo)* performance. • **en función de** according to.

funcionamiento *nm* operation, working.

funcionar *vi* to work. • **"No funciona"** "Out of order".

funcionario,-a *nm,f* civil servant.

funda *nf* **1** *(flexible)* cover. **2** *(rígida)* case. ▪ **funda de almohada** pillowcase.

fundación *nf* foundation.

fundador,-ra *nm,f* founder.

fundamental *adj* fundamental.

fundamento *nm* basis, grounds.

fundar *vt* **1** *(crear)* to found; *(erigir)* to raise. **2** *(basar)* to base, found.

fundir *vt* **1** *(un sólido)* to melt. **2** *(metal)* to cast; *(hierro)* to smelt. **3** *(bombilla, plomos)* to blow.

funeral *nm* **1** *(entierro)* funeral. **2** *(ceremonia)* memorial service.

funicular *nm* funicular railway.

furgoneta *nf* van.

furioso,-a *adj* furious.

fusible *nm* fuse.

fusil *nm* rifle.

fusilar *vt (ejecutar)* to shoot.

fusión *nf* **1** *(de metales)* fusion; *(de hielo)* thawing. **2** *(de empresas)* merger.

fútbol *nm* soccer; GB football.

futbolín *nm* GB table football, US table soccer.

futbolista *nmf* soccer player; GB footballer, football player.

futuro,-a *adj* future. ► *nm* **futuro** future.

G

gabardina *nf* raincoat.
gafas *nf pl* glasses. ▪ **gafas de sol** sunglasses.
gai *adj-nmf* gay.
gaita *nf* bagpipes *pl*.
gajo *nm (de naranja)* section.
gala *nf (espectáculo)* show: *cena de gala*, gala dinner; *traje de gala*, evening dress.
galardón *nm* award.
galaxia *nf* galaxy.
galería *nf* gallery. ▪ **galería de arte** art gallery; **galerías comerciales** GB shopping arcade *sing*; US mall.
Gales (País de) *nm* Wales.
galés,-a *adj* Welsh. ► *nm,f (hombre)* Welshman; *(mujer)* Welshwoman. ► *nm* **galés** *(idioma)* Welsh.
galgo *nm* greyhound.
gallego,-a *adj-nm,f* Galician. ► *nm* **gallego** *(idioma)* Galician.
galleta *nf* GB biscuit; US cookie. ▪ **galleta salada** cracker.
gallina *nf (ave)* hen.
gallinero *nm* **1** *(corral)* henhouse. **2** *(en teatro)* the gods.
gallo *nm* **1** *(ave)* cock, rooster. **2** *(nota falsa)* false note.
galón *nm (distintivo)* stripe.
galopar *vi* to gallop.
gama *nf (variedad)* range.

gamba *nf* GB prawn; US shrimp.
gamberro,-a *nm,f* hooligan.
gamo *nm* fallow deer.
gana *nf* wish, desire: *el equipo jugó sin ganas*, the team played half-heartedly. • **de buena gana** willingly; **de mala gana** reluctantly; **dar la gana** to want: *no me da la gana*, I don't want to; **tener ganas de** to want, feel like.
ganadería *nf* **1** *(cría)* livestock farming. **2** *(ganado)* livestock.
ganado *nm* livestock.
ganador,-ra *nm,f* winner.
ganancia *nf* gain, profit.
ganar *vt* **1** *(premio, concurso)* to win. **2** *(dinero)* to earn. **3** *(a un contrincante)* to beat. • **salir ganando** to do well.
gancho *nm* hook.
ganga *nf* bargain.
gangrena *nf* gangrene.
gángster *nm* gangster.
ganso *nm* goose; *(macho)* gander.
garaje *nm* garage.
garantía *nf* guarantee.
garbanzo *nm* chickpea.
garganta *nf* **1** throat. **2** *(desfiladero)* gorge.
garra *nf (de león, oso, etc.)* claw; *(de águila, halcón, etc.)* talon.
garrafa *nf* container.
gas *nm* gas.
gasa *nf* gauze.

gaseosa *nf* fizzy lemonade.

gaseoso,-a *adj* **1** *(estado)* gaseous. **2** *(bebida)* carbonated, fizzy.

gasoil *nm* diesel, diesel oil.

gasóleo *nm* diesel, diesel oil.

gasolina *nf* GB petrol; US gas, gasoline. • **echar gasolina** to put some petrol in. ▪ **gasolina normal** two-star petrol; **gasolina sin plomo** lead-free petrol; **gasolina súper** four-star petrol.

gasolinera *nf* GB petrol station; US gas station.

gastar *vt* **1** *(dinero)* to spend. **2** *(usar)* to use.

gasto *nm* **1** *(de dinero)* expenditure, expense. **2** *(de agua, luz)* consumption. • **con todos los gastos pagados** all expenses paid.

gastronomía *nf* gastronomy.

gatear *vi* to crawl.

gatillo *nm (de arma)* trigger.

gato,-a *nm,f (animal)* cat. ▶ *nm* **gato** *(de coche)* jack. • **a gatas** on all fours.

gaviota *nf* gull.

gazpacho *nm* cold tomato soup.

gel *nm* gel.

gelatina *nf* **1** *(sustancia)* gelatine. **2** *(de fruta)* jelly.

gemelo,-a *adj-nm,f (hermano)* twin. ▶ *nm* **gemelo** *(músculo)* calf muscle. ▶ *nm pl* **geme-** los **1** *(de camisa)* cufflinks. **2** *(prismáticos)* binoculars.

gen *nm* gene.

generación *nf* generation.

general *adj* general. ▶ *nm (oficial)* general. • **en general** in general; **por lo general** generally.

generar *vt* to generate.

género *nm* **1** *(clase)* sort: *es único en su género*, it's unique of its kind. **2** *(gramatical)* gender. **3** *(especie)* genus. **4** *(en literatura)* genre. **5** *(tela)* cloth. **6** *(producto)* merchandise. ▪ **géneros de punto** knitwear.

generoso,-a *adj* generous.

genético,-a *adj* genetic.

genial *adj* brilliant.

genio *nm* **1** *(carácter)* temper: *tiene mal genio*, he's bad tempered. **2** *(persona)* genius. **3** *(criatura imaginaria)* genie.

gente *nf* people.

gentileza *nf* **1** *(elegancia)* grace. **2** *(cortesía)* politeness. • **por gentileza de** by courtesy of.

gentío *nm* crowd.

genuino,-a *adj* genuine, real.

geografía *nf* geography.

geología *nf* geology.

geometría *nf* geometry.

geranio *nm* geranium.

gerente *nmf (hombre)* manager; *(mujer)* manager, manageress.

germen *nm* germ.

gerundio *nm* gerund.

gesticular *vi* to gesticulate.
gestión *nf* 1 *(negociación)* negotiation. 2 *(de negocio)* administration, management. 3 *(trámite)* step.
gesto *nm* 1 *(gen)* gesture. 2 *(con la cara)* expression.
gestor,-ra *nm,f* agent.
gestoría *nf* business agency.
gigante,-a *adj-nm,f* giant.
gimnasia *nf* gymnastics. • **hacer gimnasia** to exercise, work out. ▪ **gimnasia rítmica** rhythmic gymnastics.
gimnasio *nm* gym(nasium).
ginebra *nf* gin.
ginecólogo,-a *nm,f* GB gynaecologist; US gynecologist.
gira *nf* *(artística)* tour.
girar *vi* 1 *(dar vueltas)* to rotate, revolve; *(rápidamente)* to spin. 2 *(torcer)* to turn. 3 *(conversación)* GB to centre around; US to center round.
girasol *nm* sunflower.
giro *nm* 1 *(vuelta)* turn. 2 *(de dinero, postal)* money order. 3 *(frase idiomática)* turn of phrase.
gitano,-a *adj-nm,f* gypsy.
glaciar *nm* glacier.
glándula *nf* gland.
global *adj* total.
globo *nm* 1 *(esfera)* globe, sphere. 2 *(de aire)* balloon. ▪ **globo ocular** eyeball; **globo terráqueo** globe.
glóbulo *nm* 1 globule. 2 *(en sangre)* corpuscle.

gloria *nf* 1 *(triunfo, honor)* glory. 2 *(fama)* fame.
glorieta *nf* 1 *(rotonda)* GB roundabout; US traffic circle. 2 *(en jardín)* arbour, bower.
glorioso,-a *adj* glorious.
glucosa *nf* glucose.
gobernar *vt* *(país)* to govern.
gobierno *nm* *(de país)* government.
gol *nm* goal. • **marcar un gol** to score a goal.
golf *nm* golf.
golfo *nm* *(bahía)* gulf.
golondrina *nf* swallow.
golosinas *nf* GB sweets; US candy *sing.*
goloso,-a *adj* sweet-toothed.
golpe *nm* 1 *(porrazo)* blow, knock. 2 *(ruido)* knock, bang. 3 *(en coche)* bump. 4 *(desgracia)* blow. • **de golpe** suddenly; **no dar golpe** not to do a thing. ▪ **golpe de Estado** coup d'état.
golpear *vt* to hit.
goma *nf* 1 *(material)* rubber. 2 *(de borrar)* GB rubber; US eraser. 3 *(tira elástica)* elastic band.
gomina *nf* hair gel.
gordo,-a *adj* 1 *(persona, cara)* fat. 2 *(libro, jersey)* thick. 3 *(accidente, problema)* serious. ▶ *nm* **gordo** *(en lotería)* first prize, jackpot.
gorila *nm* gorilla.
gorra *nf* *(con visera)* cap; *(de bebé)* bonnet. • **de gorra** *fam* free.

gorrión *nm* sparrow.

gorro *nm* **1** *(de lana)* hat. **2** *(de bebé)* bonnet.

gota *nf* **1** *(de líquido)* drop. **2** *(enfermedad)* gout.

gotera *nf* leak.

gótico,-a *adj* Gothic.

gozar *vi* to enjoy oneself.

grabación *nf* recording.

grabado *nm* **1** *(técnica)* engraving. **2** *(ilustración)* engraving, print.

grabadora *nf* recorder.

grabar *vt* **1** *(en piedra)* to engrave. **2** *(sonido, imagen)* to record. **3** INFORM to save.

gracia *nf* **1** *(donaire)* gracefulness. **2** *(encanto)* charm. **3** *(chiste)* joke. • **dar las gracias a ALGN** to thank SB; **gracias a** thanks to; **hacer gracia** to be funny; **¡muchas gracias!** thank you very much!

gracioso,-a *adj* funny.

grada *nf* **1** *(peldaño)* step. **2** *(asiento)* row of seats.

grado *nm* degree.

graduable *adj* adjustable.

graduación *nf* **1** *(acción)* adjustment. **2** *(militar)* rank.

graduar *vt* **1** *(regular)* to adjust. **2** *(ordenar)* to grade. • **graduarse la vista** to have one's eyes tested.

gráfico,-a *adj* graphic. ▶ *nm* **gráfico** graph. ■ **gráfico de barras** bar chart.

gragea *nf* pill.

gramática *nf* grammar.

gramo *nm* gram, gramme.

gran *adj* → grande.

granada *nf* **1** *(fruta)* pomegranate. **2** *(bomba)* grenade.

granate *adj-nm (color)* maroon.

grande *adj* **1** *(de tamaño)* big, large. **2** *(de número, cantidad)* large. **3** *(de importancia)* great.

granel *adv.* **a granel** *(sólidos)* loose, in bulk; *(líquidos)* in bulk.

granero *nm* granary, barn.

granizada *nf* hailstorm.

granizado *nm* slush.

granizar *vi* to hail.

granizo *nm* hail.

granja *nf* farm.

granjero,-a *nm,f* farmer.

grano *nm* **1** *(de arroz)* grain; *(de café)* bean. **2** *(en la piel)* spot, pimple.

grapa *nf* **1** *(para papel)* staple. **2** *(bebida)* grappa.

grapadora *nf* stapler.

grasa *nf* **1** *(comestible)* fat. **2** *(lubricante, suciedad)* grease.

gratinar *vt* to brown under the grill.

gratis *adv* free.

gratuito,-a *adj* free.

grava *nf* **1** *(piedras)* gravel. **2** *(piedra machacada)* broken stone.

grave *adj* **1** *(accidente, enfermedad)* serious: **está muy grave**, she's very seriously ill. **2** *(situación)* difficult. **3** *(voz)* deep, low.

gravedad *nf* **1** *(de la Tierra)* gravity. **2** *(importancia)* seriousness.

Grecia *nf* Greece.

griego,-a *adj-nm,f* Greek. ► *nm* **griego** *(idoma)* Greek.

grieta *nf* crack, crevice.

grifo *nm* GB tap; US faucet.

grillo *nm* *(insecto)* cricket.

gripe *nf* flu, influenza.

gris *adj-nm* GB grey; US gray.

gritar *vi* *(gen)* to shout; *(chillar)* to cry out, scream.

grito *nm* **1** *(gen)* shout. **2** *(de dolor)* cry. **3** *(de miedo)* scream. • **ser el último grito** to be the latest fashion.

grosella *nf* redcurrant. ■ **grosella silvestre** gooseberry.

grosero,-a *adj* **1** *(vulgar)* coarse, rough. **2** *(maleducado)* rude.

grosor *nm* thickness.

grúa *nf* **1** crane. **2** *(para averías)* breakdown van; *(por mal aparcamiento)* tow truck. • **"No aparcar, se avisa grúa"** "Any vehicles parked here will be towed away".

grueso,-a *adj* **1** *(objeto)* thick. **2** *(persona)* fat, stout.

grumete *nm* cabin boy.

grumo *nm* **1** *(de salsa)* lump. **2** *(de sangre)* clot.

gruñido *nm* **1** *(de cerdo)* grunt. **2** *(de perro)* growl.

grupo *nm* group. ■ **grupo de noticias** newsgroup.

gruta *nf* cave.

guante *nm* glove.

guantera *nf* glove compartment.

guapo,-a *adj* *(hombre)* good-looking; *(mujer)* pretty, beautiful.

guarda *nmf* *(vigilante)* guard; *(de zoo)* keeper. ■ **guarda de seguridad** security guard; **guarda jurado** armed security guard.

guardabarros *nm* mudguard.

guardabosque *nmf* forest ranger.

guardaespaldas *nm* bodyguard.

guardameta *nmf* goalkeeper.

guardar *vt* **1** *(en su sitio)* to put away. **2** *(mantener)* to keep. **3** *(para otra ocasión)* to save. **4** INFORM to save. • **guardar cama** to stay in bed; **guardar silencio** to remain silent.

guardarropa *nm* *(en museo, discoteca)* cloakroom.

guardería *nf* crèche, nursery.

guardia *nmf* *(vigilante)* guard. ► *nf* **1** *(servicio)* turn of duty. **2** *(tropa)* guard. • **estar de guardia** to be on duty. ■ **guardia urbana** local police.

guarida *nf* **1** *(de animales)* den. **2** *(de personas)* hideout.

guarnición *nf* **1** *filete con guarnición de patatas fritas*, steak with chips. **2** *(militar)* garrison.

guarro,-a adj 1 (sucio) dirty, filthy. 2 (indecente) disgusting, revolting.

guay adj fam GB cool; US neat.

guerra nf war.

guerrillero,-a nm,f guerrilla.

guía nmf (persona) guide. ► nf (libro) guidebook: *una guía de Madrid*, a guide to Madrid. ■ **guía telefónica** telephone directory.

guiar vt (instruir, orientar) to guide, lead: *nos guió por la ciudad*, he took us round the city.

guinda nf cherry.

guindilla nf (chilli) pepper.

guiñar vt to wink.

guiñol nm puppet theatre.

guion o **guión** nm 1 hyphen. 2 (de discurso) notes. 3 (de película) script.

guionista nmf scriptwriter.

guiri nmf arg foreigner.

guisado,-a adj cooked, prepared. ► nm **guisado** stew.

guisante nm pea.

guisar vt (cocinar) to cook; (carne, pescado) to stew.

gulso nm stew.

güisqui nm whisky.

guitarra nf guitar. ■ **guitarra eléctrica** electric guitar.

guitarrista nmf guitarist.

gusano nm (de tierra) worm; (de mariposa) caterpillar. ■ **gusano de seda** silkworm.

gustar vi to like: *me gusta*, I like it; *le gusta leer*, she likes

reading. • **gustar más** to prefer: *¿cuál te gusta más?* which do you prefer?; **cuando guste** fml whenever you want.

gusto nm 1 (sentido) taste. 2 (sabor) GB flavour; US flavor: *no le noto el gusto* I can't taste it. 3 (placer) pleasure: *tenemos el gusto de invitarles a la boda*, we are pleased to invite you to the wedding. • **con mucho gusto** with pleasure; **dar gusto** to be nice; **estar a gusto** to feel comfortable; **tanto gusto** pleased to meet you.

H

haba nf broad bean.

haber aux to have. ► nm 1 (cuenta corriente) credit. 2 (posesiones) property. • **haber de** to have to, must: *he de salir*, I have to go out; **hay** there is/there are: *hay dos habitaciones*, there are two bedrooms; **hay que** you have to: *hay que tener mucho cuidado*, you have to be very careful.

hábil adj 1 (diestro) skilful. 2 (despabilado) clever.

habilidad nf skill.

habitación *nf* **1** *(cuarto)* room. **2** *(dormitorio)* bedroom.

habitante *nmf* inhabitant.

hábito *nm* habit.

habitual *adj* **1** *(normal)* usual. **2** *(cliente, visitante)* regular.

habla *nf* **1** *(facultad)* speech. **2** *(idioma)* language.

hablar *vi* **1** *(gen)* to talk. **2** *(en situaciones formales)* to speak. ► *vt (idioma)* to speak. • **¡ni hablar!** certainly not!

hacer *vt* **1** *(crear, producir, causar)* to make: **hacer la comida**, to make lunch. **2** *(actividad, estudios, trayecto)* to do: **hacer los deberes**, to do one's homework; **hicimos 250 km**, we did 250 km. ► *vi (tiempo meteorológico)* to be: **hace calor**, it's hot. ► *vpr* **hacerse** *(convertirse en)* to become, turn, get. • **hace 1** *(tiempo pasado)* ago: **compré la bici hace tres años**, I bought the bike three years ago. **2** *(tiempo que dura)* for: **tengo la bici desde hace tres años**, I've had the bike for three years.

hacha *nf* axe.

hacia *prep* **1** *(dirección)* towards. **2** *(tiempo)* about, around.

hacienda *nf* *(finca)* estate. ▪ **hacienda pública** public funds, public finances.

hada *nf* fairy. ▪ **hada madrina** fairy godmother.

halcón *nm* falcon.

hallar *vt* to find. ► *vpr* **hallarse** *(estar)* to be.

hamaca *nf* hammock.

hambre *nf* **1** *(apetito)* hunger. **2** *(escasez)* famine. • **tener hambre** to be hungry.

hamburguesa *nf* hamburger.

harina *nf* flour.

harto,-a *adj* **1** *(repleto)* full. **2** *fam (cansado)* fed up.

hasta *prep* **1** *(tiempo)* until, till: **hasta ahora**, until now. **2** *(lugar)* as far as: **te acompañaré hasta la iglesia**, I'll go with you as far as the church. ► *conj* even: **hasta mi hermano pequeño podría hacerlo**, even my little brother could do it. • **¡hasta luego!** see you later!; **hasta que** until.

haya *nf* *(árbol)* beech.

hazaña *nf* deed, exploit.

hebilla *nf* buckle.

hechizo *nm* spell, charm.

hecho,-a *adj (manufacturado)* made. ► *nm* **hecho 1** *(realidad)* fact. **2** *(suceso)* event. • **bien hecho** *(bistec)* well done; **de hecho** in fact.

hectárea *nf* hectare.

helada *nf* frost.

heladería *nf* GB ice-cream parlour; US ice-cream parlor.

helado *nm* ice cream.

helar *vi* to freeze.

helecho *nm* fern.

hélice *nf* propeller.

helicóptero *nm* helicopter.

hembra *nf* female.
hemisferio *nm* hemisphere.
hemorragia *nf* GB haemorrhage; US hemorrhage.
heredar *vt* to inherit.
hereditario,-a *adj* hereditary.
herencia *nf* 1 *(bienes)* inheritance. 2 *(genética)* heredity.
herida *nf* *(con arma)* wound;
(en accidente) injury.
herido,-a *adj* *(con arma)*
wounded; *(en accidente)* injured.
herir *vt* *(con arma)* to wound;
(en accidente) to injure.
hermano,-a *nm,f* *(hombre)*
brother; *(mujer)* sister.
hermoso,-a *adj* beautiful.
hernia *nf* hernia, rupture.
héroe *nm* hero.
heroína *nf* 1 *(mujer)* heroine.
2 *(droga)* heroin.
herradura *nf* horseshoe.
herramienta *nf* tool.
herrero *nm* blacksmith.
hervir *vt-vi* to boil.
hidratante *adj* moisturizing.
hidroavión *nm* seaplane.
hidrógeno *nm* hydrogen.
hiedra *nf* ivy.
hielo *nm* ice.
hiena *nf* hyena.
hierba *nf* 1 *(césped, pasto)*
grass. 2 *(para cocinar)* herb.
hierbabuena *nf* mint.
hierro *nm* iron. ▪ **hierro colado** cast iron; **hierro forjado**
wrought iron.

hígado *nm* liver.
higiene *nf* hygiene.
higo *nm* fig. ▪ **higo chumbo**
prickly pear.
higuera *nf* fig tree.
hijo,-a *nm,f* *(chico)* son; *(chica)*
daughter; *(sin especificar)* child.
hilera *nf* row.
hilo *nm* 1 *(de coser)* thread. 2
(lino) linen. 3 *(telefónico)* wire.
▪ **hilo musical** piped music.
himno *nm* hymn. ▪ **himno
nacional** national anthem.
hincar *vt* to drive in.
hincha *nmf* fan, supporter.
hinchar *vt* to inflate, blow up.
hinchazón *nf* swelling.
hipermercado *nm* hypermarket.
hípico,-a *adj* *(club)* riding.
hipo *nm* hiccups.
hipócrita *nmf* hypocrite.
hipódromo *nm* racetrack,
racecourse.
hipopótamo *nm* hippopota-
mus.
hipoteca *nf* mortgage.
hispano,-a *adj* 1 *(de España)*
Spanish, Hispanic. 2 *(de América)* Spanish-American. ▶ *nm,f*
(de América) Spanish American; US Hispanic.
hispanoamericano,-a *adj*
Spanish American.
histérico,-a *adj* hysterical.
historia *nf* 1 *(estudio del pasado)* history. 2 *(relato)* story.
historial *nm* *(médico)* record.

histórico,-a *adj* historical.
hobby *nm* hobby.
hockey *nm* hockey. ▪ **hockey sobre hielo** ice hockey; **hockey sobre hierba** hockey.
hogar *nm* home. • **sin hogar** homeless.
hoguera *nf* bonfire.
hoja *nf* 1 (*de planta*) leaf. 2 (*de papel, metal*) sheet. 3 (*de libro*) page. 4 (*de cuchillo*) blade. ▪ **hoja de afeitar** razor blade.
hojalata *nf* tin.
hojaldre *nm & nf* puff pastry.
hola *interj* hello!, hi!
Holanda *nf* Holland.
holandés,-esa *adj* Dutch. ► *nm,f* Dutch person. ► *nm* **holandés** (*idioma*) Dutch.
hombre *nm* man. ▪ **hombre de negocios** businessman.
hombro *nm* shoulder.
homenaje *nm* tribute, homage.
homicidio *nm* homicide, murder.
homogéneo,-a *adj* homogeneous.
homosexual *adj-nmf* homosexual.
hondo,-a *adj* deep.
honesto,-a *adj* honest.
hongo *nm* (*planta*) fungus; (*como comida*) mushroom.
honor *nm* GB honour; US honor.
honrado,-a *adj* honest.
hora *nf* 1 (*60 minutos*) hour. 2 (*tiempo*) time: ¿*qué hora es?*, what time is it?; ¿*tiene hora, por favor?*, have you got the time? 3 (*cita*) appointment: *mañana tengo hora con el dentista*, I have an appointment with the dentist for tomorrow. • **de última hora** last-minute: *noticias de última hora*, breaking news. ▪ **hora punta** 1 (*tráfico*) rush hour. 2 (*electricidad, teléfonos*) peak time; **horas de oficina** business hours; **horas extras** overtime.
horario *nm* 1 (*de trenes, clases*) timetable. 2 (*de trabajo, consulta*) hours. ▪ **horario de atención al público** opening hours.
horca *nf* gallows.
horizontal *adj* horizontal.
horizonte *nm* horizon.
hormiga *nf* ant.
hormigón *nm* concrete. ▪ **hormigón armado** reinforced concrete.
hormigueo *nm* prickling sensation.
hormona *nf* hormone.
horno *nm* 1 (*de cocina*) oven. 2 (*de fábrica*) furnace. • **al horno** 1 (*manzana, patata, pescado*) baked. 2 (*pollo*) roast.
horóscopo *nm* horoscope.
horquilla *nf* hairgrip.
horrible *adj* horrible, dreadful.
horror *nm* 1 (*miedo*) horror. 2 *fam* (*muchísimo*) an awful lot.

horroroso,-a adj **1** (atroz) horrible. **2** (malísimo) dreadful.

hortalizas nf pl vegetables.

hortensia nf hydrangea.

hospedarse vpr to stay.

hospital nm hospital.

hospitalidad nf hospitality.

hostal nm small hotel.

hostelería nf hotel and catering industry.

hostia nf **1** (oblea) host. **2** fam (golpe) thump. ▶ interj ¡**hostia**! fam (enfado) damn it!, bugger!; (sorpresa) bloody hell!

hotel nm hotel.

hoy adv **1** (día) today. **2** (actualmente) now. • **hoy en día** nowadays; **hoy por hoy** at the present time.

hoyo nm hole.

hoz nf sickle.

hucha nf money box.

hueco nm hollow.

huelga nf strike. ▪ **huelga de celo** work-to-rule.

huella nf **1** (de pie) footprint; (de animal, máquina) track. **2** (vestigio) trace, sign. ▪ **huella dactilar** fingerprint.

huérfano,-a adj-nm,f orphan.

huerta nf (de verduras) vegetable garden; (de frutales) orchard.

huerto nm (de verduras) vegetable garden; (de frutales) orchard.

hueso nm **1** (del cuerpo) bone. **2** (de aceituna, cereza) GB stone; US pit.

huésped,-da nm,f guest.

huevo nm egg. ▪ **huevo duro** hard-boiled egg; **huevo escalfado** poached egg; **huevo estrellado** fried egg; **huevo frito** fried egg; **huevo pasado por agua** soft-boiled egg; **huevos revueltos** scrambled eggs.

huida nf escape, flight.

huir vi **1** (escapar) to escape, flee. **2** (evitar) to avoid: **huir de algo**, to avoid STH.

humanidad nf humanity.

humanitario,-a adj humanitarian.

humano,-a adj human.

humedad nf **1** (en la atmósfera) humidity. **2** (en pared, suelo) damp.

húmedo,-a adj **1** (tiempo, clima) humid. **2** (pelo, tierra) damp.

humilde adj humble.

humillar vt to humiliate.

humo nm smoke.

humor nm **1** (ánimo) mood. **2** (gracia) GB humour; US humor. ▪ **humor negro** black comedy.

hundir vt **1** (gen) to sink. **2** (mano, puñal) to plunge. ▶ vpr **hundirse 1** (gen) to sink. **2** (edificio) to collapse. **3** (empresa) to go under. **4** (bolsa, precio) to plummet.

huracán nm hurricane.

I

ida *nf.* • **billete de ida** GB single; US one-way ticket; **billete de ida y vuelta** GB return ticket; US round-trip ticket.
idea *nf* idea.
ideal *adj-nm* ideal.
idéntico,-a *adj* identical.
identificar *vt* to identify.
ideología *nf* ideology.
idioma *nm* language.
idiota *nmf* idiot.
ídolo *nm* idol.
idóneo,-a *adj* suitable, fit.
iglesia *nf* church.
ignorancia *nf* ignorance.
ignorar *vt (no saber)* not to know, be ignorant of.
igual *adj* 1 *(idéntico)* the same. 2 *(en jerarquía)* equal. ▶ *nm (signo)* equals sign. ▶ *adv* 1 *(quizá)* maybe: **igual no vienen**, they may not come. 2 *(de la misma manera)* the same: **piensan igual**, they think the same. • **dar igual** not to matter; **es igual** it doesn't matter; **igual de...** as... as: **soy igual de alto que tú**, I'm as tall as you.
ilegal *adj* illegal.
ileso,-a *adj* unharmed, unhurt.
iluminación *nf* lighting.
iluminar *vt* to light up, illuminate.

ilusión *nf* 1 *(esperanza)* hope. 2 *(imagen falsa)* illusion. • **hacerle ilusión algo a** ALGN: **me hace mucha ilusión que vengas**, I'm really looking forward to you coming.
ilustración *nf* illustration.
ilustre *adj* illustrious, distinguished.
imagen *nf* 1 *(gen)* image. 2 *(en televisión)* picture.
imaginación *nf* imagination.
imaginar(se) *vt-vpr* to imagine.
imán *nm* magnet.
imbécil *nmf* idiot, imbecile.
imitación *nf* 1 *(copia)* imitation. 2 *(parodia)* impression.
imitar *vt* 1 *(copiar)* to imitate, copy. 2 *(gestos)* to mimic, *(como diversión)* to do an impression of, GB take off.
impaciente *adj* impatient.
impar *adj* odd.
imparcial *adj* impartial.
impasible *adj* impassive.
impedir *vt* 1 *(imposibilitar)* to prevent. 2 *(dificultar)* to impede, hinder.
imperativo *nm* imperative.
imperdible *nm* safety pin.
imperfecto,-a *adj (defectuoso)* flawed, imperfect. ▶ *nm* **imperfecto** imperfect, imperfect tense.
imperio *nm* empire.
impermeable *adj* waterproof. ▶ *nm* raincoat.

impersonal *adj* impersonal.

implantar *vt* **1** *(corazón, cabello)* to implant. **2** *(reforma)* to introduce.

implicar *vt (conllevar)* to imply.

imponer *vt* **1** *(castigo, tarea)* to impose. **2** *(respeto, miedo)* to inspire. ► *vpr* **imponerse** **1** *(hacerse obedecer)* to impose one's authority. **2** *(vencer)* to win.

importación *nf* import. • **de importación** imported.

importancia *nf* importance.

importante *adj* important.

importar *vi* **1** *(tener importancia)* to matter: *no me importa*, I don't care. **2** *(molestar)* to mind: *¿te importaría cerrar la ventana?*, would you mind closing the window? ► *vt* to import. • **no importa** it doesn't matter.

importe *nm* **1** *(coste)* cost. **2** *(cantidad)* amount.

imposible *adj* impossible.

impotente *adj* impotent.

imprenta *nf* **1** *(arte)* printing. **2** *(taller)* printer's, printing house.

imprescindible *adj* essential, indispensable.

impresión *nf* **1** *(sensación)* impression. **2** *(de texto)* printing.

impresionante *adj* impressive, striking.

impresionar *vt* **1** *(causar admiración a)* to impress. **2** *(conmover)* to touch, move.

impreso,-a *adj* printed. ► *nm* **impreso** *(formulario)* form.

impresora *nf* printer. ▪ **impresora de chorro de tinta** inkjet printer; **impresora láser** laser printer.

imprevisto,-a *adj* unforeseen, unexpected.

imprimir *vt* to print.

improbable *adj* improbable.

improvisar *vt-vi* to improvise.

imprudente *adj (irreflexivo)* imprudent, rash; *(al conducir)* careless, reckless.

impuesto *nm* tax, duty. ▪ **impuesto sobre el valor añadido (IVA)** value added tax *(VAT)*; **impuesto sobre la renta** income tax.

impulso *nm* **1** *(deseo súbito)* impulse, urge. **2** *(fuerza, velocidad)* momentum. **3** *(estímulo)* boost.

inadmisible *adj* unacceptable.

inaguantable *adj* intolerable, unbearable.

inalámbrico,-a *adj* cordless.

inauguración *nf* opening, inauguration.

inaugurar *vt* to open, inaugurate.

incapaz *adj* **1** *(no capaz)* incapable. **2** *(incompetente)* incompetent.

incendiar *vt* to set on fire, set fire to. ► *vpr* **incendiarse** to catch fire.

incendio *nm* fire. ▪ **incendio provocado** arson.
incentivo *nm* incentive.
incesante *adj* incessant, unceasing.
incidente *nm* incident.
incierto,-a *adj* **1** *(dudoso)* uncertain, doubtful. **2** *(desconocido)* unknown.
incinerar *vt (basura)* to incinerate; *(cadáver)* to cremate.
incisivo *nm (diente)* incisor.
incitar *vt* to incite.
inclinación *nf* **1** *(pendiente)* slant, slope. **2** *(tendencia)* inclination.
inclinar *vt (ladear)* to tilt; *(cuerpo)* to bow; *(cabeza)* to nod.
incluir *vt* to include.
incluso *adv-conj-prep* even.
incógnita *nf* **1** unknown quantity. **2** *(misterio)* mystery.
incoherencia *nf* incoherence.
incoloro,-a *adj* colourless.
incómodo,-a *adj* **1** *(gen)* uncomfortable. **2** *(molesto)* awkward.
incomunicado,-a *adj* **1** *(aislado)* isolated; *(por la nieve)* cut off. **2** *(preso)* in solitary confinement.
inconfundible *adj* unmistakable.
inconsciente *adj* unconscious.
inconveniente *nm (desventaja)* drawback; *(dificultad)* problem.

incorporar *vt* to incorporate. ▶ *vpr* **incorporarse 1** *(levantarse)* to sit up. **2** *(a puesto, regimiento)* to join.
incorrecto,-a *adj* incorrect.
increíble *adj* incredible.
incremento *nm* increase.
incubadora *nf* incubator.
incurable *adj* incurable.
indecente *adj* indecent.
indeciso,-a *adj* indecisive.
indefenso,-a *adj* GB defenceless; US defenseless.
indefinido,-a *adj* **1** *(impreciso)* undefined, vague. **2** *(ilimitado)* indefinite.
indemnización *nf* **1** *(acción)* indemnification. **2** *(compensación)* compensation, indemnity.
independencia *nf* independence.
independiente *adj* independent.
indicación *nf* **1** *(señal)* sign. **2** *(observación)* hint.
indicador *nm (gen)* indicator; *(uso técnico)* gauge.
indicar *vt* to indicate, show.
indicativo,-a *adj-nm* indicative.
índice *nm* **1** *(gen)* index. **2** *(dedo)* index finger, forefinger. ▪ **índice de precios al consumo** retail price index.
indicio *nm* sign, indication.
indiferente *adj* indifferent.
indígena *adj-nmf* native.

indigente *nmf* destitute person.

indigestión *nf* indigestion.

indignar *vt* to infuriate, make angry. ► *vpr* **indignarse** to get angry.

indio,-a *adj-nm,f* Indian.

indiscreto,-a *adj* 1 *(falto de discreción)* indiscreet. 2 *(falto de tacto)* tactless.

indispensable *adj* indispensable, essential.

indispuesto,-a *adj* indisposed, unwell.

individual *adj (gen)* individual; *(habitación, cama)* single.

individuo *nm* person, individual.

indulto *nm* pardon.

indumentaria *nf* clothing, clothes.

industria *nf* industry.

industrial *adj* industrial.

inercia *nf* inertia.

inesperado,-a *adj* unexpected.

inevitable *adj* inevitable, unavoidable.

infalible *adj* infallible.

infancia *nf* childhood.

infantería *nf* infantry. ■ **infantería de marina** marines.

infantil *adj* 1 *(libro, enfermedad)* children's. 2 *(educación, población)* child.

infarto *nm* heart attack.

infección *nf* infection.

infeccioso,-a *adj* infectious.

infectar *vt* to infect.

infeliz *adj* unhappy.

inferior *adj* 1 *(gen)* lower. 2 *(en calidad)* inferior.

infierno *nm* hell.

infinitivo *nm* infinitive.

infinito,-a *adj* infinite.

inflación *nf* inflation.

inflamable *adj* inflammable.

inflamación *nf* inflammation.

inflar *vt* 1 *(globo, neumático)* to inflate, blow up. 2 *(hechos, noticias)* to exaggerate.

influencia *nf* influence.

influir *vi* to influence.

información *nf* 1 *(datos)* information. 2 *(oficina)* information desk. 3 *(noticias)* news.

informal *adj* 1 *(ambiente, reunión)* informal. 2 *(ropa)* casual.

informar *vt* to inform.

informática *nf* computer science, computing.

informático,-a *adj* computer, computing. ► *nm,f* computer expert.

informativo,-a *adj* informative. ► *nm* **informativo** news bulletin.

informe *nm* report.

infracción *nf (fiscal, de circulación)* GB offence; US offense; *(de ley)* infringement.

infusión *nf* infusion: *infusión de manzanilla*, camomile tea; *infusión de menta*, mint tea.

ingeniero,-a *nm,f* engineer.

ingenioso,-a *adj (inteligente)* ingenious, clever; *(con chispa)* witty.

ingenuo,-a *adj* naïve, ingenuous.

ingerir *vt* to consume, ingest.

Inglaterra *nf* England.

ingle *nf* groin.

inglés,-esa *adj* English. ► *nm,f (persona)* English person. ► *nm* **inglés** *(idioma)* English.

ingrediente *nm* ingredient.

ingresar *vt* **1** *(dinero)* to deposit, pay in. **2** *(paciente)* to admit. ► *vi (en colegio)* to enter; *(en club etc)* to become a member; *(en hospital)* to be admitted to.

ingreso *nm* **1** *(en organización)* entry. **2** *(en hospital, club, etc)* admission. **3** *(en cuenta bancaria)* deposit. ► *nm pl* **ingresos** income.

inicial *adj-nf* initial.

iniciar *vt* **1** *(introducir)* to initiate. **2** *(empezar)* to begin.

iniciativa *nf* initiative.

inicio *nm* beginning, start.

injusto,-a *adj* unjust, unfair.

inmediato,-a *adj (reacción, respuesta)* immediate. • **inmediato,-a** next to, near.

inmenso,-a *adj* immense.

inmigrante *adj-nmf* immigrant.

inmigrar *vi* to immigrate.

inmobiliaria *nf* GB estate agency; US real estate agency.

inmóvil *adj* still, motionless.

inmueble *nm* building.

inmunidad *nf* immunity.

innovación *nf* innovation.

inocente *adj* **1** *(libre de culpa)* innocent. **2** *(ingenuo)* naïve. **3** *(no culpable)* not guilty, innocent. ► *nmf (no culpable)* innocent person.

inodoro *nm* toilet.

inofensivo,-a *adj* inoffensive, harmless.

inoxidable *adj (gen)* rustproof; *(acero)* stainless.

inquietar(se) *vt-vpr* to worry.

inquieto,-a *adj* **1** *(agitado)* restless. **2** *(preocupado)* worried, anxious.

inquilino,-a *nm,f* tenant.

inscribirse *vpr* **1** *(en colegio)* to enrol. **2** *(en club, organización)* to join. **3** *(en concurso)* to enter.

inscripción *nf* **1** *(grabado)* inscription. **2** *(registro)* enrolment, registration.

insecticida *adj-nm* insecticide.

insecto *nm* insect.

inseguro,-a *adj* **1** *(falto de confianza)* insecure. **2** *(peligroso)* unsafe.

insertar *vt* to insert.

inservible *adj* useless, unusable.

insignia *nf (distintivo)* badge.

insignificante *adj* insignificant.

insinuar *vt* to insinuate, hint.
insípido,-a *adj* insipid.
insistir *vi* to insist.
insolación *nf* sunstroke.
insólito,-a *adj* unusual.
insomnio *nm* insomnia.
inspección *nf* inspection.
inspector,-ra *nm,f* inspector.
inspiración *nf* inspiration.
inspirar *vt* 1 *(aspirar)* to inhale, breathe in. 2 *(infundir)* to inspire.
instalación *nf* installation. ▶ *nf pl* **instalaciones** *(recinto)* installations; *(servicios)* facilities.
instalar *vt* to install. ▶ *vpr* **instalarse** to settle.
instantánea *nf* snapshot.
instantáneo,-a *adj* 1 *(repuesta, reacción)* instantaneous. 2 *(éxito, resultado, café)* instant.
instante *nm* moment, instant. • **al instante** immediately.
instinto *nm* instinct.
institución *nf* institution, establishment.
instituto *nm* 1 *(organismo)* institute. 2 *(de enseñanza)* GB secondary school; US high school. ▪ **instituto de belleza** beauty salon.
instrucción *nf* education. ▶ *nf pl* **instrucciones** instructions.
instrumento *nm* instrument.
insuficiencia *nf* lack, shortage. ▪ **insuficiencia cardíaca** heart failure; **insuficien-**

cia respiratoria respiratory failure.
insultar *vt* to insult.
insulto *nm* insult.
intacto,-a *adj* intact.
integración *nf* integration.
integral *adj* 1 *(total)* comprehensive. 2 *(sin refinar - pan, harina)* wholemeal; *(- arroz)* brown.
íntegro,-a *adj* 1 *(completo)* whole, entire. 2 *(honrado)* honest, upright.
intelectual *adj-nmf* intellectual.
inteligencia *nf* intelligence.
inteligente *adj* intelligent, clever.
intención *nf* intention.
intensidad *nf* *(gen)* intensity; *(de viento)* force.
intenso,-a *adj* *(gen)* intense; *(dolor)* acute.
intentar *vt* to try, attempt.
intento *nm* attempt, try.
intercambio *nm* exchange.
interés *nm* interest.
interesante *adj* interesting.
interesar *vi* to interest.
interferencia *nf* interference.
interfono *nm* intercom.
interior *adj* 1 *(jardín, patio)* interior. 2 *(estancia, piso)* inner. 3 *(bolsillo)* inside. 4 *(comercio, política)* domestic, internal. 5 *(mar, desierto)* inland. ▶ *nm* 1 *(parte interna)* inside, inner part. 2 *(de país)* interior.

interjección *nf* interjection.

intermedio,-a *adj* 1 *(nivel)* intermediate. 2 *(tamaño)* medium. ► *nm* **intermedio** intermission, interval.

intermitente *nm* GB indicator; US turn signal.

internacional *adj* international.

internauta *nmf* Net user.

interno,-a *adj* internal.

interpretación *nf* 1 *(explicación)* interpretation. 2 *(actuación)* performance. 3 *(traducción)* interpreting.

interpretar *vt (obra, pieza)* to perform; *(papel)* to play; *(canción)* to sing.

intérprete *nmf* 1 *(traductor)* interpreter. 2 *(actor, músico)* performer.

interrogación *nf (signo)* question mark.

interrogar *vt* 1 *(testigo)* to question. 2 *(sospechoso)* to interrogate, question.

interrumpir *vt* to interrupt.

interruptor *nm* switch.

interurbano,-a *adj (transporte)* intercity; *(llamada)* long-distance.

intervalo *nm* 1 *(de tiempo)* interval. 2 *(de espacio)* gap.

intervención *nf* 1 *(gen)* intervention. 2 *(operación)* operation. 3 *(discurso)* speech.

intervenir *vi* to take part. ► *vt (paciente)* to operate on.

intestino *nm* intestine.

íntimo,-a *adj* 1 *(secreto, ambiente)* intimate. 2 *(vida)* private. 3 *(amistad)* close.

intoxicación *nf* poisoning.

intranet *nm* intranet.

intriga *nf* 1 *(maquinación)* intrigue. 2 *(de película etc)* plot.

introducción *nf* introduction.

introducir *vt (meter)* to put in, insert. ► *vpr* **introducirse** to enter, get in.

intruso,-a *nm,f* intruder.

intuición *nf* intuition.

inundación *nf* flood.

inútil *adj* useless.

invadir *vt* to invade.

inválido,-a *adj (persona)* disabled, handicapped.

invasión *nf* invasion.

invención *nf* invention.

inventar *vt* to invent.

invento *nm* invention.

invernadero *nm* greenhouse, hothouse.

invernal *adj* wintry, winter.

inversión *nf (de dinero, tiempo)* investment.

inverso,-a *adj* inverse.

invertir *vt* 1 *(orden)* to invert. 2 *(dinero, tiempo)* to invest.

investigación *nf* 1 *(policial, judicial)* investigation, inquiry. 2 *(científica, académica)* research.

investigar *vt* 1 *(indagar)* to investigate. 2 *(estudiar)* to do research on.

invierno *nm* winter.
invisible *adj* invisible.
invitación *nf* invitation.
invitado,-a *nm,f* guest.
invitar *vt* to invite: *déjame que te invite a un café*, let me buy you a coffee.
inyección *nf* injection.
ir *vi* **1** *(gen)* to go. **2** *(camino etc)* to lead. **3** *(funcionar)* to work. ► *aux* **1** ir + a + *infin*: *voy a salir*, I'm going out. **2** ir + *ger*: *vas mejorando*, you're getting better; *fuimos corriendo*, we ran. ► *vpr* **irse** *(marcharse)* to go away, leave.
ira *nf* anger, rage, wrath.
iris *nm* iris.
Irlanda *nf* Ireland. ■ **Irlanda del Norte** Northern Ireland.
irlandés,-esa *adj* Irish. ► *nm,f* *(hombre)* Irishman; *(mujer)* Irish woman. ► *nm* **irlandés** *(idioma)* Irish.
irónico,-a *adj* ironic.
irregular *adj* irregular.
irritar *vt* to irritate, annoy.
isla *nf* island.
islámico,-a *adj* Islamic.
Italia *nf* Italy.
italiano,-a *adj-nm,f* Italian.
itinerario *nm* itinerary, route.
izar *vt* to hoist.
izquierda *nf* **1** *(dirección)* left: *gira a la izquierda*, turn left. **2** *(mano)* left hand; *(pierna)* left leg. **3** POL left wing.
izquierdo,-a *adj* left.

J

jabalí *nm* wild boar.
jabón *nm* soap.
jabonera *nf* soapdish.
jacinto *nm* hyacinth.
jaleo *nm* *(alboroto)* racket, din.
jamás *adv* never; *(con superlativos)* ever: *jamás he escrito un libro*, I have never written a book; *el mejor libro que jamás se haya escrito*, the best book ever written.
jamón *nm* ham. ■ **jamón de York** boiled ham; **jamón serrano** cured ham.
jaque *nm* check. ■ **jaque mate** checkmate.
jaqueca *nf* migraine, headache.
jarabe *nm* syrup.
jardín *nm* garden. ■ **jardín de infancia** nursery school.
jardinero,-a *nm,f* gardener.
jarra *nf* GB jug; US pitcher. ■ **jarra de cerveza** beer mug.
jarro *nm* GB jug; US pitcher.
jarrón *nm* vase.
jaula *nf* cage.
jefe,-a *nm,f* *(superior)* boss; *(de departamento)* head; *(de tribu)* chief. ■ **jefe de estación** station master; **jefe de Estado** Head of State.
jerarquía *nf* **1** *(gradación)* hierarchy. **2** *(categoría)* rank.

jergón *nm* straw mattress.

jeringuilla *nf* syringe.

jeroglífico *nm* 1 *(texto antiguo)* hieroglyph. 2 *(juego)* rebus.

jersey *nm* sweater, pullover, GB jumper.

jilguero *nm* goldfinch.

jinete *nm* rider, horseman.

jirafa *nf* giraffe.

jornada *nf* day.

joroba *nf (deformidad)* hump.

joven *adj* young. ► *nmf (hombre)* youth, young man; *(mujer)* girl, young woman.

joya *nf* jewel.

joyería *nf (tienda)* GB jewellery shop, jeweller's; US jewelry store, jeweler's.

joyero *nm* GB jewellery box; US jewelry box.

juanete *nm* bunion.

jubilación *nf* 1 *(acción)* retirement. 2 *(dinero)* pension.

jubilado,-a *nm,f* retired person.

jubilarse *vpr* to retire.

judía *nf (planta)* bean. ■ **judía blanca** haricot bean; **judía pinta** kidney bean; **judía verde** French bean, green bean.

judicial *adj* judicial.

judío,-a *adj* Jewish. ► *nm,f* Jew.

juego *nm* 1 *(para entretenerse)* game. 2 *(acto)* play. 3 *(en tenis)* game. 4 *(de apuestas)* gambling. 5 *(conjunto de piezas)* set. ● **a juego** matching; **hacer juego** to match.

juerga *nf fam* binge, rave-up.

jueves *nm* Thursday.

juez *nmf* judge. ■ **juez de banda** linesman; **juez de línea** linesman.

jugada *nf (en ajedrez)* move; *(en billar)* shot; *(en dardos)* throw.

jugador,-ra *nm,f* 1 *(en deportes, juegos)* player. 2 *(apostador)* gambler.

jugar *vt-vi* 1 *(gen)* to play. 2 *(apostar)* to bet.

jugo *nm* juice.

juguete *nm* toy.

juguetería *nf* toy shop.

juicio *nm* 1 *(facultad)* judgement. 2 *(sensatez)* reason, common sense. 3 *(proceso)* trial, lawsuit. ● **a mi juicio** in my opinion.

julio *nm* July.

jungla *nf* jungle.

junio *nm* June.

junta *nf* 1 *(reunión)* meeting. 2 *(conjunto de personas)* board, committee.

juntar *vt (unir)* to put together; *(piezas)* to assemble. ► *vpr* **juntarse** *(reunirse)* to get together.

junto,-a *adj* together. ► *adv.* ● **junto a** near, close to; **junto con** together with.

jurado *nm* 1 *(tribunal)* jury. 2 *(en concurso)* panel of judges, jury.

juramento *nm (promesa)* oath.
jurar *vt-vi* to swear.
justicia *nf* justice.
justificar *vt* to justify.
justo,-a *adj* **1** *(con justicia)* fair, just. **2** *(apretado)* tight. **3** *(exacto)* exact: *me dio el dinero justo*, she gave me the right money. **4** *(escaso)*: *me queda el dinero justo*, I've just got enough money left. ► *adv* **justo** exactly, precisely.
juvenil *adj-nmf (en deporte)* under 18.
juventud *nf* **1** *(edad)* youth. **2** *(conjunto de jóvenes)* young people, youth.
juzgado *nm* court.
juzgar *vt* **1** *(gen)* to judge. **2** *(en tribunal)* to try.

K

karaoke *nm* karaoke.
kárate *nm* karate.
kart *nm* go-cart.
kilo(gramo) *nm* kilo(gram).
kilométrico *nm* runabout ticket.
kilómetro *nm* kilometre, kilometer.
kiosko *nm* → quiosco.
kiwi *nm* kiwi.
Kleenex® *nm* Kleenex®, tissue.

L

la[1] *det* the.
la[2] *pron (persona, ella)* her; *(usted)* you; *(cosa, animal)* it.
la[3] *nm (nota musical)* la, A.
labio *nm* lip.
labor *nf* **1** *(trabajo)* task. **2** *(de costura)* needlework; *(de punto)* knitting.
laborable *adj* working.
laboratorio *nm* laboratory.
labrador,-ra *nm,f* farm worker.
labrar *vt (tierra, metal)* to work.
laca *nf (para pelo)* hair lacquer, hair spray.
lácteo,-a *adj* dairy, milk.
ladera *nf* slope, hillside.
lado *nm* side. • **al lado** close by, near by; **al lado de** next to, beside.
ladrar *vi* to bark.
ladrillo *nm* brick.
ladrón,-ona *nm,f* thief.
lagartija *nf* (wall) lizard.
lagarto *nm* lizard.
lago *nm* lake.
lágrima *nf* tear.
laguna *nf* pool.
lamentar *vt* to regret, be sorry about.
lamer *vt* to lick.
lámpara *nf* lamp.
lamparón *nm* stain.
lana *nf* wool. • **de lana** woollen.

lancha *nf* launch.

langosta *nf* **1** *(crustáceo)* lobster. **2** *(insecto)* locust.

langostino *nm* GB prawn; US shrimp.

lanza *nf (en torneo)* lance; *(arrojadiza)* spear.

lanzadera *nf* shuttle.

lanzamiento *nm* **1** *(de objeto)* throwing. **2** *(de cohete, producto)* launch. ■ **lanzamiento de disco** the discus; **lanzamiento de jabalina** the javelin.

lanzar *vt* **1** *(tirar)* to throw. **2** *(cohete, nave, producto)* to launch.

lapa *nf* limpet.

lápida *nf* tombstone.

lápiz *nm* pencil. ■ **lápiz de labios** lipstick.

largo,-a *adj* long. ► *nm* **largo** length: *tiene dos metros de largo*, it's two metres long. • **a lo largo de** along, throughout.

largometraje *nm* feature film, full-length film.

laringe *nf* larynx.

larva *nf* larva.

las *det* the. ► *pron (ellas)* them; *(ustedes)* you.

láser *nm* laser.

lástima *nf* pity, shame.

lastimarse *vpr* to get hurt.

lata *nf* **1** *(envase)* tin, can. **2** *fam (fastidio)* bore, nuisance. • **dar la lata** to annoy; **en lata** canned, tinned.

lateral *adj* lateral, side.

latido *nm* beat.

látigo *nm* whip.

latir *vi* to beat.

latitud *nf* latitude.

latón *nm* brass.

laurel *nm* **1** *(árbol)* bay tree. **2** *(hoja)* bay leaf.

lava *nf* lava.

lavabo *nm* **1** *(pila)* washbasin. **2** *(cuarto de baño)* bathroom. **3** *(público)* toilet.

lavadora *nf* washing machine.

lavandería *nf* laundry. ■ **lavandería automática** GB launderette; US laundromat.

lavaplatos *nm* → lavavajillas.

lavar *vt* **1** *(manos, ropa)* to wash. **2** *(platos)* to wash up. **3** *(limpiar)* to clean. ► *vpr* **lavarse** to have a wash, get washed.

lavavajillas *nm* **1** *(máquina)* dishwasher. **2** *(líquido)* washing-up liquid.

laxante *adj-nm* laxative.

lazo *nm* **1** *(lazada)* bow. **2** *(nudo)* knot.

le *pron* **1** *(objeto directo)* him; *(usted)* you. **2** *(objeto indirecto - a él)* him; *(- a ella)* her; *(a cosa, animal)* it; *(a usted)* you.

leal *adj* loyal, faithful.

lección *nf* lesson.

leche *nf* milk. ■ **leche condensada** condensed milk; **le-**

che descremada skimmed milk; **leche en polvo** powdered milk; **leche entera** whole milk.
lechón *nm* sucking pig.
lechuga *nf* lettuce.
lechuza *nf* barn owl.
lector *nm* reader.
lectura *nf* 1 *(acción)* reading. 2 *(textos)* reading matter.
leer *vt* to read.
legal *adj* legal.
legaña *nf* sleep.
legendario,-a *adj* legendary.
legislación *nf* legislation.
legislativo,-a *adj* legislative.
legislatura *nf* term of office.
legítimo,-a *adj* legitimate.
legumbre *nf* pulse.
lejano,-a *adj* distant.
lejía *nf* bleach.
lejos *adv* far, far away.
lencería *nf* 1 *(de mujer)* underwear, lingerie. 2 *(tienda)* lingerie shop.
lengua *nf* 1 *(en la boca)* tongue. 2 *(idioma)* language. 3 *(de tierra)* strip. ▪ **lengua materna** mother tongue.
lenguado *nm* sole.
lenguaje *nm* 1 *(gen)* language. 2 *(habla)* speech.
lengüeta *nf* *(de zapato)* tongue.
lente *nm & nf* lens. ▪ **lentes de contacto** contact lenses.
lenteja *nf* lentil.
lentilla *nf* contact lens.
lento,-a *adj* slow.

leña *nf* firewood.
leñador,-ra *nm,f* woodcutter.
leño *nm* log.
león,-ona *nm,f* *(macho)* lion; *(hembra)* lioness.
leopardo *nm* leopard.
leotardos *nm pl* thick tights.
lepra *nf* leprosy.
les *pron* 1 *(objeto indirecto - a ellos)* them; *(- a ustedes)* you. 2 *(objeto directo - ellos)* them; *(- ustedes)* you.
lesión *nf* injury.
lesionarse *vpr* to injure oneself, get injured.
letra *nf* 1 *(del alfabeto)* letter. 2 *(de imprenta)* type. 3 *(escritura)* handwriting. 4 *(de canción)* lyrics, words. ▪ **letra de cambio** bill of exchange, draft.
letrero *nm* sign, notice.
levadura *nf* yeast.
levantar *vt* 1 *(alzar)* to raise; *(bulto, trampilla)* to lift. 2 *(construir)* to erect, build. 3 *(sanción, embargo)* to lift. ▸ *vpr* **levantarse** 1 *(ponerse de pie)* to rise, stand up. 2 *(de la cama)* to get up, rise.
leve *adj* 1 *(ligero)* light. 2 *(poco importante)* slight, trifling.
léxico,-a *adj* lexical.
ley *nf* *(gen)* law; *(del parlamento)* act, bill.
leyenda *nf* legend.
liar *vt* 1 *(cigarrillo)* to roll. 2 *(confundir)* to confuse.
libélula *nf* dragonfly.

liberación *nf (de país)* liberation; *(de preso, rehén)* freeing, release.

liberar *vt (país)* to liberate; *(preso, rehén)* to free, release.

libertad *nf* freedom, liberty. ▪ **libertad bajo fianza** bail.

libra *nf (moneda, peso)* pound.

libre *adj* free. • **libre de impuestos** tax-free, duty-free.

librería *nf* **1** *(tienda)* GB bookshop; US bookstore. **2** *(estantería)* bookcase.

libreta *nf* notebook.

libro *nm* book. ▪ **libro de bolsillo** paperback; **libro de consulta** reference book; **libro de reclamaciones** complaints book; **libro de texto** textbook.

licencia *nf* **1** *(documento)* permit; GB licence; US license. **2** *(permiso)* permission.

licenciado,-a *nm,f* graduate.

lícito,-a *adj* licit, lawful.

licor *nm* liqueur.

licuadora *nf* liquidizer.

líder *nmf* leader.

lidiar *vt (toros)* to fight.

liebre *nf* hare.

liga *nf* **1** *(para media)* garter. **2** *(en política, deporte)* league.

ligamento *nm* ligament.

ligar *vt (salsa)* to thicken. ▶ *vi fam (conquistar)* to pick up.

ligero,-a *adj* **1** *(liviano)* light. **2** *(leve)* slight. **3** *(frívolo)* flippant, thoughtless. • **a la ligera** hastily.

light *adj* **1** *(comida)* low-calorie; *(refresco)* diet. **2** *(tabaco)* light.

lija *nf* sandpaper.

lila *adj-nf* lilac.

lima[1] *nf (utensilio)* file.

lima[2] *nf (fruta)* lime.

limitar *vt* to limit. ▶ *vi* to border.

límite *nm* **1** *(tope)* limit. **2** *(frontera)* boundary, border.

limón *nm* lemon.

limonada *nf* lemonade.

limosna *nf* alms. • **pedir limosna** to beg.

limpiacristales *nmf-nm* window cleaner.

limpiaparabrisas *nm* GB windscreen wiper; US windshield wiper.

limpiar *vt* **1** *(gen)* to clean. **2** *(con paño)* to wipe.

limpio,-a *adj* **1** *(gen)* clean. **2** *(persona)* neat, tidy.

línea *nf* **1** *(gen)* line. **2** *(tipo)* figure. • **cuidar la línea** to watch one's weight; **en línea** on-line. ▪ **línea aérea** airline; **línea continua** solid white line; **línea férrea** railway line.

lingote *nm* ingot.

lino *nm* **1** *(tela)* linen. **2** *(planta)* flax.

linterna *nf (de pilas)* GB torch; US flashlight.

lío *nm* **1** *(embrollo)* mess, muddle. **2** *(problema)* trouble.

liquidación *nf* **1** *(de deuda)* settlement. **2** *(de mercancías)* clearance sale.

líquido,-a *adj* liquid. ► *nm* **líquido** liquid.

lírico,-a *adj* lyrical.

lirio *nm* iris.

liso,-a *adj* **1** *(superficie)* smooth, even. **2** *(pelo)* straight. **3** *(color)* plain.

lista *nf* list. ■ **lista de correo** mailing list; **lista de espera 1** *(gen)* waiting list. **2** *(para avión)* standby.

listado *nm* INFORM listing.

listín *nm* telephone directory.

listo,-a *adj* **1** *(preparado)* ready. **2** *(inteligente)* clever, smart.

litera *nf* *(en dormitorio)* bunk bed; *(en barco)* bunk; *(en tren)* couchette.

literatura *nf* literature.

litoral *nm* coast.

litro *nm* GB litre; US liter.

llaga *nf* ulcer, sore.

llama[1] *nf* *(de fuego)* flame. ● **en llamas** ablaze.

llama[2] *nf* *(animal)* llama.

llamada *nf* **1** *(telefónica)* phone call. **2** *(a la puerta)* knock; *(con timbre)* ring. ■ **llamada a cobro revertido** GB reverse charge call; US collect call.

llamar *vt* **1** *(gen)* to call. **2** *(por teléfono)* to phone, call, ring. ► *vi* *(a la puerta)* to knock; *(al timbre)* to ring. ► *vpr* **llamarse** to be called, be named: *¿có-*

mo te llamas?, what's your name?; *me llamo Juan*, my name is Juan.

llano,-a *adj* *(plano)* flat.

llanta *nf* rim.

llanto *nm* crying, weeping.

llanura *nf* plain.

llave *nf* **1** *(de puerta etc)* key. **2** *(herramienta)* spanner. ● **cerrar con llave** to lock. ■ **llave de contacto** ignition key; **llave de paso 1** *(del agua)* stopcock. **2** *(del gas)* mains tap; **llave inglesa** adjustable spanner; **llave maestra** master key.

llavero *nm* key ring.

llegada *nf* **1** *(gen)* arrival. **2** *(en deportes)* finishing line.

llegar *vi* **1** *(gen)* to arrive, reach. **2** *(alcanzar)* to reach: *¿llegas al estante?*, can you reach the shelf? **3** *(ser suficiente)* to be enough: *no me llega el dinero*, I haven't got enough money.

llenar *vt* *(gen)* to fill (up); *(formulario)* to fill in. ► *vi* to be filling. ► *vpr* **llenarse** *(de gente)* to get crowded.

lleno,-a *adj* **1** *(gen)* full. **2** *(de gente)* crowded.

llevar *vt* **1** *(transportar)* to carry. **2** *(prenda)* to wear, have on. **3** *(acompañar)* to take; *(conducir, guiar)* to lead: *te llevaré al zoo*, I'll take you to the zoo. **4** *(libros, cuentas)* to keep. **5** *(dirigir)* to be in charge of, manage, run. ► *vpr* **lle-varse 1** *(coger)* to take. **2** *(premio)* to win. **3** *(estar de moda)* to be fashionable. **4** *(entenderse)* to get on.

llorar *vi* **1** *(persona)* to cry, weep. **2** *(ojos)* to water.

llover *vi* to rain.

llovizna *nf* drizzle.

lluvia *nf* rain.

lo *det* the. ► *pron (él)* him; *(usted)* you; *(cosa, animal)* it.

lobo,-a *nm,f (macho)* wolf; *(hembra)* she-wolf.

local *adj* local. ► *nm* premises.

localidad *nf* **1** *(pueblo)* village; *(ciudad)* town. **2** *(asiento)* seat. **3** *(entrada)* ticket. • **"No hay localidades"** "Sold out".

loción *nf* lotion.

loco,-a *adj* mad, crazy.

locomotora *nf* engine, locomotive.

locura *nf* madness, insanity.

locutor,-ra *nm,f* announcer.

lodo *nm* mud, mire.

lógico,-a *adj* logical.

lograr *vt* **1** *(trabajo, beca)* to get, obtain. **2** *(objetivo)* to attain, achieve.

lomo *nm* **1** *(de animal)* back. **2** *(de cerdo)* loin. **3** *(de libro)* spine.

lona *nf* canvas.

loncha *nf* slice.

longaniza *nf* pork sausage.

longitud *nf* **1** *(largo)* length. **2** *(geográfica)* longitude.

loro *nm* parrot.

los *det* the. ► *pron (ellos)* them; *(ustedes)* you.

lote *nm* **1** *(de productos)* lot. **2** *(en informática)* batch.

lotería *nf* lottery.

lubina *nf* bass.

lucha *nf* **1** *(pelea)* fight, struggle. **2** *(deporte)* wrestling.

luchar *vi* **1** *(pelear)* to fight. **2** *(como deporte)* to wrestle.

luego *adv* **1** *(más tarde)* later. **2** *(después de algo)* then. ► *conj* therefore, then.

lugar *nm* **1** *(sitio)* place. **2** *(posición)* position. • **en lugar de** instead of.

lujo *nm* luxury. • **de lujo** luxury.

luna *nf* **1** *(astro)* moon. **2** *(cristal - de ventana)* window pane; *(- de vehículo)* GB windscreen; US windshield. ■ **luna de miel** honeymoon; **luna llena** full moon.

lunar *adj* lunar. ► *nm* **1** *(en la piel)* mole; *(postizo)* beauty spot. **2** *(en tejido)* spot, polka-dot.

lunes *nm* Monday.

lupa *nf* magnifying glass.

luto *nm* mourning.

luz *nf* **1** *(gen)* light. **2** *fam (electricidad)* electricity. • **dar a luz** to give birth to. ■ **luces de carretera** full-beam headlights; **luces de cruce** dipped headlights; **luces de posición** sidelights.

M

macarrones *nm pl* macaroni.

macedonia *nf* fruit salad.

maceta *nf* plant pot, flowerpot.

macho *nm* **1** *(animal)* male. **2** *(pieza)* male piece, male part.

macizo,-a *adj* **1** *(sólido)* solid; *(fuerte)* well-built. ▶ *nm* **macizo** *(montañoso)* massif.

madera *nf* **1** *(gen)* wood; *(para la construcción)* timber.

madre *nf* mother.

madrina *nf* **1** *(de bautizo)* godmother. **2** *(de boda)* matron of honour.

madrugada *nf* **1** *(después de medianoche)* early morning. **2** *(alba)* dawn. • **de madrugada** in the small hours.

madrugar *vi* to get up early.

madurar *vt (fruta)* to ripen. ▶ *vi* to mature.

maduro,-a *adj* **1** *(persona)* mature. **2** *(fruta)* ripe.

maestro,-a *nm,f* teacher.

magdalena *nf* sponge cake.

magia *nf* magic.

magistrado,-a *nm,f* judge.

magnetófono *nm* tape recorder.

magnífico,-a *adj* magnificent, splendid.

mago,-a *nm,f* magician, wizard.

mahonesa *nf* mayonnaise.

maíz *nm* maize; US corn.

majestad *nf* majesty.

mal *adj* **1** *(desagradable, adverso)* bad. **2** *(enfermo)* ill. ▶ *adv* badly, wrong. • **menos mal que...** thank goodness...

maldición *nf* curse.

maldito,-a *adj fam* damned, bloody.

maleducado,-a *adj* rude, bad-mannered.

malentendido *nm* misunderstanding.

malestar *nm* **1** *(incomodidad)* discomfort. **2** *fig (inquietud)* uneasiness.

maleta *nf* suitcase, case. • **hacer la maleta** to pack.

maletero *nm (de coche)* GB boot; US trunk.

maletín *nm* briefcase.

maleza *nf* weeds.

malgastar *vt (tiempo)* to waste; *(dinero)* squander.

malherido,-a *adj* seriously injured.

malhumor *nm* bad temper.

malla *nf* **1** *(red)* mesh. **2** *(prenda)* leotard.

Mallorca *nf* Majorca.

malo,-a *adj* **1** *(perjudicial, imperfecto)* bad. **2** *(malvado)* wicked. • **estar malo,-a** to be ill.

maltratar *vt (animal)* to illtreat, mistreat; *(persona)* to batter.

malva *adj-nm (color)* mauve.
malvado,-a *nm,f* villain.
mama *nf (de mujer)* breast; *(de animal)* udder.
mamá *nf fam* GB mum(my); US mom(my).
mamar *vi (niño)* to suck.
mamífero *nm* mammal.
mampara *nf* screen.
manada *nf (de elefantes)* herd; *(de lobos)* pack.
manantial *nm* spring.
mancha *nf (de sangre, aceite, comida)* stain; *(de bolígrafo)* mark; *(en la piel)* spot.
manchar *vt-vi* to stain. ▶ *vpr* **mancharse** to get dirty.
manco,-a *adj* one-handed.
mandar *vt* 1 *(ordenar)* to order. 2 *(enviar)* to send.
mandarina *nf* tangerine.
mandíbula *nf* jaw.
mando *nm* 1 *(autoridad)* command. 2 *(para mecanismos)* control. ▪ **mando a distancia** remote control.
manecilla *nf (de reloj)* hand.
manejable *adj* manageable, easy-to-handle.
manejar *vt* to handle, operate.
manera *nf* way, manner. • **de manera que** so that; **de ninguna manera** by no means; **de todas maneras** anyway, in any case. ▪ **manera de ser** character, the way SB is.
manga *nf* sleeve.
mango[1] *nm (asa)* handle.

mango[2] *nm (fruta)* mango.
manguera *nf* hose.
manía *nf* 1 *(ojeriza)* dislike. 2 *(obsesión)* mania.
manicomio *nm* mental hospital.
manifestación *nf* 1 *(de protesta, etc.)* demonstration. 2 *(expresión)* manifestation. 3 *(declaración)* statement.
manifestar *vt (opinión)* to express, state; *(sentimiento)* to show. ▶ *vpr* **manifestarse** *(en la calle)* to demonstrate.
manilla *nf (de reloj)* hand.
manillar *nm* handlebars.
maniobra *nf* GB manoeuvre; US maneuver.
manipular *vt* to manipulate.
maniquí *nm (muñeco)* dummy. ▶ *nmf (modelo)* model.
manivela *nf* crank.
manjar *nm* delicacy.
mano *nf* 1 *(de persona)* hand. 2 *(de pintura, etc.)* coat. • **dar la mano** *(saludar)* to shake hands; **de segunda mano** secondhand. ▪ **mano de obra** GB labour; US labor.
manojo *nm* bunch.
mansión *nf* mansion.
manso,-a *adj* tame, docile.
manta *nf* 1 *(para abrigarse)* blanket. 2 *(pez)* manta ray. ▪ **manta de viaje** travelling rug.
manteca *nf* fat. ▪ **manteca de cacao** cocoa butter; **manteca de cerdo** lard.

mantecado *nm* shortbread.

mantel *nm* tablecloth.

mantener *vt* **1** *(conservar)* to keep. **2** *(guardar)* to store. **3** *(sostener)* to support, hold up. **4** *(ideas)* to defend.

mantenimiento *nm* maintenance.

mantequilla *nf* butter.

manual *adj-nm* manual.

manuscrito *nm* manuscript.

manzana *nf* **1** *(fruta)* apple. **2** *(de casas)* block.

manzanilla *nf* **1** *(flor)* camomile. **2** *(infusión)* camomile tea. **3** *(vino)* manzanilla sherry.

manzano *nm* apple tree.

mañana *nf* *(parte del día)* morning. ► *nm* *(porvenir)* tomorrow, the future. ► *adv* tomorrow. • **hasta mañana** see you tomorrow; **pasado mañana** the day after tomorrow.

mapa *nm* map.

maquillaje *nm* make-up.

máquina *nf* machine. ▪ **máquina de afeitar** razor, shaver; **máquina de escribir** typewriter; **máquina de fotos** camera; **máquina tragaperras** slot machine.

maquinilla *nf*. ▪ **maquinilla de afeitar** razor.

mar *nm & nf* **1** *(gen)* sea. **2** *fam* very, a lot: *lo pasamos la mar de bien*, we had a great time. • **en alta mar** on the high seas;

hacerse a la mar to put to sea. ▪ **mar adentro** out to sea.

maravilloso,-a *adj* wonderful, marvellous.

marca *nf* **1** *(señal)* mark, sign. **2** *(de comestibles, productos del hogar)* brand; *(de otros productos)* make. **3** *(récord)* record. • **de marca** top-quality: *ropa de marca*, designer clothes. ▪ **marca de fábrica** trademark; **marca registrada** registered trademark.

marcador *nm* scoreboard.

marcar *vt* **1** *(señalar)* to mark. **2** *(hacer un tanto)* to score. **3** *(a otro jugador)* to mark. **4** *(pelo)* to set. **5** *(al teléfono)* to dial.

marcha *nf* **1** *(caminar)* march. **2** *(partida)* departure. **3** *(música)* march. • **a marchas forzadas** against the clock; **salir de marcha** to go out. ▪ **marcha atlética** walking race; **marcha atrás** reverse gear.

marcharse *vpr* to leave. • **¡marchando!** coming up!

marchitarse *vt-vpr* to wither.

marco *nm* frame.

marea *nf* tide. ▪ **marea alta** high tide; **marea baja** low tide; **marea negra** oil slick.

mareado,-a *adj* **1** *(con náuseas)* sick. **2** *(aturdido)* dizzy, giddy. **3** *(borracho)* tipsy.

marearse *vpr* *(sentir náuseas)* to get sick; *(sentirse aturdido)* to feel dizzy.

mareo *nm* **1** *(con náuseas)* sickness. **2** *(aturdimiento)* dizziness.

marfil *nm* ivory.

margarina *nf* margarine.

margarita *nf* daisy.

margen *nm & nf* **1** *(gen)* margin. **2** *(extremidad)* border, edge. **3** *(de río)* bank.

marginar *vt* to leave out.

marido *nm* husband.

marinero *nm* sailor.

marino,-a *adj* marine. ► *nm* **marino** seaman.

marioneta *nf* puppet, marionette.

mariposa *nf* butterfly.

mariquita *nf* ladybird.

marisco *nm* shellfish, seafood.

marisma *nf* salt marsh.

marisquería *nf* seafood restaurant.

marítimo,-a *adj* maritime.

mármol *nm* marble.

marrón *adj-nm* brown.

martes *nm* Tuesday.

martillo *nm* hammer.

mártir *nmf* martyr.

marzo *nm* March.

mas *conj* but.

más *adv* **1** *(gen)* more: *más pequeño*, smaller; *más caro*, more expensive, dearer; *¿no quieres más?*, don't you want more? **2** *(superlativo)* most: *el más caro*, the most expensive; *el más pequeño*, the smallest. **3** *(de nuevo)* any-more: *no voy más a ese sitio*, I'm not going there anymore. **4** *(con pronombre)* else: *¿algo más?*, anything else? ► *pron* more. ► *nm (signo)* plus. • **de más** spare, extra; **más bien** rather; **más o menos** more or less; **ni más ni menos** no less; **por más (que)** however much.

masa *nf* **1** *(de volumen)* mass. **2** *(de pan)* dough.

masaje *nm* massage.

máscara *nf* mask.

mascarilla *nf* **1** *(cosmética)* face pack. **2** *(de médico)* face mask.

masculino,-a *adj* **1** *(no femenino)* male. **2** *(para hombres)* men's. **3** *(sustantivo)* masculine.

masticar *vt-vi* to masticate, chew.

mástil *nm* **1** mast. **2** *(de bandera)* flagpole.

mata *nf (arbusto)* bush. ▪ **mata de pelo** mop of hair.

matadero *nm* slaughterhouse, abattoir.

matamoscas *nm (insecticida)* flykiller; *(pala)* flyswatter.

matar *vt-vi* to kill.

matasellos *nm* postmark.

mate *adj (sin brillo)* matt.

matemáticas *nf pl* mathematics.

materia *nf* **1** *(sustancia)* matter. **2** *(asignatura)* subject. ▪ **materia prima** raw material.

material *adj-m* material. ▪
material de oficina office
stationery.
materno,-a *adj* maternal: *leche materna*, mother's milk.
matiz *nm* **1** *(color)* shade, tint.
2 *fig (variación)* nuance.
matorral *nm* bushes, thicket.
matrícula *nf* **1** *(en curso)* registration. **2** *(número)* GB registration number; GB license num-
ber; *(placa)* GB number plate;
US license plate. ▪ **matrícula
de honor** honours.
matricular(se) *vt-vpr* to register; GB enrol; US enroll.
matrimonio *nm* **1** *(ceremonia, institución)* marriage. **2**
(pareja) married couple.
maullido *nm* miaow.
maxilar *adj* maxillary. ▶ *nm*
jaw.
máximo,-a *adj* maximum.
mayo *nm* May.
mayonesa *nf* mayonnaise.
mayor *adj* **1** *(comparativo)* big-
ger, greater, larger; *(persona)*
older; *(hermanos, hijos)* elder.
2 *(superlativo)* biggest, great-
est, largest; *(persona)* oldest;
(hermanos, hijos) eldest. • **al
por mayor** wholesale.
mayordomo *nm* butler.
mayoría *nf* majority, most. ▪
mayoría de edad adulthood.
mayorista *nmf* wholesaler.
mayúscula *nf* capital letter.
mazapán *nm* marzipan.

mazorca *nf* cob.
me *pron* **1** *(como objeto)* me. **2**
(reflexivo) myself.
mecánico,-a *adj* mechani-
cal. ▶ *nm,f* mechanic.
mecanismo *nm* mechanism.
mecanógrafo,-a *nm,f* typist.
mecedora *nf* rocking chair.
mecha *nf* **1** *(de vela)* wick. **2**
(de bomba) fuse. ▶ *nf pl* **me-
chas** *(en el pelo)* highlights.
mechero *nm* lighter.
medalla *nf* medal.
media *nf* *(promedio)* average.
▶ *fpl* **medias** *(hasta la cintura)* tights; *(hasta la pierna)*
stockings.
mediano,-a *adj* **1** *(de tamaño)*
middle-sized. **2** *(de calidad)*
average, medium.
medianoche *nf* midnight.
mediante *adj* by means of.
medicamento *nm* medicine.
medicina *nf* medicine.
médico,-a *adj* medical. ▶ *nm,f*
doctor, physician.
medida *nf* **1** *(unidad)* measure.
2 *(disposición)* measure, step. •
a medida que as; **hecho a
medida** made-to-measure.
medio,-a *adj* **1** *(mitad)* half. **2**
(intermedio) middle. **3** *(promedio)* average. ▶ *nm* **medio 1**
(mitad) half. **2** *(centro)* middle.
▶ *adv* half. ▶ *nm pl* **medios**
means. • **a medias 1** *(sin terminar)* half done, half fin-
ished. **2** *(entre dos)* between

the two: *lo pagamos a medias*, we went halves on it. ■ **media pensión** half board; **medio ambiente** environment; **medio de transporte** means of transport; **medios de comunicación** the mass media.

mediocre *adj* mediocre.

mediodía *nm* 1 *(las doce)* noon, midday. 2 *(hora del almuerzo)* lunchtime.

medir *vt* 1 *(tomar medidas)* to measure. 2 *(calcular)* to gauge.

médula *nf* marrow. ■ **médula espinal** spinal cord.

medusa *nf* jellyfish.

megáfono *nm* megaphone, loudspeaker.

mejilla *nf* cheek.

mejillón *nm* mussel.

mejor *adj-adv* 1 *(comparativo)* better. 2 *(superlativo)* best. ● **a lo mejor** perhaps, maybe; **mejor dicho** rather; **tanto mejor** so much the better.

mejorar *vt* to improve. ► *vi-vpr* **mejorar(se)** 1 *(reponerse)* to recover, get better. 2 *(el tiempo)* to clear up.

melena *nf* 1 *(de persona)* long hair. 2 *(de león, caballo)* mane.

mellizo,-a *adj-nm,f* twin.

melocotón *nm* peach.

melodía *nf* melody.

melón *nm* melon.

membrana *nf* membrane.

membrete *nm* letterhead.

membrillo *nm (fruto)* quince; *(dulce)* quince jelly.

memoria *nf* 1 *(gen)* memory. 2 *(informe)* report. ► *nf pl* **memorias** *(biografía)* memoirs. ● **de memoria** by heart.

mencionar *vt* to mention.

mendigo,-a *nm,f* beggar.

mendrugo *nm* hard crust of bread.

menestra *nf* vegetable stew.

menisco *nm* meniscus.

menopausia *nf* menopause.

menor *adj* 1 *(comparativo)* smaller, lesser; *(persona)* younger. 2 *(superlativo)* smallest, least; *(persona)* youngest. ► *nmf* **menor (de edad)** minor. ● **al por menor** retail.

Menorca *nf* Minorca.

menos *adj* 1 *(comparativo - con incontables)* less; *(- con contables)* fewer. 2 *(superlativo - con incontables)* the least; *(con contables)* the fewest. ► *adv* 1 *(comparativo - con incontables)* less; *(- con contables)* fewer. 2 *(superlativo - con incontables)* the least; *(con contables)* the fewest. 3 *(para hora)* to: *las tres menos cuarto*, a quarter to three. ► *prep (excepto)* except, but. ► *nm* minus. ● **a menos que** unless; **al menos** at least; **por lo menos** at least.

mensaje *nm* message.

menstruación *nf* menstruation.

mensual *adj* monthly.
menta *nf* mint.
mental *adj* mental.
mente *nf* mind.
mentir *vi* to lie, tell lies.
mentira *nf* lie.
mentiroso,-a *nm,f* liar.
mentón *nm* chin.
menú *nm* menu.
menudo,-a *adj* **1** *(pequeño)* small, tiny. **2** fine: *¡menudo lío!*, what a fine mess! • **a menudo** often, frequently.
meñique *nm* little finger.
mercadillo *nf* market, street market.
mercado *nm* market. ■ **mercado de valores** stock-market.
mercancía *nf* goods.
mercería *nf* *(tienda)* GB haberdasher's; US notions store.
merecer(se) *vt-vi* to deserve.
merendar *vi* to have an afternoon snack, have tea.
merendero *nm* picnic spot.
merengue *nm* meringue.
merienda *nf* afternoon snack.
mérito *nm* merit, worth.
merluza *nf* hake.
mermelada *nf* *(de cítricos)* marmalade; *(de otras frutas)* jam.
mero *nm* grouper.
mes *nm* month.
mesa *nf* *(de salón, comedor)* table; *(de despacho)* desk. • **poner la mesa** to set the table;

quitar la mesa to clear the table.
meseta *nf* tableland, plateau.
mesilla *nf* small table. ■ **mesilla de noche** bedside table.
mesón *nm* inn, tavern.
mestizo,-a *adj* of mixed race, half-breed.
meta *nf* **1** *(portería)* goal; *(de carreras)* finishing line. **2** *fig (objetivo)* aim, goal.
metal *nm* metal.
metálico,-a *adj* metallic. • **pagar en metálico** to pay cash.
meter *vt* **1** *(introducir)* to put. **2** *(punto)* to score. ▶ *vpr* **meterse 1** *(entrar)* to get in. **2** *(entrometerse)* to interfere, meddle. • **meterse con** ALGN **1** *(burlarse)* to tease SB. **2** *(atacar)* to pick on SB.
método *nm* method.
metralleta *nf* submachine gun.
metro¹ *nm* *(medida)* GB metre; US meter.
metro² *nm* *(transporte)* GB underground, tube; US subway.
mexicano,-a *adj-nm,f* Mexican.
México *nm* Mexico.
mezcla *nf* **1** *(acción - de razas, colores)* mixing; *(- de cafés, tabacos)* blending. **2** *(producto - de razas, colores)* mixture; *(- de cafés, tabacos)* blend.
mezclar *vt* **1** *(razas, colores)* to mix; *(cafés, tabacos)* blend. **2** *(desordenar)* to mix up.

mezquita *nf* mosque.
mi¹ *adj* my.
mi² *nm (nota)* E.
mí *pron* **1** me. **2** *(mí mismo,-a)* myself.
michelín *nm fam* spare tyre.
microbio *nm* microbe.
micrófono *nm* microphone.
microondas *nm* microwave.
microscopio *nm* microscope.
miedo *nm* fear. • **tener miedo** to be afraid.
miel *nf* honey.
miembro *nm* **1** *(socio)* member. **2** *(extremidad)* limb.
mientras *conj* **1** while. **2** *(condición)* as long as, while. ▶ *adv* meanwhile. • **mientras tanto** meanwhile, in the meantime.
miércoles *nm* Wednesday.
mierda *nf* shit.
miga *nf* crumb.
migración *nf* migration.
migraña *nf* migraine.
mil *num* thousand.
milagro *nm* miracle
milenio *nm* millenium.
milímetro *nm* GB millimetre; US millimeter.
militar *adj* military. ▶ *nm* military man, soldier. ▶ *vi* POL to be a militant.
milla *nf* mile.
millón *nm* million.
mimar *vt* to spoil.
mimbre *nm* wicker.

mina *nf* **1** *(gen)* mine. **2** *(de lápiz)* lead.
mineral *adj-nm* mineral.
miniatura *nf* miniature.
minifalda *nf* miniskirt.
mínimo,-a *adj (gasto)* minimal; *(cantidad, temperatura)* minimum. • **como mínimo** at least.
ministerio *nm* GB ministry; US department.
ministro,-a *nm,f* GB minister; US secretary.
minoría *nf* minority.
minorista *nmf* retailer.
minúscula *nf* small letter.
minusválido,-a *adj* handicapped, disabled.
minutero *nm* minute hand.
minuto *nm* minute.
mío,-a *adj* my, of mine. ▶ *pron* mine.
miope *adj* short-sighted.
miopía *nf* shortsightedness.
mirada *nf* look.
mirador *nm* viewpoint.
mirar *vi* **1** *(ver)* to look at. **2** *(observar)* to watch.
misa *nf* mass.
miseria *nf* **1** *(desgracia)* misery. **2** *(pobreza)* extreme poverty.
misil *nm* missile.
misión *nf* mission.
mismo,-a *adj* **1** *(igual)* same. **2** *(enfático - propio)* own; *(- uno mismo)* oneself: *lo haré yo **mismo***, I'll do it myself. ▶

pron same. ► *adv* right: **aquí mismo**, right here.

misterio *nm* mystery.

mitad *nf* **1** half: **la mitad de una botella**, half a bottle. **2** *(en medio)* middle: **en mitad de la carretera**, in the middle of the road.

mitin *nm* rally.

mito *nm* myth.

mocasín *nm* loafer, moccasin.

mochila *nf* rucksack, backpack.

moco *nm* mucus.

moda *nf* fashion. ● **pasado de moda** old-fashioned.

modales *nm pl* manners.

modelo *adj-nm* model. ► *nmf* fashion model.

módem *nm* modem.

moderar *vt* to moderate.

moderno,-a *adj* modern.

modesto,-a *adj* modest.

modificar *vt* to modify,.

modista *nmf (que confecciona)* dressmaker; *(que diseña)* fashion designer.

modo *nm* manner, way. ● **de cualquier modo** anyway; **de ningún modo** by no means; **de todos modos** anyhow, in any case; **en cierto modo** to a certain extent.

módulo *nm* module.

moflete *nm fam* chubby cheek.

moho *nm* GB mould; US mold.

mojar *vt (empapar)* to wet; *(humedecer)* to dampen.

molde *nm* GB mould; US mold.

moler *vt (café)* to grind.

molestar *vt-vi* to disturb, bother. ► *vpr* **molestarse 1** *(tomarse el trabajo)* to bother. **2** *(ofenderse)* to get upset.

molestia *nf* **1** *(incomodidad)* nuisance, bother. **2** *(dolor)* slight pain, discomfort. ● **"Rogamos disculpen las molestias"** "We apologize for any inconvenience".

molido,-a *adj (café)* ground.

molinillo *nm* grinder, mill.

molino *nm* mill.

molusco *nm* GB mollusc; US mollusk.

momento *nm* **1** *(gen)* moment, instant. **2** *(época)* time. ● **de momento** for the time being; **por el momento** for the time being.

momia *nf* mummy.

monarquía *nf* monarchy.

monasterio *nm* monastery.

mondadientes *nm* toothpick.

moneda *nf* **1** *(unidad monetaria)* currency, money. **2** *(pieza)* coin.

monedero *nm* purse.

monitor,-ra *nm,f (profesor)* instructor. ► *nm* **monitor** *(pantalla)* monitor.

monja *nf* nun.

monje *nm* monk.

mono,-a *adj (bonito)* pretty, cute. ► *nm* **mono 1** *(animal)* monkey. **2** *(prenda)* overalls.

monopatín *nm* skateboard.
monótono,-a *adj* monotonous.
monstruo *nm* monster.
montacargas *nm* GB goods lift; US freight elevator.
montaje *nm* **1** *(de aparato, mueble)* assembly. **2** *(de película)* cutting, editing. **3** *(de obra teatral)* staging.
montaña *nf* mountain. ■ **montaña rusa** big dipper.
montañismo *nm* mountain climbing, mountaineering.
montar *vi* **1** *(a vehículo)* to mount, get on. **2** *(caballo, bicicleta)* to ride. ▶ *vt* **1** *(cabalgar)* to ride. **2** *(nata)* to whip; *(claras)* whisk. **3** *(máquinas)* to assemble. **4** *(negocio, exposición)* to set up. **5** *(película)* to edit, mount. **6** *(obra de teatro)* to stage.
monte *nm* mountain, mount.
montón *nm* **1** *(pila)* heap, pile. **2** *fam (gran cantidad)* loads great, quantity.
montura *nf (de gafas)* frame.
monumento *nm* monument.
moño *nm (de pelo)* bun.
moqueta *nf* fitted carpet.
mora *nf* **1** *(de moral)* mulberry. **2** *(zarzamora)* blackberry.
morado,-a *adj* dark purple. ▶ *nm* **morado 1** *(color)* dark purple. **2** *(golpe)* bruise.
moral *adj* moral. ▶ *nf* **1** *(reglas)* morality, morals. **2** *(ánimo)* morale, spirits.

morcilla *nf* black pudding.
morder *vt-vi* to bite.
mordisco *nm* bite.
moreno,-a *adj* dark. ▶ *nm* **moreno** suntan. ● **ponerse moreno** to tan.
morir(se) *vi-vpr* to die.
moro,-a *adj* **1** *(norteafricano)* Moorish. **2** *(musulmán)* Muslim.
morro *nm* **1** *fam (de persona)* mouth, lips. **2** *(de animal)* snout, nose.
morsa *nf* walrus.
mortadela *nf* mortadella.
mortal *adj* **1** *(persona)* mortal. **2** *(mortífero)* lethal.
mortero *nm* mortar.
mosaico *nm* mosaic.
mosca *nf* fly.
moscardón *nm* blowfly.
mosquearse *vpr fam (enfadarse)* to get cross.
mosquito *nm* mosquito.
mostaza *nf* mustard.
mosto *nm* grape juice.
mostrador *nm* counter. ■ **mostrador de facturación** check-in desk.
mostrar *vt (enseñar)* to show. ▶ *vpr* **mostrarse** to be: *se mostró muy interesado*, he was very interested.
mote *nm* nickname.
motín *nm* riot.
motivar *vt* **1** *(causar)* to cause, give rise to. **2** *(estimular)* to motivate.

motivo *nm* **1** *(causa)* motive, reason. **2** *(de dibujo, música)* motif. • **con motivo de** on the occasion of.

moto *nf fam* motorbike.

motocicleta *nf* motorbike.

motor,-ra *adj* motor. ► *nm* **motor** *(no eléctrico)* engine; *(eléctrico)* motor. ▪ **motor de búsqueda** search engine.

motora *nf* small motorboat.

motorista *nmf* motorcyclist.

mover(se) *vt-vpr* to move.

móvil *adj* movable, mobile. ► *nm* **1** *(teléfono)* mobile (phone), cellular phone. **2** *(motivo)* motive, inducement.

movimiento *nm* movement.

mozo,-a *nm,f (chico)* boy, lad; *(chica)* girl, lass.

muchacho,-a *nm,f (chico)* boy, lad; *(chica)* girl, lass.

muchedumbre *nf* crowd.

mucho,-a *adj* **1** *(frases afirmativas - singular)* a lot of, much; *(- plural)* a lot of, many. **2** *(frases negativas e interrogativas - singular)* much; *(- plural)* many. ► *pron (singular - frases afirmativas)* a lot, much; *(- frases negativas e interrogativas)* much; *(plural)* many. ► *adv* **mucho 1** *(gen)* a lot: *lo siento mucho,* I'm very sorry. **2** *(comparaciones)* much. **3** *(mucho tiempo)* a long time. **4** *(frecuentemente)* often, much.

mudanza *nf* removal.

mudarse *vpr* **1** *(gen)* to change. **2** *(de residencia)* to move.

mudo,-a *adj* dumb.

mueble *nm* piece of furniture.

mueca *nf* grimace

muela *nf* tooth.

muelle¹ *nm (en puerto)* dock.

muelle² *nm (resorte)* spring.

muerte *nf* death.

muerto,-a *adj* dead. ► *nm,f* dead person. • **estar muerto de hambre** to be starving.

muestra *nf* **1** *(ejemplar)* sample. **2** *(señal)* proof, sign.

muestrario *nm* collection of samples.

mujer *nf* **1** woman. **2** *(esposa)* wife. ▪ **mujer de la limpieza** cleaning lady.

mulato,-a *adj-nm,f* mulatto.

muleta *nf* crutch.

mulo,-a *nm,f (macho)* mule; *(hembra)* she-mule.

multa *nf* fine.

multinacional *adj-nf* multinational.

múltiple *adj* **1** *(numeroso)* multiple. **2** *(muchos)* many, a number of.

multiplicar(se) *vt-vpr* to multiply.

multitud *nf* multitude, crowd.

mundial *adj* world(wide). ► *nm* world championship.

mundo *nm* world. • **todo el mundo** everybody.

municipal *adj* municipal.

municipio *nm* municipality.
muñeca *nf* **1** *(del brazo)* wrist. **2** *(juguete)* doll.
muñeco *nm* **1** *(monigote)* dummy. **2** *(juguete)* doll. ▪ **muñeco de nieve** snowman; **muñeco de peluche** soft toy.
mural *adj-nm* mural.
muralla *nf* wall.
murciélago *nm* bat.
murmurar *vi* to murmur.
muro *nm* wall.
muscular *adj* muscular.
músculo *nm* muscle.
museo *nm* museum.
musgo *nm* moss.
música *nf* music. ▪ **música de fondo** background music.
músico,-a *adj* musical. ▶ *nm,f* musician.
muslo *nm* thigh.
musulmán,-ana *adj-nm,f* Muslim, Moslem.
mutuo,-a *adj* mutual.
muy *adv* very.

N-Ñ

nabo *nm* turnip.
nácar *nm* mother-of-pearl.
nacer *vi* **1** *(persona, animal)* to be born. **2** *(río)* to rise.
nacimiento *nm* **1** *(de persona, animal)* birth. **2** *(de río)* source.

nación *nf* nation.
nacional *adj* **1** *(bandera, equipo, seguridad)* national. **2** *(productos, mercados, vuelos)* domestic.
nada *pron* nothing, not... anything. ▶ *adv* not at all: **no es nada fácil**, it isn't at all easy. • **como si nada** as if nothing had happened; **–de nada** –don't mention it.
nadar *vi* to swim.
nadie *pron* nobody, not... anybody.
naipe *nm* card.
nana *nf* lullaby.
naranja *nf* orange.
naranjada *nf* orangeade.
narcótico *nm* narcotic.
nariz *nf* nose.
narración *nf* **1** *(acción)* narration, account. **2** *(relato)* story
nata *nf* **1** *(para montar)* cream. **2** *(de leche hervida)* skin.
natación *nf* swimming.
natal *adj* of birth. ▪ **ciudad natal** home town.
natillas *nf pl* custard.
nativo,-a *adj-nm,f* native.
natural *adj* **1** *(color, estado, gesto)* natural. **2** *(fruta, flor)* fresh. **3** *(yogur)* plain.
naturaleza *nf* nature.
naufragio *nm* *(de barco)* shipwreck.
náusea *nf* nausea, sickness. • **sentir náuseas/tener náuseas** to feel sick.

náutico,-a *adj* nautical.

navaja *nf* **1** *(cuchillo)* penknife, pocketknife. **2** *(molusco)* razor-shell. ∎ **navaja de afeitar** razor.

nave *nf* **1** *(barco)* ship. **2** *(de iglesia)* nave. ∎ **nave espacial** spaceship; **nave industrial** industrial building.

navegador *nm* browser.

navegar *vi* to navigate, sail. • **navegar por Internet** to surf the Net.

Navidad *nf* Christmas: *¡Feliz Navidad!*, Merry Christmas!

necesario,-a *adj* necessary.

neceser *nm* GB toilet bag; US toilet kit.

necesidad *nf* **1** *(falta)* need. **2** *(cosa esencial)* necessity. • **hacer sus necesidades** to relieve oneself.

necesitar *vt* to need. • **"Se necesita camarero"** "Waiter required".

negar *vt* **1** *(acusación, afirmación)* to deny. **2** *(permiso, solicitud)* to refuse. ▶ *vpr* **negarse** to refuse.

negativo,-a *adj* negative.

negociación *nf* negotiation.

negociar *vi* **1** *(comerciar)* to trade, deal. **2** *(hablar)* to negotiate.

negocio *nm* **1** *(comercio, actividad)* business. **2** *(transacción)* deal, transaction.

negro,-a *adj* **1** *(color, raza, pelo)* black. **2** *(tono, ojos, piel)* dark. ▶ *nm* **negro** *(color)* black.

nervio *nm* nerve.

nervioso,-a *adj* nervous.

neto,-a *adj* net.

neumático *nm* GB tyre; US tire.

neutro,-a *adj* **1** *(neutral)* neutral. **2** *(género)* neuter.

nevada *nf* snowfall.

nevar *vi* to snow.

nevera *nf* fridge, refrigerator.

ni *conj* **1** *(en doble negación)* neither… nor: *no tengo tiempo ni dinero*, I have neither time nor money. **2** *(ni siquiera)* not even: *ni por dinero*, not even for money.

nido *nm* nest.

niebla *nf* fog.

nieto,-a *nm,f (gen)* grandchild; *(niño)* grandson; *(niña)* granddaughter.

nieve *nf* snow.

ningún *adj* → ninguno,-a.

ninguno,-a *adj* no, not… any. ▶ *pron* **1** *(hablando de varias personas o cosas)* none: *ninguno de nosotros vio nada*, none of us saw anything. **2** *(hablando de dos personas o cosas)* neither: *ninguno de los dos funciona*, neither of them works. **3** *(nadie)* nobody, no one: *ninguno lo vio*, nobody saw it, no one saw it.

niñera *nf* nursemaid, nanny.

niño,-a *nm,f (gen)* child; *(chico)* boy; *(chica)* girl; *(bebé)* baby.

níspero *nm* medlar.

nivel *nm* 1 *(en una escala, jerarquía)* level. 2 *(calidad)* standard.

no *adv* 1 no, not. 2 *(prefijo)* non: *la no violencia*, nonviolence. ▶ *nm* no. • *..., ¿no?* tag question: *lo viste, ¿no?*, you saw it, didn't you?

noble *adj* noble.

noche *nf* night. • **buenas noches** 1 *(saludo)* good evening. 2 *(despedida)* good night; **esta noche** tonight; **por la noche** at night.

nochebuena *nf* Christmas Eve.

nochevieja *nf* New Year's Eve.

noción *nf* notion.

nocivo,-a *adj* harmful.

nogal *nm* walnut tree.

nómada *nmf* nomad.

nombre *nm* 1 *(gen)* name. 2 *(sustantivo)* noun. • **en nombre de** on behalf of. ■ **nombre de pila** first name, Christian name; **nombre y apellidos** full name.

nómina *nf (sueldo)* pay.

noria *nf (de feria)* big wheel.

norma *nf* rule.

normal *adj* 1 *(común, usual)* normal. 2 *(nada especial)* ordinary.

norte *adj-nm* north.

nos *pron* 1 *(complemento)* us. 2 *(reflexivo)* ourselves. 3 *(recíproco)* each other.

nosotros,-as *pron* 1 *(sujeto)* we. 2 *(complemento, con preposiciones)* us.

nota *nf* 1 *(anotación)* note. 2 *(calificación)* GB mark; US grade. 3 *(cuenta)* GB bill; US check. 4 *(musical)* note.

notar *vt* 1 *(percibir)* to notice. 2 *(sentir)* to feel. • **se nota que...** you can see that....

notario,-a *nm,f* notary.

noticia *nf* news: *una noticia*, a piece of news.

novato,-a *nm,f* novice, beginner.

novecientos,-as *num* nine hundred.

novedad *nf* 1 *(cosa nueva)* novelty. 2 *(cambio)* change.

novela *nf* novel.

noveno,-a *num* ninth.

noventa *num* ninety.

noviazgo *nm* engagement.

noviembre *nm* November.

novio,-a *nm,f* 1 *(chico)* boyfriend; *(chica)* girlfriend. 2 *(prometido - chico)* fiancé; *(- chica)* fiancée. 3 *(en boda - hombre)* bridegroom; *(- mujer)* bride.

nube *nf* cloud.

nublado,-a *adj* cloudy, overcast.

nuboso,-a *adj* cloudy.

nuca *nf* nape of the neck.

nuclear *adj* nuclear.
núcleo *nm* nucleus.
nudillo *nm* knuckle.
nudo *nm* knot.
nuera *nf* daughter-in-law.
nuestro,-a *adj* our, of ours.
► *pron* ours.
nueve *num* nine; *(en fechas)*
ninth.
nuevo,-a *adj* new. • **de nuevo** again.
nuez *nf* walnut. ▪ **nuez de
Adán** Adam's apple; **nuez
moscada** nutmeg.
nulo,-a *adj* invalid.
numerar *vt* to number.
número *nm* 1 *(gen)* number.
2 *(de zapatos)* size.
nunca *adv* 1 *(en negativa)* never. 2 *(en interrogativa)* ever. •
casi nunca hardly ever; **nunca más** never again.
nutria *nf* otter.
nutritivo,-a *adj* nutritious,
nourishing.
ñoqui *nm* gnocchi.
ñu *nm* gnu.

O

o *conj* or. • **o... o...** either... or..;
o sea that is to say.
oasis *nm* oasis.
obedecer *vt* to obey.
obediente *adj* obedient.

obeso,-a *adj* obese.
obispo *nm* bishop.
objetivo,-a *adj* objective. ►
nm **objetivo** 1 *(fin)* aim, goal.
2 *(de ataque)* target. 3 *(lente)*
lens.
objeto *nm* object.
oblicuo,-a *adj* oblique.
obligación *nf* obligation.
obligar *vt* to oblige, force.
obligatorio,-a *adj* compulsory, obligatory.
obra *nf* 1 *(de arte, ingeniería)*
work; *(de literatura)* book; *(de
teatro)* play. 2 *(acto)* deed. 3
(edificio en construcción) building site. ► *nf pl* **obras** *(en casa)*
building work; *(en la calle)* road-
works. ▪ **obra maestra** masterpiece.
obrero,-a *nm,f* worker.
obsequio *nm* gift.
observación *nf* observation.
observar *vt* 1 *(mirar)* to observe. 2 *(notar)* to notice.
obsesión *nf* obsession.
obstáculo *nm* obstacle, hin-
drance.
obstante. • **no obstante** however, nevertheless.
obstruirse *vpr* to get blocked
up.
obtener *vt* to obtain.
obús *nm* shell.
obvio,-a *adj* obvious.
oca *nf* goose.
ocasión *nf* 1 *(momento)* occasion. 2 *(oportunidad)* opportu-

nity, chance. **3** *(ganga)* bargain. • **de ocasión 1** *(segunda mano)* secondhand. **2** *(barato)* bargain.

ocaso *nm* sunset.

occidental *adj* western.

occidente *nm* the West.

océano *nm* ocean.

ochenta *num* eighty.

ocho *num* eight; *(en fechas)* eighth.

ochocientos,-as *num* eight hundred.

ocio *nm (tiempo libre)* leisure.

octavo,-a *num* eighth.

octubre *nm* October.

oculista *nmf* ophthalmologist.

ocultar *vt* to hide.

ocupación *nf* occupation.

ocupado,-a *adj* **1** *(persona)* busy. **2** *(asiento)* taken; *(aseos, teléfono)* engaged.

ocupar *vt* **1** *(conquistar)* to occupy. **2** *(llenar)* to take up.

ocurrir *vi* to happen, occur. ► *vpr* **ocurrirse**: *no se le ocurrió preguntar*, it didn't occur to her to ask.

odiar *vt* to hate.

odio *nm* hatred.

odontólogo,-a *nm,f* dental surgeon, odontologist.

oeste *nm* west.

ofender *vt* to offend.

ofensiva *nf* offensive.

oferta *nf* **1** *(propuesta, ganga)* offer. **2** *(en concurso)* bid, tender. • **de oferta** on offer.

oficial *adj* official. ► *nm* **1** *(militar)* officer. **2** *(empleado)* clerk. **3** *(obrero)* journeyman.

oficina *nf* office.

oficinista *nmf* office worker.

oficio *nm (trabajo manual especializado)* trade; *(profesión)* profession.

ofimática *nf* office automation.

ofrecer *vt* **1** *(dar - premio, trabajo)* to offer; *(- banquete, fiesta)* to hold. **2** *(presentar - posibilidad)* to give; *(- dificultad)* to present.

oído *nm* **1** *(sentido)* hearing. **2** *(órgano)* ear.

oír *vt* to hear.

ojal *nm* buttonhole.

ojeras *nm pl* bags under the eyes.

ojo *nm* **1** *(órgano)* eye. **2** *(agujero)* hole. • **a ojo** at a rough guess. ■ **ojo de buey** porthole; **ojo de la cerradura** keyhole.

ola *nf* wave.

oleaje *nm* swell.

óleo *nm (material)* oil paint; *(cuadro)* oil painting.

oler *vt-vi* to smell. • **olerse algo** to suspect STH.

olfato *nm* sense of smell.

oliva *nf* olive.

olivo *nm* olive tree.

olla *nf* pot. ■ **olla a presión** pressure cooker.

olmo *nm* elm.

olor *nm* smell.

olvidar *vt* **1** *(gen)* to forget. **2** *(dejar)* to leave.

olvido *nm (lapsus)* oversight.

ombligo *nm* navel.

once *num* eleven; *(en fechas)* eleventh.

onceavo,-a *num* eleventh.

onda *nf* wave.

ondear *vi (bandera)* to flutter.

opaco,-a *adj* opaque.

opción *nf* option.

ópera *nf* opera.

operación *nf* operation.

operador,-ra *nm,f* operator.
■ **operador turístico** tour operator.

operar *vt* to operate.

opinar *vt* to think. ► *vi* to express an opinion.

opinión *nf (juicio)* opinion. • **cambiar de opinión** to change one's mind.

oponer *vt (resistencia)* to offer. ► *vpr* **oponerse 1** *(estar en contra)* to oppose. **2** *(ser contrario)* to be opposed.

oportunidad *nf* **1** *(ocasión)* opportunity. **2** *(ganga)* bargain. **3** *(conveniencia)* advisability.

oposición *nf* **1** *(enfrentamiento)* opposition. **2** *(examen)* competitive examination.

oprimir *vt* **1** *(tecla, botón)* to press. **2** *(persona, pueblo)* to oppress.

optativo,-a *adj* optional.

óptica *nf* **1** *(tienda)* optician's. **2** *(ciencia)* optics.

optimismo *nm* optimism.

opuesto,-a *adj* opposite.

oración *nf* **1** *(rezo)* prayer. **2** *(frase)* clause, sentence.

orador,-ra *nm,f* speaker.

oral *adj* oral. • **por vía oral** to be taken orally.

orangután *nm* orang-utan.

órbita *nf* **1** *(de satélite)* orbit. **2** *(de ojo)* socket.

orca *nf* killer whale.

orden *nm (disposición)* order. ► *nf* **1** *(mandato, asociación)* order. **2** *(judicial)* warrant. • **del orden de** GB in the order of; US on the order of. ■ **orden del día** agenda; **orden público** law and order.

ordenado,-a *adj* tidy.

ordenador *nm* computer. ■ **ordenador portátil** laptop.

ordenar *vt* **1** *(arreglar)* to put in order; *(habitación)* to tidy up. **2** *(mandar)* to order.

ordeñar *vt* to milk.

ordinario,-a *adj* **1** *(corriente)* ordinary. **2** *(grosero)* vulgar, common.

orégano *nm* oregano.

oreja *nf* ear.

organigrama *nm (de empresa)* organization chart; *(de procedimiento, sistema)* flow chart.

organismo *nm* **1** *(ser viviente)* organism. **2** *(entidad pública)* organization, body.

organización nf organization.
organizar vt to organize.
órgano nm organ.
orgullo nm pride.
orgulloso,-a adj proud.
orientación nf 1 (dirección) orientation. 2 (guía) guidance.
oriental adj eastern.
orientar vt 1 (dirigir) to orientate. 2 (guiar) to guide. ▶ vpr **orientarse** 1 (encontrar el camino) to find one's way about.
oriente nm east.
orificio nm orifice.
origen nm origin: *de origen español*, of Spanish extraction.
original adj-nm original.
orilla nf 1 (borde) edge. 2 (del río) bank; (del mar) shore.
orina nf urine.
orinal nm (de adulto) chamber pot; (de niño) potty.
oro nm gold.
orquesta nf 1 (clásica, sinfónica) orchestra. 2 (banda) dance band.
orquídea nf orchid.
ortiga nf nettle.
ortografía nf spelling.
oruga nf caterpillar.
os pron 1 (complemento directo) you. 2 (complemento indirecto) to you. 3 (reflexivo) yourselves. 4 (recíproco) each other.
oscuridad nf darkness.
oscuro,-a adj 1 (lugar, color) dark. 2 (origen, explicación) obscure. • **a oscuras** in the dark.

oso nm bear. ■ **oso de peluche** teddy bear; **oso hormiguero** anteater.
ostentar vt 1 (exhibir) to flaunt. 2 (poseer) to hold.
ostra nf oyster.
otoño nm GB autumn; US fall.
otorgar vt (conceder) to grant; (premio) to award.
otro,-a adj 1 (con sustantivo en singular) another; (precedido de determinante o adjetivo posesivo) other: *vino otra persona en su lugar*, another person came in his place; *la otra silla era más cómoda*, the other chair was more confortable. 2 (con sustantivo en plural) other: *entre otras cosas*, amongst other things. ▶ pron 1 (singular) another, another one. 2 **el otro, la otra** (cosa, persona) the other one. 3 **los otros, las otras** (cosa) the other ones, the others; (personas) the others. • **otro tanto** as much.
ovación nf ovation.
ovalado,-a adj oval.
ovario nm ovary.
oveja nf sheep
óvulo nm ovule.
oxidado,-a adj rusty.
oxígeno nm oxygen.
oyente nmf (de la radio) listener. ▶ nm pl **oyentes** audience.
ozono nm ozone. ■ **capa de ozono** ozone layer.

P

pabellón *nm* **1** *(edificio - aislado)* block, section; *(- anexo en feria)* pavilion. **2** *(de la oreja)* outer ear. ■ **pabellón deportivo** sports hall.

paciencia *nf* patience.

paciente *adj-nmf* patient.

pacífico,-a *adj* peaceful.

pacto *nm* pact, agreement.

padecer *vt-vi* to suffer.

padre *nm* father.

padrenuestro *nm* Lord's Prayer.

padrino *nm* **1** *(de bautizo)* godfather. **2** *(de boda)* man who gives the bride away.

paella *nf* paella.

paga *nf* pay; *(de niños)* pocket money. ■ **paga extra** bonus.

pagar *vt* *(compra, entrada)* to pay for; *(sueldo, alquiler, cuenta)* to pay; *(deuda)* to pay off.

página *nf* page.

pago *nm* payment. ■ **pago por visión** pay per view.

país *nm* country.

paisaje *nm* **1** *(terreno)* landscape. **2** *(vista)* scenery.

paja *nf* straw.

pajarería *nf* pet shop.

pajarita *nf* **1** *(lazo)* bow tie. **2** *(de papel)* paper bird.

pájaro *nm* bird. ■ **pájaro carpintero** woodpecker.

pala *nf* **1** *(para cavar)* spade. **2** *(de pelota)* bat.

palabra *nf* word. ● **tener la palabra** to have the floor. ■ **palabra clave** keyword.

palabrota *nf* swearword.

palacio *nm* palace. ■ **palacio de congresos** conference centre (US center); **palacio de deportes** sports centre (US center).

paladar *nm* palate.

palanca *nf* lever. ■ **palanca de cambio** gear lever, gearstick.

palangana *nf* washbasin.

palco *nm* box. ■ **palco de autoridades** royal box.

pálido,-a *adj* pale.

palillo *nm* **1** *(mondadientes)* toothpick. **2** *(de tambor)* drumstick. ■ **palillos chinos** chopsticks.

paliza *nf* **1** *(zurra)* beating, thrashing. **2** *(derrota)* defeat. **3** *fam (pesadez)* bore.

palma *nf* **1** *(planta)* palm tree. **2** *(de la mano)* palm.

palmera *nf* palm tree.

palo *nm* **1** *(vara)* stick. **2** *(mástil)* mast. ● **a palo seco** on its own. ■ **palo de golf** golf club.

paloma *nf* dove, pigeon.

palomitas *nf pl* popcorn.

palpitación *nf* palpitation.

pamela *nf* sun hat.

pan *nm* *(alimento)* bread; *(hogaza)* round loaf; *(barra)* French loaf. ■ **pan de molde** sliced bread; **pan integral** whole-meal bread; **pan rallado** bread-crumbs.

pana *nf* corduroy.

panadería *nf* bakery, baker's.

panal *nm* honeycomb.

pancarta *nf* placard.

páncreas *nm* pancreas.

panda *nm* panda.

pandereta *nf* small tambour-ine.

panel *nm* panel.

panfleto *nm* pamphlet.

pánico *nm* panic.

panorama *nm* panorama, view.

pantalla *nf* **1** *(gen)* screen. **2** *(de lámpara)* shade.

pantalón *nm* trousers. ■ **pantalón corto** shorts; **pantalón vaquero** jeans.

pantano *nm* *(ciénaga)* marsh; *(embalse)* reservoir.

pantera *nf* panther.

pantorrilla *nf* calf.

pañal *nm* GB nappy ; US diaper.

paño *nm* **1** *(tela)* cloth, mater-ial. **2** *(trapo para polvo)* duster. ■ **paño de cocina** tea cloth, tea towel.

pañuelo *nm* **1** *(para sonarse)* handkerchief. **2** *(complemen-to)* scarf. ■ **pañuelo de pa-pel** tissue.

papa *nm* *(pontífice)* pope.

papá *nm* *fam* dad, daddy. ■ **Papá Noel** Father Christmas.

papagayo *nm* parrot.

papel *nm* **1** *(material)* paper. **2** *(hoja)* piece of paper, sheet of paper. **3** *(en obra, película)* role, part. ■ **papel de aluminio** aluminium foil; **papel de fu-mar** cigarette paper; **papel de lija** sandpaper; **papel de plata** silver paper, tinfoil; **pa-pel higiénico** toilet paper; **papel pintado** wallpaper.

papelera *nf* **1** *(en oficina)* wastepaper basket. **2** *(en la calle)* GB litter bin; US litter basket.

papelería *nf* stationer's.

paperas *nf pl* mumps.

papilla *nf* **1** *(para enfermo)* pap. **2** *(para bebé)* baby food.

paquete *nm* *(de libros, ropa)* package, parcel; *(de tabaco, folios, galletas)* packet; *(de azúcar, harina)* bag. ■ **paque-te postal** parcel.

par *adj* even. ▶ *nm* *(pareja)* pair. ● **a la par 1** *(al mismo tiempo)* at the same time. **2** *(juntos)* to-gether; **de par en par** wide open; **sin par** matchless.

para *prep* **1** *(finalidad)* for, to, in order to: *para ahorrar di-nero*, (in order) to save mon-ey. **2** *(dirección)* for, to: *el tren para Toledo*, the train to To-ledo; *para adelante*, for-wards; *para atrás*, back-wards. **3** *(tiempo, fechas límites)* by: *déjalo para luego*, leave it for later. ● **para entonces**

parir

by then; **para que** in order that, so that; **¿para qué?** what for?

parabrisas *nm* GB windscreen; US windshield.

paracaídas *nm* parachute.

parachoques *nm (de coche)* GB bumper; US fender.

parada *nf* 1 *(gen)* stop. 2 DEP save. ▪ **parada de taxis** GB taxi stand; US cab stand.

parado,-a *adj* 1 *(quieto)* still, motionless. 2 *(desempleado)* unemployed. • **salir bien/ mal parado de algo** to come off well/badly out of STH.

parador *nm* hotel.

paraguas *nm* umbrella.

paraíso *nm* paradise. ▪ **paraíso fiscal** tax haven.

paraje *nm* spot, place.

paralelo,-a *adj* parallel.

parálisis *nf* paralysis. ▪ **parálisis cerebral** cerebral palsy.

paralítico,-a *adj-nm,f* paralytic.

paralizarse *vpr* 1 *(miembro)* to be paralysed. 2 *(actividad)* to come to a standstill.

parapente *nm (deporte)* paragliding; *(paracaídas)* paraglider.

parar(se) *vt-vi-vpr (gen)* to stop. • **ir a parar** to end up; **sin parar** nonstop, without stopping.

pararrayos *nm* lightning conductor.

parásito *nm* parasite.

parche *nm* patch.

parchís *nm* GB ludo; US Parcheesi®.

parcial *adj* partial. ▶ *nm (examen)* mid-term exam.

parecer *vi* 1 *(por cómo se percibe)* to seem; *(por su aspecto externo)* to look. 2 *(opinar)* to think: **si te parece bien…**, if it's all right with you… 3 *(aparentar)* to look as if: **parece que va a llover**, it looks as if it's going to rain. ▶ *vpr* **parecerse** 1 to look alike, be alike: **Hugo y su hermano se parecen**, Hugo and his brother look alike. 2 to look like: **Hugo se parece a su padre**, Hugo looks like his father. ▶ *nm (opinión)* opinion. • **al parecer** apparently.

parecido,-a *adj* similar.

pared *nf* wall.

pareja *nf* 1 *(gen)* pair. 2 *(de personas)* couple. 3 *(de baile, compañero)* partner. • **hacer buena pareja** to be two of a kind. ▪ **pareja de hecho** unmarried couple.

parentesco *nm* kinship, relationship.

paréntesis *nm* 1 *(signo)* parenthesis, bracket. 2 *(pausa)* break, interruption. • **entre paréntesis** in brackets.

pariente,-a *nm,f* relative.

parir *vi* to give birth.

parking *nm (público)* GB car-park; US parking lot; *(particular)* garage: *una plaza de parking*, a parking space.

parlamento *nm* parliament.

paro *nm* 1 *(desempleo)* unemployment. 2 *(interrupción)* stoppage. 3 *(dinero)* unemployment benefit. • **estar en el paro** to be out of work, be unemployed. ▪ **paro cardiaco** cardiac arrest.

párpado *nm* eyelid.

parque *nm* park. ▪ **parque de atracciones** funfair; **parque infantil** children's playground; **parque natural** nature reserve; **parque temático** theme park.

parqué *nm* parquet.

parra *nf* grapevine.

párrafo *nm* paragraph.

parrilla *nf* grill. • **a la parrilla** grilled. ▪ **parrilla de salida** starting grid.

parrillada *nf* mixed grill.

parte *nf* 1 *(gen)* part. 2 *(en contrato)* party. 3 *(de un partido)* half. • **a partes iguales** in equal shares; **de parte de** on behalf of, from; **¿de parte de quién?** who's calling?; **en ninguna parte** nowhere; **por todas partes** everywhere; **por una parte...**, **por otra** on the one hand..., on the other hand... ▪ **parte facultativo** medical report;

parte meteorológico weather report.

participación *nf* 1 *(colaboración)* participation. 2 *(de lotería)* share.

participante *nmf* participant.

participar *vi (tomar parte)* to take part, participate. ▶ *vt (notificar)* to notify, inform.

participio *nm* participle.

partícula *nf* particle.

particular *adj* 1 *(específico)* particular. 2 *(especial)* special. 3 *(privado)* private. • **sin otro particular** yours faithfully.

partida *nf* 1 *(salida)* departure, leave. 2 *(documento)* certificate. 3 *(de juego)* game.

partidario,-a *nm,f* supporter.

partido *nm* 1 *(grupo)* party, group. 2 *(partida)* game, match. • **sacar partido de** to profit from; **tomar partido** to take sides. ▪ **partido amistoso** friendly match.

partir *vt* 1 *(separar)* to divide, split. 2 *(romper)* to break, crack. ▶ *vi (irse)* to leave, set out, set off. ▶ *vpr* **partirse** to split up, break up. • **a partir de hoy** from today onwards.

partitura *nf* score.

parto *nm* (child)birth, delivery. ▪ **parto provocado** induced labour (US labor); **parto sin dolor** painless childbirth.

pasa *nf* raisin.

pasadizo *nm* passage.

pasado,-a *adj* **1** *(anterior)* past, gone by: *el lunes pasado*, last Monday. **2** *(último)* last. **3** *(carne)* overdone. ► *nm* **pasado** *(momento anterior)* past; *(de un verbo)* past tense. ● **pasadas las…** after…; **las… pasadas** gone…: *son las cuatro pasadas*, it's gone four.

pasaje *nm* **1** *(billete)* ticket. **2** *(pasajeros)* passengers *pl.* **3** *(calle)* passage, alley. **4** *(de texto)* passage.

pasajero,-a *adj* passing. ► *nm,f* passenger.

pasamanos *nm* handrail.

pasamontañas *nm* balaclava.

pasaporte *nm* passport.

pasar *vi* **1** *(gen)* to pass. **2** *(entrar)* to come in, go in. **3** *(cesar)* to come to an end. **4** *(límite)* to exceed: *pasa de la edad que piden*, he is over the age they are asking for. **5** *(ocurrir)* to happen. **6** *fam (mostrar poco interés)* not to be bothered. ► *vt* **1** *(entregar)* to pass. **2** *(página)* to turn. **3** *(límite)* to go beyond. **4** *(aventajar)* to surpass, beat. **5** *(adelantar)* to overtake. **6** *(tiempo)* to spend. ► *vpr* **pasarse 1** *(excederse)* to go too far, exaggerate. **2** *(pudrirse)* to go off. **3** *(ir)* to go by,

walk past. ● **pasar por** to be considered; **pasarlo bien/ mal** to have a good/bad time; **¿qué pasa?** what's the matter?, what's wrong?

pasarela *nf (de barco)* walkway; *(de modelos)* catwalk.

pasatiempo *nm* pastime, hobby.

Pascua *nf (cristiana)* Easter; *(judía)* Passover. ► *nf pl* **Pascuas** Christmas.

pase *nm* **1** *(gen)* pass, permit. **2** *(de película)* showing.

pasear *vt* to walk. ► *vi-vpr* **pasear(se)** to go for a walk.

paseo *nm* **1** *(a pie)* walk, stroll; *(en coche)* drive; *(en bici, a caballo)* ride. **2** *(calle)* avenue, promenade. ● **dar un paseo** to go for a walk. ■ **paseo marítimo** sea front, promenade.

pasillo *nm (de casa)* corridor; *(de avión)* aisle.

pasión *nf* passion.

pasivo,-a *adj* passive. ► *nm* **pasivo** liabilities.

paso *nm* **1** *(al caminar)* step, footstep. **2** *(camino)* passage, way. ● **a dos pasos** just round the corner; **abrirse paso** to force one's way through; **"Ceda el paso"** "Give way"; **de paso 1** on the way: *me pilla de paso al trabajo*, it's on my way to work. **2** in passing: *lo dijo de paso*, he mentioned it in passing; **estar de paso** to be passing through; **"Prohibido el paso"** "No entry". ■ **paso a nivel** GB level crossing; US grade crossing; **paso de cebra** zebra crossing; **paso de peatones** pedestrian crossing; **paso elevado** GB flyover; US overpass; **paso subterráneo** underpass.

pasta *nf* 1 *(masa)* paste; *(de pan)* dough. 2 *(fideos, macarrones, etc.)* pasta. 3 *(pastelito)* cake. 4 *fam (dinero)* dough, money. ■ **pasta dentífrica** toothpaste.

pastar *vt-vi* to pasture, graze.

pastel *nm* 1 *(tipo bizcocho)* cake; *(tipo empanada)* pie, tart. 2 *(colores, etc.)* pastel.

pastelería *nf* cake shop.

pastilla *nf* 1 *(medicamento)* tablet, pill. 2 *(de jabón)* cake, bar.

pasto *nm* pasture.

pastor,-ra *nm,f (hombre)* shepherd; *(mujer)* shepherdess.

pata¹ *nf* 1 *(gen)* leg. 2 *(garra)* paw. 3 *(pezuña)* hoof. ● **a cuatro patas** on all fours; **a la pata coja** hopping; **meter la pata** *fam* to put one's foot in it; **patas arriba** upside down. ■ **patas de gallo** crow's feet.

pata² *nf (ave)* female duck.

patada *nf* kick.

patata *nf* potato. ■ **patatas fritas** 1 *(de bolsa)* GB crisps;

US potato chips. 2 *(de sartén)* GB chips; US French fries.

paté *nm* paté.

patente *adj* patent, evident. ▶ *nf* patent.

paterno,-a *adj* paternal.

patín *nm* 1 skate. 2 *(de agua)* pedalo. ■ **patines de ruedas** roller skates; **patines en línea** rollerblades.

patinaje *nm* skating. ■ **patinaje artístico** figure skating; **patinaje sobre hielo** ice skating.

patinar *vi* 1 *(con patines)* to skate. 2 *(vehículo)* to skid.

patinazo *nm (con el coche)* skid.

patinete *nm* scooter.

patio *nm* 1 *(de casa)* patio. 2 *(de escuela)* playground. ■ **patio de butacas** GB stalls; US orchestra.

pato *nm* duck.

patria *nf* homeland.

patrimonio *nm* heritage, patrimony. ■ **patrimonio de la humanidad** world heritage.

patriotismo *nm* patriotism.

patrocinar *vt* to sponsor.

patrón,-ona *nm,f* 1 *(santo)* patron saint. 2 *(jefe)* employer, boss. 3 *(de barco)* skipper. ▶ *nm* **patrón** 1 *(de modista)* pattern. 2 *(modelo)* standard.

patrulla *nf* patrol.

pausa *nf* pause.

pavo *nm* turkey. ■ **pavo real** peacock.

payaso *nm* clown.

paz *nf* peace. • **dejar en paz** to leave alone; **hacer las paces** to make up, make it up.

peaje *nm* toll.

peatón *nm* pedestrian.

peca *nf* freckle.

pecado *nm* sin.

pecera *nf (redonda)* fishbowl; *(rectangular)* aquarium, fish tank.

pecho *nm* **1** *(tórax)* chest. **2** *(de mujer - busto)* bust; *(- seno)* breast. • **dar el pecho** to breast-feed.

pechuga *nf* breast.

peculiar *adj* peculiar.

pedal *nm* pedal.

pedazo *nm* piece, bit. • **hacer pedazos** to break to pieces.

pedestal *nm* pedestal.

pediatra *nmf* pediatrician.

pedido *nm* order. • **hacer un pedido** to place an order.

pedir *vt* **1** *(gen)* to ask for. **2** *(mendigar)* to beg. **3** *(mercancías, en restaurante)* to order: *¿qué has pedido de postre?*, what did you order for dessert?

pedo *nm fam (ventosidad)* fart. • **estar pedo** *fam* to be drunk.

pega *nf fam (dificultad)* snag.

pegamento *nm* glue.

pegar[1] *vt* **1** *(adherir - gen)* to stick; *(- con pegamento)* to glue. **2** *(arrimar)* to put. ▶ *vi (combi-*

nar) to match: *ese color no pega en el salón*, that colour doesn't look right in the living room. ▶ *vpr* **pegarse** *(adherirse)* to stick.

pegar[2] *vt* **1** *(golpear)* to hit. **2** *(dar)* to give: *deja ya de pegar gritos*, stop shouting. ▶ *vpr* **pegarse** *(golpearse)* to hit each other.

pegatina *nf* sticker.

peinado *nm* hair style.

peinar *vt (con peine)* to comb; *(con cepillo)* to brush. ▶ *vpr* **peinarse** to comb one's hair.

peine *nm* comb.

peladilla *nf* sugared almond.

pelar *vt* **1** *(fruta, verdura)* to peel. **2** *(persona)* to cut SB's hair. ▶ *vpr* **pelarse 1** *(perder piel)* to peel. **2** *(cortarse el pelo)* to get one's hair cut.

peldaño *nm* step.

pelea *nf* fight, quarrel.

pelear(se) *vi-vpr* **1** *(gen)* to fight, quarrel. **2** *(a golpes)* to come to blows.

peletería *nf* fur shop, furrier's.

pelícano *nm* pelican.

película *nf* film. ▪ **película de acción** adventure film; **película de miedo** horror film; **película de suspense** thriller; **película del oeste** western; **película muda** silent movie.

peligro *nm* danger.

peligroso,-a *adj* dangerous.
pelirrojo,-a *adj* red-haired. ▶ *nm,f* redhead.
pellizco *nm* pinch.
pelo *nm* 1 *(gen)* hair. 2 *(de barba)* whisker. 3 *(de animal)* coat, fur. • **no tener pelos en la lengua** to speak one's mind; **por los pelos** by the skin of one's teeth; **tomarle el pelo a ALGN** to pull SB's leg; **venir a pelo** to be just what SB needs.
pelota *nf* ball. • **en pelotas** *fam* naked; **hacer la pelota a ALGN** *fam* to suck up to SB. ▪ **pelota vasca** pelota.
pelotón *nm* squad.
peluca *nf* wig.
peluche *nm* plush.
peluquería *nf* hairdresser's.
peluquín *nm* hairpiece.
pelusa *nf* fluff.
pelvis *nf* pelvis.
pena *nf* 1 *(tristeza)* grief, sorrow. 2 *(lástima)* pity. 3 *(castigo)* penalty, punishment. • **valer la pena** to be worth while.
penalti *nm* penalty.
pendiente *adj* 1 *(por resolver)* pending. 2 *(deuda)* outstanding. 3 *(atento): estaba pendiente de todos los detalles*, none of the details escaped him, he missed nothing. ▶ *nf* slope. ▶ *nm* earring.
pene *nm* penis.

penetrar *vt* 1 *(atravesar)* to penetrate. 2 *(líquido)* to permeate.
península *nf* peninsula.
pensamiento *nm* 1 *(idea, facultad)* thought. 2 *(mente)* mind. 3 *(flor)* pansy.
pensar *vt-vi* to think. • **¡ni pensarlo!** no way!, don't even think about it!; **sin pensar** without thinking.
pensión *nf* 1 *(dinero)* pension. 2 *(residencia)* boarding house. ▪ **media pensión** half board; **pensión completa** full board; **pensión de jubilación** retirement pension.
pensionista *nmf* pensioner.
pentágono *nm* pentagon.
pentagrama *nm* stave, staff.
penúltimo,-a *adj-nm,f* penultimate.
peña *nf (roca)* rock.
peón *nm* 1 *(trabajador)* unskilled labourer. 2 *(en damas)* man. 3 *(en ajedrez)* pawn.
peor *adj-adv* 1 *(comparativo)* worse. 2 *(superlativo)* worst.
pepinillo *nm* gherkin.
pepino *nm* cucumber.
pepita *nf* 1 *(de fruta)* seed, pip. 2 *(de metal)* nugget.
pequeño,-a *adj* 1 *(de tamaño)* little, small. 2 *(de edad)* young, small: *tengo dos hermanos pequeños*, I have to younger brothers. • **de pequeño,-a** as a child.

perla

pera *nf* pear.

percance *nm* mishap.

percatarse *vpr* to notice.

percebe *nm* goose barnacle.

percha *nf (individual)* hanger; *(de gancho)* coat hook.

perchero *nm (en la pared)* coat rack; *(de pie)* coat stand.

percibir *vt (notar)* to perceive.

perdedor,-ra *nm,f* loser.

perder *vt* **1** *(gen)* to lose. **2** *(malgastar)* to waste. **3** *(tren, avión etc)* to miss. ► *vi* **1** *(salir derrotado)* to lose. **2** *(empeorar)* to go downhill. ► *vpr* **perderse 1** *(extraviarse)* to go astray, get lost. **2** *(acontecimiento)* to miss.

pérdida *nf* **1** *(extravío)* loss. **2** *(de tiempo, dinero)* waste. **3** *(escape)* leak. • **no tener pérdida** to be easy to find: *no tiene pérdida*, you can't miss it.

perdido,-a *adj* **1** *(gen)* lost: *objetos perdidos*, lost property. **2** *(desperdiciado)* wasted.

perdigón *nm* pellet.

perdiz *nf* partridge.

perdón *nm* **1** *(indulto)* pardon. **2** *(de pecado)* forgiveness. • **con perdón** if you'll pardon the expression; **pedir perdón** to apologize; **¡perdón!** sorry!; **¿perdón?** pardon?, sorry?

perdonar *vt* **1** *(error, ofensa)* to forgive. **2** *(deuda)* to let off. **3** *(excusar)* to excuse.

perdurar *vt* to last, endure.

peregrino,-a *nm,f* pilgrim.

perejil *nm* parsley.

perenne *adj* perennial, perpetual: *árbol de hoja perenne*, evergreen tree.

pereza *nf* laziness, idleness.

perfección *nf* perfection.

perfecto,-a *adj* **1** *(ideal)* perfect. **2** *(rematado)* complete: *un perfecto desconocido*, a complete stranger.

perfil *nm* profile.

perforar *vt* **1** *(gen)* to perforate. **2** *(uso técnico)* to drill, bore.

perfume *nm* perfume, scent.

perfumería *nf* perfumery, perfume shop.

periferia *nf* **1** *(gen)* periphery. **2** *(afueras)* outskirts.

perilla *nf* goatee.

perímetro *nm* perimeter.

periódico,-a *adj* periodic. ► *nm* **periódico** newspaper.

periodista *nmf* journalist.

periodo *nm* period.

periquito *nm* parakeet; *(australiano)* budgerigar.

periscopio *nm* periscope.

perito *nm* expert.

perjudicar *vt* to damage, harm.

perjudicial *adj* harmful.

perjuicio *nm (moral)* injury; *(material)* damage.

perla *nf (joya)* pearl. ▪ **perla cultivada** cultured pearl.

permanecer *vi* to remain.
permanente *adj* permanent,
lasting. ► *nf (del pelo)* perm.
• **hacerse la permanente** to
have one's hair permed.
permiso *nm* **1** *(autorización)*
permission. **2** *(documento)* permit. **3** *(soldado)* leave. • **con su
permiso** if you'll excuse me.
■ **permiso de conducir** driving licence.
permitir *vt* to permit, allow,
let. ► *vpr* **permitirse** to take
the liberty of.
pero *conj* but.
peroné *nm* fibula.
perpendicular *adj-nf* perpendicular.
perra *nf* bitch.
perro *nm* dog. • **"Cuidado
con el perro"** "Beware of
the dog". ■ **perro callejero**
stray dog; **perro guardián**
guard dog.
persecución *nf* **1** *(seguimien-
to)* pursuit. **2** *(represión)* persecution.
perseguir *vt* **1** *(delincuente,
presa)* to pursue, chase. **2** *(pretender)* to be after.
persiana *nf (gen)* blind; *(enro-
llable)* roller blind; *(de tablas)*
shutter.
persistente *adj* persistent.
persona *nf* person: *una persona, dos personas*, one person, two people. ■ **persona
mayor** adult, grown-up.

personaje *nm* **1** *(en libro, etc)*
character. **2** *(persona famosa)*
celebrity.
personal *adj* personal. ► *nm*
personnel, staff.
personalidad *nf* **1** *(carácter)*
personality. **2** *(persona famosa)*
public figure.
perspectiva *nf* **1** *(gen)*
perspective. **2** *(posibilidad)*
prospect. **3** *(vista)* view.
persuadir *vi* to persuade,
convince.
pertenecer *vi* to belong
pertenencias *nf pl* belongings.
pértiga *nf* pole.
perverso,-a *adj* perverse.
pesa *nf* weight: *hacer pesas*,
to do weight training.
pesadilla *nf* nightmare.
pesado,-a *adj* **1** *(gen)* heavy.
2 *(aburrido)* dull, tiresome,
boring.
pésame *nm* condolences, expression of sympathy. • **dar
el pésame** to offer one's
condolences.
pesar *vt-vi (gen)* to weigh. ►
vi **1** *(tener mucho peso)* to be
heavy. **2** *(sentir)* to be sorry,
regret. ► *nm* **1** *(pena)* sorrow,
grief. **2** *(arrepentimiento)* regret. • **a pesar de** in spite of,
despite.
pesca *nf* fishing. ■ **pesca de
arrastre** trawling; **pesca sub-
marina** underwater fishing.

pescadería *nf* fishmonger's.
pescadilla *nf* small hake.
pescado *nm* fish.
pescador *nm* fisherman.
pescar *vi* to fish.
pesebre *nm* (de Navidad) crib.
pesimista *adj* pessimistic. ▶
  nmf pessimist.
pésimo,-a *adj* very bad.
peso *nm* 1 (gen) weight. 2
  (balanza) scales, balance. 3
  DEP shot: *lanzamiento de peso*, shot put; *levantamiento
  de peso*, weight-lifting.
pestaña *nf* 1 (del ojo) eyelash. 2 (de cartón) flap.
peste *nf* 1 (epidemia) plague.
  2 (mal olor) stink, stench.
pestillo *nm* bolt.
pétalo *nm* petal.
petanca *nf* petanque.
petardo *nm* (cohete) banger.
petición *nf* request.
petirrojo *nm* robin.
peto *nm* bib.
petróleo *nm* oil, petroleum.
petrolero *nm* oil tanker.
pez *nm* fish.
pezón *nm* nipple.
pezuña *nf* hoof.
pianista *nmf* pianist.
piano *nm* piano: *yo toco el
  piano*, I can play the piano. ■
  piano de cola grand piano.
piar *vi* to chirp.
piara *nf* herd of pigs.
pica *nf* 1 (lanza) pike. 2 (de toros) goad.

picado,-a *adj* 1 (ajo, cebolla)
  chopped; (carne) GB minced;
  US ground. 2 (mar) choppy. 3
  (vino) sour. 4 (diente) decayed.
  5 fam (ofendido) offended. •
  caer en picado to plummet.
picadura *nf* 1 (de mosquito,
  serpiente) bite; (de abeja, avispa) sting. 2 (tabaco) cut tobacco.
picante *adj* 1 (sabor) hot, spicy.
  2 (pícaro) spicy, naughty.
picaporte *nm* 1 (llamador)
  door knocker. 2 (pomo) door
  handle.
picar *vt* 1 (mosquito, serpiente)
  to bite; (abeja, avispa) to
  sting. 2 (algo de comer) to nibble. 3 (cebolla, patata, etc) to
  chop; (carne) GB to mince; US
  to grind; (hielo) to crush. ▶ vi
  1 (sentir escozor) to itch. 2
  (tomar algo de comer) to nibble. 3 (estar picante) to be
  spicy. ▶ vpr **picarse** 1 (fruta)
  to begin to go rotten. 2 (diente) to begin to decay. 3 (mar)
  to get choppy. 4 (enfadarse)
  to take offence (US offense).
pícaro,-a *adj* 1 (malicioso) mischievous. 2 (astuto) sly, crafty.
pichón *nm* young pigeon.
picnic *nm* picnic.
pico *nm* 1 (de ave) beak. 2 (de
  montaña) peak. 3 (herramienta) pick, pickaxe. 4 (cantidad)
  small amount: *tres mil y pico*, three thousand odd.

picor *nm* itch.

picotear *vt* **1** *(ave)* to peck at. **2** *(persona)* to nibble.

pie *nm* **1** foot: *fuimos a pie*, we went on foot; *con los pies descalzos*, barefoot. **2** *(de página)* bottom. **3** *(de columna, lámpara)* base, stand. • **al pie de la letra** literally; **dar pie a** to give, rise to; **ponerse de pie** to stand up. ▪ **pie de atleta** athlete's foot; **pies planos** flat feet.

piedad *nf* **1** *(devoción)* piety. **2** *(compasión)* pity, mercy.

piedra *nf* **1** *(gen)* stone. **2** *(de mechero)* flint. ▪ **piedra pómez** pumice stone; **piedra preciosa** precious stone.

piel *nf* **1** *(de persona)* skin. **2** *(de animal - gen)* skin; *(- de vaca, elefante)* hide; *(- de foca, zorro, visón)* fur. **3** *(cuero - tratado)* leather; *(- sin tratar)* pelt. **4** *(de fruta - gen)* skin; *(- de naranja, manzana, patata)* peel. ▪ **piel de gallina** goose pimples.

pienso *nm* fodder.

pierna *nf* leg.

pieza *nf* piece. ▪ **pieza de recambio** spare part.

pigmento *nm* pigment.

pijama *nm* pyjamas.

pila *nf* **1** *(eléctrica)* battery. **2** *(de bautismo)* font.

píldora *nf* pill.

pillar *vt* *(atrapar)* to catch; *(atropellar)* to run over. ▶ *vpr*

pillarse to catch: *me he pillado el dedo con la puerta*, I caught my finger in the door.

pilotar *vt* *(avión)* to pilot; *(coche)* to drive.

piloto *nmf* *(de avión, barco)* pilot; *(de coche)* driver. ▶ *nm (luz - de coche)* tail light, rear light; *(- de aparato)* pilot light. ▶ *adj* pilot: *piso piloto*, show flat. ▪ **piloto automático** automatic pilot.

pimentón *nm* paprika.

pimienta *nf* pepper.

pimiento *nm* pepper. ▪ **pimiento morrón** sweet red pepper.

pinar *nm* pine grove.

pincel *nm* brush, paintbrush.

pinchadiscos *nmf fam* DJ, disc jockey.

pinchar *vt* **1** *(con objeto punzante)* to prick. **2** *(rueda)* to puncture. **3** *(globo, pelota)* to burst. **4** *fam (teléfono)* to tap. ▶ *vpr* **pincharse 1** *(persona)* to prick oneself. **2** *(rueda)* to puncture. **3** *(globo, pelota)* to burst.

pinchazo *nm* **1** *(punzada)* prick. **2** *(de rueda)* puncture, flat.

pincho *nm* **1** *(espina)* thorn, prickle. **2** *(aperitivo)* tapa, bar snack. ▪ **pincho moruno** kebab.

ping-pong® *nm* ping-pong®.

pingüino *nm* penguin.

plano

pino *nm* pine tree.

pintada *nf* piece of graffiti.

pintalabios *nm* lipstick.

pintar *vt* to paint. ► *vpr* **pintarse** to make oneself up.

pintaúñas *nm* nail varnish.

pintor,-ra *nm,f* painter.

pintoresco,-a *adj* picturesque.

pintura *nf* 1 *(arte)* painting. 2 *(color, bote)* paint. 3 *(cuadro)* picture.

pinza *nf* 1 *(de cangrejo)* claw. 2 *(para la ropa)* peg. ► *nf pl* **pinzas** *(de cocina)* tongs; *(de manicura)* tweezers.

piña *nf* 1 *(fruta)* pineapple. 2 *(de pino)* pine cone.

piñón *nm (de pino)* pine nut.

piojo *nm* louse.

pionero,-a *adj* pioneering.

pipa¹ *nf (de tabaco)* pipe.

pipa² *nf* 1 *(de fruta)* pip, seed. 2 *(de girasol)* sunflower seed.

piragua *nf* canoe.

pirámide *nf* pyramid.

pirata *nm* pirate.

piropo *nm* compliment.

pirueta *nf* pirouette, caper.

piruleta *nf* lollipop.

pirulí *nm* lollipop.

pisada *nf* 1 *(acción)* footstep. 2 *(huella)* footprint.

pisapapeles *nm* paperweight.

pisar *vt* to tread on, step on.

piscina *nf* swimming-pool.

piso *nm* 1 *(planta, suelo)* floor. 2 *(vivienda)* apartment; GB flat.

pista *nf* 1 *(rastro)* trail, track. 2 *(indicio)* clue. 3 *(de atletismo)* track; *(de tenis)* court; *(de esquí)* slope, ski run. 4 *(de circo)* ring. 5 *(de aterrizaje)* runway. ■ **pista de baile** dance floor.

pistacho *nm* pistachio.

pistola *nf* pistol.

pistón *nm* piston.

pitar *vi (con silbato)* to blow a whistle; *(con claxon)* to blow one's horn. ► *vt (abuchear)* to boo at.

pitido *nm* whistle.

pitillera *nf* cigarette case.

pitillo *nm* cigarette.

pito *nm* whistle.

pizarra *nf* 1 *(roca)* slate. 2 *(de escuela)* blackboard.

pizca *nf* bit; *(de sal)* pinch.

pizza *nf* pizza.

placa *nf* 1 *(lámina)* plate. 2 *(inscrita)* plaque. 3 *(de policía)* badge. 4 *(de cocinar)* ring.

placer *nm* pleasure.

plaga *nf* plague, pest.

plan *nm* plan, project. ■ **plan de estudios** syllabus.

plancha *nf* 1 *(de metal)* plate, sheet. 2 *(para planchar)* iron.

planchar *vt (gen)* to iron; *(traje, pantalón)* to press.

planear *vt* to plan. ► *vi (avión)* to glide.

planeta *nm* planet.

planificar *vt* to plan.

plano,-a *adj* flat, even. ► *nm* **plano** 1 *(mapa)* plan, map. 2

(en filmación) shot. ▪ **primer plano** *(foto)* close-up.

planta *nf* **1** *(gen)* plant. **2** *(del pie)* sole. **3** *(piso)* floor. ▪ **planta baja** GB ground floor; US first floor.

plantación *nf* plantation.

plantar *vt (en tierra)* to plant; *(semilla)* to sow. ● **dejar a AL-GN plantado** to stand SB up.

plantear *vt* **1** *(problema)* to set out. **2** *(pregunta)* to pose, raise. ▸ *vpr* **plantearse 1** *(pensar)* to think about. **2** *(cuestión)* to arise.

plantilla *nf* **1** *(de zapato)* insole. **2** *(patrón)* model, pattern. **3** *(personal)* staff.

plasma *nm* plasma.

plástico,-a *adj* plastic. ▸ *nm* **plástico** plastic.

plata *nf* silver.

plataforma *nf* platform. ▪ **plataforma de lanzamiento** launchpad; **plataforma petrolífera** oil rig.

plátano *nm* **1** *(fruta)* banana. **2** *(árbol)* plane tree.

platea *nf* stalls.

platillo *nm* **1** *(plato)* saucer. **2** *(de balanza)* pan. **3** *(instrumento)* cymbal. ▪ **platillo volante** flying saucer.

plato *nm* **1** *(gen)* dish. **2** *(en comida)* course. ● **fregar los platos** to wahs the dishes; GB to do the washing-up, wash up.

plató *nm* set.

playa *nf* beach.

playeras *nf pl* tennis shoes.

plaza *nf* **1** *(de pueblo, ciudad)* square. **2** *(mercado)* marketplace. **3** *(sitio)* space. **4** *(asiento)* seat. **5** *(empleo)* position, post. ▪ **plaza de toros** bullring; **plaza mayor** main square.

plazo *nm* **1** *(de tiempo)* period. **2** *(pago)* GB instalment; US instalment.

plegable *adj* folding.

plegar *vt* to fold.

pleito *nm* litigation, lawsuit.

pleno,-a *adj* full, complete.

pliegue *nm* **1** *(doblez)* fold. **2** *(en ropa)* pleat.

plomo *nm* **1** *(metal)* lead. **2** *(de la luz)* fuse: *se fundieron los plomos,* the fuses blew.

pluma *nf* **1** *(de ave)* feather. **2** *(de escribir)* quill pen; *(estilográfica)* fountain pen.

plumero *nm* feather duster.

plural *adj-nm* plural.

población *nf* **1** *(habitantes)* population. **2** *(ciudad)* city, town; *(pueblo)* village. ▪ **población activa** working population.

poblado,-a *adj* **1** *(zona)* populated. **2** *(barba)* thick. ▸ *nm* **poblado** settlement.

pobre *adj* poor.

pobreza *nf* poverty.

pocilga *nf* pigsty.

poco,-a *adj (singular)* little, not much; *(plural)* few, not many. ► *pron (singular)* little; *(plural)* not many. ► *adv* little, not much. ● **dentro de poco** soon; GB presently; **hace poco** not long ago; **poco a poco** little by little; **por poco** nearly.

podar *vt* to prune.

poder *vt* 1 *(gen)* can. 2 *(tener permiso para)* can, may: *¿puedo fumar?*, may I smoke? 3 *(en conjeturas)* may, might: *puede que esté enfermo*, he may be ill, he might be ill. ► *nm (capacidad, facultad)* power. ● **no poder con** not to be able to cope with; **no poder más** to be unable to do any more; **¿se puede?** may I come in?

podio *nm* podium.

podrido,-a *adj* rotten.

poema *nm* poem.

poesía *nf* 1 *(género)* poetry. 2 *(poema)* poem.

poeta *nmf* poet.

poetisa *nf* poetess.

polar *adj* polar.

polémico,-a *adj* polemic.

polen *nm* pollen.

policía *nf* police. ► *nmf (hombre)* policeman; *(mujer)* policewoman.

polideportivo *nm* GB sports centre; US sports center.

polígono *nm* polygon. ● **polígono industrial** industrial estate.

polilla *nf* moth.

política *nf* 1 *(ciencia)* politics: *se dedica a la política*, he's in politics. 2 *(método)* policy.

político,-a *adj* political. ► *nm,f* politician.

póliza *nf* certificate, policy.

polizón *nm* stowaway.

pollería *nf* poultry shop.

pollo *nm* chicken. ■ **pollo asado** roast chicken.

polo *nm* 1 *(gen)* pole. 2 *(helado)* GB ice lolly; US Popsicle®. 3 *(jersey)* polo shirt.

polvo *nm* 1 *(en aire, muebles)* dust. 2 *(en farmacia, cosmética)* powder. ● **estar hecho polvo** *fam* to be knackered. ■ **polvos de talco** talcum powder.

pólvora *nf* gunpowder.

polvorón *nm* crumbly shortcake.

pomada *nf* cream.

pomelo *nm* grapefruit.

pomo *nm* knob, handle.

pómulo *nm* cheekbone.

ponche *nm* punch.

poner *vt* 1 *(gen)* to place, put, set. 2 *(instalar)* GB to install; US to instal. 3 *(encender)* to turn on, put on. 4 *(huevos)* to lay. 5 *(estar escrito)* to say: *¿qué pone en ese letrero?*, what does that sign say? 6 *(establecer)* to open: *han puesto un bar*, they've opened a bar. 7 *(programa, película)* to show. **8 poner + adj** to make: *me pone enfermo*, he makes me sick. ▶ *vpr* **ponerse 1** *(sombrero, ropa)* to put on. **2** *(sol)* to set. **3** *(volverse)* to become, get, turn. **4** *(al teléfono - cogerlo)* to answer the phone; *(- acudir)* to come to the phone: *dígale que se ponga*, tell her to come to the phone. ● **ponerse a + inf** to start to + *inf*.

popa *nf* stern.

popular *adj* popular.

por *prep* **1** *(causa)* because of: *llegaron tarde por la nieve*, they were late because of the snow; *lo hice por ti*, I did it for you. **2** *(tiempo)* at, in; *(duración)* for: *por la noche*, at night; *vino por poco tiempo*, he didn't stay for long. **3** *(lugar)* along, in, on, by, up, down: *iremos por la autopista*, we'll go by motorway. **4** *(medio, agente)* by: *por avión*, by air. **5** *(distribución)* per: *cinco por ciento*, five per cent. **6** *(en multiplicación)* times. **7** *(medidas)* by: *mide tres metros por dos*, it measures three metres by two. ● **¿por qué?** why?; **por supuesto** of course; **por tanto** therefore.

porcelana *nf* **1** *(material)* porcelain. **2** *(vajilla)* china.

porcentaje *nm* percentage.

porche *nm* porch.

porción *nf* **1** *(parte)* portion, part. **2** *(cuota)* share.

poro *nm* pore.

porque *conj* because.

porquería *nf* dirt, filth.

porra *nf* club; *(de policía)* GB truncheon; US nightstick.

portaaviones *nm* aircraft carrier.

portada *nf* **1** *(de libro)* title page. **2** *(de revista)* cover. **3** *(de periódico)* front page. **4** *(de disco)* sleeve.

portador,-ra *nm,f* bearer; *(de virus)* carrier.

portaequipajes *nm* luggage rack.

portal *nm* **1** *(entrada)* doorway; *(vestíbulo)* entrance hall. **2** *(de Internet)* portal.

portarse *vpr* to behave, act.

portátil *adj* portable. ▶ *nm* *(ordenador)* laptop, portable.

portavoz *nmf* *(gen)* spokesperson.

portería *nf* **1** *(de edificio)* porter's lodge. **2** *(en fútbol)* goal.

portero,-a *nmf* **1** *(de edificio)* doorkeeper, porter. **2** *(guardameta)* goalkeeper. ■ **portero automático** entry phone.

porvenir *nm* future.

posada *nf* lodging-house, inn.

posar *vi* to pose. ▶ *vpr* **posarse 1** *(pájaro)* to alight, perch, sit. **2** *(sedimento)* to settle.

posdata *nf* postscript.

poseer *vt* to own, possess.

posesión *nf* possession.
posesivo,-a *adj* possessive
posibilidad *nf* possibility.
posible *adj* possible. • **hacer todo lo posible** to do one's best.
posición *nf* position.
positivo,-a *adj* positive.
poso *nm* 1 *(de mineral)* sediment. 2 *(de café, vino)* dregs.
posponer *vt* to postpone, delay, put off.
postal *adj* postal. ► *nf* postcard.
poste *nm* post.
póster *nm* poster.
posterior *adj* 1 *(de atrás)* back, rear. 2 *(más tarde)* later.
postre *nm* dessert.
postura *nf* 1 *(posición)* posture, position. 2 *(actitud)* attitude, stance.
potable *adj* drinkable.
potaje *nm* stew.
potencia *nf* power.
potente *adj* powerful.
potro,-a *nm,f* colt, foal. ► *nm* **potro** *(para gimnasia)* vaulting horse.
pozo *nm* 1 *(de agua, petróleo)* well. 2 *(en mina)* shaft.
práctica *nf* practice. ► *nf pl* **prácticas** training.
practicar *vt* 1 *(idioma, profesión)* GB to practise; US to practice. 2 *(deporte)* to play, do. ► *vi* GB to practise; US to practice.

práctico,-a *adj* practical.
pradera *nf* prairie.
prado *nm* meadow.
precaución *nf* precaution. • **conducir con precaución** to drive carefully.
precedente *adj* preceding, prior, foregoing. ► *nm* precedent. • **sin precedentes** unprecedented.
precinto *nm* seal.
precio *nm* price. ■ **precio de fábrica** factory price; **precio de venta al público** retail price.
precioso,-a *adj* 1 *(valioso)* precious. 2 *(bello)* beautiful.
precipicio *nm* precipice.
precipitación *nf* 1 *(prisa)* rush, haste, hurry. 2 *(lluvia)* precipitation.
precipitarse 1 *(apresurarse)* to be hasty. 2 *(obrar sin reflexión)* to act rashly.
precisión *nf* precision,.
preciso,-a *adj* 1 *(exacto)* precise, exact, accurate. 2 *(necesario)* necessary.
precocinado,-a *adj* precooked.
precoz *adj* 1 *(niño)* precocious. 2 *(envejecimiento, eyacualción)* premature.
predecir *vt* to predict, foretell.
predicar *vt* to preach.
predicción *nf* prediction; *(meteorológica)* forecast.

predominio *nm* predominance.

preferencia *nf* preference. • **tener preferencia** *(al volante)* to have right of way.

preferir *vt* to prefer.

prefijo *nm* prefix; *(telefónico)* code.

pregunta *nf* question.

preguntar *vt* to ask. ▶ *vpr* **preguntarse** to wonder.

prehistoria *nf* prehistory.

prejuicio *nm* prejudice.

prematuro,-a *adj* premature.

premiar *vt* 1 *(otorgar premio a)* to award a prize to. 2 *(recompensar)* to reward.

premio *nm* 1 *(en concurso, sorteo)* prize. 2 *(recompensa)* reward. ▪ **premio gordo** jackpot.

prenda *nf* 1 *(de vestir)* garment. 2 *(garantía)* pledge.

prender *vt* 1 *(agarrar)* to seize. 2 *(sujetar)* to attach. ▶ *vi* *(fuego etc)* to catch.

prensa *nf* press. ▪ **prensa amarilla** gutter press; **prensa del corazón** gossip magazines.

prensar *vt* to press.

preocupar(se) *vt-vpr* to worry.

preparación *nf* preparation.

preparado,-a *adj* ready, prepared.

preparar *vt* to prepare. ▶ *vpr* **prepararse** to get ready.

preparativos *nm pl* preparations, arrangements.

preposición *nf* preposition.

presa *nf* 1 *(cosa prendida)* prey. 2 *(embalse)* dam.

presencia *nf* presence. ▪ **buena presencia** smart appearance.

presenciar *vt* *(asistir)* to be present at; *(contemplar)* to witness.

presentación *nf* 1 *(gen)* presentation. 2 *(de personas)* introduction.

presentador,-ra *nm,f* presenter, host.

presentar *vt* 1 *(gen)* to present. 2 *(mostrar)* to display, show. 3 *(personas)* to introduce. ▶ *vpr* **presentarse** *(comparecer)* to present oneself; *(candidato)* to stand.

presente *adj-nm* present. • **tener presente** to bear in mind.

preservar *vt* *(proteger)* to protect; *(conservar)* to preserve.

preservativo *nm* condom.

presidencia *nf* 1 *(de nación)* presidency. 2 *(en reunión)* chairmanship.

presidente,-a *nm,f* 1 *(de nación, club, etc)* president. 2 *(en reunión - hombre)* chairman; *(- mujer)* chairwoman.

presidir *vt* 1 *(nación)* to be president of. 2 *(reunión)* to chair.

presión *nf* pressure. ▪ **presión arterial** blood pressure.

presionar vt 1 (apretar) to press. 2 (coaccionar) to put pressure on.

preso,-a nm,f prisoner.

préstamo nm (acción) lending; (dinero) loan.

prestar vt 1 (dejar prestado) to lend, loan; (pedir prestado) to borrow. 2 (servicio) to do, render. 3 (ayuda) to give. 4 (atención) to pay. ► vpr **prestarse 1** (ofrecerse) to lend oneself. 2 (dar motivo) to cause.

prestigio nm prestige.

presumir vi to be vain.

presupuesto nm (cálculo anticipado) estimate; (coste) budget.

pretender vt 1 (querer) to want to. 2 (intentar) to try to.

prevenir vt 1 (prever) to prevent. 2 (advertir) to warn.

previo,-a adj previous.

previsión nf forecast.

previsto,-a adj: *su llegada está prevista para las cinco*, he is expected to arrive at five; *había previsto todo*, she had thought of everything. • **según lo previsto** according to plan.

prima nf 1 bonus. 2 → primo, -a.

primavera nf spring.

primer num → primero,-a.

primera nf 1 (clase) first class. 2 (marcha) first gear.

primero,-a num first. ► adv **primero** first. • **a primeros de mes** at the beginning of the month. ■ **primeros auxilios** first aid.

primitivo,-a adj primitive.

primo,-a adj 1 (materia) raw. 2 (número) prime. ► nm,f cousin.

princesa nf princess.

principal adj main, chief. ► nm (piso) first floor.

príncipe nm prince.

principiante,-a nm,f beginner.

principio nm 1 (inicio) beginning, start. 2 (norma) principle. • **al principio** at first; **en principio** in principle.

prioridad nf priority.

prisa nf hurry. • **darse prisa** to hurry, hurry up; **tener prisa** to be in a hurry.

prisión nf (lugar) prison, jail. • **en prisión preventiva** remanded in custody.

prisionero,-a nm,f prisoner.

prismáticos nm pl binoculars.

privado,-a adj private.

privar vt 1 (despojar) to deprive. 2 (prohibir) to forbid. ► vpr **privarse** to do without.

privilegio nm privilege.

proa nf prow, bow.

probabilidad nf probability.

probable adj probable, likely.

probador nm changing room.

probar vt 1 (demostrar) to prove. 2 (comprobar) to try, test. 3 (vino, comida) to taste, try. 4 (prendas) to try on.

problema *nm* problem.

procedencia *nf* **1** *(de persona, producto)* origin, source. **2** *(de tren)* point of departure.

proceder *vi (venir de)* to come.

procedimiento *nm* procedure, method.

procesar *vt* **1** *(dato, texto)* to process. **2** JUR to prosecute.

procesión *nf* procession.

proceso *nm* **1** *(gen)* process. **2** JUR trial.

proclamar *vt* to proclaim. ►
vpr **proclamarse**: *se proclamó campeona*, she won the championship.

procurar *vt (intentar)* to try.

producción *nf* production.

producir *vt* **1** *(gen)* to produce. **2** *(causar)* to cause. ►
vpr **producirse** to happen.

productividad *nf* productivity.

producto *nm* product.

productor,-ra *adj* productive. ► *nm,f* producer.

profesión *nf* profession.

profesional *adj-nmf* professional.

profesor,-ra *nm,f* teacher; *(de universidad)* lecturer.

profundidad *nf* depth.

profundo,-a *adj* **1** *(agujero, piscina)* deep. **2** *(pensamiento, misterio, etc)* profound.

programa *nm* **1** GB programme; US program. **2** INFORM program.

programación *nf* programming.

programador,-ra *nm,f* INFORM programmer.

programar *vt* **1** GB to programme; US to program. **2** INFORM to program.

progresar *vi* to progress.

progreso *nm* progress.

prohibición *nf* prohibition.

prohibir *vt (gen)* to forbid; *(por ley)* to prohibit, ban.

prolongar *vt (en el tiempo)* to prolong; *(de longitud)* to extend.

promedio *nm* average.

promesa *nf* promise.

prometer *vt* to promise.

prometido,-a *nm,f (hombre)* fiancé; *(mujer)* fiancée. • **estar prometidos** to be engaged.

promoción *nf* **1** *(gen)* promotion. **2** *(curso)* class, year.

pronombre *nm* pronoun.

pronóstico *nm* **1** *(gen)* forecast. **2** *(médico)* prognosis.

pronto *adv* **1** *(inmediatamente)* soon. **2** *(rápidamente)* quickly. **3** *(temprano)* early. • **de pronto** suddenly; **¡hasta pronto!** see you soon!; **tan pronto como...** as soon as...

pronunciar *vt* **1** *(palabra)* to pronounce. **2** *(discurso)* to make.

propaganda *nf* **1** POL propaganda. **2** *(anuncios)* advertising.

propiedad *nf* **1** *(derecho)* ownership. **2** *(objeto)* property. • **hablar con propiedad** to speak properly.

propietario,-a *nm,f* owner.

propina *nf* tip.

propio,-a *adj* **1** *(perteneciente)* own: *en defensa propia*, in self-defence. **2** *(indicado)* proper, appropriate. **3** *(particular)* typical, peculiar: *es muy propio de él*, it's very typical of him. **4** *(mismo - él)* himself; *(- ella)* herself; *(- cosa, animal)* itself: *el propio autor*, the author himself.

proponer *vt* to suggest, propose.

proporción *nf* proportion.

proporcionar *vt* to supply, give.

propósito *nm* intention. • **a propósito** *(adrede)* on purpose.

propuesta *nf* proposal.

prórroga *nf* **1** *(de un plazo)* extension. **2** *(en deporte)* GB extra time; US overtime.

prosa *nf* prose.

prospecto *nm* *(de propaganda)* leaflet; *(de medicina)* directions for use.

prosperar *vi* to prosper, thrive.

protagonista *nmf* **1** *(de película)* main character. **2** *(de obra de teatro)* lead.

protección *nf* protection.

proteger *vt* to protect.

proteína *nf* protein.

protesta *nf* protest.

protestar *vi* **1** to protest. **2** *(quejarse)* to complain.

provecho *nm* profit, benefit. • **¡buen provecho!** enjoy your meal!

proveedor,-ra *nm,f* supplier, purveyor.

provenir *vi* to come.

proverbio *nm* proverb, saying.

provincia *nf* province.

provisional *adj* provisional.

provisto,-a *adj* provided.

provocar *vt* **1** *(irritar)* to provoke. **2** *(causar)* to cause.

próximo,-a *adj* **1** *(cercano)* near, close. **2** *(siguiente)* next: *el mes próximo*, next month.

proyección *nf* **1** *(gen)* projection. **2** *(de película)* screening.

proyectil *nm* projectile.

proyecto *nm* **1** *(plan)* plan. **2** *(estudio, esquema)* project. ■ **proyecto de ley** bill.

prudente *adj* *(sabio)* sensible, wise, prudent; *(cuidadoso)* careful.

prueba *nf* **1** *(demostración)* proof. **2** *(examen)* test. **3** *(deportiva)* event. **4** *(de delito)* piece of evidence. • **hacer la prueba** to try; **poner a prueba** to put to the test. ■ **prueba de alcoholemia** breath test.

psicología *nf* psychology.

psiquiatra *nmf* psychiatrist.
publicar *vt* to publish.
publicidad *nf* 1 *(difusión)* publicity. 2 *(anuncios)* advertising; *(en televisión)* adverts.
público,-a *adj* public. ▸ *nm* **público** *(espectadores)* audience.
puchero *nm* cooking pot.
pudrirse *vpr* 1 *(gen)* to rot. 2 *(comida)* to go bad.
pueblo *nm* village, small town.
puente *nm* 1 bridge. 2 *(fiesta)* long weekend. ▪ **puente aéreo** air shuttle; **puente de mando** bridge.
puerro *nm* leek.
puerta *nf* door. ▪ **puerta de embarque** boarding gate.
puerto *nm* 1 *(de mar - pequeño)* harbour; *(- grande)* port. 2 *(de montaña)* mountain pass. 3 INFORM port. ▪ **puerto deportivo** marina.
pues *conj* 1 *(ya que)* since, as. 2 *(por lo tanto)* then, therefore. 3 *(enfático)* well: *pues bien*, well then; *¡pues claro!*, of course!
puesta *nf*. ▪ **puesta a punto** tuning; **puesta de sol** sunset; **puesta en marcha** 1 *(de vehículo)* starting. 2 *(de proyecto)* implementation.
puesto *nm* 1 *(lugar)* place. 2 *(de mercado)* stall; *(de feria etc.)* stand. 3 *(empleo)* position, post. ● **puesto que** since.
pulga *nf* flea.

pulgar *nm* thumb.
pulmón *nm* lung.
pulmonía *nf* pneumonia.
pulpo *nm* octopus.
pulsar *vt* to press.
pulsera *nf* bracelet.
pulso *nm* pulse. ● **echar un pulso** to arm-wrestle; **tener buen pulso** to have a steady hand.
pulverizador *nm* spray, atomizer.
puma *nm* puma.
punta *nf (extremo - de dedo, lengua)* tip; *(- de aguja, cuchillo, lápiz)* point. ● **sacar punta a** *(lápiz)* to sharpen.
puntería *nf* aim.
punto *nm* 1 *(gen)* point. 2 *(de puntuación)* GB full stop; US period. 3 *(en costura, cirugía)* stitch. ● **en punto** sharp, on the dot; **estar en su punto** to be just right; **hasta cierto punto** up to a certain point. ▪ **punto de encuentro** meeting point; **punto de vista** point of view; **punto muerto** 1 *(cambio de marchas)* neutral. 2 *(en negociaciones)* impasse, deadlock; **punto y aparte** full stop, new paragraph; **punto y coma** semicolon; **puntos suspensivos** GB dots; US suspension points.
puntuación *nf* 1 *(en ortografía)* punctuation. 2 *(en competición)* scoring; *(total)* score.

puntual *adj* punctual.
puñado *nm* handful.
puñal *nm* dagger.
puñetazo *nm* punch.
puño *nm* 1 *(mano)* fist. 2 *(de prenda)* cuff.
pupila *nf* pupil.
pupitre *nm* desk.
puré *nm* purée. ■ **puré de patatas** mashed potatoes.
puro,-a *adj* 1 *(sin mezclar)* pure. 2 *(mero)* sheer, mere. ► *nm* **puro** cigar.
pus *nm* pus.
puzzle *nm* puzzle.

Q

que[1] *pron* 1 *(sujeto - persona)* who, that; *(- cosa)* that, which. 2 *(complemento - persona)* whom, who; *(cosa)* that, which. 3 *(complemento - de tiempo)* when; *(- de lugar)* where.
que[2] *conj* 1 *(después de verbos)* that. 2 *(con comparativos)* than: *es más alto que su padre*, he is taller than his father.
qué *pron* what? ► *adj* 1 *(en exclamativas)* how, what: *¡qué bonito!*, how nice! 2 *(en interrogativas)* which?
quebrar *vi* to go bankrupt.
quedar *vi* 1 *(faltar)* to remain, be left. 2 *(sentar)* to look: *te queda muy bien*, it suits you. 3 *(estar situado)* to be: *¿por dónde queda tu casa?*, whereabouts is your house? ► *vpr* **quedarse** to remain, stay, be.
queja *nf* 1 *(protesta)* complaint. 2 *(de dolor)* moan, groan.
quejarse *vpr* 1 *(protestar)* to complain. 2 *(gimiendo)* to moan, groan.
quemadura *nf* 1 *(gen)* burn. 2 *(de agua hirviendo)* scald.
quemar *vt* 1 *(gen)* to burn. 2 *(incendiar)* to set on fire. ► *vi (estar muy caliente)* to be burning hot. ► *vpr* **quemarse** 1 to burn oneself. 2 *(al sol)* to get burnt.
querer *vt* 1 *(amar)* to love. 2 *(desear)* to want.
querido,-a *adj* dear, beloved.
queso *nm* cheese.
quiebra *nf* bankruptcy.
quien *pron* 1 *(sujeto)* who. 2 *(complemento)* who, whom. 3 *(indefinido)* whoever, anyone who.
quién *pron* 1 *(sujeto)* who. 2 *(complemento)* who, whom. ● *¿de quién?* whose?
quienquiera *pron* whoever.
quieto,-a *adj* still.
quilla *nf* keel.
química *nf* chemistry.
químico,-a *adj* chemical.
quince *num* fifteen; *(en fechas)* fifteenth.

quiniela *nf* football pools.
quinientos,-as *num* five hundred.
quinto,-a *num* fifth.
quiosco *nm* kiosk. ■ **quiosco de periódicos** newspaper stand.
quirófano *nm* GB operating theatre; US operating room.
quiste *nm* cyst.
quitamanchas *nm* stain remover.
quitanieves *nm* GB snowplough; US snowplow.
quitar *vt* to remove, take out, take off. ▶ *vpr* **quitarse 1** *(apartarse)* to move away. **2** *(desaparecer)* to go away, come out: *se me han quitado las ganas*, I don't feel like it any more. **3** *(ropa)* to take off. ● **de quita y pon** detachable.
quizá *adv* perhaps, maybe.
quizás *adv* perhaps, maybe.

R

rábano *nm* radish.
rabia *nf* **1** *(enfermedad)* rabies. **2** *(enfado)* rage, fury.
rabo *nm* tail
racha *nf* **1** *(de viento)* gust. **2** *(período)*: *una buena racha*, a run of good luck.

racimo *nm* bunch.
ración *nf* **1** *(porción)* portion. **2** *(parte que toca)* share.
racional *adj* rational.
racista *adj-nmf* racist.
radar *nm* radar.
radiactivo,-a *adj* radioactive.
radiador *nm* radiator.
radical *adj-nmf* radical.
radio[1] *nm* **1** *(de círculo)* radius. **2** *(de rueda)* spoke.
radio[2] *nf* *(medio)* radio.
radio[3] *nm* **1** *(hueso)* radius. **2** *(elemento químico)* radium.
radiocasete *nm* radio-cassette.
radiografía *nf* **1** *(técnica)* radiography. **2** *(imagen)* X-ray.
ráfaga *nf* **1** *(de viento)* gust. **2** *(de disparos)* burst.
raíl *nm* rail.
raíz *nf* root. ● **a raíz de** as a result of. ■ **raíz cuadrada** square root.
rallado,-a *adj* grated. ● **pan rallado** breadcrumbs.
rallar *vt* to grate.
rama *nf* branch.
rambla *nf* *(paseo)* boulevard, avenue.
ramo *nm* **1** *(de flores)* bunch. **2** *(ámbito)* field, section.
rampa *nf* ramp.
rana *nf* frog.
rancho *nm* *(granja)* ranch.
rango *nm* rank, class.
ranura *nf* **1** *(canal)* groove. **2** *(para monedas, fichas)* slot.

rapaz *nf (ave)* bird of prey.
rape *nm (pez)* angler fish.
rápido,-a *adj* quick, fast. ▶ *nm pl* **rápidos** *(del río)* rapids.
raptar *vt* to kidnap.
raqueta *nf* 1 racket. 2 *(para nieve)* snowshoe.
raro,-a *adj* 1 *(poco común)* rare. 2 *(peculiar)* odd, strange. • **raras veces** seldom.
rascacielos *nm* skyscraper.
rascar *vt* to scratch.
rasgo *nm* 1 *(línea)* stroke. 2 *(facción)* feature. 3 *(peculiaridad)* characteristic. • **a grandes rasgos** in outline.
rasguño *nm* scratch.
raso *nm (tejido)* satin. • **al raso** in the open air.
raspa *nf (de pescado)* bone.
raspar *vt (rascar)* to scrape; *(quitar rascando)* to scrape off.
rastrillo *nm* rake.
rastro *nm* 1 *(pista)* trail. 2 *(señal)* trace. 3 *(mercado)* flea market.
rata *nf* rat.
ratero,-a *nm,f* pickpocket.
ratificar *vt* to ratify.
rato *nm (momento)* while. • **pasar el rato** to kill time.
ratón *nm* mouse.
raya[1] *nf* 1 *(línea)* line. 2 *(de color)* stripe: *a rayas*, striped. 3 *(del pantalón)* crease. 4 *(del pelo)* parting. • **pasarse de la raya** to overstep the mark; **tener a raya** to keep in line.

raya[2] *nf (pez)* skate.
rayado,-a *adj* 1 *(con rayas)* striped. 2 *(disco)* scratched.
rayar *vt* 1 *(líneas)* to draw lines on, line, rule. 2 *(superficie)* to scratch.
rayo *nm* 1 *(de luz)* ray, beam. 2 *(en el cielo)* flash of lightning. ▪ **rayo de sol** sunbeam.
raza *nf* 1 *(humana)* race. 2 *(animal)* breed.
razón *nf* reason. • **no tener razón** to be wrong; **"Razón aquí"** "Enquire within"; **tener razón** to be right.
razonable *adj* reasonable.
re *nm (nota)* D; *(en solfeo)* re, ray.
reacción *nf* reaction.
reaccionar *vi* to react.
reactor *nm* 1 *(nuclear etc.)* reactor. 2 *(avión)* jet plane.
real[1] *adj (auténtico)* real.
real[2] *adj (regio)* royal.
realidad *nf* reality. • **en realidad** really, in fact.
realización *nf (de tarea)* carrying out; *(de propósito)* achievement.
realizar *vt* 1 *(propósito, sueño)* to realize. 2 *(tarea)* to accomplish, carry out, do.
reanimar(se) *vt-vpr* to revive.
reanudar *vt* to renew, resume.
rebaja *nf* reduction. ▶ *nf pl* **rebajas** sales.
rebajar *vt* 1 *(precio, coste)* to reduce; *(color)* to tone down 2 *(nivel)* to lower.

rebanada *nf* slice.
rebaño *nm* *(de cabras)* herd; *(de ovejas)* flock.
rebasar *vt* to exceed.
rebeca *nf* cardigan.
rebelde *nmf* rebel.
rebelión *nf* rebellion, revolt.
rebobinar *vt* to rewind.
rebotar *vi* *(balón)* to bounce.
rebote *nm* rebound.
rebozar *vt* *(con pan rallado)* to coat in breadcrumbs; *(con huevo)* to batter.
rebuznar *vi* to bray.
recado *nm* 1 *(mensaje)* message. 2 *(encargo)* errand.
recaída *nf* relapse.
recambio *nm* *(de maquinaria)* spare part, spare; *(de pluma, bolígrafo)* refill.
recapacitar *vi* to reflect.
recargable *adj* *(mechero)* refillable; *(batería)* rechargeable.
recargar *vt* 1 *(arma)* to reload; *(mechero)* to refill; *(batería)* to recharge. 2 *(sobrecargar)* to overload.
recargo *nm* extra charge.
recaudación *nf* *(dinero)* takings.
recaudar *vt* *(impuestos)* to collect; *(dinero)* to raise.
recepción *nf* reception.
recepcionista *nmf* receptionist.
receptor *nm* TV receiver.
receta *nf* 1 *(médica)* prescription. 2 *(culinaria)* recipe.

rechazar *vt* to reject, turn down.
rechazo *nm* rejection.
rechoncho,-a *adj* chubby.
recibidor *nm* entrance hall.
recibimiento *nm* reception, welcome.
recibir *vt* 1 *(carta, señal, etc.)* to get, receive. 2 *(persona)* to meet.
recibo *nm* 1 *(resguardo)* receipt. 2 *(factura)* invoice, bill.
reciclable *adj* recyclable.
reciclar *vt* 1 *(materiales)* to recycle. 2 *(profesionales)* to retrain.
recién *adv* recently, newly: *pan recién hecho*, freshly baked bread. • **"Recién pintado"** "Wet paint". ▪ **recién casados** newlyweds; **recién nacido** newborn baby.
reciente *adj* recent.
recinto *nm* *(gen)* premises; *(cerrado)* enclosure.
recipiente *nm* container.
recíproco,-a *adj* reciprocal.
recital *nm* recital.
recitar *vt* to recite.
reclamación *nf* 1 *(demanda)* claim, demand. 2 *(queja)* complaint, protest.
reclamar *vt* *(pedir)* to demand. ▶ *vi* *(quejarse)* to complain.
recluso,-a *nm,f* prisoner.
recluta *nmf* 1 *(voluntario)* recruit. 2 *(obligado)* conscript.
recobrar(se) *vt-vpr* to recover.

recogedor *nm* dustpan.

recoger *vt* **1** *(coger del suelo)* to pick up. **2** *(ordenar)* to tidy up. **3** *(ir a buscar)* to fetch, pick up.

recolectar *vt* *(cosecha)* to harvest; *(dinero)* to collect.

recomendación *nf* recommendation.

recomendar *vt* to recommend.

recompensa *nf* reward, recompense.

reconocer *vt* **1** *(gen)* to recognize. **2** *(a paciente)* to examine. **3** *(un error)* to admit.

reconocimiento *nm* **1** *(gen)* recognition. **2** *(chequeo médico)* examination, check up

reconstruir *vt* to reconstruct.

récord *adj-nm* record. • **batir un récord** to break a record.

recordar *vt-vi* to remember.

recorrer *vt* to travel round.

recorrido *nm* **1** *(trayecto)* journey. **2** *(distancia)* distance travelled.

recortar *vt* to cut (out).

recorte *nm* **1** *(de periódico)* press clipping. **2** *(de presupuesto)* cut.

recreativo,-a *adj* recreational.

recreo *nm* **1** *(entretenimiento)* recreation, amusement. **2** *(en la escuela)* playtime.

recta *nf* **1** *(línea)* straight line. **2** *(en carretera)* straight (piece of road). ▪ **recta final** final straight.

rectángulo *nm* rectangle.

rectificar *vt* to rectify.

recto,-a *adj* **1** *(derecho)* straight. **2** *(honesto)* just, honest. ▶ *nm* **recto** rectum. ▶ *adv* straight on.

recuadro *nm* box.

recuento *nm* recount.

recuerdo *nm* **1** *(imagen mental)* memory. **2** *(regalo)* souvenir. ▶ *nm pl* **recuerdos** *(saludos)* regards; *(en carta)* best wishes.

recuperar(se) *vt-vpr* to recover.

recurrir *vi* *(acogerse - a algo)* to resort to; *(- a alguien)* to turn to. ▶ *vt* *(una sentencia)* to appeal against.

recurso *nm* **1** *(medio)* resort. **2** JUR appeal. ▶ *nm pl* **recursos** resources, means.

red *nf* **1** *(de pesca, Internet)* net. **2** *(sistema)* network.

redacción *nf* **1** *(escrito)* composition. **2** *(oficina)* editorial office. **3** *(redactores)* editorial staff.

redactor,-ra *nm,f* editor.

redada *nf* raid.

redondear *vt* *(cantidad)* to round off; *(por encima)* to round up; *(por debajo)* to round down.

redondo,-a *adj* **1** *(circular)* round. **2** *(perfecto)* perfect, excellent: *un negocio redondo*, an excellent business deal. ▶ *nm* **redondo** *(de carne)* topside. • **a la redonda** around.

reducir vt (disminuir) to reduce. ➤ vi (al conducir) to change down.

reembolso nm (pago) reimbursement; (devolución) refund. • **contra reembolso** cash on delivery.

reemplazar vt to replace.

referencia nf reference.

referirse vpr (aludir) to refer: ¿a qué te refieres?, what do you mean?

refinar vt to refine.

reflejar vt to reflect.

reflejo nm 1 (imagen) reflection. 2 (destello) gleam. ➤ mpl **reflejos** 1 (reacción) reflexes. 2 (en el pelo) highlights.

reflexionar vt to reflect.

reflexivo,-a adj (verbo etc.) reflexive.

reforma nf 1 (cambio) reform. 2 (de edificio) alteration: *"Cerrado por reformas"*, "Closed for alterations".

refrán nm proverb, saying.

refrescar vt 1 (bebida) to cool, chill. 2 (memoria) to refresh. ➤ vi (tiempo) to turn cool: *por la noche refresca*, the nights are cool. ➤ vpr **refrescarse** 1 (tomar el fresco) to take a breath of fresh air. 2 (con agua) to freshen up.

refresco nm soft drink.

refrigerador nm fridge.

refuerzos nm pl (tropas) reinforcements.

refugiado,-a adj-nm,f refugee.

refugiarse vpr to take refuge.

refugio nm shelter, refuge.

regadera nf watering can.

regalar vt to give: *me lo han regalado*, I was given it, it was a present.

regaliz nm liquorice.

regalo nm gift, present. • **de regalo** free.

regar vt 1 (plantas) to water. 2 (terreno) to irrigate. 3 (calle) to hose down.

regata nf regatta.

regate nm dribble.

régimen nm 1 (de comida) diet. 2 (político) régime. • **estar a régimen** to be on a diet.

regimiento nm regiment.

región nf region.

registrar vt 1 (inspeccionar) to search, inspect. 2 (datos) to register.

registro nm 1 (inspección) search, inspection. 2 (inscripción) registration. 3 (oficina) registry; (libro) register.

regla nf 1 (norma) rule. 2 (instrumento) ruler. 3 (menstruación) period. • **en regla** in order; **por regla general** as a rule.

reglamento nm regulations.

regresar vi to return, come back, go back.

regreso nm return.

regular adj 1 (habitual) regular. 2 (pasable) so-so, average. ➤ vt to regulate.

rehén *nmf* hostage.
rehusar *vt* to refuse, decline.
reina *nf* queen.
reinar *vi* to reign.
reincidir *vi* to relapse.
reiniciar *vt* to reboot.
reino *nm* kingdom.
reintegro *nm* **1** *(de dinero de cuenta)* withdrawal. **2** *(de dinero pagado)* reimbursement.
reír(se) *vi-vpr* to laugh.
reivindicar *vt (derecho)* to demand, claim; *(propiedad)* to claim; *(atentado)* to claim responsibility for.
reja *nf* grille.
rejilla *nf* **1** *(de ventilación)* grille. **2** *(de chimenea)* grate.
relación *nf* **1** *(gen)* relation. **2** *(listado)* list. **3** *(de pareja)* relationship. ■ **relaciones públicas** public relations.
relacionar *vt (vincular)* to relate, connect. ▸ *vpr* **relacionarse** *(tener amistad)* to get acquainted.
relajación *nf* relaxation.
relajarse *vpr* to relax.
relámpago *nm* flash of lightning.
relativo,-a *adj* relative.
relato *nm* story, tale.
relevar *vt (sustituir)* to relieve.
relevo *nm* **1** *(acto, persona)* relief. **2** DEP relay. ● **tomar el relevo** to take over.
relieve *nm* relief. ● **poner de relieve** to emphasize.

religión *nf* religion.
religioso,-a *adj* religious.
rellano *nm* landing.
rellenar *vt* **1** *(volver a llenar)* to refill. **2** *(cuestionario)* to fill in. **3** *(ave)* to stuff; *(pastel)* to fill.
relleno *nm (de aves)* stuffing; *(de pasteles)* filling.
reloj *nm (de pared, mesa)* clock; *(de pulsera)* watch. ● **contra reloj** against the clock. ■ **reloj de arena** hourglass; **reloj de sol** sundial; **reloj despertador** alarm clock; **reloj digital 1** *(de pulsera)* digital watch. **2** *(de pared, mesa)* digital clock.
relojería *nf (tienda)* watchmaker's shop.
remar *vi* to row.
rematar *vt* **1** *(acabar)* to finish off. **2** DEP *(con cabeza)* to head; *(con pie)* to shoot.
remate *nm* **1** *(final)* end. **2** DEP *(con cabeza)* header; *(con pie)* shot.
remedio *nm* **1** *(medicamento)* remedy, cure. **2** *(solución)* solution.
remesa *nf (de mercancías)* consignment, shipment.
remite *nm* sender's name and address.
remitente *nmf* sender.
remitir *vt* **1** *(enviar)* to remit, send. **2** *(tormenta)* to abate; *(fiebre)* to go down.
remo *nm* **1** *(pala)* oar; *(de canoa)* paddle. **2** *(deporte)* rowing.

remojo *nm* soaking. • **poner algo en remojo** to leave STH to soak.

remolacha *nf* beetroot. ■ **remolacha azucarera** sugar beet.

remolcar *vt* to tow.

remolino *nm* 1 *(de agua)* whirlpool; *(de aire)* whirlwind. 2 *(de pelo)* GB tuft; US cowlick.

remolque *nm* trailer. • **a remolque** in tow.

remontar *vt* 1 *(río)* to go up. 2 *(superar)* to overcome. ► *vpr* **remontarse** *(datar)* to go back, date back.

remordimiento *nm* remorse.

remoto,-a *adj* remote.

remover *vt* 1 *(líquido, salsa)* to stir. 2 *(tierra)* to turn over. 3 *(tema)* to bring up again.

renacuajo *nm* tadpole.

rencor *nm* GB rancour; US rancor.

rendido,-a *adj* exhausted.

rendija *nf* crack.

rendimiento *nm* 1 *(de máquina)* output. 2 *(de persona)* performance.

rendir *vt* *(producir)* to yield, produce. ► *vt-vi* *(dar fruto)* to pay. ► *vpr* **rendirse** to surrender.

reno *nm* reindeer.

renovar *vt* 1 *(contrato, actividad)* to renew. 2 *(casa)* to renovate.

renta *nf* 1 *(ingresos)* income. 2 *(beneficio)* interest. 3 *(alquiler)* rent. ■ **renta per cápita** per capita income.

rentable *adj* profitable.

renunciar *vt* 1 *(dejar)* to give up; *(abandonar)* to abandon; *(rechazar)* to refuse. 2 *(dimitir)* to resign.

reñir *vi* *(discutir)* to quarrel, argue. ► *vt* *(reprender)* to scold.

reparación *nf* *(arreglo)* repair.

reparar *vt* *(arreglar)* to repair, mend.

repartir *vt* 1 *(distribuir)* to deliver. 2 *(entregar)* to give out; *(correo)* to deliver.

reparto *nm* 1 *(gen)* delivery. 2 *(actores)* cast.

repasar *vt* 1 *(lección, texto)* to revise, go over. 2 *(máquina, cuenta)* to check.

repelente *adj* repellent.

repente *nm*. • **de repente** suddenly.

repercusión *nf* repercussion.

repertorio *nm* repertoire.

repetición *nf* repetition.

repetidor *nm* relay, booster station.

repetir *vt-vi* to repeat.

repisa *nf* shelf.

repleto,-a *adj* full up.

réplica *nf* 1 *(respuesta)* answer. 2 *(copia)* replica.

repollo *nm* cabbage.

reportaje *nm* *(en televisión)* report; *(prensa)* feature.

reportero,-a *nm,f* reporter.
reposar *vt-vi* to rest.
reposo *nm* rest. • **dejar en reposo** to leave to stand.
repostar *vi (coche)* to fill up; *(avión)* to refuel.
repostería *nf* confectionery.
representación *nf* 1 *(imagen, sustitución)* representation. 2 *(teatral)* performance. 3 *(delegación)* delegation.
representante *nmf* representative.
representar *vt* 1 *(ilustrar, sustituir)* to represent. 2 *(obra de teatro)* to perform. 3 *(edad)* to look: *no representa esa edad*, she doesn't look that age.
reprimir *vt* to repress.
reproche *nm* reproach.
reproducir(se) *vt-vpr* to reproduce.
reptar *vi* to crawl.
reptil *nm* reptile.
república *nf* republic.
repuesto *nm* spare part.
repugnante *adj* repugnant.
reputación *nf* reputation.
requesón *nm* cottage cheese.
requisito *nm* requisite.
resaca *nf* hangover.
resbalar(se) *vi-vpr* 1 *(deslizarse)* to slide. 2 *(sin querer)* to slip.
resbalón *nm* slip.
rescatar *vt* 1 *(salvar)* to rescue. 2 *(recuperar)* to recover.

rescate *nm* 1 *(de persona)* rescue. 2 *(dinero)* ransom.
resentimiento *nm* resentment.
reserva *nf* 1 *(de plazas)* booking, reservation. 2 *(provisión)* reserve. 3 *(vino)* vintage. 4 *(de animales)* reserve. ▶ *nmf (deportista)* reserve, substitute. • **sin reservas** unreservedly, wholeheartedly.
reservar *vt (plazas)* to book, reserve. ▶ *vpr* **reservarse** *(conservarse)* to save oneself.
resfriado *nm (con congestión)* cold; *(poco importante)* chill.
resfriarse *vpr* to catch a cold.
resguardo *nm (recibo)* receipt.
residencia *nf* residence. • **residencia de ancianos** residential home; **residencia de estudiantes** GB hall of residence; US dormitory.
residir *vi* 1 *(habitar)* to reside, live. 2 *(radicar)* to lie: *es ahí donde reside el problema*, that's where the problem lies.
residuo *nm* residue. • **residuos radiactivos** radioactive waste.
resignarse *vpr* to resign oneself.
resina *nf* resin.
resistencia *nf* 1 *(de material)* resistance. 2 *(de persona)* endurance. 3 *(oposición)* reluctance, opposition.

resistente *adj* resistant.
resistir *vt* **1** *(no ceder, aguantar)* to withstand. **2** *(tolerar)* to stand, bear. ▶ *vpr* **resistirse 1** *(negarse)* to refuse. **2** *(forcejear)* to resist. **3** *(oponerse)* to offer resistance.
resolver *vt* *(problema)* to solve.
respaldo *nm* **1** *(de asiento)* back. **2** *(apoyo)* support, backing.
respectivo,-a *adj* respective.
respecto *nm*. • **al respecto** on the matter, about; **con respecto a** with regard to, regarding.
respetar *vt* to respect.
respeto *nm* respect.
respiración *nf* breathing. ▪ **respiración boca a boca** mouth-to-mouth resuscitation.
respirar *vi* to breathe.
responder *vt-vi* to answer, reply.
responsabilidad *nf* responsibility.
responsable *adj* responsible.
respuesta *nf* *(contestación)* answer, reply; *(reacción)* response.
resta *nf* substraction.
restablecerse *vpr* *(recuperarse)* to recover, get better.
restante *adj* remaining.
restar *vt* to subtract.
restauración *nf* **1** *(de muebles etc.)* restoration. **2** *(hostelería)* catering.

restaurante *nm* restaurant.
resto *nm* **1** *(lo que queda)* rest. **2** *(en matemáticas)* remainder. ▶ *nm pl* **restos** *(gen)* remains; *(de comida)* leftovers.
resultado *nm* result.
resultar *vi* **1** *(funcionar)* to work. **2** *(ocurrir, ser)* to turn out to be. **3** *(salir)* to come out: *resultar herido*, to be wounded. • **resulta que** it turns out that.
resumen *nm* summary. • **en resumen** in short.
resumir *vt* to summarize.
retablo *nm* altarpiece.
retina *nf* retina.
retirada *nf* **1** withdrawal. **2** MIL retreat.
retirar *vt* *(apartar)* to withdraw. ▶ *vpr* **retirarse 1** *(tropas)* to retreat. **2** *(apartarse)* to withdraw. **3** *(jubilarse)* to retire.
retiro *nm* **1** *(jubilación)* retirement. **2** *(pensión)* pension.
reto *nm* challenge.
retocar *vt* to touch up.
retorcer *vt* *(doblar)* to twist. ▶ *vpr* **retorcerse** *(de dolor)* to writhe; *(de risa)* to double up.
retorno *nm* return.
retransmisión *nf* broadcast.
retransmitir *vt* to broadcast.
retrasar *vt* **1** *(salida, proceso)* to delay, put off. **2** *(reloj)* to put back. ▶ *vi-vpr* **retrasar-(se) 1** *(ir atrás)* to fall behind.

riesgo

2 *(llegar tarde)* to be late. **3** *(reloj)* to be slow.
retraso *nm* **1** *(de tiempo)* delay. **2** *(subdesarrollo)* backwardness.
retrato *nm* **1** portrait. **2** *(foto)* photograph. ▪ **retrato robot** identikit picture.
retrete *nm* toilet, lavatory.
retroceder *vi* to go back.
retrovisor *nm* rear-view mirror.
reuma *nm* rheumatism.
reunión *nf* meeting.
reunir(se) *vt-vpr (personas)* to meet; *(cosas)* to get together.
revelado *nm* developing.
revelar *vt* **1** *(descubrir)* to reveal. **2** *(fotos)* to develop.
reventar(se) *vt-vpr (estallar)* to burst.
reventón *nm* **1** *(de tubería)* burst. **2** *(de neumático)* blowout.
reverencia *nf (inclinación)* bow; *(flexión de piernas)* curtsy.
revés *nm* **1** *(reverso)* back, reverse. **2** *(bofetada)* slap. **3** *(contrariedad)* misfortune. **4** *(en tenis etc.)* backhand. ● **al revés 1** *(todo lo contrario)* on the contrary. **2** *(en orden inverso)* the other way round. **3** *(lo de dentro fuera)* inside out. **4** *(lo delantero detrás)* back to front. **5** *(boca abajo)* upside down, the wrong way up.

revisar *vt (teoría, edición)* to revise; *(cuenta)* to check.
revisión *nf (de teoría, edición)* revision. ▪ **revisión médica** checkup.
revisor,-ra *nm,f* ticket inspector. ▪ **revisor ortográfico** spellchecker.
revista *nf* **1** *(publicación)* magazine, review. **2** *(espectáculo)* revue.
revolcarse *vpr* to roll about.
revolución *nf* revolution.
revólver *nm* revolver.
revolver *vt* **1** *(remover)* to stir; *(agitar)* to shake. **2** *(desordenar)* to mess up.
revuelta *nf (revolución)* revolt, riot.
revuelto *nm* scrambled eggs.
rey *nm* king. ▪ **los Reyes Magos** the Three Kings, the Three Wise Men.
rezagarse *vpr* to fall behind.
rezar *vi* to pray.
riachuelo *nm* stream.
riada *nf* flood.
ribera *nf* **1** *(de río)* bank. **2** *(de mar)* seashore.
rico,-a *adj* **1** *(gen)* rich. **2** *(sabroso)* tasty, delicious.
ridículo,-a *adj* ridiculous.
riego *nm* irrigation, watering. ▪ **riego sanguíneo** blood circulation.
riel *nm* rail.
rienda *nf (brida)* rein.
riesgo *nm* risk, danger.

rifar *vt* to raffle.
rifle *nm* rifle.
rígido,-a *adj* rigid.
rigor *nm* GB rigour, US rigor.
rima *nf* rhyme.
rímel *nm* mascara.
rincón *nm* corner.
rinoceronte *nm* rhinoceros.
riña *nf* 1 *(pelea)* fight. 2 *(discusión)* quarrel.
riñón *nm* kidney.
río *nm* river. • **río abajo** downstream; **río arriba** upstream.
risa *nf* laugh.
ritmo *nm* 1 *(compás)* rhythm. 2 *(velocidad)* pace, speed.
rito *nm* rite.
rival *nmf* rival.
rizado,-a *adj* curly.
rizo *nm* curl.
robar *vt* *(banco, persona)* to rob; *(objeto)* to steal; *(casa)* to burgle, break into.
roble *nm* oak tree.
robo *nm* *(a banco, persona)* robbery; *(de objeto)* theft; *(en casa)* burglary.
robot *nm* robot.
roca *nf* rock.
roce *nm* 1 *(señal - en superficie)* scuff mark; *(- en piel)* chafing mark. 2 *(contacto físico)* light touch.
rocío *nm* dew.
rodaja *nf* slice.
rodaje *nm* 1 *(de película)* filming, shooting. 2 *(de vehículo)* running-in.

rodar *vi* *(dar vueltas)* to roll, turn. ► *vt* 1 *(película)* to shoot. 2 *(coche)* to run in.
rodear *vt* 1 *(cercar)* to surround, encircle. 2 *(desviarse)* to make a detour.
rodeo *nm* 1 *(desvío)* detour. 2 *(elusión)* evasiveness.
rodilla *nf* knee.
roedor *nm* rodent.
rogar *vt* 1 *(suplicar)* to beg. 2 *(pedir)* to ask, request.
rojo,-a *adj* red. ► *nm* **rojo** red.
rollo *nm* 1 *(de tela, papel)* roll. 2 *fam* *(aburrimiento)* drag, bore, pain.
románico,-a *adj-mn* Romanesque.
romántico,-a *adj-nm,f* romantic.
rombo *nm* rhombus.
romero *nm* rosemary.
rompecabezas *nm* 1 *(juego)* puzzle. 2 *(problema)* riddle.
rompeolas *nm* breakwater.
romper(se) *vt-vpr* *(gen)* to break; *(papel, tela)* to tear; *(cristal)* to smash. ► *vt* *(relaciones)* to break off.
ron *nm* rum.
roncar *vi* to snore.
ronda *nf* 1 *(patrulla)* patrol. 2 *(de policía)* beat. 3 *(de bebidas, cartas)* round.
rondar *vt-vi* 1 *(vigilar)* to patrol. 2 *(merodear)* to prowl around. 3 *(cifra)* to be about.
ronquido *nm* snore.

ropa *nf* clothes. ■ **ropa interior** underwear.

rosa *adj-nm (color)* pink. ▶ *nf (flor)* rose.

rosado *adj-nm (vino)* rosé.

rosal *nm* rosebush.

rosca *nf (de tuerca)* thread.

roscón *nm* ring-shaped roll or cake.

rosquilla *nf* doughnut.

rostro *nm fml* face.

roto,-a *adj* broken.

rotonda *nf* roundabout.

rótula *nf* knee-cap.

rotulador *nm* felt-tip pen.

rótulo *nm* **1** *(etiqueta)* label. **2** *(letrero)* sign. **3** *(anuncio)* poster, placard.

rotura *nf* **1** *(de objeto)* breakage. **2** *(de hueso)* fracture.

roulotte *nf* caravan.

rozadura *nf* scratch.

rozar *vt-vi (tocar ligeramente)* to touch, brush. ▶ *vt (raer)* to rub against: *el zapato me rozaba*, my shoe was rubbing.

rubéola *nf* German measles, rubella.

rubí *nm* ruby.

rubio,-a *adj (hombre)* blond; *(mujer)* blonde.

ruborizarse *vpr* to blush.

rúbrica *nf* **1** *(firma)* flourish. **2** *(título)* title.

rueda *nf (de vehículo)* wheel. ■ **rueda de recambio** spare wheel.

ruedo *nm* bullring.

ruego *nm* request.

rugby *nm* rugby.

rugir *vi* to roar.

ruido *nm* noise.

ruina *nf* ruin: *al borde de la ruina*, on the brink of ruin; *el edificio amenazaba ruina*, the building was about to collapse. ▶ *nf pl* **ruinas** ruins. ● **en ruinas** in ruins.

ruiseñor *nm* nightingale.

rulo *nm (para pelo)* curler.

rumba *nf* rumba.

rumbo *nm* course, direction. ● **con rumbo a** bound for; **sin rumbo** aimlessly.

rumiante *adj-nm* ruminant.

rumor *nm* **1** *(noticia, voz)* GB rumour; US rumor. **2** *(murmullo)* murmur.

rumorearse *vi* GB to be rumoured; US to be rumored.

rupestre *adj (planta)* rock; *(pintura)* cave.

ruptura *nf* **1** *(de acuerdo)* breaking. **2** *(de relación)* breaking-off; *(de matrimonio)* break-up.

rural *adj* rural, country.

Rusia *nf* Russia.

ruso,-a *adj* Russian. ▶ *nm,f (persona)* Russian. ▶ *nm* **ruso** *(idioma)* Russian.

rústico,-a *adj* rustic.

ruta *nf* route.

rutina *nf* routine.

rutinario,-a *adj* monotonous.

S

sábado *nm* Saturday.
sabana *nf* savannah.
sábana *nf* sheet.
saber *nm* knowledge. ► *vt-vi* *(conocer)* to know. ► *vt* **1** *(poder)* can: *sabe tocar el piano*, she can play the piano. **2** *(tener noticias de)* to hear: *hace mucho que no sé nada de ellos*, I haven't heard anything from them for ages. **3** *(enterarse)* to find out: *cuando supe que era su cumpleaños...*, when I found out it was her birthday... ► *vi* *(tener sabor a)* to taste. ► *vi* *(tener sabor a)* to taste. • **a saber** *fml* namely; **hacer saber** to inform; **saber mal a ALGN**: *le supo mal que se fueran sin ella*, she was upset that they went without her; **que yo sepa** as far as I know.
sabio,-a *adj* learned, wise.
sable *nm* sabre.
sabor *nm* **1** *(gusto)* taste. **2** *(gusto añadido)* GB flavour, US flavor. • **tener sabor** to taste.
sabroso,-a *adj* tasty.
sacacorchos *nm* corkscrew.
sacapuntas *nm* pencil sharpener.
sacar *vt* **1** *(poner fuera)* to take out. **2** *(extraer)* to extract, pull out: *fui al dentista a*

sacarme una muela, I went to the dentist to have a tooth out. **3** *(moda)* to introduce, bring out: *han sacado un nuevo disco*, they have brought out a new record. **4** *(entrada, pasaporte)* to get: *he sacado las entradas para el concierto*, I've bought the tickets for the concert. **5** *(tenis)* to serve; *(fútbol - al principio)* to kick off; *(durante el partido)* to take the kick. • **sacar adelante 1** *(proyecto)* to carry out. **2** *(hijos)* to bring up.
sacarina *nf* saccharine.
sacerdote *nm* priest.
saciar *vt* *(hambre)* to satiate; *(sed)* to quench.
saco *nm* **1** *(bolsa)* sack, bag. **2** *(contenido)* sackful, bagful. ▪ **saco de dormir** sleeping bag.
sacramento *nm* sacrament.
sacrificarse *vpr* to make sacrifices.
sacrificio *nm* sacrifice.
sacudir *vt* *(agitar)* to shake.
safari *nm* safari.
sagrado,-a *adj* **1** *(religioso)* holy. **2** *(que merece respeto)* sacred.
sal *nf* **1** *(condimento)* salt. **2** *(gracia)* wit. ▪ **sal de mesa** table salt; **sales de baño** bath salts.
sala *nf* **1** *(habitación)* room. **2** *(sala de estar)* living room. **3** *(de hospital)* ward. **4** *(de tribu-*

nal) courtroom. **5** *(cine)* cinema. ∎ **sala de espera** waiting room; **sala de estar** living room; **sala de fiestas** nightclub, discotheque.

salado,-a *adj* **1** *(con sal)* salted. **2** *(con demasiada sal)* salty. **3** *(no dulce)* GB savoury; US savory.

salamandra *nf* salamander.

salar *vt* to salt.

salario *nm* salary, wages.

salchicha *nf* sausage.

salchichón *nm* salami.

saldo *nm* **1** *(de una cuenta)* balance. **2** *(liquidación)* sale.

salero *nm* *(recipiente)* saltcellar.

salida *nf* **1** *(acto)* departure. **2** *(de personas)* exit, way out; *(de aire, gas)* vent; *(de agua)* outlet. **3** *(de autopista)* exit. **4** DEP start. **5** *(excursión)* trip, outing. ∎ **salida de emergencia** emergency exit; **salida del sol** sunrise; **salida nula** false start; **salidas internacionales** international departures; **salidas nacionales** domestic departures.

salir *vi* **1** *(ir de dentro para afuera)* to go out. **2** *(venir de dentro para fuera)* to come out. **3** *(partir)* to leave: *el autobús sale a las tres*, the bus leaves at three. **4** *(aparecer)* to appear: *salir en los periódicos*, to be in the newspapers. **5** *(resultar)* to turn out, to be: *la*

tarta te ha salido perfecta, the cake has turned out perfect. **6** *(del trabajo, colegio)* to leave, come out. **7** *(producto)* to come out, be released. **8** *(sol)* to rise. ► *vpr* **salirse** **1** *(soltarse, desviarse)* to come off. **2** *(líquido)* to leak, leak out. ● **salir a** ALGN to take after SB; **salir adelante** to be successful; **salir con** ALGN to go out with SB; **salir ganando con algo** to do well out of STH; **salir perdiendo** to lose out.

saliva *nf* saliva.

salmón *nm* salmon.

salmonete *nm* red mullet.

salón *nm* **1** *(en casa)* living room, lounge. **2** *(público)* hall. ∎ **salón de actos** assembly hall; **salón de belleza** beauty salon; **salón recreativo** amusement arcade.

salpicadero *nm* dashboard.

salpicar *vt* to splash.

salpicón *nm*. ∎ **salpicón de marisco** seafood salad.

salsa *nf* **1** sauce. **2** *(baile)* salsa.

salsera *nf* gravy boat.

saltamontes *nm* grasshopper.

saltar *vi* **1** *(botar)* to jump. **2** *(al agua)* to dive. **3** *(desprenderse)* to come off. ► *vt (valla etc.)* to jump (over). ► *vpr* **saltarse** **1** *(ley etc)* to ignore. **2** *(omitir)* to skip, miss out.

salto *nm* **1** *(gen)* jump. **2** *(de trampolín)* dive. • **dar un salto** to jump. ▪ **salto con pértiga** pole vault; **salto de agua** waterfall, falls *pl*; **salto de altura** high jump; **salto de cama** negligée; **salto de esquí** ski-jump; **salto de longitud** long jump; **salto mortal** somersault.

salud *nf* health. ▶ *interj* **¡salud!** *(al brindar)* cheers!; *(al estornudar)* bless you!

saludar *vt-vi* to say hello to. • **le saluda atentamente 1** *(si no conocemos el nombre)* yours faithfully. **2** *(si conocemos el nombre)* yours sincerely.

saludo *nm* **1** *(gen)* greeting. **2** *(entre militares)* salute. ▶ *nm pl* **saludos** best wishes.

salvación *nf* salvation.

salvaje *adj* *(gen)* wild; *(pueblo)* savage, uncivilized. ▶ *nmf* savage.

salvamanteles *nm* table mat.

salvamento *nm* rescue.

salvar *vt* to save, rescue. ▶ *vpr* **salvarse** *(sobrevivir)* to survive. • **¡sálvese quien pueda!** every man for himself!

salvavidas *nm* life belt.

salvo *prep* except, except for. • **estar a salvo** to be safe and sound; **ponerse a salvo** to reach safety; **salvo que** unless.

san *adj* → santo,-a.

sanción *nf* **1** *(multa)* fine. **2** *(castigo)* sanction: *una sanción de cuatro partidos*, a four-game suspension.

sandalia *nf* sandal.

sandía *nf* watermelon.

sándwich *nm* sandwich.

sangrar *vt-vi* to bleed.

sangre *nf* blood. • **a sangre fría** in cool blood. ▪ **sangre fría** sangfroid, calmness.

sangría *nf* *(bebida)* sangria.

sanidad *nf* public health.

sanitarios *nm pl* bathroom fittings.

sano,-a *adj* healthy. • **sano y salvo** safe and sound.

santo,-a *adj* **1** *(lugar, vida, misa)* holy. **2** *(con nombre)* Saint. **3** *(para enfatizar)* blessed: *todo el santo día*, the whole day long. ▶ *nm,f* saint.

sapo *nm* toad.

saque *nm* **1** *(tenis)* service. **2** *(fútbol)* kick-off. ▪ **saque de banda** throw-in; **saque de esquina** corner.

sarampión *nm* measles.

sardina *nf* sardine.

sargento *nm* sergeant.

sarpullido *nm* rash.

sartén *nf* GB frying pan; US skillet.

sastre,-a *nm,f* *(hombre)* tailor; *(mujer)* dressmaker.

satélite *nm* satellite.

satén *nm* satin.

satisfacción *nf* satisfaction.

satisfacer *vt* to satisfy.
satisfecho,-a *adj* satisfied.
sauce *nm* willow. ▪ **sauce llorón** weeping willow.
sauna *nf* sauna.
saxofón *nm* saxophone.
sazonar *vt* to season.
se[1] *pron* **1** *(reflexivo - a él mismo)* himself; *(- a ella misma)* herself; *(- a usted mismo)* yourself; *(- a ellos mismos)* themselves; *(- a ustedes mismos)* yourselves. **2** *(recíproco)* one another, each other. **3** *(en pasivas e impersonales)*: *se dice que...*, it is said that...; *se suspendió el partido*, the match was postponed; *se habla español*, Spanish spoken.
se[2] *pron (objeto indirecto - a él)* him; *(- a ella)* her; *(cosa)* it; *(- a usted/ustedes)* you; *(- a ellos/ellas)* them.
secador *nm* dryer. ▪ **secador de pelo** hair-dryer.
secadora *nf* clothes-dryer, tumble-dryer.
secar *vt (pelo, ropa, piel)* to dry; *(lágrimas, vajilla)* to wipe.
sección *nf* **1** *(división)* section. **2** *(en tienda, oficina)* department.
seco,-a *adj* **1** *(no mojado)* dry. **2** *(frutos, flores)* dried. **3** *(golpe, ruido)* sharp. ● **a secas** simply, just; **en seco** sharply, suddenly.
secretaría *nf* secretary's office.

secretario,-a *nm,f* secretary: *secretario,-a de dirección*, executive secretary.
secreto,-a *adj* secret. ► *nm* **secreto** secret.
secta *nf* sect.
sector *nm* **1** *(zona)* area. **2** *(de la industria)* sector.
secuela *nf* consequence.
secuencia *nf* sequence.
secuestro *nm* **1** *(de persona)* kidnapping. **2** *(de avión)* highjacking.
secundario,-a *adj* secondary.
sed *nf* thirst. ● **tener sed** to be thirsty.
seda *nf* silk. ▪ **seda dental** dental floss.
sedal *nm* fishing line.
sedante *adj-nm* sedative.
sede *nf* **1** *(de organización)* headquarters; *(de empresa)* head office. **2** *(del gobierno)* seat. **3** *(de acontecimiento)* venue.
seducir *vt* to seduce.
segar *vt* to reap.
segmento *nm* segment.
seguido,-a *adj* **1** *(acompañado)* followed. **2** *(consecutivo)* consecutive: *dos días seguidos*, two days running. ► *adv* straight on. ● **en seguida** at once, immediately.
seguidor,-ra *nm,f* follower.
seguir *vt* **1** *(gen)* to follow. **2** *(continuar)* to continue. ► *vi* **1** *(proseguir)* to go on: *siga to-*

do recto hasta la plaza, go straight on until you come to the square. **2** *(permanecer)* to remain: *siguió de pie*, he remained standing. **3** *(estar todavía)* to be still: *sigue enfermo*, he's still sick.

según *prep (de acuerdo con)* according to. ▶ *adv* **1** *(depende de)* depending on: *según lo que digan*, depending on what they say. **2** *(como)* just as: *todo quedó según estaba*, everything stayed just as it was. **3** *(a medida que)* as: *según iban entrando se les daba una copa*, as they came in they were given a drink.

segundero *nm* second hand.

segundo,-a *num* second. ▶ *nm* **segundo** second.

seguridad *nf* **1** *(contra accidentes)* safety. **2** *(contra robos, ataques)* security. **3** *(certeza)* certainty. **4** *(confianza)* confidence. • **con toda seguridad** definitely. ▪ **Seguridad Social** National Health Service.

seguro,-a *adj* **1** *(físicamente)* safe. **2** *(estable)* secure. **3** *(fiable)* reliable: *un método muy seguro*, a very reliable method. **4** *(cierto)* definite: *aún no es seguro que venga*, it's not definite that he's coming yet. **5** *(convencido)* confident, sure, certain: *estoy seguro de que no va a defraudarnos*, I'm sure he won't let us down. ▶ *nm* **seguro 1** *(contrato, póliza)* insurance. **2** *(mecanismo)* safety catch, safety device. ▶ *adv* *(sin duda)* for sure, definitely: *lo sé seguro*, I know for sure. • **seguro que...** I bet...

seis *num* six; *(en fechas)* sixth. • **son las seis** it's six o'clock.

seiscientos,-as *num* six hundred.

seísmo *nm* earthquake.

selección *nf* selection. ▪ **selección nacional** national team.

seleccionar *vt* to select.

selecto,-a *adj*: *un club selecto*, an exclusive club; *vinos selectos*, fine wines, choice wines; *ante un público selecto*, before a selected audience.

sellar *vt* to seal.

sello *nm* **1** *(de correos)* stamp. **2** *(de estampar, precinto)* seal. **3** *(distintivo)* hallmark. ▪ **sello discográfico** record label.

selva *nf* jungle.

semáforo *nm* traffic lights.

semana *nf* week. ▪ **Semana Santa** Easter.

semanal *adj* weekly.

semanario *nm* weekly magazine.

sembrar *vt (con semillas)* to sow; *(con plantas)* to plant.

semejante *adj (parecido)* similar. ▶ *nm* fellow being.

semen *nm* semen.

señorita

semestre *nm* six-month period; *(en educación)* semester.
semifinal *nf* semifinal.
semilla *nf* seed.
senado *nm* senate.
senador,-ra *nm,f* senator.
sencillo,-a *adj* 1 *(fácil)* simple. 2 *(persona)* natural, unaffected.
sendero *nm* path.
seno *nm* *(pecho)* breast.
sensación *nf* 1 *(percepción)* feeling. 2 *(efecto)* sensation.
sensacional *adj* sensational.
sensato,-a *adj* sensible.
sensibilidad *nf* sensitivity.
sensible *adj* sensitive.
sentar *vi* 1 *(comida)* to agree: *el chocolate no me sienta bien*, chocolate doesn't agree with me. 2 *(ropa)* to suit: *esa corbata te sienta bien*, that tie suits you. 3 *(hacer efecto)* to do: *un poco de aire fresco te sentará bien*, a bit of fresh air will do you good. ▶ *vpr* **sentarse** to sit down.
sentencia *nf* *(condena)* sentence. • **dictar sentencia** to pass sentence.
sentido *nm* 1 *(vista, oído, etc)* sense. 2 *(dirección)* direction: *una calle de sentido único*, a one-way street. 3 *(juicio)* consciousness. 4 *(significado)* meaning. • **perder el sentido** to faint; **recobrar el sentido** to regain consciousness;

tener sentido to make sense. ▪ **sentido común** common sense; **sentido del humor** sense of humour (US humor).
sentimiento *nm* feeling.
sentir *vt* 1 *(lamentar)* to regret. 2 *(oír)* to hear. ▶ *vt-vpr* **sentir(se)** to feel. • **¡lo siento!** I'm sorry!; **sentirse mal** to feel ill.
seña *nf* sign. ▶ *nf pl* **señas** address. • **hacer señas** to signal, gesture.
señal *nf* 1 *(indicio)* sign. 2 *(marca)* mark. 3 *(signo)* signal. 4 *(por teléfono)* tone: *no había señal*, there was no dialling tone. ▪ **señal de tráfico** road sign.
señalar *vt* 1 *(indicar)* to show. 2 *(marcar)* to mark: *señálalo en rojo*, mark it in red. 3 *(hacer notar)* to point to. 4 *(con el dedo)* to point at.
señor *nm* 1 *(hombre)* man; *(caballero)* gentleman. 2 *(en tratamientos)* sir; *(delante de apellido)* Mr: *el señor Pérez*, Mr Pérez.
señora *nf* 1 *(mujer)* woman; *(dama)* lady. 2 *(esposa)* wife. 4 *(en tratamientos)* madam; *(delante de apellido)* Mrs: *la señora Gómez*, Mrs Gómez; *señoras y señores*, ladies and gentlemen.
señorita *nf* 1 *(mujer joven)* young lady. 2 *(delante de ape-*

llido) Miss: *la señorita López*, Miss López. **3** *(profesora)* teacher.

separación *nf* **1** *(acción)* separation. **2** *(espacio)* gap.

separar *vt* to separate. ▸ *vpr* **separarse** *(de una persona)* to separate, split up.

sepia *nf* cuttlefish.

septiembre *nm* September.

séptimo,-a *num* seventh.

sepultar *vt* to bury.

sepultura *nf* grave.

sequía *nf* drought.

ser *vi* **1** *(gen)* to be. **2** *(pertenecer)* to belong: *el cuadro es de Picasso*, the painting is by Picasso. **3** *(material)* to be made of: *la mesa es de madera*, the table is made of wood. ▸ *aux* to be. ● **a no ser que** unless; **a poder ser** if possible; **de no ser por...** had it not been for...; **érase una vez** once upon a time; **es más** furthermore; **sea como sea** in any case. ■ **ser humano** human being; **ser vivo** living creature.

sereno,-a *adj* calm.

serial *nm* serial.

serie *nf* series.

serio,-a *adj* **1** *(persona, enfermedad)* serious. **2** *(formal)* reliable.

serpiente *nf* snake. ■ **serpiente de cascabel** rattlesnake.

serrar *vt* to saw.

serrín *nm* sawdust.

servicio *nm* **1** *(atención)* service. **2** *(criados)* servants. **3** *(juego)* set. **4** *(tenis)* serve, service. **5** *(retrete)* toilet. ■ **servicio a domicilio** home delivery service; **servicio militar** military service.

servidor *nm* INFORM server.

servilleta *nf* napkin, serviette.

servir *vt* **1** *(comida)* to serve: *¿ya le sirven?*, are you being served? **2** *(bebida)* to pour: *¿te sirvo yo?*, shall I pour? ▸ *vi* **1** *(ser útil)* to be useful. **2** *(trabajar)* to serve. ▸ *vpr* **servirse 1** *(comida)* to help oneself: *sírvase usted mismo*, help yourself. **2** *(utilizar)* to use. ● **servir de** to be used as; **servir para** to be used for.

sesenta *num* sixty.

sesión *nf* **1** *(reunión)* session, meeting. **2** *(de película)* showing.

seso *nm* brain, brains.

seta *nf* mushroom; *(no comestible)* toadstool.

setecientos,-as *num* seven hundred.

setenta *num* seventy.

setiembre *nm* September.

seto *nm* hedge.

sexo *nm* sex.

sexto,-a *num* sixth.

short *nm* shorts.

si[1] *conj* if. ● **si bien** although; **si no** otherwise.

si² *nm (nota musical)* ti, si, B.

sí¹ *pron (él)* himself; *(ella)* herself; *(cosa)* itself; *(uno mismo)* oneself; *(plural)* themselves.

sí² *adv* **1** *(en respuestas)* yes. **2** *(sustituye al verbo)*: **ella no irá, pero yo sí**, she won't go, but I will. ▶ *nm* yes

sida *nm* AIDS.

sidra *nf* cider.

siempre *adv* always. • **para siempre** forever; **siempre que** whenever; **siempre y cuando** provided, as long as.

sien *nf* temple.

sierra *nf* **1** *(herramienta)* saw. **2** *(cordillera)* mountain range.

siesta *nf* siesta, afternoon nap.

siete *num* seven; *(en fechas)* seventh. ▶ *nm (rasgón)* tear.

sifón *nm (bebida)* soda water.

sigla *nf* acronym.

siglo *nm* century.

significado *nm* meaning.

significar *vt* to mean.

signo *nm (señal)* sign.

siguiente *adj* following, next.

sílaba *nf* syllable.

silbar *vi* **1** *(con los labios, viento)* to whistle. **2** *(abuchear)* to hiss.

silbato *nm* whistle.

silbido *nm* whistle.

silencio *nm* silence. • **guardar silencio** to keep quiet.

silicona *nf* silicone.

silla *nf* chair. ▪ **silla de montar** saddle.

sillín *nm* saddle.

sillón *nm* armchair.

silueta *nf* **1** *(contorno)* silhouette. **2** *(figura)* figure: **te realza la silueta**, it shows off your figure.

silvestre *adj* wild.

símbolo *nm* symbol.

simétrico,-a *adj* symmetric.

similar *adj* similar.

simpático,-a *adj* nice.

simple *adj* **1** *(sencillo)* simple. **2** *(puro)* mere: **con una simple llamada**, with just a phone call.

simultáneo,-a *adj* simultaneous.

sin *prep* **1** *(gen)* without. **2** *(por hacer)*: **está sin planchar**, it has not been ironed. • **sin embargo** however.

sincero,-a *adj* sincere.

sindicato *nm* trade union.

sinfonía *nf* symphony.

singular *adj* **1** *(único)* singular, single. **2** *(excepcional)* extraordinary. **3** *(raro)* peculiar.

siniestro *nm (accidente)* accident. • **fue declarado siniestro total** it was declared a write-off.

sino *conj* but.

sinónimo *nm* synonym.

sintético,-a *adj* synthetic.

síntoma *nm* symptom.

sintonizar *vt* to tune in to.

sinvergüenza *nmf* cheeky devil.

siquiera *conj.* • **ni siquiera** not even.

sirena *nf* 1 *(alarma)* siren. 2 *(ninfa)* mermaid.

sirviente,-a *nm,f* servant.

sistema *nm* system.

sitio *nm* 1 *(lugar)* place. 2 *(espacio)* space, room.

situación *nf* situation.

situar *vt* to situate, locate.

sobaco *nm* armpit.

soborno *nm* 1 *(acción)* bribery. 2 *(regalo)* bribe.

sobra *nf* excess, surplus. ► *nf pl* **sobras** leftovers. • **de sobra** more than enough.

sobrar *vi* 1 *(quedar)* to be left over. 2 *(sin aprovechar)* to be more than enough. 3 *(estar de más)* to be superfluous.

sobre *prep* 1 *(encima)* on, upon: *el jarrón está sobre la mesa*, the vase is on the table. 2 *(por encima)* over, above: *el helicóptero volaba sobre la ciudad*, the helicopter flew over the city. 3 *(acerca de)* on, about: *hablar sobre algo*, to talk about STH. 4 *(alrededor de)* around, about: *llegaré sobre las once*, I'll get there at about eleven o´clock. ► *nm* 1 *(de carta)* envelope. 2 *(envoltorio)* packet: *sopa de sobre*, packet soup. 3 *(paquete pequeño)* sachet: *sobre de azúcar*, sachet of sugar. • **sobre todo** above all, especially.

sobremesa *nf (charla)* after-lunch chat; *(hora)* afternoon.

sobresaliente *nm (calificación)* A, first.

sobresalir *vi* 1 *(destacarse)* to stand out. 2 *(estar saliente)* to stick out. 3 *(abultar)* to protrude.

sobrevivir *vi* to survive.

sobrino,-a *nm,f (chico)* nephew; *(chica)* niece.

sobrio,-a *adj* sober, temperate.

social *adj* social.

sociedad *nf* society. ■ **sociedad anónima** GB limited company; US incorporated company; **sociedad limitada** private limited company.

socio,-a *nm,f* 1 *(de un grupo)* member. 2 *(de empresa)* partner.

sociología *nf* sociology.

socorrer *vt* to help, aid.

socorrista *nmf (en la playa)* lifeguard.

socorro *nm* help, aid, assistance. ► *interj* ¡socorro! help! • **pedir socorro** to ask for help.

soda *nf* soda water.

sofá *nm* sofa, settee.

software *nm* software.

soga *nf* rope.

soja *nf* soya bean.

sol¹ *nm* 1 *(astro)* sun. 2 *(luz)* sunlight, sunshine. • **tomar el sol** to sunbathe.

sol² *nm (nota)* sol, G.

solapa *nf* **1** *(de chaqueta)* lapel. **2** *(de sobre, libro)* flap.

solar¹ *adj* solar

solar² *nm (terreno)* plot.

soldado *nm* soldier.

soldar *vt (unir)* to weld; *(con estaño)* to solder.

soledad *nf* **1** *(estado)* solitude. **2** *(sentimiento)* loneliness.

solemne *adj* solemn.

soler *vi* **1** *(presente)* to be in the habit of doing: *soler hacer*, to usually do. **2** *(pasado)*: *solía ir a correr*, he used to go running.

solicitar *vt* **1** *(pedir)* to request. **2** *(trabajo)* to apply for.

solidaridad *nf* solidarity.

sólido,-a *adj* solid.

solitario,-a *adj* **1** *(sin compañía)* solitary. **2** *(sentimiento)* lonely. **3** *(lugar)* deserted. ▶ *nm* **solitario** solitaire.

sólo *adv* only.

solo,-a *adj* **1** *(sin compañía)* alone: *vive sola*, she lives alone. **2** *(solitario)* lonely: *se siente muy solo*, he feels very lonely. **3** *(único)* one, single: *una sola persona*, one single person. ▶ *nm* **solo** **1** *fam (café)* black coffee. **2** *(canción)* solo. ▶ *adv* **solo** only.

solomillo *nm* sirloin.

soltar *vt* **1** *(dejar suelto)* to let go of. **2** *(poner en libertad)* to set free, release. **3** *(desatar)* to undo, unfasten. ▶ *vpr* **soltarse** **1** *(desatarse)* to come undone. **2** *(desprenderse)* to come off.

soltero,-a *nm,f (hombre)* bachelor; *(mujer)* single woman.

solución *nf* solution.

solucionar *vt* to solve.

sombra *nf* **1** *(lugar sin sol)* shade. **2** *(silueta)* shadow. ▪ **sombra de ojos** eye shadow.

sombrero *nm* hat.

sombrilla *nf (de mano)* parasol; *(de playa)* sunshade.

someter *vt* **1** *(subyugar)* to subdue. **2** *(exponer)* to subject: *someter algo a prueba*, to put STH to test. ▶ *vpr* **someterse** **1** *(rendirse)* to surrender: *el país tuvo que someterse al invasor*, the country had to surrender to the invader. **2** *(tratamiento etc.)* to undergo.

somier *nm* bed base.

somnífero *nm* sleeping pill.

sonajero *nm* rattle.

sonámbulo,-a *adj-nm,f* sleepwalker.

sonar *vi* **1** *(con timbrazos)* to ring; *(con campanadas)* to strike; *(con pitido)* to beep. **2** *(ponerse en marcha)* to go off. **3** *(conocer vagamente)* to sound familiar: *su cara me suena*, her face is familiar. ▶ *vpr* **sonarse** to blow one's nose.

sonda *nf* probe.
sondeo *nm* poll.
sonido *nm* sound.
sonreír *vi* to smile.
sonrisa *nf* smile.
soñar *vt-vi* to dream.
sopa *nf* soup.
sopera *nf* soup tureen.
soplar *vi* to blow.
soportar *vt* 1 *(sostener)* to support. 2 *(aguantar)* to put up with: *¿cómo lo soportas?*, how can you put up with him? 3 *(tolerar)* to stand: *no soporto a esta chica*, I can't stand this girl.
soprano *nmf* soprano.
sorbete *nm* sorbet.
sorbo *nm* sip.
sordo,-a *adj* 1 *(persona)* deaf. 2 *(sonido, dolor)* dull.
sordomudo,-a *adj* deaf and dumb. ► *nm,f* deaf mute.
sorprendente *adj* surprising.
sorprender *vt* to surprise.
sorpresa *nf* surprise.
sortear *vt* 1 *(echar a suertes)* to draw lots for; *(rifar)* to raffle. 2 *(obstáculos)* to get round.
sorteo *nm* *(de lotería)* draw; *(rifa)* raffle.
sortija *nf* ring.
soso,-a *adj* 1 *(sin sabor)* tasteless. 2 *(sin sal)*: **está soso**, it needs salt. 3 *(aburrido)* dull.
sospecha *nf* suspicion.
sospechar *vt* to suspect.

sospechoso,-a *nm,f* suspect.
sostén *nm* 1 *(apoyo)* support. 2 *(prenda)* bra, brassiere.
sostener *vt* 1 *(aguantar)* to support, hold up. 2 *(sujetar)* to hold. 3 *(conversación, reunión)* to have. 4 *(opinión)* to maintain, affirm.
sótano *nm* 1 *(usado como almacén)* cellar. 2 *(planta)* basement.
stop *nm* stop sign.
su *adj* *(de él)* his; *(de ella)* her; *(de usted/ustedes)* your; *(de ellos)* their; *(de animales, cosas)* its.
suave *adj* 1 *(piel, tela, color, voz)* soft. 2 *(superficie)* smooth. 3 *(brisa, persona)* gentle. 4 *(clima, sabor, detergente)* mild.
suavizante *nm* 1 *(para ropa)* fabric softener. 2 *(para pelo)* conditioner.
subasta *nf* auction.
subcampeón,-ona *nm,f* runner-up.
subida *nf* 1 *(ascenso)* ascent; *(a montaña)* climb. 2 *(pendiente)* slope. 3 *(aumento)* rise.
subir *vi* 1 *(a coche)* to get in; *(a tren, autobús, avión)* to get on. 2 *(aumentar)* to rise. ► *vt* 1 *(escalar)* to climb. 2 *(mover arriba)* to carry up, take up. 3 *(incrementar)* to put up. ► *vpr*
subirse 1 *(a coche)* to get in; *(a tren, autobús, avión)* to get on; *(a caballo)* to mount. 2

(trepar) to climb. **3** *(elevar)* to pull up: *súbete los calcetines*, pull your socks up.

submarinismo *nm* scuba diving.

submarino *nm* submarine.

subrayar *vt* **1** *(con una línea)* to underline. **2** *(recalcar)* to emphasize.

subsidio *nm* subsidy, aid. ■ **subsidio de desempleo** unemployment benefit.

subterráneo,-a *adj* subterranean, under-ground.

suburbano,-a *adj* suburban.

suburbio *nm* *(barrio pobre)* slum area; *(barrio de las afueras)* poor suburb.

subvención *nf* subsidy, grant.

suceder *vi* **1** *(acontecer)* to happen. **2** *(seguir)* to follow. ► *vt* *(sustituir)* to succeed.

sucesivo,-a *adj* consecutive, successive. ● **en lo sucesivo** from now on.

suceso *nm* **1** *(hecho)* event, happening. **2** *(incidente)* incident.

sucesor,-ra *nm,f* **1** *(en un puesto)* successor. **2** *(heredero)* heir; *(heredera)* heiress.

suciedad *nf* dirt.

sucio,-a *adj* dirty.

sucursal *nf* branch office.

Sudamérica *nf* South America.

sudamericano,-a *adj* South American.

sudar *vi* to sweat.

sudor *nm* sweat.

sudoroso,-a *adj* sweaty.

suegro,-a *nm,f* *(hombre)* father-in-law; *(mujer)* mother-in-law.

suela *nf* sole.

sueldo *nm* salary, pay.

suelo *nm* **1** *(en la calle)* ground; *(de interior)* floor. **2** *(tierra)* soil.

suelto,-a *adj* *(no sujeto)* loose; *(desatado)* undone. ► *nm* **suelto** *(cambio)* small change.

sueño *nm* **1**(*ganas de dormir)* sleepiness: *tengo mucho sueño*, I´m very sleepy. **2** *(lo soñado)* dream.

suero *nm* **1** *(de la sangre)* serum. **2** *(solución salina)* saline solution.

suerte *nf* **1** *(fortuna)* luck. **2** *(azar)* chance: *fue la suerte la que me llevó hasta ti*, it was fate that led me to you. ● **tener suerte** to be lucky; **tener mala suerte** to be unlucky.

suéter *nm* sweater.

suficiente *adj-pron* enough.

sufrir *vt* **1** *(padecer)* to suffer. **2** *(ser sujeto de)* to have; *(operación)* to undergo. *sufrir un accidente*, to have an accident.

sugerir *vt* to suggest.

suicidarse *vpr* to commit suicide.

suicidio *nm* suicide.

sujetador *nm* bra, brassiere.

sujetar *vt* 1 *(agarrar)* to hold. 2 *(fijar)* to fix, secure.

sujeto,-a *adj (fijo)* fastened. ▶ *nm* **sujeto** 1 *(de verbo)* subject. 2 *(persona)* fellow.

suma *nf* sum, amount.

sumar *vt* to add up.

sumergir *vt (meter en líquido)* to submerge; *(con fuerza)* to plunge; *(rápidamente)* to dip. ▶ *vpr* **sumergirse** *(submarinista)* to go underwater, dive; *(submarino)* to dive.

suministrar *vt* to provide, supply.

suministro *nm* supply.

súper *nm* 1 *fam (supermercado)* supermarket. 2 *(gasolina)* GB four-star petrol; US regular.

superar *vt* 1 *(exceder)* to surpass, exceed. 2 *(obstáculo etc)* to overcome. 3 *(récord)* to break. 4 *(prueba)* to pass.

superficie *nf* surface.

superior *adj* 1 *(de arriba)* upper. 2 *(mayor)* greater. 3 *(mejor)* superior.

supermercado *nm* supermarket.

superviviente *nmf* survivor.

suplemento *nm* supplement.

suplente *adj-nmf* substitute.

suplicar *vt* to beg.

suponer *vt* 1 *(creer)* to suppose. 2 *(dar por sentado)* to assume. 3 *(acarrear)* to entail.

supositorio *nm* suppository.

suprimir *vt (noticia)* to suppress; *(ley, impuestos)* to abolish; *(palabras, texto)* to delete.

supuesto,-a *adj* 1 *(falso)* supposed, assumed. 2 *(presunto)* alleged. • **por supuesto** of course.

sur *adj-nm* south.

surgir *vi* to arise, appear.

surtido *nm* assortment.

surtidor *nm* 1 *(fuente)* fountain. 2 *(chorro)* jet, spout. ■ **surtidor de gasolina** GB petrol pump; US gas pump.

suscribir *vt* 1 *(contrato)* to sign. 2 *(opinión)* to subscribe. ▶ *vpr* **suscribirse** *(a una revista)* to subscribe to.

suscripción *nf* subscription.

suspender *vt* 1 *(aplazar)* to postpone. 2 *(examen)* to fail. 3 *(cancelar)* to suspend.

suspense *nm* suspense.

suspensión *nf* 1 *(de coche)* suspension. 2 *(cancelación)* suspension.

suspenso *nm* fail.

suspiro *nm* sigh.

sustancia *nf* substance.

sustantivo *nm* noun.

sustitución *nf* 1 *(transitoria)* substitution. 2 *(permanente)* replacement.

sustituir *vt* 1 *(transitoriamente)* to substitute. 2 *(permanentemente)* to replace.

susto *nm* fright, scare.

suyo,-a *adj (de él)* of his; *(de ella)* of hers; *(de usted/ustedes)* of yours; *(de ellos)* of theirs. ▸ *pron (de él)* his; *(de ella)* hers; *(de usted/ustedes)* yours; *(de ellos,-as)* theirs.

T

tabaco *nm* 1 *(planta, hoja)* tobacco. 2 *(cigarrillos)* cigarettes: *el tabaco es malo para la salud*, smoking damages your health. ■ **tabaco negro** black tobacco; **tabaco rubio** Virginia tobacco.

tábano *nm* horsefly.

taberna *nf* pub, bar.

tabique *nm* partition wall. ■ **tabique nasal** nasal bone.

tabla *nf* 1 *(de madera pulida)* board; *(de madera basta)* plank. 2 *(índice)* table. ▸ *nf pl* **tablas** *(ajedrez)* stalemate, draw. ■ **tabla de planchar** ironing board; **tabla de surf** surfboard; **tabla de windsurf** sailboard.

tablero *nm* board. ■ **tablero de ajedrez** chessboard.

tableta *nf* 1 *(de chocolate)* bar. 2 *(pastilla)* tablet.

tablón *nm* plank. ■ **tablón de anuncios** notice board.

taburete *nm* stool.

tachar *vt* to cross out.

taco *nm* 1 *(para calzar)* wedge. 2 *(para tornillo)* Rawlplug®. 3 *(de entradas)* book; *(de billetes)* wad. 4 *(de billar)* cue. 5 *(de jamón, etc)* cube, piece. 6 *(en botas de fútbol)* stud. 7 *fam (palabrota)* swearword.

tacón *nm* heel.

táctica *nf* tactics.

tacto *nm* 1 *(sentido)* touch. 2 *(textura)* feel. 3 *(delicadeza)* tact.

tal *adj* such: *en tales condiciones*, in such conditions; *tal día*, such and such a day; *te llamó un tal García*, someone called García phoned you. ▸ *pron (cosa)* something; *(persona)* someone, somebody. ● **con tal de que** so long as, provided; **¿qué tal?** how are things?; **tal como** just as; **tal cual** just as it is; **tal vez** perhaps, maybe.

taladro *nm (herramienta)* drill; *(barrena)* gimlet.

talar *vt* to fell, cut down.

talco *nm* talc.

talento *nm* talent.

talla *nf* 1 *(estatura)* height; *(altura moral etc)* stature. 2 *(de prenda)* size: *¿qué talla usas?*, what size are you? 3 *(escultura)* carving, sculpture. ● **dar la talla** *(ser competente)* to measure up.

tallarines *nm pl* noodles.

taller *nm* **1** *(de artesano, profesional)* workshop. **2** *(de pintor)* studio. **3** *(industrial)* factory. ■ **taller de coches** garage.

tallo *nm* stem, stalk.

talón *nm* **1** *(de pie, calzado)* heel. **2** *(cheque)* GB cheque; US check.

tamaño *nm* size.

también *adv* also, too, as well.

tambor *nm* **1** *(instrumento)* drum. **2** *(de lavadora)* drum. **3** *(de detergente)* drum, giant size pack.

tampoco *adv* neither, nor, not… either.

tampón *nm* **1** *(de entintar)* inkpad. **2** *(absorbente)* tampon.

tan *adv* **1** so; *(después de sustantivo)* such: *no quiero una moto tan grande*, I don't want such a big motorbike; *¡son unos chicos tan malos!*, they are such naughty boys. **2** *(con adjetivos o adverbios)* so: *no comas tan deprisa*, don't eat so quickly. **3** *(comparativo)* as… as: *es tan alto como tú*, he's as tall as you are. **4** *(consecutivo)* so: *pasó tan deprisa que no lo vi*, he went by so fast that I didn't see him. ● **tan sólo** only.

tanda *nf* **1** *(conjunto)* batch, lot. **2** *(serie)* series, course. **3** *(turno)* shift.

tanque *nm* tank.

tanto,-a *adj* **1** *(con incontables)* so much; *(con contables)* so many. **2** *(en comparaciones - incontables)* as much; *(- contables)* as many. **3** *(en cantidades aproximadas)* odd: *tiene treinta y tantos años*, he's thirty something. ▶ *pron (incontables)* so much; *(contables)* so many. ▶ *adv* **1** *(cantidad)* so much. **2** *(tiempo)* so long. **3** *(frecuencia)* so often. ▶ *nm* **1** *(punto)* point. **2** *(cantidad imprecisa)* so much, a certain amount. ● **a las tantas** very late; **al tanto** informed, up to date; **no es para tanto** it's not that bad; **por lo tanto** therefore; **¡y tanto!** oh yes!, certainly! ■ **tanto por ciento** percentage.

tapa *nf* **1** *(cubierta - de caja, olla)* lid; *(-de tarro)* top. **2** *(de libro)* cover. **3** *(de comida)* appetizer.

tapar *vt* **1** *(cubrir)* to cover. **2** *(abrigar)* to wrap up. **3** *(cerrar - olla, tarro)* to put the lid on; *(- botella)* to put the top on. **4** *(ocultar)* to hide; *(vista)* to block. ▶ *vpr* **taparse** *(cubrirse)* to cover oneself up; *(abrigarse)* to wrap up.

tapete *nm* table runner.

tapia *nf* **1** *(cerca)* garden wall. **2** *(muro)* wall.

tapicería *nf* upholstery.

tapiz *nm* tapestry.

tapón nm 1 (de goma, vidrio) stopper; (de botella) cap, cork; (de lavabo, bañera) plug. 2 (en baloncesto) block.

taquilla nf 1 (de tren, etc.) ticket office, booking office; (de teatro, cine) box-office. 2 (en vestuario, colegio) locker.

tardar vt (emplear tiempo) to take: *tardé tres años*, it took me three years. ► vi (demorar) to take long: *se tarda más en tren*, it takes longer by train.

tarde nf 1 (hasta las seis) afternoon. 2 (después de las seis) evening. ► adv late. • **llegar tarde** to be late; **más tarde** later; **¡buenas tardes!** 1 (más temprano) good afternoon. 2 (hacia la noche) good evening.

tarea nf task, job.

tarifa nf 1 (precio) tariff, rate; (en transporte) fare. 2 (lista de precios) price list • **pagar con tarjeta** to pay by credit card. ■ **tarjeta de embarque** boarding card; **tarjeta de visita 1** (personal) GB visiting card; US calling card. 2 (profesional) business card; **tarjeta telefónica** phone card; **tarjeta postal** postcard.

tarro nm (recipiente) jar, pot.

tarta nf (pastel) cake; (de hojaldre) tart, pie.

tartamudo,-a nm,f stutterer, stammerer.

tartera nf lunch box.

tasa nf 1 (precio) fee, charge. 2 (impuesto) tax. 4 (índice) rate.

tasca nf bar, pub.

tatuaje nm tattoo.

taxi nm taxi, cab.

taxímetro nm taximeter, clock.

taxista nmf taxi driver, cab driver.

taza nf 1 (recipiente) cup. 2 (de retrete) bowl.

tazón nm bowl.

te pron 1 (complemento directo) you; (complemento indirecto) you, for you. 2 (reflexivo) yourself.

té nm tea: *té con limón*, lemon tea.

teatro nm 1 (sala) GB theatre; US theater. 2 (género) drama. • **hacer teatro** to play, act.

tebeo nm comic.

techo nm ceiling. • **los sin techo** the homeless.

tecla nf key.

teclado nm keyboard.

técnica nf 1 (tecnología) technology. 2 (habilidad) technique, method.

técnico,-a adj technical. ► nm,f technician.

tecnología nf technology.

teja nf (en tejado) tile.

tejado nm roof.

tejanos nm pl jeans.

tejido *nm* **1** *(tela)* fabric, material. **2** *(en anatomía)* tissue.

tejón *nm* badger.

tela *nf* **1** *(tejido)* material, fabric, cloth; *(retal)* piece of material. **2** *(cuadro)* painting.

telaraña *nf* cobweb, spider's web.

tele *nf fam* telly, TV.

telecomunicaciones *nf pl* telecommunications.

telediario *nm* news.

teleférico *nm* cable car.

telefonista *nmf* telephone operator.

teléfono *nm* **1** *(aparato)* telephone, phone. **2** *(número)* phone number. • **contestar al teléfono** to answer the phone; **estar hablando por teléfono** to be on the phone; **llamar a** ALGN **por teléfono** to phone SB, ring SB. ▪ **teléfono inalámbrico** cordless telephone; **teléfono móvil** mobile phone, US cellular phone; **teléfono público** public phone.

telegrama *nm* telegram, cable.

telenovela *nf* soap opera.

telesilla *nf* chair lift.

telespectador,-ra *nm,f* viewer.

telesquí *nm* ski lift.

teletexto *nm* Teletext®.

televisar *vt* to televise.

televisión *nf* **1** *(sistema)* television. **2** *fam (aparato)* television set. • **ver la televisión** to watch television.

televisor *nm* television set.

télex *nm* telex.

telón *nm* curtain.

tema *nm* **1** *(asunto)* subject. **2** *(canción)* song. ▪ **temas de actualidad** current affairs.

temblar *vi* **1** *(de frío)* to shiver; *(de miedo)* to tremble. **2** *(voz)* to quiver.

temblor *nm* tremor, shudder. ▪ **temblor de tierra** earthquake.

temer *vt* to fear, be afraid of.

temor *nm* fear.

temperamento *nm* temperament, nature.

temperatura *nf* temperature.

tempestad *nf* storm.

templado,-a *adj (agua, comida)* lukewarm; *(clima, temperatura)* mild, temperate.

templo *nm* temple.

temporada *nf* **1** *(en artes, deportes, moda)* season. **2** *(período)* period, time: *voy a pasar una temporada en casa de mis abuelos*, I´m going to live with my grandparents for a time. ▪ **temporada alta** high season; **temporada baja** low season.

temporal *adj* temporary. ▶ *nm* storm.

temprano *adv* early.

tenazas *nf pl* pincers; *(para la comida)* tongs.

tendedero *nm (cuerda)* clothesline; *(lugar)* drying place.

tendencia *nf* tendency, inclination.

tender *vt* 1 *(puente)* to build; *(vía, cable)* to lay. 2 *(ropa, colada)* to hang out. 3 *(mano)* to stretch out, hold out. 4 *(emboscada, trampa)* to lay. ► *vi* to tend. ► *vpr* **tenderse** *(tumbarse)* to lie down.

tendero,-a *nm,f* shopkeeper.

tendón *nm* tendon, sinew.

tenedor *nm* fork.

tener *vt* 1 *(posesión)* to have, have got. 2 *(coger)* to take: **ten esto**, take this. 3 *(sensación, sentimiento)* to be, feel: **tengo calor**, I´m hot; **tengo hambre**, I'm hungry; **tengo sed**, I'm thirsty. 4 *(edad, tamaño)* to be: **tiene diez años**, he's ten, he's ten years old. 5 *(celebrar)* to hold: **tener una reunión**, to hold a meeting. ► *aux* **tener que** 1 *(obligación- a otra persona)* to have to. 2 *(- a uno mismo)* must.

teniente *nm* lieutenant. ■ **teniente de alcalde** deputy mayor.

tenis *nm* tennis. ■ **tenis de mesa** table tennis.

tenista *nmf* tennis player.

tenor *nm (cantante)* tenor.

tensión *nf* 1 *(gen)* tension. 2 *(sanguínea)* pressure. ■ **tensión arterial** blood pressure.

tenso,-a *adj* 1 *(cable, cuerda)* taut. 2 *(persona, músculo)* tense. 3 *(relaciones)* strained.

tentación *nf* temptation.

tentáculo *nm* tentacle.

tentativa *nf* attempt.

teñir *vt* to dye.

teoría *nf* theory.

terapia *nf* therapy.

tercer *num* → tercero,-a.

tercero,-a *num* third. ■ **tercera edad** old age.

tercio *nm* third.

terciopelo *nm* velvet.

terco,-a *adj* obstinate, stubborn.

terminal *adj* terminal. ► *nf* 1 *(gen)* terminal. 2 *(de autobuses)* terminus.

terminar *vt-vi (acabar)* to finish. ► *vi (ir a parar)* to end up, end. ► *vpr* **terminarse** 1 *(finalizar)* to finish, be over. 2 *(agotarse)* to run out: **se nos ha terminado el papel**, we've run out of paper.

término *nm* 1 *(final)* end, finish. 2 *(plazo, palabra)* term. ● **en otros términos** in other words; **en primer término** in the foreground; **en términos generales** generally speaking; **poner término a algo** to put an end to STH; **por término medio** on average. ■ **término municipal** municipal area.

termita *nf* termite.

termo *nm* thermos (flask).

termómetro *nm* thermometer.

termostato *nm* thermostat.

ternera *nf* veal.

ternero,-a *nm,f* calf.

ternura *nf* tenderness.

terraplén *nm* embankment.

terraza *nf* 1 (*balcón*) terrace. 2 (*azotea*) roof terrace. 3 (*de un café*): **en la terraza de un bar**, outside a bar.

terremoto *nm* earthquake.

terreno *nm* 1 (*tierra*) piece of land, ground; (*solar*) plot, site. 2 (*superficie*) terrain. 3 (*de cultivo*) soil; (*campo*) field. 4 (*ámbito*) field, sphere. ■ **terreno de juego** pitch.

terrestre *adj* 1 (*vida, transporte*) land, terrestrial. 2 (*animal, vegetación*) land.

terrible *adj* terrible, awful.

territorio *nm* territory.

terrón *nm* lump.

terror *nm* terror.

terrorismo *nm* terrorism.

tertulia *nf* gathering. ■ **tertulia televisiva** talk show.

tesis *nf* thesis.

tesoro *nm* 1 (*cosas de valor*) treasure. 2 (*del Estado*) treasury, exchequer.

test *nm* test. ■ **test de embarazo** pregnancy test.

testamento *nm* will, testament. • **hacer testamento** to make one's will.

testículo *nm* testicle.

testificar *vt-vi* to testify.

testigo *nmf* witness. ▶ *nm* DEP baton.

testimonio *nm* testimony. ■ **falso testimonio** perjury.

tetera *nf* teapot.

tetilla *nf* (*de biberón*) teat.

tetina *nf* teat.

tetrabrik® *nm* carton.

textil *adj* textile.

texto *nm* text.

ti *pron* you.

tía *nf* (*pariente*) aunt.

tibia *nf* tibia, shinbone.

tibio,-a *adj* tepid, lukewarm.

tiburón *nm* shark.

tic *nm* tic, twitch.

tiempo *nm* 1 (*período, momento*) time. 2 (*meteorológico*) weather. 3 (*parte de partido*) half. 4 (*gramatical*) tense. • **a tiempo** in time; **al mismo tiempo** at the same time; **del tiempo** 1 (*fruta*) in season. 2 (*bebida*) at room temperature; **¿qué tiempo hace?** what's the weather like? ■ **tiempo libre** spare time; **tiempo muerto** time out.

tienda *nf* 1 GB shop; US store. 2 (*de campaña*) tent. ■ **tienda de comestibles** grocer's.

tierno,-a *adj* 1 (*blando*) tender, soft. 2 (*reciente*) fresh.

tierra *nf* 1 (*superficie sólida*) land. 2 (*terreno cultivado*) soil, land. 3 (*sustancia*) earth, soil. **4** *(zona de origen)*: **en mi tierra**, where I come from. **5** *(suelo)* ground. **6 la Tierra** *(planeta)* the Earth. • **tierra adentro** inland; **tomar tierra** to land. ■ **tierra firme** terra firma.

tieso,-a *adj* **1** *(rígido)* stiff, rigid. **2** *(erguido)* upright, erect.

tiesto *nm* flowerpot.

tifón *nm* typhoon.

tigre *nm* tiger.

tijeras *nf pl* scissors.

tila *nf* lime-blossom tea.

timar *vt* to swindle.

timbre *nm* **1** *(de la puerta)* bell. **2** *(sello)* stamp. • **llamar al timbre** to ring the bell.

tímido,-a *adj* shy.

timo *nm* swindle, fiddle.

timón *nm* *(de barco)* rudder.

tímpano *nm* eardrum.

tinta *nf* ink.

tinte *nm* **1** *(colorante)* dye. **2** *(tintorería)* dry-cleaner's.

tinto,-a *adj* *(vino)* red. ▶ *nm* **tinto** red wine.

tintorería *nf* dry-cleaner's.

tío *nm* *(pariente)* uncle.

tiovivo *nm* merry-go-round, roundabout.

típico,-a *adj* typical.

tipo *nm* **1** *(clase)* sort, kind. **2** *(de interés, etc.)* rate. **3** *(de hombre)* build, physique; *(de mujer)* figure.

tira *nf* strip. • **la tira** *fam* a lot, loads.

tirada *nf* **1** *(impresión)* print run. **2** *(jugada)* throw. • **de una tirada** in one go.

tirado,-a *adj* **1** *fam* *(precio)* dirt cheap. **2** *fam* *(problema, examen)* dead easy. • **dejar tirado a** ALGN to leave SB in the lurch.

tirador *nm* *(de puerta)* knob; *(de cajón)* handle.

tirantes *nm pl* **1** *(de vestido)* straps. **2** *(de pantalón)* GB braces; US suspenders.

tirar *vt* **1** *(lanzar)* to throw; *(tiro)* to fire; *(bomba)* to drop. **2** *(dejar caer)* to drop. **3** *(desechar)* to throw away. **4** *(derribar)* to knock down; *(casa, árbol)* to pull down; *(vaso, botella)* to knock over. ▶ *vi* **1** *(cuerda, puerta)* to pull: *tira de la cadena*, pull the chain. **2** *(en juegos)*: *tira tú*, it's your turn, it's your go. **3** *fam* *(funcionar)* to work, run. **4** *(disparar)* to shoot. ▶ *vpr* **tirarse** *(lanzarse)* to throw oneself. ■ **tira y afloja** give and take.

tirita® *nf* GB plaster; US Band-aid®.

tiritar *vi* to shiver, shake.

tiro *nm* **1** *(lanzamiento)* throw. **2** *(disparo, ruido)* shot. **3** *(herida)* bullet wound. **4** *(de caballos)* team. **5** *(de chimenea)* draught. • **a tiro 1** *(de arma)* within range. **2** *(a mano)* within reach; **sentar como**

un tiro a ALGN **1** *(comida)* not to agree with SB. **2** *(comentario)* to make SB really upset. ∎ **tiro al blanco** target shooting; **tiro con arco** archery.

tirón *nm* **1** *(acción)* tug: *sufrió un tirón en un músculo*, he pulled a muscle. **2** *(robo)* bag-snatching. ● **de un tirón** *fam* in one go.

tiroteo *nm* shooting.

títere *nm* puppet, marionette.

titular *adj* appointed, official. ► *nmf* **1** *(en deporte)* first-team player. **2** *(de cuenta, pasaporte)* holder. ► *nm (de prensa)* headline. ► *vpr* **titularse** *(obra, película)* to be called.

título *nm* **1** *(gen)* title. **2** *(académico)* degree; *(diploma)* certificate, diploma. **4** *(acción)* bond, security.

tiza *nf* chalk.

toalla *nf* towel.

toallero *nm* towel rail.

tobillo *nm* ankle.

tobogán *nm* slide.

tocadiscos *nm* record player.

tocador *nm (mueble)* dressing table. ∎ **tocador de señoras** powder room.

tocar *vt* **1** *(gen)* to touch. **2** *(hacer sonar - instrumento, canción)* to play; *(- timbre)* to ring; *(- bocina)* to blow, honk; *(- campanas)* to ring. ► *vi* **1** *(corresponder)* to be one's turn: *¿a*

quién le toca ahora?, whose turn is it now? **2** *(caer en suerte)* to win.

tocino *nm* **1** *(grasa)* lard. **2** *(carne)* bacon.

todavía *adv* **1** *(tiempo -en frases afirmativas)* still; *(-en frases negativas)* yet. **2** *(para reforzar)* even: *esto todavía te gustará más*, you'll enjoy this even more.

todo,-a *adj* **1** *(gen)* all. **2** *(por completo)* whole: *participó toda la clase*, the whole class took part. **3** *(cada)* every: *todos los veranos*, every summer. **4** *(enfático)* quite. ► *pron* **1** **todo** *(sin exclusión)* all, everything. **2 todos,-as** everybody, everyone. ► *adv* all. ● **del todo** completely; **estar en todo** to be really with it; **todos nosotros/ vosotros/ ellos** all of us/you/ them.

todoterreno *nm* all-terrain vehicle.

toldo *nm* awning.

tolerancia *nf* tolerance.

tolerar *vt* to tolerate.

toma *nf* **1** *(acción)* taking. **2** *(dosis)* dose. **3** *(captura)* capture. **4** *(grabación)* recording. **5** *(de imágenes)* take. ∎ **toma de contacto** initial contact; **toma de corriente** power point; **toma de posesión** takeover; **toma de tierra** GB earth wire; US ground wire.

tomar vt 1 (gen) to take. 2 (comida, bebida, baño) to have: ¿quieres tomar algo?, would you like a drink? ► vpr **tomarse** (vacaciones, comentario) to take. • **tomarla con ALGN** to have it in for SB; **tomar por** to take for.

tomate nm tomato. • **ponerse como un tomate** to go as red as a beetroot.

tómbola nf tombola.

tomillo nm thyme.

tomo nm volume.

ton. • **sin ton ni son** without rhyme or reason.

tonel nm barrel, cask.

tonelada nf ton.

tónica nf 1 (bebida) tonic. 2 (tendencia) tendency, trend.

tónico nm tonic.

tono nm 1 (de sonido, voz) tone. 2 (de color) shades. • **a tono con** in tune with; **bajar el tono** to lower one's voice; **subir el tono** to speak louder.

tontería nf 1 (dicho, hecho) silly thing, stupid thing. 2 (insignificancia) little thing.

tonto,-a adj silly.

tope nm 1 (límite) limit, end. 2 (objeto) stop: el tope de la puerta, the doorstop. • **a tope** 1 fam (lleno) packed. 2 (al máximo) flat out.

tópico nm commonplace, cliché. • **de uso tópico** for external use.

topo nm mole.

toquilla nf shawl.

tórax nm thorax.

torbellino nm whirlwind.

torcedura nf sprain.

torcer vt 1 (cuerda, brazo) to twist. 2 (inclinar) to slant. ► vi (girar) to turn: tuerce a la derecha, turn right. ► vpr **torcerse** 1 to sprain: se torció el tobillo, she sprained her ankle. 2 (plan) to fall through.

tordo nm (pájaro) thrush.

torear vt-vi (toro) to fight.

torero,-a nm,f bullfighter.

tormenta nf storm.

tornado nm tornado.

torneo nm tournament.

tornillo nm screw.

torniquete nm tourniquet.

torno nm (de carpintero) lathe; (de alfarero) potter's wheel. • **en torno a** 1 (alrededor de) around. 2 (acerca de) about, concerning.

toro nm bull.

torpe adj (patoso) clumsy.

torre nf 1 (de edificio) tower. 2 (de ajedrez) rook, castle. ■ **torre de control** control tower.

torrente nm torrent.

torrija nf French toast.

torta nf 1 (dulce) cake. 2 fam (bofetón) slap. • **ni torta** not a thing; **pegarse una torta** to give oneself a bump.

tortazo nm 1 (bofetón) slap. 2 (golpe) thump.

tortícolis *nf* stiff neck.

tortilla *nf* GB omelette; US omelet. ▪ **tortilla de patatas** Spanish omelette; **tortilla francesa** plain omelette.

tórtola *nf* dove.

tortuga *nf* 1 *(de tierra)* GB tortoise; US turtle. 2 *(marina)* turtle.

tortura *nf* torture.

tos *nf* cough. ▪ **tos ferina** whooping cough.

toser *vi* to cough.

tostada *nf* piece of toast.

tostadora *nf* toaster.

tostar *vt (pan)* to toast; *(café)* to roast.

total *adj-nm* total.

tóxico,-a *adj* toxic.

trabajador,-ra *adj* hardworking. ► *nm,f* worker.

trabajar *vi-vt* to work.

trabajo *nm* 1 *(gen)* work. 2 *(tarea)* task, job. 3 *(empleo)* job. 4 *(para clase)* essay, project. ▪ **trabajos manuales** handicrafts.

tracción *nf* traction. ▪ **tracción delantera/trasera** front/rear-wheel drive.

tractor *nm* tractor.

tradición *nf* tradition.

tradicional *adj* traditional.

traducción *nf* translation. ▪ **traducción automática** machine translation; **traducción simultánea** simultaneous translation.

traducir *vt* to translate.

traductor,-ra *nm,f* translator.

traer(se) *vt-vpr* to bring. ● **traerse algo entre manos** to be busy with STH; **me trae sin cuidado** I couldn't care less; **traérselas** *fam* to be really difficult.

traficante *nmf* dealer, trafficker.

tráfico *nm* traffic.

tragaperras *nf* slot machine.

tragar(se) *vt-vpr* 1 *(comida, medicina)* to swallow. 2 *(creer)* to fall for it.

tragedia *nf* tragedy.

trago *nm* 1 *(sorbo)* swig. 2 *(bebida)* drink. ● **echar un trago** to have a drink; **pasar un mal trago** to have a bad time of it.

traicionar *vt* to betray.

traidor,-ra *nm,f* traitor.

tráiler *nm* 1 *(película)* trailer. 2 *(vehículo)* GB articulated lorry; US trailer truck.

traje *nm* 1 *(de hombre)* suit. 2 *(de mujer)* dress. ▪ **traje de baño** bathing suit, bathing costume; **traje de etiqueta** evening dress; **traje de luces** bullfighter's costume; **traje espacial** spacesuit.

trama *nf (argumento)* plot.

tramar *vt (preparar)* to plot: *estarán tramando algo*, they must be up to something.

trámite *nm* 1 *(paso)* step. 2 *(negociación)* procedure. 3 *(formalismo)* formality: *es puro trámite*, it's purely a formality.

tramo *nm* 1 *(de carretera)* stretch, section. 2 *(de escalera)* flight.

trampa *nf* 1 *(para cazar)* trap. 2 *(engaño)* trap, trick. ● **hacer trampas** to cheat.

trampolín *nm* 1 *(de piscina)* springboard, diving board. 2 *(de esquí)* ski jump.

tramposo,-a *nm,f* cheat.

tranquilidad *nf* 1 *(paz)* quiet, piece. 2 *(calma)* calm.

tranquilizante *nm* tranquillizer.

tranquilizar(se) *vt-vpr (alguien nervioso)* to calm down; *(alguien preocupado)* to set one's mind at rest.

tranquilo,-a *adj* 1 *(persona, voz, mar)* calm. 2 *(lugar, momento)* quiet, peaceful. ● **dejar a ALGN tranquilo** to leave SB alone; **¡tranquilo!** 1 *(cálmate)* take it easy! 2 *(no te preocupes)* don't worry!

transatlántico,-a *adj* transatlantic. ► *nm* **transatlántico** liner.

transbordador *nm* ferry. ■ **transbordador espacial** space shuttle.

transbordo *nm (de pasajeros)* change; *(de equipajes)* transfer. ● **hacer transbordo** to change.

transcurrir *vi* to pass, elapse.

transeúnte *nmf* passer-by.

transferencia *nf* transfer.

transformador *nm* transformer.

transformar(se) *vt-vpr* to change.

transfusión *nf* transfusion.

transición *nf* transition.

transistor *nm* transistor.

transitivo,-a *adj* transitive.

tránsito *nm* 1 *(tráfico)* traffic. 2 *(acción)* passage, transit.

transmisión *nf* 1 *(gen)* transmission. 2 *(de radio etc)* broadcast.

transmisor,-ra *adj* transmitting. ► *nm,f* transmitter.

transmitir *vt* 1 *(gen)* to transmit. 2 *(por radio etc.)* to broadcast.

transparencia *nf* 1 *(gen)* transparency. 2 *(diapositiva)* slide.

transparentarse *vpr (blusa, vestido)* to be see-through.

transparente *adj* transparent.

transpirar *vi* to perspire.

transportar *vt (gen)* to transport; *(en barco)* to ship.

transporte *nm* transport.

transportista *nmf* haulier.

tranvía *nm* GB tram; US streetcar.

trapecio *nm (de circo, gimnasia)* trapeze.

trapecista *nmf* trapeze artist.
trapo *nm (paño)* cloth. ► *nm pl* **trapos** clothes. ■ **trapo de cocina** tea towel; **trapo del polvo** dust cloth.
tráquea *nf* trachea.
tras *prep* **1** *(después de)* after: *día tras día*, day after day. **2** *(detrás de)* behind: *se escondió tras la puerta*, she hid behind the door.
trasero,-a *adj* back, rear.
trasladar *vt* **1** *(desplazar)* to move. **2** *(de cargo etc.)* to transfer. ► *vpr* **trasladarse 1** *(persona)* to go. **2** *(mudarse)* to move.
traslado *nm* **1** *(mudanza)* move. **2** *(de cargo)* transfer.
trasnochar *vi* to stay up late.
traspasar *vt* **1** *(atravesar)* to go through, pierce. **2** *(negocio, jugador)* to transfer. • **"Se traspasa"** "For sale".
traspaso *nm* **1** *(de negocio)* sale. **2** *(de jugador, competencias)* transfer. **3** *(precio)* takeover fee.
trasplante *nm* transplant.
trastero *nm* lumber room.
trasto *nm (cosa)* piece of junk. ► *nm pl* **trastos** *(utensilios)* tackle.
trastorno *nm* **1** disruption; *(molestia)* inconvenience. **2** *(enfermedad)* disorder.
tratado *nm* **1** *(pacto)* treaty. **2** *(estudio)* treatise.

tratamiento *nm* **1** *(gen)* treatment. **2** *(título)* title, form of address. ■ **tratamiento de textos** word processing.
tratar *vt* **1** *(gen)* to treat. **2** *(asunto, relación)* to deal with. ► *vi (relacionarse)* to be acquainted. ► *vpr* **tratarse 1** *(ser cuestión)* to be about: *tratándose de ti...*, seeing as it's you... **2** *(tener relación)* to be friendly with. • **tratar de 1** *(intentar)* to try to. **2** *(dirigirse a)* to address as: *nos tratamos de usted*, we address each other as "usted". **3** *(versar)* to be about.
trato *nm* **1** *(de personas)* manner, treatment. **2** *(contacto)* contact. **3** *(acuerdo)* agreement. **4** *(comercial)* deal. • **cerrar un trato** to close a deal; **¡trato hecho!** it's a deal! ■ **malos tratos** ill-treatment.
través *nm.* • **a través de 1** *(mediante)* through. **2** *(de un lado a otro)* across.
travesía *nf* **1** *(viaje)* voyage, crossing. **2** *(calle)* street.
trayecto *nm* **1** *(distancia)* distance, way. **2** *(recorrido)* route: *el autobús cubría el trayecto Madrid-Burgos*, the bus was doing the Madrid-Burgos run. **3** *(viaje)* journey: *el trayecto entre Barcelona y Mallorca*, the journey between Barcelona and Majorca.

trayectoria *nf* **1** *(recorrido)* trajectory. **2** *(evolución)* line, course. ▪ **trayectoria profesional** career.

trébol *nm* **1** *(hierba)* clover. **2** *(naipes)* club.

trece *num* thirteen; *(en fechas)* thirteenth.

tregua *nf* **1** MIL truce. **2** *(descanso)* respite, rest.

treinta *num* thirty; *(en fechas)* thirtieth.

tremendo,-a *adj* **1** *(terrible)* terrible, dreadful. **2** *(muy grande)* tremendous.

tren *nm* **1** *(ferrocarril)* train. **2** *(ritmo)* speed, pace: *a este tren no llegaremos*, we won't get there at this speed. ▪ **tren de cercanías** suburban train; **tren de aterrizaje** undercarriage; **tren de lavado** car wash.

trenza *nf* GB plait; US braid.

trepar *vt-vi* to climb.

tres *num* three; *(en fechas)* third. ▪ **tres en raya** GB noughts and crosses; US tic-tac-toe.

trescientos,-as *num* three hundred.

tresillo *nm* three-piece suite.

triángulo *nm* triangle.

tribu *nf* tribe.

tribuna *nf* **1** *(plataforma)* platform, rostrum. **2** stand.

tribunal *nm* **1** *(gen)* court. **2** *(de examen)* board of examiners.

triciclo *nm* tricycle.

trigo *nm* wheat.

trillizo,-a *nm,f* triplet.

trimestre *nm* **1** *(académico)* term. **2** *(tres meses)* quarter.

trinchar *vt* to carve.

trinchera *nf* trench.

trineo *nm* *(de perros)* sleigh; *(para jugar)* sledge.

trío *nm* trio.

tripa *nf* **1** *(estómago)* stomach. **2** *(panza)* belly.

triple *adj-nm* triple. ▪ **triple salto** triple jump.

tripulación *nf* crew.

tripulante *nmf* crew member.

tripular *vt* to man.

triste *adj* sad.

tristeza *nf* sadness.

triturar *vt* *(ajo, minerales)* to crush; *(-papel)* to shred.

triunfar *vi* **1** *(tener éxito)* to succeed. **2** *(ganar)* to win.

triunfo *nm* **1** *(victoria)* triumph, victory; *(en deportes)* win. **2** *(éxito)* success. **3** *(naipes)* trump.

trocear *vt* to cut up.

trofeo *nm* trophy.

trombón *nm* trombone.

trompa *nf* **1** *(instrumento)* horn. **2** *(de elefante)* trunk.

trompeta *nf* trumpet.

tronco *nm* trunk.

trono *nm* throne.

tropa *nf* troops, soldiers.

tropezar(se) *vi-vpr* to trip.

tropical *adj* tropical.

trote *nm* *(de caballo)* trot.

trozo *nm* piece, chunk.
trucha *nf* trout.
truco *nm* trick. • **coger el truco** to get the knack.
trueno *nm* clap of thunder.
tu *adj* your.
tú *pron* you.
tuberculosis *nf* tuberculosis.
tubería *nf (de agua)* pipe; *(de gas, petróleo)* pipeline.
tubo *nm* tube. ▪ **tubo de ensayo** test tube; **tubo de escape** exhaust pipe; **tubo digestivo** alimentary canal.
tuerca *nf* nut.
tuerto,-a *adj* one-eyed.
tulipán *nm* tulip.
tumba *nf* 1 *(mausoleo)* tomb. 2 *(fosa)* grave.
tumbarse *vpr* to lie down.
tumbona *nf (de playa)* deckchair; *(para tumbarse)* lounger.
tumor *nm* GB tumour; US tumor.
túnel *nm* tunnel. ▪ **túnel de lavado** car wash.
túnica *nf* tunic.
tupé *nm* quiff.
turbina *nf* turbine.
turbio,-a *adj* cloudy.
turismo *nm* 1 *(actividad)* tourism. 2 *(industria)* tourist trade, tourist industry. 3 *(coche)* car.
turista *nmf* tourist.
turístico,-a *adj* tourist.
turnarse *vpr* to take turns.

turno *nm* 1 *(en cola, lista)* turn. 2 *(de trabajo)* shift.
turrón *nm* nougat.
tutor,-ra *nm,f* 1 JUR guardian. 2 *(profesor)* tutor.
tuyo,-a *adj* of yours. ▶ *pron* yours.

U

u *conj* or.
UCI *abr (Unidad de Cuidados Intensivos)* ICU, intensive care unit.
úlcera *nf* ulcer.
último,-a *adj* 1 *(gen)* last. 2 *(más reciente)* latest: *las últimas noticias*, the latest news. 3 *(más alejado)* furthest; *(de más abajo)* bottom, lowest; *(de más arriba)* top; *(de más atrás)* back: *vive en el último piso*, he lives on the top floor. 4 *(definitivo)* final: *mi última oferta*, my final offer. • **a la última** up to date; **estar en las últimas** 1 *(moribundo)* to be at death's door. 2 *(arruinado)* to be down and out; **por último** finally.
ultramarinos *nm pl (tienda)* grocer's; *(comestibles)* groceries.
umbral *nm* threshold.
un,-a *det* a, an. ▶ *adj* one.

unanimidad *nf* unanimity.
undécimo,-a *num* eleventh.
único,-a *adj* **1** *(solo)* only. **2** *(extraordinario)* unique.
unidad *nf* **1** unit. **2** *(cohesión)* unity.
uniforme *adj (velocidad, ritmo)* uniform; *(temperatura, superficie)* even. ► *nm* uniform.
unión *nf* union.
unir *vt* **1** *(juntar)* to join. **2** *(enlazar)* to link.
universal *adj* universal.
universidad *nf* university.
universitario,-a *adj* university. ► *nm,f (en curso)* university student; *(con título)* university graduate.
universo *nm* universe.
uno,-a *adj (número)* one. ► *pron* **1** one. **2** *(impersonal)* one, you: *en estos casos, uno no sabe qué hacer*, you don't know what to do in these situations. ► *nm (número)* one; *(en fechas)* first. ► *adj pl* **unos,-as** some. **3** *(aproximado)* about, around: *seremos unos veinte*, there will be around twenty of us. • **de uno en uno** one by one; **es la una** it's one o'clock.
untar *vt (crema, pomada)* to smear; *(mantequilla, queso)* to spread.
uña *nf* nail.
urbanización *nf* **1** *(proceso)* urbanization. **2** *(conjunto residencial)* housing development, housing estate.
urbano,-a *adj* urban.
urgencia *nf* **1** *(prisa)* urgency. **2** *(asunto)* emergency. ► *nf pl* **urgencias** casualty.
urgente *adj* **1** *(llamada, asunto)* urgent. **2** *(carta)* express.
urna *nf* **1** *(para votar)* ballot box. **2** *(para cenizas)* urn. **3** *(para objetos valiosos)* glass case.
urraca *nf* magpie.
urticaria *nf* rash.
usado,-a *adj* **1** *(gastado)* worn out, old. **2** *(de segunda mano)* secondhand, used.
usar *vt* **1** *(utilizar)* to use. **2** *(prenda)* to wear. • **de usar y tirar** disposable.
uso *nm* **1** *(utilización)* use. **2** *(de prenda)* wearing: *es obligatorio el uso del cinturón de seguridad*, seat belts must be worn.
usted *pron fml* you.
usual *adj* usual, customary.
usuario,-a *nm,f* user.
utensilio *nm* **1** *(de cocina)* utensil. **2** *(herramienta)* tool.
útero *nm* uterus.
útil *adj* useful.
utilización *nf* use.
utilizar *vt* to use, utilize.
uva *nf* grape.
UVI *abr (Unidad de Vigilancia Intensiva)* ICU, intensive care unit.

V

vaca *nf* **1** *(animal)* cow. **2** *(carne)* beef.

vacaciones *nf pl* holiday; GB holidays; US vacation. • **irse de vacaciones** to go on holiday (US vacation).

vacante *nf* vacancy.

vaciar *vt* **1** *(recipiente)* to empty. **2** *(contenido)* to pour away, pour out.

vacilar *vi* to hesitate.

vacío,-a *adj* **1** *(recipiente, lugar)* empty. **2** *(no ocupado)* unoccupied. ▶ *nm* **vacío 1** *(abismo)* void, emptiness. **2** *(en física)* vacuum. • **envasado al vacío** vacuum-packed.

vacuna *nf* vaccine.

vacunar *vt* to vaccinate.

vado *nm* **1** *(de río)* ford. **2** *(en calle)* garage entrance. ▪ **"Vado permanente"** "Keep clear".

vagabundo,-a *nm,f* tramp.

vagina *nf* vagina.

vago,-a[1] *nm,f* idler, loafer.

vago,-a[2] *adj (impreciso)* vague.

vagón *nm* **1** *(para pasajeros)* GB carriage, coach; US car. **2** *(para mercancías)* GB wagon, goods van; US boxcar, freight car. ▪ **vagón restaurante** restaurant car.

vaho *nm* steam; GB vapour; US vapor. ▶ *nm pl* **vahos** MED inhalation.

vaina *nf* **1** *(de espada)* sheath, scabbard. **2** *(de guisante, judía)* pod.

vainilla *nf* vanilla.

vaivén *nm* swaying, swinging.

vajilla *nf* **1** *(gen)* dishes, crockery. **2** *(juego completo)* dinner service.

vale *nm (de compra)* voucher. ▶ *interj* OK, all right.

valer *vi* **1** *(tener valor)* to be worth. **2** *(costar)* to cost: *¿cuánto vale?*, how much is it? **3** *(ser válido)* to be valid. **4** *(servir)* to be useful, be of use: *no vale para director*, he's no use as a manager. • **no vale** it's no good; **vale más…** it's better…: *más te vale no llegar tarde*, you'd better not arrive late.

válido,-a *adj* valid.

valiente *adj* brave.

valioso,-a *adj* valuable.

valla *nf* **1** *(cerca)* fence, barrier. **2** *(en atletismo)* hurdle. ▪ **valla publicitaria** GB hoarding; US billboard.

valle *nm* valley.

valor *nm* **1** *(gen)* value. **2** *(precio)* price. **3** *(coraje)* courage; GB valour; US valor. ▶ *nm pl* **valores** *(financieros)* securities, bonds. • **¡qué valor!** what a nerve!; **sin ningún valor** worthless, worth nothing.

valorar *vt* to value.

válvula *nf* valve.

vender

vampiro *nm* vampire.
vanguardia *nf* **1** *(en arte etc.)* avant-garde. **2** MIL vanguard.
vano,-a *adj* **1** *(inútil)* vain, useless. **2** *(ilusorio)* illusory, futile. • **en vano** in vain.
vapor *nm* steam; GB vapour; US vapor. • **al vapor** steamed.
vaquero *nm* GB cowherd; US cowboy. ▶ *nm pl* **vaqueros** jeans.
variable *adj* variable.
variante *nf (carretera)* bypass.
variar *vt-vi* to vary, change. • **para variar** for a change.
varicela *nf* chickenpox.
variedad *nf* variety. ▶ *nf pl* **variedades** *(espectáculo)* variety show.
varilla *nf* **1** *(palito)* stick, rod. **2** *(de paraguas)* rib.
varios,-as *adj* some, several.
variz *nf* varicose vein.
varón *nm* male, man.
vasija *nf* vessel.
vaso *nm* **1** *(de cristal)* glass. **2** *(de papel, plástico)* cup. **3** *(sanguíneo)* vessel.
vasto,-a *adj* vast, immense.
vatio *nm* watt.
vaya *interj* **1** well! **2** *(con sustantivos)* what a…: *¡vaya casa!*, what a house!
vecino,-a *nm,f* **1** *(de edificio, calle)* GB neighbour; US neighbor. **2** *(habitante - de barrio)* resident; *(- de ciudad)* inhabitant.

veda *nf* close season.
vegetación *nf* vegetation.
vegetal *adj-nm* plant.
vegetariano,-a *adj-nm,f* vegetarian.
vehículo *nm* vehicle.
veinte *num* twenty; *(en fechas)* twentieth.
vejez *nf* old age.
vejiga *nf* bladder.
vela¹ *nf (de cera)* candle. • **pasar la noche en vela** to have a sleepless night.
vela² *nf (de barco)* sail.
velada *nf* evening.
velarse *vpr (foto)* to get fogged.
velatorio *nm* wake, vigil.
velero *nm* sailing boat.
veleta *nf* weathercock.
vello *nm* hair.
velo *nm* veil.
velocidad *nf* **1** *(rapidez)* speed, velocity. **2** *(marcha)* gear.
velódromo *nm* cycle track.
veloz *adj* fast, quick, swift.
vena *nf* vein.
vencedor,-ra *nm,f* winner.
vencer *vt* **1** *(derrotar)* to beat. **2** *(militarmente)* to defeat. ▶ *vi* **1** *(gen)* to win. **2** *(deuda)* to fall due.
venda *nf* bandage.
vendaje *nm* bandaging.
vendar *vt* to bandage.
vendedor,-ra *nm,f (hombre)* salesman; *(mujer)* saleswoman.
vender *vt* to sell. • **"Se vende"** "For sale".

vendimia *nf* grape harvest.
veneno *nm* (*químico, vegetal*) poison; (*de animal*) venom.
venenoso *adj* poisonous.
venganza *nf* revenge.
vengarse *vpr* to take revenge.
venir *vi* 1 (*gen*) to come. 2 (*estar*) to be: *mi teléfono viene en la guía*, my phone number is in the book. • **venir bien** to be suitable: *¿te viene bien esta tarde?*, does this afternoon suit you?; **venir mal** not to be convenient: *a esa hora me viene mal*, that time isn't convenient; **venirse abajo** 1 (*edificio*) to collapse, fall down. 2 (*persona*) to go to pieces; **¡venga!** come on!
venta *nf* 1 (*transacción*) sale, selling. 2 (*hostal*) roadside inn. • **"En venta"** "For sale".
ventaja *nf* advantage.
ventana *nf* window. • **doble ventana** double-glazed window.
ventanilla *nf* 1 (*de coche, sobre, en banco*) window. 2 (*de cine*) box office.
ventilador *nm* fan.
ventilar *vt* (*habitación, ropa*) to air.
ventisca *nf* snowstorm, blizzard.
ventosa *nf* sucker.
ver *vt* 1 (*percibir, mirar*) to see. 2 (*televisión*) to watch. ► *vpr* **verse** (*con ALGN*) to meet,

see each other: *nos vemos bastante a menudo*, we see each other quite often. • **a ver** let's see; **hacer ver algo** to pretend STH; **¡hay que ver!** would you believe it!; **no poder ver** not to be able to stand: *no puede ver a su primo*, she can't stand her cousin; **véase** see.
veraneante *nmf* summer resident.
veranear *vi* to spend the summer.
veraneo *nm* GB summer holiday; US summer vacation.
verano *nm* summer.
veras *adv*. • **de veras** really, truly.
verbena *nf* (*fiesta*) dance.
verbo *nm* verb.
verdad *nf* 1 truth. 2 (*confirmación*): *es bonita, ¿verdad?*, she's pretty, isn't she? • **de verdad** 1 (*en serio*) really. 2 (*como debe ser*) real.
verdadero,-a *adj* true, real.
verde *adj* 1 (*color, tela, ojos*) green. 2 (*fruta*) unripe. 3 *fam* (*chiste*) blue, dirty. ► *nm* (*color*) green. • **poner verde a ALGN** *fam* to run SB down.
verdulería *nf* greengrocer's.
verdura *nf* vegetables *pl*.
veredicto *nm* verdict.
vergüenza *nf* 1 (*culpabilidad*) shame. 2 (*bochorno*) embarrassment.

verificar *vt* to verify.

verja *nf* railing.

vermut *nm* vermouth.

verruga *nf* wart.

versión *nf* version. • **en versión original** original language version.

verso *nm* verse.

vértebra *nf* vertebra.

vertebral *adj* vertebral.

vertedero *nm* dump, tip.

vertical *adj-nf* vertical.

vértice *nm* vertex.

vértigo *nm* vertigo.

vesícula *nf* vesicle.

vespa® *nf* scooter.

vestíbulo *nm* hall.

vestido *nm* dress. ▪ **vestido de noche** evening dress; **vestido de novia** wedding dress.

vestimenta *nf* clothes.

vestir *vt* 1 *(llevar)* to wear. 2 *(a alguien)* to dress. ▶ *vpr* **vestirse** to get dressed.

vestuario *nm* 1 *(ropa)* wardrobe, clothes. 2 *(camerino)* dressing room; *(en gimnasio etc.)* GB changing room; US locker room.

veterano,-a *adj-nm,f* veteran.

veterinario,-a *nm,f* GB veterinary surgeon, vet; US veterinarian.

vez *nf* 1 *(ocasión)* time. 2 *(turno)* turn. • **a la vez** at the same time; **a veces** sometimes; **alguna vez** 1 *(en afirmación)* sometimes. 2 *(en pregunta)* ever; **de vez en cuando** from time to time; **dos veces** twice; **en vez de** instead of; **muchas veces** often; **otra vez** again; **rara vez** seldom, rarely; **tal vez** perhaps, maybe.

vía *nf* 1 *(camino)* road, way; *(calle)* street. 2 *(de tren - raíl)* track, line; *(- andén)* platform. • **por vía oral** to be taken orally. ▪ **vía de acceso** slip road; **vía pública** thoroughfare; **vías respiratorias** respiratory tract.

viable *adj* viable.

viajante *nm* commercial traveller.

viajar *vi* to travel.

viaje *nm* journey, trip. • **¡buen viaje!** have a good journey!; **estar de viaje** to be away; **irse de viaje** to go on a journey, go on a trip. ▪ **viaje de novios** honeymoon.

viajero,-a *(pasajero)* passenger, *(aventurero)* traveller.

víbora *nf* viper.

vibrar *vi* to vibrate.

viceversa *adv* viceversa.

vicio *nm* 1 *(corrupción)* vice, corruption. 2 *(mala costumbre)* bad habit.

víctima *nf* victim.

victoria *nf* 1 *(gen)* victory, triumph. 2 *(en partido)* win.

vid *nf* vine.

vida nf 1 (de ser vivo) life. 2 (medios) living: *se gana la vida como escritor*, he earns a living as a writer. • **en mi/ tu/su/la vida** never.

vídeo nm video. • **grabar algo en vídeo** to tape STH.

videocámara nf camcorder.

videocasete nm video cassette.

videoclip nm video.

videoclub nm video shop.

videojuego nm video game.

vidriera nf (obra artística) stained glass window.

vidrio nm glass.

viejo,-a adj (persona) old, aged; (cosa) old. ► nm,f (hombre) old man; (mujer) old woman. • **hacerse viejo** to get old.

viento nm wind

vientre nm belly, abdomen.

viernes nm Friday.

viga nf 1 (de madera) beam, rafter. 2 (de acero) girder.

vigente adj in use, in force.

vigilante nmf (hombre) watchman; (mujer) watchwoman.

vigilar vt-vi 1 (ir con cuidado) to watch. 2 (con armas) to guard.

vigor nm GB vigour; US vigor. • **en vigor** in force.

villa nf 1 (casa) villa. 2 (pueblo) small town.

villancico nm Christmas carol.

vinagre nm vinegar.

vinagreras nf pl cruet stand.

vinagreta nf vinaigrette.

vino nm wine. ▪ **vino blanco** white wine; **vino de Jerez** sherry; **vino rosado** rosé wine; **vino tinto** red wine.

viña nf vineyard.

viñedo nm vineyard.

viñeta nf 1 (dibujo) cartoon. 2 (tira) comic strip.

violar vt 1 (acuerdo, derecho) to violate. 2 (persona) to rape.

violencia nf violence.

violento,-a adj violent.

violeta adj-nm (color) violet. ► nf (flor) violet.

violín nm violin.

violinista nmf violinist.

violonchelo nm cello.

virgen adj 1 (persona) virgin. 2 (cinta) blank. 3 (en estado natural) unspoilt. ► nf virgin.

virtual adj virtual.

virtud nf virtue.

viruela nf smallpox.

virus nm virus.

visado nm visa.

vísceras nf pl viscera.

visera nf (de gorra) peak; (de casco) visor.

visible adj visible.

visión nf sight, vision. • **ver visiones** to dream, see things.

visita nf 1 (acción) visit. 2 (visitante) visitor, guest.

visitante nmf visitor.

visitar vt 1 (ir a casa de) to visit. 2 (enfermo) to see.

visón *nm* mink.
víspera *nf* **1** *(día anterior)* day before. **2** *(de fiesta)* eve.
vista *nf* **1** *(sentido)* sight, vision. **2** *(panorama)* view. • **con vistas a 1** *(jardín, calle)* overlooking. **2** *(beneficios, resultados)* with a view to; **conocer de vista** to know by sight; **estar a la vista** to be evident; **hasta la vista** good-bye, so long; **salta a la vista que...** it is obvious that...
visto,-a *adj* seen. • **por lo visto** as it seems; **ser lo nunca visto** to be unheard of. ▪ **visto bueno** approval.
vitamina *nf* vitamin.
vitrina *nf* **1** *(en casa)* glass cabinet, display cabinet. **2** *(de exposición)* glass case, showcase. **3** *(escaparate)* shop window.
viudo,-a *nm,f* *(hombre)* widower; *(mujer)* widow.
viva *interj* hurrah!
víveres *nm pl* food, provisions.
vivero *nm* **1** *(de plantas)* nursery. **2** *(de peces)* fish farm.
vivienda *nf* **1** *(alojamiento)* housing, accommodation. **2** *(morada)* home; *(- casa)* house; *(- piso)* GB flat; US apartment.
viviente *adj* living, alive.
vivir *vi* to live. ▶ *vt (pasar)* to live through: *los que vivieron la guerra*, those who

lived through the war. • **vivir de** to live on: *vive de su pensión*, she lives on her pension.
vivo,-a *adj* **1** *(con vida)* alive, living. **2** *(color)* bright, vivid. **3** *(animado)* lively. • **en vivo** *(programa)* live.
vocabulario *nm* vocabulary.
vocación *nf* vocation.
vocal *adj* vocal. ▶ *nf (letra, sonido)* vowel. ▶ *nmf (de comité)* member.
vodka *nm* vodka.
volante *nm* **1** *(de vehículo)* steering wheel. **2** *(documento)* note: *pedí un volante para el especialista de la piel*, I asked to be referred to the skin specialist.
volar *vi* to fly. ▶ *vt (hacer explotar)* to blow up. • **volando** in a rush: *tuve que desayunar volando*, I had to eat my breakfast in a hurry.
volcán *nm* volcano.
volcar *vt* to knock over. ▶ *vi* to overturn. ▶ *vpr* **volcarse** *(entregarse)* to devote oneself.
voleibol *nm* volleyball.
voltereta *nf* somersault.
volumen *nm* volume. • **bajar/subir el volumen** to turn the volume down/up. ▪ **volumen de negocios** turnover.
voluntad *nf* **1** *(de decidir)* will. **2** *(propósito)* intention, purpose. **3** *(deseo)* wish.

voluntario,-a *adj* voluntary. ► *nm,f* volunteer.

volver *vt* **1** *(dar vuelta a)* to turn (over); *(hacia abajo)* to turn upside down; *(de fuera a dentro)* to turn inside out. **2** *(convertir)* to turn, make: *me vuelve loco*, he drives me mad. ► *vi (regresar)* to come back, go back. ► *vpr* **volverse 1** *(darse la vuelta)* to turn (round): *se volvió hacia mí*, he turned towards me. **2** *(convertirse)* to turn, become: *se ha vuelto loco*, he's gone mad. • **volver en sí** to recover consciousness, come round; **volverse atrás** to back out.

vomitar *vi* to vomit, be sick.

vosotros,-as *pron* you. ▪ **vosotros,-as mismos,-as** yourselves.

votación *nf* vote, voting.

votar *vi* to vote.

voto *nm* vote.

voz *nf* **1** *(gen)* voice. **2** *(grito)* shout: *no me des esas voces*, don't shout! • **a media voz** in a whisper; **en voz alta** aloud; **en voz baja** in a low voice.

vuelo *nm* flight. ▪ **vuelo sin motor** gliding.

vuelta *nf* **1** *(giro)* turn: *da una vuelta a la llave*, give the key one turn. **2** *(en un circuito)* lap. **3** *(paseo a pie)* walk, stroll: *ir a dar una vuelta*, to go for a walk. **4** *(paseo en coche)* drive. **5** *(regreso)* return: *la vuelta la haremos en tren*, we'll come back by train. **6** *(dinero de cambio)* change: *quédese con la vuelta*, keep the change. • **a la vuelta** on the way back; **dar la vuelta 1** *(alrededor)* to go round. **2** *(girar)* to turn round. **3** *(de arriba abajo)* to turn upside down. **4** *(de dentro a fuera)* to turn inside out; **estar de vuelta** to be back. ▪ **vuelta al mundo** round-the-world trip; **vuelta ciclista** cycle race.

vuestro,-a *adj* your, of yours. ► *pron* yours.

vulgar *adj* **1** *(grosero)* vulgar. **2** *(corriente)* common, general.

W-X

Walkman® *nm* Walkman®.

wáter *nm fam* toilet.

waterpolo *nm* water polo.

W.C. *abr (retrete)* WC, toilet.

web *nf* **1** *(sitio)* website. **2** *(página)* webpage.

whisky *nm* whisky; *(irlandés)* whiskey.

windsurf *nm* windsurfing.

xenofobia *nf* xenophobia.

xilófono *nm* xylophone.

Y

Z

y *conj* **1** *(gen)* and. **2** *(con hora)* past: *son las tres y cuarto*, it's a quarter past three. **3** *(con números)*: *cuarenta y cuatro*, forty-four.

ya *adv* **1** *(con pasado)* already: *ya lo sabía*, I already knew. **2** *(con presente)* now: *es preciso actuar ya*, it is vital that we act now. **3** *(ahora mismo)* immediately, at once. **4** *(luego)* later: *ya veremos*, we'll see. **5** *(uso enfático)*: *ya lo sé*, I know; *ya entiendo*, I see. • **ya no** not any more, no longer; **ya que** since.

yacimiento *nm* bed, deposit. ▪ **yacimiento arqueológico** archaeological site.

yate *nm* *(a motor)* pleasure cruiser; *(de vela)* yacht.

yegua *nf* mare.

yema *nf* **1** *(de huevo)* yolk. **2** *(del dedo)* fingertip.

yerno *nm* son-in-law.

yeso *nm* **1** *(mineral)* gypsum. **2** *(en construcción)* plaster.

yo *pron* **1** *(sujeto)* I. **2** *(objeto, con preposición)* me. • **yo mismo** myself.

yoga *nm* yoga.

yogur *nm* yoghurt.

yóquey *nm* jockey.

yugular *adj-nf* jugular.

yunque *nm* anvil.

zafiro *nm* sapphire.

zamarra *nf* sheepskin jacket.

Zambia *nf* Zambia.

zambullirse *vpr* to dive.

zanahoria *nf* carrot.

zancada *nf* stride.

zancadilla *nf* *(para caer)* trip.

zanja *nf* ditch, trench.

zapatería *nf* GB shoe shop; US shoe store.

zapatilla *nf* slipper. ▪ **zapatillas de deporte** trainers.

zapato *nm* shoe. ▪ **zapatos de tacón** high-heeled shoes.

zar *nm* tsar, czar.

zarpa *nf* paw.

zarpar *vi* to set sail.

zarza *nf* bramble.

zarzamora *nf* *(planta)* blackberry bush; *(fruto)* blackberry.

zócalo *nm* skirting board.

zona *nf* area, zone. ▪ **zona azul** pay-and-display parking area; **zona verde** park.

zoo *nm* zoo.

zoología *nf* zoology.

zoológico *nm* zoo.

zorro,-a *nm,f* *(animal)* fox.

zueco *nm* clog.

zumbido *nm* **1** *(de insecto)* buzzing. **2** *(de motor)* humming.

zumo *nm* juice.

zurda *nf* *(mano)* left hand.

zurdo,-a *adj* left-handed.